70°   65°   60°

ATLANTIC

N

San Salvador

Crooked I.

Mayaguana

Caicos Is

Turks

Gt. Inagua

OCEAN

25°

Puerto Plata

Samaná

HAITI

DOMINICAN REP.

20°

Virgins

Puerto Rico

St. Maarten →   Anguilla

St. Croix   Saba   Barbuda

St. Kitts

Nevis   Antigua

Montserrat

Guadeloupe

Dominica

15°

a   n   S   e   a

Martinique

St. Lucia

St. Vincent   Barbados

Aruba   Curaçao

Bonaire   470 m.

Grenadines

Grenada

Tobago

Santa Marta

MAIN

Margarita

Trinidad

ISH

La Guaira

10°

VENEZUELA

D. de Fontaine

A CRUISING GUIDE TO
THE CARIBBEAN AND THE BAHAMAS

Including the North Coast of South America,
Central America, and Yucatan

A CRUISING GUIDE TO
THE CARIBBEAN AND THE BAHAMAS

Including
The North Coast of South America,
Central America, and Yucatan

Jerrems C. Hart and
William T. Stone

CONTRIBUTORS
Jolyon Byerley   THE WINDWARDS AND LEEWARDS
Alexander C. Forbes   THE VIRGIN ISLANDS
Kit S. Kapp   THE SPANISH MAIN

DODD, MEAD & COMPANY · NEW YORK

Library of Congress Cataloging in Publication Data

Hart, Jerrems C
    A cruising guide to the Caribbean and the Bahamas.

    Bibliography: p.
    Includes index.
    1. Caribbean area—Description and travel—1951—
—Guide-books. 2. Yachts and yachting—Caribbean area.
I. Stone, William T., joint author. II. Title.
F2171.2.H37 917.29'04'5 75-43577
ISBN 0-396-07284-4

PICTURE ACKNOWLEDGMENTS

Credits for photographs and route and sketch charts

J. E. Allen: pages 54, 149, 182, 193, 196, 197, 198, 209, 211, 462, 465, 466, 467, 468, 471, 479, 481, 497, 502, 508, 510, 542, 543, 553, 554

Bahamas Ministry of Tourism: pages 109, 124

CSY Ltd.: pages 337, 339, 346, 351, 359

Dorothy De Fontaine: endpapers; pages 32, 69, 75, 547

Fishergate Reproduction: pages 85, 135, 144, 153, 199, 287, 370, 390, 410, 420, 441, 459, 532

Alexander C. Forbes: pages 190, 218, 222, 223, 224, 227, 229, 234, 235, 236, 238, 240, 242, 244, 246, 248, 250, 251, 253, 255, 257, 258, 260, 261, 263, 264, 265, 266, 268, 269, 270, 271, 273, 275, 277, 279, 281, 283, 314, 492, 493, 525, 528

R. K. Franks: pages 33, 87

J. C. Hart: pages 51, 63, 111, 117, 123, 126, 129, 139, 141, 146, 148, 163, 191, 267, 302, 303, 307, 341, 342, 353, 362, 366, 375, 377, 449, 451, 527, 548, 552

Kim Hart: page 138

Hart's Camera (Curaçao): pages 403, 404, 405

Instituto Panameño de Turismo: page 429

Kit S. Kapp: pages 388, 392, 418, 422, 427, 436, 471

Nelson McClary: pages 472, 477, 482, 489, 490, 494, 499, 500, 503, 511, 512

V. E. B. Nicholson & Sons: pages 317, 319, 325

Jay Stone: page 276

U. S. Sailing Directions: pages 167, 177

Venezuelan Tourist Corporation: page 383

FOREWORD

Gold, sugar, a pinch of salt, and a heavy measure of luxurious climate: these have most influenced the fortunes of the Caribee Islands and the Spanish Main from the time of the Spaniards, who came seeking a shorter trade route to Asia and found treasure instead, to the current invasion of tourists who come by planeloads and shiploads to spend their leisure time and money in a balmy climate that changes little from day to day and season to season.

Mexico and Peru soon ran out of gold, the sugar industry has been a fickle provider through the years, and the development of inland mines has almost brought an end to salt panning. But the unclouded sun and the steady trade winds go on and on, providing the most cogent reason to come to this region of climatic perfection, where the greatest benefits are health rather than wealth.

Yachtsmen have for years been aware of these attributes, but until the last decade or so there have been few with adequate experience, staunch enough vessels, and sufficient time at their disposal to make the relatively long open-water hops necessary to reach this coveted cruising region. Until recently, too, the logistical problems of keeping supplied with water and fuel, and of finding people and places for repairs and maintenance, have been a decided obstacle.

The amazing growth of the chartering business, more general affluence, the realization that a career can be interrupted without undue loss, the explosion in yacht building, and the concurrent expansion of the ranks of knowledgeable yachtsmen, have brought great changes. But only certain pockets of the Caribbean and Bahamas have been affected: specifically, the northern and central Bahamas, eastern Puerto Rico, the Virgin Islands, and the island chain from Antigua to Grenada. In fact, when the Caribbean is viewed as a whole, yachts are just beginning to spread their sails over this region, which is some 1,700 miles wide and almost a thousand miles from north to south. This book is written expressly to break down the boundaries of these pockets of yachting activity. If it succeeds, it will lead to a multitude of individual discoveries like those that have surprised us and given us pleasure. It is such private discoveries that are the very essence of cruising, even if it takes a guidebook to get you there!

Other guides for yachtsmen zero in on relatively small segments of the vast area we cover here. We list all those guides in the Appendix and we urge you to use them when in those regions, for they will probably cover more anchorages than we do; furthermore, you will benefit, when moving from place to place, by a different emphasis and viewpoint.

Whenever other guides have preceded us, we have tried to complement rather than compete. If we have omitted some anchorage that appears elsewhere, just keep on comparing, for you will probably find some places here that have not been mentioned elsewhere. We make no excuses nor any exalted claims for our coverage except to say that wherever you choose to sail in the great Caribbean basin, you will not be far from some harbor or sheltered anchorage mentioned in this book.

Beyond a mere digest of ports and places in this part of the world, we have tried to give you a comprehensive résumé of the elements that constitute a successful cruising plan for these waters. For instance, if you have never before sailed below latitude 25° N, it is difficult to adjust to the constancy of the trade winds. You are in a belt above the equator in which air is constantly flowing in from the north to fill space being vacated by heated, rising air masses while, at the same time, this flow of surface air is being deflected to the right as a result of the earth's rotation. This constancy of wind direction, which is around 80% NE or E for most of the region, means in turn that open bays and headlands, when properly oriented, provide shelter that wouldn't even be considered in the temperate parts of the globe. Besides their convenient directional constancy, the trades seldom blow over Force 5, and calms are infrequent. The rise and fall of the tide is less than 2 feet in most places, and fog is unknown. In fact, the conditions are so perfect we might say that though the sea may never be completely forgiving to the careless sailor, it is more relenting here.

It's not all peaches and cream, however, for you will be far from civilization as we are accustomed to it; you will need to plan for every contingency, to try to make your boat a self-sustaining entity, to realize that you will from time to time be thrown upon your own resourcefulness. Then, too, you may be disturbed by unpleasant racial incidents or by thievery provoked by poverty and growing disrespect for law (which is by no means confined to the Caribbean).

The area is understandably too vast for minutely detailed, up-to-date coverage by a mere pair of authors. We don't pretend to have been everywhere, but we've found others who have. For the Virgin Islands, we enlisted the aid of Alex Forbes, who has a home and has operated a charter-boat fleet there, and who has written his own guidebook to this immensely popular cruising ground. Jolyon Byerley, who has skippered charter boats out of Antigua ever since the Nicholsons initiated the chartering scheme in the West Indies, knows the Windwards and Leewards like the back of his hand, and writes both entertainingly and authoritatively about them. We are honored to have him as a collaborator. And to have Kit Kapp, who started out as a charter-boat skipper out of St. Thomas and eventually concentrated his attentions on the Spanish Main from Venezuela to Panama and beyond. He has since led expeditions into the area under the aegis of the Explorers' Club of New York to study Indian cultures, seek out lost historic sites, and conduct hydrographic surveys. As we began to develop information on this part of the Caribbean, people kept saying, "You'd better get in touch with Kit Kapp, he knows this area better than anybody." In addition to his chapters on Venezuela, Colombia, and the San Blas, Kit has also contributed valuable piloting advice drawn from his cruising experience along the Costa Rican and Nicaraguan coasts. We're happy to have him on our team, and you will be, too, when you see how he has covered his territory.

Beyond these diligent collaborators, we have picked the brains of a score of other people who have recently sailed in the Caribbean, some of whom have spent enough time in certain places to give us very authoritative information indeed. The following are among those who have entered into rather exhaustive correspondence or meetings with us.

Bob and Ginnie Higman, who have by now nearly closed the loop in their Caribbean circumnavigation in *Tormentor III*, have been particularly helpful in their letter-writing about such places as Mona Island, La Parguera, Trinidad and Tobago, Venezuela, and Providencia, for they are quick to sense the things that other yachtsmen need to know. For the big and beautiful island of Jamaica, which is being covered here for the first time ever, we have leaned heavily on the expert advice of Bob Fletcher, veteran sailor out of Mobay, and his son-in-law, Tom Robson. Dick Steele, who cruised his *Bonhomme Richard* from California all around the Caribbean and back again, has been generous with his time in answering our questions about a number of places around the circuit. Jacque Kappes of *Liberty Belle* has shared with us her insight of Haiti. We have also been greatly assisted in our coverage of this mysterious land and the southern coast of the Dominican Republic by Jack Laird, who cruised the area in his powerboat *Miss Applejack*. Tony and José de Pablo, with true Hispanic graciousness, put themselves and their *Bertram* at our disposal for a proper survey of the lovely southeast coast of the Dominican Republic and its budding riviera near La Romana. Michael Ronan and Sr. Christian de Lemos, of Puerto Plata, helped us explore little-known harbors on the north coast of the Dominican Republic.

Nelson and Jane McClary, who cruised the Gulf of Honduras in their 72-foot *Josefine*, a ketch-rigged Baltic trader, have made a major contribution to our coverage of the Bay Islands and the Rio Dulce, generously sharing their intimate knowledge gained in five years of sailing those waters. They have allowed us to draw liberally upon Jane's writing and Nelson's superb photography. We are deeply in their debt, too, for additional information on the coastal waters of Belize. Our thanks also to Dave Kimball, a member of the McClarys' crew, who has given us highlights of his own unique exploration of the 118-mile barrier reef of Belize. We are grateful to Dorwin Teague for permission to quote from a published article on his cruise in this offbeat area.

Dr. Carlos Nouel, Venezuelan yachtsman and distinguished physician of Caracas, introduced us to the fine yacht-club facilities on the coast of Venezuela and, with his friend Dr. Victor Montoya, helped answer our many questions about government requirements for yachts visiting the offshore islands and mainland ports.

In the Netherlands Antilles, Mr. "Henk" Hendrikse, chief of the Harbor Safety Office at Willemstad, Curaçao, was especially helpful in showing us points of interest to visiting yachtsmen and explaining the impressive search and rescue services maintained in the Dutch islands.

We are indebted to several yachtsmen-writers who have permitted us to quote liberally from their books or published articles, especially to Eric Hiscock for his sage advice on successful ocean voyaging, to Samuel Eliot Morison for permission to quote from his extensive writings on Columbus, to Bill Robinson for use of his commentaries in *Yachting* on passage-making to the Caribbean, and to Donald M. Street for permission to cite parts of his revised edition of *A Cruising Guide to the Lesser Antilles*.

We are grateful to John Van Ost for permission to use material from Caribbean Sailing Yachts publications, including harbor charts prepared for CSY charterers. We are also indebted to several Commodores of the Seven Seas Cruising Association who have cheerfully answered our queries about some of the out-of-the-way areas they have visited and let us reproduce letters that appeared originally in the SSCA *Bulletin*.

Following are others, not mentioned in the text, who have helped us in special ways or enhanced our coverage of certain places—and even this list is incomplete:

Bob Sparkman, on the subject of insurance

Corky Roberts in Barbados

C. L. Mofford and Dr. Paul Chevalier in Trinidad

Bill Rood and Capt. Alberto Arvele in Santo Domingo

Frank T. Bonnin in Ponce

Esther Burnham of *Eventide* and *Chickadee*

Liam Maguire of Pine Cay in the Caicos group

James L. Madden of *Gesture II*

Stanley Livingston, Jr., of *Manukai*

Morton Gibbons-Neff of *Prim*

Aubrey Graves of *Haligonian*

The Nicholsons of English Harbour

Edgard du Prey of Martinique

Marguerite Britter in Grenada

George T. Eggleston in St. Lucia

John Miles

Howard H. MacGowan

Dick Avery in St. Thomas

Charles Cary in Tortola

Capt. Jan Oenes in Curaçao

Daniel Valin, Roger Le Breton, Yves-Michel Barbe, and Serge Lodeon, all of Martinique

The Alburys of Man o' War Cay

Ralph Christianson of San Juan

Jack Vincent and Nick Zinkowski of Culebra

James L. Radawski of Roatán

Betty Wittmer of S.S.C.A.

Phil and Nancy Dean of *Morelle*

Jack Allen of *Belinda*

Pearce Coady of *Cleopatra's Barge*

Wells Morse of *Legend*

Ken Court of *Mamari*

Walter C. ("Wiki") McNiel of *Tropic Bird*

Dud and Barbara Dewey of *Nimbus*

Still others have helped us with valuable criticism, editorial review, and special research. These include Bill Robinson and others on the staff of *Yachting*; Bob and Dorothy Franks, who assisted in the updating of the Virgin Islands chapter; F. G. Walton Smith, President, and May Smith, Secretary, of The International Oceanographic Foundation; Frederick Johnson, Director of the Cruising Information Center of the Peabody Museum, Salem, Massachusetts; the library staff at Mystic Seaport; and Clinton F. Lloyd, a former shipmate and member of C.C.A., who directed us to the logs of many interesting voyages in the Cruising Club of America archives at Mystic Seaport.

Readers will recognize Dorothy De Fontaine's familiar hand and style in the endpapers of this book, together with several route charts. Kit Kapp has embellished his chapters on the Spanish Main with handsome sketch charts of places that are not detailed in any published charts. In the Virgin Islands, we have reproduced Alex Forbes' clear and concise sketch charts, which originally appeared in his *Virgin Islands Cruising Guide*, published in 1970. Jack Allen's distinctive sketch charts are scattered liberally throughout this book, to guide you into places not clearly shown in the government charts. Jack, a lifelong cruising yachtsman himself, understands how to present the details other yachtsmen need to know. We are glad to have been able to draw upon these talents to help remove some of the uneasiness that goes with cruising in unfamiliar waters.

Institutions that have assisted us with research, in addition to those mentioned above, include: The Marine Historical Association, Mystic Seaport, Mystic, Connecticut; the Cruising Club of America; and Yachting Publishing Corporation (particularly for permission to republish selected photographs from their outstanding collection of slides and prints on the Bahamas and Caribbean).

To all who have helped us in large measure or small, we extend our sincere thanks. We hope to make new friends among our readers, for we need the continuing cooperation of those who sail these waters to add to our store of knowledge, to correct us where we've been wrong, to amplify where we've been too brief, and to add deserving places that we may have missed.

Try as we did to make this Guide accurate and dependable, it is of course manifestly impossible to guarantee our directions, many of which are a synthesis of information beyond our own experience, nor do we claim that our personal observations and recommendations are either infallible or complete. There may be some, too, who will misinterpret our text despite our earnest attempts to be exact. Therefore those who follow this Guide are warned to use it with all the caution that becomes a good seaman for, after all, this is a guide, not a bible. Sketch charts and excerpts from government charts are intended as aids to piloting by eye and are not necessarily accurate enough to be used with rules and protractors.

JERREMS C. HART
WILLIAM T. STONE

CONTENTS

Contents

CHAPTER ONE

Plans, Preparations, and Cruising Conditions

Objectives

Not counting the zigs and zags that are part of any thorough cruise, the circuit from southern Florida out through the Antilles to Grenada, back along the Spanish Main to the Panama Canal, thence through the western Caribbean and the Yucatan Channel to Key West, is almost 4,000 miles. Only a fortunate few will have the time for such an ambitious expedition. The rest will content themselves with various goals to the east and south, working their way out the hard way against the trades, then coasting home in comfort with wind and sea abaft the beam.

The successive objectives of such a plan are fairly well defined because each is separated by a significant body of open water.

Once Around, Clockwise

First, the Gulf Stream, 50 miles wide and often rough, must be crossed to reach the turquoise waters of the Bahamas. Then, running in the shelter of the larger islands, there is smooth sailing as far as George Town in the Exumas. Proceeding further east to the Caicos group, the islands dwindle in size and become too scattered to provide a lee, and fueling and repair facilities almost disappear.

From South Caicos, itself only an outpost, the next major objective is Puerto Rico, along the aptly named "Thorny Path." It skirts the rugged north coast of the Dominican Republic with only two intermediate shelters, at Puerto Plata and Samaná Bay, then leads 65 miles across the Mona Passage, where winds and countercurrents are apt to produce nasty conditions resembling those in the Gulf Stream. After this, the partial lee of Puerto Rico seems especially welcome; at least, the land breezes off this big island tend to dull the force of the trade winds, so that only in the afternoon do they reach their maximum onshore strength. In the appropriate chapters that follow, we will have more to say about how to manage the winds off these big islands.

Most cruisers who have come this far are heading at least for the Virgin

1

Islands, through relatively sheltered waters. The next hurdle is the 85-mile Anegada Passage to St. Martin, after which you will have "turned the corner" of the prevailing winds and can expect easier sailing down the string of islands to Grenada, which has for years been the terminus of most Caribbean cruises. Barbados and Tobago are seldom visited because they lie upwind of Grenada—but the more adventurous, seeking new lands to discover, have begun to extend their cruising west to Isla Margarita and the other islands off the Venezuelan coast, and they bring back tales of unspoiled beauty, plenty of comfortable anchorages, and pleasant people.

Those who continue along the Spanish Main, now with the wind and sea squarely astern, are usually bound for the Panama Canal. The Dutch islands of Bonaire, Curaçao, and Aruba are dividends along the way, and the paradisiacal San Blas archipelago is to be explored just before reaching the Canal Zone.

Cruising the western Caribbean is usually confined to the island stepping-stones of San Andrés, Providencia, Swan, and Cozumel in the course of passaging north from the Canal. Coasting along the shores of Costa Rica and Nicaragua, where the trades tend to be deflected so that they blow more on the nose than on the beam, is infrequently attempted. This whole side of the Caribbean is of course a lee shore and thus not to be trifled with. On the other hand, Roatán, in the Gulf of Honduras, is well worth including in a cruise plan, and a growing number of hardy souls are snaking their way through the maze of cays that make up the barrier reef skirting Belize (formerly British Honduras). The wind pattern allows this virgin cruising area also to be approached comfortably from Key West or in the course of a swing through the Bahamas to Haiti, Jamaica, and the Caymans.

Except for the Thorny Path, the only easting in this clockwise cruising plan is the return to Florida through the Yucatan Channel, but there the trades are occasionally foiled by weather fronts that move across the Gulf of Mexico. We have slipped through that channel in between the usual procession of winter northers, while the wind was southerly and before it had time to swing into the north and northeast with its full intensity. Also, the north-flowing current, which later turns east, is a substantial help.

If you are simply seeking the easiest way through the Caribbean to the Panama Canal, we recommend taking the Windward Passage rather than the seemingly more direct route by way of the Yucatan Channel. Because the winds in the Bahamas tend to be more variable than further south, you should have little windward work down to Inagua, where you should expect steady reaching winds for the rest of the way. This track will take you to Jamaica, where you will find it convenient to stop at Port Antonio or Port Royal (Kingston) for provisions, water, and fuel. To break up the trip still further, you might want to detour slightly to anchorages among the cays of the Pedro, Serranilla, and Serrana Banks.

This track is roughly equal in distance to a southbound passage through the Yucatan Channel (bucking a substantial current), with the usual stops at Swan Island, Providencia, and San Andrés—about 1,250 miles.

The Hard Way

Yachtsmen coming from the temperate zones, accustomed to winds and tidal currents from every point of the compass, find it hard to adjust to the regularity of the trade winds and the predominately one-way ocean currents in the Caribbean. But the sheer discomfort and futility of trying to beat your way against them cannot be overemphasized. Many have set a counterclockwise course from the Panama Canal to Grenada and have had horrendous tales to tell of head seas encountered, and some have aborted their plans and headed north to Jamaica.

One hardy sailor who did it tells us: "The coasts of Colombia and Venezuela at that time of the year [January] are almost impossible; three boats before us were dismasted."

Another yachtsman remarks:

From Cartagena to Aruba was by far the worst part of our trip except for the tehuantepecer we hit. The current, the wind and, most of all, the choppy seas are dead against you. We made Aruba before dark one night, and it took us 12 hours to get the last 6 miles, with wind, current, and seas pounding us to death. Aruba offers no abatement of wind on the lee side, only a little less sea.

Chuck and Bobbie Bryant of the cutter *Cygnus* reported in the *Bulletin* of the Seven Seas Cruising Association:

Having sailed from the Canal to Grenada, west to east into the trades off the South American coast in May, 1968, and again in September, 1971, we would never do it again! From much research and our own two experiences, and talk with many yachtsmen who have done it or tried to, the only month to even consider is November.

We can add no more explicit advice than that of Kit Kapp, who has made six eastbound passages, in all seasons, from Panama to the Leeward Islands. In fact, he recommends that the owner of a small yacht should seriously consider shipping her from the Canal as deck cargo on a freighter to Trinidad, to save wear and tear on the gear—in spite of the costs of a cradle and the transportation itself.

For those who persist, Kapp offers this experienced counsel:

a. Plan to make your passage from April to December, but preferably in October and November.

b. Allow plenty of time.

c. Be sure your engine is in good condition, because you will have to power much of the way.

d. Carry all the fuel you can and top off tanks wherever possible.

e. Secure all hatches, ports, and deck gear for heavy sea conditions, and by no means tow your dinghy. Have an extra hook handy on deck.

f. Plan to live on sandwiches and other snacks when underway, because cooking may be physically impossible.

g. Plan to make short hops from shelter to shelter as the weather allows; and plan your departures to take advantage of the daily cycle of the winds in a particular area. This may mean an evening departure when the trades have abated; or leaving in the very early morning, when near mountainous terrain, to take advantage of the land breezes.

Here is the way Kit would establish the successive legs:

1. The Canal Zone to Holandes Cays in the San Blas Islands, taking refuge at Isla Grande if necessary.

2. San Blas directly to Isla Tesora light and Cartagena, but bearing off to shelter in the San Bernadino or Rosario Islands if the weather is too much.

3. Cartagena to Santa Marta, which could be one of the roughest legs.

4. Santa Marta to Cape La Vela, taking refuge in Bahía Cinto if necessary. Keep within 2 or 3 miles of shore for an easier sea and less current, especially beyond Ríohacha.

5. Cape La Vela to Aruba, taking refuge in Bahía Honda if necessary. Skirt the Guajira Peninsula, about 2 or 3 miles off, to Punta Espada, then run southeasterly across the Gulf of Venezuela until you are well under the lee of the Paraguana Peninsula before turning northerly toward Punta Salina. Stay in the lee of the land, about 4 miles off, to Punta Macolla, thence take up a course for a point to the east of Oranjestad on Aruba.

6. Aruba to Bonaire, taking refuge in Curaçao if necessary.

7. Bonaire to Puerto La Cruz. Make a long tack to the southeast, using the La Guaira area for refuge in adverse weather. Otherwise, upon reaching the coast, tack to the northeast for shelter at Los Roques, or try for the west end of Isla La Tortuga. When the weather improves, carry on to Puerto La Cruz for a well-earned rest.

8. Puerto La Cruz to Bahía Guamache on Isla Margarita. Favor the coastline to the vicinity of Cumaná, then head north, using the lee of Isla Cubagua, thence to Bahía Guamache.

9. Isla Margarita to Grenada, taking refuge in Islas Los Testigos only if necessary. In heavy weather, the prudent course would be southeasterly to

Carúpano (or perhaps Esmeralda Bay), then to Puerto Santo, Cabo Tres Puntas, and northeast to Grenada.

Weather Wisdom

To understand the weather picture better, and for details of conditions to be expected in different parts of the Caribbean, *Sailing Directions for the West Indies,* Vol. I and II, should be studied. British *Pilots*, Vol. 70, 71, 71A, and 69A, give similar information. However, we think, the most valuable tool for planning a cruise around the Caribbean is *Atlas of Pilot Charts, Central American Waters and South Atlantic Ocean,* Publication 106 of the U.S. Naval Oceanographic Office.* Therein, by means of easy-to-read wind roses, current arrows, and comments about average conditions, you can almost "see" the weather pattern on a month-to-month basis. Remember, however, that these are averages and do not show the effects of "extended northers" during the winter that may reach as far as the Panama Canal or the Windwards.

Also, one must consider the effects of occasional "easterly waves," which are troughs of low pressure traveling from east to west across the Caribbean and causing a northerly slant to the winds ahead of them and a southerly flow behind them. These easterly waves with their wind and rain are in fact the very conditions under which tropical storms and hurricanes develop.

Wind and Sea

Everyone who sails the open sea takes a profound and quite understandable interest in trying to gauge wind and sea conditions, especially after the whitecaps have begun to form. From the deck of a small craft, the sea usually looks much worse than it really is; through a camera lens, however, the converse is always true. In this book we have used both the Beaufort Scale and wind speed in knots, though we favor the former because it spans a range of speed, and the wind is never constant.

We've included several pictures (see page 7) by the late Winston Megoran. We think they show the sea as it really is. We are indebted to *Yachting Monthly* (London) for letting us reproduce them here. Bear in mind that these are ocean seas, far from land; the wind has had time to build them to their full height. In constricted places, on banks and alongshore where the water suddenly becomes shallow, and when strong tidal or ocean currents such as the Gulf Stream are opposing the wind, then steeper, shorter, and more dangerous seas will result. We all know, too, that high waves are interspersed with lower ones, that they march across the sea in series, and that there can be wind waves on top of old

*Now published by the Defense Mapping Agency Hydrographic Center. See Bibliography.

swells, sometimes coming from two directions at once. With all these factors to consider, it takes a fine eye to make a proper estimate of a given sea condition. The pictures on the opposite page may help.

BEAUFORT WIND SCALE

Beaufort Number (force)	Limits of Wind Speed in knots.	Descriptive Terms.	Sea Criterion.
0	Less then 1	Calm	Sea like a mirror
1	1–3	Light air	Ripples with the appearance of scales are formed but without foam crests.
2	4–6	Light breeze	Small wavelets, still short but more pronounced. Crests have a glassy appearance and do not break.
3	7–10	Gentle breeze	Large wavelets. Crests begin to break. Foam of glassy appearance. Perhaps scattered white horses.
4	11–16	Moderate breeze	Small waves, becoming longer; fairly frequent white horses.
5	17–21	Fresh breeze	Moderate waves, taking a more pronounced long form; many white horses are formed. (Chance of some spray.)
6	22–27	Strong breeze	Large waves begin to form; the white foam crests are more extensive everywhere. (Probably some spray.)
7	28–33	Near gale	Sea heaps up and white foam from breaking waves begins to be blown in streaks along the direction of the wind.
8	34–40	Gale	Moderately high waves of greater length; edges of crests begin to break into spindrift. The foam is blown in well-marked streaks along the direction of the wind.
9	41–47	Strong gale	High waves. Dense streaks of foam along the direction of the wind. Crests of waves begin to topple, tumble and roll over. Spray may affect visibility.
10	48–55	Storm	Very high waves with long overhanging crests. The resulting foam in great patches is blown in dense white streaks along the direction of the wind. On the whole the surface of the sea takes a white appearance. The tumbling of the sea becomes heavy and shocklike. Visibility affected.
11	56–63	Violent storm	Exceptionally high waves. (Small and medium-sized ships might be for a time lost to view behind the waves.) The sea is completely covered with long white patches of foam lying along the direction of the wind. Everywhere the edges of the wave crests are blown into froth. Visibility affected.
12	64+	Hurricane	The air is filled with foam and spray. Sea completely white with driving spray; visibility very seriously affected.

Force 2

Force 4

Force 5

Force 6

Force 8

Hurricanes

Since the West Indies and the ocean to the east are the spawning grounds of hurricanes, the incidence of these ultimate storms must be considered in your cruising timetable. On the other hand, lest the fear of being caught in a hurricane becomes too inhibiting, consider that there are only four or five in a normal year and that the area of Force 12 winds averages little more than 100 miles from the eye or storm center and only occasionally as much as 200 miles. Then realize that although the season officially lasts from June through November, the percentage incidence by month is: September 36%, August 29%, October 19%, July 7%, June 5%, and November 3%. Note, too, that these statistics include *all* Atlantic hurricanes, many of which reach this designation in the Gulf of Mexico and would be classed only as tropical storms or perhaps just "disturbances" in the Caribbean Sea.

As we have seen, the most dangerous months are August, September, and October, and the greatest percentage of these "high season" storms reach their hurricane intensity in the western half of the Caribbean. Furthermore, they invariably trend to the northeast and north. Therefore, the further south and east you are during the height of the season, the less likely you are to be clobbered.

Considering the advanced state of the art of finding and continuously plotting hurricanes, as practiced by the National Hurricane Center in Miami, no alert yachtsman should find himself at sea in the path of one of these killer storms. In such an unfortunate event, however, he will obviously want to do what he can to mitigate the consequences. In the tropics, these storms tend to move quite slowly, perhaps 300 miles a day, so there is a chance to move out of the most destructive path. Having in mind that a hurricane is spiraling counterclockwise with the winds drawing toward the vortex, the semicircle to the right of the storm's path (as might be seen from an observation plane) is the most dangerous, since the winds are stronger to the extent of the storm's forward movement.

To help you avoid a hurricane or to make the best of a bad situation, here are some helpful hints:

Precursory signs:
Two days before—long, heavy swells, 4–5 per minute instead of 12–15. Thunderstorm clouds.
Day before—bright skies, above normal temperature, little or no cumulus clouds seen, unusual wind direction, barometer drops below 29.53 inches.
Immediate signs:
High cirrus ("mares'-tails") followed by cirrostratus clouds, halos around sun and moon. Then altostratus turning to altocumulus, becoming cumulus congestus, black, with rising wind.

Maneuvering:

1. Determine bearing of storm from swell and wind direction. Bearing is wind direction plus 115°.

2. If wind hauls to right (clockwise), you are in the dangerous semicircle. Bring wind on starboard bow (45° relative) and make best speed.

3. Use radar, if available.

4. If wind remains steady and barometer continues falling, you are in direct path. Bring wind on starboard quarter (160° relative) and make best speed toward the "safe" semicircle.

5. Never try to cross direct path of storm.

6. If in the "safe" semicircle, bring wind on starboard quarter (130° relative) and make best possible speed.

The Boat

Without making any attempt to detail *the* perfect boat for cruising the Caribbean, there are some parameters into which such a craft should fit. In the first place, winds of 30 knots and waves of 8 feet on top of huge ocean swells are not uncommon. A seascape so awesome (or gruesome, whichever way you are inclined to look at it) is not the usual fare by any means, but any extended Caribbean cruise will include some passages of that sort. Under such head-on conditions, a sailboat under 35 feet or a powerboat much under 40 feet would, to say the least, be highly uncomfortable. Draft, too, has much to do with seaworthiness, whether sail or power, and we have no hesitation in recommending 4½ feet or more, even for the Bahamas. In fact, we have cruised through the Bahamas with 3½ feet and with 6 feet and have found ourselves excluded from only a few choice places because of the deeper draft. In the rest of the Caribbean, draft is not really an important consideration, and deeper draft will give you a stiffer, steadier boat.

Tank capacities should be sufficient for at least a week on water and 500 miles on fuel (750 miles in the western Caribbean) if power is the only propulsion, and this is where most boats designed for U.S. coastal cruising fall far short. Know in advance what your limits are and plan to carry extra rubber or plastic tanks on deck to make up the deficiencies. To some Spartan sailors, 20 gallons of water might be enough, but such a ration would hardly last a day on a powerboat with pressure taps all over the boat and sailors used to daily showers.

A powerboat with a range of 200 miles at cruising speed may well go two or three times as far at some slower speed, a factor that can best be determined by adding a flowmeter to the fuel system. An auxiliary, working out against the trades, will want to use power on many occasions, at least as far as the Virgins. In determining range, however, it must be remembered that speed is not the only factor. Head-sea and wind conditions will materially affect consumption, and a reserve of 20% should be allowed for such contingencies.

Bear in mind that little painted anchors with bits of vinyl-covered chain don't "go" in the West Indies. You may learn a lot about anchoring out there, but you need to be equipped with the right ground tackle before you leave. Without going into a long dissertation on this subject, which is well covered in seamanship books, we suggest you take two different types of patent anchors (a Danforth and a plow, for instance), each with a nylon rode and 10–12 feet of chain, plus a spare to replace one of the standard anchors in case of loss or breakage—we have seen Danforths come up off a coral bottom looking like a piece of spaghetti.

The more opening portlights, hatches, windsails, and awnings you have, the better, for the tropical sun beating down mercilessly on an unshaded, poorly ventilated boat can take all the pleasure out of island cruising. Awnings should be not only the width of the boat but should extend well forward and aft, not just over the cockpit, for it is surprising how much a shaded deck will lower the temperature below decks. Side curtains are another benefit. The most effective cowl ventilators have really big mouths, and dorade boxes are best fitted with two exterior openings so that you can swap the ventilator for a deckplate to get straight-through ventilation when in port.

Insect screens are a distinct convenience but not an absolute necessity; the bugs are at their worst for only a couple of hours around sunset and can be held more or less at bay with liberal use of repellents. We have found that the smoldering-incense repellent made in the Orient is especially effective. The trouble with screens is that they seriously cut down the flow of air on quiet nights.

A life raft with survival rations, water, and flares should of course be a part of every equipment list.

Charts and Other Published Aids

Although all U.S. charts, domestic and foreign, are now under a uniform numbering system, they are far from uniform in detail, accuracy, symbols, scale, and general appearance. The familiar and beautifully detailed coastal charts formerly produced by the Coast and Geodetic Survey, with their yellow land areas and water areas of shaded blue, will take you through Puerto Rico and the Virgin Islands. In all other regions, you will be depending on U.S. Navy charts. Some have been prepared from aerial surveys; others are adaptations of charts, mostly British, that derive from surveys a hundred years old or older.

Islands that once were British (the whole Caribbean, for that matter) are well charted by the British Admiralty, as the French islands are by the French government. In our place descriptions, however, we show British Admiralty (BA) or French charts only where we consider them superior to their U.S. counterparts in detail or scale.

The BA charts have one distinct advantage—they fold to a uniform 20½ by 28 inches. You can stow them in a drawer of modest size and use them conveniently on a smallish chart table. Also, they can be ordered in folio groups that include every published chart for a given area. If you decide to use British charts and are not pressed for time, order them from Capt. O. M. Watts Ltd., 49 Albemarle St., London, W.1. It may take four months for them to arrive by ship, but that is preferable to ordering them from U.S. agents; their stock is usually incomplete, and they add handling charges.

By all means stock up on the charts you'll need before you leave the States, but if you change your route or are still missing a chart or two, the following sources will probably have U.S., BA, or French charts of their immediate cruising areas:

Bahamas: Yacht Haven, or John S. George in Palmdale shopping area, both
    in Nassau
Jamaica: R. S. Gamble & Son Ltd., Harbour St. in Kingston
Virgin Islands: Bosun's Locker in St. Thomas
St. Barts: Alma
Antigua: Carib Marine, English Harbour
Martinique: Librairies Antillaises, Fort-de-France
St. Vincent: Survey Department in Kingstown
Bequia: Lulley's
Grenada: Stevens & Co., Prickly Bay
Trinidad: R. Landry & Co., Ltd., 12 Borde St., Port-of-Spain
Panama: Islamorada in Panama City (very extensive stock, as they supply big
    ships transiting the Canal)

The charts referenced KSK (numbers 1–9) are large-scale charts of certain popular or convenient areas along the coasts of Venezuela, Colombia, and Panama (also one of Port Royal on Roatán Island, Honduras). The key to these charts along the San Blas Coast and the Gulf of Darien is the orientation chart in Chapter 16. Complete information about these charts, including a list of places where you can get them, appears in the Appendix.

In Grand Bahama and the Abaco Islands, chart reference numbers with the prefix B or H are enlarged versions of Harry Kline's sketch charts, which appear in the *Yachtsman's Guide to the Bahamas*. They are fully cataloged in that publication.

Aside from their climatological data, the *Sailing Directions* offer only limited help to yachtsmen, and some of their scary admonitions should not be taken too seriously if you are to persevere in your Caribbean cruising. After all, they are written primarily for big ships, and before that for clumsy sailing vessels; the best places for small craft, where the water may be a couple of fathoms or less, are usually not mentioned. If they are, reference is made to the need for "local knowledge," that elusive ingredient that never seems to be around in extreme situations when you really need it.

The nearest thing to local knowledge in these waters comes in several spiral-bound yearly guidebooks that give detailed directions, supported by numerous sketches, for getting into most of the important harbors and anchorages from the Bahamas to Grenada, excluding the Leewards. The "granddaddy" of these guides is *Yachtsman's Guide to the Bahamas,* which is absolutely indispensable in those waters. Neither the U.S. nor the Admiralty charts give any detail whatsoever for the circuitous routes among the islands and cays. Elsewhere, the official charts are much more helpful from the standpoint of scale and detail, but still, the informal guides will time and again take you into places you might otherwise fear to enter.

The monthly *Bulletin* of the Seven Seas Cruising Association contains very valuable cruising information in the form of letters from members and others. The coverage is world-wide, but almost every issue includes some advice useful to those cruising in the Caribbean and Bahamas. Membership is confined to those who move about under sail and who live aboard, but subscriptions are open to nonmembers. Write to S.S.C.A., Box 14514, North Palm Beach, Fla. 33408.

Aids to Navigation

You will have little occasion to use buoyage in the course of your navigation. In the first place, buoys are few and far between. Second, they are usually found only in the entrances to commercial ports, where they mark depths and dangers that seldom concern small craft. In the few places where you do find them in your travels, remember to forget the "red, right, returning" jingle— unless you are in the waters of the Bahamas, Mexico, Cuba, Hispaniola, Puerto Rico, or the U.S. Virgins. These are the only areas where the U.S. buoyage system generally applies. As a general rule, the buoys around the French and formerly British islands will be the opposite color and shape of the U.S. system. Don't make quick judgments about buoys; always refer to the chart and use your common sense.

But never mind. Buoy tending in the West Indies is rather lackadaisical at best, and many will be so covered with guano as to be indistinguishable anyway.

Since big ships depend on radar and other electronic positioning devices, lighthouses tend to receive the same lack of attention; their reliability is nowhere near as important as it once was. So never be upset if you fail to see a light you had planned to use in your overnight sailing.

Navigation Equipment

In the clockwise circuit of the Caribbean we have just described, most of your navigation will be in the coastwise category, and since the offshore legs are generally less than 300 miles, a carefully maintained DR track should suffice to put you close to your target, especially if you are in a powerboat or sailing steadily off the wind. Upwind sailing, particularly with head or crosscurrents to contend with, is another matter, however, and we recommend that every sailboat carry a sextant, even if you are only able to cope with noon sights for latitude. After all, that was the only technique known to seamen until the perfection of the chronometer.

In the choice of electronic navigation equipment, every yacht cruising the Caribbean should have at least a depth finder and an RDF set. At the other extreme, either Omega or Loran-C would be the ultimate if the budget can stand it. Despite its imprecision and the problem of getting readouts near sunrise and sunset, Loran-A is a useful tool for the long hops, but this system is being phased out in mid-1980 in favor of the more accurate and more expensive Loran-C. Unfortunately, Loran-C has a glaring blank space in its skywave coverage, right in the middle of the western Caribbean where it might be most needed.

Since fog is nonexistent in the Bahamas and Caribbean, radar may seem unnecessary, but we well recall standing on and off the reef-strewn coast of Hispaniola during 30 hours of heavy rain and zero visibility when that bright orange picture of our position would have been very welcome indeed. Even in perfect weather, radar is a distinct boon every time you make a landfall; in fact, a radar set with moderate range, say 24 miles, coupled with a carefully kept DR track, should (with a depthfinder) be all the electronics you really need to find your way in Caribbean waters, especially among the high islands and along the mountainous coasts of the Spanish Main.

Radio Communications

Simply from a safety standpoint, we would not put to sea without radio; it's also nice to be aware of what's going on at home and fun to be able to keep in touch with friends you've made along the way. And there may be crew changes to be arranged and spare parts to be ordered and expedited.

With the AM bands (the old Double Sideband) being phased out in the U.S. in 1977 (1978 elsewhere) in favor of VHF-FM and Single Sideband, radio communications in the islands are in a state of flux. It should be remembered that the diligent Federal Communications Commission controls operations only in Puerto Rico and the U.S. Virgins, so that DSB use in other, uncontrolled parts of the Caribbean is apt to carry on for an indeterminate period.

In addition to the universal frequencies of 2182, 2638, and 2738 kHz in the AM bands, you may want to consider the following crystals, depending on the capacity of your set to accept them and your intended cruising areas:

2198 kHz—Nassau marine operator (VPN2).
2009 kHz—St. Thomas marine operator (WAH).
2030 kHz—Virgin Islands working frequency, replacing 2638 kHz for the "Children's Hour."
2527 kHz—The working frequency used by all yachts and shore facilities up and down the Windwards and Leewards.

If you already have an AM set, don't let it out of your hands, because it is the only way to maintain adequate communication with other yachts and shore stations in the area covered by this Guide. SSB is useful only for calling the States through WOM in Miami and the High Seas Operator; the service is excellent for that purpose, but you will be out of range most of the time on the commonly used ship-to-ship and ship-to-shore frequencies in the A3 mode.

For keeping in touch with the States through WOM, you will want channels 4-1 and 8-1 if you cruise as far as the Virgins, Jamaica, or Roatán, and 13-1 if you want to be sure to get through when cruising farther afield. Having WOM also enables you to receive the weather forecasts for the Caribbean and the Gulf of Mexico at 0500, 1100, 1700, and 2200 Greenwich Mean Time.

If you have an SSB set, which is inherently low-powered, you will have discovered that the AM channels 2182, 2638, and 2738 kHz have extremely limited range, so that in an emergency in a remote sea area, your chances of being heard on 2182 kHz are just a matter of luck. Until the U.S. Coast Guard switches to SSB and begins to monitor one or more channels, you can reach them over long distances only through WOM.

Before you can legally have SSB aboard, you are required to have a VHF-FM set that operates in the 156-162 mHz range. Because of its clarity, freedom from interference, uncomplicated installation, and low power drain, VHF-FM holds the greatest promise for short-range communication between yachts and shore facilities. Between yachts, especially sailing yachts with masthead antennas, excellent reception is assured to about 22–24 miles; if you are talking to a shore station with an antenna atop an island mountain peak, reception at 50–80 miles is not unusual.

Besides the mandatory VHF-FM channels 16 and 06, we suggest 68, which has become common aboard yachts for intership and ship-to-shore talking. Although the pattern is slow and not very uniform in its development, marinas and yacht clubs tend to select 09 or 69 for their working frequency. Marine operator service is available on channel 26 via WAH in St. Thomas and North Post Radio (9YL) on the northeast coast of Trinidad.

Insurance

This subject is very much in the hot-potato category, since there are no specific guidelines under which yacht underwriters operate, and they are all very individualistic in their thinking.

When they come to assessing their risk, your own experience and competence is extremely important to them, since you will be voyaging long distances in open ocean and in relatively primitive areas far removed from repair facilities. Assuming you have proved yourself experienced and resourceful through your previous record as a policyholder, your first step toward widening the cruising limits of your policy should be to present to your broker a detailed plan of your cruising intentions, including the countries and ports you will visit, and when; where and when you will lay up out of commission, if at all, and where your boat will be during the hurricane season.

Depending on political conditions at the time, underwriters may look with disfavor on certain countries, even to the point of suspending insurance if you enter one that happens to be on their current blacklist. In the recent past, Haiti, the Dominican Republic, and Grenada have been in this category.

The more complete your plan and the more knowledge of the Caribbean and its pitfalls you can display, the more reasonable your premium is apt to be. If, for instance, you have recognized certain problems and show that you have added certain gear and equipment or taken other logical steps to counter them, your plan will find favor.

If this sounds as if you must plead your case before an underwriter, that's exactly what happens! Yet you will or should have thought out all such details anyway, so it is just a matter of pulling it all together for a condensed presentation. As one broker said to us, "Any indication of knowledge is good!" Remember that the underwriter wants your premium as much as you want his insurance, but he wants his commitment to be safe. After all, there are not so many far-ranging cruising people that his business will be seriously affected if he turns down a few applications or occasionally makes himself uncompetitive.

Ship's Paperwork

You will, of course, be sure that your numbering certificate, or license-of-vessel if it is documented, is up to date. You should also review the renewal procedure if renewal will come up in the course of your cruise. Those papers are essential when you return to the U.S., but we've noted that foreign officials seem little interested in the license or document and tend to zero in on the crew list.

The crew list should contain names and middle initials, where and when born, citizenship, passport number (if any), and rating aboard the yacht, i.e., mate, cook, stewardess, and so on. Never list any of the ship's company as passengers; this implies commercialism and may complicate the procedures and cause extra charges. Since you will have to give up two or more copies in each country you enter, it's a good idea to run off a batch of these lists when you have access to a copy machine.

To foreign officials, the next most important paper (called *zarpe* in Spanish) is your clearance document from your last port. This is why it is so important to "clear" as well as "enter" in each country. You will have to do this about thirty times if you run the whole circle of the Bahamas and the Caribbean, and you'll also have to check in with officials in each and every major port in some of the fussy countries. All of this becomes tiresome, annoying, and occasionally costly; sometimes it involves detouring or backtracking if the official port of entry happens to lie beyond the harbor where you want to put in for the night. You must, for example, enter St. Lucia at Castries before you can anchor at Pigeon Island. Unfortunately, this routine is just one of the facts of the cruising life.

To be correct, you must enter at a port of entry (which we indicate in the appropriate sections of this guide), drop anchor, hoist your Q flag and courtesy flag, and await developments. Incidentally, do maintain a complete inventory of courtesy ensigns, because some officials take real offense when they see a yacht without one. In fact, we have even heard of fines being levied for this oversight. If the whole town knows you are there and why, and nothing happens after a reasonable time, the master will probably be safe in going ashore with his papers to seek out the officials. However, he should instruct his crew to stay on board. Where we or others have observed the routines in various ports, we have reported them in the appropriate sections, but even so, you may run afoul of the law, depending on the individual who happens to be in charge at the time.

For instance, when *Yellow Bird* and her sister ship, *Gitano*, entered Cozumel early one morning, their Q flags flapping at the starboard yardarms, we skippers settled down to a leisurely breakfast, then waited at least an hour before hiring a taxi to go to the office of the Port Captain nearer town. Upon completing our business there, we returned to our yachts to find three uniformed, armed, and impatient officers itching to put us under arrest for going ashore without permission, despite the fact that in every other port in Mexico it had been the practice for the skipper to go ashore with the papers. So it seems that you cannot always make yourself conveniently available to the officials and be correct at the same time. In this Cozumel incident, our friends aboard *Gitano* were fluent in Spanish and the confrontation was soon straightened out with smiles all around.

There is, however, very good reason for all this madness: the smuggling of drugs is now a very urgent problem throughout the Caribbean. That reminds us of the case of a powerboat, stolen in Palm Beach, that had been left at Chub

Cay in the Berry Islands when we happened to be there. The thieves had had no problem entering at Chub because they were able to produce the ship's papers. They said they would return to pick up the boat, but apparently were scared off, or maybe the boat had already served their illicit purposes. In any case, the moral of that story is never to leave your ship's papers where they can be easily found.

Personal Documents

Although passports are not specifically required by many of the countries you are likely to visit, we strongly urge that you and each of your crew carry one, for then there can be no question of your identity. Otherwise, you will have to carry positive proof of citizenship—in the case of a U.S.-born person, a birth or baptismal certificate or an expired passport. A naturalized citizen should carry his certificate of naturalization; a person born outside the U.S. should have a State Department Certificate of Birth. For extended cruising, we think a passport is easier in the end.

Immigration regulations are always subject to change, but in 1974 the U.S. State Department advised that the following countries required visitors to have passports: Canary Islands, Colombia, Costa Rica, Dominican Republic, Honduras, Jamaica, Nicaragua, Panama, and Venezuela.

Tourist cards are issued to visitors for limited stays in Guatemala, Haiti, and Mexico. The other Caribbean countries are said to permit entry upon proof of citizenship, but we must emphasize that the requirements as interpreted by a major official in a minor port may be quite different from the official requirements at a major international airport. If difficulties develop, you cannot win through bluff or argument, especially when faced with a language barrier, but you may gain your point through a smiling and conciliatory attitude or perhaps a discreet tip.

For long stays in any country, different regulations usually apply. Check the embassy or a consulate of the country involved.

Except in rare cases when you are acting on respected current advice, we do not recommend that you go to the trouble of obtaining papers to enter a certain country by going to one of their consulates in the U.S. or elsewhere. The procedure is time-consuming and frequently costly—and the papers are not likely to carry much weight at the other end.

Occasionally a country will require an International Certificate of Vaccination against yellow fever.

Since you may want to rent a car, bring your driver's license. They are valid wherever we have been, although in some places (such as Barbados and Antigua) a local operator's license will be issued and a fee charged, presumably in deference to the local taxi organization.

To stay out of trouble, do not sign on any seagoing hitchhikers. If you do, be sure of their background and carefully examine their personal documents. Remember that as master you are responsible for a member of your crew with inadequate or false papers; remember too that most countries do not allow you to discharge a crew member who does not carry an onward or return air ticket. Keep in mind particularly that drug-running is a very real menace all over this area and has brought about yacht hijackings and several mysterious missing-at-sea cases. In fact, the U.S. Coast Guard now urges yachts in the Bahamas and Caribbean to be sure to keep some trusted person aware of their itinerary and crew complement, to be wary of calls for assistance in apparent distress situations, and to report such circumstances by radio before being lured into a possible trap.

When you have changes in your crew list (friends arriving to replace others, for instance), make this situation clear to the immigration officials at the port where the changes will take place. Also, be sure your incoming friends have round-trip tickets, subject of course to refund later. Otherwise they may not be able to talk their way past the immigration desk at the airport.

Dogs and Cats

Animals from home or picked up en route have become members of many a yacht's company. Some cruising people think they're a nuisance, which they can be; others appreciate their trusting and usually quiet companionship in all sorts of places and all sorts of weather. To bring a pet along is a choice for some; for others there's really no choice at all.

Unfortunately, island people develop insular attitudes, one of them being a lurking fear of animal diseases, such as rabies, which might come to their island by way of some pestilential animal from a disease-ridden mainland. Thus, on some islands pets are definitely banned; a few easy-going places have no restrictions at all; others have prohibitions that are not necessarily enforced; still others admit pets under certain stipulations that may or may not be enforced, depending on where you enter and who's in charge at the time. From country to country, we have found these regulations even harder to nail down than the entry requirements relating to the human species.

So this is definitely a grey area—but we *can* state that the French islands of Guadeloupe and Martinique present no problem, whereas most of the formerly British islands do not allow transient dogs or cats ashore under any circumstances. This is the case at Antigua, St. Kitts, Nevis, St. Lucia, St. Vincent, Trinidad and Tobago, Barbados, and Grand Cayman. Grenada requires a prior permit from the Ministry of Agriculture in St. George's (at least there is no blanket prohibition). Bermuda requires a health certificate issued no later than 10 days before arrival and a rabies vaccination certificate not over a year

old. You are also supposed to have obtained prior written permission. The Bahamas will give you no trouble if you have a health certificate issued no later than 24 hours before arrival (which is sometimes a neat trick for a slow boat or one delayed by weather) as well as a rabies vaccination certificate. Lacking the required papers, you may or may not be able to satisfy the authorities by saying you won't let the pet ashore.

Pets are not allowed ashore at all in Panama and the Canal Zone.

Puerto Rican regulations call for a health certificate and rabies vaccination certificate dated not more than 10 days and 30 days, respectively, before departure to the island, while the U.S. Virgins require the usual health certificate plus a certificate indicating a rabies vaccination not less than 2 weeks nor more than 6 months prior to arrival.

Before entering the British Virgins, request a permit by writing to the Chief Agricultural Officer at Road Town, Tortola. Enclose an up-to-date health certificate.

Elsewhere, the regulations almost invariably stipulate certificates of rabies vaccination within 6 months to a year, together with a health certificate, and some call for prior permission or signatures from a consulate, or both (for a fee, of course).

As far as the leisurely cruising yachtsman is concerned, these regulations are more easily written out than complied with. He can only hope that the officials will be reasonable in his case, bearing in mind that the rules are directed primarily toward imported livestock and the flying tourist's pet. In any case, it is obvious that wherever you cruise, your pet must have a health certificate issued at your point of departure from the States, and a certificate to prove its rabies vaccination, dated as recently as possible. We suggest you also carry a statemer that the animal has not been exposed to rabies within the last 6 months. route, wherever you may find reliable veterinary services we advise that a f health certificate be obtained and the rabies vaccination renewed if nece$

All of the above is for the sake of officialdom. For your dog's sake, we $ recommend a daily dosage of one of the standard medicines for c heartworm, a usually fatal disease carried by mosquitos and theref lent almost everywhere. Cats seem to be immune.

Electricity

Heavy dependence on electricity is a mistake. Anchoring and shore power, where it is available at all, is likely to b load imposed on the dock's wiring. Since bottled g everywhere, cooking need not depend on electricity. P user of precious amps and so vital in warm climes.

heavy-duty compressor system, belt-driven by the main engine for a few hours a day, that stores cold by means of eutectic plates in a heavily insulated custom cabinet. We first saw such refrigeration systems in the West Indies ten years ago, and they have been popular there ever since.

Down among the islands, variations in voltage and frequency are more the rule than the exception. To avoid damage to motors, large yachts that depend heavily on shore power would do well to install a separate transformer through which the incoming voltage can be adjusted to the normal 115 or 230 volts. It should be remembered that battery chargers, even though they may be rated for 50 to 60 cycles, do not operate at the same efficiency at the lower frequency. Some makes of charger are more sensitive than others in this respect; in fact, some will not function at all at the 50 cycles common in the formerly British islands.

Standing Watches

The tedium of watchkeeping on steady passages of two days or more can be mitigated by instituting a watch list, so that each member of the crew can plan his or her days' eating, sleeping, reading, odd jobs, or just plain loafing. Somehow the time seems to slip by more easily when the yacht runs on a fixed schedule.

We have found the following watch lists comfortable for 3-man or 4-man crews in which one member, whom we list as "C", does all the cooking and consequently spends only about half as much time on watch.

3-MAN	1200 1530	1530 1730	1730 2200	2200 2400	0000 0400	0400 0800	0800 0900	0900 1100	1100 1200
1st day	A	C	B	C	A	B	C	A	B
alternate day	B	C	A	C	B	A	C	B	A

4-MAN	1200 1500	1500 1700	1700 2000	2000 2300	2300 0200	0200 0600	0600 1000	1000 1100	1100 1200
1st day	X	C	B	A	B	X	A	C	B
alternate day	B	C	X	A	X	B	A	C	X

In the 3-man list, A and B stand 9½ hours each per day and the cook 5 hours. The 4-man routine, A, B, and X each stand 7 hours and the cook only 3 hours.

Mooring

Outside of the Bahamas and the Virgins, you'll very seldom find marinas with larger piers and handy pilings. Nor will you be inclined to go alongside

commercial docks, because of dirty walls and pilings or a heavy surge. This means you will have to get used to docking as it has been done in the Mediterranean for centuries: you set a bow anchor out and then back down so your stern is a couple of feet from the pier or quayside and your stern lines crossed.

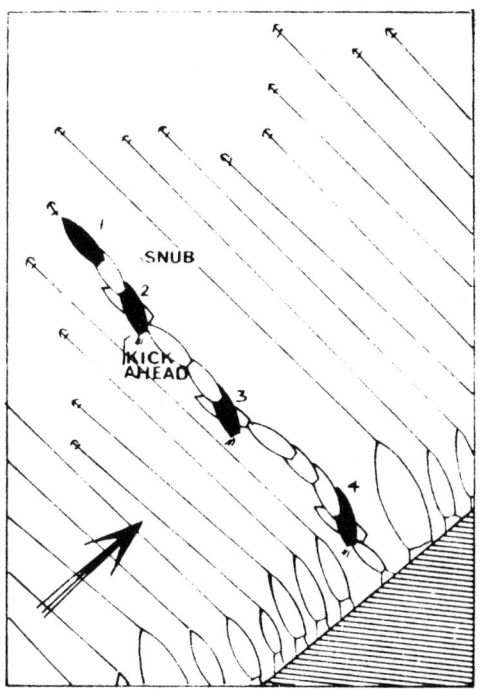

The Mediterranean moor

Ordinarily this is a simple maneuver, except for judging the distance off for setting your anchor. You will do well to overestimate this rather than underestimate it. Calculate your scope using the HW depth multiplied by at least 5 with chain and 7 with rope. Actually, we like to drag the anchor under power for the last 10–15 feet to be sure it's securely set.

In a crosswind, this can be tricky, but here again you had best overallow for leeway, since you can always pause during the maneuver to let the wind straighten you out. Normally the bow will fall off more than the stern, in which case you snub your rode temporarily to straighten her up. This is an especially useful tactic with an auxiliary, which will seldom back straight anyway.

In the Mediterranean, stern gangplanks (usually collapsible) are standard equipment, with sturdy swivel fittings at the transom, rollers or wheels for the pier end, and an adjustable topping lift for raising the gangplank clear of the pier at night or under surge and wave conditions. For some reason, this very convenient apparatus is seldom seen in the Caribbean. If you think you can get by with some kind of jury rig like an old plank, a swimming ladder, or a network of stern lines, you will be following the crowd, but for convenience as well as safety we recommend fitting a substantial gangplank before you leave the States.

Medical Matters

The size of its cruising area should also be a measure of the size of a small ship's medicine chest—not only for the sake of the crew but for those you find along the way, from a Panamanian native on a faraway islet with a badly slashed foot to a professional skipper with a debilitating case of Montezuma's Revenge.

Here is what we have aboard *Yellow Bird*. Use it as a basis for discussion with your own doctor, who in any case will have to prescribe some of it:

Common Remedies
Solarcaine spray (for sunburn and other painful skin conditions)
Tincture of merthiolate, 1:1000
Phisoderm (antibacterial cleanser for wounds)
Sodium bicarbonate (antacid)
Boric acid powder
Eye drops
BFI first-aid powder
Milk of magnesia tablets
Aromatic ammonia, capsules or spirits
Fleet enemas
Seasickness remedies
Bacitracin ointment (for superficial infections)
Aspirin

Prescription Medications
Polycillin, 250 mg. (for respiratory tract infections)
Benadryl antihistamine (one 3-4 times a day)
Hydrocortisone, 1% topical ointment (for skin allergies)

Azulfidine, 0.5 gm. (for dysentery)
Bismuth-paregoric-pectin tablets (for mild dysentery)
Gantrisin, 0.5 gm. (for cystitis)
Gantrisin opthalmic ointment (for "pink eye")
Codeine, ½-grain (for pain, every four hours)
Decadron tablets (for bursitis)
Darvon (for pain)

Instruments and Supplies
Fever thermometers
Resusitube
Eye cup
Scissors
Butterfly closures
Ace bandages
Gauze bandages and pads, large assortment
Adhesive tape
Band-Aids, large assortment
Petrolatum gauze (for burns)
Vaseline dressings (for burns)
Cotton balls

A comprehensive first-aid manual should of course be a part of every yacht's library.

No matter how inviting they may seem, avoid washing or swimming in slow-moving fresh-water streams or pools in Hispaniola, Puerto Rico, Martinique, St. Lucia (except the hot sulphur springs at Soufrière), and Guadeloupe. Although the whole Caribbean area is considered suspect, these islands in particular are known to harbor a debilitating parasitic disease called bilharziasis; its scientific name is *Schistosomiasis mansoni.* It derives from human or animal feces and requires hosting by snails that collect in slow-moving water. The larvae of such infected snails can penetrate the human skin to spread the disease through the blood stream; it eventually affects the liver in particular.

Everybody knows enough not to eat the fruit of the manchineel tree, but not that it drips its poison, too. Don't stand under one in the rain!

White sea urchins can be eaten, but the black ones are dangerous to touch and, unfortunately, all too prevalent in some of the most inviting swimming areas. If you tangle with one of these seagoing porcupines, you won't have to rush for the medicine chest, because the antidote is handy wherever you are. A quick application of urine will do wonders; its acid will neutralize the nitrogen in the urchin's poison.

Ciguatera was the term given to fish poisoning back in the days of Columbus, and it has ever since been a recognized health problem all over the eastern Caribbean and (to a lesser extent) the Bahamas. The greatest number of cases from the greatest variety of fish are reported in the Virgins and the other islands north of Antigua. The disease is not well understood, but is thought to be caused by toxin present in algae ingested by the fish—any species of fish. However, barracuda and amberjack are most often blamed, owing to their heavy diet of smaller, possibly toxin-carrying fish. The principal symptoms of fish-poisoning are vomiting, cramps and diarrhea, a tingling sensation in the face and extremities, and pain and weakness in the joints. The best treatment is to induce vomiting.

Spares

Before you leave the mainland of abundance for the islands of scarcity, make sure you are adequately equipped with the things that no amount of ingenuity or talent with tools can replace. Make a careful study of the systems aboard your boat and, in a purposefully pessimistic frame of mind, consider the possible failures, item by item, that could delay your cruise and bring expensive consequences. Never mind if it seems to be a part or assembly beyond your capability to fix; you may very well find someone with sufficient experience to do the job, but he will be helpless if he doesn't have the parts.

Remember that customs duties are the primary source of tax income for many of the islands, so that importations are a costly business. The nature of the rates are such that some cajoling and perhaps a little bribery may be needed to obtain the most favorable one for your particular case. Then, when you add in radiotelephone charges, air-freight, agency fees, and impatience and anxiety, you will probably conclude that a generous stock of spare parts is good insurance for your peace of mind as well as your pocketbook.

Following is a checklist of items we consider essential to the spare-parts lockers of a well-found boat. If at first it seems excessive, think carefully about each potential trouble spot before you delete anything. On the other hand, if the list suggests additional things you think you might need, by all means pick them up before you depart.

Engine
Alternator
Regulator
Starter solenoid
Starter assembly (or at least the clutch and spring unit)
Injectors or spark plugs
Washers for injectors
Water-pump assembly (or at least a repair kit) with impellers
Copper tubing for fuel lines (with cutting and flanging tools)
Oil-filter elements
Fuel-filter elements
Air-cleaner elements
Instrument gauges (water temperature, oil pressure, and so on)
Zincs for cooling system
Gasket kit
Fuel pump
Thermostat
Radiator hose
Drive belts

Sailing Gear and Rigging
Winch handles
Halliards, made up with fittings
Wire forestay and backstay, made up with fittings
Shackles
Turnbuckles
Mast tangs
Cotter pins
Baggeywrinkle
Sailcloth (dacron-canvas repair panels)
Assorted rope for running rigging

Electrical
Battery (with acid and distilled water)
Battery terminals
Assorted wire (with cutting and crimping tool)
Assorted terminals and connectors
Tape
Fuses or circuit breakers
Lamps
Running lights (replacement housing or assembly)

Plumbing
Water-pressure-system pump, complete
Assorted hose
Hose clamps
Bilge-pump diaphragms
Water-heater element
Assorted "O" rings
For toilets: joker valve, impeller, seals, gaskets, complete pump assembly

Electronic

Spares kit for radar (by manufacturer)

Spares kit for autopilot (by manufacturer)

Fuses

Flasher lamp for depthfinder

Refrigeration

Freon gas in 1-lb. cans (built-in valve required in system)

Brushes for compressor motor

Drier

Solenoid valve

Drive belt

For Twin-screw Powerboats

Pair of handed propellers (with puller tool)

Shaft

Strut

Deck Equipment

Docklines

At least 2 spare anchors (preferably of different types)

Spare anchor rode (250 feet)

Fenders and fender board

Wiper blades

PART I

Routes to the Caribbean

CHAPTER TWO

Passaging from the U.S. East Coast

The Choice of Route

Whatever the points of departure or destination of an offshore passage, certain basics must be kept foremost in mind in choosing the route. Eric Hiscock sums them up in his book *Voyaging Under Sail:* "The essentials when planning a voyage are to make the greatest use of fair winds and avoid dangerously bad weather by choosing a suitable course and being in the right place at the right time."

Making maximum use of fair winds is a relatively simple matter once you reach the Caribbean, where the NE trades blow with predictable regularity much of the year. But it's not so simple to select the right route at the right time for a small-boat passage to the Caribbean in the often unpredictable North Atlantic. Particularly careful planning is required for a successful passage from the East Coast, where weather conditions in the Bermuda-Hatteras region are controlling factors much of the year. Those who embark casually with dreams of sailing off into the sunrise are due for a rude awakening unless they have diligently studied their Pilot Charts and alternative routes.

Every seasoned mariner benefits from the experiences of other sailors. Sir Francis Chichester prepared himself for his epic single-handed circumnavigation by reading every log and printed account of sailing over the clipper-ship routes that he could lay his hands on. Skippers who are serious about taking the sea lanes to the Caribbean will do well to follow his example. Too often, bad advice is picked up along the waterfront at the last minute before departure, leading to mistakes that cannot be corrected once you are on your own offshore. On the other hand, with careful advance planning, there is no reason why a well-found boat, starting at the right time of the year on a suitable route with a competent crew, cannot make a successful passage to the islands.

In the following pages, we have made extensive use of logs and published records of many yachts that made successful voyages as a result of sound planning and seamanlike execution. We cite other passages that turned out less successfully—or disastrously, in a few cases—either because the boat was unsuitable for that kind of voyage, or the crew was ill-prepared, or because it was the wrong time of year to attempt that particular route.

In planning a departure from the northeast coast of the United States or Canada, your first decision must be whether to make a direct offshore passage to your chosen destination in the Caribbean, or whether to begin your voyage with a coastwise or Intracoastal Waterway passage to more southerly departure points. Several basic factors will determine the initial choice, the most important being: (1) suitability and readiness of your boat and crew for an offshore passage, (2) how much time you can afford to spend getting to your destination, and (3) whether you can get away at the time of year best suited for the course of your choice. Once these decisions have been made, you will be ready to consider alternative departure points and destinations, and to look more closely into the route options that are best for different times of the year. For those who have time for extended cruising, the options may be more numerous than one would suspect; they include several offshore routes, either direct or by way of Bermuda, and a number of alternative island-hopping routes for the cruising skipper who can afford to plan a more leisurely schedule through the Bahamas and along the coasts of Hispaniola.

If one is planning an offshore passage from anywhere north of Cape Hatteras, weather conditions, timing, and good judgment are the primary ingredients of a successful voyage. Unfortunately, it's not always convenient to leave at the time most suitable for an easy passage south—spring and early summer, when cruising happens to be at its best in northern coastal waters. Conversely, late autumn, when most cruising skippers feel the strongest urge to head south, is apt to be just the wrong time. And those who postpone their departure to winter months are asking for trouble, if not inviting disaster.

Bill Robinson, writing in the August, 1969, issue of *Yachting*, rightly warned that departure for southern waters via the offshore route is foolhardy in the late fall and early winter. Reviewing seasonal weather patterns, he states:

> The only really good season for passage in a small yacht . . . is late spring and early summer, and even here there can be freak storms or out-of-character weather, such as the hurricane that delayed the start of the 1968 Bermuda race by one day. From midsummer on, hurricanes have to be considered. Many a lucky voyager has skipped between them, but their usual track out of the Caribbean is to parallel the North American continent between the mainland and Bermuda. True, modern reporting methods give many days' warning in most cases, but sometimes things develop too rapidly and the storm starts moving too fast for a small boat to clear the danger area.

The hurricane season begins to taper off in late October, and by November the percentage incidence of tropical storms has dropped to 3 percent, as noted on page 8, but before the end of November, autumn gales take over quickly, followed by winter conditions that are highly unfavorable, if not dangerous, for an offshore passage in the North Atlantic. Winter passages from New York or New England ports should be ruled out as too hazardous for most small yachts from December through March, when the chances of escaping a combination of gale-force winds and freezing cold somewhere north of Bermuda and east of Hatteras are slim indeed.

Coast Guard search and rescue files contain the records of many yachts lost during winter gales on the North Atlantic track to the West Indies. Scarcely a year passes without the loss or disappearance of one or more vessels, and there need be no mystery about the so-called "Bermuda Triangle," where weather-breeding conditions alone are sufficient to explain most of such losses.

These seasonal weather patterns leave two periods in which conditions are likely to be especially favorable for offshore passage-making: the spring and early summer months mentioned by Bill Robinson, and a brief period in the fall between the end of the hurricane season and the onset of winter gales. Both periods offer a variety of route options.

OFFSHORE COURSES AND DISTANCES

Distances are considerably less important than winds, currents, and regional weather conditions in planning your course, whatever the time of year. In spring and early summer, yachts starting from New York or New England may find it to their advantage to detour by way of Bermuda, breaking the long, direct passage with a stopover for provisions and perhaps a change of crew. The extra distance is slight, and a favorable wind slant at the outset may get you across the Gulf Stream sooner and give you the easting you'll need to pick up the NE trades south of Bermuda. The basic objective is to reach the vicinity of 65° W and 25° N as expeditiously as possible, taking advantage of the westerlies at the outset and hopefully avoiding calms and head winds in the variable belt before the trades set in.

The direct distance between New York and St. Thomas is about 1,400 nautical miles, and there's very little difference whether you start from New London, Newport, or any departure point west of Cape Cod. Bermuda is only about 160 miles east of the rhumb line for St. Thomas, and if you are lucky enough to pick up northerly or westerly winds, the longer route might prove to be faster.

The traditional course for the Bermuda race is 635 miles from Brenton Reef Light to St. David's Head, with the larger classes usually finishing in 3½ to 4 days, the smaller yachts in 4 to 5½ days, and a few stragglers requiring up to 6 days. Not everyone races to Bermuda, however, and the average cruising

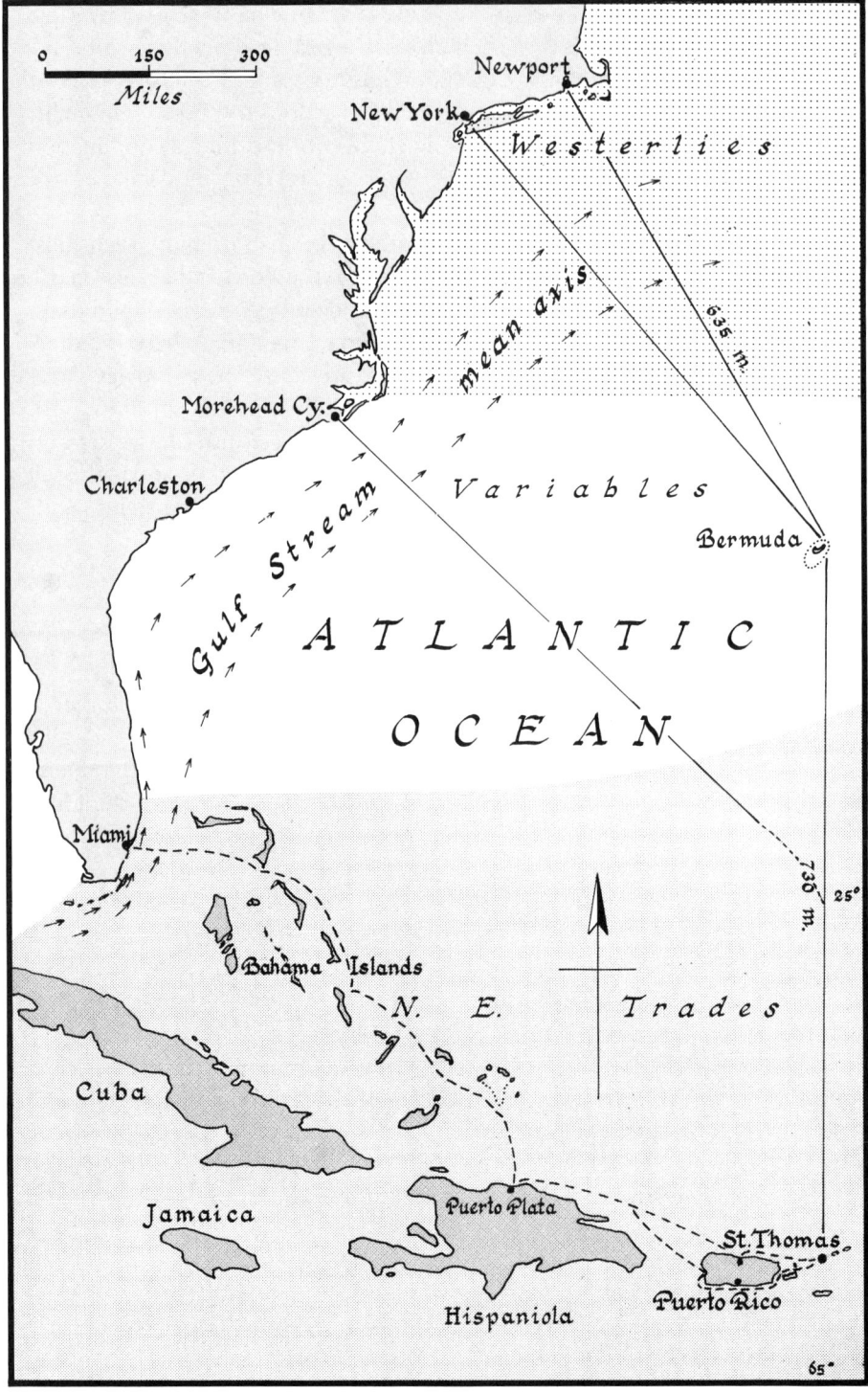

auxiliary is almost sure to take longer, even with the use of power in periods of calm that may be encountered in spring and summer. Six to 8 days is not unusual, even for a well-sailed 30-to-40-foot auxiliary that encounters several days of calm or squalls and head winds in the Gulf Stream.

Even the racing fleet often has a rough time crossing the Gulf Stream. The Bermuda–Azores high, with its clockwise circulation of air, gives no assurance of constant winds once you reach the Stream, the northern edge of which lies about 170 to 180 miles southeasterly of Newport. Frequent squalls and sudden windshifts are more often the rule than the exception where the warm waters of the Stream meet the cold waters of the North Atlantic, and low-pressure disturbances have given the ocean racers trouble more than once in recent years. Under such conditions, small cruising auxiliaries, often sailing with a family crew, may have problems in the Stream and even have some difficulty locating Bermuda or making a successful landfall when visibility is poor.

Most cruising boats plan to make their landfall off St. David's Head, as the ocean racers do. However, this can be dangerous in stormy weather, as the

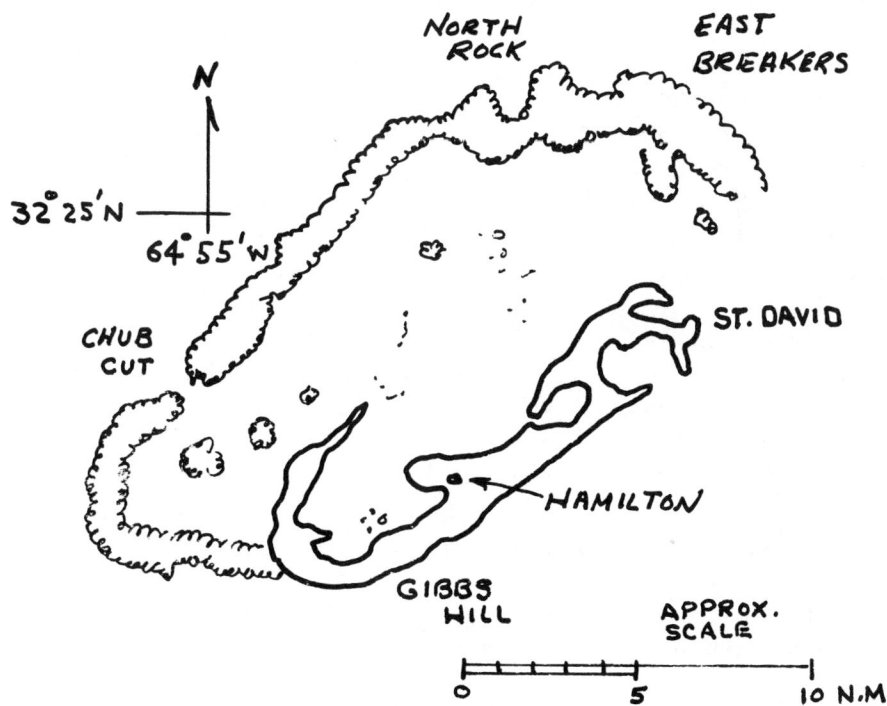

BERMUDA

racing fleet itself discovered in the 1972 race; three boats were dismasted in high winds and mountainous seas close to the reefs that rise steeply from the 100-fathom curve. A dozen other boats withdrew or failed to finish that race, and under similar conditions, most cruising boats would be well advised to stand clear of the islands and their dangerous reefs until conditions have improved. When visibility is good, it is not too difficult to sight Bermuda's two powerful lights at night, or to establish a radio fix from the RDF signals at Gibb's Hill and Kindley Field before sighting land. Cruising skippers visiting Bermuda for the first time should study their *Sailing Directions* carefully before entering St. George's or Hamilton Harbour, both of which may be reached through connecting channels leading from The Narrows at the northeast end of the island group.

The course from Bermuda to St. Thomas is almost due S, about 750 miles on the rhumb line, with variable winds for almost half the way until you pick up the NE trades between 25° and 22° N. latitude. With a little luck and the use of power in periods of calm, cruising boats usually manage to reach Virgin Island Passage between Culebra and St. Thomas in 6 or 7 days under favorable conditions in spring and early summer. When you reach the trades, it can be a glorious reach in May or June, and often into July if long-range weather predictions indicate no hurricanes in the Caribbean. But don't attempt such a passage in August or September, when tropical storms are always a threat and may come up without sufficient warning to take evasive action. In his *Cruising Guide to the Lesser Antilles*, Donald M. Street recalls one year "when a hurricane formed due E of Anguilla and flattened that island before *any* warning was sent out. There was so little advance notice that boats in St. Thomas harbor did not even have time to get to Hurricane Hole, St. John, only 20 miles away."

Long-range weather predictions cannot always be trusted for offshore passages; freak storms may develop quickly at any time, especially during the fall and winter months. In late October and November, many amateur skippers and professional yacht-delivery captains prefer to make short coastwise passages from New York or New England to Norfolk, and then run down the Intracoastal Waterway to Morehead City, N.C., or Charleston, S.C., before jumping off for St. Thomas or other destinations in the islands. Of course, under the right conditions, it is also possible to make successful voyages starting from Chesapeake Bay, although on that course you have Cape Hatteras and its outlying shoals under your lee, which can be dangerous in a northeast blow.

Looking over the logs of vessels we have known or sailed aboard leads us to the conclusion that there is really no such thing as a "normal" passage at any time of the year. There are records of fast passages and slow passages, of uneventful voyages and hazardous voyages, during the same periods year after year. A few examples follow of what we have experienced or been told over the years.

Starting from Annapolis, Md., two experienced sailor friends of ours, John Miles and Al Hinnegan, departed from the Chesapeake in early November a few years ago for St. Thomas. After a slow start (it took them 30 hours to reach Norfolk), they picked up a fresh southwesterly breeze that carried them safely past Hatteras directly on course for the Virgins. The westerlies held until they picked up the NE trades about 30 hours before reaching the Virgins—8 days and 12 hours from Cape Henry. Two years later, Hinnegan and two other Chesapeake sailors, Russell Potter and Whitney Dodge, attempting to take a 33-foot fiberglass sloop from Newport, R.I., to the Virgins in December, lost their lives in a winter gale in the North Atlantic. Hinnegan's body was recovered by the Coast Guard cutter *McCullock* 39 days after their departure, following a search by Coast Guard, Navy, and Air Force planes that had spent 980 hours covering 589,000 square miles of the North Atlantic.

Many fast and safe passages have been made from Morehead City and Charleston to St. Thomas, a distance of about 1,200 miles, in 7 or 8 days. But not all such voyages are successful. Early in November, 1970, the staunchly-built, 52-foot classic schooner *Integrity* departed from Morehead City with favorable long-range forecasts for a passage to the Virgin Islands. With a professional skipper and delivery crew aboard, she was quickly overtaken by heavy weather south of Cape Hatteras. Knocked down and rolled completely over by a mammoth maverick sea, she was dismasted, lost some of her hatches, took on water, and eventually was abandoned when the Yugoslav freighter *Belakraina* came alongside and offered to remove the captain and crew. The offer was accepted and *Integrity* was left a derelict. She was picked up later by a converted Brixham-trawler yacht about 150 miles northeast of the island of Grand Turk and towed to that port for salvage.

Aubrey Graves, a Chesapeake yachtsman, sailed from Morehead City on October 19, 1970, for the Virgins with equally favorable weather forecasts, planning to take his 45-foot Nova Scotia schooner *Haligonian* on the generally preferred course, ESE for about 600 miles to the 65th meridian, where the NE trades are supposed to carry one due S to St. Thomas. *Haligonian,* like *Integrity*, ran into gale winds south of Hatteras, but with less serious consequences. When she began to take water and the main electric bilge pump burned out, the prospect of beating offshore for possibly another 10 days or so seemed less and less attractive the more the crew pondered it. Good judgment prevailed, and a quick but painful decision was made to head back toward the coast under reefed main and jib. Finally, under jib alone, they made a safe but exposed nighttime anchorage in the lee of Frying Pan Shoal, where the Coast Guard advised them to await daylight before entering Cape Fear River.

Delivery skippers, who have been taking yachts to the islands at all seasons for a number of years now, have developed much practical information from their experiences. One of them is Bruce Cameron, who began deliveries for Patrick

Ellam, Inc., in 1970, making a number of noteworthy passages that led him to reevaluate various routes and departure dates.

Writing in *Yachting* (August, 1971) Cameron noted that "during the fall migration that year many boats experienced particularly grueling weather, and the islands were full of salty tales of those who made it—and some who did not."

The following excerpts are from Cameron's notes on five passages all made during 1970 from different departure points:

New York—Morehead City—Tortola (Feb.–Mar.)

This winter passage in a Carib-41 was made in unusually good weather—2 days to Norfolk in a bone-chilling northwester, 3 days on the Waterway to Morehead City, and several days wait there for another NW breeze. Sailed the second leg to Tortola in 7 days, near record time, with the nor'wester carrying us to the Gulf Stream; but the remainder of the trip was a wet, gruelling fight to keep above the rhumb line, with winds from the east (Force 5).

New York—Bermuda—Tortola (June–July)

This summer trip, also made in a Carib-41, took 4 days to Bermuda under power much of the time in glassy calms, with fresh SW breeze on final day. The passage from Bermuda to Tortola was made in 7 days, starting with southerlies that carried us 150 miles E of the rhumb line on starboard tack; then picked up easterly trades sooner than usual and by 25° N we were reaching along in warm breezes normally found further south.

Morehead City—St. Thomas (November)

This fall passage was made in *Djinn*, a superb 63-foot S & S sloop, in 7 days after waiting 18 hours in Morehead to check weather with Coast Guard. Boats that had left a few days earlier had experienced moderate gales and a menacing low system was coming in from the west. With locally west winds, we decided to leave before the low arrived, reasoning that the westerly would carry us out to the Stream and *Djinn* being a fast passage-maker would be far offshore before the low system reached the Carolinas. The predictions held true. We carried the westerly beyond the Stream, when it increased to Force 6 and we reefed down for a night. We stayed E of the rhumb line and picked up the trades about 22.5° N.

Charleston—San Juan (Dec.–Jan.)

This winter delivery of a new Columbia 43 began further south than usual because of a weather pattern similar to that encountered with *Djinn*. Our wait in Charleston was 6 days, as unsettled conditions continued with a series of lows moving in from the west (one producing 60-70-knot winds). The National Weather Service office in Charleston was most helpful, making some sage predictions on our particular problem, with a real feeling for a sailor's concerns. They advised us to wait out the unsettled period when local conditions looked quite innocent. . . . When we finally took off the trip was slow: 30 hours of westerly winds which gradually decreased to motoring weather, eventually followed by SE winds, shifting more easterly about 21° and never exceeding Force 4. The trip took nearly 11 days.

In drawing conclusions, Bruce Cameron did not suggest any ideal route or schedule, but offered several basic recommendations:

A late spring or early summer departure makes for an easy and fast trip via Bermuda. School vacations ease the crew problem in this period.

Winter and indeed fall trips can be very hard. The trades are sometimes south of east and about 24° N. Get a lot of early easting. However, in the fall early southing is advisable to get out of the more gale-ridden middle Atlantic.

Care in getting a weather forecast before leaving is mandatory particularly in the "off" seasons. A look at a current map is invaluable. The National Weather Service is excellent for this information whereas the TV and newspaper maps may be outdated. Leaving when conditions are right, not on a schedule, requires more time. Thus the "off" season time for the trip is longer.

A radio contact with other yachts is useful. In the fall this is easy to establish with the many yachts leaving.

Have extra food and drink for at least 20 days total. Running out is not fun.

Carry as much fuel as possible and at least enough to get adequate sea room when leaving the Carolinas (two days worth).

Enjoy it! It is a great passage if you do it right.

From the viewpoint of the cruising skipper, a few additional comments on route selection may be in order. The professional captain and the amateur skipper have an identity of purpose only when each is expected to get from Point A to Point B as quickly as possible. The professional delivery captain usually is. But there are many situations in which the owner-skipper has choices not open to the delivery captain. For one, he can afford to wait longer for settled weather. He can change his plans more easily and choose another port of departure with greater freedom. If the outlook is poor for an offshore passage from Charleston he can continue down the Intracoastal to Florida and still have a chance to make his easting from the Bahamas. Finally, if time is not a controlling factor, he can consider an altogether different route by cruising southeast into the Caribbean through the Bahamas.

ROUTES VIA THE BAHAMAS

A number of interesting routes are available to the cruising skipper who is not pressed for time and can afford the luxury of leisurely island-hopping through the 600-mile chain of the Bahamas to Caicos, Grand Turk, or Great Inagua at the southern end of the chain, where he is only an overnight passage away from the north coast of Hispaniola. For those who cannot afford to tarry in the Bahamas, other options are open. Deep-water sailors may prefer a direct passage to San Juan or St. Thomas from departure points several hundred miles southeast of Florida.

The direct distance from Palm Beach or Miami to St. Thomas is approximately 1,000 miles, although the actual sailing track is substantially longer when you zig-zag through the islands or encounter headwinds much of the way on the offshore passages. Most yacht-delivery skippers avoid these routes because they are too time-consuming and are likely to prove a hard upwind battle. Yet there are often advantages for cruising boats that can wait for the right weather to start from a preferred departure point, and there are special rewards for those who can linger long enough in the Bahamas to savor the distinctive combination of bank and deepwater cruising in those lovely islands.

In this chapter, we are concerned with routes to the Caribbean from and through the Bahamas, rather than with descriptions of the individual islands. They are discussed in separate chapters of Part II covering the Bahamas, Caicos and Grand Turk, and Hispaniola on the Thorny Path to the Lesser Antilles. We have travelled the island-hopping routes under both sail and power, making the passage between Florida and the Virgin Islands in both directions and at different times of the year. We have made the eastbound passage in November and early December and encountered northeast winds that made it a close reach most of the way to Caicos and Hispaniola, but not the hard beat to windward one is likely to experience in late December or January. Furthermore, we have studied the logs of other vessels that followed much the same routes, and of some that made direct offshore passages from various departure points. The following is a synthesis of those experiences.

Northern and Central Bahamas to Virgin Islands

Many cruising boats have made successful passages from the northern and central Bahamas direct to the Virgins by waiting for a moderate norther to give them their necessary easting early in the voyage, making it possible to carry the NE trades all the way to their destination. Northers occur regularly from December through March. Some of them are too boisterous for comfort or safety in a small cruising boat; others, lighter at the start, may peter out before you are far enough east to pick up the trades. You can run offshore from any point in the Bahamas; the further south you depart the more likely you are to start with a light northerly that dies out entirely before the trades come in.

Abaco to the Virgin Islands

When we were at Man-O-War Cay in January, 1974, Stanley Livingston's 50-foot yawl *Manukai* was waiting for a norther to make a direct passage to the British Virgins, where her owner planned to join the Cruising Club of America, of which he was then vice-commodore, for its winter cruise in those islands. Unfortunately, a sudden death in the family prevented the owner from being aboard when the norther arrived in mid-January, and *Manukai* departed with a young but experienced crew. The breeze was relatively light at the outset but freshened as it moved around from N to NE, giving them boisterous winds and seas along the way. The unusual feature of the voyage was that *Manukai* was on the port tack for the whole passage, with the exception of about 3 hours before making its landfall on Jost van Dyke. The passage was made without incident in 7 days and 1 hour. In 1975, *Manukai* followed much the same course, but took 9 days in lighter airs.

The steamer track from Florida ports and Nassau to the eastern Caribbean is by way of the Northeast Providence Channel and is favored by some sailing auxiliaries and long-range cruising power yachts. The direct distance from Hole-in-the-Wall Light at the NE end of Providence Channel is about 660 miles to San Juan, or 710 miles to St. Thomas, but the ESE course makes it a close beat for sailing vessels after a northerly swings into the east. During the winter months, this is likely to be a rough trip even for true seagoing powerboats. In spring and early fall, when the prevailing winds are E to SE, this route often involves tedious hours of tacking upwind into the long Atlantic seas, or exasperating periods of calm in the oily swells. We know of an Alberg-35 with a husband and wife crew that alternated between light head winds, variables, and flat calms for 11 days until the engine failed within sight of Puerto Rico. At that point, without a zephyr of breeze, and without power, an onshore current carried them across a fringing reef and deposited the boat on a beach north of San Juan. After several months of arduous repair work on the damaged hull and engine, this doughty retired couple continued their cruise to the Virgin Islands, where they spent a pleasant winter.

Southern Bahamas to the East

After island-cruising through the Bahamas as far southward as George Town, Great Exuma (see Chapter 5), there are several other departure points from which cruising boats have made direct ocean voyages to Puerto Rico or the

Virgin Islands. These are from Cape Santa Maria at the northern end of Long Island; out through Crooked Island Passage; or, farther down, through Mayaguana Passage, Caicos Passage, or Turks Island Passage, each of which provides a deep-sea track frequented by eastbound and westbound commercial traffic. For sailing vessels, a departure eastward from any of these passages is sure to involve a long, hard beat to windward, even when you start with a norther (and as we've noted, they are more likely to be short-lived the farther south you start).

If you start offshore from Caicos or Grand Turk, at the southern end of the island chain, you encounter another hazard: the treacherous shallows of the Mouchoir and Silver Banks, which extend more than 150 miles southeast of Grand Turk and have been the graveyard of many good ships since the days of Spanish galleons. The few successful eastbound voyages that we know about through these passages have been made when N to NNE winds continued long enough to carry vessels almost all the way to Puerto Rico. Such conditions are unusual, and more often than not cruising boats have abandoned the ocean voyage entirely or returned to the Bahamas in search of an easier route to the east.

Under settled conditions, the island-hopping route from the southern Exumas to the Caicos Bank, a direct distance of about 250 miles, can be made in a series of daylight runs with overnight anchorages at each of the major islands along the way. When you have reached South Caicos, you are only about 110 miles NW of Puerto Plata, the only port of entry on the north coast of the Dominican Republic, within two or three days sailing distance of Puerto Rico.

The best seasons for taking this route are spring and fall, when conditions are generally favorable for fast runs across the three deep ocean passages, with good visibility for landfalls on the larger islands. We have made the eastbound trip from Long Island to the Caicos Bank in three or four days under sail in late November, with NE winds giving us a fair breeze during daylight and only a few hours of windward work approaching West Caicos. Other cruising boats have encountered frustrating head winds and steep seas that made it an uphill battle, taking a week or more to reach Caicos. Still others have tired of the windward beating, and given up the battle or headed for Great Inagua, southwest of Caicos and Grand Turk.

Powerboats can plan their daily runs with considerable precision, making landfalls earlier in the day and finding a good anchorage for the night in protected harbors on most of the islands. But those who follow this course, whether by sail or power, should realize that conditions in the open passages may be quite different from those in the sheltered sounds of the central Bahamas, and that finding a safe harbor may be difficult or impossible in gale force winds and heavy rain.

On the other hand, sailing the windward side of these outer out-islands is an exhilarating experience in a fair breeze. The 1,000-fathom line is only a few miles offshore, and the barrier reefs are close enough that you can see the surf breaking and piling up on the sandy beaches beyond. Harbors and anchorages on each of these islands are described in Part II, and the approaches should be studied carefully on the largest scale government charts, harbor plans, and sketch charts before entering. Here we list only the principal harbors and approximate distances between them, for planning daily runs.

Clarence Harbour, Long Island (26253, 26240) is about 40 miles SE of Cape Santa Maria, which is the northern tip of Long Island, and can usually be reached in one day from George Town, Exuma. It is exposed to the north but offers protection in prevailing trades. Water and fuel available.

Portland Harbour, Crooked Island (26240, 26252 Plan E) is another 40 miles ESE across Crooked Island Passage, with Bird Rock Lighthouse often visible many miles out at sea. Columbus anchored here on October 19, 1492, but better anchorages nearby are described in Chapter Five.

Major's Cay Harbour (26240) lies 14 miles ESE of Bird Rock Light on the north coast of Crooked Island, and is entered through a narrow break in the reef that should not be attempted in stormy weather. (See page 136 for anchorages.)

Atwood Harbour, Acklin's (26240) is 12 miles E of Major's, marked by a new light at the harbor entrance. It's a tiny harbor exposed to the northeast, but a good jumping-off place for Mayaguana.

Abraham Bay, Mayaguana (26252, Plan F) lies approximately 50 miles across Mayaguana Passage. This may be a long windward leg if the trades are from E to ESE. Several anchorages are described in Part II. On an eastbound passage in *Brer Fox*, we sailed north of Mayaguana on a 30-hour overnight run direct from Crooked Island to Providenciales on Caicos Bank with NNE to NE winds all the way. A lucky break!

Providenciales and West Caicos (26260) lie approximately 45 miles SE of Abraham Bay across Caicos Passage, where a night run in good weather may be preferable to a daytime crossing. Even under the best conditions, it's not easy to identify the entrance to the west side of Caicos Bank; the entrance is completely surrounded by reefs correctly described in the *Sailing Directions* as "extremely dangerous." A landfall in midmorning after a night run is easier and safer than a late-afternoon arrival, when a low sun makes it difficult or impossible to read water depths. At night, we would only dare to enter through the reef at Ft.

George Cut on the northwest coast of Providenciales, described in Chapter 3. Directions for entering and crossing the 50-mile-wide Caicos Bank at various points are also discussed in that chapter.

Cockburn Harbour, South Caicos (26261, Plan) is the best jumping-off point for Hispaniola and Puerto Rico. The protected anchorage here is preferable to the open roadstead at Grand Turk, 20 miles across Turks Island Passage.

The Thorny Path, via Hispaniola

In recent years, an increasing number of eastbound cruising yachts have followed the old sailing route by way of Hispaniola, which was "out of bounds" during the troubled years of the Trujillo and Duvalier dictatorships in the Dominican Republic and Haiti. Frederic Fenger sailed the mountainous north coast of Hispaniola before World War I, making his way to the Virgin Islands with a young bride and an aging 52-foot schooner. He has recorded his upwind passage in *The Cruise of the Diablesse,* now a cruising classic. Many recent voyagers have found the route a thorny path indeed, beating much of the way into the teeth of boisterous winter trades, with few protected harbors along the way; others have experienced relatively easy overnight runs to Puerto Plata and interesting coastwise cruising to Samaná Bay and across the Mona Passage to Puerto Rico.

Cruising conditions in Hispaniola are fully described in Chapter 7, including approaches and entry procedures for all major harbors in both Haiti and the Dominican Republic. Here we will make only general observations about routes and offshore weather conditions in the open passages, drawn from our own experiences and those of others.

Once you are clear of the island-hopping to Caicos and are approaching the large, high, land mass of Hispaniola, a powerboat skipper's tactics will differ from a sailor's. The object is to avoid the prevailing wind as much as possible. Yet both sail and power boats can take advantage of special wind conditions that prevail around all the large mountainous islands, and learn to avoid some of the strongest headwinds. More often than not, we have found the winds to be more moderate at night along the coasts of Hispaniola and Puerto Rico, when the cooled air is flowing down off the hills and out to sea. Sometimes this offshore flow is enough to counter the trade winds completely, providing a welcome spell of coastwise running in calm conditions under a starry sky with the brooding mountains close by and only the ever present swell to disturb one's balance. Having carefully noted the courses and distances while making the daylight approach to an overnight anchorage, we often got under way at 0200 or 0300 in the morning and tried to time our arrival at the next stop before the trades really piped up in the early afternoon. With a fast powerboat, there is considerable flexibility in such tactics. Sailboat tactics naturally will differ on the longer passages, but we've also taken advantage of the offshore winds at night by getting an early start or, when conditions are favorable, continuing alongshore in the evening breeze.

The open water passage from Caicos to Puerto Plata in the Dominican Republic is approximately 110 miles SSE, usually made in an overnight run by sailboat or trawler-type yacht, and often in a daylight run by a fast seagoing powerboat. In winter months, it is generally a rough passage, with 10-to-12-foot seas when the trades are blowing hard. Long-range weather forecasts are hard to come by. (There's a Loran slave station operated by the Coast Guard at South Caicos, but they do not respond to calls on 2182 kHz or provide any regular weather check.)

Conditions may also change suddenly, as we discovered on a passage in December, 1971. Although we had been unable to get any regional weather forecast before leaving Caicos, a moderate northeast breeze promised a fast overnight passage on a comfortable reach. But that hopeful promise failed to materialize. A low-pressure system was soon upon us, with severe squalls and heavy rain that reduced visibility to near zero. We furled the main before dark and ran off comfortably enough under our low-cut No. 3 ("mule") genoa and mizzen, logging 7 knots until midnight, when the squalls became almost constant, with sudden shifts in wind direction and velocity. Backwinded by one such shift, the boat fell off into a trough, momentarily losing steerageway and fouling the taffrail log line around the rudder. It took us several hours to clear that fouled line and reset the log, during which time we could only guess our speed and distance run.

By daybreak of December 7, the storm was generating Force 8 winds and building up 15-foot seas with breaking tops. There was no letup in the torrential rain, which obscured everything outside the boat. By that time, we estimated we should be approaching Cape Isabela at the northern tip of Hispaniola, some 20 miles NW of Puerto Plata.

The coast of Hispaniola is mountainous here, rising steeply from the sea to bold headlands visible for more than 30 miles in good weather. The 100-fathom curve lies less than 1½ miles off Cape Isabela and trends irregularly southeastward, following the steep, reef-fringed coastline toward Puerto Plata, the only real port on the north coast of the Dominican Republic.

With less than a half-mile visibility between rain squalls and no accessible radio or other navigational aids to guide us, our only safe course was to stand offshore before getting too close to the breaking reefs. So we tacked on and off soundings for almost 7 hours, waiting for a break in the storm. When there was no change by early afternoon, we feared we'd have to put through another night under these conditions, beating off a dangerous lee shore. Then, through a sudden break in the rain-laden storm clouds, we caught a fleeting glimpse of

Mt. Isabela de Torres rising from the sea some 15 miles to the southwest. This was the 2,600-foot mountain that guided Columbus to Puerto Plata in 1493, and it gave us an unmistakable landmark from which to set our course. Although the squalls continued intermittently, we ran our distance with assurance and three hours later were at anchor behind the sheltering reefs of Puerto Plata's harbor.

Puerto Plata to Puerto Rico

Although the direct distance from Puerto Plata across Mona Passage to the west end of Puerto Rico is only about 200 miles, the time required to make good that distance in a cruising auxiliary may range anywhere from 35 to 40 hours under good conditions, and up to twice as long when the trades are right on the nose, as they are likely to be much of the year. We were fortunate to pick up moderate NNE winds after a welcome two-day layover at Puerto Plata. This gave us a favorable slant to clear Cape Cabron at the northeast tip of Hispaniola with only two short offshore tacks around the headlands of Cape Macorís and Cape Viejo Francés. There are no good harbors on this section of the coast, but one can find shelter at Santa Barbara inside Samaná Bay. Most sailboats prefer to continue southeastward across Mona Passage to the west end of Puerto Rico, where wind and sea conditions should determine whether you ought to take the north or the south coast around that large island. Our eastbound passage in December, 1971, was favored by NE winds that made it possible to continue up the north coast to San Juan, doing the last 8 hours under power and sail. From Puerto Plata to San Juan our taffrail log showed we had sailed 310 miles over the bottom, mostly hard on the wind, in 58 hours, about 4 hours better than our return over a somewhat shorter route in light SE winds with periods of calm in April.

SUMMARY

How much time should one allow for the entire island-hopping route from Florida to Puerto Rico? The answer, of course, depends on what kind of boat you have and how much time you can spare for overnight stops and gunkholing along the way. Our logged distance under sail was just over 1,000 miles; we made it in three weeks, anchoring almost every night in the Bahamas, with 2-day layovers at George Town, Caicos and Puerto Plata. A larger cruising auxiliary could do the same eastbound route, with fewer stopovers, in two weeks or less with favorable NNE to NE winds, but if the trades are E to SE, as they frequently are in the spring and early summer, this passage might take a month or more for the average small sailing vessel.

Cruising powerboats make the same voyage in considerably less time, of course. A recap of *Out Islander*'s log on an eastbound passage from Miami to Ponce, Puerto Rico from March 21 to April 1, 1967, gives the following daily runs:

	Winds	*Nautical Miles*
Miami to Chub Cay	ESE 4, diminishing through the day	129
Chub to Compass Cay	Variable light breezes, smooth	105
Compass to Clarence Town, Long Island	N 2 to 3, smooth sea	125
Clarence Town to Abraham Bay, Mayaguana	NE 3, little swell	122
Mayaguana to Cockburn Harbour, S. Caicos	ENE 4 in the afternoon	113
S. Caicos to Puerto Plata	E 4, 4–5' seas. Dep. 0537, arr. 1243	115
Puerto Plata to Samaná	SE 3–4, confused swells. Dep. 0400, arr. 1135	118
Samaná to Puerto Real via Mayagüez	Heavy rain squalls at first, then E 3–4 but 6' to 7' seas in western half of Mona Passage	146
Puerto Real to Ponce	SE 4 along S coast of P.R.	46
	Total miles	1,019

To our way of thinking, the island-hopping route offers something more than just one way to get your boat to the Caribbean. It is a unique cruising experience in itself, providing opportunities for those who are making the trip for the first time to test their navigational skills in relatively short inter island passages, and offering more experienced skippers a wide variety of offshore and coastwise cruising in areas that are off the beaten track.

CHAPTER THREE

Passaging from the U.S. West Coast and through the Panama Canal

More than 3,000 miles lie between San Diego and the Panama Canal. You'll hug the coast for most of it: miles upon miles of uninhabited coastline along the desolate and treeless peninsula of Baja California, then a 290-mile open-water hop across the Sea of Cortez to lively and splashy Puerto Vallarta; then along a stretch of coast marked by low cliffs, with a backdrop of magnificient mountains—and then to pleasure-crazy Acapulco. Beyond that resort of resorts lie a thousand miles of seemingly endless beaches, lagoons, and occasional volcanos until you reach the mud, silt, and breathless heat of the Costa Rican port of Puntarenas.

Next comes the crenated coast of Panama, pocked with islands, splashed with verdant jungle growth, and almost uninhabited, to the most southerly point of the passage—just over 7° N—at Cape Mala, a name that needs no interpretation. Here the trade winds, now released to flow unhindered across the low isthmus, rush to meet you in one violent blast, as though to prove that the Pacific isn't always pacific. And here, having trended east as much as south along the entire coast of Central America, your course turns north to Balboa, the western end of the Panama Canal.

Just to show how distorted the geography of this passage can be in the mind's eye of most people, ask anyone what major U.S. city lies due north of the Canal. The usual answers will be New Orleans or even Houston. It's hard to realize that Miami is actually a little *west* of the meridian of Cristóbal and that it's only 1,226 more miles to Key West by the shortest route.

Between San Diego and the Canal, the usual stops for provisioning, fueling, rest, and relaxation are:

San Diego	0 miles
Cabo San Lucas	760 "
Puerto Vallarta	291 "
Acapulco	452 "
Acajutla (El Salvador)	665 "
Puntarenas (Costa Rica)	425 "
Balboa	469 "
	3,062 "

Mexican tourist cards for each of the crew should be obtained at a Mexican tourist or consular office before leaving California. Whether or not you really like fishing, fish are so plentiful in Mexican waters that you definitely should pick up a fishing permit along with your tourist card. A sierra mackerel on your dinner table, less than an hour out of the water, is a delicious treat. We have provided our dinner after only 50 yards of trolling with the dinghy!

The months during which this coast can be most safely run are limited by the hurricane season, which begins in late June or July and carries through October. Standard practice among cruising people who know this area well is to leave San Diego around November 1 and be back in June. Winds are northwest most of the time down as far as Cape Corrientes or maybe a little farther, but after that you are in the lee of the mountainous backbone of Central America and will feel only the light sea and land breezes blowing on and off the coast as the land mass alternately heats and cools the air above it.

There's a chance of strong winds down the Pacific side of Baja, and there are three other places where you may take a drubbing: the dreaded Gulf of Tehuantepec, the somewhat less feared Gulf of Papagayo—in both gulfs the winds come in hard and suddenly from the northeast, amplified by the topography of the coast—and the bash to the Canal after leaving the shelter of Cape Mala.

The tehuantepecer in particular must be treated with utmost respect. It is extremely local and difficult to forecast, and its wind velocity may go from Force 2 to 8 within a matter of minutes. The firmly accepted strategy of all who pass that way is "to keep a foot on the beach," in order to avoid the vicious sea that builds up only a mile or so offshore. We saw a yacht that had been literally sandblasted by following the beach so closely, and were told the crew had had to don snorkel masks to protect their eyes. Nevertheless, this is the tactic to follow.

Another bane of this coast that needs mentioning is the incessant Pacific swell. West Coast sailors take it in stride, sometimes with boomed-out stabilizing devices, but it remains a novel discomfort to sailors from the Atlantic coast. Sometimes the judicious setting of a stern anchor may turn the roll into a pitch, but the flukey night breezes tend to foil that tactic. In any case, most anchorages that are not completely enclosed will subject you to swell, and you'll frequently find it a good reason to keep going through 24 hours rather than roll all night at anchor in an open bight.

San Diego to Acapulco (18000, 21005, 21011, 21014, 21017, 21020)

Since it is not within the scope of this book to report on all the ports and anchorages along the Central American coast, we will detail only those places that are particularly convenient or otherwise popular for reasons of provisioning, repairs, fueling, or just plain scenery. And we will make only passing reference to the voyage down the outside of the Baja Peninsula, since several other guidebooks cover the subject more than adequately.

Taking advantage of the prevailing northwesterlies, some boats that have the stamina will run the whole Baja segment in one hop anyway. As a matter of fact, there are only three well-protected harbors on this coast anyway: Ensenada, which is only 65 miles below San Diego; Turtle Bay, a canning port 20 miles south of the turn of the coast at Cedros Island; and Magdalena Bay, a beautiful spot 170 miles short of Cabo San Lucas, where there is a tidy naval base at Puerto Cortez. Other shelters along this shore, behind huge beds of kelp in some cases, are generally open to the south and west and always open to the unceasing swell.

Cabo San Lucas (21123), with its pierced and jagged rocks standing out into the sea and its backdrop of treeless mountains, is at first bleak and barren. It softens as you round the corner into a lovely bay of restless water with a curving beach and a cluster of low-rise resort hotels.

The trick here is to find bottom for anchoring on the 4–5 fathom ledge that fronts the beach. The best place is a cable or two E of the Camino Real Hotel, where you can run in very close to the beach. To avoid the effluent and flies, stay away from the cannery when it is operating.

A deepwater channel has been dredged alongside the cannery into a basin that serves as the terminal for the ferry to Puerto Vallarta. A marina, which occupies the rest of the area (formerly the airstrip), provides all-weather protection for at least a portion of the usual yacht fleet.

Puerto Vallarta (21321) has become, since the building of a modern marina, the most prominent yachting center on the Central American coast. Although no place in Mexico will fill all your needs, Puerto Vallarta is a better bet than most, and the services of Juan Arias, an attentive ship's agent, are one of the features here. For a reasonable fee, he can arrange whatever you need and leave you more time to enjoy a resort that, despite all the hotels and the army of tourists that fly in every day, has managed to retain much of the flavor of "a little Spanish town."

When Bruce Crabtree was there in his power yacht *Crabby Too,* in March of 1974, he reported:

> Dredging in the marina where the concrete slips are located is completed, and the main basin is dredged to 32 feet. The dredge was working again on the east side of the basin so that a launching ramp, ways for a boatyard, and also the terminal for the ferry to Cabo San Lucas can be constructed. As things stand now, all services and facilities excepting hauling out are availa-

ur exhaust system before and after Mexico and you'll see what we mean.
fortunately, Mexico has a long, long coastline; you can only take what comes
be thankful.

Acapulco to Puntarenas (21023, 21026, 21540)

ong this 1,090-mile stretch of sparsely inhabited coast, upon whose almost
ss sandy shore the surf beats heavily, you will be very much on your own
ovisions and repairs; assistance of *any* kind is hard to come by. There is a
ation in the quiet and the wildness of the shoreline, and in the majesty of
ountains, some of them volcanos, that provide the backdrop for this
al scene. This is how we wrote at the time of our reactions to this
ettable cruising experience:

entimes porpoises came to play with *Yellow Bird*, to scratch their backs
stem, to snort in our faces as we hung over the bow watching them, and
w us how they could jump clear of the water while swimming on their
I'll never forget the sight of them at night, their writhing bodies
d in plumes of phosphorescence against the blackness of the sea.
nt many hours in the landward doorway of *Yellow Bird*'s darkened
ouse, the miles sliding away in the muted thunder of the bow wave
its unceasing curl, plowed up phosphorescent sparks to vie with the
a half-moon hanging in an absolutely clear sky. My watch lasted no
l, for there was always something to occupy mind and eye: the faint
of the beach less than a mile away, the loom of jagged peaks against
ear that the stars sparkled almost all the way to the horizon ahead,
anywhere beyond the arc of our mast and stern lights, a coastline
d since the cooling of the earth's crust.
ere nights when I welcomed the cool breeze off the land after the
of the day, a breeze sometimes scented with wood smoke from
tches of forest fires occasionally to be seen on the mountainsides.
abin was the regular flash of the radar as it swept across the
. A cup of hot bouillon was always at hand in the galley to fortify
, and routine called for scanning the engine instruments, al-
never wavered, and occasionally a trip to the heart of the ship
hts were extra bright, the heat intense but dry, and the tur-
ined on and on, uncomplainingly.

21421) stands on the very corner of the forbidding Gulf of
Ángel, you listen anxiously for the weather broadcasts from
o or seek local advice from the natives. Anchor anywhere in

ble, and hopefully the new boatyard will fill that bill. The treatment of
yachtsmen at P.V. is so much better than at other Mexican ports that it is
becoming extremely crowded within the marina and even space along the
wall in the original basin is coming at a premium.

In the roster of international resorts, Puerto Vallarta has clearly become one
of the "in" places—ever since Liz and Dick were here during the filming of
"Night of the Iguana." The luxury hotels are in the outskirts; the fancy shops,
bistros, and restaurants have become cleverly integrated within the old town,
often behind the original facades. The cobbled streets, all dips and bumps, have
no effect on the burro traffic but are deadly on shock absorbers and tailpipes. A
river of wondrously clear water runs through the west end of town. Down on its
boulders and shale, every day is laundry day, even for some gringo inhabitants
who like the old way of doing things. Above the river, helter-skelter in tiers, are
the balconied apartments of the newcomers to town. Mexicans cheekily call the
place "Gringo Gulch."

Yelapa (21017) is only 16 miles west of Puerto Vallarta and so unimportant as
a port, or even a shelter, that perhaps it shouldn't be included here. Yet this tiny
Indian hamlet—a slender waterfall drops gracefully off the forested cliff
behind it—rates an overnight stop.

No roads lead to Yelapa. The only access is by yacht or the dozens of launches
and excursion boats that ply from Puerto Vallarta every morning. Even without
its waterfall, Yelapa would be a unique attraction, because there are no cars, no
jeeps—in fact, no wheels at all. With its thatched roofs, dark interiors and dirt
floors, and every yard a livestock pen, Yelapa is likely to remain a classic
example of Mexican rusticity for some time.

Beyond the haphazard collection of huts, the simple church, and a maze of
stone corrals for the animals, the path to the waterfall (the one with the most
burro droppings) is a boulder-strewn trail that joins the brook itself amid all the
claustrophobia of the jungle. The exquisite waterfall plunges out of deep,
green foliage high above into a perfectly round pool, all Tahiti-like and delightfully cool to swim in after the hot walk up.

But before you see all this, you have to anchor, a feat to be accomplished
under the hypercritical eye of every other yachtsman in the cove. If you can set
your anchor and end up with safe swinging room in less than three passes,
you'll probably be champ for that day. On our fourth try, we finally got a fluke
to catch in the rocky bottom off the beach in front of Steve's Restaurant, just N
of the excursion boat's mooring. There seem to be three deep ledges around
the harbor, narrow enough and slippery enough to tax your anchoring skill (or
luck) to the limit. The rest of the cove is almost bottomless. But never mind, the
excursion is well worth the trouble.

Chamela Bay (21321) is the next shelter that rates a large-scale chart after Puerto Vallarta 100 miles away. Entering is simple, even in moonlight, and the logical anchorage is in the NW corner of the bay in 6–7 fathoms. Chamela is a wild and lonely place; the swell breaks with a resounding thrump upon its huge semicircle of beach.

Tenacatita Bay (21341) is only 27 miles beyond Chamela, but one is tempted to use it because a large-scale chart is available. Round the center rock and anchor in perfect quiet NNW of Squall Point. The river mouth here is typical jungle scenery, and the mosquito invasion we endured after sunset was beyond description.

Manzanillo Bay (21342) offers a popular and convenient anchorage—in populated surroundings, for a change. Rather than go into the crowded commercial harbor, Bruce Crabtree of *Crabby Too* recommends anchoring off the luxurious Las Hadas Hotel on the NW tip of the bay. He reports:

> Breakwaters built by the resort complex provide an all-weather anchorage for boats up to 50–60 feet, Med-style now, but I think they plan to install slips. The main breakwater extends far enough eastward to provide another outside anchorage for a dozen or so larger boats, if you don't mind being buzzed by the ski boats. Las Hadas (connoting a fairyland) is a treat in itself; their main swimming pool is larger than some lakes I've seen, with a suspension bridge across it and a swim-in, walk-in bar serving banana daiquiris in brandy snifters.

> Others report that a thatched-roof marina building is in progress, complete with showers, washing machines, and a marine store.

Isla Grande (21381) is a place of rare beauty. It offers reasonable protection from wind and surge. Anchor in the sandy cove off the beach shelter with the currugated roof, or move on 9 more miles to the following place with a tongue-twisting name.

Zihuatanejo (21382) affords excellent protection, and it's an interesting town to roam around in. It is at present a Mexican resort for Mexicans, but some say it will in time become another Acapulco. You are expected to check in at the Port Captain's office on the beach.

Acapulco (21401) is practically a must stop, if only because it is the last real civilization until Puntarenas, Costa Rica. Acapulco is like a transplant from the

French Riviera with a sprinkling of rusticity, and you have to lik enjoy Mexico's top resort.

The Club de Yates is the usual choice, although there is p anchor off in the same part of the bay if you are willing to ta thievery. Enter inside Roqueta Island and keep rounding perfectly sheltered cove in front of the yacht club opens up. all the inner slips, so visitors must moor Med-style to the ou The ski boats kick up quite a chop during the heat of the da place is comfortable and usually free of any swell.

The club has a popular swimming pool, a bar, a so-so re docks, and electrical fittings that do not accept U.S. plug forth at the entrance, as if to remind you that the grea and the poor is an incentive to crime.

Acapulco Ya

The most convenient place to ta' Puntarenas is at the yacht club in Ac fuel is in order here. The petrol monopoly called Pemex (Petroleos diesel we've found anywhere, pro

the western part of the harbor and adjust your sea legs for the constant swell that rolls in around the point.

Many yachts clear Mexico here in order to avoid putting in at Salina Cruz. We and others have found the officials cordial and efficient, but not above accepting a favor or two in return for their graciousness.

Guatulco (BA439) appears to be a much better anchorage and lies only 25 miles E of Puerto Ángel, but we understand that official clearance may not be taken here. The entrance is straightforward toward the shrine at the head of the bay. In the Seven Seas Cruising Association *Bulletin*, Eric Hiscock of *Wanderer IV* had this to say of the place:

> The bay, which has no known dangers, is well sheltered from all but SE winds, and we did not experience there the swell which we found so tiresome in most Mexican anchorages. A comparatively new light structure on Bufadero Point is a help in locating the place but its light, like so many others along this coast, was not working. There is on the sand beach at the head of the bay a blue shrine shaded by palms whose fronds provide the only touch of green in a brown and barren landscape (we were there in April in the dry season), and around the shrine are the huts of a small fishing community.

You should check in with the Port Captain who has a house on the hill at the W side of the bay. This is a branch office for Puerto Ángel.

Salina Cruz (21442) is a necessary stop if you have not already cleared Mexico at Acapulco or Puerto Ángel. Otherwise it seems foolhardy to stop at the very head of the gulf out of which the tehuantepecers come. If you happen to be enjoying good weather in your progress along the beach, you had best get through the area as quickly as possible—and if you are overtaken by the dread wind near Salina Cruz, you still might just as well continue, because you will be putting the wind more and more on your stern while moving steadily away from the area of most intense storms.

Windy and unattractive Salina Cruz is actually two separate ports, both of them crowded with shrimpers whose maneuvering and mooring habits may be a bit rough around a spic-and-span yacht. Anchor preferably in the outer harbor, which is cleaner though subject to surge, and report to its Port Captain. He will be found in town, past the plaza and across from the new church.

To refuel, you'll have to enter the inner harbor, which is full of garbage and oil. Since this miserable basin is also a free port, you must find another Port Captain and go through the paper shuffle again.

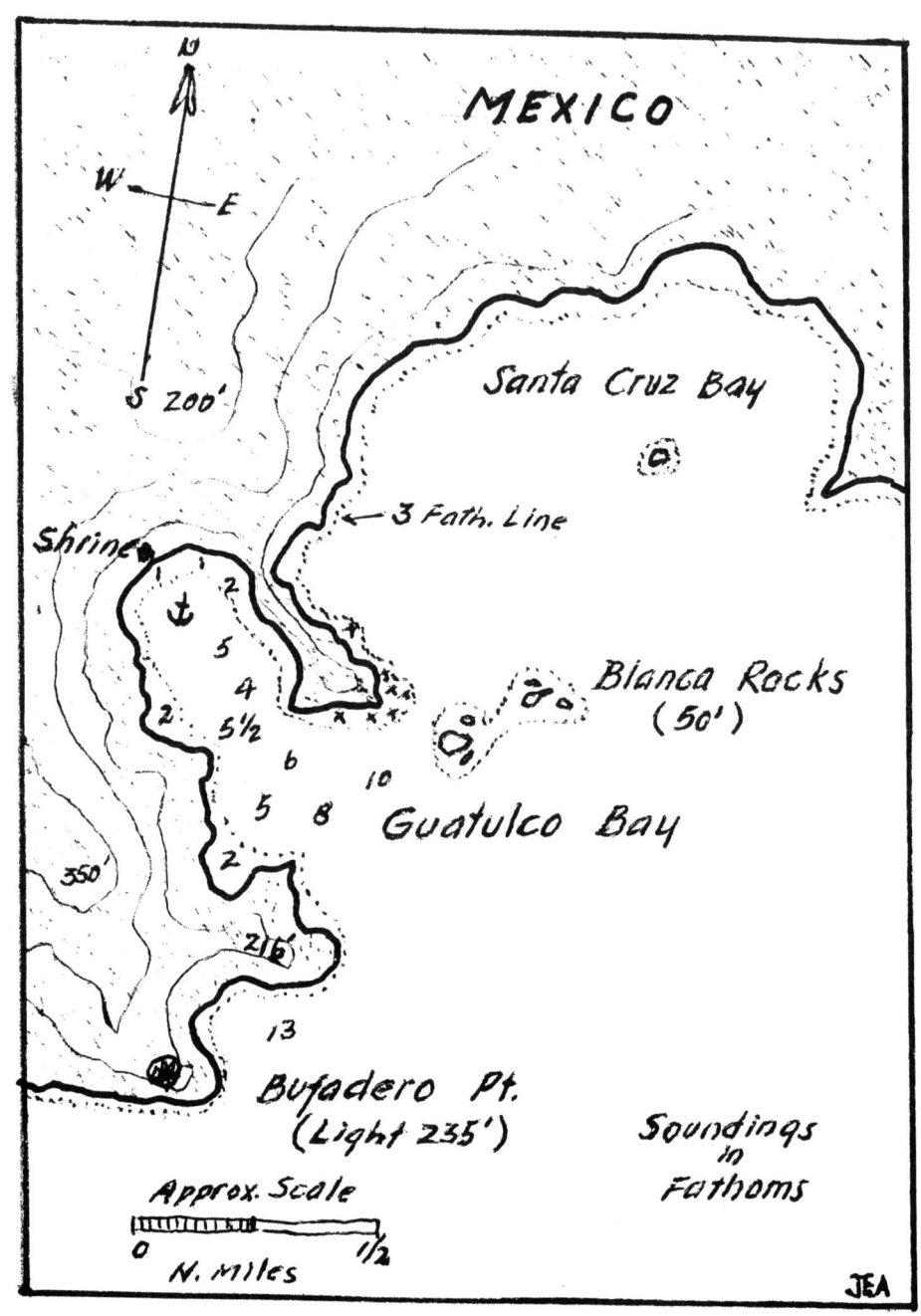

Guatulco Bay, Mexico

Acajutla (21481), in El Salvador, offers slightly more protection than the wide-open roadsteads of Champerico and San José in Guatemala, particularly if there happens to be a freighter at the pier to make a lee. Moor stern-to at the pier or anchor N of the warping buoys. Since the bottom is rocky, you would do well to use chain if possible and also a tripline. Yachtsmen have been very hospitably received here, both by officials and populace. It is a very poor town, where you will sense the curiosity rather than the envy of the people.

Fuel and water may be had, but all supplies are minimal.

Gulf of Fonseca (21521) is bordered by El Salvador, Honduras, and Nicaragua. La Unión, in Honduras, is the only port of significance, and it is hardly worth the run up to the head of the gulf to visit this impoverished, dirty, and appallingly hot town.

If you simply want rest or temporary shelter use Moneypenny Anchorage, just inside the gulf in Nicaraguan territory. There you will find good protection in the lee of the volcano about 4 cables E of the hook. Nicaraguans are said to be unfriendly to yachtsmen, but you probably won't be molested if you do not go ashore.

If you know your Hornblower stories, you'll remember it was here that the illustrious, always resourceful captain captured the Spanish ship *Navidad* and, strictly following his orders, turned her over to the ruthless dictator El Supremo, who later gave him cause to rue his action.

Playa del Cocos (21540), in Costa Rica, is an unprepossessing village straggling along a pretty beach. A reef, covered at high tide, makes out from the center of the beach. Anchor to either side of the reef on the good holding bottom. Coming from the north, Cocos is the first entry port for Costa Rica, so you are expected to look up the Port Captain at his office on the beach. Do not be surprised or disturbed to find the office closed, however; since Costa Rica eliminated entry fees for yachts, all incentive for paperwork has vanished.

Elsewhere in these parts, Bahía Elena (Port Parker) and Nacascola in Culebra have had rave notices.

Puntarenas (21544, 21545), the largest port between Acapulco and the Panama Canal, is much frequented by U.S. and Canadian tuna boats, able to handle most repairs and refits, and a more than adequate provisioning stop.

Anchor off the steel pier in the vague hope that customs and immigration will come out to you. However, you will probably be asked to moor alongside a barge in the L of the pier, an operation that can safely be accomplished only near slack water, because the current runs up to 4 knots here. The Port Offices are in the warehouse building one block N of the pier, one flight up. The pier vicinity is too exposed for extended anchorage, and dinghies are not supposed to land on the bathing beach.

Puntarenas, meaning sandy point, is a long sliver of land separating the last couple of miles of a muddy river estuary from the Gulf of Nicoya. Hiring a pilot might be prudent if you're entering the river for the first time, but you *can* do it yourself. Wait for three-quarters tide and rising. Swing wide around the sand spit off the bathing beach and approach the bar and the point at right angles, passing the point not more than 40 yards off as you cross the bar through the tide rips. Then move over close to the beach and the groins as you proceed up the obvious channel.

We do not recommend the anchorage off the town; in fact, yachts have from time to time been restricted from using it because the river traffic is heavy here and yachts have been damaged. Also, the only place to land your dinghy is at the filthy ferry dock, where it or the outboard may be stolen.

Before attempting to proceed upstream to the Costa Rica Yacht Club or Pacific Marina for the first time, you had best have a shoreside look at the channel at low tide, when all the mud flats are exposed. (The tidal range is 9–10 feet.) From the ferry dock, for instance, you will see that the channel angles across to the other shore close to where a creek enters the river. Stay about 30–40 yards off that mangrove shore until you come near another creek almost directly across from Pacific Marina, then move into mid-channel and stay there until you reach the C.R.Y.C., where you will be assigned a mooring in over 6 feet LW with little swinging room. At three-quarters tide you should have nothing less than 11 feet all the way to the anchorage.

The club is adequate but in no sense luxurious, and caters mostly to outboards and small sailboats. Swarms of mosquitos come out of the mangroves after sunset.

Pacific Marina, just downstream from the yacht club, has recently changed hands and will now, perhaps, receive a much-needed sprucing up. Do not count on more than 5 feet of water here at low tide.

Sam Manley's Shipyard is famous along this coast, so famous that you may not be able to get on his schedule for a haulout. His steady customers are the fishing fleet, anyway. We've been told there is another yard called Pescarnes that has a modern railway.

An expatriate from Boston, Joe Hoskins, has set up an electronics shop near Pacific Marina and usually monitors 2738 kHz at 0730, 1230, and 1600 under the call name "Marlec."

Lovers of dairy products are in a dairy country; try the Dos Pinos ice cream available in Puntarenas.

Having finished your errands and other business in the dust and enervating heat of Puntarenas, we suggest you move 8 miles SW across the gulf to Ken Hayes' place at Jesusita Island, where the water is clear and smooth, a breeze is usually stirring, bugs are absent, and where you will be intrigued by the friendly and informal atmosphere of this strictly unpretentious resort.

In the same vicinity and also well protected is Joe and Nancy Hill's place, Hacienda Nicoyana, where in fact you can safely leave your boat if you have to go home for a spell. We understand now that you may be able to go directly to Hayes' or Hills' places and ferry over to Puntarenas with your papers for presentation to the Port Captain. This would be more pleasant than anchoring off Puntarenas and just as convenient in the end. When you come into the Gulf, call Joe Hoskins on 2738 kHz for the latest information on procedures.

An expedition to San José, the capital of Costa Rica, is highly refreshing. Only 20 mintues by rickety DC-3 from Puntarenas, San José is 3,700 feet up in the mountains and mercifully cool. It is also the cleanest city we have ever seen, bar none. For a down-to-earth impression of this pretty country, take the open-windowed train for the return trip. For 4½ hours and 85 winding miles, slabbing down mountainsides and across lofty wooden trestles (the kind one sees in movie wrecks), with stops at every hamlet and *finca* all the way down, the scenery is so overpowering that you may be glad to get back to sea again.

Puntarenas to the Panama Canal (21544, 21560, 21580, 21601, 21602)

In contrast with the endless miles of generally unindented coastlines of Guatemala, El Salvador, and Nicaragua, the Costa Rican and Panamanian coasts as far as Cape Mala present a delightful cruising world. It is well worth a slower pace in your day-to-day progress toward the Caribbean. The tehuantepecers and the papagayos are behind you, and you can do a lot of lazy powering in an area of calms and doldrums amid a profusion of luscious jungle scenery.

Golfito (21563) may be safely entered at night. The lights and other aids are reliably maintained by United Brands, since Golfito is a loading port for the famous Chiquita bananas. The harbor is landlocked, clean, and thoroughly delightful—and a good spot for provisioning.

Anchor near the fuel dock or just inside the bay and N of the channel near the yellow house where "Captain Tom" lives. He is an interesting American who literally went on the beach here some 18 years ago and has been greeting visiting yachtsmen ever since.

You may obtain your *zarpe* for Panama from the Port Captain, whose office is in the same building as the L.A.C.S.A. ticket office.

Isla Gámez (21581), in Panama, is only a speck of an islet with a beach of glaring white sand (so different from the dark sand that fringes most of Central

America), a stand of palms and other dense tropical foliage, and a thatched pavilion near the beach.

To reach this little piece of paradise, owned since 1958 by Ed and Jean Niemeier of Poulsbo, Washington, round Parida Island clockwise with careful attention to the chart, which is accurate. Do not attempt this approach in failing light; there are a number of rocky bars to avoid.

Bahía Honda (21583) is a quiet anchorage in any weather, deep in the cove to the left of the small uninhabited island that lies dead ahead as you enter this landlocked bay. Stay off the shore until you are well down into the bay in order to avoid a reef on your port hand. In sharp contrast to Gámez, the sand is black here and the jungle so dense that it's impossible to move off the beach without a machete. Villagers will probably come out in their *canoas* to sell you fruit; they appear to need the money even more than you may need their produce.

This entire area between Isla Parida and Isla de Coiba is worth some slow and serious cruising if you are addicted to wild jungle scenery and lonely gunkholes.

Naranjas Cove (21580) lies near the slot between the island and the point of the same name. Although it offers no real protection and the bottom is rocky, it is the last anchorage before turning the corner toward Cape Mala. Anchor off the beach with the house, as close as your sounder dictates.

Benao Cove (21601) provides ideal protection and pretty surroundings when the north wind is howling around Cape Mala, which from all reports seems to be more often than not. We spent two delightful days here while 50-knot winds blew down from the green hills and raised a 2-foot chop only a hundred yards off the beach. A handful of huts perch on the hills above the curving shore, and several times we saw horsemen cantering heavily along the strand.

Cape Mala to the Panama Canal (21601, 21605) is usually dead to windward for the last 90 miles of the passage, except in the fall when some southerlies and variables can be expected. A steady head current on this side of the Gulf of Panama sets up some bad rips off Cape Mala itself. As we mentioned, we waited a couple of days at Benao for the wind to ease off; we still had very rough conditions after rounding the cape, but maybe we had become too softened by the nonweather we had experienced most of the way down the Central American coast.

Instead of making directly for Taboga Island, near the Canal entrance, the sailing skipper will be inclined to slant across the gulf, have a look at the Pearl Islands, and catch the northwesterly set of the current to the Canal.

Las Perlas Islands (21606, 21607, 21608, 21609) are a logical close-reach target for sailors; the course takes advantage of their lee and the favorable current to the Canal. We are indebted to Bob Tonks of *Seguin* for letting us extract the following, which he wrote originally for the S.S.C.A. *Bulletin*:

We think the Perlas compare favorably with the Virgins but are almost completely unspoiled, although one of the most northern islands, Contadora, is undergoing considerable development with an airstrip, a hotel made up of a series of house trailers (that are to be replaced), R/T service to the mainland, crushed ice, and a small store. There are also quite a few vacation houses. The only signs of habitation in the other islands are the small group of cottages on the southern tip of Isla del Rey and several small native villages.

It didn't rain while we were there in February, the nights were cool, and there were no insects. Sometimes it was hazy, but at other times clear enough to see the mainland. The winds with any authority were usually between N and W, light in the morning, coming up to perhaps 18 knots in the afternoon. A hardly perceptible swell from the SW caused some surf but usually not enough to prevent an easy landing.

There is an abundance of beautiful white beaches for swimming and the water is probably in the mid or lower 70's, but not clear enough for snorkeling. As a note of caution we did see some sharks and a hotel guest at Contadora had an accident with a sting ray while we were there. Fish were jumping all over the place.

Rocks are scattered all over. "Rocks awash at low tide" and "Rocks covered at high water." There is even said to be a buoyed rock which is noted on the chart as "missing"! We saw the rock, so assume it must be the buoy that's missing. We found two rocks that we don't think are shown on the chart but since they were inside the blue 5-fathom line we formed the habit of staying outside this curve or coming to anchor very cautiously since the water wasn't clear enough for eyeball piloting.

The following are all good anchorages, and there are many more we didn't have time to investigate:

Cove, NW corner of Santelmo Bay, Isla del Rey
Contadora, SE side. The chart seems misleading, as we found we could go much further W than seemed indicated.
Passage between Islas Chapera and Pajaros
Ensenada Playa Brava, Isla Pedro Gonzales
Bahía Playa Grande, Isla San Jose
Between Isla del Rey and Isla Espiritu Santo

The Panama Canal

The Canal is one of the great engineering wonders of our age, even by today's standards. The huge locks, three pairs up and three down, are 1,000 feet long and 110 feet wide, enclosed by lock gates 7 feet thick that are designed to be nearly buoyant. The deep land cuts and the miles of dredging and filling of swamps were accomplished 60 years ago, long before the advent of the mammoth earth-moving equipment of today. The entire operation was carried out under an intense sun, oppressive humidity, through the worst kind of tropical growth, and amid swarms of mosquitos carrying malaria.

Transiting the Canal is a fascinating, even awesome experience for the crew, but for the skipper the logistics and the concern for his vessel tend to detract from the thrill. Many conflicting stories have come to us about crossing the Isthmus by yacht. Some people have breezed through with no apparent fuss or bother; others have complained bitterly about the inconveniences, the arbitrariness of the officials, and the delays. And some have suffered unrecompensed damage to their boats.

There are surely good reasons for many of these complaints, but you must remember that the Canal was built for big ships and that the 300 yachts or so that pass through each year are really a nuisance. First, they are relatively fragile; second, a highly paid pilot (or an advisor, for vessels 65 feet or under), must be assigned to every vessel to make sure that accidents do not interrupt the clocklike precison of the traffic, which averages some 40 to 50 ships a day.

Now a word about the Canal Zone and the Panama Canal Company. The Zone is a 10-mile wide strip of land that comes as close to an autonomous domain as any U.S. possession could. Retired army officers have by custom been its governors through the years, and it is one of the very few government entities that has made money instead of passing it out at taxpayers' expense. Thus Zone officials can afford to do things their way with minimum interference from Washington; and they do just that, despite occasional gripes from some U.S. citizens who happen to be yachtsmen and find themselves inconvenienced by some of the regulations, which are admittedly baffling.

One of the most universal yachtsman's gripes is the prohibition against using your outboard anywhere within the Zone's waters. We questioned the Canal authorities about this regulation, and were told that the "safety and protection of all concerned" requires licensing of all operators in charge of powered craft and that "treaty commitments (with Panama) prohibit Canal authorities from examining transients and issuing them motorboat operators' licenses." You may conclude what you will from this, especially about the treaty with Panama, but just keep right on rowing your dinghy when you're in the Zone.

Relations between the Zone and Panama have been delicate, to say the least, for years and have in fact become severely strained recently as an inevitable

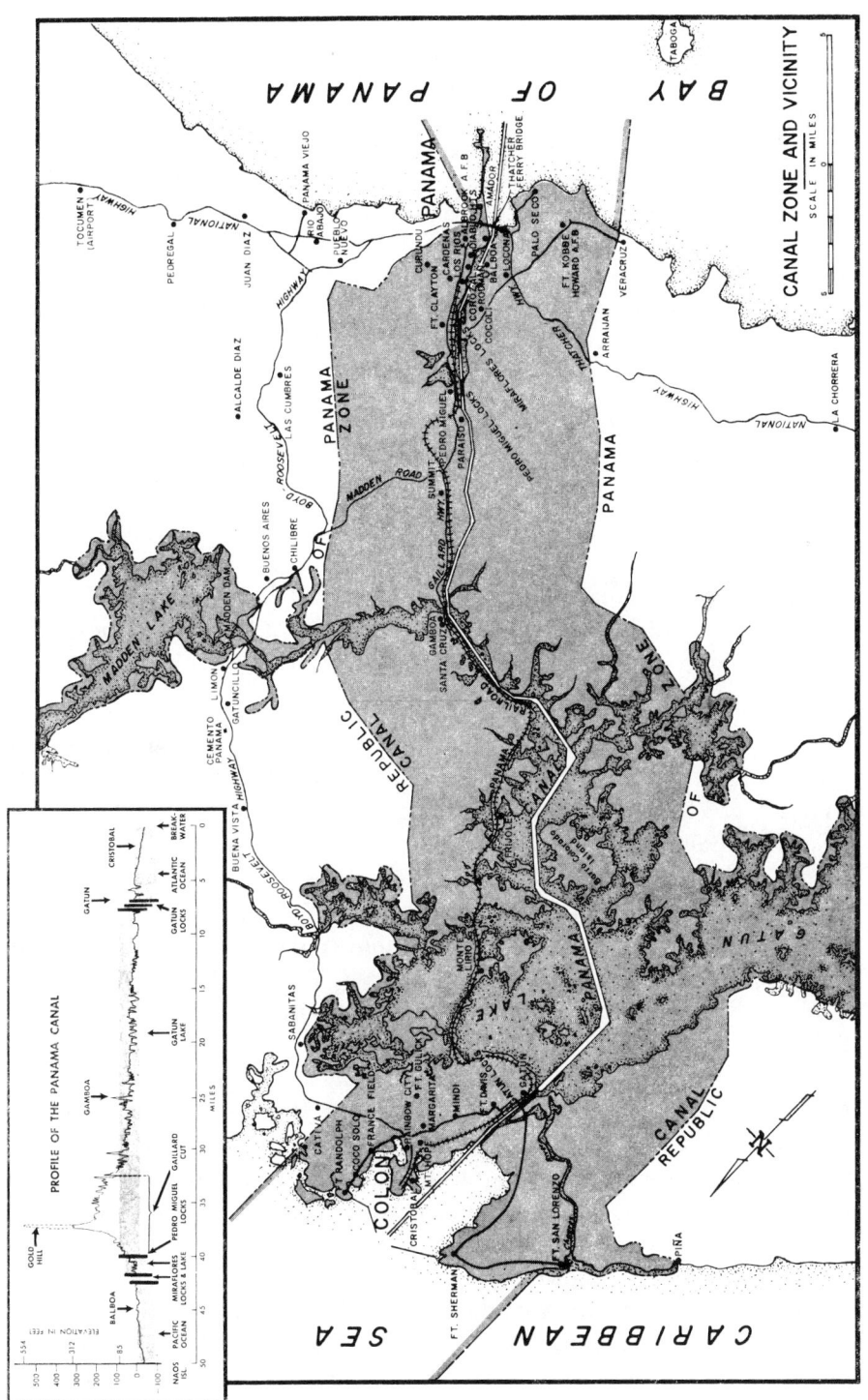

CANAL ZONE AND VICINITY

SCALE IN MILES

BAY OF PANAMA

PANAMA

PANAMA ZONE

REPUBLIC OF PANAMA

CANAL ZONE

GATUN LAKE

CANAL REPUBLIC

CARIBBEAN SEA

TOCUMEN (AIRPORT)

PEDREGAL

ALCALDE DIAZ

PANAMA VIEJO
RIO ABAJO
PUEBLO NUEVO
JUAN DIAZ

BUENOS AIRES
CHILIBRE
LAS CUMBRES

MADDEN LAKE

MADDEN DAM
LIMON
GATUNCILLO
CEMENTO PANAMA

SABANITAS

COLON
CRISTOBAL
CATIVA
RANDOLPH
COCO SOLO
ORANGE FIELD
RAINBOW CITY
FT. DAVIS
MARGARITA
MINDI
FT. LESSEPS
FT. SHERMAN
FT. SAN LORENZO
PIÑA

LA CHORRERA

ARRAIJAN
VERACRUZ

FT. KOBBE
HOWARD A.F.B.
PALO SECO
BALBOA
AMADOR
THATCHER FERRY BRIDGE
LA BOCA
DIABLO HEIGHTS
COROZAL
LOS RIOS
ALBROOK A.F.B.
ANCON
FT. CLAYTON
CURUNDU
CARDENAS
PEDRO MIGUEL
PARAISO
SUMMIT
GAMBOA
SANTA CRUZ

MIRAFLORES LOCKS
PEDRO MIGUEL LOCKS
MADDEN ROAD
GAILLARD HWY.
BOYD ROOSEVELT HIGHWAY
TRANS-ISTHMIAN HIGHWAY

NATIONAL HIGHWAY

RAILROAD

BUENA VISTA HIGHWAY

PROFILE OF THE PANAMA CANAL

GOLD HILL
GAMBOA
CRISTOBAL
GATUN
ATLANTIC OCEAN
GATUN LOCKS
GATUN LAKE
BREAK-WATER
PEDRO MIGUEL LOCKS
GAILLARD CUT
MIRAFLORES LOCKS & LAKE
BALBOA
PACIFIC OCEAN
NAOS ISL.

ELEVATION IN FEET
500 400 300 200 100 0 -100
554 312 85 30

MILES
0 5 10 15 20 25 30 35 40 45

result of the worldwide popular furor over any situation that smacks of co-
lonialism. Panama, which has the United States to thank for its independence
from Colombia, and in fact for its very existence, now wants the Canal—lock,
stock, and barrel. Not wanting to aggravate this state of affairs, the United
States has for years steered all the commercial benefits of the Zone, except the
proceeds of the Canal operation itself, to Panama. Hence there are no stores
within the Zone except PX establishments closed to transients; visitors must do
their shopping in Panama City on the Pacific side or Colón on the Atlantic.

Being denied the facilities that one might expect in a U.S. possession makes
refitting and victualing a little more awkward, but Panama is still a likely place
for most repairs and for receiving spares sent from the States.

Taboga Island (21603) is the usual staging area for yachts coming from the
"South Sea," as the early English used to call the Pacific side, and is a pleasant
spot to spend the couple of days needed to complete arrangements for transit.
Ferries run the 9 miles into Balboa regularly, but not late into the evening.

Proceed well into the anchorage off the hotel, as far as your draft will allow
with due consideration for the 16-foot range of the tide, which, incidentally,
uncovers the sand spit between the hotel and the little island to the east and
thereby helps to keep the anchorage smoother than one might expect.

Balboa (21604) is another possible layover. You may anchor off Flamenco
Island, with your Q flag flying, and communicate your desires on channel 12
VHF-FM or 2182 kHz to the signal station on the hill. You are still a couple of
miles from Balboa and the Canal offices, and as previously mentioned, you are
not allowed to use a powered dinghy anywhere within the formal limits of the
Canal. A Company launch will ferry you from Flamenco anchorage into the
operations office and back for $42, which of course makes Taboga infinitely
cheaper and almost as convenient.

The only other alternative is to try to engage in advance a mooring at the
Balboa Yacht Club (tel. 52-2524). This is easier said than done during the
winter season, for the club is of course privately owned and its first obligations
are to its members who live and work in the Zone. If you are lucky enough to get
a visitor's mooring, you will enjoy the club's hospitality, the free launch service,
the company at the bar, the two American Legion Restaurants (one formal, the
other not so), and the showers and washer-dryers. Ice and fuel are available too.
Your stay will, however, be limited to 10 days or less, at the club's discretion.

Having obtained clearance to use the club's mooring area, you are allowed to
proceed there under your own power, but no further. To avoid the shallows off
the club, do not turn in until you have passed Buoy "16."

Balboa Yacht Club has a railway capable of hauling about 25 tons. Some

Balboa Yacht Club

cruisers get their bottom work done by tying alongside the old barge across the Canal and taking advantage of the 16-foot tidal range.

Note that dogs and cats are not allowed ashore in the Zone.

If you need to fill the gaps in your chart drawers when passing from ocean to ocean, you will find in Panama City an efficient and well-stocked chart outlet called Islamorada, located about a block from El Panama Hotel.

The Canal Transit (21604) takes only a day for the 50-mile run, but you will need to allow two days more for all the arrangements. Go first to the Port Captain's office near Pier 18 in Balboa for customs and immigration clearance, and if you are making any crew changes here, this is the time to bring up the subject. If you plan to refuel at Balboa Yacht Club (refueling is more convenient here than at Cristóbal), you will need a clearance from customs. Ask the yacht club to make out a Petroleum Release Form for you.

Next stop will be the operations people upstairs. They will set up a date with an admeasurement team to come with sticks and tapemeasures to determine certain vital statistics concerning your vessel that are important (and intelligible) only to the Canal Administration, their tonnage formula being different from any other anywhere in the world. In our case, we had taken the trouble to obtain a Panama Canal Certificate from the Coast Guard in San Diego;

nonetheless, *Yellow Bird* had to be measured all over again, at additional expense to us. Fortunately for the handful who make the transit more than once, this formality applies only to maiden transits, since all vessels' statistics are kept on file.

You will also be obliged to sign a waiver that quite effectively relieves the Panama Canal Company from responsibility for any damage to your vessel while in the Zone. This you must sign; otherwise, make up your mind to go around the Horn.

Having established a day for transiting, or at least having made the waiting list, and having been duly measured, you will then be sent to the Collector's Office in another part of town to pay the tariff. It will probably be about $35–$55 for an ordinary-sized yacht. The amount is calculated from the tonnage and other more baffling measurements reported by the admeasurers, plus incidentals and, usually, a contingency fee. You need not know the formula because you will have to pay whatever they tell you anyway. And in cold cash. Not even American Express checks are accepted. In any case, the amount, whatever it may be, should seem modest enough when compared with the $6,000 or more that an 8,000-ton freighter is charged. If it develops that you have overpaid according to the Company's computations later, you may expect a refund by mail.

When the appointed morning finally comes for transiting, your advisor or pilot will come aboard, and you must by all means be ready to get under way; you will be fined $100 if for any reason you are not prepared. Give your advisor or pilot coffee at once (all professional seamen drink coffee almost continuously) and be sure to prepare lunch for him, even if you are accustomed only to munching crackers at noon. Lunch is a part of the contract.

Until recently, a top-licensed pilot was assigned to every vessel that moved in the canal, despite the fact that the tolls paid by yachts barely met the cost of one hour of a pilot's wages. In a sensible economy move, an *advisor* is now put aboard vessels 65 feet and under. These advisors, duly licensed by the Canal Authorities, are non-U.S. citizens employed by the Canal to handle small craft, including the Governor's boat. As their title implies, they advise the yacht's master what to do and how to do it, but the skipper is in control and has full responsibility for his vessel.

The turbulence when the water starts to flow into the first lock has to be seen to be believed. We advise devoting one of the preliminary days to a preview— from the deck of someone else's boat. Some other yacht is usually looking for an extra hand to cope with the lines, and there can be no better way to see for yourself how the transit is done. The train, which runs at about 2-hour intervals and costs $1.25, will take you back from the other end of the Canal, and you'll have had an interesting day of sightseeing in the bargain.

We are told the turbulence is worst in the first lock because of the reaction of

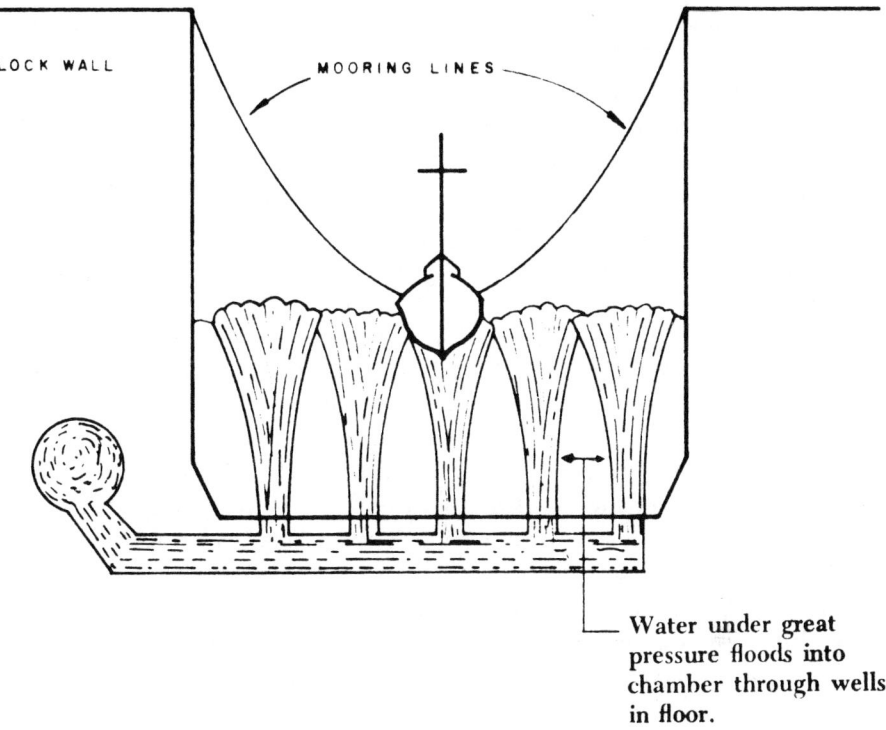

LOCK WALL   MOORING LINES

Water under great pressure floods into chamber through wells in floor.

Flooding lock chamber (cross-section view). Four-foot diameter wells in floor admit water from conduits into chamber. Great pressure boils surface but fills huge chamber in less than 15 minutes.

fresh water from above meeting salt water, of different specific gravity, at sea level. In any case you will be literally tossed about like a cork, so be sure your lines are carefully tended. You are expected to have four 100-foot lines aboard (with eyes for 12-inch bollards) and one crewman for each; otherwise you will be required to hire a Company linehandler or enlist the aid of one or more fellow yachtsmen.

Never let anybody, from the highest official down, talk you into going through the locks in any fashion other than (a), alongside another, larger vessel of low freeboard, or (b), "center-lock," which means putting a line out from each bow and each quarter, as opposed to "side-tie," tying to the wall, as the term implies. With proper attention to fendering it would be satisfactory, in fact desirable, to side-tie to a tugboat, say, but tying to the top of a wall maybe 30 feet high gives you no leverage with your lines and no chance to keep your bow and stern from slamming into the concrete with alternate surges of churning water.

Why have four linehandlers? Because as soon as you are roughly in position, four messenger lines will be heaved from the lock walls to which you attach your own hawsers, and this whole operation of securing must be done smartly before the lock starts to fill.

If your pilot or advisor doesn't think of it for you (and he should), ask if you can be moved ahead of the big ship that will be occupying the lock with you; otherwise you'll be in for a buffeting from the propeller wash as the ship moves out ahead of you.

You can count on the second and third "up" locks to be progressively less turbulent, and in the "down" locks there is so little water action that the lines can be hand held while the attendants "walk" you into the next chamber.

The high point of the canal system, 85 feet above sea level, is also the trip's high point of interest. Going north, you plunge into the 9-mile-long Gaillard Cut, the result of excavating more than 230 million cubic yards of earth, a volume equal to a 12-foot-square shaft cut through the center of the earth. The Cut was once plagued by continual landslides, but the soft volcanic material has been pushed back so that the Cut now runs between gradually sloping green-clad hills and is not quite so spectacular as it appeared in early photographs.

After leaving this high backbone of the Isthmus, you enter beautiful Gatun Lake, the vast reservoir that provides the water to fill the locks after each spilling. Just to make you and your little yacht feel inconsequential, reflect that every transit involves the dumping of 52 million gallons from Gatun Lake into the Atlantic and Pacific Oceans, or enough water to meet the daily needs of a city of 350,000.

Surrounded by seemingly impenetrable jungle scenery, Gatun Lake would be an ideal place to relax and fish and explore for a few days. However, since you can't move about without a pilot or an operating license, only the locals are allowed to make full use of Gatun Lake's 163 square miles of rare beauty. If you have a deckwash system, take advantage of the unlimited fresh water for showers for the crew and for washing the encrusted Pacific salt off your boat.

Cristóbal (26068) used to be called Limón Bay in the days of Drake, Hawkins, and Morgan. It has now been staunchly breakwatered to produce the sheltered ports of Cristóbal in the Canal Zone and Colón in Panama.

Anchorage Area F, an expansive, fairly shallow area in the SE corner of the bay, delineated by amber and red buoys, is also called "The Flats." It is the only place in this end of the Zone where yachts may anchor if there is no room at the Panama Canal Yacht Club. Area F would be all right if it weren't for that annoying prohibition against using an outboard, for it's a long, long row to shore, especially when the afternoon trades are up. Just try that in your little inflatable! If you're entering from the Atlantic, this is where you must go, flying your Q flag, to wait until a boarding officer shows up.

The Panama Canal Yacht Club (more commonly known as the Cristóbal

Yacht Club) is very cooperative, and we think the surroundings are more attractive than at Balboa (although large mosquitos are not unknown). The tidal range of only 2 feet is easy to cope with compared with 16 feet on the Pacific side. The facilities include a bar, restaurant, showers, and laundromat with dryer; there are also two railways, one for boats up to 30–35 feet and 10 tons, and a larger one for vessels up to about 25 tons. Here, as in Balboa, the big problem is to obtain a berthing assignment at the club (issued by the Customs Inspector) since it is full much of the time. And when and if you do get in, your stay is assured for only five days, although the permission may be extended if the docks are not in heavy demand.

When we passed through with *Yellow Bird*, our pilot arranged a berthing for us at the small-craft landing between Piers 8 and 9 in the commercial port itself, primarily because we had to take on several hundred gallons of diesel. This berth was convenient to the Port Captain's office and only a short walk to the yacht club or into Colón, where we found an excellent *supermercado*. Good water was available at the landing, and we took on our fuel conveniently from a tank truck. And incidentally, for truck delivery you must order exactly the amount you need and pay for it in advance. If you miscalculate the order, that's too bad. There's no rebate for what you cannot take on, and they won't bring more.

If that special berthing setup sounds too good to be true, it must be said that it has a very serious drawback. Big ships take on bunker oil on each side of you, and the piping under the piers is corroded and shot full of holes. Very black and very cloying spilled oil sloshes about continuously between the piers and far up on your topsides. The wakes from Navy liberty launches roaring in and out at all times of the day and night don't help matters either. The filthy water is also very bad on dinghy bottoms if you happen to row in from The Flats. Pollution is also a problem at the yacht club, but only under certain wind and current conditions. It's never as bad as at the ship piers.

Quite frankly, we suggest dropping your advisor or pilot after the transit and proceeding directly to an anchorage off the Club Nautico in Colón. We offer directions in Chapter Sixteen.

CHAPTER FOUR

Passaging from Europe by the Trade-Wind Route

For nearly 500 years, sailing vessels have been navigating along a well-established Atlantic track from the Madeira or Canary Islands to the isles of the Caribees and the Spanish Main—the trade-wind route. Columbus found and established it on his four voyages, and it has been followed ever since by all manner of ancient and modern mariners. Probably no other sailing route in the world, not even the clipper-ship routes, has had more consistent use or been travelled by a greater variety of windships.

The recommended route for the trade-wind passage, as Eric Hiscock states it in *Voyaging Under Sail*, is "to make 25°N in 25°–30°W, then to 18°N in 40°W, and thence to destination; but the season of the year must be taken into consideration when judging how far south it will be necessary to go to ensure holding the trades." Columbus found that the trades become steady and strong out of the northeast at about 20°N—about 500 miles, say, southwest of the Canaries. But many voyagers, including the Admiral himself, have found (as we'll see) that neither the direction nor the strength of the trades are always to be relied on. You can sail from the Canaries to the Caribbean in 21 days, as Columbus himself did. You can also take a month and a half or more to make the same passage.

Getting to the Madeiras or the Canaries is, of course, your first step. Many westward passages along the trade-wind route over the last 25 years have been made by yachts returning from trans-Atlantic races or from participating in British or continental yachting events. So we restrict our advice, limited though it is, to considerations involved in getting from the English Channel and Gibraltar to the sunny islands off Africa that will be your last landfall before the New World.

To the Madeira and Canary Islands

The Madeiras lie about 1,250 miles southeast of Falmouth; the Canaries are about 250 miles farther south. The passage requires from 10 to 25 days, largely depending on the kind of weather you encounter in the Bay of Biscay. As Hiscock points out in *Voyaging Under Sail*, the north-to-northeast wind known as the Portuguese trades predominate during the summer from Cape Finisterre southward, but tend to become variable in September and October, with an increasing proportion of southwest winds and a higher percentage of gales during the fall months. Therefore, Hiscock suggests that if time permits, it may be better to leave from the English Channel earlier and spend more time in the Madeiras or Canaries before making a late-fall or early-winter departure on the trade-wind route to the Caribbean.

Over the years, many cruising yachts have preferred to sail first to Spain or Portugal, or Gibraltar, stopping off for final preparations on the continent before leaving for the islands. Gibraltar is about 1,100 miles from Falmouth, a passage of 10–14 days; it's 760 miles farther to the Canaries. Older cruising boats took anywhere from 10 days to two weeks to get from the Channel to Gibraltar, and another week or 10 days to get to the Canaries. With favorable winds, modern yachts may take 5 or 6 days for the relatively short offshore passage to the Canaries, although light airs and headwinds may be encountered at any time.

In considering the passage from Madeira or the Canaries, it is important to bear in mind that these island groups are about 250 miles apart, and that the major islands of the Canaries extend east and west for approximately that distance, and north and south about 60 to 75 miles. Thus a passage departing from Lanzarote at the northwest end of the island group may be a couple of hundred miles longer than a passage starting from the easternmost islands. Tenerife and Grand Canary lie approximately in the center of the archipelago, between 27°30′ and 28°30′N and between 16° and 17°W, some distance above the northern limits of the northeast trades. La Luz, the port for Las Palmas on Grand Canary, has little to attract yachts; the harbor is a bunkering port, and the surface of the water is often coated with oil. So in recent years, more yachts have been making their departure from Lanzarote, Tenerife, or Santa Cruz de

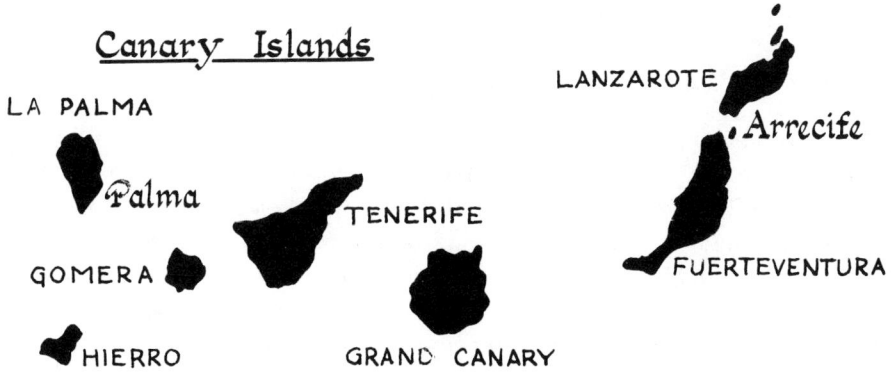

Departure points from the Canaries

la Palma (not to be confused with Las Palmas, Grand Canary) at the northeast end of the group.

Fewer yachts depart from the Madeiras; from them, it usually takes several days longer to reach the steady trade-wind belt. The port of Funchal on the main island of Madeira offers a convenient stopping point, however, and recent visitors report that cruising yachts are made very welcome. A pilot meets boats outside the harbor and helps them find anchorage—usually with bow and stern anchors, although sometimes moorings may be available. The Club Naval offers showers and other facilities, and you can leave your dinghy safely there.

Comparative Times on Trade-Wind Routes

Celestial navigation was in its infancy when Columbus made his historic voyages, and the Admiral had only the crudest methods for determining his position at sea or even his speed. But once he reached the latitude of the southeast trades, his ancient and cumbersome ships often made surprisingly fast passages. They compare favorably with those of many modern cruising yachts. We've found it interesting and instructive to compare some of the routes followed by the early explorers and make a random check of passage times made by contemporary yachts over much the same routes at different seasons.

We summarize the passage times of the four Columbus voyages in Table A, page 71, showing the point of departure from the Canary Islands, the date of departure, the destination or point of arrival in the West Indies, the distance in nautical miles, and the number of days at sea. In part II we compare passage times by a representative group of modern yachts, compiled in part from a number of trade-wind crossings recorded by Eric Hiscock, who has kindly permitted us to quote from his *Voyaging Under Sail*, supplemented by records of more recent passages by yachts with which we happen to be familiar.

Observations on the Voyages of Columbus

There has been no dearth of information about the trade winds and their vagaries since the days of Prince Henry the Navigator, when Portuguese mariners found their way southward along the west coast of Africa and westward to the Madeiras and Azores long before Columbus. As Samuel Eliot Morison notes in *The Southern Voyages* (the second volume of *The European Discovery of America*), considerable data-gathering had been going on since about 1430, when Prince Henry "set up a sort of information service where shipmasters might consult the latest charts and pick up useful data about winds and currents."

Table A.

I. The Four Voyages of Christopher Columbus

Vessel & Master	Point of departure	Date or month	Destination or landfall	Distance* (Naut. Mi.)	Days at sea
Santa Maria Columbus (1st voyage)	Gomera, Canary Is.	9 Sept. 1492	San Salvador Bahamas	2800*	34
Marie Galante Columbus (2nd voyage)	Ferro, Canary Is.	12 Oct. 1493	Dominica	2500*	21
Santa Maria de Gaia Columbus (3rd voyage)	Gomera, Canary Is.	26 June 1498	Trinidad (via Cape Verdes)	2800*	32
La Capitana Columbus (4th voyage)	Grand Canary	25 May 1502	Martinique	2600*	21

II. Selected Passages by Modern Yachts, 1931–1973

Uldra 31' gaff yawl Dennis Puleston	Tenerife Canary Is.	22 Oct. 1931	Antigua	2900*	29
Moonraker 29' gaff cutter E.A. Pye	Madeira	9 Oct. 1949	Barbados	2960	30
Diotema 30' gaff cutter V/Adm. Goldsmith	Canary Is.	29 Oct. 1949	Barbados	2700*	44
Omoo 45' gaff ketch L. Van de Weile	Canary Is.	17 Oct. 1951	Barbados	2700*	23
Sopranino 20' sloop P.J. Ellam	Canary Is.	11 Jan. 1951	Barbados	2700*	28

* In this tabulation we follow the method used by Hiscock to determine distance run: when data are available, "the distances are those arrived at by adding together the days' runs; they are not necessarily the shortest distances. When such figures are not available the distances measured along the usual sailing ship routes have been taken from the small scale ocean charts; such measurements are only approximate," and are followed by an asterisk. For further information on passages by some of the yachts mentioned by Hiscock, see *Voyaging Under Sail*, Appendix I and II.

II. Selected Passages by Modern Yachts (continued)

Vessel & Master	Point of departure	Date or month	Destination or landfall	Distance* (Naut. Mi.)	Days at sea
Wanderer III 30' sloop Eric Hiscock	Canary Is.	11 Oct. 1952	Barbados	2700*	26
Viking 33' Swed. ketch No engine S. Holmdahl	Canary Is.	15 Oct. 1952	Barbados	2700*	32
Beyond 43' cutter T.C. Worth	Canary Is.	6 Nov. 1952	Barbados	2700*	21
Havfruen III 60' gaff ketch (built 1897) T. H. Carr	Madeira	11 Nov. 1954	Barbados	2960	23
Kochab 39' yawl J. F. Evans	Madeira	2 Nov. 1956	Barbados	2960	33
Dyna 58' S/S yawl Clayton Ewing	Tenerife Canary Is.	22 Jan. 1961	Barbados	2800*	14.8
Rena 45' ketch Cmdr. Vancil	Madeira	11 Nov. 1962	Grenada	3000*	26
Widgee 29' sloop D. Guthrie (singlehanded)	Madeira	27 Sept. 1965	Antigua	2988	26
Mamari 28' ketch Ken Court	Grand Canary	3 Jan. 1968	Barbados	2730	25.5
Sheldrake 42' ketch C. Stisted	Grand Canary	3 Jan. 1968	Barbados	2800*	29
Wanderer IV 49½' ketch Eric Hiscock	Grand Canary	Oct. 1968	Barbados	2777	26.9
Dyna II 51½' sloop Clayton Ewing	Lanzarote Canary Is.	20 Jan. 1970	Grenada	3000*	18.5
Gesture II 48' Swan slp. Jas. Madden	Lanzarote Canary Is.	Oct. 1972	Grenada	3150	17.1

II. Selected Passages by Modern Yachts (continued)

Vessel & Master	Point of departure	Date or month	Destination or landfall	Distance* (Naut. Mi.)	Days at sea
Legend 48′ Swan slp. Wells Morss	Lanzarote Canary Is.	Oct. 1972	Grenada	3100	16.9
Prim 40′ cutter M. Gibbons-Neff	Lanzarote Canary Is.	7 Nov. 1972	Grenada	3150	18.3
Xanadu 48′ ketch F. Bates McKcc	Canary Is.	4 Dec. 1973	Barbados	2700*	21.5

Columbus studied many of these early maps and charts and picked up much practical information on his own previous voyages along the African coast and into the North Atlantic. He learned a lot about prevailing winds and also much about ships and their sailing characteristics from the Portuguese, who had already developed the lateen-rigged caravel, which could sail closer to windward than the old square-riggers. Columbus had learned from his Portuguese tutors, in Morison's words, "how to handle a caravel in head wind and sea, how to claw off a lee shore, and what kind of sea stores to take on a long voyage." So his discovery of the trade-wind route to the West Indies was grounded in his earlier experience, though it took him four voyages over a period of 12 years (1492–1504) to learn how to use the trades to best advantage.

Several particulars about the four voyages of Columbus are worth recalling when comparing the routes and passage times of modern yachts. Apart from the primitive state of celestial navigation in the 15th century, Columbus and other early navigators lacked any accurate knowledge of seasonal weather patterns in the tropics. That made it impossible for them to determine the best times of the year to plan their departure in order to avoid tropical storms. Yet even on his first voyage, the Admiral had a seamanlike plan for avoiding headwinds in the northern latitudes and taking advantage of the prevailing northeast trades on the westward passage. By the time of his final voyage, he had encountered enough hurricanes to predict thc probable months of their occurrence and to plot the general pattern of these revolving tropical storms. As a result of his intuitive sea sense and his increasing knowledge of the behavior of the trades, his fastest passages followed a course very close to the preferred route of present-day deep-water skippers.

In comparing the passage times of ancient and modern sailing vessels, there is another factor that present-day navigators are likely to overlook: on all his voyages, Columbus sailed in company with other ships of various types and sizes, keeping in touch night and day as far as possible. On the first voyage, contrary to later experience, Columbus left the Canaries with a fresh easterly wind that carried the little fleet (*Santa Maria, Niña,* and *Pinta*) a distance of approximately 1,163 nautical miles in the first 10 days—not bad going, when you consider that the fleet kept in sight every day, the fastest vessel rounding up to allow the slower ones to come within hailing distance toward sundown. The best day's run on that voyage was 182 miles, according to Morison, and for 5 consecutive days the fleet averaged 141 miles per day.

On his second voyage, from the Canaries to Dominica, Columbus followed the same procedure with a large fleet of 17 vessels. He made a remarkably fast passage—21 days—considering that the entire fleet kept their stern lights in sight of one another throughout the hours of darkness. On his fourth voyage, Columbus made an even faster passage—21 days from Grand Canary to Martinique, a route about 100 miles longer than that of the second voyage. That 21-day passage established a mid-Atlantic crossing record that stood for years.

On both of these very fast voyages, Columbus set a course from the Canaries of W by S until he picked up the steady trades after leaving the frequent calms and variables encountered near the Canaries. He had learned that the trades became steady and strong when he reached about 20°N, where he set his course westward to the islands. The exhilaration which must have been experienced by the early explorers, as well as by those who followed into this fair-wind belt, is vividly described by Morison in his *Southern Voyages*:

> Sailing before the trades in a square-rigger is a sailor's dream of the good life at sea. You settle down to the pleasant ritual, undisturbed by shifts of wind and changes of weather; and the ocean crossing seems to have been pure joy for everyone who loved the sea. There is the constant play of light and color on the bellying square sails (gold at sunset, silver in the moonlight, black in starlight, white as the clouds themselves at noon). The sea, flecked with whitecaps, is of a gorgeous deep blue, the schools of flying fish spring like a flash of silver from the bow wave.

But Columbus, like other mariners who followed him, discovered that the trade-wind belts are neither easily predictable nor precisely defined. The first and third voyages of Columbus were slow passages, caused by long periods of light airs, calms, or headwinds, usually encountered at the northern or southern limits of the northeast trades. On his first voyage, the fleet ran into light variable winds and rain, lasting several days, during which they averaged about 46 miles a day; they made only 234 miles in 5 days. This was at the northern limits of the trades, since the fleet had been steering a magnetic course W from the Canaries, which was about W by S true, owing to the variation that Columbus had no way of suspecting when he set out from the Canaries, but noted and compensated for during the course of the voyage, much to the consternation of his crew. Columbus is said to be the first navigator to have recognized and dealt with westerly variation.

On his third voyage, in the summer of 1498, Columbus encountered 8 days of calms after his little fleet of three vessels left the Cape Verde Islands, where they had stopped briefly seeking fresh meat and cattle. This time they sailed a SW magnetic course, which carried them to about 9°30′N in 29°W near the southern limits of the trades, where the equatorial current put them into the doldrums.

Modern Trade-Wind Passages

As our tabulation shows, modern sailing vessels have encountered conditions very similar to those experienced by Columbus, making both faster and slower passages over much the same routes during the past 45 years or more. The slowest passage recorded by Hiscock was the 44-day crossing made by the 30-foot, gaff-rigged cutter *Diotema*, sailed by Vice-Admiral Sir Lennon Goldsmith in 1949. This Hanna-designed vessel ran into 7 days of calm and 4

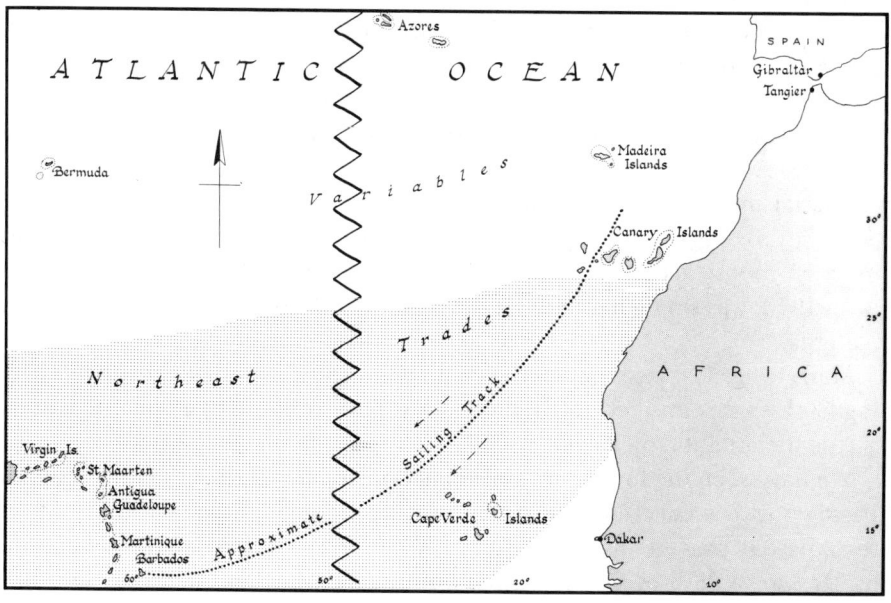

The trade-wind route

days of head winds along the usually reliable trade-wind route. So modern ocean-sailing skippers, for all their sophisticated navigational equipment, ocean charts, and sail inventories, would be happy to do as well as Columbus on his two fastest voyages. Most of the modern boats on our list were equipped with auxiliary engines, which they were free to use for limited periods during calms or light winds, although (with a few exceptions) we don't know just how much they were actually used.

We have not tried to determine what yacht has made the fastest westbound passage by the southern route. It is possible that several pre-war or early post-war ocean-sailing yachts made a faster crossing than the 21-day passage by Tom Worth and his wife in their 43-foot cutter *Beyond* in 1952, but this is the fastest recorded by Hiscock up to that time. The yacht was designed by Laurent Giles & Partners and built of aluminum alloy in England in 1951, and continued her fast southern crossing by making a voyage around the world.

The Cruising Club of America has been awarding its Blue Water Medal since 1923 in recognition of noteworthy voyages made in small boats by amateur sailors of all nationalities. Many winners of this coveted award have made passages to the West Indies by the trade-wind route as part of more extended voyages or circumnavigations. In 1947, Ernesto Uriburu of Argentina won the award in his 50-foot ketch *Gaucho*, after sailing from Buenos Aires to the Mediterranean, and then returning across the Atlantic following the route of Columbus from Palos, Spain, to San Salvador, and then to New York. Sten and Brita Holmdahl of Sweden won the award in 1954 for their circumnavigation in *Viking*, whose trade-wind passage to the islands is included in our tabulation, while Eric and Susan Hiscock were similarly honored the following year for their circumnavigation in *Wanderer III*; part of their voyage was the Atlantic crossing by the southern route.

Special mention, apart from his other awards, must be made of the ten Atlantic crossings made by James W. Crawford, Jr., seven of which were made in his 61-foot steel cutter *Angantyr*. One extraordinary passage of his, in *Angantyr* in 1970, was single handed: he did it alone in 19 days, from the Canaries to Antigua.

Many other fast passages by the trade-wind route have been made by Cruising Club yachts entitled to fly the CCA's Transoceanic Pennant for voyages across the Atlantic or Pacific.

We have seen the logs of several small cruising boats which made creditable passages with small crews and without racing sail inventories. One of these was the 25½-day passage made in January, 1968, from Grand Canary to Barbados by *Mamari*, a 28-foot wooden ketch built in New Zealand in 1956. This little vessel was owned and sailed by Kenneth E. Court, a naval architect who was completing four years of extended cruising from Hawaii to the Chesapeake by way of the Indian Ocean, the Red Sea, and the Mediterranean. He used twin staysails to good effect under a variety of light to moderate easterly winds, logging 136 miles for the best day's run in 26–28 knots, completing the passage 3½ days ahead of *Sheldrake*, a 40-foot ketch that departed Grand Canary the same day.

Some of the fastest passage times were recorded by a group of Cruising Club yachts returning by the southern route after the race to Spain in 1972. *Gesture II*, a 48-foot Swan sloop owned and sailed by James L. Madden, and *Legend*, another Swan 48, owned and skippered by Wells Morss, departed from Arricite, Lanzarote, about the same time at the end of October, 1972, and reached Grenada within a few hours of each other. *Gesture* held a southerly course to 22°N before turning westward, averaging 7½ knots and making higher speeds when the trades held strong and true. Madden used power for only 2 hours in a brief spell of light winds toward the end of the 3,150 mile course, which he covered in 17 days, 2 hours. *Legend* followed a similar course, but stopped briefly at Grand Canary, and then ran even further south to 17° before swinging westward. Her elapsed time from Lanzarote to Grenada (not counting the stopover at Grand Canary) was 16 days, 22½ hours.

Other fast passage times were recorded by CCA yachts returning by the southern route that year, including Commodore Dick Nye's *Carina*, Jim Mullen's *Southern Star*, Lynn Williams' *Dora IV*, Gene Sydnor's *Etoile*, and John Wilson's *Holger Danske*. In all, 11 Cruising Club yachts were awarded the Parkinson trophy for their trans-Atlantic passages in 1972, the largest number in any single year up to that time.

Among the most interesting CCA records we have seen are those of Past Commodore Clayton Ewing, who has given us the following personal account of three very fast passages he has made since 1961 returning across the Atlantic in the three *Dynas*:

The first passage was in *Dyna I*, a 58-foot yawl built in 1957 by the Burger Boat Co. in Manitowoc, Wisconsin, and designed by Sparkman and Stephens. Incidentally, she was the first welded-aluminum sailboat built in this country.

We departed Santa Cruz, Tenerife, at 1800 hours on January 22, 1961, and anchored at Barbados at 1030 local time on the morning of February 6, which, according to my arithmetic, is 14 days, 19 hours, 30 minutes, taking into account the 3-hour difference in local time. This, of course, was a fast passage. I doubt that we ever had less than 20 knots of wind, nor more than 35. We departed Santa Cruz with a fresh wind under a double-reefed mainsail and a working jib "wung" out on a spinnaker pole. A couple of days later, we took out the reef and went to a storm spinnaker, and a few days after that to a full-sized spinnaker. The wind was always between northeast and southeast the entire passage, and we carried either the working jib, on a spinnaker pole, or a spinnaker at all times.

There was a crew of eight aboard, including my wife, Janet. We had three two-man watches, three hours on and six off, which made an easy passage of it, with plenty of rest for everyone. We always had a helmsman, and we always carried the mainsail without any self-steering devices or twin-jib arrangements, as we did on the subsequent passages.

The second passage was in *Dyna II*, a smaller boat, a 51.5-foot aluminum sloop, also designed by Sparkman and Stephens, and built by Palmer Johnson of Sturgeon Bay, Wisconsin, in 1968. This time, we departed Lanzarote in the Canary Islands on January 20, 1970, at about 1300 hours, and tied up at the Stevens Marina in St. George's, Grenada, at approximately 2350, February 7. The elapsed time was therefore 18 days, 13 hours, 50 minutes (counting the three-hour difference in local time). The distance is a couple of hundred miles greater than from Tenerife to Barbados. This passage was also fast, with winds of 20 to 30 knots the first few days. We reached south with a number 2 genoa and a small reef in the mainsail the first three days, as I recall, before the wind moderated sufficiently to permit us to use a full-size jib and main. At about 19°N, we changed course to a more westerly direction, and from that point on, sailed with spinnakers of various sizes. The last three days of the passage, the wind diminished to perhaps 10 or 12 knots, and finally died out completely in the lee of Grenada.

In these first two passages, upon departing the Canary Islands, we sailed SSW magnetic to a point below 20° latitude before altering course to a more westerly heading toward our destination. I strongly recommend that anyone making the passage, at least in January, follow this procedure, because it almost assures one of fresh easterly winds across to the West Indies.

The third passage was made in *Dyna III*, a 55-foot Sparkman and Stephens yawl, built of fiberglass by Nautor in Finland. Again we had a crew of eight and followed the same plan in terms of watches, steering, and so forth. We sailed from Bayona, Spain, on August 2, 1972, to Madeira, where we lay over for about 36 hours, but I don't have the exact date of our arrival. My recollection is that it was 4 days from Bayona to Madeira.

From Madeira, we sailed southwest to approximately 22°N in relatively light air before changing course to the westward. This time our destination was Bermuda. Being August, this was the hurricane season, and there were hurricanes to the south of us. We watched the weather very carefully, of course, and made weather maps of the North Atlantic at least once and usually twice a day, using the NSS weather broadcasts, which gave us complete knowledge of the hurricanes, their direction, strength, and location at regular intervals. Our plan for avoiding them was to sail along the southerly edge of the Bermuda high, which we did, and then finally angled up toward Bermuda. This, however, produced much lighter air all the way than we had had on the previous two passages, but it kept us out of the hurricane areas.

Again, I do not recall the exact date of our arrival in Bermuda, but it must have been August 26 or 27. We laid over there for about 30 hours and then proceeded to the Virginia Capes, up the Chesapeake, and anchored at my home on the Choptank River at about 2300 hours on September 1. Total time for the passage was 30 days. The distance, of course, was well over a thousand miles greater than the previous two passages, and the wind materially lighter, although we did have a very nice four-day run from Bermuda to the Choptank River.

PART II

The Clockwise Circuit

CHAPTER FIVE

The Bahamas

If the level of the sea surrounding the Bahamas could somehow be lowered twenty or thirty feet, you would see a mesa of pink-white sand with several plunging, water-filled canyons cutting into or through it. Here and there a string of limestone and coral nubbins would protrude slightly above the mesa; those are the islands and cays that would remain after the water had poured back. No wonder that Ponce de Leon, when he sailed through here in 1513, called the region *Bajamar,* meaning shallow water.

These scattered islands, which barely break the surface of the sea, are entirely different from the massive and sometimes towering islands that ring the Caribbean Sea, and sailing among them is a different experience. The beauty of the Greater and Lesser Antilles lies mostly in the height, the grandeur, and the verdure of the islands themselves; the beauty of the Bahamas lies in the incredible transparency and reflected colors of the water surrounding them. Because they are so low, and so rocky and porous, the islands of the Bahamas support no rivers; no run-off of any kind brings silt and mud to mar the clarity of the water.

Sailing across this slightly submerged plateau, or bank, on a breezy day with whitecaps and cloud shadows racing across the surface, is a fascinating, almost mesmerizing, experience. But it calls for a closely kept DR track and a careful watch on the needle or flasher of the depthfinder. Land may lie only five miles away, yet still be unseen. For miles and miles the sandy bottom may be a steady 10 or 12 feet down, then rise almost imperceptibly until you would swear you were gliding over a 6-inch film of water.

Conning your way through such waters is called "eyeball navigation," an acquired knack, but one you will learn quite quickly if you will but swallow your first fears and apply your powers of observation to the limit. How strange it is that sailors who confidently follow their charts among unseen dangers in murky waters elsewhere will "freeze" when similar underwater hazards are clearly visible twenty feet or more below the surface!

Some dangers stand out unmistakably: the dark brown or sickly yellow of a coral ledge or the jet blackness of an isolated coral head. True, there may be plenty of water over these conspicuous dangers, but until your ability to judge depth has developed through experience, it is only prudent to go around them—or proceed carefully over them if the sketch chart definitely shows a safe track. Fleeting cloud shadows are a real problem, for they completely obliterate the subtle distinction between good water and bad. The local pilots call these shadows "flyers," and even they are confused by the temporary blackouts.

By far the most difficult aspect of "eyeballing" is judging depth over a sandy bottom, where the only clue to gradual shallowing lies in the almost imperceptible change from light green to yellow and then to that whitish cast of water that will scarcely float a dinghy. Then there are places, sometimes far out of sight of any points of reference, where "sand bores" predominate—parallel ridges of sand scoured by the current through which safe channels run but which also result in dead ends. This kind of bottom, which most often occurs near the edges of the banks before the sudden drop to very deep water, presents, we think, the greatest challenge to the neophyte as well as to the experienced Bahamian pilot. When we come through one of these indistinct channels and see the deep water only a hundred yards away, we must confess to a feeling of frustration, because the bores seem to interlock in a mazelike way to block our progress to the blue water. You especially want to have the tide on the rise during such passages, so that a harmless grounding on the sand will mean only a short wait.

Now a word about the tides on the banks. While the tide and current tables give enough data to calculate the flow in the cuts and the state of the tide at some important junctions, the effect of the tidal currents far out on the banks is anybody's guess. Recalling our very first experience in Bahamian waters—running across the Little Bahama Bank from Mangrove Cay toward Sale Cay, a distance of only 30 miles—we found ourselves set 3 miles to the north, and we had been traveling at better than 20 knots! Many times we have been set more than 2 miles from our DR in the 16-mile run from Cat Cay to Sylvia Beacon.

To try to understand the currents on the banks, imagine, if you will, an upside-down plate in a tub of water with a string attached to the plate's center. As you lift the string the water will fall off the plate equally all around. Then imagine the same experiment with an irregular hors d'oeuvre dish and with the string off center, and you'll get some idea of the irregularity of the currents flowing on and off the banks. All we know is that the water flows with considerable velocity, but we cannot know the angle or direction of the flow because we don't know where the center is.

With some experience, it is possible to see the more obvious dangers on a cloudy day. For the tricky passages you must have sun—and the higher and the more behind you the better. Unless you are following definite guidebook or sketch-chart tracks, you will have to consider the position of the sun at critical junctures in your day-to-day cruising plans.

Unlike Gaul, the Bahamas are divided in four parts, at least for the purpose

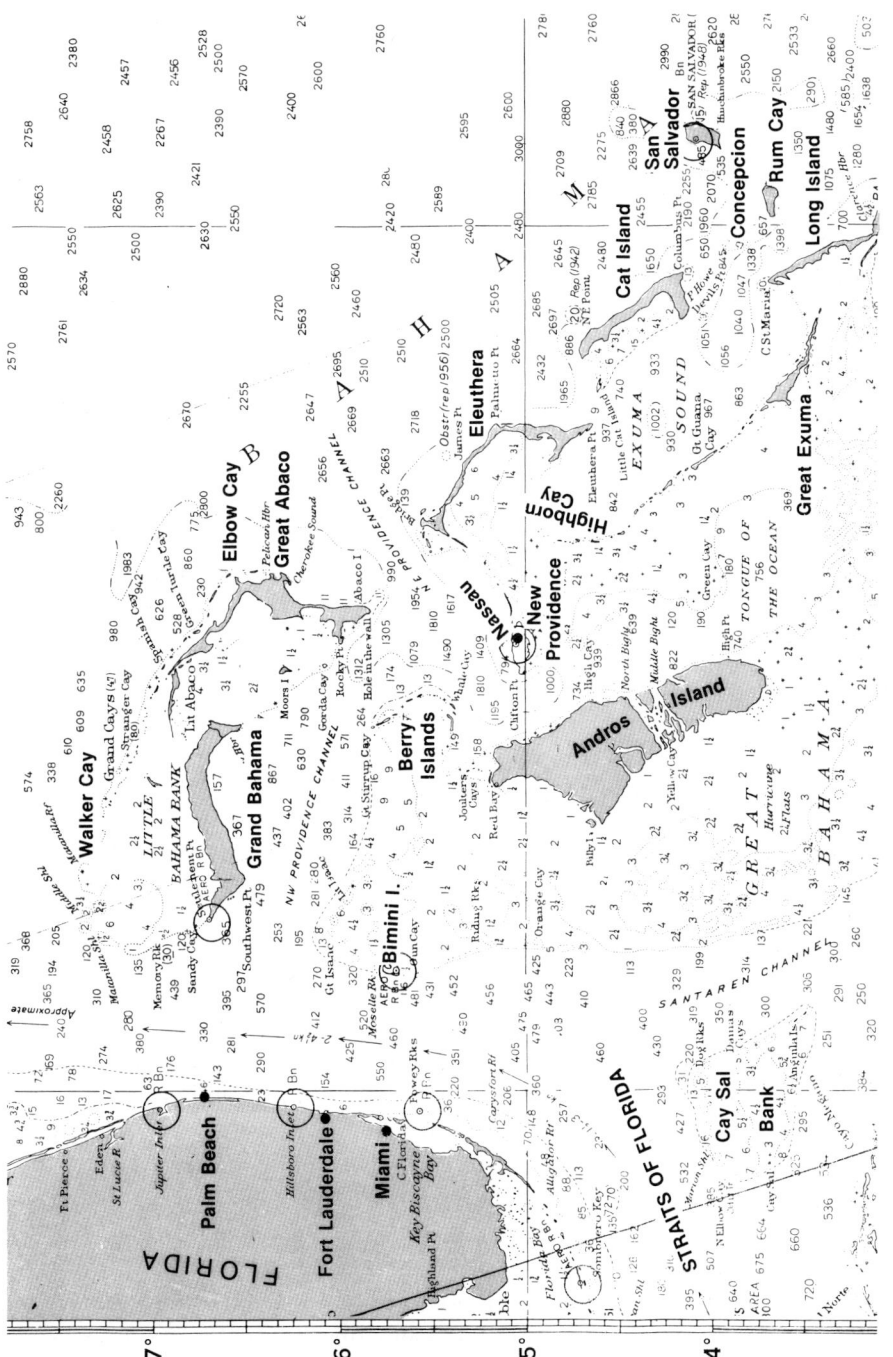

The Northern and Central Bahamas

of this book, and the parts do not lend themselves to a straightforward cruising sequence in their 500-mile trend southeasterly from Florida. Through the Virgins and down the Lesser Antilles, you can cover all the major islands with only a little backtracking. But in the Bahamas, a number of digressions are required to see them all; in fact, a series of loops are necessary, which we will cover, as logically as possible, in four parts.

First are the islands of Grand Bahama and Abaco, which occupy the Little Bahama Bank and serve as the northern approaches. Second are the central approaches via Bimini and Cat Cay through the Berry Islands to the center of things at Nassau, and in this part we will include Andros, the biggest of the Bahama Islands but one of the least visited. Third is the figure-8 loop of the central Bahamas, which leads across to Spanish Wells and continues down the lee of the long, thin sliver of Eleuthera, across to the gorgeous Exuma chain, down to the popular terminus at George Town, and across deep Exuma Sound to the sheltered bights of drowsing Cat Island and back to Nassau. The fourth and last part includes the remaining islands southeast of Cat and Little Exuma Islands. They are seldom visited except by yachts on passage to Puerto Rico, Haiti, or Jamaica. Their full exposure to the prevailing easterlies and, up to now, the lack of yacht facilities have discouraged visitors. Though nothing has been done about the weather, more and more yachts will probably sail along these southernmost Bahamas to get to the budding facilities in the Caicos Islands beyond.

THE LITTLE BAHAMA BANK (26320)

Most northerly of the Bahama chain, the Little Bahama Bank stands apart from the rest of the islands to the south, separated by the deep ocean straits of Northwest and Northeast Providence Channels. As a cruising area it ranks high by any standard, offering its own distinctive combination of reefs, cays, and sandy beaches, interspersed with more than the usual number of snug harbors and historic settlements.

Only by comparision with the Great Bahama Bank can this northern tier of islands and banks be characterized as "little." Within its own boundaries, the Little Bank occupies a vast area of some 6,000 square miles of pale green waters, fringed to the north and east by one of the longest barrier reefs in the Western Hemisphere and bordered on the south by Great Abaco and Grand Bahama, the second and third largest islands in all the Bahamas.

For those cruising the Bahamas for the first time, the northern bank provides a convenient starting point for a more extended cruise. As we note below, the 55-mile Gulf Stream crossing between Palm Beach and West End, Grand Bahama, is one of the easiest routes to the islands, longer by a few miles than the Miami–Bimini–Cat Cay route, but with a better landfall channel for entering at

West End. Crossing the Little Bank to the Abaco Cays is generally easier—at least for sailboats—than making the long run from Bimini across the 90-mile stretch of the Great Bahama Bank to the Berry Islands and beyond to the Central Bahamas. There are no navigational problems, and the main routes across the bank to some harbor of protection are relatively short. If you are looking for a cruising ground close enough to reach easily in your own boat, yet remote enough to be off the main tourist tracks and interesting enough to invite exploration by sail or power, keep your head pointed eastward across the Little Bank to the Abaco Cays.

The Abaco Cays

Situated in the northeastern half of the bank, the Abacos are sheltered from the open Atlantic by the long barrier reef that extends for 140 miles from Mantanilla Shoal to Little Harbour, with the wooded coastline of Great and Little Abaco closing in on the southeast side of the bank for the last 50 miles of that distance. Lying between the "mainland" of Great Abaco and the chain of low coral cays behind the barrier reef are the protected bank waters of the Sea of Abaco, forming the heart of this historic maritime area.

The Abaco Cays are sea islands with a heritage. First settled during the American Revolution by Loyalists from the Carolinas and southern New England, the islands remained isolated seafaring communities for more than 150 years. Today they are no longer isolated; Abaco airports are less than an hour's

The Abaco Cays

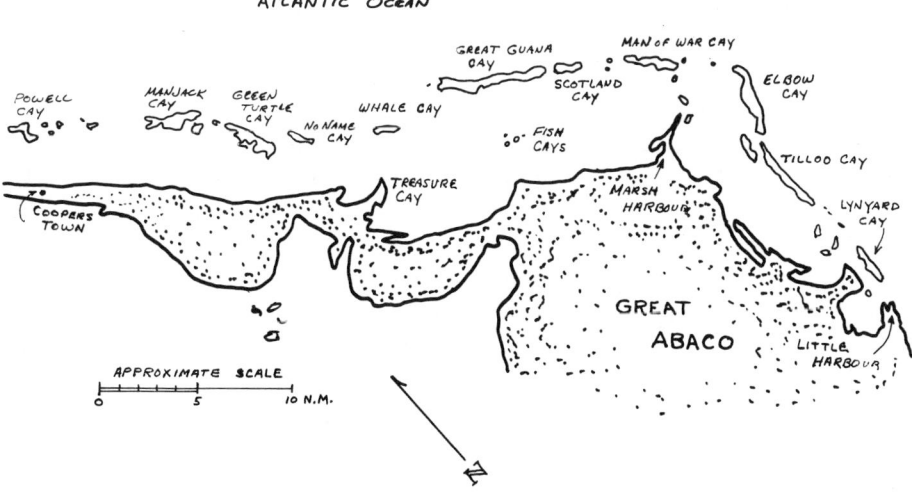

flying time from Nassau or Florida. But in the prim little settlements at Hope Town, Man-O-War Cay, and New Plymouth, most of the inhabitants are descendants of the early settlers, bearing English names like Albury, Lowe, Russell, and Sweeting. The settlements all front on the water, with small frame houses clustered together around the harbors and along narrow streets and pathways reminiscent of Nantucket or Stonington in an earlier age. Communication between the settlements is entirely by boat (except for the ubiquitous C/B radio-telephone) and most of the villages are close enough to be within easy reach of each other by small craft in almost any weather.

This is the heart of a unique cruising area. It lacks the high hills of the Virgin Islands or the lush tropical verdure of the Grenadines, but it surpasses both in its miles of white sandy beaches and pale blue and green waters in which one soon learns to pilot safely by eye. Over the past 20 years, we've cruised many other parts of the Bahamas and West Indies, each with its own particular charms, but we have yet to find any area we enjoy revisiting more than the nearby Abacos. We are drawn not just by the sparkling waters, the unspoiled beaches, or even the proximity of so many snug harbors, although all of these attractions contribute to the enjoyment of cruising the area. For us, this particular corner of the Little Bahama Bank is unique in the distinctive charm of its settlements and the simple integrity of its people, who have retained their Anglo-Saxon character through two centuries of a rapidly changing world. The Abacos, it's said, have an ambience all their own.

Planning an Abaco Cruise

If you are planning to cruise the Abacos in your own boat, don't try to do it all in a week, even though you may feel you're pressed for time on a fast passage to other parts. Though it is possible to transit the area under power in two or three daylight runs, with overnight stops at Green Turtle or Marsh Harbour, and continuing outside in another day's passage to Eleuthera, we don't recommend any such timetable. If you plan to charter in the Abacos, a week's cruise may allow you to do the Green Turtle–Marsh Harbour circuit, but it won't give you half the time you'll wish you'd had for leisurely cruising. Our suggestion is to allow 10 days as a minimum, and more if possible. An increasing number of yachtsmen make the Abacos their winter base, leaving their boats at one of the yards in the area. Others who arrive in the Abacos on the first leg of an extended cruise, expecting to pass on in a week, often linger several months before feeling the urge to move. So be flexible, and allow your plans to change from day to day.

In the following sections, we describe briefly the highlights of an Abaco cruise, looking at some of the harbors and settlements that we enjoy revisiting and you might include in a 10-day itinerary. For sailing directions across the bank and piloting in and out of the harbors, you must keep the *Yachtsman's Guide* handy for ready reference in the pilothouse or cockpit; a set of Harry Kline's blown-up sketch charts—14 of which cover the Abacos—are always useful to have aboard. We indicate the appropriate charts for each area. Follow them carefully, and you shouldn't have any piloting problems, although we have noted a few channels where we've been able to carry a greater depth than indicated on the charts. But use your depth finder or lead line, and don't get careless!

Approaching the Abacos from West End, most cruising powerboats allow two days for the 125-mile run across the bank to the Marsh Harbour–Hope Town area, while smaller sailing auxiliaries often take three days, with overnight stops at Great Sale and Green Turtle Cays. The bank waters on this route range from 1½ to 3½ fathoms over clear sandy bottom with virtually no hidden dangers.

Marsh Harbour, Great Abaco (H-8) is the supply center for the "Hub of Abaco," the maritime triangle bounded by Man-O-War Cay to the north and Hope Town and Elbow Cay to the east. Two airlines schedule daily flights to and from Florida and Nassau; local ferry service to Man-O-War and Hope Town is provided by the Alburys' reliable all-weather water taxis.

The Town Dock on the south shore of the main harbor is a convenient starting point for the Golden Harvest shopping center with its food market, laundromat, and liquor store, and is within easy walking distance of several banks, hardware stores, the post office, and other shops and service establishments. The Union Jack Motel and restaurant are just back of the dock, and the new Conch Inn, with its marina, snack bar, and first-class restaurant are less than half a mile up the harbor. The marina has slips for a dozen cruising-size vessels drawing up to 6 feet, fuel pumps for gas and diesel, and water and ice. Caribbean Sailing Yachts is based at the head of the harbor, with some 30 bareboat charter yachts cruising the area. While Marsh Harbour is protected from the prevailing easterly winds, it is exposed to the W and NW and very uncomfortable in the early stages of a winter norther. Most cruising yachts prefer Hope Town or Man-O-War for an overnight anchorage, though the shopping is not as good.

Hope Town (H-9) is surely the most photographed harbor in the Bahamas. Its candy-striped lighthouse and completely landlocked harbor make it a popular anchorage for all boats cruising the area. It is headquarters for Abaco Bahamas Charters, Ltd., who operate a fleet of bareboat charter yachts in the 30-to-40-foot range. The Hope Town Sailing Club welcomes visiting yachtsmen to participate in its occasional regattas for cruising boats, and to join its Saturday evening BYOB gatherings at the clubhouse near the waterfront. Hope Town

Harbour Lodge, with its unpretentious Bahamian decor, has a good restaurant, a swimming pool, and an ocean beach with snorkeling on the reefs offshore. Groceries are obtained at Vernon's on the Queen's Highway and several other small stores in the settlement. Look for homemade bread at Bessie's Bakery. Gasoline and diesel fuel are available at the Lighthouse Marina and dock; it's on your right at the harbor entrance just below the 120-foot lighthouse. If you don't mind climbing the 101 steps to the top, this century-old lighthouse with its weighted mechanism for turning the lights is worth a visit. The view from the top is lovely.

With Hope Town as a base, we have often spent several delightful days exploring the inside passage leading south between Elbow Cay and Lubbers Quarters, where there's a good shelling beach. Six feet can be taken into White Sound, with anchorage inside. Then, if you continue on around Tilloo Bank, through the marked passage leading inside North Bar Channel, you come to Lynyard Cay and Little Harbour on the Abaco mainland about 16 miles south of Hope Town. Here you'll find some fascinating coral reefs off Sandy Cay and in the Pelican Cays Underwater Preserve, maintained by the Bahamas National Trust.

Little Harbour, Abaco (H-11) is one of our favorite Abaco anchorages and perhaps the most intriguing harbor we have visited in the northern Bahamas. But we cannot broadcast its special attractions without endangering its secret charms, including its isolation and enduring tranquility. Enter if you dare, but only on a rising tide at the top of the flood, and then only if you draw less than 6 feet. Then find an anchorage, if you can, off the sandy crescent beach. For those who cannot get into Little Harbour itself, nearby Lynyard Cay offers surprisingly good shelter even when it's blowing hard out of the SE.

Visit the Johnston Studio, where some of Randolph Johnston's famous bronze castings may be on display, along with Margot's ceramic art and son Pete's bronze whales and porpoises. Randolph Johnston is one of the few artists in the world to use the ancient lost-wax process of casting bronze, which he does with his own smelter and self-made equipment.

There's a good close-in coral reef right off the beach at the entrance to Little Harbour, and "blue holes" in the bight of Old Robinson.

Man-O-War Cay (H-7), 4½ miles north of Marsh Harbour and about the same distance W of Hope Town, keeps alive the Abaco boatbuilding tradition and is justly proud of its reputation. Entering the narrow, 60-foot wide channel at the east end of Dickey Cay, you are midway between two harbors: one opens up sharply to the right, the other leads northward into a crowded anchorage and a colorful waterfront lined with docks, boatyards, and marine railways.

Here you'll find all manner of yachts and local craft tied alongside or moored in the channel.

A new U-shaped marina and fuel dock is home port for the Albury ferry service and provides slips for up to 30 yachts; the largest can berth an 80-footer. The entrance channel and berths will carry 6 feet at MLW.

You will find Alburys in all parts of the Bahamas, but at one time or another most of them came from Man-O-War, and almost half of the families living on the island today bear that family name. Marcel and Ritchie Albury operate the ferry fleet of fine, sturdy M-O-W-built powerboats that ply between Marsh Harbour, Hope Town, Guana, and Scotland Cays; they manage the fuel dock and new marina, and Ritchie's wife Sylvia surpervises the Dock-n-Dine restaurant, the only public eating place in the settlement.

The William Albury Shipyard, founded in 1888, built many fine Abaco schooners in the days when power tools were unknown. Its two railways can haul yachts up to 60 feet and 6 feet draft. "Uncle Will" Albury, who died in 1972, ran the yard for half a century, building large wood yachts and motor sailers to yacht standards. Under Scott Weatherford, the yard continues to do excellent repair work, and is prepared to accept orders for custom-built motor sailers.

The Edwin Albury Boat Yard, a few steps down the waterfront, now the largest yard, has two marine railways, carpenter shop, new machine shop, engine repair facilities, shore storage space, and several moorings in the harbor. Edwin, too, has built auxiliary yachts and motor sailers, and one of his recent boats, the 42-foot motor sailer *Mallolo,* is berthed in the harbor. Edwin's father, Maurice Albury, has a small shop at the top of the hill, where he builds classic Abaco sailing dinghies famous for their sailing qualities and fine construction.

The sail loft nearby is run by "Uncle Norman" Albury, his wife, Selina, and their daughter, Lois. They make highly prized duffle bags, yachting jackets, hats, and other hand-sewn canvas accessories. Norman, now well into his seventies, is still the best walking source of news on the island. You'll soon notice that the older people around here, in talking, will drop an 'h' whenever it comes along and add one where it doesn't belong. Haziel Albury, principal of the three-unit school, has been postmaster and lay preacher on Sundays. Willard and Benny Albury, in their yard near Edwin's, turn out wood-hulled outboards using local Madeira frames; they still compete successfully with fiberglass boats throughout the islands. No visit to Man-O-War is complete without making the rounds of these active yards and shops.

If the harbor in front of the town is crowded, as it is likely to be, visiting yachts can find an equally protected anchorage, with more swinging room, in 12 to 15 feet of water in the eastern branch. A number of yachts owned by American residents are moored there.

Great Guana and Scotland Cays (H-4), between Man-O-War and Green Turtle, offer several anchorages for overnight or midday visits. The lagoon between the two islands has a spectacular sandy beach and natural pool that's worth exploring, but if your boat draws over 3 feet you'll have to anchor outside, near the pier at the eastern entrance.

Guana settlement is built around a crescent beach in Guana Cove, with a town dock at the northwest corner adjacent to the marina-pier of Guana Harbour Club, where visiting yachts can usually find a berth in no more than 6 feet at MLW. The harbor is wide open to winds from SE to SW, however, and under such conditions you may want to get out in a hurry. You will find better protection in the west harbor behind the small rocky cay. The ocean beach, a quarter-mile walk from the harbor, is one of the best in the Abacos.

Whale Cay Passage (H-13) is strongly advised for yachts drawing 5 feet or more when making the passage between Guana and Green Turtle, to avoid grounding on the long, shallow sand bank (with less than 6 feet over it at high tide) that extends right across the sound to the mainland of Abaco. You might get through on the last hour of a rising tide by running close in behind Whale Cay, or by taking the intricate "Don't Rock" passage off Treasure Cay, but the outside course assures you deep water and is not much longer. Follow directions in the *Yachtsman's Guide* and you should have no trouble in settled weather. But beware of northers, which can make the passage impossible when winds from NW to NE exceed 30 knots, or when a distant storm builds up steep rollers that break angrily across the channel bars at both ends of Whale Cay. This condition, which occurs even in relatively calm weather when the ocean swells reach a certain height, is appropriately called a "rage." Even in light wind conditions we have encountered 12-foot swells, not breaking and therefore not dangerous. It's worth remembering this in planning a one-week cruise, as you might find yourself stranded on the wrong side of Whale Cay in a rage lasting several days.

Green Turtle Cay (H-6) is one of the most appealing of the Abaco cays, rivaling Man-O-War and Hope Town as a port of call. It is higher than most of the others, rising to nearly 100 feet, and has an indented shoreline on the south opening into two landlocked bays known as White Sound and Black Sound. There is a small harbor in the settlement of New Plymouth. Over a century ago, New Plymouth had a population of 1,500; blockade running during the Civil War made the island suddenly prosperous, but today the settlement has declined to less than 500 permanent residents.

Green Turtle is a port of entry, and the Commissioner is helpful to yachtsmen cruising the area. Three clubs or lodges offer shore accommodations and yacht services: Bluff House, atop an 80-foot headland, and the nearby Green Turtle Club, both in White Sound, and The Other Shore Club on Black Sound. All have fuel docks, slips, and the usual facilities. Six feet can be taken into Black Sound, but if you draw over 5½ feet you will have to enter White Sound at the top of the tide.

There's an inn on the main street of New Plymouth, several well-stocked stores, and the Blue Bee Bar at the south end of town—the only place in the outer Abaco cays where "package goods" are sold. The mailboat and island trading steamers tie up alongside Government Dock at the NW end of the settlement, where there is usually room for one or two cruising boats to land for shopping.

The Cays between Green Turtle and Walker's (H-1, H-2, H-3)

On a 10-day to 2-week cruise, few boats get much beyond Green Turtle, although this is a convenient place to lay over for a day or more to fish the reefs or explore the cays to the west, where some of the better coves and beaches are. But watch out if a norther is making up, as there is not much protection westward of Green Turtle until you get to the end of the bank at Walker and Grand Cays.

Manjack Cay is just W of Green Turtle. In addition to the Crab Cay anchorage at the south end (shown in *Yachtsman's Guide*), try the cove at the north tip of Manjack, with its half-moon beach. The cove can be entered from the NW with 6 feet, but it's exposed from the W to N.

Powell Cay has one of the best shelling beaches in the area. It's on the south side of this privately owned but uninhabited island, where a former settler has left a well-built pier. Don't leave plastic garbage bags ashore as too many thoughtless visitors have done. The anchorage off the pier is good in a moderate norther but exposed to the S and SW.

Allan's Pensacola Cay has one of the best harbors west of Green Turtle, off a sandy beach near the 250-foot radio mast. You can take 6 feet into this anchorage at LW but it's uncomfortable in a norther. The "hurricane hole" at the SE end of the cay carries only 4 feet at high water.

Carter Cays are four low islands about 20 miles NW of Allan's Pensacola, outside the usual cruising range from Green Turtle but providing overnight anchorage for vessels crossing the banks. A strong tidal current runs through the anchorage near the tracking station, and there's no protection in a norther.

Grand Cays and Walker Cay are the two northernmost islands in the chain. Grand Cays is a port of entry, with a small settlement around the inner harbor. Walker's Cay Club is a top sportfishing resort, with modern marina, swimming pool, restaurant and bar, all quite plush and not inexpensive. The approach channel is marked by day beacons and will carry 5 feet to the marina, which has a similar controlling depth. Walker's is a good departure point for northbound vessels to ride the axis of the Gulf Stream to Charleston or Morehead City. We've made Charleston from Walker's in 48 hours under working sails.

Great Sale and Little Sale Cays are two islands lying halfway between West End and Green Turtle on the direct route across the bank, providing a convenient overnight stop for sailing vessels and low-speed, displacement powerboats. Best anchorage in the prevailing easterlies is the long harbor at the S end of Great Sale, between the scissors-like prongs of lowland forming the bight, but it is exposed to the S and W.

In mild weather out of the S, we spent a very comfortable night anchored in the lee of Little Sale Cay just E of the light and close in under the 40-foot cliffs, where there is a prominent cleft. There is 9 feet 60 yards off, and the sandy bottom provides powerful holding and peace of mind. This is a useful alternative to Great Sale Harbour which is wide open to winds from SSE to SW.

Mangrove Cay, halfway between Great Sale and West End, Grand Bahama, has no harbor but provides good anchorage ½-mile off its N end in 8 to 10 feet.

Little Abaco and Hawksbill Cays provide the only anchorages on the north coast of Little Abaco. There is a temporary shelter in a cove behind some rocks a few hundred yards off the west end of Little Abaco, but it's no place to lie overnight in unsettled weather. The Hawksbill Cays provide better protection and are closer to the direct route across the bank, with the settlement of Fox Town close by to the S. "Center of the World Rock" is 3 miles E of the Hawksbills.

Mainland of Great Abaco (H-3, H-4)

The north coast of Great Abaco from Angel Fish Point at the western end to Treasure Cay 20 miles eastward carries deep water close inshore with only one settlement, Cooperstown, and no harbors to beckon the cruising yachtsman. Gasoline and diesel fuel are available at Cooperstown, where crayfish and other products of the sea may usually be found at one of the small stores or houses along the waterfront. The government pier and nearby fuel dock are exposed to all winds except those from the S—an uncomfortable place to lie when there's a chop. Not recommended for an overnight berth.

Treasure Cay is the largest resort development in the Abacos, with Treasure Cay Inn and Marina offering all possible shoreside facilities: swimming pool, golf and tennis, two restaurants and bar, commissary, rest rooms and showers. The dredged channel leading to the marina supposedly carries 6 feet, but watch for shoaling on both sides. Drawing 6 feet, and at the top of the tide, *Yellow Bird* grazed bottom twice. The area around the entrance to the channel has shoaled badly and needs dredging. There are slips and moorings for maybe 40 boats, with plenty of water for washing down and the best drinking water in the Abacos. The 5-mile beach is superb.

Cherokee Sound and Settlement lies 20 miles S of Marsh Harbour and 6 miles S of Little Harbour. It's perhaps the most isolated and remote settlement in Abaco, without any direct road or land connection with other parts of the Abaco mainland. Once an important shipbuilding and fishing community, its population has dwindled to less than a hundred older natives; most of the young people have migrated to other parts in search of employment. The entrance to Cherokee Sound is through a narrow break in the reef, leading into a shallow bank beyond Duck Cay where the controlling depth is not over 4 feet. Nevertheless, you will find a protected anchorage in 6 to 8 feet between Mangrove and Riding Cay, about ¾ of a mile from the settlement, which you can only reach by dinghy. If you can find someone to pilot you in, Cherokee is well worth a visit; but we don't recommend trying it alone for the first time except under ideal sea and light conditions. (We have heard from a Cherokee mariner that you can anchor close behind Cherokee Point, in 6 feet of water, after entering through an opening in the reef that is plainly visible in good weather; but we haven't had an opportunity to verify this ourselves.)

The coast between Cherokee and Hole-in-the-Wall provides no shelter of any kind, and coastal vessels keep well off to avoid the rocky shoals near Guineaman Bay. The only possible anchorage is at the very southern tip of Abaco in the tiny bight appropriately called Hole-in-the-Wall. Here you might find temporary shelter if caught in a norther, but in our estimation it's a dubious anchorage at any time. The surge is constant, and it's no place to be if the wind shifts into the south.

The Bight of Abaco (H-12)

This is the great unknown cruising ground of the Abacos, seldom visited by local boatmen and rarely by cruising yachts. Occupying the entire SE side of the bank, it covers an area five times as large as Abaco Sound and has its own distinctive character. Here you will be very much on your own in a strange group of islands and cays with low profiles and distant horizons. The Bight is full of contrasts and surprises: it looks remote on the charts, and it is; it looks hard to reach and difficult to navigate, but it's not; it looks mostly shallow, but it's more often deep. It seems to have few protected harbors, yet there are many good anchorages where you can find shelter in most weather.

You can reach The Bight easily from any direction, and you can circumnavigate Great and Little Abaco including the best of The Bight in your itinerary. One should allow at least a week for such an expedition, and be prepared to hole up for a few days if you encounter heavy weather. Starting from the north, you have a choice: you can round Hole-in-the-Wall and continue clockwise around Sandy Point, then head NNW across The Bight for 60 miles to the west end of Little Abaco, where you reenter Abaco Sound across West End Bars; you can carry 6 feet there with proper respect for the tides. Or you can reverse this course, starting counterclockwise at the western end and finishing at Little Harbour or Hope Town. From Nassau, the Berry Islands, or elsewhere in the south, you can enter The Bight from the deep water of Providence Channel anywhere between Sandy Cay and Mores Island. Once inside The Bight, you will be able to take a 6-foot-draft vessel virtually anywhere except into The Marls, a shallow, impassable area at the northeast end of Great Abaco. A week's cruise could include the following islands, cays and settlements:

Sandy Point is a port of entry at the SE corner of Abaco and undoubtedly one of the most interesting and attractive settlements in the Bahamas. It's a community that makes its livelihood entirely from the sea. There are two anchorages at the north end.

Gorda Cay is a small island not far off Providence Channel, about 8 miles NE of Sandy Point, with two harbors, several anchorages, and a tiny settlement.

Mores Island is the largest island in The Bight, with a settlement called Hard Bargain (well named, not friendly) and a smaller fishing village known as The Bight, neither of which has a protected anchorage.

Woolendean Cays offer an anchorage in 5 feet of water off a sandy beach at the north end of this chain of small cays, which are used by fisherman during the crayfish season.

Joe Downer Cays are larger and somewhat higher than the Woolendeans and offer several anchorages, the best of which is off South Downer.

Norman Castle was a busy logging center early in this century from which lumber was shipped by schooners. Remains of the pier may still be seen, but wild horses and hogs are the only living creatures in the old lumber town ashore. There are two anchorages in 6 to 8 feet S of Davis Point.

Basin Harbour to Randall's Cay are a group of rocky limestone cays at the NW corner of The Bight, undoubtedly the most spectacular in the Abacos. Basin Harbour Cay rises perpendicularly, its limestone cliffs reaching a height of 50 feet and dropping off into 20 feet of water at the base. It has two harbors with protected anchorages. Between Basin Harbour and Randall's you'll find several other snug anchorages amid the rocky cays, and one in Big Cut, which carries deep water through this little archipelago. This is an interesting place to lay over for a day of exploring or bonefishing in the area.

Spence Rock and Cave Cay are your landmarks for the passage around the W end of Little Abaco, leading back into Abaco Sound and the N coast of Great Abaco. At Spence Rock you leave the deeper waters (12–24 feet) that cover most of the middle and upper Bight, to pass through one of the winding channels described in the *Yachtsman's Guide*. There are shoal spots, but if you follow directions carefully you can sound your way through with 5–5½ feet and arrive on the other side with a sense of satisfaction and, we might add, relief. Prudent navigators go through on a rising tide, preferably the last two hours of flood.

If you are looking for something different and enjoy a feeling of being alone, try The Bight for a week. But if you need marinas and shoreside facilities, keep on toward the west and you will find them on Grand Bahama Island.

GRAND BAHAMA ISLAND (26320)

Occupying the southwestern corner of the Little Bahama Bank, Grand Bahama Island looks out on the deep aquamarine waters of Northwest Providence Channel to the south and the pale-green shallows of the bank to the north. This low, pine-clad island is about 65 miles long, averaging 7 miles wide, with a land area of approximately 530 square miles, as compared with Abaco's 650.

The entire north coast is virtually inaccessible to yachts of even moderate draft and, being low and swampy, really has nothing to attract cruising boats. Some years ago we took our powerboat, *Out Islander*, drawing 3½ feet, into the uncharted maze of swashes and brown bars that lie along a general course of 125° to the northern end of Water Cay, where we anchored about 300 yards off, after searching for a pocket deep enough to leave us afloat at low tide. The channel all the way to the settlement here might have carried 3 feet, but by that time we were in no mood for further experimentation. In trying to track down some of the folklore of the area, our expedition ashore at Water Cay was eminently unsuccessful—we never saw Boomy, the man-eating ostrich, nor did we find the house of Greybeard the pirate.

Going out the next morning we ran aground, nicked a propeller, noted that the tide lags Memory Rock by 1½ to 2 hours, and while glumly waiting to float off, came to the positive conclusion that though these waters may be useful for practicing advanced eyeball navigation, the area is really only suitable for trimarans and cats. The only suitable harbors are those at West End and at Freeport–Lucaya, 20 miles eastward along the south shore, and among the cays and creeks at the extreme east end of Grand Bahama.

West End (B-2) is the principal port of entry for yachts crossing the Stream from Palm Beach. Vessels making a night passage can see the red flashing light atop the 215-foot radio-TV tower at West End from 20 miles at sea in clear weather, but in daylight the tall casuarina trees at Settlement Point are seldom visible for more than 7–8 miles. The channel to the marina is straightforward, with markers between Indian Cay and West End Point, but a strong tide runs through the cut, creating a tide-rip and very steep seas when the wind is blowing strong against the current. In a norther, the channel may become impassable.

If you're entering for the first time, don't be confused by the channel to the commercial basin, which lies to the right of the breakwater separating it from the marked channel to the yacht basin, and keep at least 75 yards N of the breakwater to avoid the shoal that makes off from North Point. The dredged cut into the marina is reported to shoal up after winter storms, but the last time we used the channel we found nothing less than 8 feet at half tide.

The marina is operated by the Grand Bahama Hotel (which seems to specialize in huge conventions and cut-rate tours) and provides all the usual facilities: fuel, water, ice, electricity, showers, travel lift, and an engine shop. Customs and immigration officials are automatically notified when a yacht enters flying its Q flag, and the crew should remain aboard until the vessel has been cleared. A food store, various shops, restaurants galore, and a lake-sized swimming pool at the Grand Bahama Hotel are all close by. So is the golf course and a commercial airport. The native settlement is ½-mile east of the hotel on the north shore.

There's an anchorage off the hotel for vessels drawing 4–5 feet. A shallow sandbank affords some protection, but this spot is exposed to winds from NW to SE and is very uncomfortable in a norther. Only shallow-draft boats should proceed past the hotel dock where the excursion stern-wheeler lies.

A deep anchorage will be found in Cross Bay between Settlement Point and the commercial harbor entrance, in 25–30 feet over a hard sand bottom. Here you will have protection from the prevailing easterlies but will be exposed to westerlies and northers. Vessels arriving at night often take temporary anchorage here to await daylight.

The channel leading northeasterly onto the bank just N of Indian Cay will carry about 7 feet LW in the vicinity of markers 3 and 4, and considerably more elsewhere, until you approach the entrance marker with the radar reflector out on the bank. Here it is best to keep S of the marker by at least 200 yards.

We have passed on and off the bank 4 miles N of Sandy Cay and have not seen any rocky bars, but at low tide there are some sand bores that will not carry 5½ feet. At better than half tide (and rising) we believe this route is safe for 6 feet for a night crossing, although radar is essential for picking up Sandy Cay, which is the one and only point of reference out here. Unfortunately the loran lines don't parallel this course for easy tracking.

Freeport (26323) is strictly a commercial port, developed as part of the Freeport bunkering and industrial complex and used by large tankers and bulk cargo vessels. It is a port of entry; the Customs Office is located close by the Port Director in the first basin to starboard on entering. However—except in an emergency, yachts should enter at Lucaya, in Bell Channel 6 miles E of Freeport. Vessels approaching from West End are warned to keep 4 miles off the coast because of shoaling on the edge of the bank (not indicated on 26320) and to keep a lookout for bunkering moorings off the harbor entrance. Half a dozen large tankers may be moored here at a time.

Lucaya–Bell Channel (B-13) is made conspicuous by several high-rise hotels visible long before you sight the sea buoy lying a mile off the beach. The controlling depth is 6 feet MLW between the sea buoy and the jetties on the 345° approach course. Slips and other yacht facilities are available at the docks of the Lucayan Beach Hotel, to port as you enter Bell Channel Bay, where you can clear customs and immigration.

The pretentious 150-slip marina on the northern side of the Bay was closed during part of the 1973–74 season but may have reopened by the time you read this. The casino at Lucaya Beach was permanently closed in 1974, but those who earnestly seek that kind of entertainment can still find it at El Casino in Freeport, a 5-mile taxi drive away.

The facilities in Bell Channel Bay are manifestly geared more to sport-fishermen and large power yachts than to more modest cruising auxiliaries.

Xanadu Princess and Running Mon Marinas, 2½ miles and ½ mile respectively E of Bell Channel, are manmade harbors entered through dredged channels, but you should plan to sound your way in because shoaling has been reported in the entrances. The few boats in these places are locals, and the facilities are generally run-down. In fact, the whole Freeport–Lucaya residential and recreational area has failed to develop as had been anticipated under the previous government.

Peterson Cay, a tiny mangrove cay 6 miles E of Bell Channel, provides one of the few sheltered anchorages in the 40-mile coastline between Lucaya and the eastern end of Grand Bahama Island. The anchorage is NE of the cay and a brown reef that breaks in onshore winds, with 4–6 feet over a sand bottom.

BIMINI, CAT CAY, THE BERRYS, NASSAU, AND ANDROS

The shortest distance (45 miles) across the Gulf Stream is from Miami to Bimini or Gun Cay, with a powerful beam current all the way. But in terms of time, it is almost the same to start off from, say, Key Largo, since you will get a lift from the current and often a better slant of wind. In the winter season, the northers seem to come through with exasperating regularity, so you may have to figure on waiting several days for the right conditions to make the crossing—and we can assure you that the Stream is no place to be during strong northerly winds, when conditions in the "hump," where the current is running at its maximum pace against the wind, must be seen to be believed. We often use the waiting time to wend further south along the Intracoastal Waterway to get that better slant when the time is right to start across.

Headed for New Providence, the various routes across the banks converge on Northwest Channel Beacon with the excellent shelter of Chub Cay just beyond, thence across another stretch of deep water where the conflicting ocean currents tend to set up a confused sea under windy conditions.

Bimini to Northwest Channel (26320)

To come in off the deep dark-blue of the Gulf Stream to the unbelievably clear waters of Bimini or Gun Cay with their vivid hues of blue and green and almost-white, to feel a softer wind in one's face and to see the restless surge chomping at the undercut coral edges of the cays, is an experience to be savored again and again, no matter how many times one crosses the Stream.

Both Bimini and Cat Cay are ports of entry, but have little else in common. Bimini is gay, a little on the honkytonk side, and completely addicted to deep-sea fishing. Cat Cay is profoundly quiet, a place of gracious homes set deep among the old palms and casuarina trees; the faint hum of golfcarts is the only sound of traffic, and big yachts and elaborate sportfishermen lie almost unobtrusively in the neat little harbor.

Bimini (26324) is shielded by a bar that projects from the southern tip of North Bimini and parallels the beach for most of the length of South Bimini. Through the years, there have been several channels across this bar, but the deepest one now, and the one currently used by the local freight boats, is to come in on a northeasterly heading toward the prominent water tower on South Bimini so as to pass just north of the rocky shoal that makes out from the shore. Once inside the bar, hold along the beach until you see the obvious channel trending toward the tip of North Bimini and leading into the busy harbor with its several full-fledged marinas.

If caught by a norther and unsure of the pass across the bar, shelter may be found just inside Round Rock at the south end of South Bimini. Another escape from the big seas of the Gulf Stream can be made into Barnett's Harbour, carefully placing yourself midway between the beacon on Picquet Rocks and the Triangle Rocks immediately north. "Harbour" is a misnomer in this case, but it is surprising how the sea flattens out as soon as you are inside the line of the bank, even though the surge is usually present.

Cat Cay (26320) is snug, secure, free of the current that sluices through Bimini, and easily accessible even to deep-draft boats. However, you must first negotiate the zig-zag of the Gun Cay Passage, which is somewhat frightening the first time through, especially when the current produces a strong rip. Approach the rocky southernmost tip of Gun Cay on a southeasterly heading and turn the corner sharply and only a boats-length away from the rocks. Stand along the low cliff for 30–50 yards and then bear away at right angles toward the tip of the conspicuous sand shoal, which you will leave close to port. These maneuvers will avoid the very shallow brown bar that runs north from the tip of Cat Cay.

Although Cat Cay is a private club, transients who observe the island's rules are entirely welcome. However, the services are expensive. Each year when we pass through here on our way to or from the islands, we look forward to seeing Jimmy, Cat Cay's large, efficient, and jovial dockmaster, who has been an important fixture of the island through good times and bad.

Routes Across the Bank (26320)

Using the corner of the prominent reef off Cat Cay Harbour as a departure point, the best passage across the upper part of the Great Bahama Bank now lies on a direct course to Russel Beacon, bypassing Sylvia Beacon. We have found just over 6 feet at one-quarter tide between 2.9 and 5 miles out from the Cat Cay reef, and another shoal area of 6–7 feet about 15 miles out. While it has been our general observation that the official charts tend to understate the depths on the banks, these particular shoals seem to conform very closely with the 1-fathom peckings on 26320.

Russel Beacon is the devil to find at the end of a 47-mile run, for you have no sure knowledge of which way the current has been setting and the mark, sitting on its 4-legged pedestal, is visible for only 4 miles even in good conditions. After running your time down, you might be lucky enough to sight some other yachts going the other way, which will give you a clue to Russel's probable position. If you should miss it altogether, you'll have an even harder time trying to locate the all-important Northwest Channel Beacon, 14 miles further, complicated by the fact that the intermediate flashing buoy which appeared on the chart in 1974 has been shifted to the north.

Seeking deeper water, we have tried the run from Bimini's North Rock straight to Mackie Shoal marker but we advise standing due east for 4 miles before taking up the direct course, in order to stay clear of the 1-fathom area accurately defined in 26320. A draft of 8 feet can easily be taken across here, and if set to the south, Mackie Shoal itself will be clearly seen, since its white water stands out sharply against the considerably deeper water around it.

Coming from the Florida Keys, we have entered the bank at Orange Cay and found 7–8 feet on the direct course from there to Russel. The entrance at South Riding Rock is also suitable for deeper-draft yachts, and either entry point affords a night's anchorage just inside the bank, although a surge is sure to be felt.

Northwest Channel Beacon, a slender light structure standing on a platform, may be safely passed about 100 yards or less to the north.

The Berry Islands (26308)

The whole bight on the inside of the crescent is shallow to the point of being nearly dry at low tide in many places. We have cruised some of the slightly navigable portions, such as the shortcut from Frazier's Hog Cay to Little Harbour, with 3½-foot draft and have felt very uncomfortable as we watched the needle of the depthfinder gradually drop, meanwhile seeing around us no perceptible "greening" of the whitish waters upon which we barely floated.

In summary, then, the Berrys offer mostly a weather shore with a number of relatively deep cuts between the low islands where shelter will be found from the seas if not from the swell.

If you're making a counterclockwise sweep around this chain, we can recommend the following anchorages.

Chub Cay (26320) lies 14 miles E of Northwest Channel Beacon, where an arm of the immensely deep Tongue of the Ocean intrudes into the bank and seems to establish all the requirements for an exciting sportfishing ground.

The big artificial basin at Chub Cay Club is easily entered under all sea conditions, day or night, and is a favorite stop for yachts after the long and rather monotonous run across the bank from Gun Cay. Unless a fishing tournament happens to be in progress, you will have no trouble finding a berth here in a functional, though not particularly pretty, setting.

Sometimes an overnight stay becomes unexpectedly extended while you wait out an easterly blow. That always produces a tumultuous sea between Chub and Nassau, owing to the convergence of currents from the Northeast and Northwest Providence Channels and from the Tongue of the Ocean.

Whale Cay (26311) offers rather meager shelter under the lighthouse at the southwestern end, but be careful to avoid the slightly submerged wreck of a barge near the middle of the cove. A better anchorage will be found in the pretty slot between Little Whale and Whale Cays, but you must respect the privacy of this place.

Frozen and Alder Cays (26311) combine to make a desolate yet beautiful anchorage in the narrow cove between them; the rocky bar that joins them on the ocean side seems to cut down most of the surge. We have found difficulty getting our anchor to bite in the grassy bottom here, and unless you can find a proper "hole," the depths are pretty skimpy for 6-foot draft.

Little Harbour (26311) is protected on the ocean side by high land and on the west by low, scraggy cays and by the shallow banks themselves. Anchoring in what might be called "the vestibule" abreast of Cabbage Cay, we lay to a strong current and rocked to a substantial swell that came in, only slightly moderated, over the bar. We envied the motorsailer of 4½-foot draft that lay way up in the inner harbor, not moving a mast in the still waters. But to get in there requires a high and rising tide and considerable skill and courage, because the channel is very ill defined.

Ten years earlier when we visited Little Harbour, it could have been called a settlement, for there were several families with dogs and poultry living there, and even some industry—in the form of a fishing smack being crafted by an old gentleman. He worked from a pile of gnarled tree shapes which, if you knew what you were looking for, and he did, would saw into rough but sound knees and frames. He's gone now, and so is old Mrs. Lightbourne; the only other inhabitant, when we were there in 1974, was in the hospital in Nassau. So don't count on anybody or anything at Little Harbour, including local knowledge to lead you into the sequestered inner basin.

Devil and Hoffman Cays (26308) are separated by a thin, rocky islet, which provides protection from the east and creates a splendid anchorage in 18 feet with good holding sand off its beach. The northern entrance is foul. Come in S of the islet exactly where two rocks are shown on 26308; but fear not, for the opening is wide, about 20 feet deep, and completely unobstructed.

Incidentally, when continuing north from here, stand out three-quarters of a mile or more. We ticked a coral head, in bad light conditions; it rose out of a seemingly safe 24-foot depth about 300 yards off the shore and a mile N of the south end of Hoffman's Cay.

Great Stirrup Cay (26258) gives you two, possibly three, choices for shelter. In winds from SW to NE, go in under the lighthouse; move around to Bertram's Cove if the wind is E or S.

This latter is an idyllic spot, complete with curving sand beach and swaying coconut palms, and reasonably protected by a long detached rock that looks like a man-made breakwater. Give the end of this rock a berth of 50 yards or more and come right in for the big and tiny rocks lying just off the beach, then swing E and move up to the beach, which shoals very gradually to 4–5 feet close in.

If you beat around in the bush about midway between the edge of the stand of coconut trees and the N end of the beach, you may find Commander Bertram's grave. The crew of H.M.S. *Tweed* buried their skipper here with tears and prayers on July 20th, 1834.

Three off-lying rocks and one solitary rock W of Bertram's Cove mark the entrance to Slaughter Harbour, which is merely the gap between Big and Little Stirrup Cays. There is no protection from the N and the relatively deep water projects like a horseshoe into the bank to the S. This wide, windswept anchorage has no advantages over picturesque Bertram's Cove.

Great Harbour Marina (26308) occupies what used to be a land-locked creek at the lower end of Great Harbour Cay. A fine, modern marina has been hacked out of the sand and limestone. The entrance from the E is through a man-made cut spanned by a man-propelled swing bridge. We understand that it once saw service on the Intracoastal Waterway near Dania, Florida. A more secure spot in a hurricane would be hard to find; at all other times, the setting is restful, gracious, and surrounded by the usual resort amenities, including an 18-hole golf course, a clubhouse high on a hill, and villas and condominiums galore.

To get to this mecca of instant leisure and luxury, run due S 2 miles from the W tip of Little Stirrup and turn southeasterly along the straight line of stakes leading across the bank. The first of these privately maintained finger markers is "3" and is located in 25°46.5′ N, 77°56.8′ W. Coming or going to Chub Cay from here, the shoals and foul ground N and W of Northwest Channel Beacon can be avoided by running a course from marker "3" or "5" to 24°29.2′ N, 78°14.8′ W, where a 2-second flasher used to be and may still show on the charts.

Great Harbour Marina is great for those who like that sort of place, but you have to have the will to go there, because it's well off the usual track to anywhere.

New Providence and Nassau (26309)

Having known Nassau in its waning days as a picturesque community—when the straw market was less commercial, when it was a common sight to see horse-drawn carriages clip-clopping and squeaking down Bay Street, and when there seemed to be some effort by the powers-that-were to retain the colonial charm that was Nassau's greatest asset—we now find the place grown into a lusty, buzzing city much less to our liking, not only along Bay Street and its byways, but on the waterfront as well. Others who have not experienced this year-to-year transition may of course have quite different impressions of Nassau. After all, Nassau is the center of all things in the Bahamas. Many a yacht comes through Gun Cay and Chub to Nassau and never goes any further, and virtually every boat cruising the central and southern Bahamas will find that their cruising plans radiate from this natural hub.

Nassau Harbour (26310) sports several full-service marinas at the E end of the harbor, but their fortunes, and consequently their attractiveness, have been changing with rather startling rapidity. All are adequate, and·Hurricane Hole on Paradise Island is currently considered the most attractive. How long this relatively small, 53-slip marina will continue to exist is a question, however, because Paradise Island is in the throes of a Miami Beach breed of development, and the area the marina occupies may soon become too valuable to justify a mere marina operation.

All the marinas, except the small and rather squalid Mermaid Marina, are an expensive taxi ride away from Bay Street, where the tourist goodies are sold, or from Palmdale Shopping Center, where provisions and other mundane needs are in good supply.

West of the bridge, along the Paradise Island shore to the pink Porcupine Club and beyond, there are plenty of places to anchor, although there may be some hazard in leaving the boat unattended in the evening. Another popular anchorage is off the British Colonial Hotel west of the cruise ship docks.

Coral Harbour (26309), on the opposite corner of the island from Nassau, was for years a focal point for cruising people until it burst its financial bubble a few years back. Now it lies a shambles in the shadow of the grey, far-from-finished high rises that were to have made it a showplace to vie with Paradise Island. The yacht basin is still the shelter that it always was, but only for anchoring, and a dismal aura of decrepitude pervades the place.

Lyford Cay (26309) is the only other marina outside of Nassau, but keep in mind that Lyford is a very private club. It may not turn away transient yachtsmen who are friends of members, but it does not encourage nonmembers to use its facilities.

The Eastern Approaches to Nassau (26309, 26306) include a mini-archipelago of islands, sparsely inhabited, that lie within plain sight of the high rises of the new Nassau. Among them are a handful of pleasant overnight anchorages; choose among them according to wind and sea conditions at the time. Of these we think the most useful are Victoria Beach at the east end of Paradise Island, the anchorage under little Spruce Cay north of Athol Island, and, most popular of all, Bottom Harbour under Rose Island. By virtue of the little horseshoe of islets that almost surround it, the last is excellent in a northerly blow and fairly good even in the prevailing southeasterlies, although some surge will be felt at high tide.

Andros Island (26308, 26303)

Although Andros is the biggest of the Bahama Islands, it has, we think, the least to offer the cruising man unless he is also an ardent fisherman.

The whole west coast is suitable only for wading, and the land itself looks like a lunar landscape. The east side is a weather shore like the Berrys, but much longer and without the safe and easy entrances from open water. Like the Abaco chain, Andros has a barrier reef, but it stands close in, and the inner channels are shallow, circuitous, inadequately charted, and pocked with coral heads and ledges. If you want to put your skill at eyeball piloting to the test, take 3½ feet down from Morgan's Bluff inside the reef, as we have done. You will find it as thrilling a venture as we did, especially the view out to sea through one of the few reef openings when the wind is blowing strongly onshore!

If you are the exploring type with a shallow-draft boat, the east side of Andros may give you pleasurable cruising, but there are so many other and easier places to cruise in the beautiful Bahamas that we find it hard to expound on the virtues of Andros.

An Unusual Departure (26303, 11161; BA 2009) for the Florida Keys via the south end of Andros has been recounted to us by John Somerhausen of the ketch *Pampero*. We include this outline of a 260-mile passage from South Bight, Andros, to Marathon, Fla., to show that the route is feasible and to give an example of how an inventive sailor may take advantage of prevailing winds, favorable currents, and isolated anchorages to get from A to B.

Actually, the Somerhausens came from Pipe Creek in the Exumas, using the marked Autec channel across the bank to South Bight, thence to Washerwoman's Cut with an overnight stop at the Autec site at Black Point Hill.

Near Washerwoman's Cut, *Pampero* anchored for the night about a mile W of Pigeon Cay, having made an eyeball approach from the S through scattered reefs. John advises that there are no white cliffs on the S end of Pigeon Cay as mentioned in the *Pilot,* also that arrival should be planned for early afternoon in order to have good light for making the anchorage.

Leaving Pigeon Cay as soon as it was light enough to see the numerous coral heads, *Pampero* followed the track recommended in 26303 as far as 23°19′ N, 77°40′ W, when course was altered for the Anguilla Cays on Cay Sal Bank. Through this critical area, John reports, the heads were easily seen from deck level and far enough apart so that only minor course alterations were needed.

Cay Sal Bank, described as a drowned coral atoll and one of only three such atoll formations in the Atlantic, is dotted around its perimeter with tiny cays and rocks; a few of these cays are long enough and high enough to offer a comfortable lee. The Bank is administered by the Bahamas, but the only habitation is on Cay Sal on the SW side of the Bank.

Pampero found a suitable overnight anchorage about 200 yards W of the northernmost of the Anguilla Cays in 20 feet, sand and rock. Thence she sailed NW across the bank to pass S of Double Headed Shot Cays, and on to Sombrero Cay and Marathon with the Florida Current full on the beam. Among these low, unreliably charted islands, any landmark is a significant advantage, and John reports that the disused lighthouse tower on Elbow Cay is visible about 10 miles off.

THE CENTRAL BAHAMAS

The most accessible islands east and south of Nassau may be reached in a figure-8 circuit without having to make any long open-water crossings. Once you have made it to Cat Island, you should, barring northers, have it all downwind back to Nassau.

We will start at the islands at the north end of Eleuthera, run down the sheltered bight to Powell Point, cross Exuma Sound at its narrowest point, and wend our way southeast amongst the exquisite Exuma chain, where water colors rival anything to be seen anywhere in the world. Then we'll cross Exuma Sound again to Cat Island, hopefully with a beam wind. Cat Island, where prosperous plantations once flourished, is now a poor and rather dejected place not much frequented by yachts. There is good sailing in its usually protected bight, but no adequate harbors for a deep-draft boat when winter northers roll in. From Little San Salvador it's a short skip across to Eleuthera again, then back to Nassau via Ship Channel at the top of Exuma Sound.

North Eleuthera (26305)

The run from Nassau to the islands of North Eleuthera offers at least a modest lee in strong northerly or easterly weather, depending on which side of Rose Island and the continuing string of rocks and cays you choose to run. The few landmarks are low and difficult to identify, so keep a close check on your DR. Current Cut is not as intricate as it may appear, but if you want to avoid it, use the wide and straightforward Fleeming Channel and enter the bank a half-mile north of Current Rock.

If you are coming from the Exumas, a direct approach may be made from Beacon Cay to North Eleuthera via the Fleeming Channel or Current Cut, providing you stand north to the deep water after passing Finley Cay. The first 8½ miles north of Beacon Cay are in 15–25 feet, after which the bottom turns rocky and sandy, with nests of coral heads all about. While these heads seem to be 10 feet down and surrounded by halos of sand, such areas must be treated with suspicion; consequently, we would not attempt this passage on a day with bewildering cloud shadows. In the vicinity of Finley Cay, the heads disappear and the bottom becomes pure white sand, occasionally 7½–8 feet deep, usually more.

Coming from the Abacos to the Spanish Wells area, the safest approach (indeed, the only approach in northerly weather or in less than perfect visibility), is via Egg Island. Be sure to establish safety bearings on Egg Island Light in order to clear the extensive and very dangerous reef that makes out from Egg Island. Nine or 10 miles will be saved, however, if conditions are right for using the break in the reef at Bridge Point on North Eleuthera. We recommend that you familiarize yourself with this route by first using it when heading north, for it is not easy to pinpoint your landfall after a 50-mile run south from Little Harbour bar.

Assuming safe conditions, here is how to enter through the reef. Steer due S for the beach just W of Bridge Point: this is the second beach visible to the east of Ridley Head. Ridley Head looks like two prominent black lumps, and Bridge Point lies under the highest land east of the Head. For still more identification, if you count from the visible land to the E, Bridge Point is the fifth prominent land hump. As you close Bridge Point, standing in toward the beach, you will see a dangerous rocky patch dead ahead. Approach this menace to within 50 yards or so before swinging toward Ridley Head. Pass another rocky patch close to port and then leave a hard-to-see iron pipe to starboard. Then swing Ridley Head wide to avoid the rocks that stand out from it 60–70 yards NW. From here, put Ridley Head on your stern and make directly for the next point, Gun Point, where there is a sand bar running 30 yards off the point with barely 7 feet LW. From here the blue channel leading to the dredged entrance into Spanish Wells will become clearly evident. See also the sketch for the passage from Spanish Wells to Harbour Island.

Royal Island Harbour (26307) is perfectly landlocked and safe in all weather. We prefer the western opening; although narrower, it has no obstructions if you hold to the center. The other, wider opening has a rock just under the surface almost in mid-channel just inside.

The once-gracious home in the center of the island now stands decrepit and forlorn, having been plundered and horribly desecrated after the caretaker was removed. Where weather and climate have not ravaged, man will.

A walk across the island along the old paths is a rewarding experience if you're interested in tropical trees and plants.

Spanish Wells (26307) is the area's focal point, and deservedly so. Having inched across the shallow bar that makes out from the old entrance (with 6-foot draft, we waited until 2 hours of rising tide before attempting it), and having sorted out the dilapidated bits of pipe that serve as markers along the curve around the shallow bars into the "new" channel—you finally see the original part of town break into view. Its tiny frame houses are all spic and span, their shutters and trim painted in bright hues of many colors, even purple.

This compact community has had only a few infusions of outside blood. Its forebears were a band of Loyalists who fled America at the time of the Revolu-

Spanish Wells, Sawyer's Marina in right foreground

tion. In recent years the village has grown to look like a small suburbia; bright stucco bungalows line the new streets of the western outskirts. An air of pride and prosperity pervades the place, and every garage has at least one car—golf carts would do just as well, because the maximum driving distance on the whole island is only 1.8 miles. "Automobiles are a disease," says Aziel Pinder, the chief pilot hereabouts, also a lay preacher and one of the most religious and inspired people we've ever met.

In any case these industrious people obviously can afford the cars, and they seem not to mind the high prices of food in their supermarkets, for they make a good living fishing for crayfish, which is in inexhaustible demand. They also farm vegetables and citrus for the Nassau market. At daybreak, the quiet of the harbor is broken by the whir of outboard skiffs speeding down the creek to the farms on adjacent Russell Island or standing out to sea to work their pots among the reefs. Other boats bang and bounce their way as far south as the Exumas in search of the highly valued crayfish.

Sawyer's Marina lies near the end of the navigable creek and a half-mile or so beyond the commercial docks, the shipyard, and the town generating plant. Sawyer's is a well-maintained full-service operation, justifiably popular but never too crowded when we've been there.

After Nassau, Spanish Wells is another world: clean, bright, affluent, and charming in a rustic sort of way. Furthermore, it's easy to get to, secure in all winds, and a natural stop when you're bound to or from the Abacos.

Harbour Island (26305) lies just beyond Spanish Wells. It provides the great adventure of this region; getting there involves threading your way along the "Devil's Backbone," where the surf thunders on the beach less than 50 yards away, and weaving among a patchwork of barely visible and murderous rocky ledges, only occasionally marked by rusted iron stakes. Indeed, the very name and customary description of this passage combine to scare off experienced and usually intrepid reef pilots. Not only is it a tricky run, but the timing and the weather conditions have to be nearly perfect. Don't try it without a local pilot aboard, unless the sea is reasonably smooth and the sun over your shoulder. That means you cannot safely go over in the early morning or back in the late afternoon, when the sun is in your eyes.

These circumstances have created a thriving profession in piloting for a few Spanish Wells seamen who know these waters like the back of their hands. Aziel Pinder is one of the best known of them. The trip around with him is an education in reef-running as well as an opportunity to learn much about the area in general, for Aziel knows it intimately from childhood and is an interesting conversationalist as well.

Now that we've echoed the usual warnings about this passage, we think it is appropriate in a guide of this kind to detail the run for the benefit of those who,

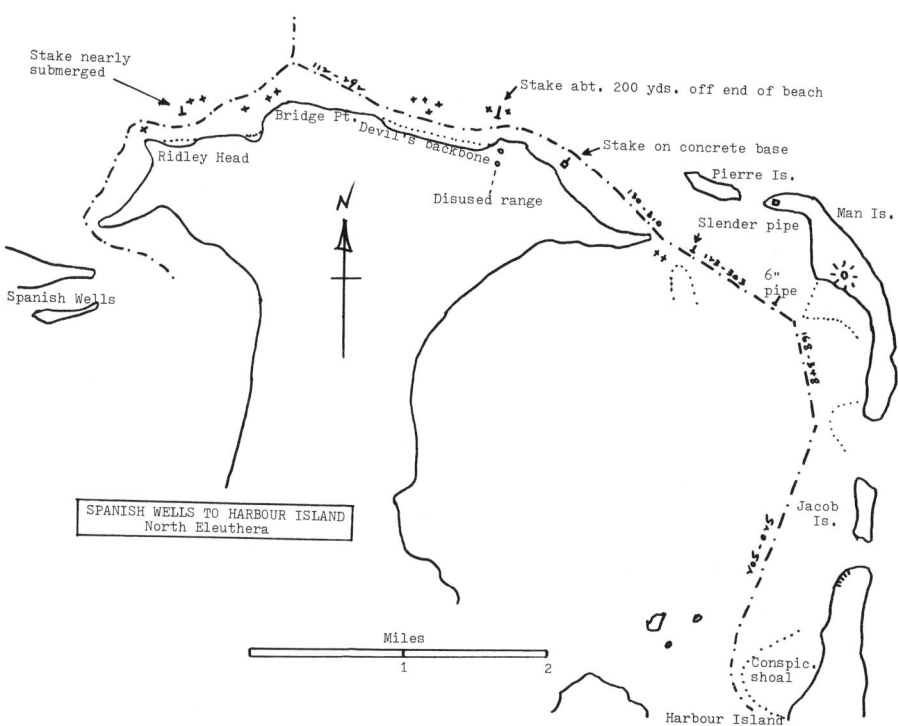

Stake nearly submerged

Stake abt. 200 yds. off end of beach

Bridge Pt. Devil's backbone

Ridley Head

Stake on concrete base

Pierre Is.

Disused range

Man Is.

Slender pipe

Spanish Wells

6" pipe

SPANISH WELLS TO HARBOUR ISLAND
North Eleuthera

Jacob Is.

Miles
1   2

Conspic. shoal

Harbour Island

under proper light and sea conditions, are tempted to pilot themselves around. Combine the following step-by-step directions with the sketch and you should have no trouble.

1. Pass Ridley Head about 150 yards off to be sure to clear the rocky bar making out NW from it.

2. Having cleared the Head, swing in toward the little beach until the iron stake is seen. Leave this to port.

3. Turn seaward gradually to pass Bridge Point about ¼-mile off, keeping a sharp eye first for coral heads to port, then two dangerous ledges to starboard.

4. Having rounded the rocks off Bridge Point, turn in toward the near end of the long beach. Follow along this beach about 50 yards off, especially near the center where the Devil's Backbone comes closest to the shore.

5. At the east end of the beach, a stake will be seen about 200 yards off the shore, also a disused Navy range on the near shore. Hold about midway between these and turn gradually toward the next point of land, being sure to keep seaward of a stake on a concrete block that is difficult to spot and marks a very dangerous ledge.

6. Pass the point about 50 yards off, heading for the S tip of Man Island until you see the first of two iron stakes that lie about 123°T. Leave both stakes to port and follow the keel marks across this shallowest part of the route, barely 6 feet LW.

7. Run slightly past the second stake until you can put the white house on Man Island astern on 168°T, holding this course until you see the sandbank making out from the cut between Jacob and Harbour Islands.

8. Meantime, the distinct shoal that makes out from Dunmore Town will come into view. Round this shoal and come in for the town roadstead.

Although it appears as Dunmore Town on the charts, this veritable relic of colonial times is locally called "Briland," which of course is a quickly slurred contraction of Harbour Island. Briland Yacht Club, which is not a club but a small resort inn, has room at the end of its dock for a couple of yachts in a good 6 feet of water, and electricity and a water faucet. You may also use either side of the town dock, the one with the pink customs house, but there are no facilities. The bottom is good holding, which is fortunate, because the whole roadstead is wide open to northers.

The Bight of Eleuthera (26305)

Continuing south from the Spanish Wells area through Current Cut—as the name implies, it is a tidal sluiceway—the vast Bight of Eleuthera offers a usually protected cruising ground somewhat reminiscent of the Mediterranean. Hatchet Bay near the center and Rock Sound at the southern end provide the only real shelters in the season of northers.

Incidentally, after passing through Current Cut, be sure to stand S along the Current Island shore to the shallow cove before doubling back toward the Eleutheran shore.

The Glass Window to Gregory Town is a pretty segment of coast. It has some sandy coves for settled-weather anchoring and some moderately high grey cliffs that drop sheer to the sea. When the wind is assuredly between NNW and ESE, stop for a swim or overnight in one of the sandy, cliff-rimmed coves adjacent the Arawak Hotel, which is 1.2 miles SE of Mutton Fish Point.

Gregory Town (26305), when it first opens up between its two steep promontories, could be a little Spanish coastal village. You may proceed with 10 feet of water or more up to the dark patch halfway in. We have not anchored overnight here, because we would expect any surge to bounce back and forth within this V-shaped cleft. A smoother anchorage would be the sandy cove ¼-mile to the NW. It carries 10 feet well in toward the beach and would be good in winds from N to SE.

Hatchet Bay (26305) is a large natural pond that has been opened to the sea by a cut, only about 20 yards wide, through the limestone cliff. The entrance is very hard to spot until you are close on it, but you can judge the location by the conspicuous white silos on the hills 2½ miles N of the cut.

Genial Harold Albury presides over the ample dock space of Hatchet Bay Plantation, where you will find water, fuel, electricity, and a nearby grocery store. It is dependable for provisioning, since there is frequent freight-boat service from Nassau. The compact bar and restaurant of the Hatchet Bay Yacht Club is a lively place in the evening, and we can recommend a dinner of the fruits of the sea.

If you prefer not to dock, we suggest you take one of the company moorings; the holding ground off the docks is unreliable. On the other hand, holding is good off the settlement of Alice Town or in the NW part of the pond, where the water is 30 feet deep in places.

Hatchet Bay for years was touted as one of the best hurricane shelters in all the Bahamas, until *Betsy* came through in 1965. Out of curiosity, we visited the scene of destruction a couple of weeks after that monster blow. The masts protruding from the waters of the anchorage and the boats on the beach told their story. To be fair about it, however, it wasn't so much the wind as the unbelievably high water that wrought most of the havoc. The southern, protecting arm of the pond was inundated, which not only let the sea in but brought with it the accumulation of years of dead foliage. This quickly clogged the seawater intakes of boats that were bravely trying to stem the onslaught of the wind by running their engines.

Governor's Harbour (26307) was once a prosperous settlement, as the houses on the hill will attest, but is now going through a period of poor fortune and half-hearted modernism, which is effectively destroying its quaintness.

The main harbor is vulnerable to northers, and the grass-covered bottom makes bad holding even in modest winds. The freight-boat dock on Cupid's Cay would be only a hazard for a yacht, and there are no other docks.

The little cove just south of Cupid's Cay appears to offer good protection from northerly and easterly winds. But the bottom is grass and rocks where the water is deepest, which means trouble in getting an anchor to set. We would be inclined to move up into Balara Bay, where the protection is less but the holding much better.

Pineapple Cays (26305) are a cluster of tiny islets less than an hour's sail below Governor's Harbour. Here the rocky shoreline gives way to an inviting beach; a backdrop of casuarina trees ends in a cliff surmounted by a resort establishment which was gutted by fire in 1975. But for the lowness of the land, it could be a Mediterranean setting.

We have anchored in 8 feet, clear sand, about 100 yards W of the small high cay nearest the beach. The semicircle of three little cays offers some protection from the SE, but the anchorage would only be safe and comfortable in winds from N through E.

Immediately E of the anchorage is the freight-boat landing for South Palmetto Point, a concrete affair with at least 10 feet at its head and 6 feet or more inside the T.

A mile S of this dock we investigated a deep basin behind a concrete mole called Rogue's Cove, where in 1974 there were about two dozen fiberglass house-barges occupying what once must have been a pretty spot. Fortunately for the esthetics of the place, the barge-renting project has failed and a new lessor has taken over. He has plans to move at least half the barges out to make room for yachts. Until this rearrangement occurs, only a couple of medium-size boats can maneuver into this tight little basin. While the cove itself is 12–14 feet deep, a sandy bar just outside the entrance has only 5 feet LW. This will be an unlovely spot until all the ugly barges are removed, but the shelter is faultless from all directions.

Tarpum Bay (26305) is a neat little settlement straggling along the shallow shoreline for almost a mile. It is approachable only by dinghy, since the anchorage is a half-mile offshore, just off a partly exposed rocky bar. The anchorage gives 10 feet and a sand bottom. In any but the prevailing southeasterly weather, the anchorage would be untenable.

Rock Sound (26305) is the commercial center of Eleuthera. In the heyday of the development activities of the late Arthur Vining Davis, it was a very busy place, but the town now seems to have returned to its earlier somnolence, and you will probably find it pleasant if not exactly quaint. Half a mile up the road is a modern shopping center. By Out Island standards, it is well stocked.

In approaching Rock Sound, you will see Starve Rocks at the base of the Sound long before you can pick up the latticed structure of the light on Poison Point. Head toward these rocks on 151°M until the prominent new buildings on the rise of land bear about 098°M. Head for these buildings until you are past Sound Point, then steer for the southernmost pier at the settlement. Yachts usually anchor off this first pier, which makes out from the church. For best holding, anchor well off the pier end, since the bottom is rocky closer in.

Eleuthera's fairly good road system may tempt you to take a sightseeing tour of the spectacular scenery on the windward side and some of the posh resorts that have sprouted on the lower third of the island. If you hire a taxi here or on any of the Out Islands, establish the fare before you get in. These drivers are used to tourists, know perfectly well what the traffic just *might* bear, and have no qualms about charging $50 for a 25-mile ride.

Kemp Pt. to Powell Pt. Exit Channel (26305) is difficult to discern and dangerous in poor light because of the isolated coral heads at the eastern end. A generally straight blue-water channel runs between 24°52.75′ N, 76°16.7′ W and a barely above-water sandspit that lies in 24°53.0′ N, 76°20.0′ W, or about 040°T from Powell Point. The following bearings will locate the eastern end of this channel until the Cape Eleuthera people get around to placing a buoy there, a project that definitely had been authorized when we were last there:

286°T on Wood Cay, the only one of the Schooner Cays with trees;

232°T on Powell Point Light;

042°T tangent on Tarpum Head.

From this position, a course of 253°T will put the sandspit fine on the port bow with 11–15 feet of water all the way. To reach the eastern end of this channel when coming from Rock Sound, you must run a dogleg along the course you came in on until Tarpum Head bears 020°T, when you will turn due W with the prominent hill behind the settlement on your stern.

Take time to establish your position firmly at the eastern end of this channel; otherwise you can become exasperatingly enmeshed in blue channels leading in the right direction but resulting in dead ends.

Port of Palms at Cape Eleuthera (26305), with its man-made lagoon against a man-made setting of tall-waving palms and clusters of villas and condominiums, has everything you would expect in a modern Florida marina— evidence of the $35 million that has already been spent on this embryonic residential resort. If you like to plug into a really adequate power supply and use all the water you like, this is the place for you. It is also the strategic link in a circular cruise from Nassau through the best of the Exumas, followed by a comfortable reach in normal weather across Exuma Sound to Port of Palms and the protection of Eleuthera Island; it's easy then to get back on schedule to Nassau from, say, Hatchet Bay, even in strong northeasterly winds.

The *cuisine* at the main pavilion is reasonably *haute* and correspondingly expensive; the tennis courts are top quality, and the fine golf course shows the adequacy of the water supply. Incidentally, we think the water from the ample wells on the property is the best tasting in the whole Bahamas.

Davis Harbour (26305, 26301) used to be the only refuge along the rather exposed southwestern coast of Eleuthera, but since the opening of the marina at Cape Eleuthera, it is little used now except by a few sportfishing boats. Furthermore, the Cotton Bay Club, of which it is a part, is not as active as it once was, and the channel has been shoaling to the extent that nearly high tide would be required to bring 6 feet in.

The entrance is barely distinguishable, lying about 1 mile N of the tripod beacon that marks the channel into the creek at the settlement of Wemyss (pronounced "Wims").

The Exuma Islands (26300, 26305, 26301)

Some 30 miles southeast of Nassau, over sandy banks that are only occasionally too rough for comfort, lie the Exumas, a string of closely connected and mostly uninhabited islands. They act as a buffer to the ocean swells of Exuma Sound and are lapped on their lee side by waters of indescribable color and clarity. The upper 60 miles down to Galliot Cut are navigable on the banks side by yachts of any normal draft. Five feet can carry a little further to Rudder Cut, but beyond that point the route for all but 3-foot draft runs outside to Elizabeth Harbour.

The banks are pure white sand, generally 12 feet or more well off the land. Passage close under the lee of the islands, however, is barred by a series of shoals at each major cut between the cays, shoals which sometimes stand as far as 4 miles out onto the banks. The extremities of these shoals have always presented a piloting problem, because they are not at all defined in the government charts and only rather casually shown in the Kline sketch charts. Too many times we have steered a course from one of the cuts toward what appeared to be the tip of one of these finger shoals, only to find it curling still further to the west and north so that we had to backtrack to get around it.

To eliminate these claustrophobic situations, we have plotted the tips of the most prominent shoals between Norman's Spit and Conch Cut. You too may find it helpful to plot these approximate positions on your 26305:

Wax Cay Bank (when coming to or from Norman's Cay): 24°33.5′ N, 76°49.5′ W; also 24°32.7′ N, 76°49.25′ W.

Hawksbill Bank (when passing inside Elbow Cay): 24°29.4′ N, 76°52.0′ W.

Cistern Bank (when rounding the "elbow" of the banks): 24°25.8′ N, 76°47.0′ W.

Warderick Wells Banks (when running through that cut): 24°22.3′ N, 76°42.9′ W; also 24°21.9′ N, 76°39.3′ W.

Bell Island Shoal: 24°17.2′ N, 76°36.8′ W.

Conch Cut Shoal (when using that cut): 24°15.5′ N, 76°35.8′ W.

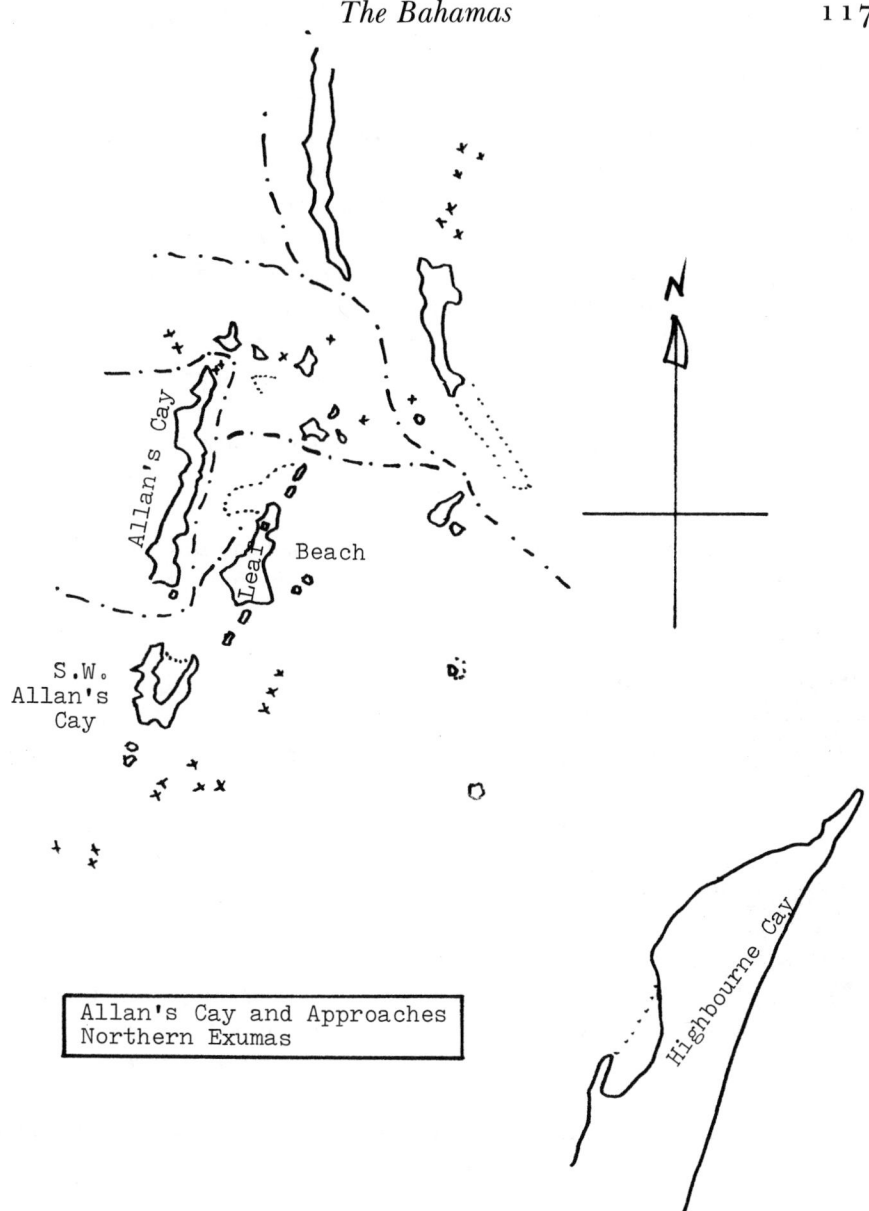

Allan's Cay and Approaches
Northern Exumas

    While shallow-draft boats can safely shortcut these extremities, there is not much distance to be saved. And be careful—the shallowest water is just before the dropoff. There are no significant coral heads along the above stretch, but there is a brown bar off Pipe Cay in 24°13.9′ N, 76°32.5′ W. It is about 300 yards long and oriented E–W. There *may* be 8–10 feet of water over it.

Allan's Cay (26257) is a pleasant slot, rimmed by a series of rocks and low islets, inhabited only by yachts. There is little protection from the wind, but you will find good holding if you pick a sandy spot. The usual anchorage is off the beach where the vacant and delapidated house stands.

The usual entrance, which is simple and unobstructed, lies between Southwest Allan's and Allan's Cays. The northern entrance has a coral patch just outside and a bar that makes out NE from the tip of Allan's, but there is no problem coming in here if you are aware of these dangers. You can also enter via the obvious blue water channel from the E, just N of the pair of caylets N of Leaf Cay. This channel comes right across what is shown in 26257 as a coral reef that uncovers at low water! Our sketch also shows the easily seen channel that leads from the Sound to the banks just N of Allan's Cay Harbour.

Unfortunately, these lovely cays have become a garbage dumping ground for the ingrates who have begun to trickle into these beautiful waters. On the beaches and in the potholes you will find their rubbish, carefully bagged to last as eyesores for a decade or more.

Highbourne Cay (26305) has always been a lively, friendly crossroads. It's the favorite first or last stop when sailing to or from Nassau, and is therefore often crowded, especially when yachts bunch up here during a norther. Although the basin is being dredged deeper and slightly larger by the indulgent American owner of the cay, himself a yachtsman, you should be prepared to use two anchors to minimize your swinging radius. Furthermore, a large yacht should be prepared either to anchor or dock when the harbor is busy, as the situation may dictate.

Coming in, keep to the right of the inner harbor range; some boat ends up on the shallow bar W of the range almost every evening. Stay away from the outermost leg of the concrete mole when a norther is impending, but if you get caught there in such a situation, put out a breast anchor before it gets too rough.

Because of the fierce current and the usual surge, we do not recommend anchoring in the Cut when the basin is full. In the usual easterly weather, it is better to anchor N of the Cut along the W shore of Highbourne; in westerly weather you would be better off at Allan's.

Fuel is available if you can get near the dock where the island freight boat *Bessie Virginia* usually lies. The dock is wired with 110V and 220V electricity, and there is a well-stocked commissary on the island. The music that emanates almost every evening from Cheap Charlie's Oar House at the head of the dock is exclusively Highbourne: calypsos you've never heard before, long on beat and a revelation in harmonics, and all the more fun because of it.

Norman's Cay (26305) has plenty of anchoring room but is rather exposed from all directions, although most of the sea is broken up by outlying rocks and caylets. The dock will accommodate three or four good-sized yachts up to 5½-foot draft but take care to avoid the 4½-foot spot about 20 yards N of the dock.

Anchor well off the pier over the sandy bottom. Closer in you will have grass and coral that can mangle a Danforth.

The club facilities include an excellent and justly popular bar and restaurant and a small but adequately stocked commissary.

Shroud Cay Anchorage (26305) is tucked in behind three prominent rocks making out from the westernmost shoulder of Shroud Cay. Go straight in for the tiny beach and anchor in 8 feet within 80 yards of it. No good in winds from S through W to N.

A well-worn trail leads over the hill to a well that is still used by passing vessels. We have not tasted the water, but a yachtsman we met said he filled his tanks from it and found it better than Nassau water, which is easy to believe. An adjacent shallow pool in the rocks has been used for bathing.

Shroud Cay Harbour (26305) is entered ½-mile NE of Pigeon Cay, where you will find a deep pool just inside with 4½ feet LW at the entrance. This is the place where Dr. Cottman rode out a hurricane tied to the mangroves that are the major part of the scenery here.

Hawksbill Cay (26305) gives good protection from the prevailing easterlies at the S end of the cay under the high bluff topped by a cairn. When approaching from the S, to avoid the bank that makes out from the cut, do not head in for the anchorage until the cairn bears about 060°. Watch for the dozen jet-black coral heads scattered about the sandy bight; some have less than 2 feet over them, but they are easily seen.

For a thrilling experience in eyeball piloting, pass out into Exuma Sound through the gut at the S end of Hawksbill by taking the southernmost dark-blue channel on courses SE and E, leaving the tiny but prominent rock ahead of you close to port. We advise going through here with a head current to give you time to sort out your moves, because the current really sluices through. In good light, it is not hazardous for skippers who can read the water, and the colors in this area are perhaps as vivid as we have seen anywhere.

After negotiating the gut, head for the small rock SW of Little Cistern and take up 128°T to pass inside Cistern Cay or head out through the wide pass into Exuma Sound.

A tight little anchorage in smooth weather will be found at Little Cistern Cay, just off the pretty little beach on its NW side. A large rocky bar just inside the entrance is easily seen. Leave it to port.

Inside Passage, Cistern Cay to Warderick Wells (26305, 26253) is perfectly safe in good light and slight sea conditions, but not for boats much over 4-foot draft because of the bar at the NW end of Long Rock.

Between Cistern Cay and the little cay just SW of it, the water is quite shoal, and another shoal makes out to the west from the little cay. We advise swinging wide to the west around that shoal, then turning easterly down the obvious blue channel and holding 100–200 yards off the chain of rocks that extends toward Long Rock. Especially favor the most easterly of these rocks in order to avoid a brown bar you will see to starboard. After crossing Wide Opening and the sand bar at Long Rock, follow the west shore of Long Rock and take up 128°T from its southern tip (with a few minor swings as the eye dictates) to the deep-blue channel at the north end of Warderick Wells Cay.

On paper these directions may not seem very explicit, but we can assure you that when you are on the scene they will make sense. With a little practice in eyeball piloting—and you will never learn until you try—the necessary twists and turns will become as easy as taking a walk in the woods, but as we say elsewhere, avoid the intricate places on days that are overcast, when there are fleeting cloud shadows, and when the sea is rough. If you stay way out on the banks between Highbourne and Staniel, you'll have no problems and few decisions, but you'll miss the rare intimacy of the Exumas, which sets them so much apart from other islands in other places.

Warderick Wells, north (26305) has a wild beauty about it that makes it one of the most popular anchorages in the Exumas. If you climb the high hill (high by Bahamian standards) with the cairn on it, a shimmering sea studded with cays will be spread out before you, and you'll have a fascinating view of where you've been and where you're headed.

In making the entrance, stand in about one-third the distance from the eastern shore until you see a grassy vein in the bottom. Following this close to port will keep you off the brown bar that makes out from the little beach to the east. From then on, the deep-water crescent of the harbor is obvious. In dead center, before the channel bears off SW, lies the wreck of a burned fiberglass sailboat, a sorry black shape against the sandy bottom.

We like best the anchorage at the extremity of the deep channel, just off the small beach. There you can power your dinghy right into the shore, instead of making a long wade to get to the larger beach under the cairn. You'll find one of the wells for which this ship-watering place is named by following an indistinct trail from the east end of that smaller, westernmost beach.

Although we think the "Bahamian moor"—two anchors lying to the opposing sets of the current—is a practice that is being overdone, this is one place where it must be used, and the anchors must be set precisely in the center of the narrow channel.

Warderick Wells, south (26305) is less frequented than the north, but offers more protection; it lies in a narrow slot between the SE end of Warderick Wells Cay and an off-lying, unnamed cay. A sandbar fills the center of this slot, and anchorage may be taken in either leg of the V. The easiest access is from Exuma Sound, and even in Force 4 conditions, this can mean a few uncomfortable miles when the current is ebbing through the cuts. There are no dangers when approaching the slot from the N.

To enter this harbor from the deep water at the north end of Hall's Pond Cay, steer about 323°T for the easternmost caylet, which extends out toward Hall's Pond Cut. Run in close to this string of tiny cays and follow the blue channel northwesterly. Shortly you will come to a pass through which you will see a sandy cay with some palm trees. Turn to starboard here and favor the cay on your port hand, take the very next opening to port through deep water, then swing very wide to starboard for the opening into the harbor. The sandbar lies immediately inside, and you can anchor in the *cul de sac* to the right, or take the left fork to anchor in the tideway off a beach, or continue out to sea at the other end.

Exuma Cays Club (26305), at the north end of Hall's Pond Cay, is not a comfortable place to lie. During our stay at the dock, we were up several times during the night to tend to the lines and fenders against the considerable surge during a period of only moderate easterlies.

The passage from here through the cut to Exuma Sound is straightforward, but to gain the banks with 6-foot draft is a more exacting exercise in eyeball piloting than we enjoy, although with lesser draft it is quite simple. The sandy islet that bears 186°T from the clubhouse is not even shown in 26305, but is the key to this channel. We cannot give precise directions because there are no distinct natural ranges and no landmarks ahead; we can only advise that you take up 182°T from the S end of the sandy islet and swing gradually through a slow curve for about 1¼ miles until you are heading 223°T. At this position, you will be clear of the shallowest water and will have the N end of Conch Cut bearing 097°T and the N end of Hall's Pond Cay bearing 009°T.

Sampson Cay (26305) doesn't get the traffic that Staniel Cay enjoys, but has always been one of our favorite stops, in large part tribute to the geniality of Don Schmidt, who manages the club, and the excellent fish and lobster dinners he produces. Especially we relish his conch fritters.

The wharf alongside the attractive stone clubhouse will take 4½ feet LW and the center finger pier 6 feet.

A basin has been dredged in back of the club; there are a couple of piers and a very narrow channel leading in. Once inside, after considerable maneuvering,

6 feet can lie alongside, but the entrance can only be negotiated within an hour of normal high tide, and only after getting precise directions from Don. Except in this back basin, Sampson is no place to be when it blows hard out of the SW as a prelude to a norther.

The Inside Channel from Sampson to Staniel comes in off the banks at High Twin Cays, threads among some small cays, and runs down through the slot (a popular anchorage) between Big and Little Major's Spots. The water colors are a delight to the eye, and the deep water is so obvious that skippers having only rudimentary eyeballing experience can, with the aid of the accompanying sketch, make it easily when the light is right. The only place requiring special care and some fast wheel-spinning is the right angle turn around the last (flat) rock of the three making N from Fowl Cay, but the deep blue of the water and the fast-running current mark the safe channel. The only shallow portion of this route lies between Twin Cays and Dennis Cay, and even this is good for 7 ½ feet LW over a clear sandy bottom.

Passages like this are the very essence of Exumas cruising.

Staniel Cay (26305), like so many halfway points, is the focal point of the Exumas. The docks at the yacht club are modern in every way, the clubhouse at the end of the pier is as comfortable as it is casual, and Bob Chamberlain puts on a good buffet of things-of-the-sea every night. His partner in this well-established venture, Joe Hocher, is the only resident engineer we've known who also tends bar and minds the radio (*Mizpah* is the call name) while still keeping all systems "go." Unless you have a major mechanical or electrical problem, the chances are good that Joe can solve just about anything for you through ingenuity and the facilities of his new machine shop out back.

One of the earliest Bahama charter captains, Bob Chamberlain liked Staniel and its people so much that he settled down there and has built up a club that is the quintessence of unaffected island retreats. Bob flies his own plane on charter, and when he isn't supervising the cooking or shuttling in the sky between Ft. Lauderdale, Nassau, and Staniel, he may be tending bar also.

Staniel Cay Yacht Club now has a competitor in Happy People Marina a few cables S. The approach is both straightforward and buoyed, the docks are well built and have all the facilities, and the local people who run it obviously know what is needed to make it attractive to yachtsmen. Furthermore, with a name like that they must be on the right track. The associated bar and restaurant are on "main street," in the center of the settlement's activity.

The one disadvantage at Staniel is its exposure to the W. However, the people there know their weather, and when a big blow is expected from that direction they will tell you to forsake their dock for a quieter anchorage (or a mooring) in the basin immediately to the N, or further up to the slot between

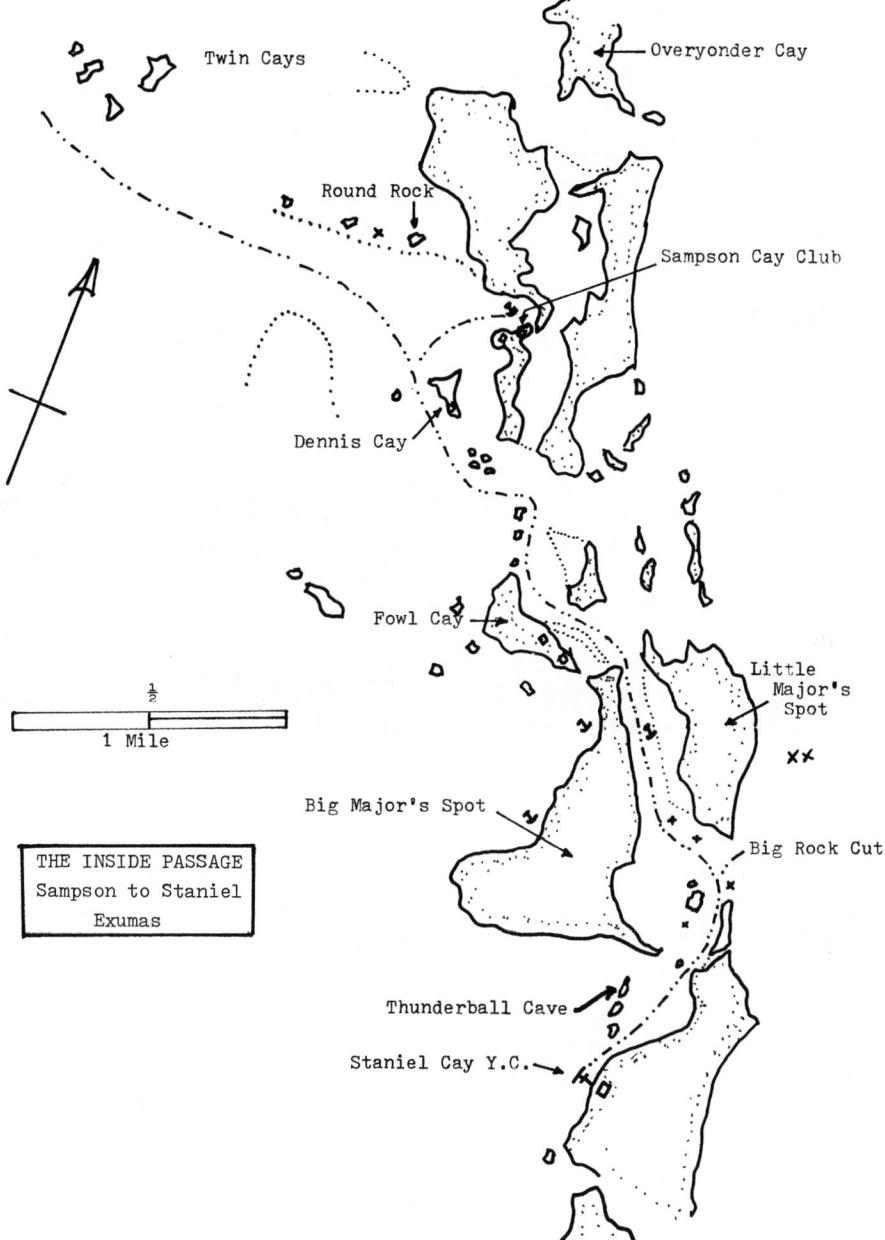

Twin Cays

Overyonder Cay

Round Rock

Sampson Cay Club

Dennis Cay

Fowl Cay

Little Major's Spot

$\frac{1}{2}$

1 Mile

Big Major's Spot

Big Rock Cut

THE INSIDE PASSAGE
Sampson to Staniel
Exumas

Thunderball Cave

Staniel Cay Y.C.

Big and Little Major's Spots, where the land is relatively high to the W and the sandy bottom assures good holding. Run well up into the slot to avoid the heavy swell that comes through the cut when the wind has veered NE.

Snorkel into Thunderball Cave (so named after the James Bond movie) and

Staniel Cay Yacht Club, Big Major's Cay in background

bob to the surface in an eerie cavern illuminated by several shafts of daylight that pass through holes in its limestone dome. The main entrance is at the W side of the last of the three islets that make out from the club dock toward Little Major's Spot.

This shallow grotto with its several entrances is a snorkeler's paradise; in fact, it is the Bahamas' answer to the Blue Grotto at Capri and the Emerald Grotto at Amalfi, but with infinitely more light and sea life. At low water, you can swim right in; at high water, an easy dive will bring you under the arch of the wide opening. Better time your visit for a period close to slack water, because the current, which runs right through the grotto, is ferocious.

On the NE side of the islet, a huge brain coral lies in 15 feet, surrounded by myriad splendrous fish that make their home around this natural wonder, which is now protected as a part of the Exuma Cays Land and Sea Park administered by the Bahamas National Trust.

Black Point Settlement (26305) is simply a huge bay with fair protection, except from the SW, but not much else to commend it. Ask any native worker you see up and down the Exumas where he comes from, and he'll probably tell you he's from Black Point; in fact, most of the outboards you see buzzing up and down the inside passages in all kinds of weather are Black Point commuters.

Little Farmer's Cay (26305) is a typical Out Island community, much like Staniel 25 years ago, with little to show what keeps it alive and kicking. However, the people seem happy and exude a friendliness that stems, perhaps, from the village patriarch, Captain Henry Moxey, and his charming wife. Born in remote Ragged Island, which is famous for the fine Bahamian seamen it has produced, Captain Moxey came to Little Farmer's in 1914, married a local girl, and made his living sailing the world's seas, eventually earning a master's license for ships to 15,000 tons. Now in his eighties, his sight is failing, but he can still point out the channels in and out of his island and rattle off the courses from there to Ragged Island via the banks. If you go to Little Farmer's, by all means make it a point to meet and talk with this fine gentleman.

The entrance from Exuma Sound leaves the islet in the center of the cut to starboard, as is obvious. But just inside, you will have to swing toward the orange roof of the church (and school) or hug the shore of Big Farmer's in order to avoid the long, shallow sandbank that lies roughly N–S and is difficult to see against a low afternoon sun.

In approaching the S entrance from the banks track, steer about 035° M for the white beach and palm trees after you have closed to within ½-mile of the tip of Little Farmer's. Otherwise the flats between the island and the main banks channel seem to be a uniform 8–9 feet LW, so that one may turn in for this entrance on 045° to 085° M, giving care only to the shoals on either hand when close in to the cay. Give the SE tip of Little Farmer's a berth of 150–200 yards and watch for the southern tip of the sandbank previously mentioned, which occupies the center of the channel toward the cut.

We have anchored in the mouth of the cove (which shallows abruptly) at the N end of Big Farmer's, or close in to the beach just around the SE tip of Little Farmer's when a norther was forecast. The freight boat lies at the head of the settlement dock, and 6 feet could anchor just inside the harbor mouth with a line ashore if need be.

Captain Moxey assured us there is 6 feet LW through the N entrance, steering WSW after turning the N tip of Little Farmer's, or sweeping wide around the bar making out from Great Guana Cay, then trending N toward the rock called "The Oven."

Considering its several anchorage options, depending on the forecast, the quaintness of the settlement, and the easy access from the banks or the Sound, we think Little Farmer's deserves more yacht traffic than it gets.

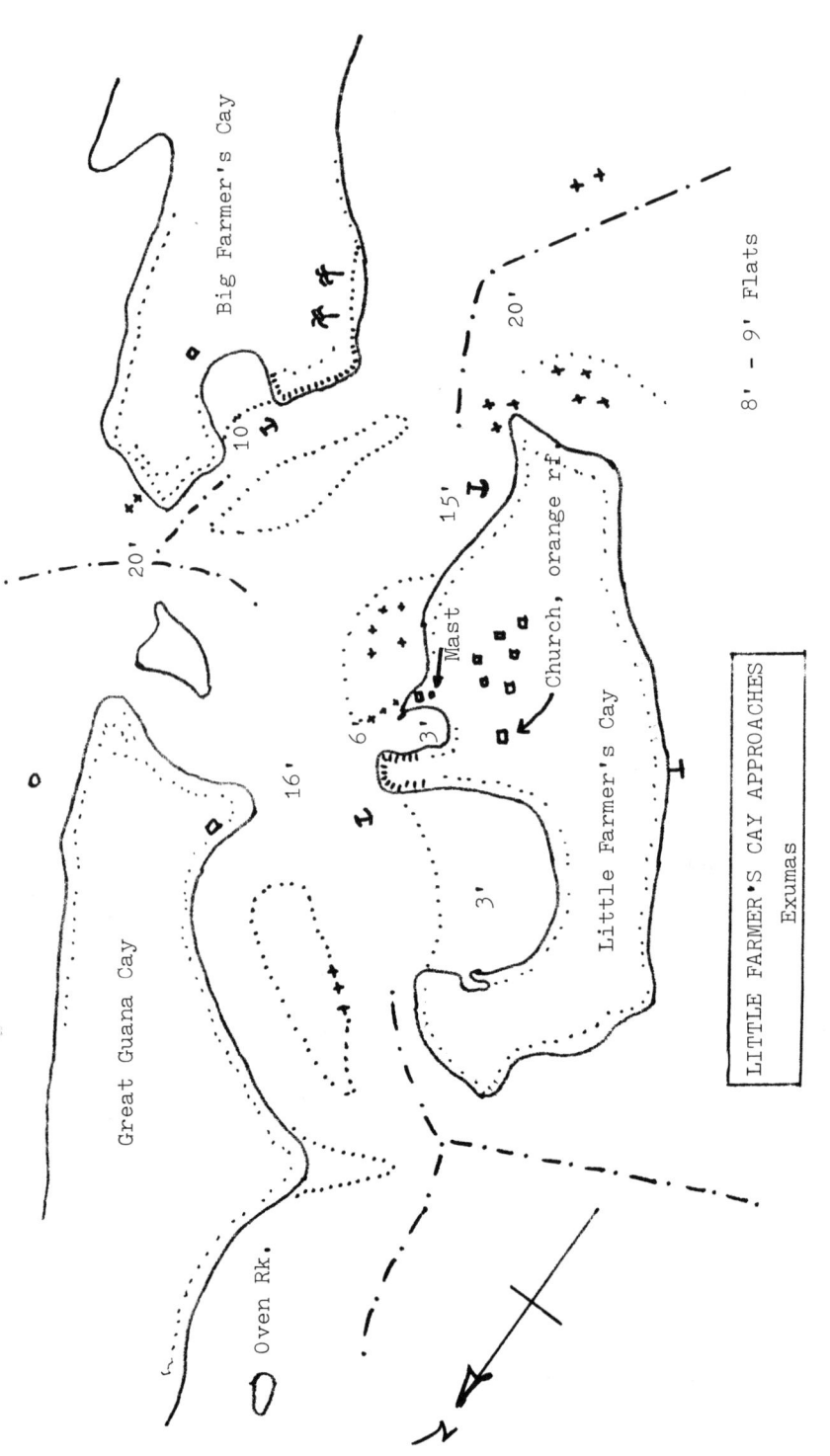

Big Farmer's Cay

Great Guana Cay

Oven Rk.

Little Farmer's Cay

Church, orange rf

Mast

8' — 9' Flats

20'

15'

10'

20'

16'

6'

3'

3'

N

LITTLE FARMER'S CAY APPROACHES
Exumas

Cave Cay (26301) has an anchorage just off the opening into the shallow pond. It's popular largely because Galliot and Cave Cay Cuts are the last openings off the banks for deep-draft vessels bound for George Town. In fact, all but multihulls and similar skimming types have to run outside from Rudder Cut, and even they are usually obliged to go outside at Square Cay Cut.

To reach the anchorage area, you will have to pass between the shoals that make out from Little Galliot and Cave Cays, steering a slight "S" where these shoals overlap at a point due S from the center of the cay with the white cliffs.

Darby Island Anchorage (26301) will keep you snug through a vicious norther. We spent two days there a few years back waiting for one of them to blow itself out. Lying to bow and stern anchors, and with a network of lines to the concrete dock, we could sit quietly in the center of our web and watch the palms of the old plantation writhe in the breeze while wild pigs swam back and forth across the creek on their foraging expeditions.

More recently, we nudged aground twice in the late-afternoon light, trying to bring 6 feet around the point that leads directly to the creek. We probably should have held close to the left hand shore. We noticed, too, that a chain is now barring the entrance to the innermost basin, where the dock is located.

Rat Cay Anchorage (26301) lies just inside the cut of that name and is a delightful place to tarry when the Sound is reasonably smooth; otherwise a bad surge comes in from two sides. Like so many places in the Exumas, this anchorage is devoid of signs of life, and the scrub-covered rockly islet that forms the breakwater ends in a wispy sandspit that covers and uncovers with the tide.

The opening faces N and is just N of the outlying and conspicuous Three Sisters Rocks (not shown in 26301). Rat Cay may be distinguished by the conical, white-slabbed hillock that lies just W of the rather narrow opening, and just offshore is a small rock awash. Move in toward this rock and the entrance will open up.

Just inside the SE tip of Rat Cay is an ill-defined sand bar. Otherwise the water is deep close along the Rat Cay shore, inside Pigeon Cay, to a very pleasant anchorage off a nice beach on the N shore.

Children's Bay Cay (26301) is called Williams Cay in 26301 and is currently owned by the Heinzes of "57 Varieties" fame. Anchorage may be taken in the cove on the NW side of the island, just beyond the dock on the point. The approach is straightforward across the opening between Rat and Children's Bay Cays.

In a period of strong easterlies, this makes a convenient and beautiful stopover in the course of an "outside" run between Galliot and Elizabeth Harbour.

Although Dick Ellis, the caretaker at Children's Bay, says you can pass out into the Sound close under the shore of Children's Bay Cay, we do not recommend any use of the cut between Rat and Children's Bay.

Elizabeth Harbour, Great Exuma (26302) encompasses the whole area in the lee of Stocking Island, including George Town, which is the leading settlement in this part of the Bahamas.

The town itself is neither quaint nor progressive, and seems a little messier each time we go there. Furthermore, the waterfront is quite shallow except near the commercial dock and is fully exposed to the prevailing wind—there's enough fetch across the bay to let a substantial chop build up. In your dinghy, however, you can pass under the road bridge to the calm of the pond behind the town.

Most yachts anchor in the first of the four basins that make up Stocking Island Harbour and make day trips over to town for provisioning, either by mother ship or by dinghy if the harbor is smooth enough. The holding ground is not to be trusted until you have made sure your anchor is truly set. We have noted that the bottom is better just inside the opening rather than further inside the cove, where your natural impulse would lead you.

We have sounded the dredged but unmarked channel leading into basin No. 2 and have found it safe for 6 feet at half tide or better. The deepest water is midway between the rocky bar to starboard and the caylet to port, when heading in toward the white boathouse of the Twyman place. The third basin to the west has a rocky bar across the entrance, which you should investigate by small boat before attempting to take 4 feet or more inside.

The channel into the large lagoon to the east is so intricate that we do not recommend it for anything but outboards. Just inside the channel, however, is the place to pick up the trail over the hill to one of the most beautiful beaches in all the Bahamas, and we say this advisedly. Take cleaning material to remove the tar from your feet before going back aboard.

The eastern exit from Elizabeth Harbour is quite simple once you have located the single stake that marks the pass between two dangerous bars in midchannel off Crab Cay. Be sure to leave this marker to starboard going out. Steer from here slightly inside the end of Man-O-War Cay to avoid a cluster of heads to port midway along this stretch, until you see a conspicuous rocky bar dead ahead. Leave this close to starboard and swing toward Mid Channel and North Channel Rocks. When fairly close up to Mid Channel Rocks, you may turn safely out to sea.

This entrance is considerably more difficult from seaward, so take time to plot your position accurately before moving in. Pigeon Cay is conspicuous,

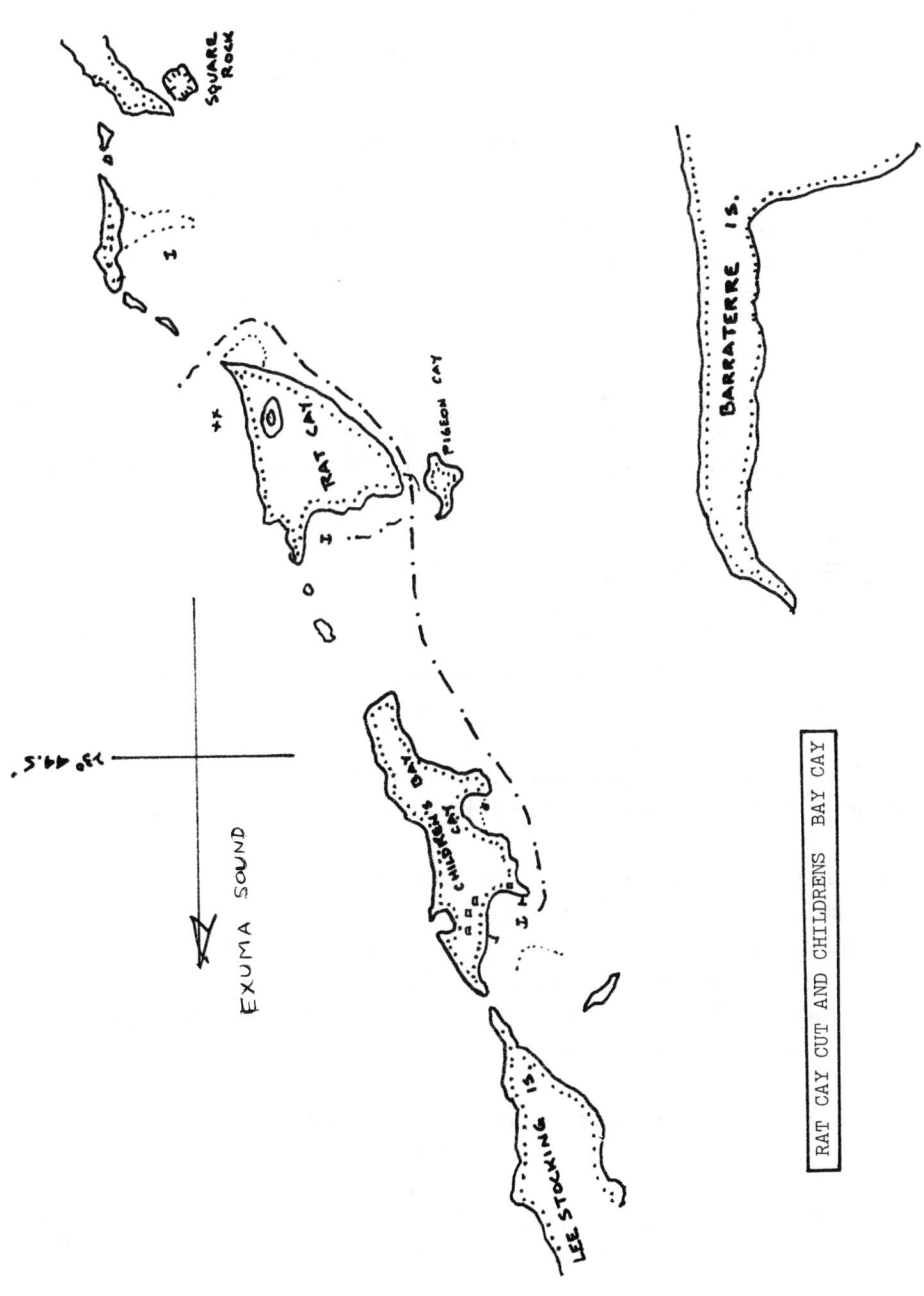

SQUARE ROCK

BARRATERRE IS.

RAT CAY

PIGEON CAY

130 44.5'

EXUMA SOUND

CHILDRENS BAY CAY

LEE STOCKING IS.

RAT CAY CUT AND CHILDRENS BAY CAY

being the most southeasterly of the outlying cays in that direction. Note the intervening line of rocks, then North Channel Rocks, followed by a wide break between them and Welk and Dog Cays, which are isolated to seaward of the chain of cays that make out from Stocking Island. A big swell often runs into this wide break.

Cat Island (26301)

Cat Island's 48 miles lie directly athwart the trades. Cat is sparsely populated, provides a thorough lee in normal weather, but has only two harbors, Hawksnest and Bennett's Harbour, that are secure against the westerly winds that precede winter northers.

Hawksnest Club (26301) is a small and unpretentious resort that has recently come under new management. A dredged channel, safe for 6 feet near HW, leads through the creek into a completely landlocked yacht basin with all the usual facilities. Since mangroves are all about, the no-see-ums at sunset are a daily menace.

The New Bight (26301) is a rather dilapidated place along the road, its landscape strewn here and there with junked cars, piles of bottles, and other assorted refuse. There is, however, an interesting stone building that appears to be the remains of an old plantation gatehouse. It stands at the foot of a road that later becomes a trail leading to a miniscule chapel of organic architecture, reminiscent of the Mediterranean, which stands atop a 200-foot hill.

The radio mast and the chapel on the hill can be seen from afar. The bottom shoals gradually and 6-foot draft will have to anchor some 150 yards off the dock.

The only real reason to stop at New Bight is to visit the chapel, bell tower, living quarters, and the trailside edifices representing the Stations of the Cross, built by the hands of the late Father Jerome, a Catholic priest, when he was in his sixties. His successor is Father Oswald, a Canadian. The walk is easily accomplished in 20 minutes and, in addition to the charm of the chapel itself, the view in all directions is rewarding. After passing the portal inscribed "Mount Alverna," take the path to the right straight up past the Stations, but only after signaling your approach by striking a stone on a piece of scrap metal hanging for that purpose on a tree at the turnoff.

New Bight to Bennett's Harbour (26301) is an uncomplicated run over numerous areas of coral heads, which we automatically steer around even though there appears to be plenty of water over them.

Leaving New Bight, it is necessary to run about W by S until Fernandez Cay bears N in order to clear the extensive sandspit that makes out from Bonefish

Point. We have plotted the extremity of this shoal at approximately 2 miles 208°T from the point. From this position, a course of 318°T will take you up the coast in 3–4 fathoms with well-spaced coral heads.

To clear the shoals off Alligator Point, we have established a position 3.9 miles 260°T from that point (which is low and very difficult to see against the land). The whole bay in the approach to Bennett's Harbour is pocked with heads, but they are easy to see against the white sand bottom, provided you have proper light and sea conditions, and there is otherwise ample depth for any yacht. From the above position we steer 043°T toward Hill 103 near Dumfries until Alligator Point again comes abeam, then turn in for the N end of the beach at Bennett's Harbour.

Bennett's Harbour (26301) is big enough for maybe three modest-sized yachts securely moored bow and stern; there is no room whatsoever to swing. If you pick a day when the freight boat is not due, you can use the decrepit dock—but be prepared to use your ingenuity in making fast, for there are no bollards or cleats. However you will have lots of help; any new arrival draws a crowd!

Ashore is a town of abjectly poor but friendly and cheerful people, ready to *give* you vegetables out of their gardens on the theory that it costs them nothing.

Little San Salvador Island (26301) is blessed with a beautiful beach, good shelter from N through SE, and only a slight swell. It's easy to enter and uninhabited. Need we say more?

THE SOUTHEASTERN BAHAMAS

Long Island (26300, 26301, 26240)

The banks in the lee of the northern half of Long Island may be negotiated at either end of the crescent of reefs that sweep from Cape Santa Maria to Elizabeth Harbour's eastern entrance. Turning SE from Elizabeth Harbour, you will leave the deep water as you approach Pigeon Cay, where good light is needed to thread between the brown bars that parallel the blue channel between Pigeon Cay and Black Rocks about ½-mile to seaward. This, incidentally, is a nasty place in northeasterly weather, as the seas heap up where they abruptly meet the shallows. From here on, if you stand about a mile off the shore, you'll have no further problems (other than lobster pots) in making the sweep to the sand spit off White Cay and thence across the bank of clear sand, with uniform 12-foot depths, to Bain's Bluff, which will be clearly visible after leaving White Cay astern.

From Bain's Bluff you may go south as far as Salt Pond, visit Stella Maris, or exit the bank beyond Dove Cay and proceed into Calabash Bay.

Salt Pond (26301) is a pleasant and friendly place on the road where the island is narrowest. It provides excellent protection from all but SW winds, since the land around this comparatively wide bay is almost mountainous by Bahamian standards.

The deepest hole, and the highest land against a northerly blow, is in the NE corner of the bay, but the usual anchorage is further S off the concrete docks, where depths are just over 6 feet for about a mile out. Ashore are the grandstand for the annual Long Island Regatta and Willis Harding's well-stocked general store, where the action, if any, is.

John McKie, a cruising man who settled here and built an attractive home high on a hill above the N end of the bay, enjoys meeting the rather few yachtsmen who come to what is almost the end of navigation for these parts. Almost but not quite, for John has scouted a channel, from Salt Pond running due W to a position S of Hog Cay Cut, that makes it possible for 6-foot draft bound for Crooked and Acklin's Islands to take advantage of the lee of Long Island by proceeding from Little Exuma across to Salt Pond, then back via his channel (staying over the sea fans all the way) to pick up the relatively deep water to Nuevitas Light and thence around South Point. This avoids the very shallow water immediately S of Hog Cay Cut.

Stella Maris Marina (26301) is part of a resort complex that straddles the island about halfway between Simms and Dove Cay. From the edge of the bar S of Dove Cay, a soft mud channel carries 4½ feet LW to the artificial basin, except during periods of prolonged SE winds, when the level is likely to be 6 inches less. The final channel and the basin itself are dredged to 7 feet.

All the usual services will be found here, including water, fuel, some chandlery items, and facilities for mechanical and hull repair. Their railway will handle at least 40 feet and 5½-foot draft. Yachtsmen are invited to use the facilities of the inn located on the windward coast, and the bus transportation is gratis if you are going over the hill for dinner.

This is an ideal spot for provisioning and for crew changes, since there is an airstrip on the premises receiving scheduled flights from Nassau.

Rounding Long Island's North End (26301) involves getting off the bank at the Cape Santa Maria end of the crescent-shaped reef extending from Little Exuma, and here again, good light is essential—no cloud shadows, please! A relatively deep NW–SE channel lies close to the very shallow white sand banks that stand off Dove Cay "like the wings of a butterfly," as John McKie expresses it. Until these conspicuous banks can be seen, it is best to stand in toward Dove

Cay. Otherwise you will become enmeshed in a series of patternless sand bores carrying less than 5 feet, which extend E and SE from the breaking reef WNW of Dove Cay.

Calabash Bay, with its 2-mile sweep of gorgeous beach, will tempt you before you round Cape Santa Maria, but you will have to choose your weather carefully, because the anchorage in tenable only in winds from E to S. Even then a long, lazy swell usually finds its way in. A course of 050°M toward the most northerly of the buildings of the Cape Santa Maria Club will clear the reef to port by a wide margin, but be wary of the sand bar just inside the reef, which seems to carry about 8 feet LW. We do not recommend trying to pass inside the reef at the S end of the bay, because the sandy bottom shoals very gradually and the depths are consequently very difficult to judge.

Cape Santa Maria (26301) appears to us to be very accurately charted, certainly if one stays outside the pecked lines that show the limits of safe depths. We have steered between the two reef areas shown W of the light on 26301, then headed NE from 23°40.9', 75°21.1', in 7–10 fathoms, until seaward of the breaking reef that stands out from the E point of the cape. At 23°42.0', 75°20.0', one can safely shape a course down the coast.

Note that the charted above-water rocks on the E side of the cape are actually only awash at LW, but are always breaking.

The lagoon on the weather shore at 23°40.0' looks interesting, but we were frightened away by the numerous rocky bars that seem to extend right across the entrance.

Clarence Town (26253) makes a welcome haven after a 41-mile sail from Cape Santa Maria along a formidable and rather featureless lee shore. Open to the N, the anchorage is uncomfortable in a norther, yet safe enough if seamanlike precautions are taken; the protection is good from all other directions. Entering presents no problems, especially since the reef off the light is always breaking. If you elect to use the town dock, we suggest you anchor off the end and back down to it, eliminating the problem of having to fender against the surge.

This pretty little settlement of some 200 friendly souls is distinguished from far out at sea by not one but two imposing, twin-spired churches that seem out of all proportion to the size of the place. Even more strange, they were both built by the same man, an Anglican missionary with architectural training by the name of Hawes. He built St. Paul's Church; later, after he had converted to Catholicism and become Father Jerome, he felt the need to outdo his first effort by constructing St. Peter's. This is the same Father Jerome who, in the last years of his life, became a hermit and built with his own hands the little chapel and other buildings that stand atop the highest hill on Cat Island.

This is the last fueling stop, a tank-truck-delivery operation, until Providenciales or Pine Cay in the Caicos group.

Little Harbour (26240 or 26280) would be hard to spot were it not for the wreck of a freighter that lies in several sections along the beach. The entrance to this wild and pretty lagoon is just S of the wreck, and the southernmost of two openings. Keep to the center of this entrance to avoid ledges on each side, and sweep wide to the left to the anchorage.

Once inside, you are safe from all winds, but with big seas out of the E, the entrance would become a dangerous surfing proposition. You would be better off to run the 10 miles to Clarence Town, where the entrance is protected from easterly weather.

Crooked and Acklin's Islands (26240 or 26280)

Crooked Island, west shore (26252) offers a respectable lee in normal weather but no secure harbors.

The anchorage under Bird Rock Light at so-called Portland Harbour is easier to make than the charts and sketches indicate, for the heads stand out prominently. It has little to commend it however, except as a night's stopover when headed for Caicos. Columbus anchored here on the 19th of October, 1492, but found better protection and less surge a little further S. You will, too. Better to anchor off the first beach S of Pittstown Point and immediately N of Landrail Point, where you will have 8 feet 100 yards off, with the Marine Farm bearing 075°M and Landrail Point 192°M.

The hospitality of the people at Landrail Point settlement is almost overpowering, especially that of the Scavella family, which is prominent here. The village is particularly tidy, and the groves of citrus fruit are the pride of many of the homes.

Six miles further S, in the cut between Crooked and Fortune Islands, is French Wells anchorage, apparently a place for sailing ships to fill their casks in days gone by. While we ourselves have been scared away by the indistinctness of the sandbar at the entrance, others have had little trouble and have liked the spot well enough to spend several days roaming the deserted beaches and exploring the creeks that run into the interior. We are told that the bar is hard sand and that the place to cross is at the limit of its arc to seaward.

You may also round the S point of Fortune Island and proceed NE as far as your draft will allow. We found anchorage in 7 feet about 1½ miles NNE of Windsor Point and 300 yards off the rather unpretty beach. At least you will have a respite from the surge here.

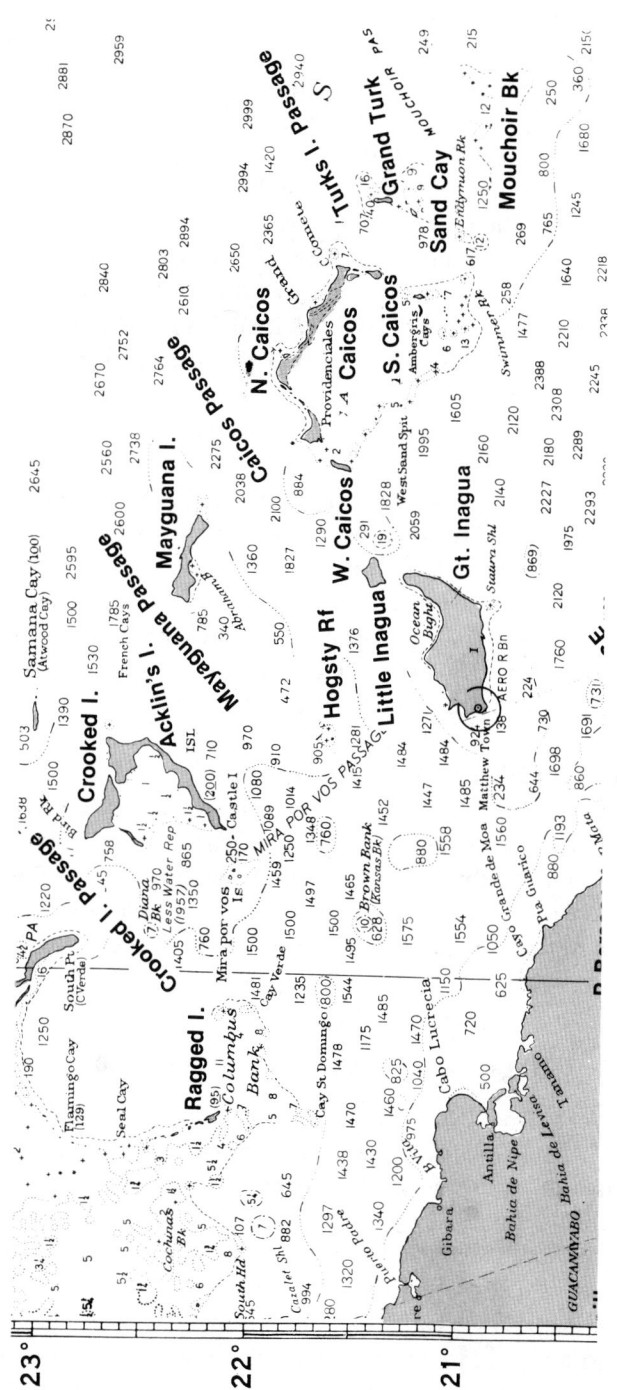

The Southeastern Bahamas

Crooked Island, north shore (26240 or 26280) is fringed by a reef extending for more than 20 miles with only an occasional break. Anchorages inside this reef will be found at McKay's Bluff, Major's Harbour, and off the village called True Blue, all having fair holding ground.

We spent a quiet night at Major's Harbour on an eastbound passage in 1971, anchored in 7 feet off a sandy half-moon beach protected by two small cays. We were well out of the constant surge that makes the other north-coast anchorages uncomfortable. The reef openings are difficult to detect in good weather and dangerous to enter when seas are breaking heavily, but we were able to locate the opening to Major's Cay Harbour by first identifying the prominent cliff at McKay's Bluff about 12 miles SE of Bird Rock, then continuing easterly for 2 miles until the next break in the reef lined up with the two small cays bearing due S. The light is unreliable and was not visible to us from the reef in daylight, but as we approached the cays it showed up in the foliage on the point to starboard.

If you enter slowly, using the leadline, you'll find 7–8 feet between the point and the small cays, shoaling rapidly in brown patches toward the beach but holding about 7 feet in the bight to starboard.

The settlement, half a mile back from the beach, boasts a tavern, but most supplies come in from the larger community of Colonel Hill, where the commissioner for the district has his office and where an airstrip links Crooked Island with Nassau and other more civilized places.

Acklin's Island (26240 or 26280) has a natural harbor at Atwood, lying 12 miles E of Major's Cay, where the reef opening is wide and more easily identified than that at Major's Cay. A new light at the entrance is better maintained and more reliable than others in this part of the Bahamas.

Although there is no settlement at Atwood, and the harbor is exposed to the N, you can usually find adequate protection close to the beach in the SW corner of the harbor.

Hogsty Reef and Great Inagua (26260)

Hogsty Reef (26252) is well worth the slight detour when bound for Inagua or the Windward Passage, since it is one of the three nearly authentic coral atolls in the North Atlantic (the others are Glover Reef off Belize in the Western Caribbean and Cay Sal Bank, which is described as a "drowned coral reef," between Cuba and the Florida Keys). By way of contrast, there are 400 or more scattered over the Pacific and Indian Oceans.

Its horseshoe shape covers an area about 3 by 5 miles, which is big enough for a healthy sea to build up in, even though the almost continuous barrier reef keeps out the ocean swells. This underwater wall rises so abruptly out of nearly mile-deep water that the breakers become visible hardly a mile away; you may not come on soundings until you are within a hundred yards or so of them.

Two low, sandy cays mark the entrance at the western side of the atoll. Northwest Cay, the larger of the two, is all of 8 feet high, with a mast for the automatic light, a lone palm tree, and a round stone beacon. Once inside, you will find a sandy bottom with a uniform 25 feet and plenty of coral heads that are easily seen.

Standing upright in a few feet of water on the NE side of the reef is a stranded Liberty ship, which came to grief during a 1963 hurricane. Unfortunately, this conspicuous mark is some 5 miles from the entrance, although it is a useful reference object from far off.

Because of the constant surge, the outer reef is dangerous for all but experienced divers, but the lagoon provides exciting snorkeling over the coral heads and the patch reefs, which abound with elkhorn coral, fish of many colors, big barracuda, spiny lobsters, and grouper and snapper for the table.

Fascinating as it may sound, however, Hogsty is not a place to put into if there is any chance of a blow.

Great Inagua (26240 or 26260, 26251) is the third largest of the Bahama Islands but is seldom visited by yachts except those en route to or from the Windward Passage. The 200-by-200-foot artificial basin just N of Matthew Town is a step in the right direction, but the entrance channel carries a bare 5 feet, and there are none of the usual facilities inside. Otherwise there is the open roadstead off Matthew Town. It is protected only when the wind hangs in its usual NE–SE arc and is open to a surge at all times. Particularly when the wind has a southerly slant, a better anchorage would be in Man-O-War Bay, close in to the coconut plantation on the northern shore.

Matthew Town exists on salt, mountains of it, extracted from the salinas behind the town. Salt brought wealth and fine homes and wide streets during a 15-year period of high production around the time of the American Civil War, but when the market slumped, Matthew Town became a ghost town. In 1938 it came to life again when three Yankee brothers by the name of Erickson reactivated the industry in so efficient a fashion that the big Morton Salt Company saw fit to buy up a controlling interest in the Ericksons' West India Chemicals Company.

Groceries are rather limited, and fueling by jerricans is a laborious operation, though you may be able to get into the inner basin for tank-truck delivery. Some repairs might be arranged if you have an urgent problem. Get your paperwork done here, because Matthew Town is a port of entry. Also, if you really must, this is a good place to contract an illness or suffer an injury since the company maintains a well-equipped hospital.

The radio beacon (-- ·· , ·· , -·) is reported to be good for at least 120 miles.

For those with time to spare and a few days of good weather, we should mention that Inagua is a naturalist's paradise, with its wild horses and cattle, freshwater turtles, lizards, varied birdlife, and especially the droves of flamingos in their sanctuary around Lake Windsor in the interior of the island.

Rum Cay and Conception Island (26300)

Rum Cay (26280, 26300, 26252) offers some protection from the prevailing SE winds and is safe from NW through N to E, but some surge is to be expected at all times. We would not want to be caught at Port Nelson in a brisk southwester.

Coming from the E or S, keep W of the dangerous reefs that encumber Sumner Point until you can make a course of 010°M on the most westerly of the villas along the shore. Approaching from the W, we found no dangers on a due E course toward the settlement dock, which we held until the two small white and most westerly houses came abeam, at which point we ran in toward the beach and anchored in 10 feet about 80 yards off this pair of houses. Note that we do *not* refer to the old houses on Cottonfield Point.

You can land your dinghy here near the airstrip and walk into town, but anoint yourself liberally with insect repellent: mosquitos and sand flies are a menace at any time of day.

In the past, the economy of Port Nelson was supported by the export of salt, sisal, and pineapples, but today the place is a ghost town of about 75 people, and

West Bay, Conception Island

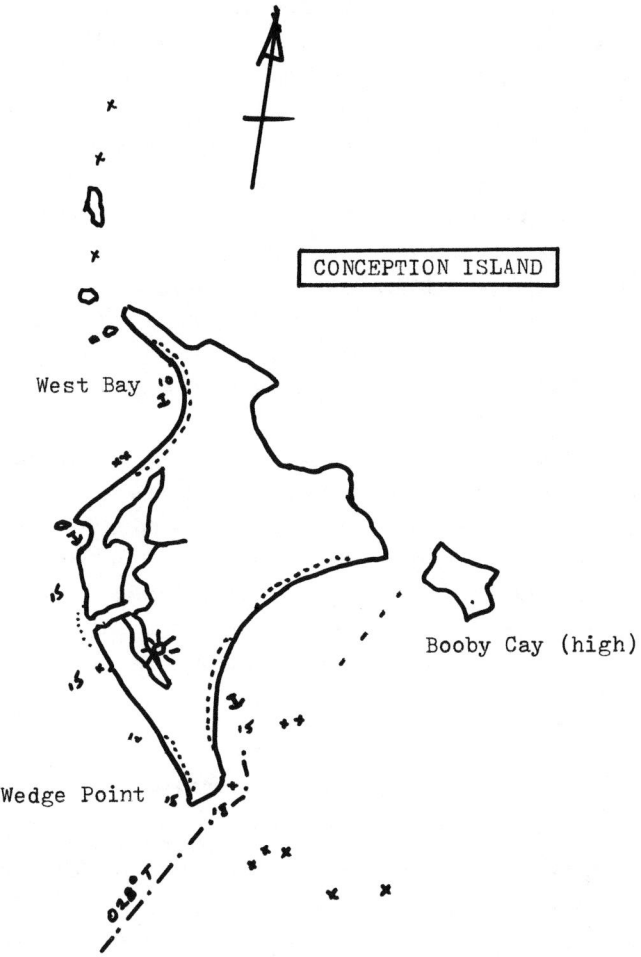

West Bay

CONCEPTION ISLAND

Booby Cay (high)

Wedge Point

nothing is grown for export even though the land seems relatively good for farming with no need to resort to pot-hole methods.

About ½-mile off the centermost of three sandy bluffs E of Sumner Point and about 200 yards S of the breaking reef itself, lies what remains of the wreck of H.M.S. *Conqueror,* the first propeller-driven British warship, which sank here in 1861. Surrounded by a forest of staghorn coral in a gully 30 feet deep, the main shaft, parts of the crankshaft, and the anchor chain and hawseholes are clearly seen. Claudie Gaitor, a superb native diver, will show you the wreck, and when you're through diving there, will find you more grouper and crayfish on the nearby heads than you can eat.

Conception Island (26280, 26300, 26301) is beautiful almost beyond conception, one of those idyllic, uninhabited places that are becoming so hard to find.

Furthermore, it would even be a reasonably secure refuge if you're overtaken by a norther when cruising this area, although you would have to be ready to shift anchorages around the island as the wind veered.

Since it is higher than the main island, Booby Cay will be your first landfall. Wedge Point at the S end of Conception is aptly named, with deep water within 100 feet of it.

To gain the bight with the 2-mile beach on the SE side of Conception, we came off soundings on a course 028°T toward the gap between Booby Cay and the main island, standing in close along the shore but avoiding the rocky bar off the second point, before turning in toward the beach, where the anchorage is protected from the W. Doubling back around Wedge Point, we found safe depths within 100 yards of the shore. On the W shore at 23°50.0' is a snug little cove with a natural breakwater to the N, but the most popular anchorage, and perhaps the prettiest, is in West Bay, where the land is high and anchorage may be taken in 11 feet within 60 yards of the perfect beach. In a 20-knot northeaster, *Yellow Bird* lay sheltered from the wind, securely anchored in good holding sand, and we experienced no surge; the sea and swell is thoroughly broken up by the reefs and shallows that extend some 5 miles to the N. We saw no uncharted dangers in an approach from the W.

Here, we think, is the perfect Bahamian isle to satisfy your urge for adventure.

San Salvador, Samana Cay, and Mayaguana Island (26280)

San Salvador (26281) is famous as the "Tierra, tierra," that Columbus first sighted in 1492. Of course, there have been different interpretations of his log, but most studies (including those of Admiral Samuel Eliot Morison) give the nod to San Salvador. The exact spot of his landing, in full regalia to meet the plenipotentiaries of the Great Khan, is less certain; in fact, there have been three monuments erected on the island to commemorate that historic event. The original marker was constructed on the northeast coast by the *Chicago Herald* newspaper; as Midwesterners, they must be excused for picking a lee shore that any seaman would be sure to avoid. The other two supposed landing places are at Cockburn Town itself and some 2 miles south of it, both, logically, in the lee of the island.

Columbus had it easy, coming as he did with the trades from Spain. It's usually a tough slug to windward coming from the Exumas or Cat Island!

A new marina has been dredged just S of the Riding Rock Inn, or about a half mile N of the settlement dock. This project is in the hands of Columbus Landings, Ltd., who are engaged in a massive land-development operation designed to convert this sleepy island into a splashy resort. Engineering plans call for a 270-by-150-foot basin and an 80-foot-wide entrance channel, all dredged to 10 feet. The approach course is 070°T on an occulting red front range and a fixed red rear range. In time, all the usual facilities will be available including fuel, a marine store, utilities, a self-service laundry, and showers.

Less elaborate plans than these have gone awry in the islands, but we can report that the basin actually existed in 1974, though there was some question about the shoaling of the channel, since the sandbanks were not adequately set back from the breakwaters. We therefore suggest you approach this new marina with caution and low hopes. After all, yachtsmen have been using the anchorage off the settlement for years.

Samana Cay (26280) boasts a good anchorage on the S coast, particularly if you are overtaken by a norther, when the harbors along the shores of Crooked and Acklin's Islands would be untenable. Approach the whitish cliff on a northeasterly heading, as shown in the sketch, and turn into the anchorage in the lee of Propeller Cay, where the bottom is good-holding sand and 10–20 feet deep. Note that the whitish cliff on the sketch is actually about a half mile W of the "White Cliff" indicated on the chart.

Crayfishing is good along the Propeller Cay shore, and the cay itself is alive with large goats that belong to the local fishermen. These fishermen round out

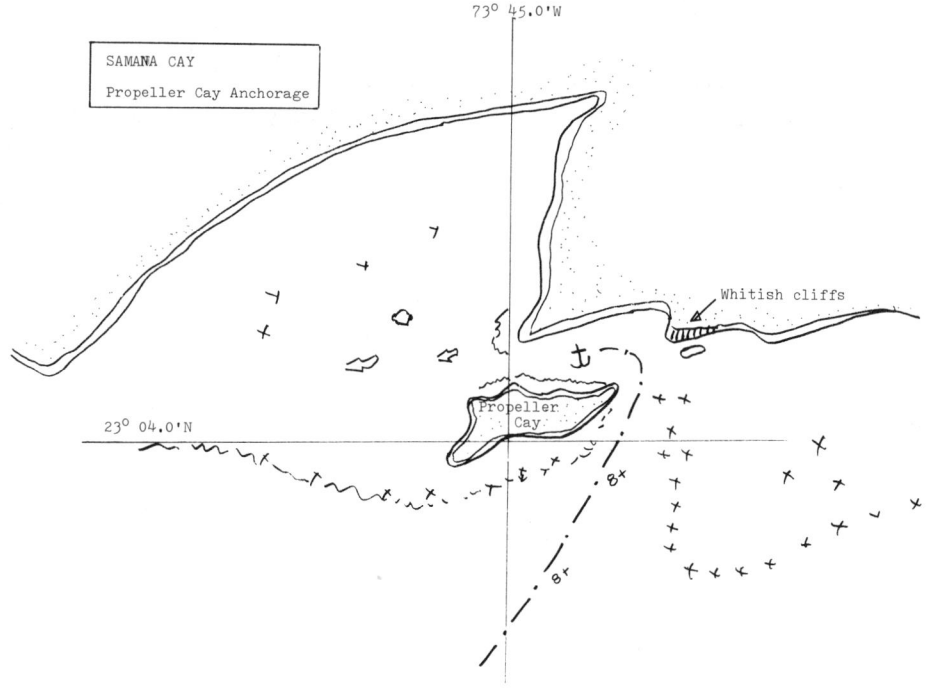

SAMANA CAY

Propeller Cay Anchorage

73° 45.0'W

Whitish cliffs

23° 04.0'N

Propeller Cay

their diet with tern eggs, which they collect twice a week by noisily driving the birds off their nests. The N shore of Samana is said to be a wonderland for avid beachcombers.

Mayaguana Island (26252, 26263) has the distinction of being minutely and recently charted; it was the site of a U.S. missile tracking station. But as you enter its expansive Abraham Bay, you will still be guided mainly by eye, because the chart soundings are so copious as to be almost bewildering.

If you arrive off the island in poor light, which is often the case because it's a long day's sail from Crooked Island or Providenciales, you will find a comfortable anchorage at Start Point, about 50 yards off the dock at the fuel storage depot there. The holding is good and the beach is kind to your dinghy. Otherwise, you will probably elect Abraham Bay, which is really much easier to enter than the busy chart would indicate. The reef opening from the SW is wide, and you need not proceed far in for protection.

The other entrance, under Guano Point, has a couple of easy turns in it, and the channel is quite distinct once you have approached the rocky bar off the light. Once through the channel, the bottom shoals rather rapidly, and you will find yourself obliged to anchor half a mile or more from the settlement, depending on your draft. At low tide, you cannot even run your outboard into the dock. There is really nothing to see or buy or do in the settlement, but you are expected to go ashore for the paperwork routine, this being the last (or first) port of entry into the Bahamas. If you don't, the officials will probably row out and fetch you in for a session in the office where the typewriter, the many forms, and the rubber stamps are. If you anchor in the W end of the Bay, you'll be too far away for them to bother with, even though they will lose a modest fee.

CHAPTER SIX

The Turks and Caicos Islands

These southeasternmost islands in the Bahamian chain are in fact Bahamian only in the geographical sense, for they hold the distinction, and in some ways the advantage, of being one of the few Crown Colonies remaining in the formerly all-powerful British Empire. Appearing as "Yucayo" on a map of the West Indies dated 1500, this remote and sparsely settled group of islands has, throughout its history, been both orphaned and fought over.

Originally settled in the 1670s by Bermudian salt rakers, it was occupied briefly by the Spanish and by the French, reluctantly joined the Bahama Colony between 1799 and 1848, later became a dependency of Jamaica until that island gained its own independence, and finally ended up as a Crown Colony of some 6,000 people presided over by a governor appointed by the Queen.

Until the last decade, the production of salt was the mainstay of these islands, but inefficient methods have taken their toll. The salinas of South Caicos, Grand Turk, and Salt Cay are now only tourist attractions, although some minor production continues on Salt Cay as a subsidized make-work project. How different from the days when Yankee trading schooners used to fill their holds with this commodity for the homeward voyage! But those were the days before refrigeration, when salt was the primary means of food preservation.

It is of course necessary to go through the usual entry and clearance procedures when passing through this archipelago. U.S. citizens do not need passports, although some proof of citizenship may be required: even a driver's license or Social Security card may suffice. However, a smallpox vaccination certificate *is* required. Providenciales, Cockburn Harbour (pronounced "CO-burn") and Grand Turk are ports of entry.

Caicos Bank (26260) is apparently shoaling gradually, judging from depths shown on early charts, but is regularly being crossed by yachts of 6-foot draft. In fact, all the routes we will describe are said to be good for 8 feet.

Even under ideal conditions, it is not easy to identify the Sand Bore Channel leading on to the W side of the Bank until you are quite close to the reef and can see the breakers on Shoe Reef on the northern side of the channel. Approach-

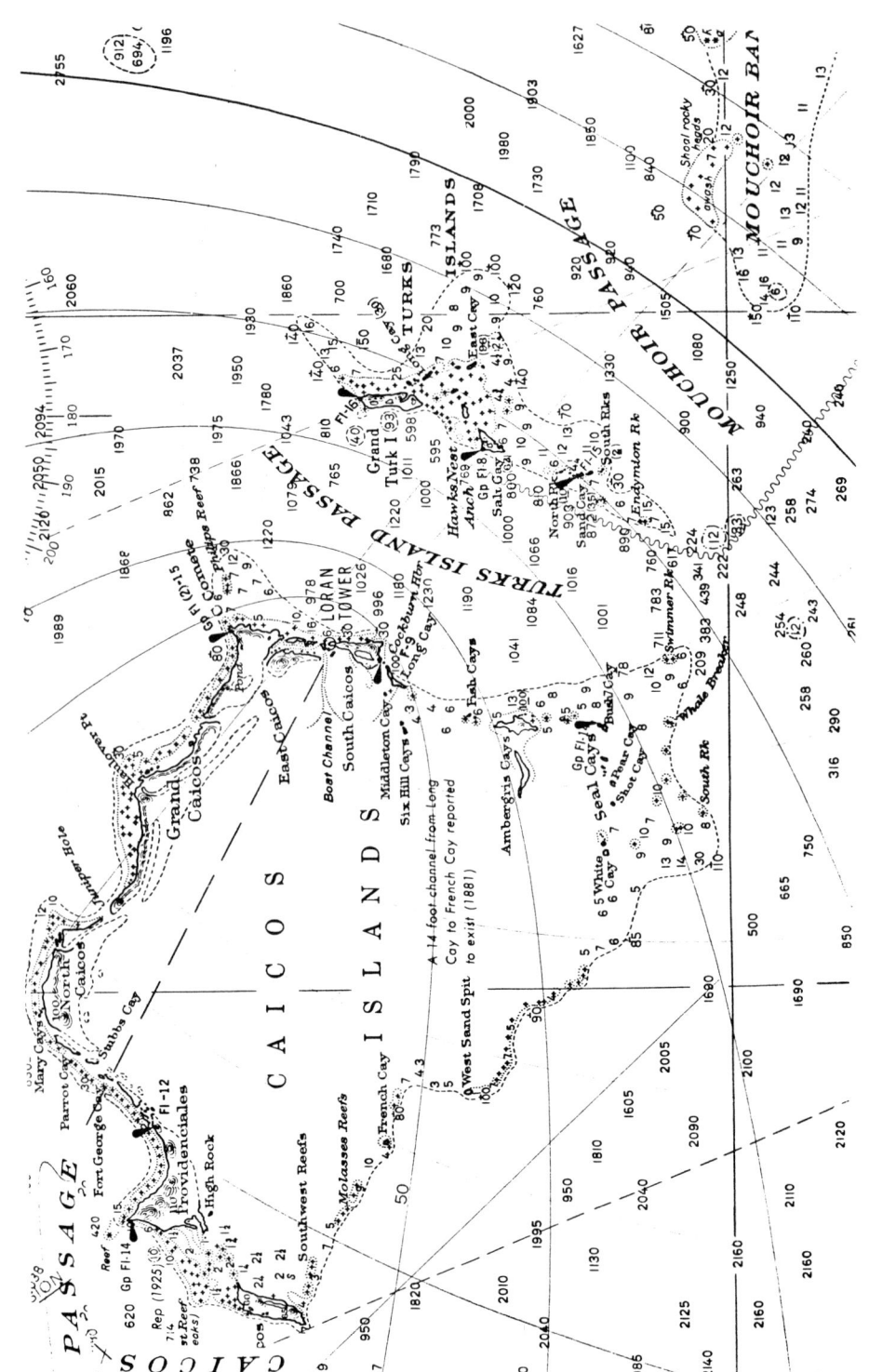

Turks and Caicos group

ing from the W, you will sight the Blue Hills of Providenciales at the N end of the island long before you pick up West Harbour Bluff at the S end, or the low profile of West Caicos Island further S.

We made our landfall N of the Shoe Reef and had to run back almost 6 miles outside the breaking coral heads before finding the opening. Once in the channel, however, we found 12–20-foot depths on an easterly heading to the rocky bluff at West Harbour, becoming 6–9 feet as we proceeded to an anchorage off a sandy beach W of Gussie Point, the next point E of West Harbour Bluff.

Alternatively, you can round the southern tip of West Caicos, where a channel over clear sand leads N to West Harbour and Gussie Point. In failing light you can anchor in reasonable comfort in this channel, which is protected by the Molasses Reef.

In our experience, the best track across the bank is 110°T from West Harbour Bluff for about 44 miles to a position just N of Six Hills Cays, where you will eyeball through the heads until you gain the deep water off the S end of Long Cay. Do not stand in too close to the tip of Long Cay, because it is necessary to round Middle Reef, which makes out SW from Long Cay. We followed this track in *Brer Fox* in 1971, only to find ourselves in very shallow water about halfway across, with no landmarks visible anywhere on the horizon. We assumed we were on Foot Shoal, which appears on both the U.S. and British charts, but soon discovered our error when we ran into even shoaler water to the N, and finally grounded gently on a soft grassy bottom inside the 1-fathom line shown on the charts. The northeasterly set of the flood current had carried us at least 4 miles N of the track in about 3½ hours running time.

Unfortunately the currents have never been studied for this or any of the Bahama banks, so you have to be alert to the possibility of being set probably, but not necessarily, to the N of this track.

Bob Wilke, who crossed with his deep-draft shrimper *Lady Jane* in 1974, advises running from Gussie Point on 135°T for 6 miles before taking up a course for the Six Hills Cays. He reports 8 feet or more all the way.

For a crash course in eyeball piloting (no pun intended), you might prefer to run SE from West Caicos along the outside of the reef (which is not continuous) to French Cay, a low scrubby island, where overnight anchorage may be taken along the western shore. From the S end of this cay, take up a course due E to the eastern edge of the bank S of Six Hills Cays. In all our Bahamas cruising we have never experienced a run so infested with ugly, black, and sprawling coral heads. In fact, it makes the Yellow Bank on the Nassau–Exumas run seem like a dredged channel. Of course, in the sunlit water the heads stand out sharply against the clear white sand, but in poor light this route would be impossible. We do not recommend this track westbound, because the sun would be in your eyes during an afternoon approach to French Cay, where the heads are the

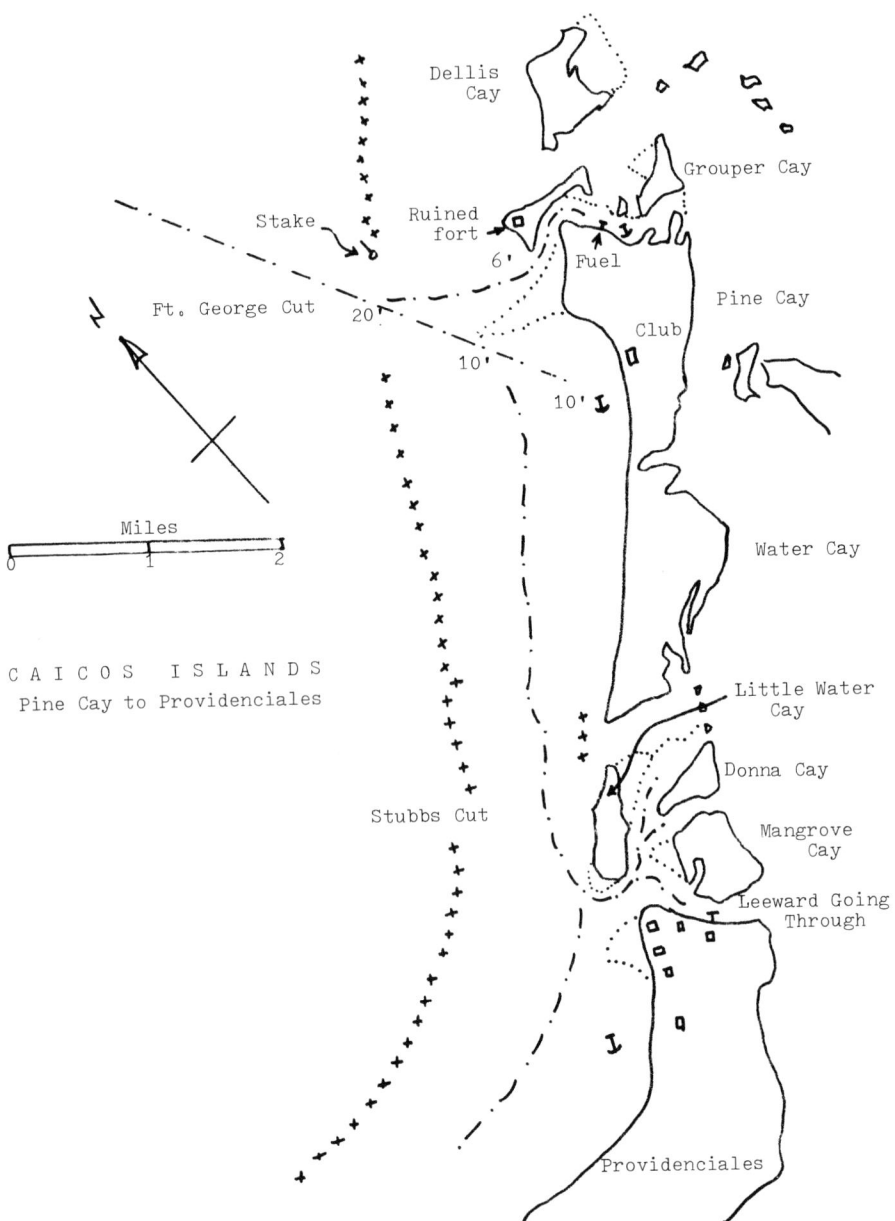

CAICOS ISLANDS
Pine Cay to Providenciales

thickest—and French Cay is not conspicuous, although it is the key to getting off the bank at the W end of the run.

Only on the Caicos Bank have we chanced to see the phenomenon known as "bank blink." Like a mirage on the desert, it seems to reflect the white water of the shoals and sandbars into the atmosphere immediately above them. On a shallow, shimmering sea over a bottom of gleaming sand, the effect is eerie, foreboding, and somewhat claustrophobic—especially when seen over the bow!

Providenciales and Pine Cay (26260) are developing at a fast pace as a residential resort area, no doubt because they enjoy the greater political security and stability of a Crown Colony. Great plans are afoot, many lots have been sold, regular air service has been instituted, and homes and commercial buildings are going up here and there. Despite the fact that these islands lie 200 miles dead to windward of Cape Santa Maria, cruising yachtsmen are steadily becoming attracted to them and liking what they find in the area.

After the long passage from Mayaguana or Great Inagua, the easiest entrance through the barrier reef is via Fort George Cut, which is about a mile wide and perfectly straightforward and safe even in poor light conditions. Inside you'll find a restful anchorage along the beautiful beach at Pine Cay. A more secure anchorage is up in the cut just beyond the Meridian Club's fuel dock, where the shallowest section, between Fort George and Pine Cays, will carry about 7 feet at half tide. From the Meridian Club beach for about ½-mile beyond Leeward Going Through, you will have easy sailing inside the reef, but from that point to the channel into Seller's Pond, there are numerous heads with plenty of water in between.

Stubbs Cut requires good light and a smooth sea, and considering the safety and convenience of Fort George Cut, we see no reason to use it until you are more familiar with the area.

It is no longer possible to continue on through the Leeward Going Through, but there is good reason to make use of the modern and well planned marina that has developed in this sheltered slot under the aegis of Bermudian Bill Kempe. The channel to it is well marked and adequate for deep-draft yachts.

The marina in Seller's Pond, where the Third Turtle Inn is located, may be approached via Seller's Cut or, with due caution, via the passage inside the protecting reef from Leeward Going Through. Immediately beyond Seller's Cut, a secondary reef (approximately N–S) makes out from the shore to the outer reef. Through this secondary reef a very narrow channel has been blasted and marked with two pairs of stakes. There is barely 4½ feet LW in this blasted channel, but most yachts can use the tide to reach the perfectly land-locked pond, where there is ample room for docking or anchoring. Carefully follow the markers that lead from the blasted channel through a forest of heads and sand bars. Even with the markers, you will need to resort to some eyeballing to get in here; if the light is poor or you are unsure of your ability to read the water, you had best circle just inside the main cut and wait for a boat to lead you in.

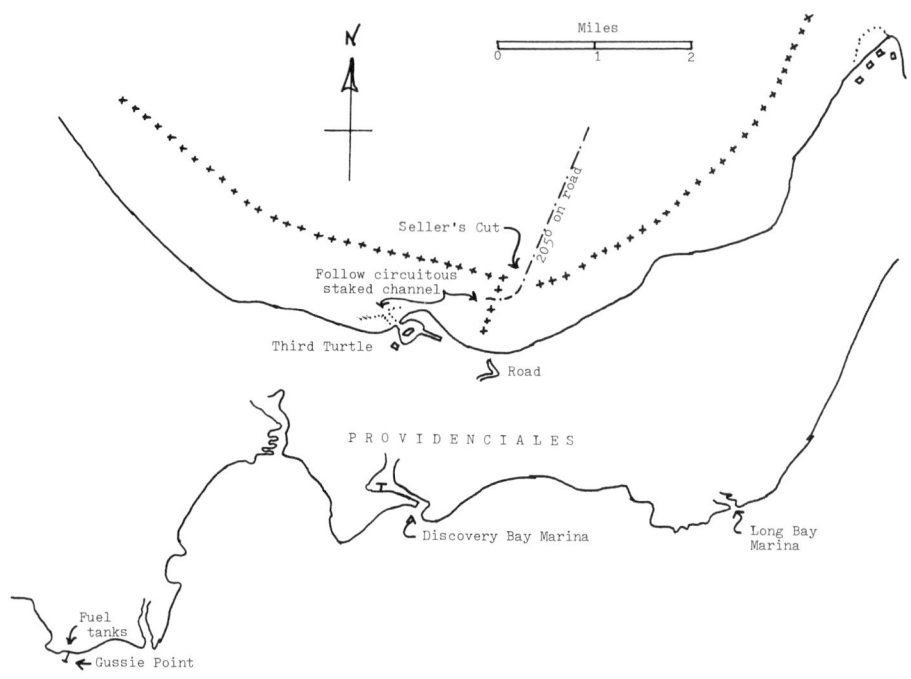

The marinas on Provo

In early 1975, two other marinas on the S shore of Providenciales were undergoing final dredging operations to open them to the sea.

Although we have circled Providenciales via Wheeland Cut and a break in the reef about ½-mile off Northwest Point, thence across Malcolm Roads and through the reef again at Wylie Cut, the lack of reference marks makes it very difficult to describe. Suffice to say that it can be done under ideal light and sea conditions.

Whitby, North Caicos (26260) is the site of a new hotel, where a marina may have been dredged before the end of 1975. Since access will be via Clarke's Cut, where the cable houses are, the following comments by Bob Brown, who was there in his 41-foot Morgan sloop *Kareme*, will be of interest:

Clarke's Cut is very dangerous. We hit bottom at better than half tide and draw 4½ feet. Eyeball navigation is OK if you have deep water, but we went close to shore and bounced off the bottom working our way back to what is reported to be a good anchorage at Bottle Creek. It was near high tide when we went in and I couldn't find enough water to anchor anywhere near Bottle Creek so we went further in and I jumped overboard to find a pool large enough to anchor without swinging into heads and shallow bottom.

Next morning while trying to get out, I ran up a dead end and went aground on coral. It took 2½ hours of back-breaking work to first pivot the boat, because my rudder was banging on coral, and then inch-by-inch to kedge off. We still bounced over the reef on departure and then waited for better than half tide to go out.

Until the area inside Clarke's Cut is thoroughly examined and the dredging is completed, the nearest anchorage to the hotel is at Sandy Point, some 4 miles W, which is reached by following the shore N of Parrot Cay. However, there is said to be a sandbar at the NE end of Parrot Cay which will carry 6 feet only at HW.

Cockburn Harbour (26261) on South Caicos gives far more protection than might appear from the chart. In fact, it is the only really secure anchorage on the E side of the Caicos Bank. The shallows to the S and W break up any sea

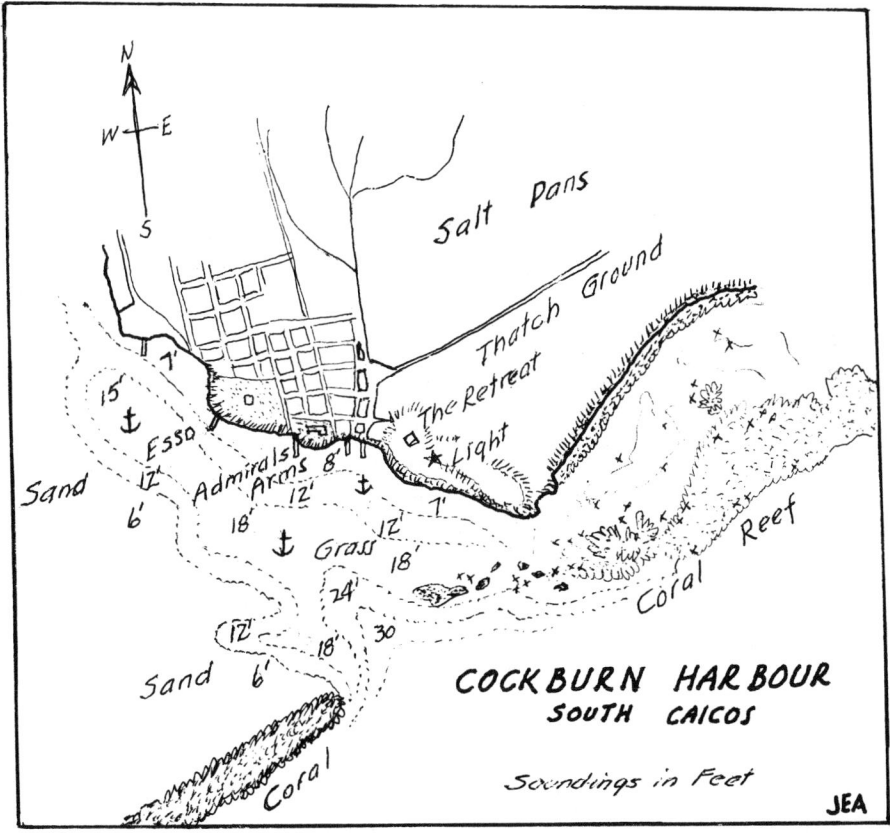

from those directions, the island itself provides a lee from northers, and in the event of a real blow from the SE, one can move across the harbor to a lee under Long Cay.

Anchor close under the cliffs on which the Admiral's Arms Inn is situated, or use their miniscule marina. You will find fuel, ice, water, laundry service, and plenty of hospitality here, and a chance to mingle and compare hobbies with private flyers who, like yachtsmen, have found South Caicos a handy stopover spot.

Since the demise of salt, the town has been gasping for some other industry to take its place. It now seems that fishing, freeze-packing, and some boat repairing and lobster-trap-making are slowly filling the void. Even so, the remaining piles of salt, the dilapidated warehouses, and the rusting relics of salt-moving equipment give a ghost-town appearance to the place.

Only limited provisions will be found in the small stores scattered here and there in the settlement.

Grand Turk (26261, 26262) is the administrative center of this island group, but holds little attraction for yachtsmen. Although the open roadstead off the town is sheltered from the prevailing easterlies, it is wide open to winds from SW to N.

The entrance to the anchorage is through a narrow opening in the reef, W of the two small piers in the center of the town and N of the mast of an old wreck that lies on the reef. In making the approach, you will first sight the radio tower S of the town and the large buildings of the missile base at the southern end of the island. The reef is only about 600 yards off the shore, so you can approach close enough in deep water to identify the wreck and the 084° range lights.

You will usually find a few boats anchored in 6–10 feet about 100 yards off the beach near the government pier. When we arrived there in 1972, we encountered a relatively moderate norther that quickly produced breaking seas on the reef and a violent surge in the harbor. Though most of the local boats and Haitian sloops remained bobbing at anchor, it didn't take us long to decide that Cockburn Harbour across the Turks Island Passage, was the best place to be under such conditions: as a matter of fact, in a really hard winter norther even the local boats seek shelter there or run down to the Hawksnest area at the SW end of Grand Turk.

Salt Cay (26261) is low, flat, and ideally suited to the production of salt, which in times past made it a prosperous place, as the remains of some grand old homes will attest. As a relic it is interesting; as an anchorage it is comfortable off the settlement only in moderate easterly weather.

Sand Cay (26261) is little more than a sand pile about 35 feet high, with a light on a frame tower. Lying about 25 miles SE of Cockburn Harbour, it makes an ideal stopover for the night when on passage to or from the Dominican Republic. Anchorage may be taken quite close up to the shelving beach.

CHAPTER SEVEN

Hispaniola

More than 480 years after its discovery in 1492, Hispaniola is only beginning to be rediscovered by cruising yachtsmen, who are finding its exotic tropical seascape just as alluring as Columbus found it on his first voyage. The Admiral called it his favorite isle in the Caribees—"the fairest land human eyes have ever seen"—and though cruising skippers who sail along the same track today may have their own favorite isles elsewhere in the Caribbean, they are not likely to quarrel too much with his descriptive eloquence.

Second-largest island of the Greater Antilles (only Cuba is larger), Hispaniola has had a more turbulent history than most of its Caribbean neighbors. Fought over and divided by France and Spain in the colonial era, raided by pirates and freebooters in the 17th and 18th centuries, ruled by native tyrants and military dictators since the 19th century, and plagued by civil strife, poverty, and political unrest, the island has nonetheless managed to continue its tortured life into the 20th century. Today, the eastern two-thirds of this 28,000-square-mile island are occupied by the Spanish-speaking Dominican Republic; French-speaking Haiti occupies the western third.

While Rafael Trujillo and "Papa Doc" Duvalier ruled the Dominican Republic and Haiti, respectively, yachts were not encouraged to visit any part of Hispaniola. But Trujillo died in 1961 and Papa Doc in 1971, and during the ensuing periods of apparent political stability, both countries have been encouraging visitors. Our own observations, on recent visits, have been reassuring, and reports from others who have cruised the area are generally favorable, though not without certain qualifications. We have received nothing but courteous treatment from officials in the major ports of entry in both Haiti and the Dominican Republic, and most of the cruising people we've met have found a friendly welcome ashore and afloat in the two countries. This doesn't mean that the area is problem-free or that cruising around Hispaniola is comparable to cruising in the American and British Virgins. It's not, for a variety of understandable reasons.

Although Hispaniola is beginning to be visited by more yachts on their way to or from the eastern Caribbean, both Haiti and the Dominican Republic are still

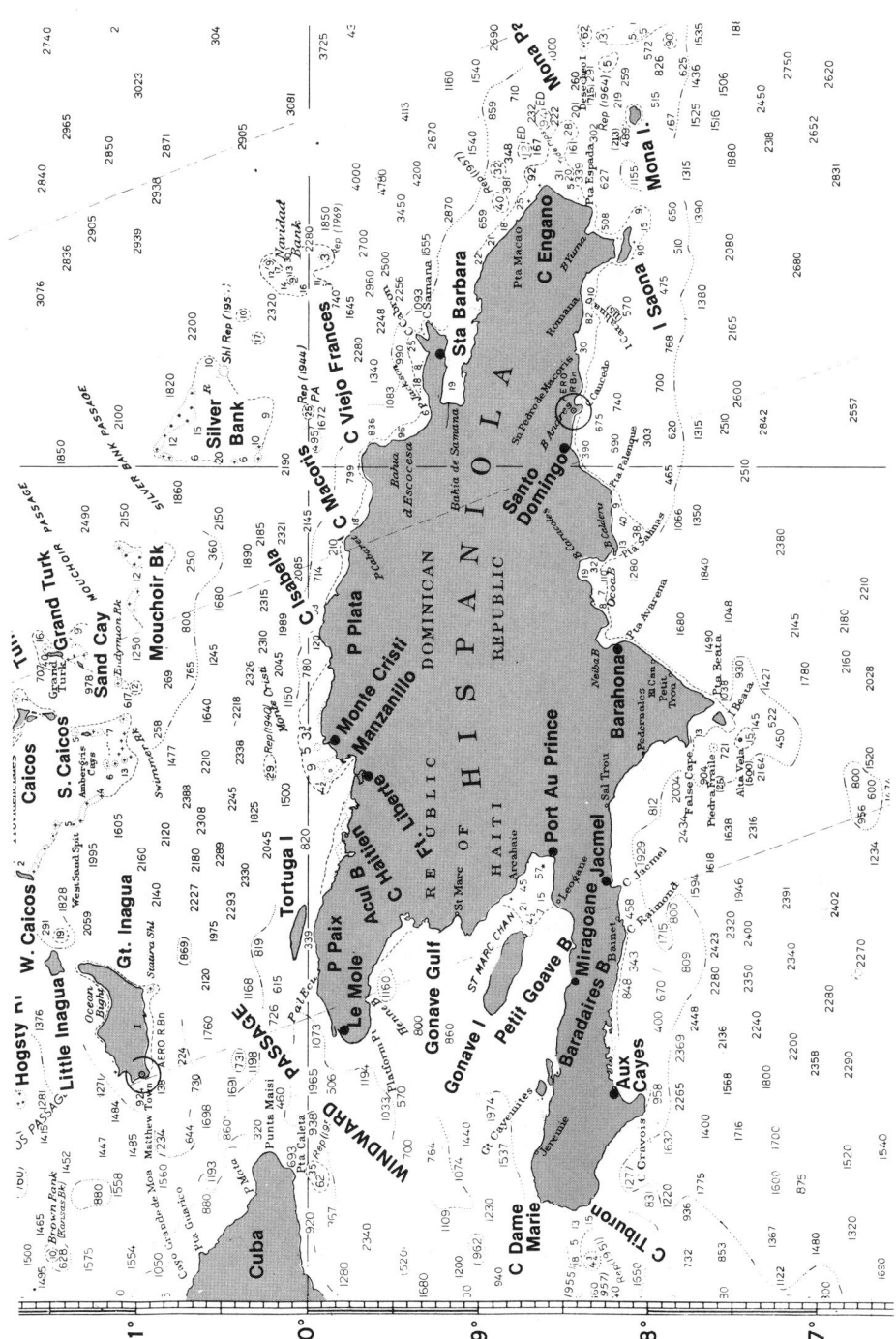

relatively remote from the main cruising centers. Few yacht facilities are to be found in even the largest ports, and there are small coastal villages that have never seen a foreign yacht. On the other side of the ledger, relatively few North American yachtsmen take the trouble to inform themselves about current conditions, customs, and traditions of the countries they intend to visit, with the result that they are often ill prepared to cope with situations that may arise along the way.

Isolated boarding incidents have occurred in the past. Several years ago a stranded U.S. powerboat was boarded by armed bandits off a remote section of the north coast of Santo Domingo. In that case, the crew was eventually rescued by a Dominican gunboat, which arrived in response to radio calls for assistance relayed through the U.S. Coast Guard in Puerto Rico, and the yacht was towed safely to Puerto Plata. Their advice to other visiting yachts was to steer clear of Hispaniola.

Another type of incident occurred when we were in Santo Domingo in February, 1973. This involved a 42-foot Chris-Craft Comanche sailing yacht that had been used to smuggle an opposition political group into the country in an abortive attempt to overthrow the Balaguer government. This yacht, *Black Jak*, had been purchased in New York by a Dominican faction in exile, taken to the Caribbean, loaded with arms at another West Indian island, and then sailed back to the Dominican Republic by 10 rebel leaders. They landed at night on a beach some 50 miles west of the capital. Headed by a former Dominican Army colonel who had opposed Balaguer in the 1965 civil strife, the rebel band apparently expected to win quick popular support once its leaders established themselves in the mountains. But the plot failed; the leaders were rounded up by the government within a week and summarily executed. The abandoned yacht was found on the beach and taken to the capital to be displayed to the press as an example of how seemingly innocent pleasure boats can be used to mount a rebellion.

After this incident, we heard several first-hand accounts of yachts being hailed and boarded by a Dominican naval vessel or patrol boat; in each case, however, the yacht was released promptly once the owner established his identity and that of his crew. The moral of these cases, it seems to us, is not that visiting yachts should have to "steer clear" of Hispaniola but that owners and crew should be prepared to cope with such situations, have their documents in order, and be able to prove their identity.

Our earlier suggestions for planning a Caribbean cruise apply particularly to Haiti and the Dominican Republic. It is essential to have clearance papers from your last foreign port, designating your intended port of entry. Make your first entry at a major port, if possible, and obtain a cruising permit if you plan to visit other ports in either country. You should have a valid identification document for every member of your crew, with evidence of citizenship; a driver's license is not acceptable. Passports, though not required for short-term tourists with return tickets, should be carried by the owner and crew members of yachts intending to cruise the area extensively.

Don't neglect to check your chart inventory before departing for Hispaniola. There are 51 U.S. coastal and harbor charts covering the island as a whole—28 for Haiti, 23 for the Dominican Republic, including large-scale plans, which are essential for entering ports and bays. You may not need them all, but the coastal reefs of Hispaniola are not a place to practice eyeball navigation without the aid of the best large-scale charts obtainable, which in this instance are considerably better than those available for the Bahamas.

In the following sections, we take a close look at coastal features, harbor entrances, and port facilities, starting with the north coast of Haiti from west to east, continuing along the north coast of the Dominican Republic to Samaná Bay and Mona Passage, as one would in making an eastbound passage to Puerto Rico and the Virgin Islands. Then we return to the west coast of Haiti, look at interesting harbors in the Gulf of Gonâve, port facilities at Port-au-Prince, and continue on around the south coasts of both Haiti and the Dominican Republic to the eastern end of the island.

THE NORTH COAST OF HAITI (26161, 26141)

The veil of mystery that enshrouds Haiti may apply even to your landfall if you are approaching from the north, for though the hills of Tortuga Island rise to 1,200 feet and the mountainous mainland reaches heights of 3,000 feet a few miles inland, the land itself may often be hidden in haze until you are quite close inshore. This condition is more than symbolic and can be confusing to navigators approaching for the first time, expecting to sight distant mountains from 30 or more miles at sea. Haze, caused by hundreds of burning charcoal fires in the hills, often shrouds much of the north coast of Hispaniola, making it difficult for those who have not experienced it before to judge distances accurately in making their approach to the coast and its fringing reefs.

Winds and currents are the major elements with which navigators must contend in approaching from the north. Yachts making the 70-mile passage between Inagua and Haiti must make allowance for the strong ocean current that has set more than one small vessel westward into the Windward Passage to an unexpected landfall on Cuba. While the *Pilot Charts* show an average westerly set of less than 1 knot most of the year, this may increase rapidly in winter months when the northeast trades are blowing their strongest. Yachts planning to enter at Cap Haïtien, the principal port of entry on this coast, should try to pass east of Tortuga, if possible, to avoid having to beat up the channel between that island and the mainland. But unless the trades are coming in steadily between NNE and NE, you may find it difficult or impossible to make the easting needed to clear Tortuga. Under those conditions, you will probably round the western end of Tortuga, as others have done, and take your punishment beating upwind through the narrow strait, with an inhospitable lee shore on the mainland.

Cap du Môle to Cap Haïtien (26161, 26141)

Yachts approaching Cap Haïtien from the western end of Tortuga or from Cap du Môle, the westernmost point in Haiti, are likely to find this 70-mile stretch of mountainous coastline rather forbidding when the winter trades are blowing boisterously. Most of the coast is bold and steep-to, with only a few bays where one might hope to find shelter. In the western half of this section, the 100-fathom line follows the rugged coast a mile or less offshore from Cap du Môle to Port-de-Paix about 35 miles ENE, or directly upwind for eastbound vessels. Tortuga Island, also high with a bold shoreline, fronts the mainland coast about 4 to 5 miles offshore in the vicinity of Port-de-Paix.

Unless you are already familiar with Haiti's inshore waters, we don't particularly recommend entering any of the small bays in this 35-mile coastal sector. However, there are several bights and indentations with anchorages used by small coastal vessels. These are described briefly below for those with previous experience in Haitian coastal waters, or for anyone cruising this area in settled weather conditions.

Juan Rabel Anchorage (26146, Plan B) is an open roadstead off the village of Magasins, about 2 miles SW of Point Juan Rabel, some 15 miles eastward from Cap du Môle. A white cliff and a long sandy beach are skirted by a reef that lies about 200 yards N of the village. Coastal vessels anchor in 10 fathoms off a shallow, foul-bottomed shorebank that extends about ¼-mile offshore.

Baie du Port à l'Écu (26146, Plan E) is a small sheltered cove less than ½-mile wide about 7½ miles eastward of Point Juan Rabel, with a deep-water approach to a high brown bluff marking the eastern entrance. There is a small village on the SW shore and good holding ground over a sand bottom S of the eastern entrance.

Baie des Moustiques (26146, Plan F) is a deep indentation about 4 miles E of Port à l'Écu, which was visited by Columbus on his first voyage. The anchorage is exposed to the N and the bottom is rocky and should be sounded before dropping the hook. The village of Cabaret is about ½-mile inland, where you will see outdoor cooking by charcoal.

Port-de-Paix (26149) is the second-largest town on the north coast of Haiti and a port of entry about halfway between Cap du Môle and Cap Haïtien. The "port" is a roadstead in the center of a small bight that recedes less than 500 yards between two entrance points about ½-mile apart, each marked by the ruins of an old fort. The anchorage off town is wide open to northerly winds but affords limited shelter in the prevailing easterlies. There is always a surge. The mud-and-sand bottom is foul in places, and holding ground poor in a blow. There is a small pier used by local boats and lighters for unloading cargo from vessels anchored in the bight. The Customs House is close by on the waterfront, and it does handle occasional foreign yachts, though we favor proceeding directly to Cap Haïtien if possible. The Bon Accueil Hotel in town has the reputation of serving fine charcoal-broiled fish dinners. Fuel and water are available, with limited provisions in the markets.

Tortuga Island (26161, 26146, Plan D)

This high, wooded island is about 20 miles long, 3 to 4 miles wide, with a bold steep-to coastline fronting Tortuga channel on its south side. The only anchorage is at Basse Terre, about 5 miles westward from the SE point, where a break in the fringing reefs affords limited protection from northers and strong easterly winds. Depths range from 3 to 6 fathoms over a sand bottom, but the holding ground is not good.

Tortuga provided a stronghold out of which operated some of the earliest buccaneer bands in the Caribbean. It is interesting to recall their history and the origin of the word that came into common use during the 1600s when the "Brethren of the Coast" established the first settlements on Tortuga. "Buccaneer" was the English version of a French word *boucanier*, one who cures meat over an open fire by the "boucan" process. The first bands to reach Tortuga arrived from St. Kitts after being driven out by a Spanish raid in the 1630s. Alec Waugh tells their story in his classic history of the West Indies, *A Family of Islands*. At the beginning, their life was relatively peaceful. They had plenty to eat. They enjoyed hunting and led a free and easy existence. Pork was their main diet, and they cut the meat in long strips which they laid over open fires (*boucans*) on gratings made of green sticks, a kind of barbecue.

The buccaneers might have been content to lead their life in the bush if they had been left alone. But the Spanish attacked Tortuga in force in 1638, driving out all the inhabitants in a violent raid. But the buccaneers came back a few months later "in far from a pacific mood, ready for revenge." They were joined during the next few decades by other freebooters from Jamaica and by traders whose ships had been intercepted by the Spanish. They too were ready for revenge and plunder. They were, in Waugh's words, "a motley crew, from many stocks, from many ways of life." In a short time they attracted still others, "the riffraff of seven nations and the seven seas; they were homeless, rootless, with families long since forgotten. They were mutineers, escaped prisoners, shipwrecked pirates; they had no country, they owed no allegiance to anyone except themselves."

Half a century later, Henry Morgan gave a different connotation to the word buccaneer when he led his well-organized raids on Spanish commerce in British ships and assembled the armadas that sacked the rich colonial cities of the Spanish Main with the backing of the British Crown. But some of Tortuga's Brethren of the Coast may well have served with Morgan in the sack of Porto Bello and the raid on Panama in 1671.

Today one hears occasional tales of cruising yachts boarded by bands of native ruffians along the rugged shores of Tortuga. We have not been able to verify any recent cases of such boardings, nor have we found anyone who claims to have discovered a good protected anchorage on the south coast of the island. The Basse Terre anchorage shown on the chart is little more than a narrow opening in the reef; it scarcely deserves to be called a roadstead, and the outer shoal is reported to be extending to the south. Several boats cruising the area have failed to find anchorage at all.

Port-de-Paix to Cap Haïtien (26141)

This 36-mile section of the coast is indented by a series of small bights and one large bay in which a number of good anchorages may be found. Here the coastal mountains recede inland but become higher, rising to peaks of nearly 4,000 feet a few miles from the coast. The 100-fathom curve continues close offshore except at the eastern end near Cap Haïtien, where reefs extend 3 to 5 miles north of the coast. There are several temporary anchorages south of Marigot Head, a prominent 500-foot-high island with four small islets around it about ½-mile offshore and 2 miles west of Limbé Point. Caution should be exercised in navigating around the islands and in Marigot Bay, as there are few charted soundings in the area. The outlying reefs and shoals begin east of Limbé Point and continue northeasterly for about 8 miles all the way to Cap Haïtien, with channels leading into deep Acul Bay to the south and Port Francis to the east. Both of these places are definitely worth exploration.

Acul Bay (26148) is the second-largest harbor on the north coast of Haiti, penetrating almost 4 miles into the surrounding hills, which provide complete protection in all weather. Large coastal vessels enter through one of the deep-water channels leading across the outer reefs (the Limbé Channel west of the reefs is the safest approach for yachts), then continue into the narrow harbor channel between a 400-foot hill behind Morro Roxo on the eastern shore and a sandspit extending off the low western shore. Cruising boats will find quiet anchorages in Lombarde Cove, just S of Morro Roxo, or further S near the head of the bay.

Port Francis (26148), known locally as "Labadie," is a lovely little bay on the western side, or "backside," of Cap Haïtien, protected by the surrounding mountains to the E and the reefs in the NW. It's a favorite anchorage for yachtsmen from "Le Cap," who find its peace and quiet a pleasant contrast to the noise and bustle of the city. The small village has good water, clean beaches, and friendly people who will charcoal-broil you a fish dinner in the native style.

Approaches to Cap Haïtien (26147)

Inbound sailing vessels that have successfully cleared the eastern point of Tortuga will have a straightforward approach to Cap Haïtien, although they'll probably have to beat part of the way unless they are lucky enough to pick up N to NE winds. In order to allow for the westerly set of the current, you may have to hold a course of 110° to keep clear of the reefs and shoals that extend northward of the cape. Power cruisers approaching from the west through Tortuga Channel or coming from Acul Bay will also have to contend with winds and currents in rounding the cape.

The final approach to the port of Cap Haïtien should always be made in daylight, as the lighthouse on Fort Picolo Point is no more reliable than most other such aids to navigation in Haiti, where unreliability is more the rule than the exception. In any case, if your approach is from the NW, take note that this lighthouse is not visible from W of a line bearing 140° as shown on chart 26141. Three mountain peaks behind Haut du Cap are conspicuous from offshore, however, and the ruins of the old fort become visible as you approach the light.

When abeam of the light, take the western channel, leaving Grand Mouton reef to port, the first two buoys to port, and the next buoy to starboard. Before you will have sighted the channel buoys, beware of what looks like a navigational aid to port: it turns out to be the mast of a sunken ship on the reef. Columbus lost his flagship *Santa Maria* on one of these harbor reefs on Christmas Eve, 1492; don't follow his example. As we've noted elsewhere, you can forget the "red, right, returning" jingle when entering most Caribbean ports, but here at Le Cap recent arrivals report that all the buoys appear to be red—from red rust, that is.

George and Jacque Kappes, reporting on a 1973 visit to Cap Haïtien in the ketch-rigged motor sailer *Liberty Belle*, provided helpful information about entry procedures and shoreside facilities. We summarize them as follows:

The Customs House is located just across the street from the commercial concrete dock, where visiting yachts may lay alongside if there's room. Native boats tie close to the foot of the dock, new arrivals in the middle, and large

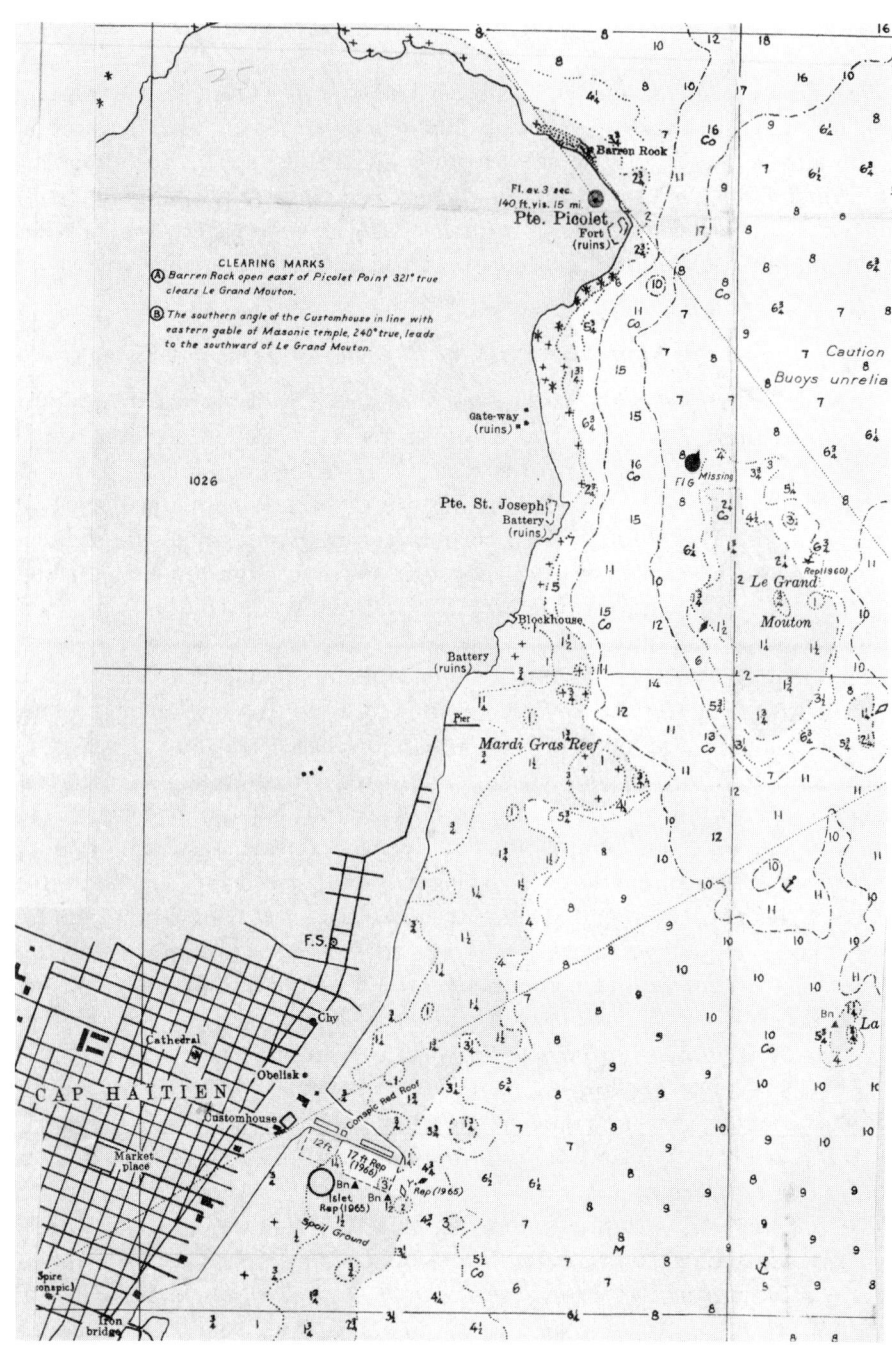

Approaches to Cap Haïtien

cruise ships and freighters at the outer end. There is usually some surge, so be prepared for liberal fendering. Customs and immigration officials are polite and helpful. They come aboard carrying guns, but don't be disturbed by that, as it's all part of the scene. With passports, health certificates, documentation papers, crew lists, and a letter from the Haitian consul in Nassau, *Liberty Belle* had no trouble clearing. But the Kappes had firearms aboard, which they declared and which were promptly taken by the authorities to be held until the yacht's departure some four months later.

If you are planning to visit other ports in Haiti, or merely do some gunkholing nearby, clearance must be obtained from the Port Captain, and you will need final clearance papers before leaving the country.

After clearing customs, most cruising boats prefer to lie out in the harbor, where anchorages may be found in 2 to 4 fathoms not far from the dock. The surge is more or less constant, but it's not too uncomfortable except in storms or severe N to NE winds. Safely anchored out, you can avoid the inquisitive stares of the scores of townsfolk, young and old, who cluster on the dock to watch every move you make.

The reactions of cruising people naturally differ, but most of the people we've seen or heard from recently have been favorably impressed by the friendliness of the Haitians, though somewhat baffled by the country itself. Bob and Ginnie Higman, cruising the coastal waters of Haiti in 1971 in *Tormentor III*, found the country "baffling, beautiful, and exasperating." They were impressed by the stark contrasts: "A country of friendliness and fear; generosity and beggary; barren mountainsides and lush tropical valleys; so much loveliness and so much poverty, too." Writing to SSCA, Ginnie acknowledged that she and her skipper husband, Bob, had two completely different sentiments about the country. "Bob hated the hassle he had to go through at every anchorage; he hated the lack of privacy, the beggary, the lack of communication, which to me were only minor inconveniences . . . it was going ashore and getting acquainted with the people that attracted me most."

For those lingering at Cap Haïtien for more than a few days, the skipper and mate of *Liberty Belle* had a number of practical suggestions. In such an environment, there are street urchins everywhere, so if you want to help the economy as well as make life ashore easier for yourself, it is best to select your own boy. He will go to market with you, carry your tote bag, and fetch ice for you from the Veau d'Or market (where it's clean). Of course, he will expect a tip, which will vary according to the size of your bag and the quality of his services. Raphael will no doubt meet you at the dock. He is a small, alert, ferrety little man with a fistful of letters of recommendation from yachtsmen who arrived before you. According to him, he can do just about anything and everything for you; but if you are inclined to accept his services, we suggest you try him out with a few small tasks under close supervision before taking all the bait.

A good friend of yachtsmen at Le Cap is Walter Bussenius, owner-manager of the Mont Joli Hotel, on the main street about a mile from the dock. Also the German consul, Carl Otto Schuet, is always helpful if you have a problem. Having lived at Cap Haïtien for over 30 years, he knows everyone and can tell you how and where to get things done. Either of these good people can advise you about water, fuel, engine repairs, or refrigerator problems.

A visit to the public market at Le Cap is an experience not to be missed. The market covers two city blocks and is roofed over, with stalls spilling out into adjacent streets. The activity is usually frenzied, with bargaining expected for every purchase.

Food is a delight, thanks to Haiti's French heritage, and there are several good eating places around town. The Brise de Mer is a pension near the Careenage where the proprietor will prepare an excellent meal of soup, crêpes, salad, main course and dessert if you call ahead. The restaurant at the Mont Joli is also good, if somewhat more expensive. Be careful of what you eat and drink, however, as dysentery ("Christophe's Revenge" as it's called locally) is not unknown. Best avoid clams, lettuce, watercress, and things grown in water. Malaria, too, is still extant, so pills such as Campoprima would not be amiss.

No one visiting Cap Haïtien should forego the pilgrimage to The Citadel, the huge fortress perched atop a mountain above the town of Milot, built by Henri Christophe, the black ruler who proclaimed himself Emperor of Haiti in 1806. "La Citadelle" took 13 years to build, and 20,000 lives were lost in the process, so it's said. Every stone, timber, cannon, and shot had to be carried up the steep mountainside by sweating, toiling humans. By one account it took 100 men two weeks to drag each of the 375 cannon to the parapets at the top. Christophe's great Citadel, which never fired a shot in anger, still stands in remarkable condition today, well worth the time and effort required to follow the narrow, winding trail to the summit, where you will be rewarded by a magnificent view of the valleys below. When we were there last, we heard the echoes of distant drums coming from different points in the valleys, intensifying the mysterious spell that seems to hang over the place.

At the base of the trail to the Citadel are the gutted remains of Christophe's palace, Sans Souci, now only a vague monument to this vain man's grandiose reconstruction of the elegance he had seen in his visits to France.

Cap Haïtien to Manzanillo Bay, D.R. (26141)

This section of the coast trends WSW for about 25 miles to the boundary between Haiti and the Dominican Republic, which is marked—appropriately, perhaps—by the muddy waters of the Massacre River. The coastline here is low and fringed by a barrier reef that rises steeply from the deep seabed with openings leading into two large bays.

Milot and ruins of the Palace of Sans Souci

Cristophe's fortress "La Citadelle" above Milot

Caracol Bay (26146, Plan A) is a shallow estuary entered through a narrow channel that meanders southward into numerous uncharted shoals. Unless you enjoy sounding the flats by dinghy (which could be rewarding), we would suggest continuing eastward for another 8 miles to Fort Liberté Bay, where you will find a number of fine anchorages in the largest all-weather bay on the entire north coast of Hispaniola.

Fort Liberté Bay (26145) is entered through a deep, narrow channel between West Point and St. Louis Redoute, a promontory on the eastern shore. The

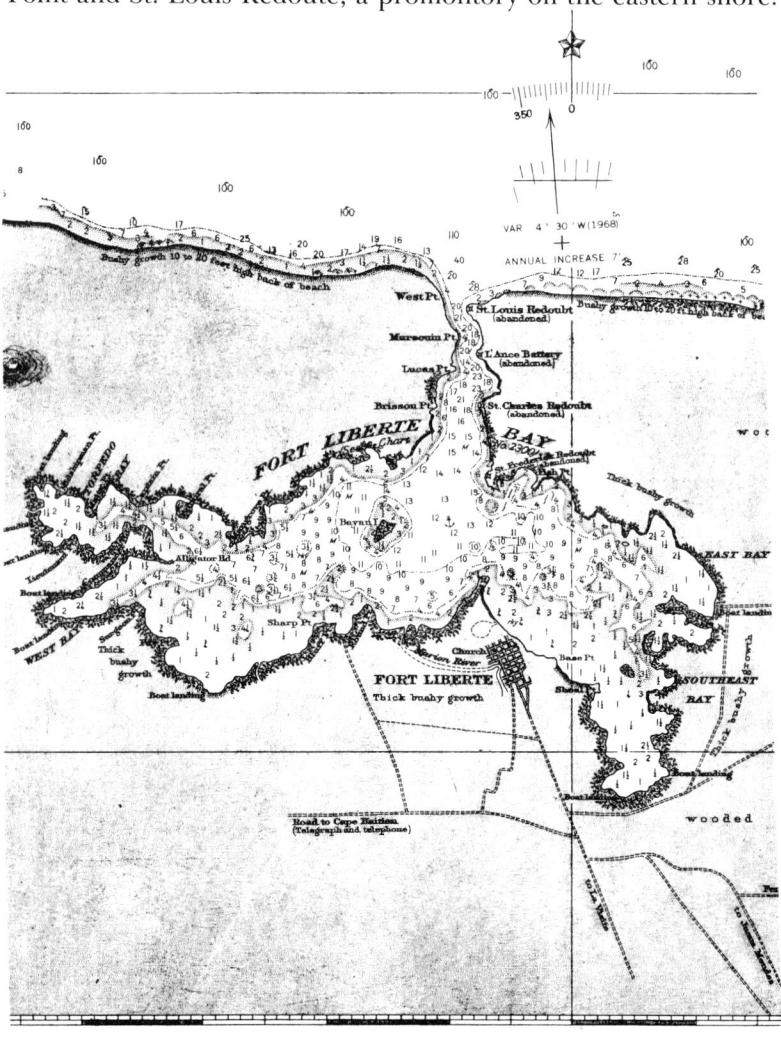

Fort Liberté Bay

ruins of an old fort are visible as you approach the entrance, and when they are directly abeam, you may safely follow midchannel until it widens into the landlocked harbor of Fort Liberté on the SE side. Or you may swing westward past a small island into another arm of the bay. The island may be passed on either side, but keep a safe distance off to avoid shoals that extend 200 yards off its NE side.

On entering the bay, it is advisable to proceed first to the town of Fort Liberté, where you must clear customs even though you may only be making a day trip from Cap Haïtien. The best time to enter is in the morning before the sea breeze starts to pipe up, as the outlying reefs and shoals show up better in calm water. Vessels are not permitted to enter at night. Depths in the Bay range from 1 to 11 fathoms, but there are a number of shoal spots around the shores and off the points. There is a pier about 360 feet long on the western side of the entrance channel and a boat-landing near a flagstaff at the NE end of the town. Cargo vessels are loaded and unloaded by lighter. Limited provisions are available in the town, but fuel and good drinking water may be hard to find. A banana plantation at the N end of town is reported to have a machine shop with facilities for engine repairs.

The frontier between Haiti and the Dominican Republic is only 5 miles E of the entrance to Fort Liberté Bay, where forts on both sides of the Massacre River are a reminder of bloody battles in years past.

THE NORTH COAST OF THE DOMINICAN REPUBLIC

Judging from the charts alone, one might conclude that the rugged north coast of the Dominican Republic is even more formidable than the Haitian coast. Starting at the Dominican border, the mountainous coastline trends ESE for 235 miles—more than twice the length of Haiti's north coast—with only a few indentations where a cruising yacht might expect shelter from the strong winter trade winds. In all, there are no more than 4 or 5 anchorages offering all-weather protection, and these are poorly spaced for cruising—there's only one overnight stopping place in the 160-mile section between Puerto Plata and Cape Engaño at the eastern tip of the island.

Yet despite its lack of good harbors, this coast is not quite as formidable as it appears on the charts, and need not be out of bounds for well-equipped sailing vessels or power yachts capable of making the long coastwise runs. Navigation is relatively straightforward, as the 100-fathom curve follows the coastline only a few miles offshore and is free of outlying dangers. Although there are virtually no aids to navigation, and few of the lights are dependable, the coastal mountains provide good landmarks that are not hard to identify from the charts. For those who have time for leisurely cruising, this area has its special attractions, as we shall see.

Manzanillo Bay to Puerto Plata (25401)

Four of the five "ports" or anchorages on the north coast are situated in the NW corner of the Dominican Republic in the 75-mile stretch between Manzanillo Bay and the principal port of entry at Puerto Plata. This historic district is closely associated with Columbus and his second-in-command, Martin Alonso Pinzon, who rendezvoused here on the first voyage and named most of the harbors and principal landmarks. Columbus returned on his second voyage to establish the first Spanish colony in the New World, which he named Isabela. The four ports, proceeding eastward, are:

Puerto Manzanillo (26142, 26144) is an open roadstead and deepwater port on the south shore of Manzanillo Bay, with a straightforward approach. The 100-fathom curve is less than a mile offshore. The harbor and town are in the process of transformation from a banana-loading port and Dominican naval station to a projected seaside resort area with the inevitable condominiums, tourist hotels, swimming beaches, and golf courses. In 1975, the project was still largely on paper; the 744-foot commercial pier was being used by banana ships, naval vessels, and smaller trading boats, which will continue to use this part of the waterfront, now occupied by the Customs House and Port Captain's office. Visiting yachts are expected to clear customs whether or not they have previously entered at Puerto Plata. Some cruising boats have reported delays before being allowed to go ashore, due apparently to naval security requirements.

Colored brochures of the future resort city, named Estero Balsa, show yacht-club marinas, with slips for visiting yachts, in the lagoon just north of the commercial pier, and nearby beaches, hotels, and residential homesites. Present plans call for construction of tourist facilities starting in 1975 and continuing for a decade or more.

Monte Cristi Bay (26143) enticed Columbus to lay over for three days in January, 1493, while he took on wood and water. He named the place Monte Cristo, and it was here that he discovered the first gold in the New World, brought to him by Indians who were panning nuggets in the nearby river now called Yaque del Norte.

Present-day mariners can follow Columbus' track across the extensive bank that fronts the coast between Manzanillo and the conspicuous promontory of El Morro, 2 miles N of the town of Monte Cristi. From the SW, the best approach is through Bradford Channel, past a group of small islands known as the Seven

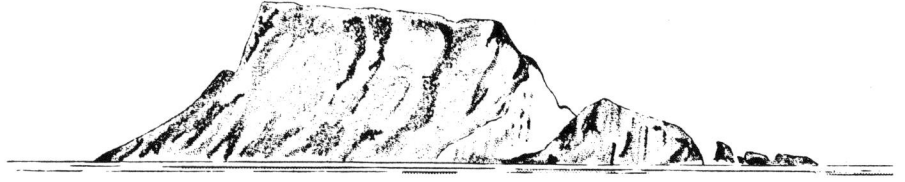

El Morro from northward

Brothers, to an anchorage a mile off the pier where the port offices are located.

Two other approaches, from the W and N, are described in the *Sailing Directions*, which gives courses and bearings based on the 825-foot summit of El Morro and a conspicuous clock tower in the town of Monte Cristi. George and Jacque Kappes, who cruised these waters in *Liberty Belle*, reported no problems in making the approach through Bradford Channel, but found shallower water inshore than indicated on the chart. They advised lying not less than a mile off, outside the shorebank, at least until you have been visited by port officials, who will come out to inspect your papers. The owner of a small sea-side tavern may accompany the officials and offer to take you ashore in his own boat. He reportedly serves good meals at his establishment. The pier is used chiefly by local craft, some of which are aground at low tide. Yachts drawing over 5 feet should check depths at the pier head before attempting to lie alongside.

The town of Monte Cristi lies about a mile inland and is reached by a causeway leading across a salt marsh. Plans for developing the bayfront beaches have been announced as part of the Manzanillo–Monte Cristi tourist project.

Cape Isabela and Puerto Blanco (25801)

Monte Cristi Bank extends eastward for more than 30 miles between El Morro and Cape Isabela, with a barrier reef fronting the coast about 1 to 2½ miles offshore for most of that distance. Most of this section of the coast is backed by a mountain range rising to more than 2,600 feet a few miles inland. While it is possible to find temporary anchorages inside the barrier reef, skippers unfamiliar with these waters are advised to stand at least 3 miles offshore until clear of the shoals north of Isabela Bay, the bight on the western side of the cape.

It was here that Columbus attempted to establish a city, which he called Isabela, but it was a poor site without a good harbor and was abandoned in less than two years. It is still a poor anchorage today, and there is no trace of the old town.

Continuing E for another 10 miles around the bold headland of Cape

Isabela, present-day cruising skippers will find perhaps the snuggest all-weather small-boat harbor on the north coast, called Puerto Blanco, about 15 miles W of Puerto Plata.

We found this delightful little harbor on a westbound passage between Puerto Rico and the Caicos Islands, when an unexpected norther caught us off Cape Isabela and led us to seek overnight shelter. Chart 25801 fails to show an inshore reef on the eastern side of the entrance which, from half a mile off, seems to overlap a corresponding reef on the western side; but as we approached on a course of 180°, a channel opened up about midway between the two shores, leading into a tight little Y-shaped harbor with one branch to port and another to starboard. We found the best anchorage to starboard in the SW branch about 200 yards off a small boat dock at the western end. The fishing village of Luperon is hidden behind a lush hillside plantation on the SW shore, with coconut palms and banana plants on its slopes.

Inquisitive visitors from the village rowed out in their homemade fishing boats (none equipped with outboards), and a party of armed soldiers from the coastal inspection post came aboard to check our papers. This is not a port of entry, but having previously entered and cleared at Puerto Plata, we were allowed to remain overnight, in the quietest and most attractive anchorage we had found on Hispaniola. We have heard from a number of other yachtsmen who have "discovered" Puerto Blanco since our visit; they have been equally enthusiastic.

The eastern branch shoals rapidly beyond the entrance, and there are unmarked shoal spots in the western branch, so yachts entering for the first time should proceed cautiously with depthfinder or leadline. You will find any number of good places to drop your hook in 8 to 12 feet over good-holding mud or sand bottom.

Puerto Plata (25803) was founded by Nicolas de Ovando in 1502 and today is the largest town on the Dominican north coast, with a population of 20,000 and a small harbor that is the only port of entry on this section of the coast. Limited yacht facilities are available in the harbor, which is being developed as a commercial port for cruise ships, tankers, and general cargo vessels.

The approach from seaward presents no difficulties in good weather, with Mt. Isabela de Torres rising to a height of 2,600 feet behind the town and the 100-fathom curve only about 2 miles off the entrance channel. (Don't count on fair weather at all times, however, because occasional storms can reduce visibility to zero, as we discovered on our first visit). The entrance channel, about 300 yards wide, leads between two reefs that break heavily in rough weather. The channel is marked on its western side by two buoys, which should be left to starboard. We found it difficult to identify the entrance range (described in the *Sailing Directions* as two light beacons in range at 218°) until after we had sighted

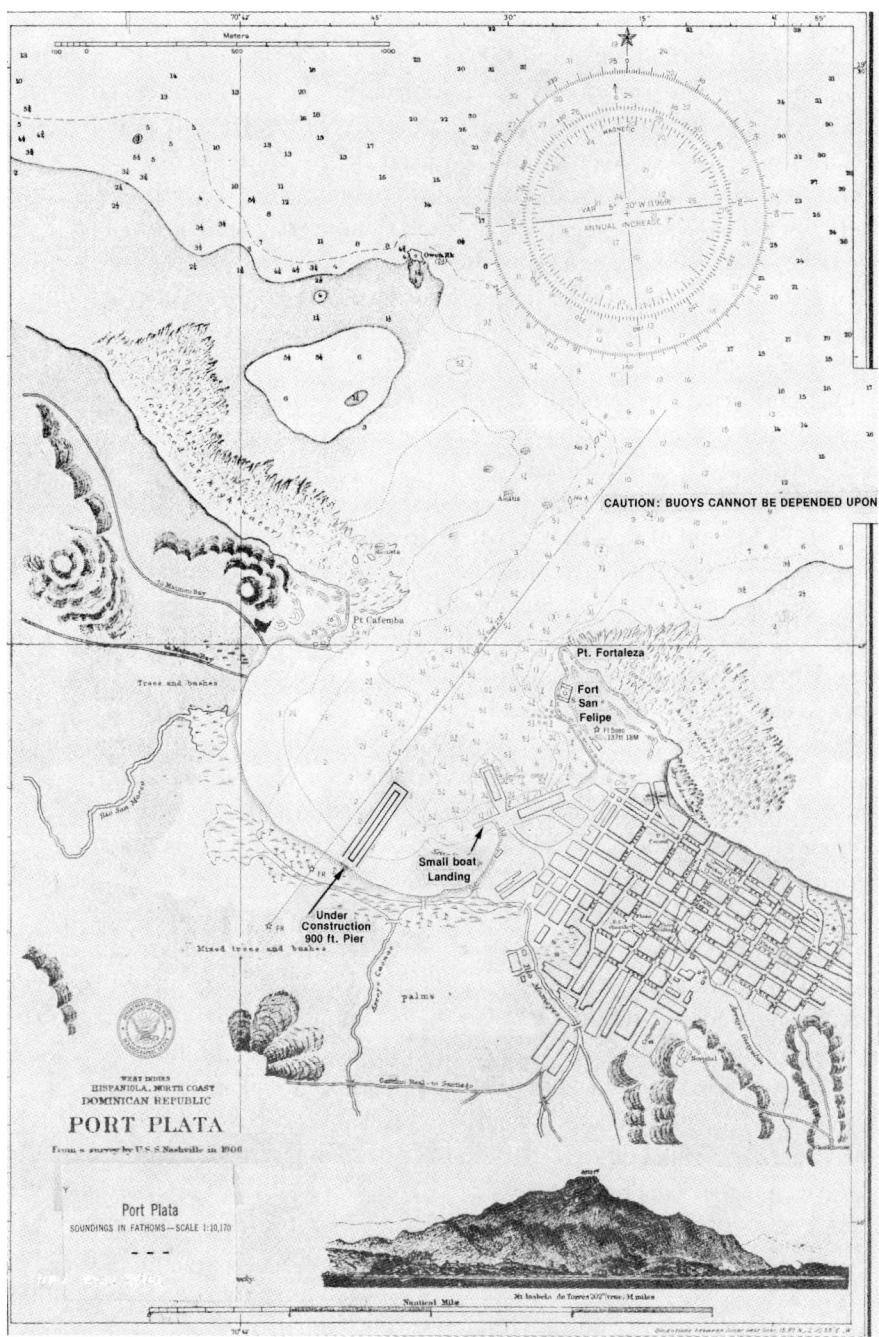

Approaches to Puerto Plata

Owen Rock on the outer edge of the shoal bank half a mile northwest of the entrance markers. When Owen Rock bears about 309°T, you can alter course to 218° and eventually distinguish the range just before entering the marked channel. The white obelisk on Point Fortaleza, at the east side of the entrance, is visible from several miles offshore, with a tall chimney about ¼-mile south.

The inner harbor is small and exposed to the trade winds that create a constant and uneasy surge throughout the anchorage. Both the British *Pilot* and U.S. *Sailing Directions* carry a cautionary note that swells from 4 to 18 feet are not uncommon between October and May. We have not encountered more than 2-to-3-foot swells on the few occasions we've been there, but each time we have found it necessary to lay two anchors to hold our bow in the general direction of the swells.

Port authorities are friendly and helpful to visiting yachts, whose numbers are increasing rapidly—from the 54 counted by the port commandant in 1970 to 140–150 a year since 1972.

On entering, yachts should proceed to the western side of the old commercial pier at the SE end of the harbor, where they will receive directions for anchoring or tieing up nearby. Port officials come aboard carrying sidearms, of course, but if your papers are in order you will be cleared quickly and given a pass to go ashore. The Customs Office is at the head of the old pier, and the Commandant's headquarters are just outside the gate surrounding the commercial dock area.

Major harbor-development work was under way in 1974–1975; construction of a new 900-foot industrial pier was about half completed, and the entire harbor and entrance channel was being dredged to a mean depth of 35 feet. A damaged cement dock adjacent to the old commercial pier has been partially repaired to provide limited landing facilities for yachts. Although the pier is lighted at night and fenced off from the street, it's generally safer to anchor out and come in by dinghy. Arriving yachts are certain to be met by Luis Bonilla, who speaks enough English to act as interpreter and usually turns up with the port authorities to offer his services as guide and "ship's provider"—at fees which he tends to adjust according to his estimate of the situation, so it's best to establish the fees in advance. Diesel fuel and gasoline can be delivered by truck.

Puerto Plata itself is well worth a visit. The ancient fort at the harbor entrance, San Felipe, dates back to 1540 and is being restored, along with other historic landmarks. The modern oceanfront boulevard, El Malecón, has been completed since our last visit in 1972, with new tourist hotels and beaches nearby. A new international airport is under construction, but was not yet completed in mid 1975; a domestic airline has daily flights to Santo Domingo, the capital, and buses run to Santiago in the interior.

Hertz and Avis rental cars are available through local travel agencies, one of which is directed by a young American, Mike Ronan, who is especially helpful to yachtsmen, being a sailor himself. Mike first came to Puerto Plata as a Peace Corps volunteer, and remained to work with another good friend of visiting boatmen, Sr. Christian de Lemos, a member of the Provincial Tourist Commission and associate in the travel firm Agencia de Viajes Cafemba. Both these gentlemen are happy to be consulted and can advise you how to get things done, or where to find a mechanic or electrician for your boat-maintenance problems.

There are several good native restaurants in the town. A short walk of only a few blocks will take you to the modern city market, where fresh food supplies are available; it's situated atop a rise commanding a fine view of the port. If you have time to lay over for a few days, take a trip by car or bus through the surrounding countryside to nearby beaches or up the wooded slopes of Mt. Isabela de Torres with its lighted statue of Christ at the summit.

Puerto Plata to Samaná Bay (25801)

Eastward of Puerto Plata, you will find no harbor providing all-weather protection for more than 100 miles, until you reach Samaná Bay and the port of Santa Barbara. For the most part, this section of the coast is steep-to, fringed by inshore reefs, and backed by mountains that present some of the most spectacular coastal scenery in the Caribbean. Several anchorages along the way afford temporary shelter from easterlies, but are exposed to the N and NE.

Sosúa (25802) lies about 10 miles SE of Puerto Plata in a tiny cove under the lee of Cape Macorís, where anchorage may be found. This is an interesting place to visit in settled weather, with a lovely sandy beach and a remarkable refugee community close by. The best anchorage is in the NE corner of the bight, just N of a coral reef, in 1 to 3 fathoms over a hard sandy bottom. The approach from the 100-fathom line less than a mile offshore is straightforward, with no dangers N of the unmarked but clearly visible reef. Northerly winds make the anchorage untenable, and there is a constant swell even in the prevailing breeze.

The refugee community at Sosúa was founded during World War II, when Rafael Trujillo made a grant of land to refugees from Nazi Germany. More than 1,000 exiles from Hitler's Third Reich settled on the land and, without previous agricultural experience, established a successful farm cooperative that has survived to this day, producing meat and dairy products for the Dominican market and for export to other parts of the Caribbean. Some of the second-generation families have migrated to the United States or returned to Europe, reducing the size of the community, but the remaining group is a vital force in the area today. There are two other communities at Sosúa, a native settlement and a residential resort community which has become popular with affluent Santo Domingans.

Port Jackson (25762) is said to provide temporary anchorage in the lee of a small cay at the head of a very large bight about 50 miles SE of Sosúa and halfway between Cape Viejo Francés and Cape Cabrón. Although it is called Port Jackson, there is no port, no harbor, no town, and very little protection except that provided by the tiny cay and the breaking reef on which it stands. It is out of the way for vessels making a coastwise passage and has nothing whatever to recommend it as an anchorage for yachts.

Port Escondido (25761) is a small bay situated at the head of a deep indentation in the coast about six miles W of Cape Cabrón. This bay is exposed to the N and W but may offer some protection when the trades are easterly. The anchorage is in a most attractive setting just off a white, palm-fringed beach backed by green hills that surround the harbor on three sides. Visiting yachts are advised to have clearance papers from their last port, as there is a small military outpost where soldiers and their families are quartered. Don't go ashore until you have been visited by the coastal inspector, who will come out with one or two soldiers to check your papers. If there are language problems, the local priest or schoolteacher may be summoned, but if your papers are in order you should receive a friendly welcome.

Proceeding eastward around Cape Cabrón you will pass one of the most spectacular coastal areas in the eastern Caribbean. White rocky cliffs rise perpendicularly from the sea to heights of more than 800 feet. Deep water carries right up to the base of the cliffs, where the ocean swells break thunderously, throwing spray and spume high in the air and echoing in huge caves and recesses in the rock. Cape Cabrón is the departure point for vessels bound for Puerto Rico and the Virgin Islands, but if you need fuel or provisions before crossing the often turbulent Mona Passage, your last port of call will be in Samaná Bay a few miles to the southeast across the deep bight of Rincón. Cape Samaná with its lighthouse perched atop a 500-foot cliff is almost as spectacular as Cabrón, and marks the northern entrance into the huge Bay of Samaná.

Santa Barbara de Samaná (25761, 25723) lies about 15 miles SW of Cape Samaná, protected by a mass of coral reefs extending most of the way across the mouth of the bay, reefs so numerous and interconnected that the chart simply calls them "foul ground." However, the approach is actually less formidable than it appears on the chart, with 5 to 6 fathoms of water across Canandaiqua Bank about a mile off the light on Balandra Head, leading into a deeper channel along the shore inside Leventado Cay and Jean Bart reef. This passage is wide and easy of access under normal weather conditions and, with due caution, could be used at night. Only when heavy ocean swells or gale-force winds create a "rage" on Canandaiqua Bank does this passage become dangerous. At such times cruising yachts should not have left the last port.

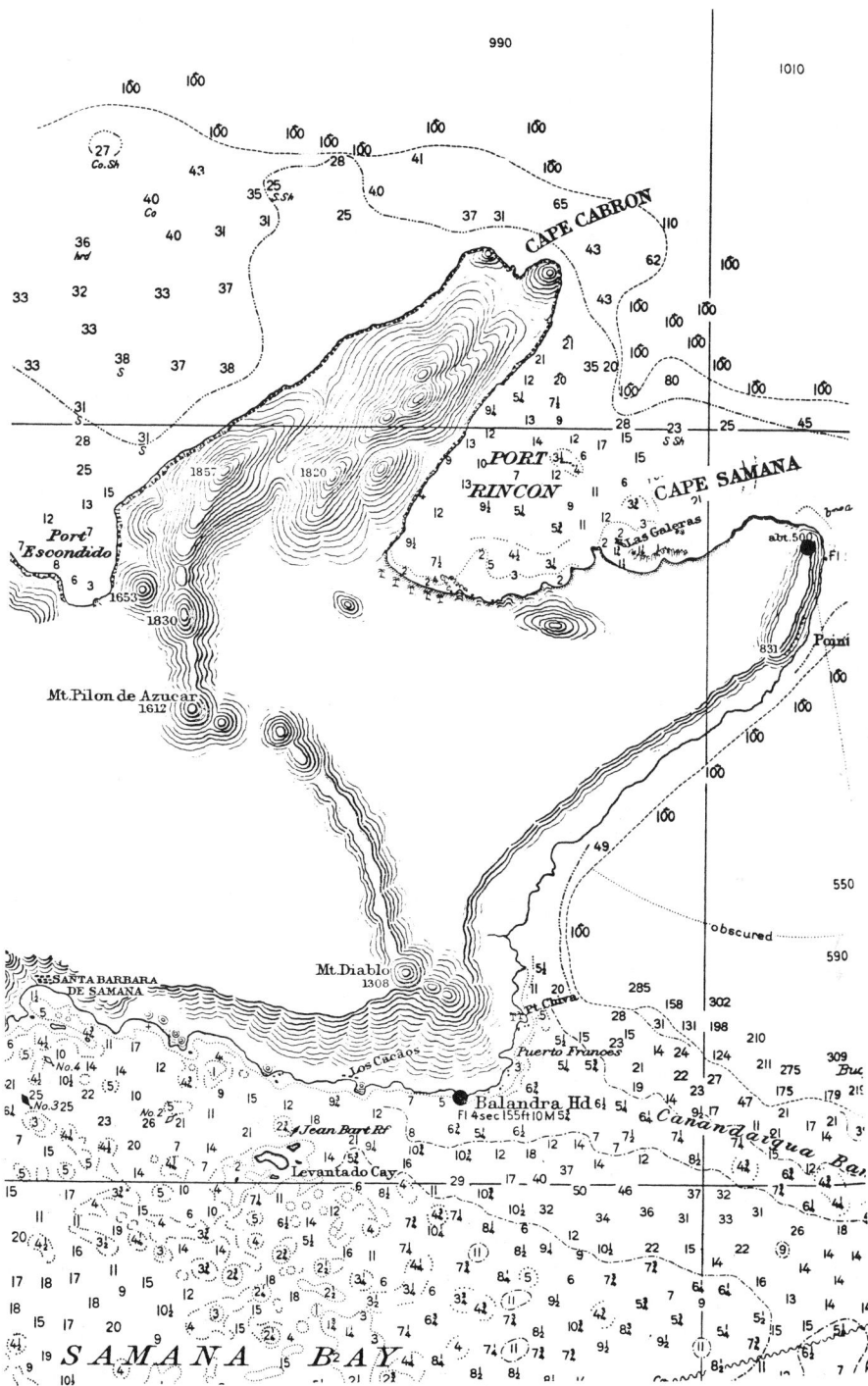

The approach to Samana Bay

This is another beautiful coastal area, well worth a visit in its own right, as well as for the excellent shelter it provides in the harbor of Santa Barbara, or simply Samaná, as it is now called. Past Balandra Head, steep hills covered with coconut and banana trees lead down to the water, with brown slashes of road attesting to their cultivation, as do the clusters of thatched roofs of the plantation workers' huts. Several small bays open up before you enter the harbor between Gorda Point and two small cays to the S.

The head of the harbor is shallow, but good anchorage will be found off the town wharf or anywhere in the center of the harbor. This is a port of entry and a naval base where the formalities are observed to the letter, so wait for the Port Commandant to pay his visit before going ashore. The main wharf area has recently been dredged to 15 feet. Good drinking water is available, and gasoline and diesel fuel (*gasoil*) can be delivered by truck or in drums to the wharf.

This picturesque old town that we visited before the 1970s has been leveled to make way for a tourist development project embracing the entire harborfront and adjacent cays. Gone are the narrow, dusty streets and alleys with their clapboard houses and shanties. A broad boulevard has been built along the waterfront, and already a high-rise hotel is in operation on the island which encloses the harbor. A hotel and marina are planned for Levantado Cay.

Nearby, however, you will find unspoiled countryside, sheltered beaches and coves, and an historic site at the Bay of Arrows where Columbus battled briefly with the first hostile Indians he had seen in the New World. They were Arawaks, normally peaceful, but they had acquired warlike ways in defending their lands against the invariably hostile Caribs.

THE WEST AND SOUTH COASTS OF HAITI

When winter trade winds make the rugged north coast of Hispaniola a Thorny Path, an alternative route around the western end of this large, mountainous island may have certain attractions for eastbound cruising yachts. Although this route is longer by almost 200 miles (300 miles if you detour to include Port-au-Prince), it has the advantage of providing better protection in a number of small bays, harbors, and sheltered anchorages in the Gulf of Gonâve and along the south coasts of Haiti and the Dominican Republic.

The huge Gulf of Gonâve lies eastward of the Windward Passage and is out of the way for vessels bound for Jamaica or the south coast of Hispaniola. But it is a starkly dramatic land and water area well worth visiting. Its bold headlands rise steeply from the sea, backed by arid mountains that reach heights of more than 5,000 feet a few miles inland, and depths plunge to 1,000 fathoms only a few miles offshore. Port-au-Prince, the populous capital of Haiti, lies at the head of the Gulf, about 100 miles east of the Windward Passage, and the mountainous Île de la Gonâve, some 30 miles long, occupies the center of the Gulf between the northern and southern approaches to the Baie de Port-au-Prince.

Winter winds are less boisterous in the gulf, though an occasional norther may sweep down to interrupt the prevailing pattern. In the Bay of Port-au-Prince, an offshore land breeze sets in at night, continuing through the morning hours until almost noon, when it is followed by a gentle sea breeeze coming in from the W and lasting until evening. This pattern extends over most of the Gulf of Gonâve and is used to advantage by native fishermen who sail westward on the morning land breeze to their fishing grounds in the gulf, returning in the afternoon with their tattered sails billowing from the sea breeze behind them. Although offshore winds are common at night in all of the larger mountainous islands, nowhere else in the Caribbean have we encountered a similar daytime pattern over so large a water area as the Gulf of Gonâve. During the summer months, winds are somewhat more variable, with more westerlies, squalls, and periods of calm extending as far west as the Windward Passage. Although Hispaniola lies in the hurricane belt, there are enough protected harbors in the gulf for cruising boats to find a safe hideout when a tropical storm comes their way.

Currents vary in different parts of the gulf, and one should always be aware of the strong set close to the shores in cruising these reef-fringed bays. In the Windward Passage, the prevailing current sets westward toward Cuba, but close to the Haitian coast it sets northward in the vicinity of Cap du Môle. In the approaches to Port-au-Prince Bay, the current is said to set NW in the St. Marc channel and E in the channel south of the island of Gonâve.

Ports of Entry in Western Haiti

If you intend to cruise for any length of time in the territorial waters of Haiti, it is essential to have an official cruising permit, or *Permis de Navigation*, authorizing you to visit other ports without restriction. This unlimited permit may be obtained only at Port-au-Prince and Cap Haïtien, although there are several other ports of entry in the Gulf (Gonaïves and St. Marc on the northern peninsula) and on the south coast (Jérémie, Jacmel, and Aux Cayes) where you may enter if necessary. Cruising skippers find out sooner or later that it's worth the extra time and mileage to make their first entry at Port-au-Prince, where customs and immigration officials are used to dealing with foreign vessels. Bob and Ginnie Higman had this advice to offer others after their three-month cruise around Haiti in *Tormentor III:*

Cruising was made much easier for us after we reached the capital and obtained papers for the rest of our voyage. M. Cadet, the Chef de Service (in

1971) typed out the one-page *Permis de Navigation* authorizing us to cruise all the territorial waters around the southern peninsula to Aux Cayes on the south coast. Up until then we'd had to obtain a new cruising paper at each town large enough to have a customs office, restricting us to anchorages only in the next governmental district. . . . and woe be to the yacht that does not rigidly observe the rule of obtaining a cruising permit for every anchorage.

Cap du Môle to Port-au-Prince (26161, 26181)

Several small bays indent the 100 miles of coast between the northwest tip of Haiti and Port-au-Prince at the head of the Gulf, providing safe anchorages for vessels making a coastwise passage with short daylight runs. Most vessels approaching from the north plan to make their landfall on Cap du Môle, but their first sight of land from seaward is more likely to be the high mountains a few miles inland behind the deep bay where Columbus first set foot on Hispaniola on December 5, 1492.

Cap St. Nicolas Môle (26262) is undoubtedly one of the most interesting bays on the northern peninsula but is seldom visited by cruising yachts, and we don't recommend anchoring overnight unless you have already obtained a cruising permit. It's not a port of entry, and the small village has no boat facilities. Furthermore, you could be detained by a boarding party with soldiers from the local army post. Jack Laird, an American yachtsman who entered Cap St. Nicolas Môle in his 57-foot power cruiser *Miss Apple Jack* after a 1969 passage from the Bahamas, was struck with its beauty and gave this interesting description of the bay and his reception:

> The Baie du Môle contains 17 old forts in various stages of deterioration. It used to be an important strategic position, as whoever controlled Le Môle controlled the Windward Passage. . . . We had rather expected to be met by some type of Coast Guard vessel, but none was there, so we went straight up to the village and anchored in 10 feet of water about 50 yards offshore. This is where Columbus was supposed to have landed centuries before. A small sailboat and two rowboats were on the beach and some of the crude houses of sticks, with palm-leaf roofs, were visible but no one was in sight.
>
> Apparently we were taken as invaders from Cuba or Mars and were expected to start blasting away with guns. . . . Eventually with a little coaxing the town folk began to appear from behind trees, bushes, huts and houses, and soon there were several hundred men, women and children on the beach just staring. Shortly one of the rowboats set out from the shore with one man rowing and another with a rifle, who turned out to be a sergeant in the army. . . . He had his instructions, as I was rowed in to the beach and walked

through the silent crowd of non-smiling faces and was taken into what I took to be the Town Hall. It was about 30 feet in diameter with sides made of small sticks placed vertically in the ground, and a roof. There was a small table and seven unpainted chairs. That was all.

With voodoo-like magic, six men came out of the woodwork. One was a good-looking army lieutenant in full uniform who spoke a "little bit" of English. One man took our passports and papers into the corner for study. As we waited the conversation was strained and difficult, but finally after about an hour I was offered *café* and I knew we were accepted as tourists. . . .

Other cruising boats have had similar experiences here and at other small towns around Haiti and the Dominican Republic where yachts are seldom seen. In encounters with local authorities, the inability of the visiting boat owner to communicate effectively often results in strained relations and misunderstandings that could be avoided if either side spoke the language of the other. Water and fuel are problems at all of the small ports and some of the larger towns as well. At Le Môle water was carried down from the mountains in buckets; there was no fuel and no dock.

Continuing southward around Cap à Foux, cruising boats may run alongshore past a succession of bold headlands and rocky promontories backed by high hills and mountains. The 100-fathom curve lies less than a mile offshore for much of the 50-mile section between Cap à Foux and the entrance to Gonaïves, the first port of entry on the northeast side of the Gulf. There are several conspicuous landmarks and a few anchorages on this coast.

Pointe la Plateforme is a white rocky bluff rising steeply to a flat table-top summit about 10 miles SE of Cap à Foux. It is easy to recognize from almost any point at sea.

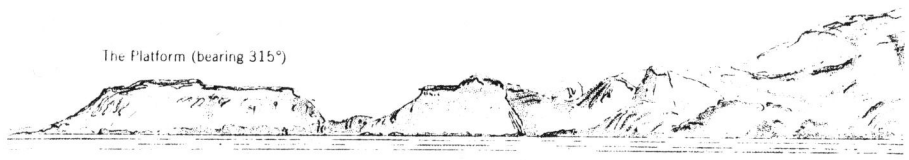

The Platform (bearing 315°)

Pointe la Plateforme, NW end of Haiti, southwestward

Baie de Henne (26161) is a deep indentation in the coast about 9 miles eastward of la Plateforme, where anchorage may be found on the E side of the bay behind the encircling hills. It is exposed to winds from the S but affords protection in the NE trades. There's a small village at the head of the bay.

Port-à-Piment (26161) is a tiny little harbor about 12 miles eastward of Baie de Henne with an anchorage used by local fishing boats but exposed to the S like others on this coast. When passing close offshore, you can identify the entrance by a conspicuous mound that rises from the flat savannah behind the cove. The nearest village is Anse Rouge, on the coast about 3½ miles to the W.

Pointe la Pierre is a bold rocky headland about 16 miles SE of Port-à-Piment. It marks the northern approach to the Bay of Gonaïves. The light on the point is usually out, but the cliffs, which rise steeply from the shorebank, are easy to identify in daylight. The bank extends only about 350 yards off the cliffs.

Baie de Gonaïves (26182)

This large bay opens up into two smaller bays that provide a number of safe anchorages. The town of Gonaïves, with a population of more than 20,000, is a port of entry used by Caribbean trading vessels and local fishing craft. The commercial harbor is exposed to the W, but vessels anchor in 6 or 7 fathoms off the town or tie up along the pier with depths of 12 feet alongside. The Customs House is near the foot of the pier. Better anchorages for cruising boats may be found in Baie Carénage to the N or Baie de l'Hôpital to the S.

Yachts are not exactly a familiar sight in Gonaïves, as Jack Laird discovered when he spent 6 hours attempting to get clearance papers for *Miss Apple Jack* in 1969.

> Since we were apparently the first pleasure boat to enter this port, no one knew exactly what to do with us and whether to allow us to come ashore. A seemingly endless parade of officials descended on *Miss Apple Jack*, starting at the lowest echelon and working up to the heads of the state. . . . The parade of officials finally ended with the arrival of the colonel in charge of the army, a special representative of the President, and a decision to pass the buck to Port-au-Prince. . . . This is not to suggest that these six hours were strained or fearful. On the contrary, it was one massive party. Our bar was open. Since it was Sunday most officials had minimal duties and therefore went home to fetch their families. All were extremely pleasant and courteous. Through all of this (as we were tied to the pier) hundreds of town folk pushed their way forward for a look-see The cops couldn't hold them back, nor was there any need, as all they wanted was to look into the goldfish bowl at us—the goldfish.

Gonaïves to Cap St. Marc

In contrast to the mountainous terrain north of Gonaïves and south of St. Marc, this 20-mile section of the coast is relatively low, with a succession of shallow bays, some of which provide anchorages for native boats.

Baie de la Tortue (26182) is encumbered with shoals and is not recommended, although local fishing craft anchor SE of Frigate Isle or at Mangrove Island off the northern entrance, about 3 miles SW of Gonaïves.

Baie de Grande Pierre (26183) is a large open bay just S of Tortue Bay with a wide and deep entrance channel leading into an anchorage with depths of 10 to 30 feet over a mud bottom. The shoreline is covered with mangroves, and there is a small village on the southeastern shore. Pointe Dessalines marks the southern entrance to the Bay.

Baie de St. Marc (26185) lies between two conspicuous points—Table au Diable on the N and Cap St. Marc about 10 miles to the S—and leads to the harbor of St. Marc 6½ miles eastward at the head of the bay. The harbor is an open roadstead exposed to westerly winds; the town is a busy coastal community of some 12,000 persons. It's said to be one of the most healthful spots in Haiti, with its sea breezes from the W and encircling mountains in the E and S. Deep water can be carried right up to the harbor, with the 100-fathom curve nowhere more than ¾-mile offshore all around the bay. In approaching the town, the twin spires of a cathedral and a flat-topped hill, Morne à Vigie, rising more than 1,000 feet, provide conspicuous landmarks. There are several small piers used by coastal vessels, but larger ships are usually moored off the town, facing westward with their stern lines anchored on the beach. This is an exposed anchorage and may be dangerous in strong westerly winds. Gas and water can be brought to the pier, but not diesel.

Approaches to Port-au-Prince (26181)

Vessels approaching the Baie de Port-au-Prince from the north will find no harbors or temporary shelter of any kind in passing through the deep ocean channel of St. Marc between the mountainous mainland and the almost equally unbroken shoreline of the island of Gonâve. The 100-fathom curve is less than a mile offshore along the northern peninsula from Cap St. Marc to Pointe Trou Forban, which marks the entrance to Port-au-Prince Bay, where the depths shoal rapidly to between 6 and 60 fathoms for the next 20 miles. As the mountains recede, the entire northeastern shoreline seems to disappear in the haze that often hangs over the low coastal plain.

Cruising yachts approaching the bay for the first time should plan to enter around midday, if possible, or at a time when visibility is good and the westerly sea breeze is behind them. We won't attempt to summarize the *Sailing Directions*, which are essential for making the final approach through the numerous reefs and shoals that protect the harbor of Port-au-Prince. No one should try to enter at night, for several obvious reasons noted by Jack Laird:

As an example of navigating here, and why you shouldn't proceed at night, the light shown on the Arcadins Islets (three small islands off the northern peninsula) is out and has been for several years. . . . Also do not depend on the harbor buoys, as they are either not there or have been changed, an indication of the difficulties our Hydrographic Office has in keeping up with local changes in many foreign lands.

Port-au-Prince Harbor (26186) is an open roadstead exposed to the W but sheltered to some extent by the fringing reefs and shoals. Pilotage is compulsory for commercial vessels, and a pilot boat is usually seen in the entrance channel or just off the quarantine anchorage adjacent to the 2,000-foot pier with a long warehouse at the outer end. The twin spires of the cathedral and two masts of the radio station provide conspicuous landmarks from the entrance channel. Once inside, most yachts will be directed to the anchorage or told where to tie up along the pier. If you don't see a pilot boat, anchor first off the south side of the pier until port officials come aboard. Advance notice of the date and expected time of your arrival helps expedite clearance procedures. The port pilots monitor channel 2738 kHz on a 24-hour basis and generally can be reached from 40 miles out, according to recent cruising visitors.

There is no really good anchorage in the commercial harbor, and the only place to tie up is the Casino Dock, whose number of small boat slips is limited. All of them were occupied when we were there in 1973. This facility is operated by Gaston Boussan, who also runs a glassbottom snorkeling boat making daily visits to Sandy Cay and outlying reefs. M. Boussan keeps a register of visiting yachts; it includes the names of well-known transatlantic sailors like Eric Tabarly and *Pen Duick III* (on a 1972 passage), and a number of U.S. yachts from Florida and Pacific Coast ports. His pier carries 6 feet alongside, with water, electricity, and fuel, and if he can't find you a slip he will be helpful in suggesting alternative anchorages. His address is P.O. Box 923, Port-au-Prince.

The American Embassy and Consulate are near the waterfront, only a few blocks from the commercial pier, and you are almost certain to find someone on the staff who is active in sailing and willing to share his knowledge of local waters and facilities. When we were there in 1973, a member of the Embassy staff was one of a group of 50 boating enthusiasts who were then organizing the Port-au-Prince Yacht Club; they hoped it would soon have a small marina and yacht facility on the bay. A new marina was being developed on the N side of the bay, about 15 miles from the capital.

Cruise ships call regularly at Port-au-Prince, and you'll see more tourists ashore here than anywhere else in Haiti. There are usually one or two sailing vessels for charter in the harbor, but they are likely to be crewed by itinerant "yotties" trying to raise enough cash to clear for their next port; their credentials should, of course, be checked out carefully.

A good friend of visiting yachtsmen and a helpful source of information is the American owner of the local Coca-Cola plant, Mr. Richard Forgham, who is also commodore of an unofficial group called the Kaka Poul Yachting and Drinking Association. Bottled water, beer, and soft drinks may be bought at the Brasserie de Couronne, operated by Mr. Forgham.

A walk around the busy, dusty streets of Port-au-Prince is always interesting. Or you can negotitate with a "share-the-taxi" driver to take you to almost any destination around town. There are several fine old hotels in the downtown area, some of them (like Sans Souci and the Oloffson) occupying colonial mansions in a garden-like setting, excellent restaurants, and all manner of outdoor markets and stalls. Filet mignon and other meats can be bought at a smaller "supermarket" called The Food Store near the Presidential Palace. Everywhere you go you are caught up in the moving streams of pedestrian traffic—barefooted, ill-clad black folk crowding the narrow streets and sidewalks, packing into the tiny, dilapidated but brightly colored buses with names such as "Mon Dieu," "Notre Dame," "Jesus Christ," and beggars and street urchins everywhere constantly reminding you of the appalling poverty of Haiti.

Port-au-Prince to Cap Dame-Marie (26181, 26191)

The south coast of the Gulf of Gonâve trends westward for approximately 120 miles to Cap Dame-Marie, closely backed by a coastal mountain range that extends to the western end of the southern peninsula. Once you have left Port-au-Prince Bay, deep water can be carried through the Gonâve (or south) channel westward to the Windward Passage, with several interesting overnight anchorages in protected coves and harbors on the peninsula, and at least one anchorage on the island of Gonâve.

Petit Goâve Bay (26187) lies about 32 miles SW of Port-au-Prince; the town of Petit Goâve is situated on the western side of the bay and a coffee mill and old fort on the southern side. The Lairds found this "a beautiful, well-kept town, slightly richer than most due to coffee growing. The officials here were most gracious and helpful and asked us to stop by on our return trip. This we did, and were utterly flabbergasted to have practically the entire town present us with a large primitive oil painting inscribed to Capt. Jack Laird and his wife 'in remembrance of their visit.'"

Miragoâne Bay (26188) is another open bay about 12 miles W of Petit Goâve, with a wide entrance that is easy to enter whether the lighted marker shown on the chart is operating or not, or is even there. There is a beautiful cathedral in

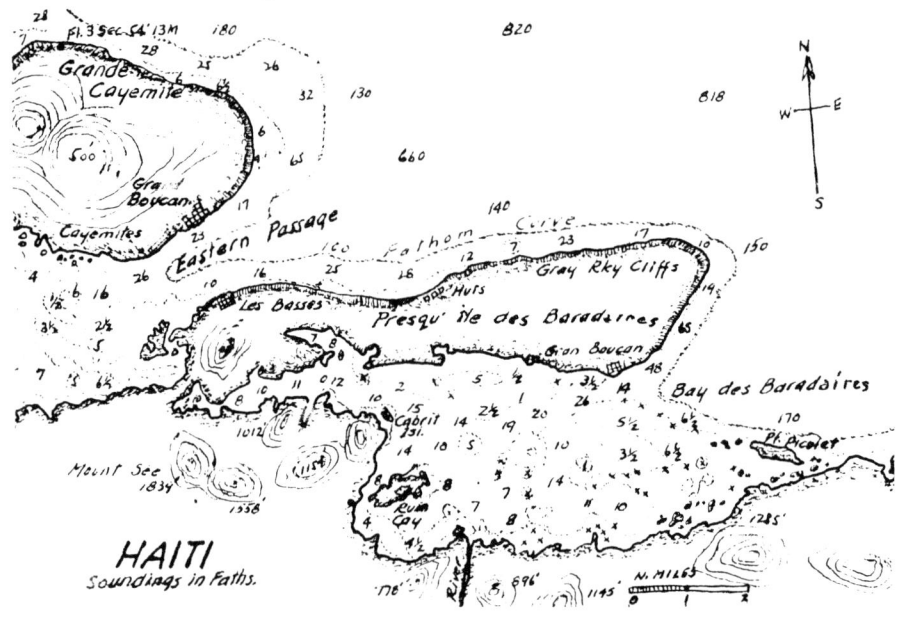

Baradaires Bay

the town on the S side of the harbor. Bauxite is shipped from this port, and the loading dock in the western part of the harbor fills the air with red dust. It should be avoided when it's operating. Better anchorage is found in the SE part of the bay.

Baradaires Bay (26189) is the largest and most interesting bay on the southern peninsula. It lies about 25 miles E of Miragoâne and is almost 10 miles long and 2 to 3 miles wide, with several primitive fishing villages around its shores and a variety of sheltered anchorages. The entrance at the N end of the bay is unmarked and less than ½-mile wide, but carries depths of over 100 feet between the reefs and shoals to the S and the small town of Gran Boucan on the northern peninsula. The water shoals rapidly about 400 yards off the town and is less than 4 feet at the small pier. Better anchorages can be found behind several rocky cays and islets 4 to 6 miles inside the bay. The most accessible are Rum Cay, a hilly, wooded island with white cliffs and bluffs about 4 miles SW of Gran Boucan, and tiny Cabrit Islet 1 mile NW of Rum Cay. Deep water can be carried all the way to the western end of the bay, with mountains rising more than 1,100 feet along the S shore. There's a fjord-like entrance into a lagoon with depths of 78 feet, well worth exploring if you can clear the 6-foot bar at the narrow entrance. Local guides can take you in a native canoe (or your own dinghy) for a fascinating trip 2 miles up the narrow Baradaires River to the town of that name.

Park Bay, Gonâve Island (26181) is the only semiprotected harbor on the N side of Gonâve channel, and it's hardly worth visiting unless you want a close look at the bare, eroding mountains of this 30-mile long island. Situated in the SE corner of the island, Park Bay is exposed to the W but sheltered by the mountains from winds from NW to SSE.

Baie de Cayemites (26190) lies a few miles NW of Baradaires Bay and provides the last chance for westbound vessels to find much shelter en route to the south coast of Haiti. Great Cayemite Island is a high thickly wooded isle a few miles NW of Baradaires, with a light on its northern shore and a deep channel between its southern shore and the mainland, leading into a large bay with a number of small islets and cays. Much of this bay is encumbered with coral reefs, shoals, and unmarked rocky heads. There are two fishing villages on either side of the eastern passage—Cayemites on the island and Les Basses on the Bec du Marsouin peninsula—both of which are exposed to winds from the E and W. Anchorages may be found at the western end of Great Cayemite in the channel separating it from Little Cayemite Island, but the passage through the reefs to the N and W is not recommended without a local pilot. The village of Corail at the SW end of the bay looks interesting, but the approach is encumbered by reefs and unmarked shoals.

Jérémie Bay (26192) lies about 12 miles southwestward of Cayemite Bay and is little more than an open roadstead exposed to the full force of the NE trades. The town of Jérémie, with a population of about 15,000, is a port of entry. It has a Customs House, a small stone pier with 6 feet at the outer end, a prominent cathedral with a clock tower, and the ruins of an old fort. Water and limited provisions are available, but the anchorage is not recommended except in settled weather. The harbor is filled with breakers in a strong breeze, and northers may come up without warning, often accompanied by heavy squalls during the summer months. Under such conditions the bay becomes unsafe. The *Sailing Directions,* while noting that the holding ground is good in the anchorage off the town, cautions vessels to "be prepared to get underway at a moment's notice." Some of our cruising friends are inclined to bypass Jérémie, although it's the last anchorage worth mentioning until after you have rounded Cap Dame-Marie at the NW end of the peninsula. However, it provides a convenient overnight stopping point for fuel and provisions if you are continuing on around the peninsula to the south coast of Haiti, where you won't find another real harbor short of Aux Cayes, about 86 miles away.

Cap Dame-Marie to Pointe de Tiburon (26191)

Several small bays indent the coast, which trends southward for 16 miles between Cap Dame-Marie and Pointe de Tiburon. Temporary anchorage may be found in any of these bays during periods of settled weather when the trades are blowing offshore, but they are completely exposed to the westward. A large triangular bank fronts this entire section of the coast, with its apex more than 12 miles offshore. Depths on the bank range between 5 and 20 fathoms, over sand and coral, in waters so clear that the bottom is plainly visible. You will find fish traps and buoys all over the bank. If you plan to anchor in any of the small bays, the large scale chart plans are essential.

Baie de Dame-Marie (26193, Plan B) lies between the cape of that name and Pointe Rousselin about 3½ miles southward, with the best anchorage off the village of Petite Rivière at the NE end of the bay. A strong current sweeps around the bay at times.

Baie de Nault (26193, Plan D) lies about 4 miles southward of Pointe Rousselin in a bight SE of Pointe à Bourry, a reddish-brown cliff that is difficult to identify from offshore. The approach from seaward is free from outlying shoals, and anchorage off the town of Anse d'Hainault affords good shelter from the trade winds during the winter months. Other bays in this section are not recommended; they are less than adequately charted, with few identifying landmarks.

Pointe de Tiburon to Cabo Beata (26191, 26201, 25841)

From the white cliffs of Tiburon to Cabo Beata in the Dominican Republic, the coast trends irregularly to the SE for about 185 miles, backed by mountains most of the way, with many small rivers and streams emptying into the sea. There are two ports of entry on the south coast of Haiti, Aux Cayes and Jacmel, and a number of good anchorages in sheltered bays within the large bight that forms the Baie des Cayes in the central section.

Yachts heading eastward from Tiburon can run along the 100-fathom curve about 2 miles offshore past a succession of high cliffs alternating with sandy beaches for almost 37 miles to Pointe-à-Gravois, where the coast recedes to Pointe l'Abacou and then opens up into the relatively protected waters of Baie de Cayes. Here eastbound vessels have a choice between standing on for a deepwater passage around Cabo Beata, about 140 miles ESE of Pointe l'Abacou, or turning N in search of an anchorage at Aux Cayes or one of the many finger bays in that area. Sailing vessels may find the offshore route rather strenuous at any time of year, as the trade winds tend to draw in along the coast, making it a long beat to windward into the steep Caribbean seas. This is particularly true in winter months, when the easterly trades blow fresh throughout the daylight hours, moderating only slightly at night if you are more than 16 miles offshore. In summer the winds are likely to be variable, with southerlies frequently interrupting the easterly flow.

The alternative inside course is made more attractive by the choice of sheltered anchorages and the kindly land breeze that comes in from the NW during the night and gradually veers around into the NE until about noon, when the sea breeze sets in from the SE and continues until evening. Strong easterly winds cause a heavy surf on the outlying islands and reefs and create a surge in the harbors, but most of the Baie des Cayes affords a welcome respite from the relentless ocean seas outside.

Baie des Cayes (26203)

This large bay is undoubtedly the most interesting cruising ground on the south coast of Haiti, and is well worth a visit. The western end of the bay is protected by Isle-à-Vache, a low, wooded island about 8 miles long and 2 to 3 miles wide, which lies about 6 miles offshore and approximately the same distance eastward of Point l'Abacou. There are two entrance channels, one to the SW of the island and the other to the NE, both of which are wide and deep. The south channel carries depths of 5 to 20 fathoms to a point about 1 mile S of the town of Les Cayes, where you must keep clear of the clearly visible reefs shown on the large-scale charts. In approaching through the eastern channel, yachts should keep well clear of the fringing reefs and small cays that extend 3 miles N of the island. There is a lovely protected anchorage on the N shore of the island. The following harbors and small bays all have reasonably good anchorages, and some offer complete protection with lovely beaches.

Les Cayes (26202) is a small commercial port in the NE corner of the bay with depths of 2 to 4 fathoms in the inner anchorage off the town. Larger ships anchor outside in 4 to 10 fathoms. There is a small pier with about 6 feet at the outer end. The best yacht anchorage is NE of the pier, where partial protection is provided by Tourterelle Battery point and its fringing reef. Provisions and water are available in the town, but visiting boats report that fuel can only be obtained "tediously from lightered drums." The town has air service three times a week to Port-au-Prince and Jacmel, and there is a small inn offering rooms and meals to travelers.

NE of the anchorage there are five deep, fingerlike bays, each of which offer all-weather protection in deep water. Jack Laird visited most of them in *Miss Apple Jack* (in 1969) and the Higmans passed this way in *Tormentor III* (in 1971) both reporting good gunkholing.

Baie de St. Louis (26205) is the largest and easternmost of the five finger openings off Aux Cayes Bay, with deep water right up to the head of the bay. The Lairds anchored here "in quiet water off a lovely beach near the town of Saint-Louis. Here we had full protection in Hispaniola's lee from the NE winds of winter. . . . The whole area is loaded with beaches, the fishing is fine, and the weather and seas seemed to prove my contention that the southern route to Puerto Rico in the winter is much preferable to the northern one with rough seas on that coast." This may depend upon how much time you have to cruise in these small bays. Those who stand offshore also encounter rough seas on the south coast.

Continuing eastward from Baie St. Louis, two more bays open up behind a long chain of protecting islands, cays, and reefs.

Baies Anglais and d'Aquin (26204) extend for 10 miles E and W, with many pretty little coves backed by mountains rising to heights of 1,200 to 2,400 feet and sheltered from the sea winds by the outlying reefs and isles, through which there are several deep channels. The best anchorages in Baie Anglais are at the NE end in the two coves behind Trompeuse Cay, and N of Grosse Cay, largest and highest of the outlying isles at the eastern end of the chain. Baie d'Aquin lies NE of Grosse Cay and offers good protection in the fingerlike arm leading to the town of Aquin at its head. The water shoals rapidly off the town, with depths of less than 6 feet over sand and mud flats. Cargo vessels anchor out in the bay in 4 fathoms and are loaded by small lighters.

Baie de Jacmel (26206) lies about 50 miles eastward of Aquin Bay, with no shelter on the bold and steep-to coast W of Cap Jacmel. The 100-fathom curve follows this section of the coast from ½-mile to 3 miles offshore, and if you start early enough in the morning you can usually carry the offshore land breeze at least part of the way. In approaching Jacmel from the westward, your only sure landmark is the end of a mountain range that drops off precipitously back of the town to form a shoulder that can be seen from a great distance at sea. Cap Jacmel is a broad headland with an isolated rock standing 25 feet high at its southern end. The bay opens just eastward of the cape and is very deep, with soundings of more than 100 fathoms to within ½-mile of the town of Jacmel at its head. An easily recognized landmark in the town is the cathedral, which has two red-topped steeples. Much of the town is built on a hillside; French architecture and flowering shrubs give it a Mediterranean atmosphere. Vessels entering the port usually anchor off the 335-foot commercial pier in 3 to 4 fathoms within sight of the Customs House, or in shoaler water on the shorebank.

This was once a rich coffee area, but several severe hurricanes have damaged the crop and reduced coffee exports from the port. The Lairds had trouble fueling and taking on water at the pier (with hundreds of sightseers looking on, as usual), but they reported the drinking water was good. They met a local coffee exporter, Mr. Masden, who was most helpful.

If you are continuing to the Dominican Republic, be sure to get your clearance papers before leaving. Jacmel is about 48 miles from the Haitian-Dominican border at Pedernales, and you should plan to enter the Dominican Republic officially at Barahona or Calderas Bay.

DOMINICAN REPUBLIC, SOUTH COAST (25841, 25842, 25849, 25721)

From Pedernales, which is not a yacht stop, you will find fair protection as far as Cabo Falso. Approaching Cabo Beata, you can expect big seas and a funnel of wind (as is the case with capes everywhere), and when you get around this obstacle you will feel the full brunt of the trades—and then some, due to the air flowing in to fill the trough caused by the air masses rising over the mountainous peninsula. Your course from Cabo Beata will be generally dictated by the winds you happen to encounter, more than likely E or ESE, and we recommend making for Calderas Bay if you can, rather than becoming further embayed by coasting down to Barahona, which is the first available shelter along that stretch of coast. Calderas Bay is only about 20 miles farther, assuming you can lay a comfortable course for it.

Thence you will do best to make for Boca Chica (bypassing Santo Domingo) and on to La Romana, which is an area definitely worth lingering in before the hop across the Mona Passage.

Bear in mind that this is a coastal area in which you can take advantage of the land breezes from W and WNW to help you with your easting.

Bahía Agujas (25841) affords excellent anchorage at the foot of the high cliffs that make out to Cabo Falso, and is to be preferred over the bay at Cabo Rojo, where there is a bauxite-loading plant.

From Agujas we recommend an early-morning departure in order to pass through the channel between Isla Beata and the cape before the trades reach their afternoon strength, since the 12-foot depths generate a heavy swell and you will have the wind dead on the nose. There is no shelter along the E side of the peninsula, and the current will be heading you, until you reach Barahona.

Barahona (25843) is a port of entry and an important sugar port with the usual commercial aspects. Water, fuel, and provisions are available and the Customs House is at the end of the 675-foot government pier. A fully protected and safe harbor for a yacht is inside the Sugar Company's area in the northern extension of the harbor.

Puerto Viejo de Azua (25844) is an attractive little bay about 15 miles NE of Barahona, with good protection behind a narrow sandy island with a 60-foot bluff and a light at its eastern end. The channel between the island and the two low-lying points leads through deep water to several good anchorages in the lagoon. A dredged channel leads to a commercial pier at the NE end.

Bahía de las Calderas (25845) affords excellent shelter, and the approach is easy even if you do not have the large-scale chart. Round Punta Calderas and head W of S toward the little village of Las Salinas in order to avoid the rocky patch on your port hand; the patch may or may not be buoyed (black). Keep out of the E end of the bay, which is reserved to the naval and air station.

Puerto Palenque (25846) is a small port offering limited protection behind a low point and fringing reef. You will find a small pier with 4–8 feet alongside and several moorings in the harbor, such as it is. Although exposed to SW and subject to some swell, it is the only shelter on this section of coast until Puerto de Haina.

Puerto de Haina (25847), another large sugar port, really offers nothing for a yacht except protection under arduous conditions.

Santo Domingo (25848 Plan) is a clean, modern city built on the rubble left after a devastating hurricane in 1930. But for this catastrophe, Santo Domingo would be a far more interesting relic of the era when it was an important way-station for Spanish explorers on their way to Central and South America during the great gold rush. Sir Francis Drake burned this gracious city in 1586, another catastrophe. The first cathedral in the New World was started here in 1514, and still stands in most of its colonial glory, and the castle of Columbus's son, Don Diego, has been painstakingly restored.

Unfortunately, the harbor of Santo Domingo is one of the Caribbean's most unattractive places for a yacht. It lies at the mouth of a river of orange-brown mud cluttered with debris both natural and unnatural. If you don't mind what this does to your topsides, proceed to the Club Nautico de Santo Domingo, on the river's W bank just before the first bridge, where you may moor in stern-to fashion to some short and very decrepit finger piers, which may have rotted away since we were there. In the immediate environs are a shanty town and a factory warehouse.

Boca Chica (25849), on the other hand, sports another Club Nautico de Santo Domingo in a lovely bight of crystal-clear green water and white sand, thoroughly protected by an offlying island and an awash reef. No wonder this was once the site of a beach villa belonging to one of the Trujillo clan.

The modern clubhouse and its bar, restaurant, pool, and manicured beach lie within a walled compound that protects this smart place from the drab, dusty village outside with its hogs and chickens roaming the streets. More than fifty local sportfishing boats occupy the main dock, but a new pier, with water lines and electricity, was nearly complete in 1974. The shower and toilet rooms are immaculate, the fuel dock will take 6-foot draft, and the club operates a 20-ton travel lift.

This attractive place is called Puerto de Andrés on the chart. You can pinpoint it from seaward by the stacks of a large sugar mill a couple of miles E of the airport. Proceed boldly past the commercial quay in the top right corner of the plan in 25849 and do not be concerned that the chart soundings end some 400 yards short of the yacht club dock; the channel will carry better than 15 feet, though you must avoid the obvious shallow bar on your port hand.

This is a fancy club, and it quite properly goes through the formality of issuing temporary memberships to members of other yacht clubs. If you are able to do so, make your arrangements in advance.

Boca Chica is about 18 miles from the capital via a beautiful landscaped superhighway.

San Pedro de Macorís (25850) is an active sugar port; we saw three large freighters loading thousands of bags of sugar while we were there. The town is rather dry and dusty, with an impressive church dominating a plaza, as one would expect in a little Spanish town. Donkey carts and even horsedrawn buggies clop through the streets. Along the boulevard fronting the water and just E of the E breakwater is an attractive hotel called the Macorix.

One might be tempted to avoid this commercial harbor, yet it is attractive in an Old World way, and spacious and easy to enter. Anchorage may be taken wherever the spirit wills, but we suggest the indent just N of Ellen Point or the area just beyond the second wharf and the Customs House. You may land a dinghy at either place; the further in you go, the less chance of any swell.

Cumayasa River (25849) is said to be navigable by yachts for at least ¼-mile from its mouth. The river is enclosed by rocky cliffs 10–15 feet high, but there are a couple of sandy beachlets for landing a dinghy. In the very heart of the sugarcane plains, this place is wild and pretty, and the water is very clear, for a river. You'll feel a surge, since the rocky walls set up a perpetual ricocheting effect.

Isla Catalina (25849), just W of La Romana, offers a good lee on its NW side.

LA ROMANA

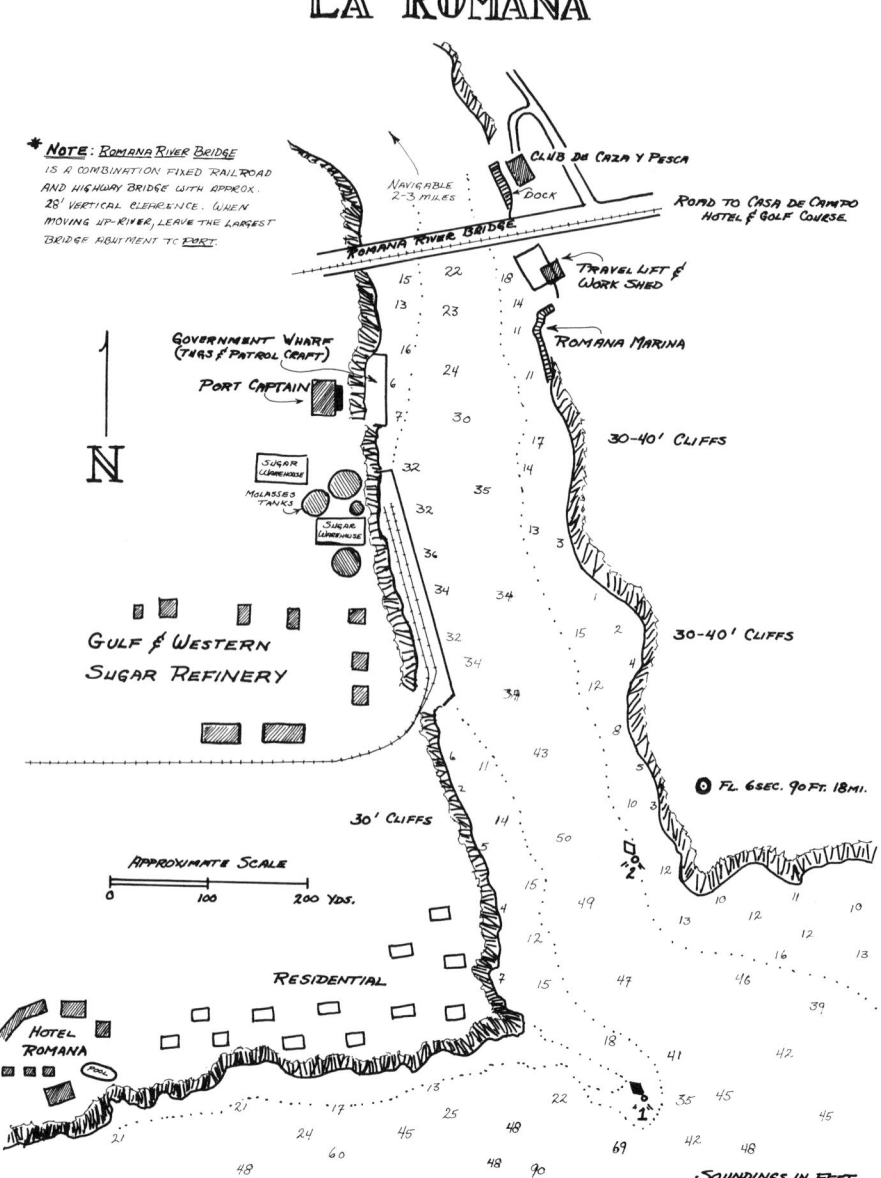

La Romana (25851) is two worlds in one: the seat of a vast cane and cattle operation by Gulf and Western Americas Corporation; a mini-Riviera growing up, under the aegis of G & W, along a shoreline of clean white sand and rustling palms.

Since the economy of most West Indian Islands is still so dependent on the cultivation of sugarcane (the southeastern plains of the Dominican Republic are one waving field of cane), perhaps a capsule history of sugar will be instructive here.

Sugar (sucrose) is a chemical found in all plant life, but is commercially derived only from sugarcane in tropical climates and from sugar beets in more temperate zones. (It was the disvovery of the value of sugar beets that, for a time, ruined the cane industry in the Caribbean.) Sugarcane is said to have originated in the South Pacific 8,000 years ago, but there was no historical reference to it until 325 B.C., when one of Alexander the Great's officers in India described its qualities.

Sugar was unknown in Europe until the 11th century. By the Middle Ages, it had become a luxury available only to the nobility. More than just a sweetener of food and drink, it was claimed to have miraculous curative powers. Cultivated by the Portuguese in Madeira and later in Brazil, it was eventually imported into the Caribbean, where the climate was ideal. Cane-cutting by hand, said still to be the most effective way to harvest, has since become the source of income for thousands upon thousands of native laborers. G & W at La Romana alone employs almost 14,000 workers in the cane fields.

As might be expected, the most conspicuous landmarks along this low coast are the stacks of the sugar mills spewing smoke by day and alight at night. La Romana is thus visible for 20 miles or more at sea.

The marina at La Romana

The Rio Romana, on which the mill and the town are situated, is only 150 yards wide, where its surprisingly clear waters spill into the sea between steep cliffs 30–40 feet high. Only 3 cables inside this fjord-like entrance, where the water runs deep to each shoreline, are the big ship wharf to port and the Romana Marina to starboard, just before the fixed bridge.

Yachts are moored Med-fashion, using their own anchors in the good holding ground, to a narrow wooden walkway built out from the base of the cliff. This marina, which is part of G & W's hotel operation, is equipped with water and 110V–220V power, but there is no clubhouse. Adjacent is a slipway with a travel lift accommodating 50 feet and 30 tons.

Passing under the combination railway-highway bridge (said to have 28 feet clearance, but don't be too sure), the river may be navigated 2–3 miles further.

Immediately beyond the bridge, on the same side as the hotel marina, is the private Club de Caza y Pesca, where 6 or 8 sportfishing boats are usually moored stern-to. This club sponsors a tournament each year that draws fishing enthusiasts from Puerto Rico, Florida, Jamaica, and sometimes as far as Venezuela. The hunting (*caza*) aspect of the club refers to the shooting of pigeons, which are prolific in the wild country to the SE. When passing upriver under the bridge, leave the solid and most substantial bridge pier to port.

At either marina, if you are obliged to moor crosswise to the channel, as most boats are, you will have to live with some roll from the swell.

The prospect of mooring in a rather narrow river mouth near a town and a sugar factory may induce some negative thoughts about La Romana, but do not be misled. The town itself is cleaner than most, the residential area near the mill where the managerial people live is prim and pleasant, and all the smoke from the mill blows off to leeward. The Romana Hotel, which actually fronts on the high mill building, was formerly a hostelry for visiting technicians and other business men, but has now been turned into a tasteful resort hotel with all the amenities and a cliffside view of the sea.

The mini-Riviera we mentioned is developing along the coast W of the river. A posh hotel of weathered wood, elegant planting in and all around it, is called Casa de Campo and is well worth a visit, if only to see the exciting horticulture. Beyond are condominium clusters with a definitely Spanish Mediterranean look, while further along the hillside are a small airstrip, a well-kept golf course, and a swimming beach.

Minitas Beach (25721), less than 3 miles E of La Romana, is a resort beach maintained by G & W, where good shelter will be found in the lee of Punta Minas (as it is named on the chart) in 8 feet or more. Sweep wide around the point if entering from the SE to avoid some rather inconspicuous rocky ledges. As the sketch shows, there are lines of reefs just off the beach, so do not move in too close.

Bayahibe (25721) is an idyllic spot. Its curving white beach and ubiquitous palms are proof positive that you don't have to cruise all the way to the South Seas to find such beauty. Constantly breaking, the few reef areas that encumber the bay are easily detected.

The calmest anchorage is off a tiny fishing village with red-roofed houses in the cove just N of the small rocky promontory. Sound your way in over the

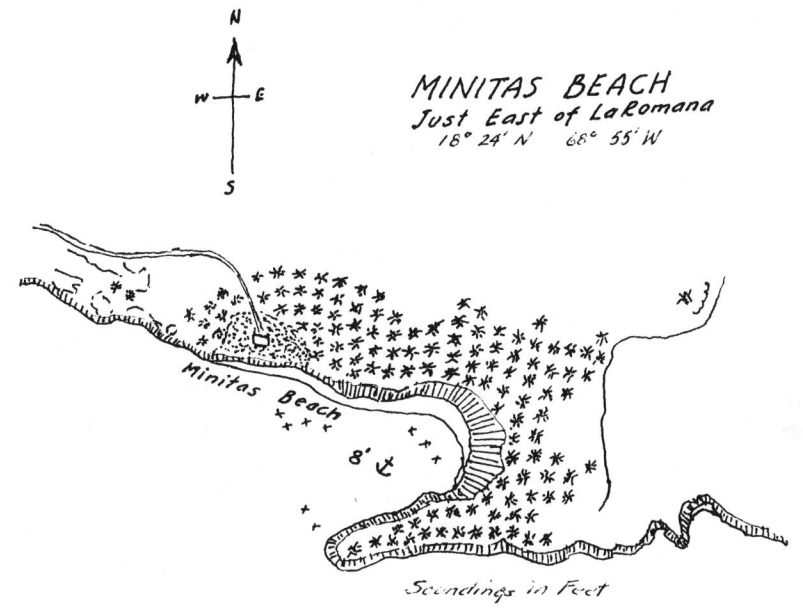

MINITAS BEACH
Just East of La Romana
18° 24' N   68° 55' W

Soundings in Feet

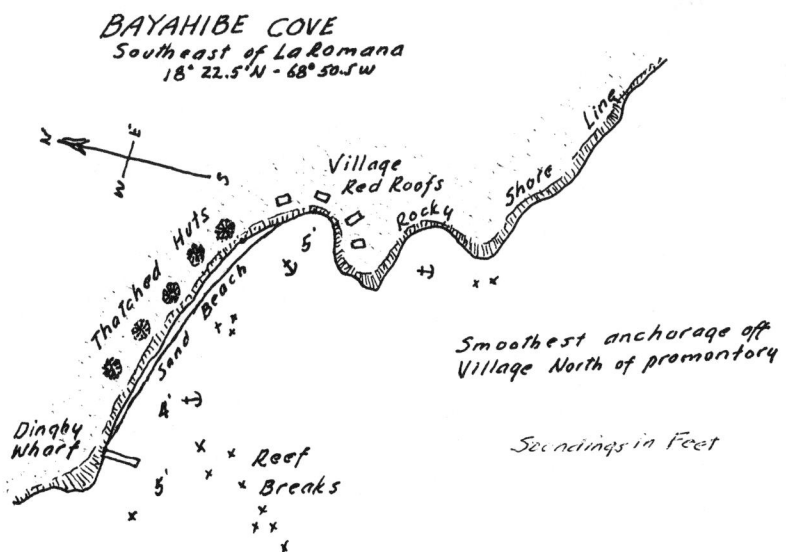

BAYAHIBE COVE
Southeast of La Romana
18° 22.5' N - 68° 50.5 W

Village
Red Roofs

Smoothest anchorage off
Village North of promontory

Soundings in Feet

gradually shoaling sandy bottom. At the NW end of the beach is the bathing area for Romana Hotel guests, who are ferried here in small launches and landed at the small pier at the furthest end of the bay.

Isla Saona and Bahía Catalinita (25721) provide a welcome place to stop and relax before or after the strenuous run across the Mona Passage. Just N of Punta Cacón is a quiet anchorage off a white sand beach, where some brightly painted buildings stand in a grove of coconut palms. The bottom is clear sand and good holding. Landing is not allowed on government-owned Isla Saona unless you have first obtained permission from the authorities in La Romana.

Sportfishing boats, with their relatively shallow draft, regularly pass inside Isla Saona en route to and from Puerto Rico. They avoid the clearly visible reef that makes out N from Punta Catuáno and pass into the open sea fairly close N of Punta Balajú. This is strictly eyeball piloting for drafts up to 3½ feet under reasonably smooth conditions—that is, as early in the morning as the light will permit. Later in the day, the sea conditions make this passage dangerous.

Anchorage may be taken just N and W of Las Calderas, where the water has a Bahama-like clarity, but deep-draft vessels will have to stay well offshore, as the bottom shoals very gradually. Fishermen living in the huts along this shore may have lobsters for sale.

The 30-mile peninsula between Isla Saona and La Romana is devoid of roads or of any access except by boat; it is almost as wild as it was in the days of Columbus, decidedly scenic, and quite sheltered from the trades. We think you'll enjoy it as we did.

CHAPTER EIGHT

Puerto Rico and Vieques Sound

MONA PASSAGE AND THE SOUTH COAST

The prevailing winds flowing around Puerto Rico are northeast in the winter and become more nearly easterly during the summer, when the Bermuda High has shifted more to the north. This wind pattern *should* produce a lee under the south coast of the island, but unfortunately the daytime wind tends to "draw" in toward the coast. The result is that you have southeasterly winds all along this coast, usually of considerable strength in the afternoon. This condition reverses itself at night, and once again we wish to emphasize the strategy of making your easting during the night and into the forenoon, in order to take advantage of the nocturnal flow of cooled air off the land. The temperature of the land cools in relation to the sea; the air mass over the land drops; this in turn forces the night air out to sea. This reversing flow pattern is a daily performance along the coasts of the large islands.

The wind that has been split and deflected by the island mass must naturally unite again. So must the wave actions that have been generated during the split, and it is this confluence of sea and swell that makes the Mona Passage such a rough body of water. For example, our log of one eastbound passage says, "Sea running 6–7 feet, but only 12–15 knot breeze." The convergence of the currents flowing along each side of Puerto Rico may also have something to do with the turbulence, but a study of the various *Sailing Directions* and *Pilot Charts* will leave you completely baffled as to what the currents may be doing to you at any particular time. The *Pilot Charts* show a current set to the northwest from January through March, and southwest or indefinite during the rest of the year; the *Sailing Directions* speak of general set to the northwest all year long. They further confound their observations by mention of tidal currents that flood SSW for 9 hours and ebb NNE for 3 hours. However, all these variable currents are usually within the ½–1-knot range and are not likely to seriously affect your reckoning.

On the other hand, there are strong local currents indicated across the bank that stands out about 22 miles from Cape Engaño. It is not by any means a shallow bank, but it does drop off sharply from 35 to over 150 fathoms, and this abrupt change in the sea bottom seems to rile the surface to the extent that, coming from the north coast of Hispaniola, you had best make a dogleg in your course toward Isla Desecheo.

This island, incidentally, makes a beautiful mark for crossing the Mona Passage, since it rises to a 715-foot peak and can be seen for almost 30 miles. Desolate and steep-sided, it lacks any landing places or even a respectable lee, and is literally fit for the birds, whose habitat it is. As if to drive us off with their threat of droppings, some of the outriders from this forest reserve and bird sanctuary picked us up long before we reached their aerie and swooped and banked around our bridge long after we had passed.

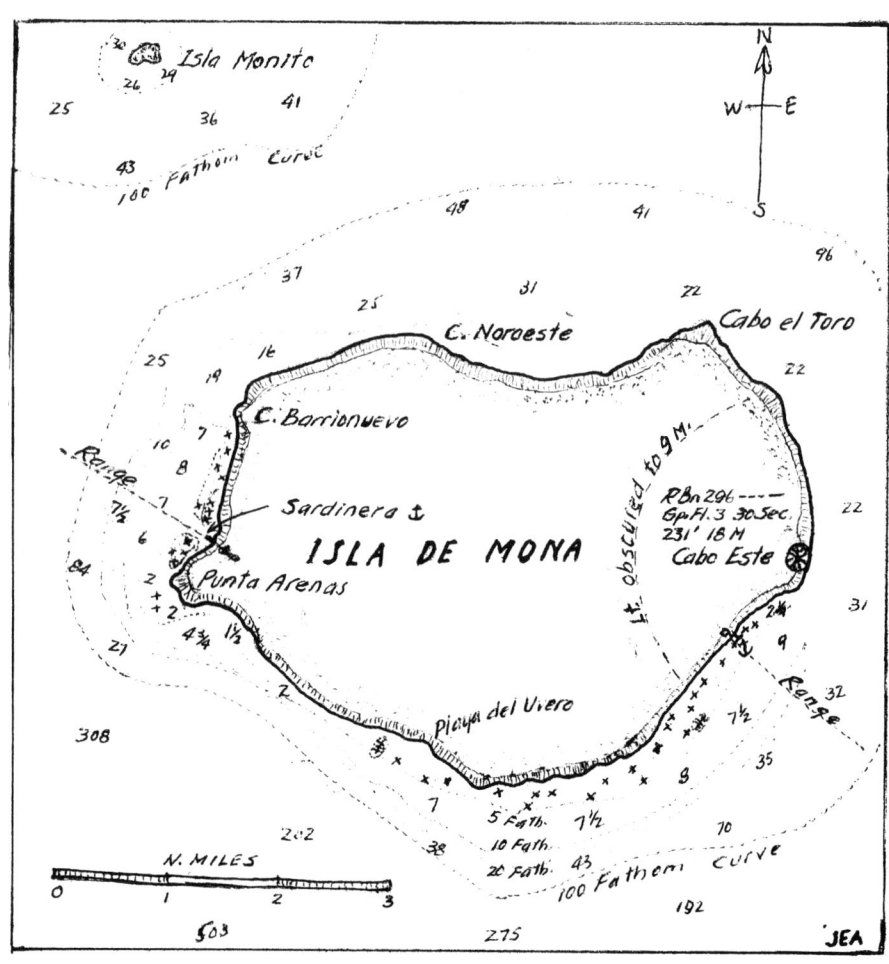

Mona Island

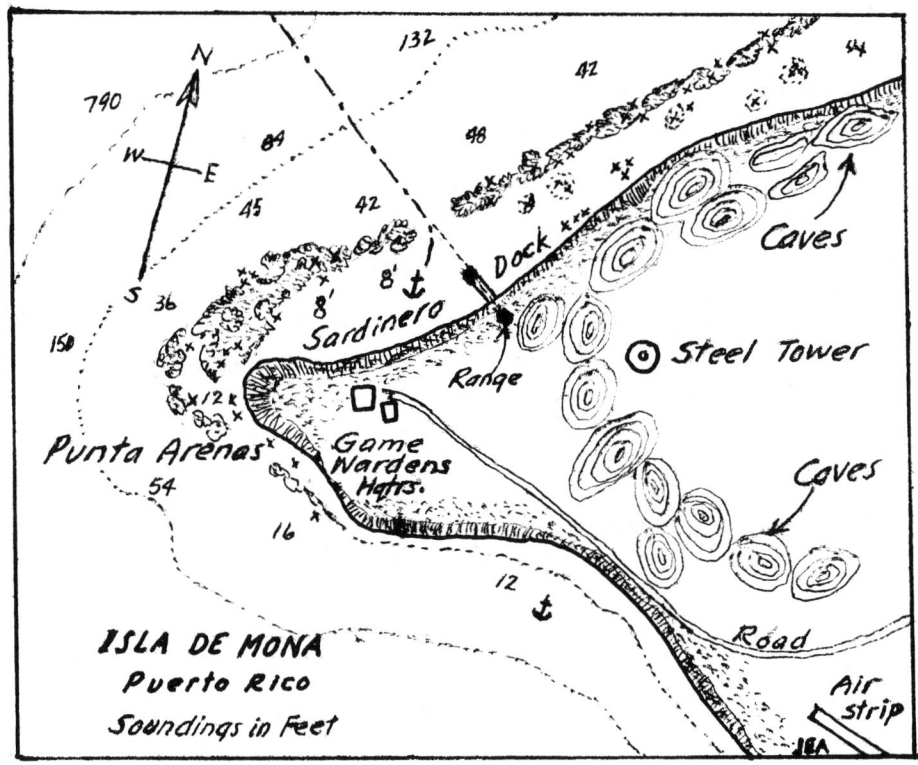

Sardinero anchorage

Mona Island (25671)

Frequently visited by sportfishing boats running between Puerto Rico and Isla Saona, this wild island offers two reef anchorages for yachts of modest draft. Mona is now operated as a commonwealth forest preserve; the only inhabitants besides the wild pigs and iguanas are a couple of wardens headquartered at Punta Arenas.

Fascinating caves riddle the island, once the dank and dripping lairs of pirates who used this strategic island as a base from which to waylay shipping that regularly used this important exit from the Caribbean. It has even been said that one could crawl the whole width of Mona underground! Of the largest of the caves near the western anchorage, Ginnie Higman of *Tormentor III* tells us:

It's on the left hand side of the road going up to the airstrip, about two blocks beyond the primitive camp at the west anchorage. There's a vaguely marked trail, and it's only about 200 feet from the road at the bottom of a climbable cliff and in a dense grove of coconuts. It was a legitimate cave with stalactites and stalagmites glistening in the glow of our flashlight. We quit when we were forced into the crawling stage. We found other caves, used by fair-sized iguanas for their homes, immediately above our anchorage.

Sardinero Anchorage at the W end is the most secure place to lie in normal weather, but would be untenable in northerly blows. These are frequent from November through February and bring in huge, breaking swells right across the entrance. Come in on a rather inconspicuous range, which consists of a front marker on the pier head and a rear marker on the land just behind. The opening in the reef is not more than 10 yards wide and will carry about 8 feetn with good-holding bottom inside.

There's good snorkeling, crayfishing, and spelunking here, but get away fast if a northerly swell develops.

Playa del Uvero may be approached as close in as your draft permits, but this is an open and emergency anchorage useful only if overtaken by northerly winds.

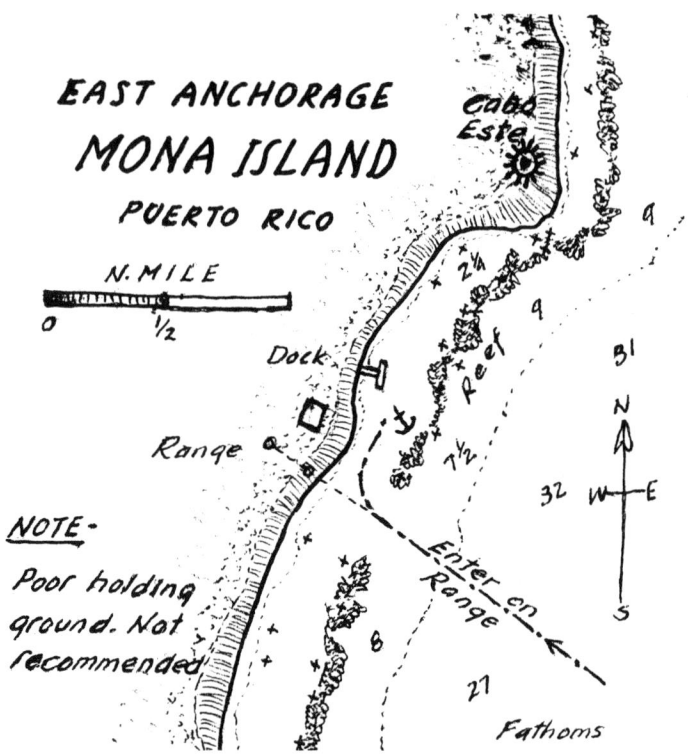

Mona Island east anchorage

East Anchorage is entered through the reef on range markers about 1 mile SW of the lighthouse. The Higmans made it in here with their 6-foot-draft ketch, *Tormentor III*, bounced around all night, and advise that the holding is poor.

Mayagüez to Ponce (25671)

Lying under the impressive Montañas de Uroyan, which rise to 2,000 feet and more, this end of Puerto Rico provides a perfect lee most of the time, with even a hurricane shelter at Puerto Real should the need arise. Here you are back in U.S. waters, where there are even buoys to occupy your attention again.

Mayagüez (25673) is really no place for a yacht to tarry because of its commercial aspect and unattractive beachfront. However, it is a must stop for Customs and Immigration formalities, unless you are prepared to carry on to Guanica, another commercial port, or to Ponce or San Juan. There is really no choice here but to proceed into the commercial dock and phone the Customs Office to request processing. To avoid an overtime charge, plan your arrival before 1630, Monday through Saturday.

The Mayagüez Yacht Club is located in 18°09.0′ N and a private marina called Club Deportivo Oeste in 18°06.2′ N.

Puerto Real (25671) is only 11 miles S of Mayagüez, and here you will avoid the persistent lazy swell. The entrance will carry 6 feet, slightly favoring the S

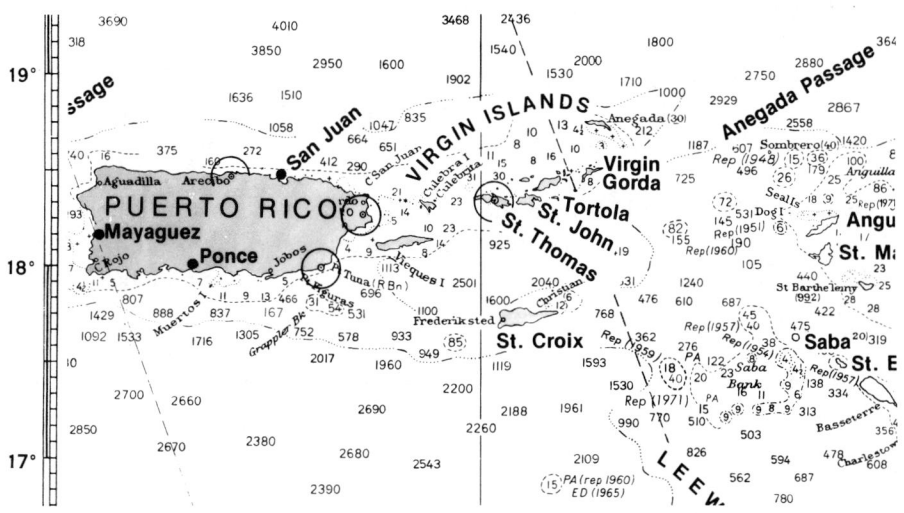

Puerto Rico and the Virgins

side, and inside this pretty little harbor the depth is ample for most yachts—but not at the docks, where we found only 3 feet over soft, harmless mud. The tidal range is only about 1 foot around Puerto Rico, so watch your groundings!

Bahía de Boqueron (25675) is simple to enter on either side of the reef that extends partway across the mouth. If you go into the pier at the end of the road for fuel, sound your way in, because it shoals to 3 feet near shore.

Cabo Rojo is a promontory with strikingly red cliffs. Like strategic capes everywhere, Cabo Rojo is likely to give you a pounding. We advise planning to round it as early as possible in the morning, since the seas will be running 5–8 feet on a normal afternoon.

La Parguera (25671) is well protected by the outlying reefs. These in turn make the entrance somewhat tricky, at least for the first time. This place is popular with local small craft, and the emphasis here is on fish. It is famous, too, for the flamelike phosphorescence of the water in the little cove immediately N of Isla Matei, which you will want to inspect by dinghy.

A group of buildings, including a prominent white hotel, stand at the end of the charted road and will be seen from seaward over the small cays that front La Parguera. Approach via the Pasa del Medio, leaving the Media Luna Reef to port and Cayo Corral to starboard, whence you may steer either way around Cayo Enrique. This track will carry 7 feet, but is narrow and requires some eyeballing as you near Isla Maguey, where it shoals considerably. Cundo's Marina with fuel, repair facilities, and a slipway is located in 67°04.0′W, but you will need local guidance to get to it the first time.

Montalva Anchorage (25671) is a gunkhole recommended by local yachtsmen. It gives 10 feet (and no facilities) in approximately 66°58.6′W. Enter through the line of reefs about 3 cables W of Cayo Don Luis.

Guanica (25679), with its high shores, makes an excellent storm shelter, but there are no yacht facilities, and the fertilizer plant on the E shore and the sugar mill in the W arm of the bay do not enhance the surroundings. Guanica is a port of entry.

Guayanilla (25681) is strictly a port for the Corco Refinery and no place for a yacht except as a storm refuge.

Ponce (25683) is Puerto Rico's Number Two city, but might well be classed Number One with yachtsmen because of the cool and pleasant situation of its yacht club and the exceptional hospitality of its members.

Situated on Cayo Gato, outside the main harbor, where the water is unpolluted, the view of sea, city, and mountains from the second story of the clubhouse is spectacular. Ponce Yacht Club has fueling facilities and a 40-ton travel lift. It is, however, available to nonmembers only in an emergency. For some, the distance to the city might be a drawback, and if you will be staying for a few days, a rental car is the only practical solution to this problem. One time when we were there, the cane fields to windward were being burned, which rained ashes on deck, but this is only a periodic nuisance.

In addition to the main channel approach, a course from the W may be laid between Punta Cucharas and Cayo Arenas (Sandy Cay), leaving Can "7" to starboard and proceeding directly to the yacht club.

Ponce to Punta Tuna (25677, 25650, 25685, 25687, 25689, 25659)

This 42-mile run along an exposed coast can be made a little more comfortable, at least for 12 of those miles, by ducking inside some of the reefs and mangrove cays that line this shore. A glance at 25687 will suggest a number of anchoring possibilites, especially along the channel leading to Central Aguirre.

This partly sheltered route, with nothing less than 10 feet, runs inside Cayo Berberia, from the red flasher off the Ponce Yacht Club to the 10-foot-or-deeper channel that runs close inside the Cayos Cabezazos, thence to the channel inside the Ratones and Barca Cays, and out through the dreadful sounding Boca del Infierno, leaving the two wrecks to port when heading out to sea.

From here there is little protection, except where the route passes inside the Guayama Reef off Punta Figuras, and very close under Punta Tuna, to take advantage of the shelter of Sargent Reef. Upon rounding Punta Tuna, you will have virtually "turned the corner" of the island and can look forward to the smoother waters of Vieques Sound.

Isla Caja de Muertos (25683 or 25685) provides a lee for anchoring off its beautiful beaches. Drop the hook just W of the light or just inside the SW tip of the larger island.

Puerto Patillas (25677) is a suitable overnight anchorage in depths of 1 to 1½ fathoms, but expect a swell. There is a dock with gasoline, water, and a small restaurant.

Palmas del Mar (25650) seemed well on its way to becoming an international resort community to rank with the tastefully contrived Old World elegance of Port Grimaud on the French Riviera, or Porto Cervo on Sardinia. An outer harbor, with partially completed breakwaters and limited mooring and berthing facilities, was already in use, and an inner harbor was being dredged and bulkheaded with slips for the residents of waterfront townhouses, as well as for transient yachtsmen. With its vast plans for a marina, boatyard, restaurants, boutiques, and all the frills that one expects in a Riviera setting, Palmas del Mar would have become an important yachting center in a previously undeveloped coastal area of Puerto Rico, and a convenient base for exploring lovely Vieques Island only 12 miles to the east.

Alas, in mid-1975, the Sea Pines Company, in order to shore up their other holdings (Hilton Head Harbor in South Carolina among them), decided to write off their $13 million Puerto Rican investment. Whether the project will be taken over by other interests before it goes to ruin remains to be seen. Inquire about the fortunes of the place before you plan to stop there.

Not yet shown in chart 25650, Palmas del Mar lies just S of Punta Candelero, about halfway between Punta Tuna and Roosevelt Roads.

THE NORTH COAST OF PUERTO RICO

Except for the large commercial harbor of San Juan, the 90-mile-long north coast has no protected bays or anchorages comparable to those on the south coast, and its ocean beaches are more exposed to the relentless northeast trades in winter. If you are coming in from the Bahamas or Hispaniola for a landfall at the northwest end of Puerto Rico, however, you will be far enough north to avoid the confusing tidal currents of Mona Passage mentioned above. From there, eastbound yachts may continue along the coast for 60 miles to San Juan, although this may be a long day's run in the strong headwinds one encounters from December through March.

If your approach is from the vicinity of Isla Desecheo, about 12 miles W of Punta Higuero at the westernmost tip of Puerto Rico, it may pay you to stand into Aguadilla Bay, which offers some protection in the prevailing easterly winds. The port has little to attract yachts, however; it is an open roadstead used by commercial vessels that load sugar and molasses from a conveyor pier while lying to mooring buoys, and the U. S. Air Force maintains a fuel pier with pipelines for handling aviation fuels. The anchorage is exposed to winds from north and west.

Punta Borinquen to San Juan (25671, 25668)

The coastline extends almost due east from Punta Borinquen, which is visible many miles at sea. When approaching this steep-to point at night, the loom of Ramey Air Force Base can be seen long before you are able to identify the Gp fl. light atop the 200-foot bluff; in fact, the navigational aid is more difficult to pick up than the bright revolving airfield light about ½-mile NE of the lighthouse. Vessels are advised to stay several miles offshore here because of a small-arms firing area near the point, and there are no landing facilities in any case.

Punta Sardina (25671) is a small promontory about 7 miles E of Punta Borinquen, with a semiprotected sandy cove and boat landing where you can enter in calm weather. The anchorage is obviously unsafe in a norther and uncomfortable in the surge created by the winter trades. But the setting is attractive, with green hills rising several hundred feet to the town of Isabela, identified by a radio tower ½-mile to the SW of the settlement.

Puerto Arecibo (25668) is the only harbor of any consequence on this coast; it is a small commercial port about 26 miles E of Punta Borinquen and 33 miles W of San Juan, providing a stopping place halfway for vessels in transit. The harbor occupies a bight protected by Punta Morillos on the E side of the promontory and by a 1,200-foot breakwater extending from it toward the SW. A well-marked, dredged channel leads from deep water to a bulkhead wharf on the S side of the breakwater, where fuel and water can usually be obtained. A pipeline on the wharf is used by barges to supply liquid chemicals to storage tanks. Fishing vessels and small craft anchor S of the wharf. Don't anchor off the town of Arecibo, on the SW side of the bight, where the water shoals and is muddy near the mouths of the Rio Grande and La Vega rivers.

Punta Palmas Altas (25668) is a low peninsula with tall palm trees and a sandy beach about 7½ miles E of Punta Morillos. A rocky reef extends W of Punta Palmas Altas, affording limited protection in easterly winds, but the tiny anchorage is exposed to the N and shoals to less than 1 fathom in places.

Punta Puerto Nuevo (25668) is a rocky promontory about 9 miles E of Palmas Altas and 15 miles W of San Juan, where boats can enter in calm weather inside the rocky islets that extend almost a mile W of the point.
   The coastline from here to San Juan is irregular, fringed in parts by reefs that extend ½-mile or more offshore. U.S. *Coast Pilot* 5 shows a danger zone. There are artillery and small-arms ranges extending up to 10 miles seaward in the vicinity of Puerto Nuevo. There is seldom any military activity in this zone, however, and coastwise vessels regularly hold a course parallel to the coast between the 20- and 100-fathom lines.

San Juan (25670), whose bay and harbor form the largest commercial port in Puerto Rico, is one of the best all-weather harbors in the entire Caribbean. The approach from sea is direct and well marked, leading close in under the ancient battlements of Morro Castle on the east side of the entrance, which connects with the high city wall that continues along the channel side of the Old City to La Fortaleza, now used as the Governor's residence. San Juan Light sits atop Morro Castle 181 feet above the entrance, and the white marble dome of the Capitol building provides a conspicuous landmark overlooking the sea about a mile east of the light.

There are several clearly marked channels leading off the entrance (or Bar Channel) to commercial piers and anchorages around the large Bay of San Juan. Cruise ships, as well as pleasure craft, turn E into San Antonio Channel between Isla San Juan and Isla Grande, leaving the Governor's palace and the Old City to port and the container-ship terminals on Isla Grande to starboard. Most yachts continue to the head of the channel, hoping to find a temporary slip available at Club Náutico or a public marina nearby. The Club is most hospitable to visiting yachtsmen and extends guest privileges to members of accredited yacht clubs, though it may be unable to provide a slip at its own limited dock facilities. The clubhouse, with its showers, bar, and fine dining rooms, is located at the SE end of Isla San Juan, close to the center of everything in old and new San Juan. Gas, diesel, water, and a 20-ton lift are under the charge of the club's capable dockmaster, who will help you call Customs if you are entering here. If you have come direct from the continental United States, you won't have to clear, as this is a U.S. port; but if you are entering from the Bahamas, the Dominican Republic, or any foreign country you should notify customs and immigration authorities as soon as you have docked. It is easier to phone them than to go to the Customs House when they are busy with commercial vessels and cruise ships, and the officials usually prefer to clear yachts at the club or nearby marina in the harbor.

Should you be unable to get a slip at the club, try the marina just across the channel at the S end of the bridge, where a number of local boats and a few transient yachts are usually moored. Most marine supplies are available in San Juan, and several small shipyards can haul yachts and do major repair work. We found one of these yards at the SW end of Isla Grande, near the old Navy airstrip, doing satisfactory maintenance and repair work on Coast Guard patrol boats and other small craft. The Coast Guard base is located on the N side of San Juan harbor at La Puntilla, near the Customs House, and its boating-safety personnel are well informed about conditions and marine facilities throughout Puerto Rican waters and eastward to the Virgin Islands. Many U.S. yachts bypass San Juan, but we have always found it a useful stopover for supplies, and the local yachtsmen could not be more friendly and helpful.

San Juan to the East End of Puerto Rico (25668, 25650)

The 30 miles of coastline between San Juan harbor and the northeast end of Puerto Rico is fringed by a long line of reefs and rocky heads. They prevent easy access to a succession of small coves and sandy, palm-lined beaches that look inviting from seaward but should not be approached without local knowledge. There is no harbor on this section of the coast, and the only boat facilities are a yacht club and marina accessible only to shoal-draft powerboats. The club and marina are located in a lagoon W of Punta Congrejos, near the San Juan International Airport, and may be entered only through a shallow inlet crossed by a bridge with 15-foot clearance—obviously no place for sailboats and larger cruisers.

Vessels making this 30-mile coastwise passage should keep well clear of the fringing reefs and rocks, as tidal currents set onshore; but you will clear all dangers by staying 2 miles or more off the coast. In periods of calm weather, this is an easy run for both sailing yachts and cruising powerboats, but during winter months, it can be a long, hard beat to windward, particularly when heavy Atlantic swells are rolling in from the northward to encounter fresh northeast trades in the shoaling waters of Puerto Rico's continental shelf. Under such conditions, it's wise to allow ample time for this long upwind passage, standing far enough offshore, if necessary, to avoid the steep confused seas that often build up off the fringing reefs. More often than not, you'll find it takes longer than you counted on to clear the rocky headland of Cabo San Juan at the northeast end of the island. Under sail, it is a good plan to leave San Juan harbor soon enough in the morning to reach Fajardo Roads by early afternoon, giving you time to explore a choice of harbors on the east coast or nearby in Vieques Sound.

THE EAST COAST AND VIEQUES SOUND (25663)

Except for cruising boats in transit between San Juan and St. Thomas, relatively few visiting yachts know much about the east coast of Puerto Rico or the numerous coves and harbors found in the chain of islands that extend eastward in the relatively protected waters of Vieques Sound. Yet this area offers a variety of sharply contrasting cruising grounds, ranging from the unspoiled beaches of Culebra and Vieques to the sophisticated resort hotels and condominiums that are rapidly transforming the eastern end of the Puerto Rican mainland.

The 10 miles of scenic coastline between Cabo San Juan and Punta Puerca, just north of the sprawling U.S. Naval Base at Roosevelt Roads, is already in process of transformation from a remote rural farming and fishing area to a water-oriented residential and resort region, with housing developments, high-rise condominiums, and large resort hotels. Along with this economic growth, the east coast is becoming the leading yachting center of Puerto Rico; new marinas and boatyards provide literally hundreds of slips for the fast-

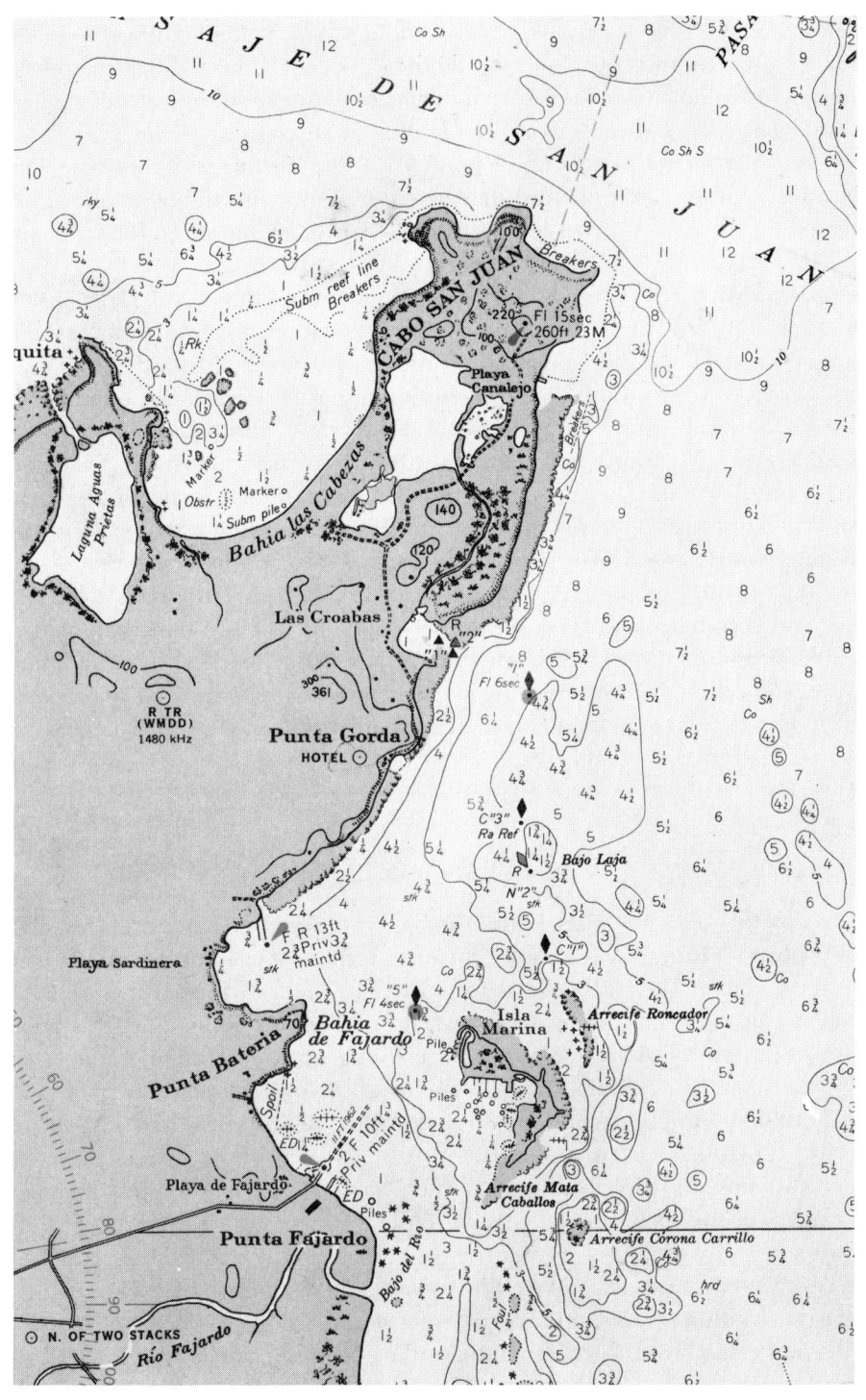

Northeast end of Puerto Rico

growing fleets of yachts that now berth permanently at this end of the island. The local yacht population has increased more than fourfold in the last decade. It includes all types of pleasure craft from large power cruisers to sportfishermen, from big ocean-racing sailboats to tiny catamarans that stage their own annual offshore race to Culebra. Although new boating facilities seem to be keeping pace with the increasing boat population, visiting yachts may find it difficult to locate a vacant slip when some of the largest marinas are fully occupied by resident boats. However, most of the harbors or marinas mentioned below make some provision for transient yachts.

Las Croabas (25667) is an ancient fishing village about a mile SSW of the lighthouse atop Cabo San Juan, but its tiny harbor is much too crowded with local fishing craft for visiting yachts to find an anchorage. If you draw less than 6 feet, you can enter the narrow marked channel into the natural basin, which has somehow retained its distinctive character amidst the changing surroundings.

El Conquistador Marina (25667) is a modern manmade yacht basin less than half a mile S of Las Croabas, operated in connection with the huge resort hotel on the hilltop above. At the marina you will find all the facilities you'd expect— swimming pool, bar, and a lift to the hotel on the cliff and its restaurants and surrounding golf courses.

Marina Puerto Chico (25667) is another relatively modern facility at the N end of Playa Sardinera, with fuel, water and electricity available. Most of the slips are occupied by local boats.

Villa Marina (25667) is a new yacht harbor and residential development which opened in 1975 on reclaimed land toward the S end of Playa Sardinera. A dredged channel entrance leads directly from Fajardo Roads into a land-locked basin with 218 slips for yachts up to 60 feet overall and 8 feet draft. All docks are of concrete construction and (believe it or not) each "will have one bath for ladies, one for gentlemen, and one for the crew," in the words of the brochure.

Isla Marina (25667), or "Isleta Marina," as it's known locally, is the oldest yacht facility in this area and is still preferred by those who enjoy lying to a mooring in the shelter of a small cay half a mile off Fajardo beach, looking back toward the towering peak of El Yunque, the impressive and dominant rainforest mountain rising 3,500 feet above the coastal plain. One of the best boatyards in Puerto Rico is here, and its marine railway and repair facilities are in demand by yachts throughout the area. Fuel, water, and electricity are available, but slips are seldom open for transient boats. Condominiums are also being built on tiny Isla Marina. There is a regular (or almost regular) launch service between Fajardo and Isla Marina.

Playa de Fajardo (25667) is a port of entry for Puerto Rico used by commercial vessels from the Virgin Islands and other Caribbean or continental ports, but it is not a yacht harbor and not the best place to find an overnight anchorage. If you need provisions from the town of Fajardo, 1½ miles inland, leave your boat at Isla Marina and take the launch to the Playa dock where you can take a taxi or "publico" to town. There is daily ferry service between Fajardo and the islands of Culebra and Vieques, much used by local residents for transporting passengers, freight, and livestock.

Roosevelt Roads (25666), the large U.S. Naval Station at the SE end of Puerto Rico, preempts Ensenada Harbor, which lies within a restricted area and may be closed to civilian navigation during periods of military activity. However, the Navy has a small yacht club at the NE end of the harbor where visitors may be welcome on invitation. After passing the Navy docks in Ensenada Honda, continue to Buoy "13," from which you can see private yachts off the Club.

Culebra and Adjacent Islands (25650)

Some of the finest cruising waters in the eastern Caribbean are found in the area between Puerto Rico and the Virgin Islands known as Vieques Sound. These are U.S. territorial waters belonging to Puerto Rico, bounded on the north by a chain of small islets and rocky cays leading eastward for 20 miles to the populated island of Culebra, thence southward about 10 miles to Vieques, largest of the group, 18 miles long and extending east and west to within 6 miles of the Puerto Rican mainland just S of Roosevelt Roads.

One reason why this attractive cruising ground remained almost unknown to cruising yachtsmen for so many years was that until July 1, 1975, much of the area had been designated a "danger zone," due to offshore gunnery, aircraft bombing practice, and unexploded ordnance around some of the islands. Your charts may still show an area northwest of Culebra as a danger zone— 204.230—where craft desiring to enter or transit must obtain clearance by contacting "Culebra Control" on 2182 kHz or by phoning the Atlantic Fleet Weapons Range at Roosevelt Roads. However, most if not all of these restrictions were removed when the Navy announced that "unqualified

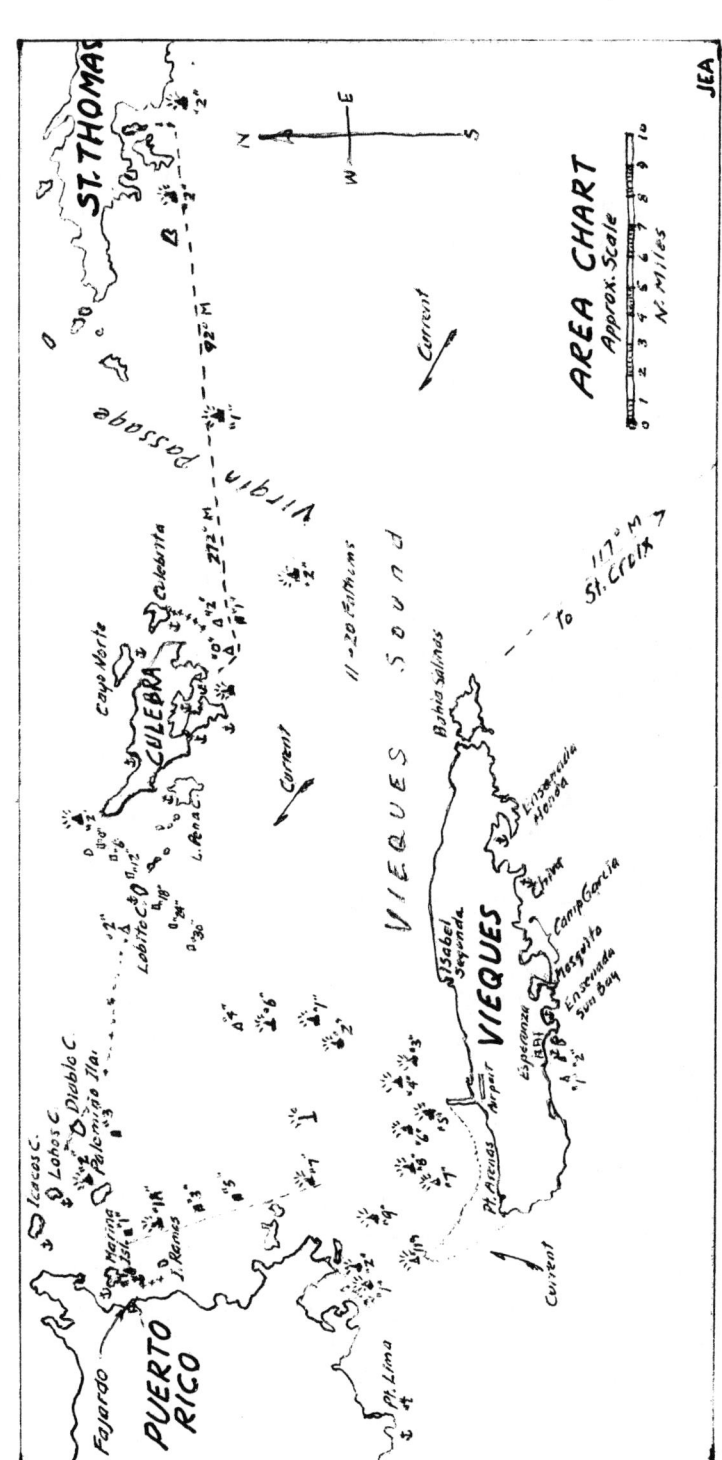

Vieques Sound

decisions" had been made to end all practice shelling on Culebra by July 1, 1975, and that similar shelling on the surrounding cays would cease by the end of 1975.

Culebra Island (25655, 25653, 25654) is one of the most intriguing islands we have found anywhere in the Caribbean. It has a superb natural harbor, any number of fine anchorages, crescent beaches backed by palm groves and fronted by sheltering coral reefs. We based here for several months in *Brer Fox* and found the quiet anchorages a pleasant change from the overcrowded harbors in some parts of the Virgin Islands only 20 miles to the eastward.

The island is only about 7 miles long and 3 to 4 miles wide, but is surrounded by a score of smaller islets, cays, and rocks with their own fringing reefs and protected coves, which make the cruising area seem much larger. Now that the entire group of islands is safe from bombing and shelling, you could spend a week going from beach to beach for swimming, fishing, and snorkeling in unspoiled surroundings. The great harbor of Ensenada Honda is big enough and deep enough to moor a fleet of warships, which is undoubtedly why President Theodore Roosevelt chose it for a naval facility at the end of the Spanish-American War; but the station has been inactive for many years, and the shoreline of the bay is backed by peaceful hillsides where cattle graze on steep slopes that rise to the 650-foot summit of Monte Resaca, near the center of the island. The harbor is entered from the southern side of the island, on a NW heading through a narrow but well-marked channel that leads between two lines of exposed coral reefs, and then opens up into a mile long bay, with depths of 30 to 40 feet almost to the town of Dewey at the NW end. Numerous smaller bays and coves lead off both sides of Ensenada Honda, providing snug anchorages under the protecting hills.

The town has a population of about 750 Spanish-speaking inhabitants and is a port of entry. The entire island is a municipality of Puerto Rico. The island people don't refer to the town as "Dewey"—the name shown on the charts— but call it Culebra; the mayor is not just mayor of the town but mayor of Culebra Island. His office is an imposing structure on the spur of a hill overlooking the two main harbors of Culebra. One of the harbors is located at the SW end of town, overlooking Bahía Sardinas, with a dock large enough to handle the Fajardo-Vieques ferries and interisland freight boats; the other is Ensenada Honda, on the eastern side of the closely built little town, and is connected with Bahía Sardinas by a small lagoon. It is, unfortunately, too shallow to allow passage for anything larger than an outboard. All yachts entering from the Virgin Islands are required to clear with Customs, and must go to the government dock on the western side of the island. The Customs office is nearby, and the formalities here have been much easier than at Fajardo or San Juan. However, we hear that the rules have changed somewhat since we

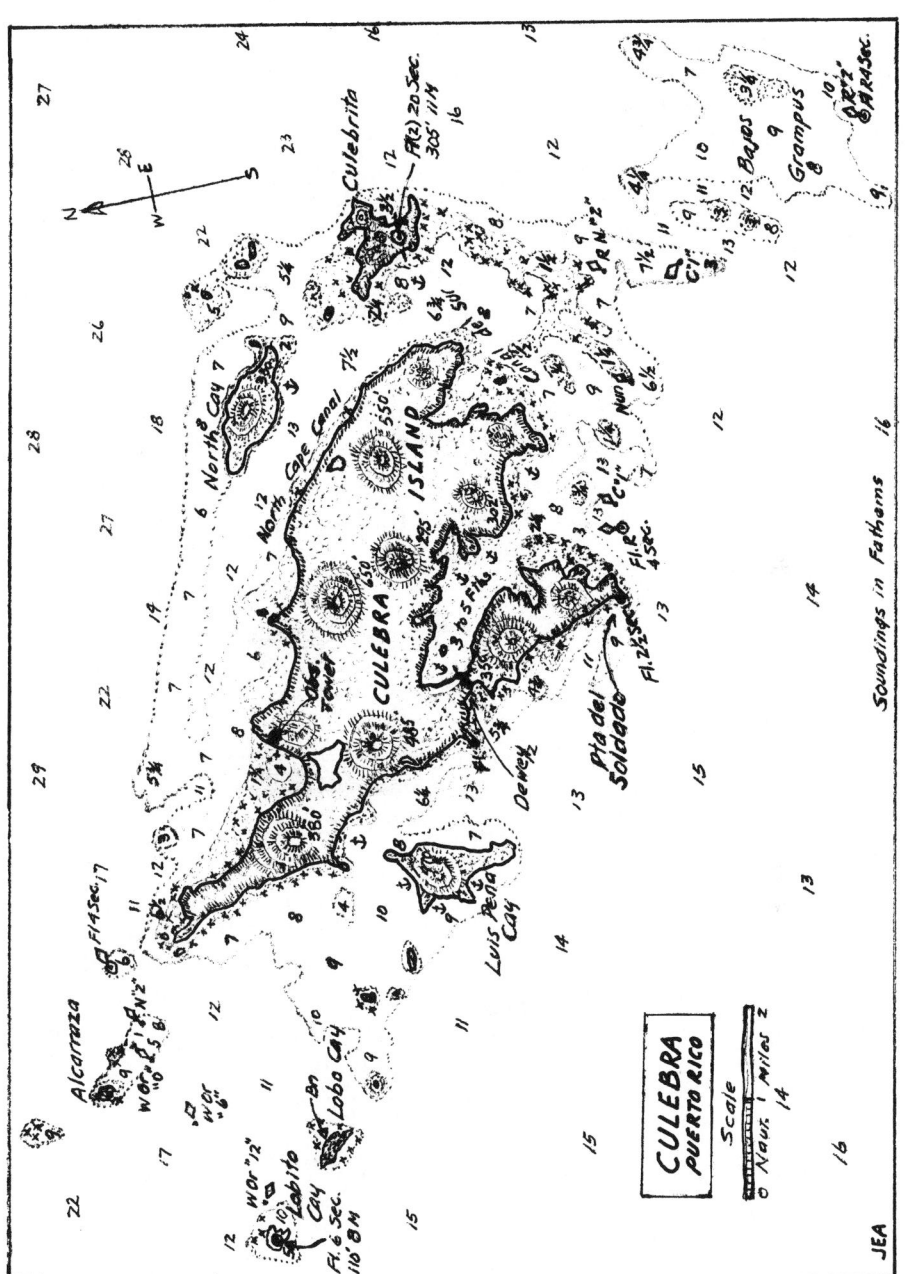

Culebra Island between Puerto Rico and St. Thomas

were last there; it is no longer possible to have Customs check you in at Ensenada Honda, and yachts of foreign registry are required to enter first at Fajardo or San Juan, an inconvenience for westbound yachts. Both harbors at Dewey have good holding ground, although there is sometimes a swell in Bahía Sardinas. If you are remaining at Culebra for more than a day or so, you'll find a wide choice of all-weather anchorages in the protected coves of Ensenada Honda and around the southeast end of the island, where there is a lovely surge-free anchorage behind the reef sheltering Puerto de Manglar. Other islands, islets, and reefs on the southern and eastern sides of Culebra form a protected passage, with several sandy beaches and sheltered daytime anchorages.

Culebra is not yet a resort island, and that has been one of its greatest charms—you may enjoy cruising without elaborate shore facilities. When we were last there (in 1973) there were no marinas, no supermarkets, and only one gas pump near the government dock on Bahía Sardinas. The Seafarer's Inn, close by the dock and facing the bay, has 8 or 10 rooms and serves excellent fish and lobster dinners—if you could only locate the owners, Druso and Jane Daubon, in time to make reservations. There is another small hotel, right in the center of town, offering native Spanish cooking, and close by are several general stores with limited provisions. The town boasts a number of small bars, and a "nightclub" called El Bole overlooking Ensenada Honda, where you can get ice.

Both harbors may be somewhat crowded with visiting yachts from the mainland of Puerto Rico on weekends or on gala occasions when Culebra is playing host to the popular sportfishing tournaments or sailing regattas held in recent years, including a recently organized multi-hull race from Fajardo to Vieques that brings top international racing skippers to the island and got special coverage in yachting magazines in 1974. Usually, however, the island and its harbors are quiet and peaceful spots.

Guest facilities are limited, but John Vincent, a former native of Maryland's Eastern Shore and onetime principal of the Culebra school, has several attractive housekeeping apartments facing Ensenada Honda, just east of the bridge across the lagoon, with a bareboat-charter yacht and several outboards at his dock. New housekeeping cottages have been built on a hillside slope called Punta Aloe, half a mile beyond the Vincent place, with a spectacular view of the harbor and the hills beyond.

There is good lobster fishing in the area, and Nick Zinkowski, a former professional diver who sailed his own fishing boat from New England to Culebra, may be able to sell you something from his commercial catch.

Further information on anchorages in the islands around Culebra is available in a new regional cruising guide entitled *Westward from the Virgins*, by Raymond N. Auger, which we list in the bibliography in the Appendix and recommend for those who plan to do more extensive cruising in Vieques Sound and the east coast of Puerto Rico.

Isla Culebrita (25653), which lies half a mile E of Culebra, is a hilly, cone-shaped little island with a lighthouse atop its 300-foot peak and a crescent beach fringed by reefs on its NW peninsula. Once used as a Navy bombing target, it is now a favorite weekend picnic spot, with several good daytime anchorages but too exposed to the N for mooring overnight.

Cayo Norte (25653), off the NE coast of Culebra, is a privately owned island with steep cliffs rising from the sea, backed by wooded hills, and fronted by a sandy beach on its S shore. There is a constant surge, and the anchorage off the SE end of the island is not recommended except in settled weather. It's best to have a local pilot on your first visit.

Cayo de Luis Peña (25655) is the largest of a chain of islands and cays extending off the NW peninsula of Culebra and formerly was in the range of fire when gunnery exercises were in progress. There used to be a Navy observation post at the top of the central peak, lighted at night. You'll find several daytime anchorages in semisheltered waters on the western side and in a sandy cove protected by coral reefs on the N coast. None of these anchorages is comfortable when swells are rolling in from the open Atlantic, and they become untenable in a norther.

Flamenco Beach, Culebra (25653) has long been one of the favorite watering places of the Culebran islanders and their ancestors before them, and no description of the island could fail to mention the symbolic role it played in the longlasting controversy between the Navy and Puerto Rico over the issue of live shelling that continued from the mid-1960s until 1975. The beach, called Flamingo in English, is the most beautiful on the island and continued to be used by the islanders and Puerto Rican visitors when it was right on the edge of the target range. Now that bombing and gunnery practice has come to an end, visiting yachtsmen are discovering that the half-moon bay and its sparkling white-sand beach are among the finest in the Caribbean. It is only a little more than 1½ miles from town and a pleasant walk through the hillside pastures beyond the airstrip. Yachts may enter the bay from the N, but the approaches are lined by dangerous reefs, and there is usually a swell during the winter months, so it is no place to be caught in a norther. Best to visit it by land.

Isla Vieques (25650, 25664)

Vieques is not only the largest of Puerto Rico's outlying islands but is actually larger than any of the U.S. or British Virgins except St. Croix, which it resembles geographically. Vieques is 18 miles long and 3–4 miles wide, with rolling hills and pastures that have made it a principal cattle producing area for Puerto Rico. The N coast is exposed to the NE trades and provides only one semi-protected harbor at the port of Isabel Segunda, about 8 miles from the western end of the island and approximately 10 miles SW of Culebra across Vieques Sound. The S coast, on the other hand, is indented by a series of small bays and sheltered coves that offer a number of good anchorages in attractive rural surroundings. Much of the western end of the island and parts of the S coast have been restricted naval areas that may be closed to navigation during periods of Navy and Marine Corps exercises, although access to some of the best harbors on the southern shore is generally available.

Isabel Segunda (25664) is the largest town on the island, with regular ferry service to Fajardo and Culebra, and daily air service by two small airlines that also serve Culebra and St. Thomas. Facilities for yachts are limited, and the anchorage off the town dock is exposed to more or less constant swells in winter. Water is available at the dock, but gas and diesel fuel have to be brought down from filling stations in town. There are several restaurants within walking distance of the dock and the old town square which dates back to Spanish colonial days.

Yachts rounding the western end of Vieques should keep well clear of the mile-long breakwater and munitions pier about halfway between Isabel Segunda and Punta Arenas at the westernmost end of the island, and don't cut corners too sharply in crossing the sandspit of Arenas Shoal, which extends more than 3 miles NW of the point. There are strong currents across this long shoal, with depths of less than 1 fathom in areas of shifting sand that are not shown on the charts. So use your sounder or leadline if you pass E of the flashing buoy at the W end of the spit.

Arenas Beach (25664) is a public playground and beach right in the middle of the restricted naval area at the western end of the island. On weekends and holidays it's a popular spot for Navy personnel from Roosevelt Roads and is used by islanders from Isabel Segunda and neighboring villages. The anchorage is exposed to a moderate swell but is safe enough for a daytime visit in settled weather.

Anchorages on South Coast of Vieques (25650) are seldom visited by cruising yachts, although there are any number of snug harbors and sheltered coves in the 10-mile coastal section between Esperanza at the west and Bahía Salina at the eastern end of the island. Here are a few that are worth a visit if you are cruising the area with time for gunkholing:

Puerto Reál (25664) is about 6 miles E of the western end of Vieques. A channel leads to the town of Esperanza, identified from seaward by the radio tower, and from closer inshore by the pier used by local fishing boats. The pier is not a safe place for yachts, and the grassy bottom provides only fair holding ground. Two small islands protect the anchorage from swells when the wind is in the SE.

Ensenada Sun Bay (25664) lies just to the E of Esperanza, with lots of anchoring room in the half-moon bay with its long public beach and bathhouse, seldom used except on weekends. There are usually swells when the SE trades are blowing.

Puerto Mosquito (25664) is a tight little hurricane hole about a mile east of Ensenada Sun Bay. It is justly famous for its phosphorescent waters, but its narrow entrance channel has a controlling depth of 3 feet that makes it inaccessible to most cruising yachts. It's worth exploring by dinghy from an anchorage just off the coral reef on the E side of the entrance.

Naval restrictions eastward from Puerto Mosquito hamper cruising or anchoring in other small bays until you reach the lighthouse at Punta Coneja, at the western entrance to another Ensenada Honda.

Ensenada Honda (25650) is, as the name implies, the largest bay on Vieques, but it is exposed to SE winds and has several shoals and rocky reefs that make it difficult to enter for the first time without a local pilot. Raymond Auger shows a sketch chart and two air photographs of bays just E of Ensenada Honda in his regional guide, *Westward from the Virgins*.

THE VIRGIN PASSAGE (25650)

Yachts bound eastward from Puerto Rico to the Virgin Islands can make the run through Vieques Sound in relatively protected waters under the lee of Culebra and its surrounding islets and reefs. Once they clear Culebrita, however, they encounter the North Atlantic swells, which tell them in no uncertain terms that they have reached the Virgin Island Passage. The distance between the easternmost point of Culebrita and the western end of St. Thomas at David Point is less than 12 nautical miles; another 6 miles takes you into the shelter of St. Thomas Harbor. Depths in Virgin Passage are not much greater than those in Vieques Sound, ranging generally from 15 to 25 fathoms, but wind and sea conditions may be totally different, when rollers from the open Atlantic pile up on the Virgin Bank to encounter steep cross-seas kicked up by the winter trades. So don't count on a fast upwind passage under sail, but plan your course to take advantage of the trades: pass close to Sail Rock if the winds are from the NE, or enter through Savana Passage when SE winds allow you to carry a northeasterly course. It's usually a glorious 3-hour sleighride downwind from St. Thomas to Culebra, but the eastbound passage may take 4 or 5 hours of wet slogging to windward.

CHAPTER NINE

The Virgin Islands

BY ALEXANDER C. FORBES

Between Puerto Rico and the Anegada Passage are the Virgin Islands, one of the world's most compact cruising areas. Lying in a 45-mile chain, the main islands are mostly mountainous, with a maze of passages between them, and indented every few miles by a tempting cove or bay. Only St. Croix is separated from the chain—by a 40-mile stretch of truly open water. The Virgins are set in a region of constant summer. Their pattern of wind and weather is predictable. Yachtsmen find it hard to fault even the most extravagant descriptions of these islands. Swimming and snorkeling are superb, and the fishing matches the best in the world.

The Virgins are owned in part by the United States and in part by Great Britain. Under the American flag are St. Thomas, St. John, St. Croix, and approximately 50 other intriguing islands and cays, many of which are uninhabited and ripe for exploring. The British Virgin Islands include Tortola, Virgin Gorda, Anegada, Jost Van Dyke, Peter Island, and about 23 smaller islands and cays. The demarcation line between the U.S. and British islands runs north to south: between Little Hans Lollik and Little Tobago, through The Narrows between St. John and Great Thatch Islands, around the eastern end of St. John, and then through the Flanagan Passage between Flanagan and Pelican Islands. All islands west of this boundary are U.S. possessions; all to the east are British.

In the U.S. Virgins, the major ports are Charlotte Amalie (rhymes with family) on St. Thomas, and Christiansted on St. Croix. Both do a booming tourist business, catering primarily to visitors from the continental United States. Both towns are amply endowed with mainland-style supermarkets and good restaurants and hotels. And they provide nearly all the usual yachtsmen's necessities.

Recently, this business has begun to overflow into the British Virgins, resulting in expanded development and services there. The major British port is Roadtown, Tortola. Although she's not so sophisticated as her American sisters, Roadtown offers an ever-growing variety of rooms, restaurants, shops, pubs, and yacht-repair facilities. Marine supply inventories on the three main islands range from sparse to adequate.

THE VIRGIN ISLANDS

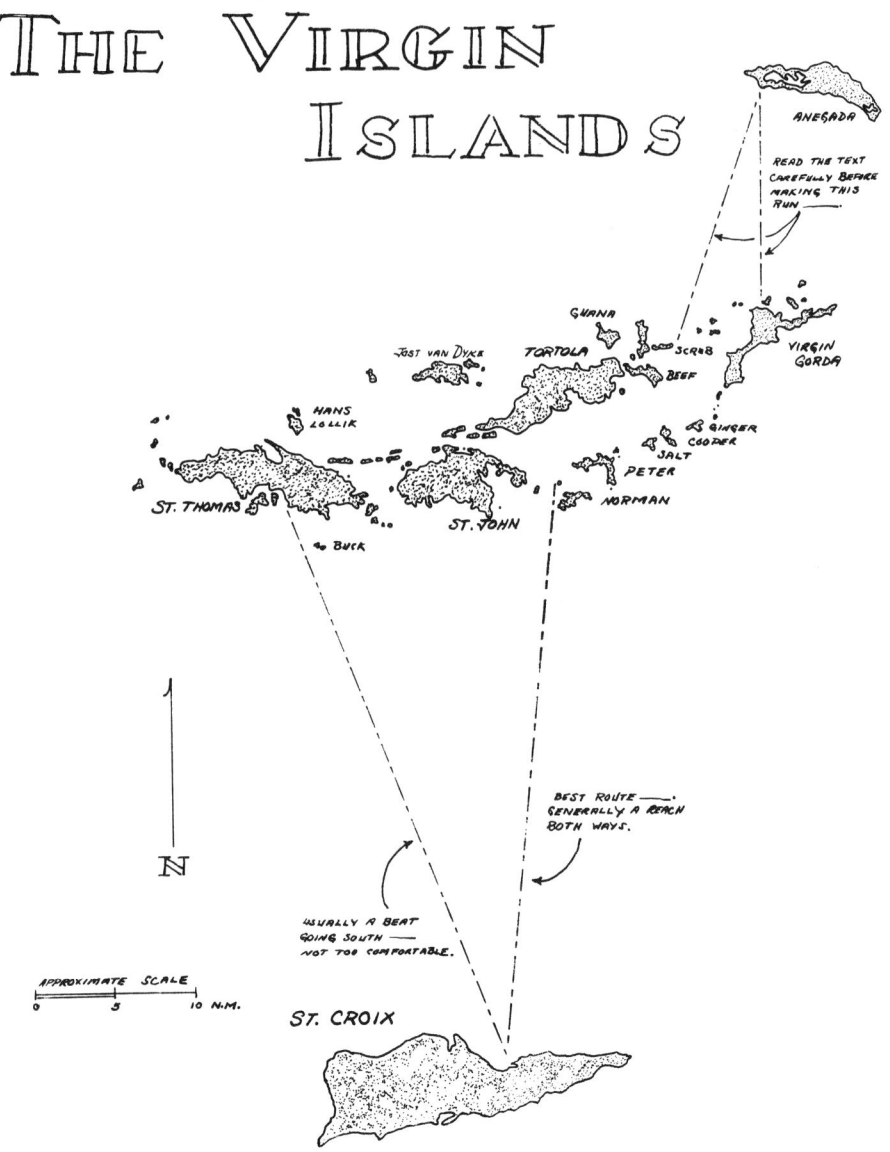

Tides and currents are a problem in only a few places. The wind is usually constant, blowing from the east. During the winter, the trade winds usually come in slightly north of east and reach velocities of 18 to 22 knots, with gusts as high as 40. During the summer, they usually veer slightly south of east and decrease to 12 to 15 knots, occasionally gusting to 25 or 30.

The seas in Pillsbury Sound and Sir Francis Drake Channel seldom exceed 2 or 3 feet, except when affected by tidal streams. Away from the lee of the islands, however, the seas can build up to formidable size. The 40-mile southerly passage from the main group of the Virgins to isolated St. Croix should be considered carefully; the passage can get quite uncomfortable when a fresh wind is blowing. So can the Virgin Passage and the Anegada Passage: none of these should be attempted in a blow by inexperienced sailors.

Customs and Immigration

In general, all vessels must clear and enter through U.S. Customs and Immigration when leaving and entering U.S. waters. This can be accomplished at Cruz Bay or Coral Harbor on St. John, Charlotte Amalie on St. Thomas, or Christiansted on St. Croix, during normal working hours on weekdays and until noon on Saturdays. Clearing at any other times involves substantial overtime charges. American flag vessels need not clear customs when leaving U.S. waters provided there are no aliens or paying passengers aboard.

When entering and leaving British waters, all vessels are likewise required to clear at West End or Roadtown on Tortola (the principal ports of entry), at Great Harbour on Jost Van Dyke, or at Spanish Town on Virgin Gorda. If you are planning to spend only a week or less in the British Virgins, you may arrange to enter and clear simultaneously, at the discretion of the customs officer. This has become an accepted practice in recent years.

Radio

The U.S. Virgins operate under FCC regulations and transmissions may be monitored by them. VHF radios are coming into wide use, in anticipation of the outlawing, at the end of 1976, of the MF, double sideband sets, which have been in use for years. In such an integrated cruising area, the British Virgins are sure to follow along with this changeover.

"Whiskey, Alpha, Hotel" is the friendly St. Thomas marine operator; his station's antennas are high on Peter Mountain. WAH is on call every day from 0800 to 2100 on 2009 kHz (MF) and 157.4 mHz (VHF), which is channel 28. WAH broadcasts a roll call at 0900, 1145, 1500, and 1800, with a weather bulletin included in the 1145 broadcast.

"The Children's Hour" is the traditional name for the period from 1200 to about 1300 when charter and private yachts in the Virgins exchange information and pass messages. The official MF frequency is now 2030 kHz, although some traffic is still carried on the former 2638 kHz frequency. Since all the shore facilities are also standing by, this is the time to place service orders and make dinner reservations.

Currents, Tides, Tidal Streams, and Rollers

The prevailing ocean current runs from east to west at ½-to-1 knot through-out the islands. Its direction and velocity can be greatly affected by tidal streams and wind. The current usually increases slightly as the wind increases from the east, though only in isolated places does it ever exceed 1½ knots. Conversely, there are certain areas where the current is considerably lighter. For example, when sailing east along the southern coast of St. Thomas, it helps to stay close to shore, since the current is considerably less and the seas easier there.

Tides in the Virgin Islands have been a source of confusion for years. The British *Pilot* states that the area experiences the standard two tides daily, while their charts (see BA 2016) mention a diurnal condition. The U.S. *Sailing Directions*, on the other hand, state that a diurnal condition prevails on the Caribbean side only and that a semidiurnal condition is found on the Atlantic side. Tide tables for the Virgins are based on San Juan, Puerto Rico, for the north side of the islands, and Galveston, Texas, for the south side. Needless to say, these tables are not too accurate. However, the standard rise and fall of the tide is only 10 to 16 inches, so there is not really much of a problem.

Tidal streams run in various directions throughout the islands, and they sometimes drastically affect both the strength and direction of the prevailing ocean current. The situation at The Narrows between St. John and Tortola is a good example of this effect. When the tide is flooding (from north to south), a tidal stream funnels through Thatch Cut and runs directly across The Narrows. Turning eastward along the St. John shoreline, this streams follows the contour of the island and finally flows into the Caribbean through the Flanagan Passage. During this period, a current in excess of 2 knots may be found close to the St. John shore; while a light westerly current, or none at all, will be found along the Tortola shore. A yacht sailing eastward through The Narrows on a flood tide will certainly benefit by staying close to the St. John shoreline, while one making a westbound passage would do well to hug the Tortola side.

Rollers are a formidable type of ground swell frequently experienced from October to May. They may continue for three or four days at a time. These swells move in from the north after several days of light east to southeast winds. They may exceed 6 feet, and have been observed to break in 9 fathoms off the northern coast of Tortola. In some places near the western end of Anegada Island, where the bottom is composed of fine sand, the formation of banks is often changed by rollers. In winter, great care must be taken when anchoring in harbors exposed to the north. Several yachts have come to grief in recent years because their skippers either ignored this hazard or were unaware of it. We indicate in this chapter all anchorages that in our opinion could be subject to this danger.

Marine Supplies

The rapidly growing yachting business has fostered the establishment of several marine supply stores. Shipyards and bareboat charter centers are also capitalizing on the demand by opening small stores in conjunction with their maintenance and repair facilities. Ice and water, once obtainable only at St. Thomas, are now generally available at all marinas and bareboat charter centers.

Fishing and Scuba Diving

The Virgin Islands offer some of the best game fishing in the world. Professional fishing guides and deep-sea fishing boats are available for charter in St. Thomas, St. Croix, and Tortola. The good fishing boats are booked well in advance of the season, so reservations need to be made early. Several places offer instruction in scuba and snorkeling and provide tours of wrecks and reefs in the area.

Route Charts

These charts show the customary routes to and from favorite anchorages. All the anchorages shown are not necessarily safe for overnight. Check the text, as well as the larger-scale charts, for greater detail when choosing an anchorage.

Where there are two or three possible routes to a particular destination, the favored routes are those that lead through the most protected water. For instance, the preferred route from the main harbor in St. Thomas to Roadtown, Tortola, under normal conditions would proceed along the coast of St. Thomas, through Current Cut, then along the west coast of St. John, leaving Johnson's Reef to port, through Fungi Passage (between Whistling Cay and Mary's Point, St. John), then through The Narrows and up to Road Harbour. You may, if you wish, go up the south coast of St. John when making this trip, but the going is likely to be more rugged because of the open water and the prevailing winds booming out of the east. If you want to cruise the south coast of St. John in normal weather, you'll find it much more enjoyable to approach from the east on a broad reach or a run. If the wind happens to be blowing out of the north, as it sometimes does in winter, cruising along the south coast of St. John will of course be quite comfortable in either direction.

The north coasts of St. Thomas and Tortola offer very little protection and may become unsafe, or at least uncomfortable, during the winter whenever the winds are blowing from north or east, or when heavy rollers are coming in. However, both of these coasts offer pleasant cruising in periods of settled weather, especially during late spring and summer, when sea conditions are

The Western Virgins

The Central Virgins

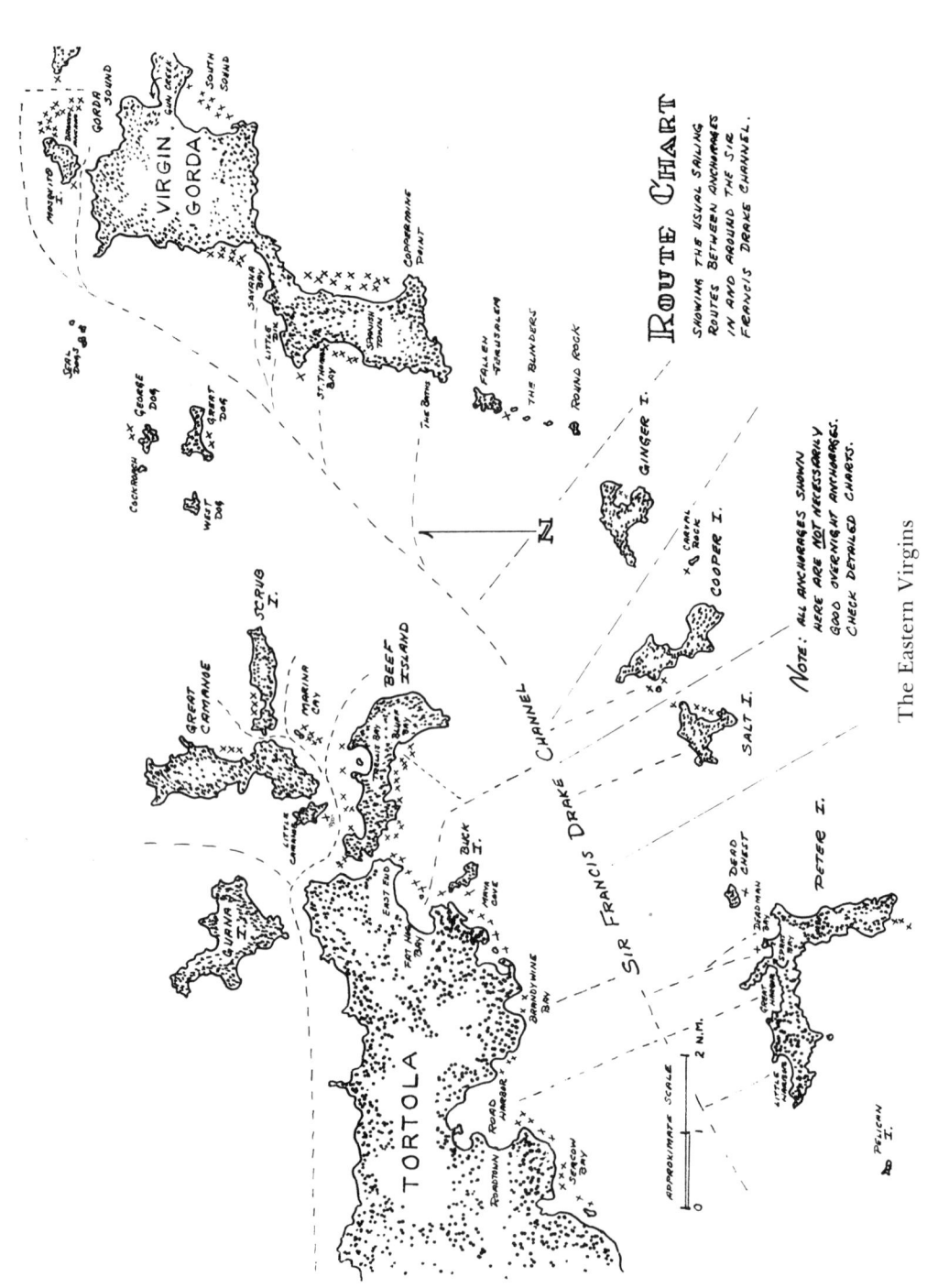

The Eastern Virgins

easier. A number of good daytime anchorages along these coasts are described in the following sections. Safe overnight anchorages are hard to find on the north side of either of the big islands, however, and Magen's Bay, on St. Thomas, is the only harbor we can recommend for an overnight stopover. Even this harbor may become untenable in a northerly blow or when ground swells are running.

The most protected, and therefore the most popular, all-weather cruising areas are those in Pillsbury Sound and Sir Francis Drake Channel, where sheltered anchorages are seldom more than a few miles apart.

THE U.S. VIRGIN ISLANDS

St. Thomas

To sit contentedly on deck in St. Thomas Harbor after a pleasant dinner ashore can be a beautiful experience, especially now that the harbor pollution has been cleaned up. The twinkling lights of Charlotte Amalie dot the steep surrounding hills, a cruise ship departs, the warm night breezes play on your face. The background of the Old World is omnipresent here, as it is everywhere in the Virgin Islands. Each European power that competed in the Caribbean has left its imprint in the islands' history, architecture, economy, and food. All are interwoven into the culture of the area.

Archeological research has shown that St. Thomas, as well as St. John and St. Croix, were inhabited by Arawak Indians for some centuries before Columbus. Although there is no mention of them in the earliest Danish records, pottery, arrowheads, stone implements, and weapons suggesting natives even earlier than the Arawaks have been found at Magen's Bay.

St. Thomas Island was discovered and named by Columbus on his second voyage, in 1493. The first colony was started by the Dutch in 1657, but they soon abandoned it and migrated to New Amsterdam (later New York).

A Danish skipper, Erik Nielsen Schmidt, who had been trading with the Danes and other Europeans living on St. Thomas, was granted permission by King Frederick III of Denmark to take control of the island as Royal Commandant and Governor. Following the King's instructions, Schmidt brought with him a Lutheran minister, one Kjelt Jensen Slagelse. Together they sailed aboard the ship *Erik* and arrived at St. Thomas around the first of January, 1666. Three months later, simply by hoisting the Danish flag and firing a salute, Governor Schmidt took possession of St. Thomas. Thereupon, he selected a suitable hill, laid out house plots, and built a fortified tower, the site of which is now known as Bluebeard's Castle.

Another fort, built on a hill to the west, was known as Kjaer's Tower until the end of the 17th century, but is now known by a beard of another color, Blackbeard. Fort Christian was built in 1680 and had a luxurious room of gilded leather used by the Governor. Other rooms were built for the use of the Lutheran and Dutch Reformed congregations. Fort Christian was rebuilt in 1870.

Governor Schmidt died just three months after the flag-raising ceremony, and Pastor Slagelse took over the conduct of the colony's affairs. The tiny settlement struggled to grow and increase its population, but the rigors of the life took its toll in European lives. Pastor Slagelse went back to Denmark and returned with settlers, soldiers, clerks, and 61 convicts in the *Fero* in 1671. This voyage took almost a year instead of the normal 6 months, and the pastor and 80 of the 128 people on board died and were buried at sea.

It was soon decided that the importation of Danish criminals was economically unsound, and the infamous slave trade began when the Danish West India Company settled in St. Thomas. Slaves were brought to work the sugarcane fields as well as to be reshipped to other areas.

Under almost continuous Danish control until 1917, St. Thomas prospered. Charlotte Amalie became a famous port, owing to liberal Danish trading laws. There is a long, but not too well documented, pirate history. Most of the buccaneers evidently preferred wealthier neighbors, such as those who lived in San Domingo, Cuba, and along the Spanish Main. However, the pirates did use St. Thomas's snug harbor to repair their vessels and sell their loot.

Beginning in 1865, the United States, which had felt the lack of a naval base in the Caribbean during the Civil War, made overtures to Denmark concerning purchase of the islands. Negotiations were carried on spasmodically over the years, but the fear that Germany might buy the islands finally brought action. The transfer, for $25 million, was completed in 1917, only two weeks after the U.S. entered World War I.

St. Thomas Harbor (25649) has two entrances. The main channel, deep enough for cruise ships, lies between Hassel Island and the eastern side of the harbor. The other, Haulover Cut, which is suitable for vessels drawing less than 10 feet, is a manmade passage between the NW end of Hassel Island and the westernmost corner of the harbor.

The approach to the main entrance is clear, although care must be taken to stay outside Triangle Reef, which lies SW of the entrance and is buoyed. Yachts may safely pass on either side of Rupert Rock, but not between the rock and the lighted buoy several hundred feet NW of it.

Of the two approaches to Haulover Cut, East Gregerie Channel, between Hassel and Water Islands, is deep and free of hazards. West Gregerie Channel, between Water Island and the mainland, is also deep and unobstructed, except for a patch of coral heads extending from Sandy Point on the NW corner of

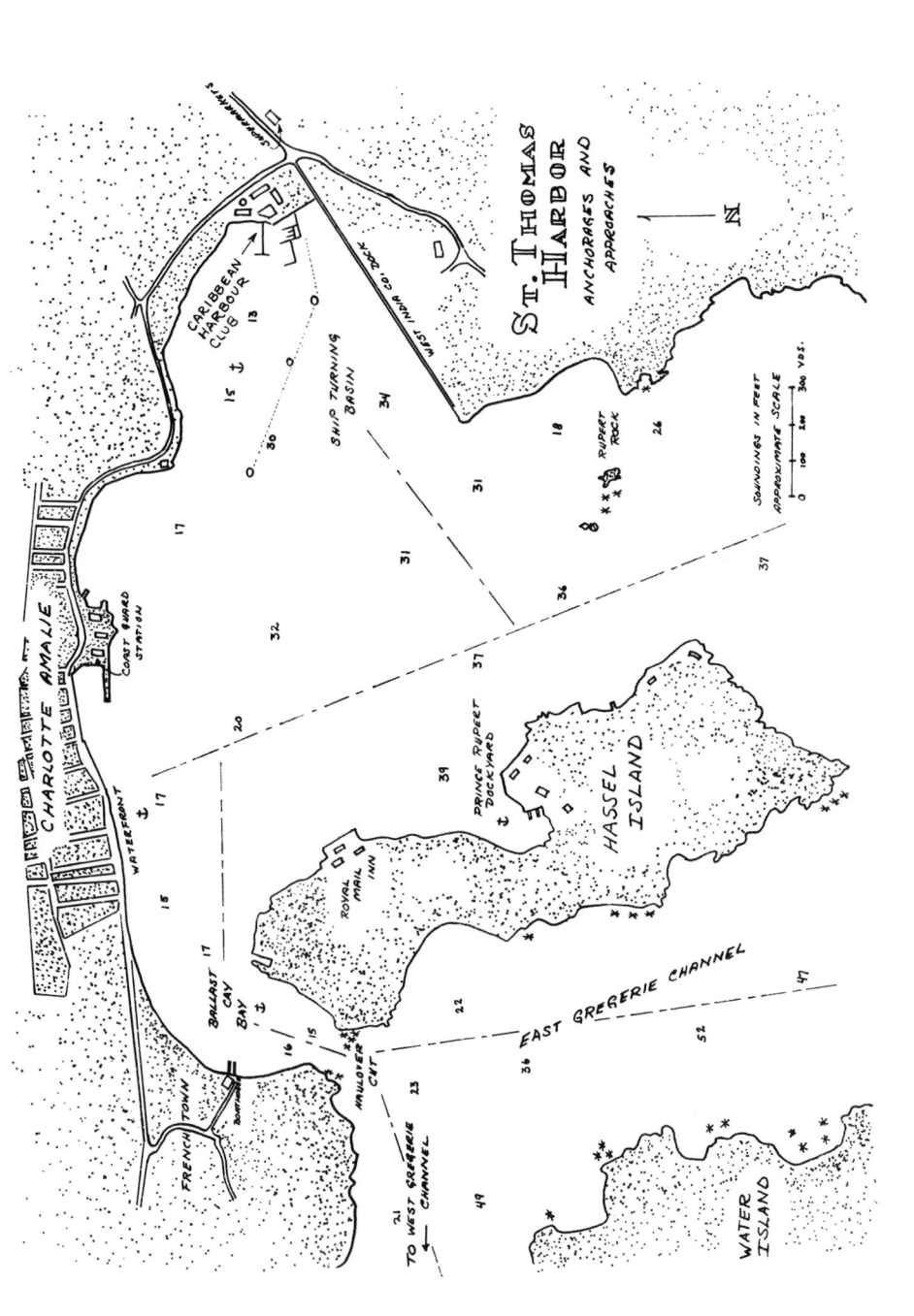

ST. THOMAS HARBOR
ANCHORAGES AND APPROACHES

N

SOUNDINGS IN FEET
APPROXIMATE SCALE
0   100   200   300 YDS.

CARIBBEAN HARBOUR CLUB

SHIP TURNING BASIN

WEST INDIA CO. DOCK

RUPERT ROCK

CHARLOTTE AMALIE

WATERFRONT

COAST GUARD STATION

FRENCHTOWN

BALLAST CAY BAY

HAULOVER CUT

TO WEST GREGERIE CHANNEL

ROYAL MAIL INN

PRINCE RUPERT DOCKYARD

HASSEL ISLAND

EAST GREGERIE CHANNEL

WATER ISLAND

Water Island to Sandy Point light buoy. These underwater heads are difficult to see. Pass W of Sandy Point, and stay in midchannel through Haulover Cut. At one time, a reef, with a marshy area behind it, connected Hassel Island to the mainland. In 1937, the government dredged the cut to promote a better circulation of water through the harbor.

St. Thomas, the largest commercial harbor in the Virgin Islands, has several yacht anchorages. Long Bay has become the most congested anchorage in the Virgins, since most of the crewed-charter fleet headquarters here, along with a colorful assortment of private yachts of every description. When anchoring here, give consideration to the numerous private moorings that infest the area; and stay well clear of the big-ship turning basin. The new Caribbean Harbour Club, which has replaced the old Yacht Haven, is located at the head of this bay and offers all the usual marina facilities, including showers and a coin laundry. In 1975, it was expanding its docks in conjunction with a large shorefront hotel.

The holding is good in midharbor, and you will have good protection under almost all conditions, with only a trace of ground swell. Because of the high mountains, the wind can be changeable, so anchor carefully.

The bulkheaded area on the northern side of the harbor is known as "The Waterfront." Commercial boats tie up here, and a few yachts moor stern-to. This is the least protected anchorage in the harbor, and if a heavy groundswell works in through the entrance, this place can become untenable. However, it's a convenient spot for taking on supplies in town, or for clearing through customs and immigration. The holding is good in mud.

Ballast Cay Bay, in the western corner of the harbor, adjacent to Haulover Cut, is the place where sailing ships used to dump their ballast before loading cargo. There's protection here for a limited number of yachts. Be sure to anchor clear of the channel, which is used by commercial traffic moving through the cut. Dick Avery's Boathouse, on the Frenchtown side, has facilities for visiting yachts. Holding is good in mud and the bay is generally smooth, except for the wash of passing commercial traffic.

Prince Rupert Dockyard, on the eastern side of Hassel Island, has a limited anchoring basin and dock space. Holding is good in mud and conditions are calm unless a ground swell works through the main harbor entrance.

Swimming is not recommended here or elsewhere in St. Thomas Harbor, although the earlier sewage-pollution problem has been largely corrected.

Honeymoon, or Druif, Bay (25649), on the western side of Water Island, is a lovely little anchorage, well away from the main harbor. The sandy beach at the head of the bay is used by residents of the island and guests of the Water Island Hotel, located on the southern bluff overlooking the bay. The usual anchorage is about 50 yards off this beach in about 20 feet, with excellent holding in sand and some grass. Although a slight ground swell is sometimes experienced, the sea is usually calm and the protection is good when the wind is out of the E.

The hotel runs a ferry service to Krum Bay, where taxis can usually be hired for a trip into town. For the convenience of snorkelers and divers, the wreck of an old iron steamship lies in about 10 feet of water just off the southern point of the harbor.

Cowpet Bay (25647) is located on the eastern end of St. Thomas, just S of Current Cut. You will recognize it by the private homes that spread across Deck Point and the garish condominium development at the head of the bay.

The Yacht Club of St. Thomas is located here, and on weekends the area teems with small class boats. Three lines of moorings are rented to club

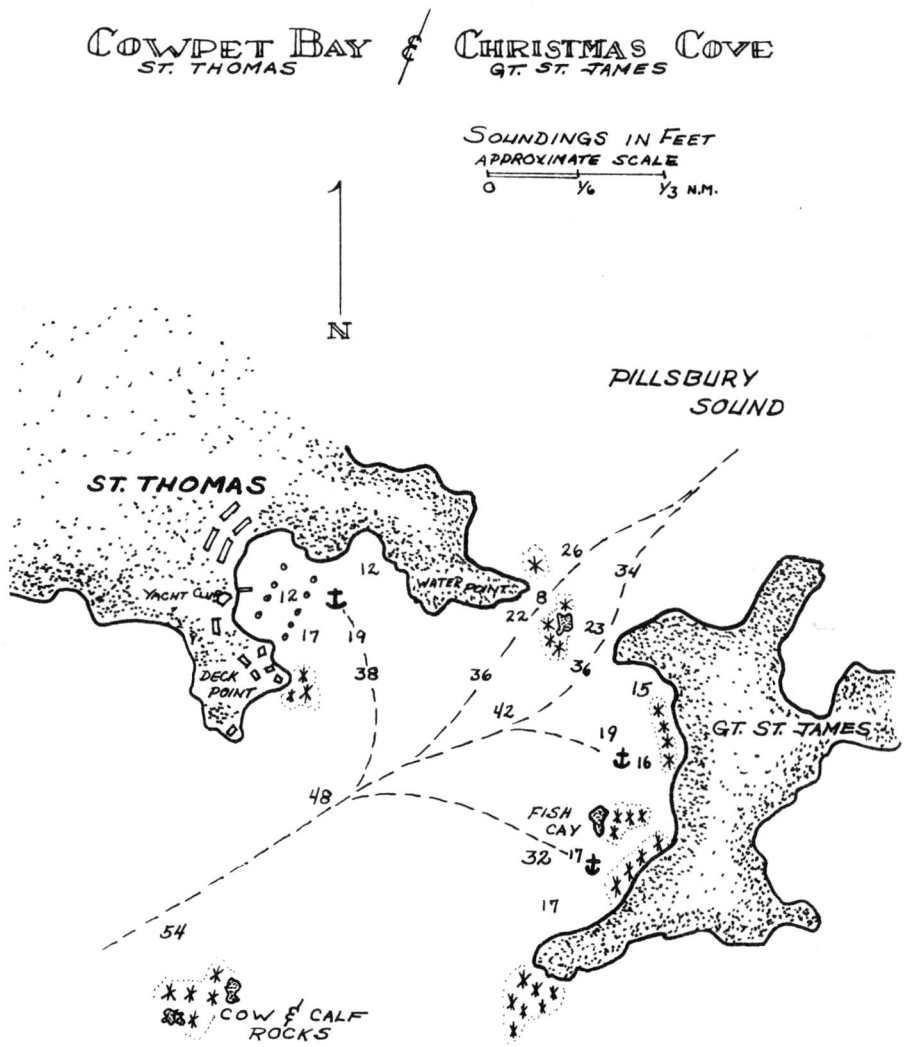

COWPET BAY & CHRISTMAS COVE
ST. THOMAS   GT. ST. JAMES

SOUNDINGS IN FEET
APPROXIMATE SCALE
0   ⅙   ⅓ N.M.

N

PILLSBURY SOUND

ST. THOMAS

YACHT CLUB

DECK POINT

WATER POINT

GT. ST. JAMES

FISH CAY

COW & CALF ROCKS

members. Visiting yachtsmen from other recognized clubs can usually arrange to use the moorings by contacting the chairman of the house committee.

There are two beaches, one in front of the Yacht Club and the other just to the N. The swimming is good, though the water is not always clear, due to the influence of the current that runs through the cut. This current is primarily responsible for the rather uncomfortable ground swell that prevails most of the year. Otherwise, this is a safe overnight anchorage with good holding in deep sand.

When the wind is blowing decidedly N of E, a comfortable anchorage will be found in either of the two indentations along the northern side of the bay.

Christmas Cove, Great St. James (25647) is immediately S of Current Cut and opposite Cowpet Bay. Anchor either N or S of Fish Cay, keeping in mind that the lay of the boat is sometimes influenced by the wind blowing through the cut in the island. The approach to either anchorage is clear of dangers, but be careful of the reef area, which extends E and slightly N of Fish Cay. The protection is good in easterly winds and the holding excellent in sand. Swimming and snorkeling are superb.

Although the shoreline of the reef area appears desolate and rocky at low tide, closer observation will unfold a teeming intertidal community of marine life.

This anchorage is popular with charter boats based in St. Thomas because it is the first or last stop when running to or from St. Thomas.

Current Cut (25647) derives its name from the strong tidal current in the passage between St. Thomas and Great St. James Islands. As you approach the cut, determine the direction of the current by looking for the rip which is almost always present. The smooth-water side of the cut is the side from which the current is coming. The rip is formed *after* the current has passed through the cut. If you see no rip, you can assume the current is slack.

Of the two passages through the cut, the eastern passage (leaving Current Rock to the W) is favored by most commercial boats. There's a minimum of 23 feet through here, with ample room for two boats to pass. If you plan to sail through when the wind is E, or S of E, expect to be blanketed by Great St. James just as you reach the narrowest part of the passage.

The western passage is neither as wide nor as deep as the other. At its shallowest point, this channel has 8 feet, but stay in midchannel, because there are rocks and reefs on both sides. The current is less on the W side of Current Rock, and there is little or no blanketing effect from Great St. James.

Pillsbury Sound (25647) is generally clear of dangers, with only a few exceptions.

In the vicinity of Cabrita Point—the headland between Great Bay and Redhook—stand well clear of the underwater rocks that extend from the point. It's wise to hold at least 100 yards off the point, for these rocks are just under the surface and practically impossible to see until you are on top of them. Then they seem to "jump" right up from the bottom. No wonder that the outermost rock is known as Jumping Rock.

The reef extending SW from Moravian Point on St. John is unmarked. While the passage through this reef may be attempted with caution by yachts drawing no more than 9 feet, the recommended route is around the outside of the reef. The route around is easily negotiated, because the outermost part of the reef is awash or breaking in all weather.

Pass inside of Shark Island off the NE coast of St. Thomas if you wish. The Brothers are clearly marked and can be left close at hand. There are no hazards around Durloe Cays except for the obvious sandbanks extending from the shore, and the water is so clear that any rocks are easily seen. Between Durloe Cays and St. John, the tide runs quite a bit stronger than between Durloe Cays and Lovango Cay.

Redhook (25647) is located at the eastern end of St. Thomas, just N of Cabrita Point. Ferries running between St. Thomas and St. John use the government dock, while the Caneel Bay ferry boats and the Park Department boats have their own dock on the S side of this bay.

Next to the government dock is the Lagoon Marina, a full service operation and an excellent source for sport-fishing information. The bottom shallows to 3 or 4 feet at the head of the bay, just W of Lagoon Marina. The holding is good in soft mud and sand.

Although the protection is fair to good, a ground swell usually runs into the harbor, which can make living aboard rather uncomfortable. Swimming is not recommended because of the generally murky water. This is a convenient anchorage if you want to pick up passengers without going all the way back to St. Thomas Harbor. Taxis can usually be found (at least during the day) for trips to town (about 30 minutes), or to the small shopping center and supermarket at Fort Milner (about 10 minutes).

Magen's Bay (25641) on the N side of St. Thomas has one of the island's loveliest beaches. The approach is straightforward and free of dangers. The best anchorage is about 100 yards from the beach in the eastern corner, where the holding is good in sand. A slight ground swell is usually present; otherwise, protection is good under most conditions, except in the winter, when rollers may make the anchorage untenable. It is not recommended as an overnight anchorage from October through May.

A restaurant of sorts dispenses hamburgers and beer during the day.

St. John

Practically uninhabited until 1717, although under Danish sovereignty, St. John suddenly felt the effect of the boom in sugar, and within ten years most of the island was taken up with prosperous plantations—109 of them, to be exact. The population had risen to about 200 whites and over 1,000 slaves. A dry summer in 1733 reduced the food supply and caused much discontent, which, along with other harsh conditions, resulted in a bloody slave revolt that left most of the whites on the island dead, except those who were able to find refuge at the plantation at Caneel Bay.

The slaves roamed the island for five months. Then a force of 200 Frenchmen from Martinique arrived to help restore order on the island, but it never seemed the same after the massacre.

The abolition of slavery in 1848 brought a definite end to what little was left of the sugar economy of St. John, and the island remained very sparsely populated and poverty-stricken until Laurance S. Rockefeller began to buy up property.

Mr. Rockefeller has long been interested in the Virgin Islands, and his commercial operations (Rockresorts) there include Caneel Bay Plantation, on St. John, and Little Dix Bay Hotel, with its associated yacht harbor, on Virgin Gorda. In 1956, Mr. Rockefeller gave over half of St. John to the U.S. for use as a National Park. The park area has been gradually expanded, and now more than two-thirds of this heavily wooded island, with its mountain trails, sandy beaches, and wonderland of submerged reefs, is under the management of the Park Service and open for all to enjoy. The southwest corner of the island, and some waterfront property on the west side of Coral Bay, are privately owned and may be headed for aggressive development.

While in park waters, there are a number of regulations that must be observed; breaking these rules may bring heavy fines. National Park Rangers may at any time board any vessel to examine documents and licenses or simply to inspect the vessel.

Here are some of these regulations:

1. No damaging, breaking off, or removing any underwater growth or formation (coral, sea fans) or in any other way impairing the natural beauty of the underwater scene.

2. Anchors must not cause damage to underwater features.

3. No tampering with wrecks without a written permit from the Park Department.

4. No boat may anchor or maneuver within waters containing marked underwater trails.

5. No water skiing.

6. No rubbish or other refuse may be discarded.

7. Cats or dogs are not allowed ashore at Hawksnest, Trunk Bay, and Cinnamon Bay. Elsewhere, pets must be on leash at all times.

8. Do not moor boats to trees or other vegetation ashore.

9. Keep beaches clean. No beach fires permitted.

For additional information contact the Ranger Stations at Redhook, Cruz Bay, or Lameshur Bay; or the Superintendent, Virgin Islands National Park, Box 1707, Charlotte Amalie, St. Thomas, V.I. 00801.

Cruz Bay (25647), on the western side of St. John, is the major harbor and the largest town on the island. It boasts a telephone service, a small hospital, a bank, a department store, a grocery store, and the Park Service Headquarters, where you can get charts and park literature. Last but not least, there is an excellent bakery, where chocolate-chip cookies and brownies may be purchased. The Administrator's home and office are located on the headland in the center of the harbor, and the U.S. Customs and Immigration offices are across the street from the town jetty.

The town is usually quiet, except on Friday and Saturday nights. Taxis are available at the head of the jetty for tours around this lovely island.

The approach to Cruz Bay is partly obstructed by a reef that extends N from Galge Point, but a lighted marker marks the northernmost edge of this reef. Pass N of this marker, favoring the northern side of the entrance.

Once inside, a safe anchorage will be found about 50 yards off the end of the town jetty, or in the northern part of the bay. The holding is good, in sand. Be wary of the southern portion of the bay, as the bottom shoals rapidly.

The jetty is used by the ferries from St. Thomas, as well as by all the rest of the commercial traffic, and cannot be recommended for a yacht. The protection is good, and except for the wash created by the commercial traffic, the anchorage is calm.

Caneel Bay (25647), less than a mile NE of Cruz Bay, is the site of the well-known Caneel Bay Plantation, one of the loveliest and best-run hotels in the Virgins. This elegant establishment was conceived by Laurance Rockefeller and tastefully designed and built about the time the Virgin Islands National Park came into being. Advance reservations are necessary to dine in this splendorous setting overlooking a fleet of anchored yachts and, in the distance, the line of islands that enclose Pillsbury Sound.

On the rise of land behind the main hotel, you can walk among the ruins of

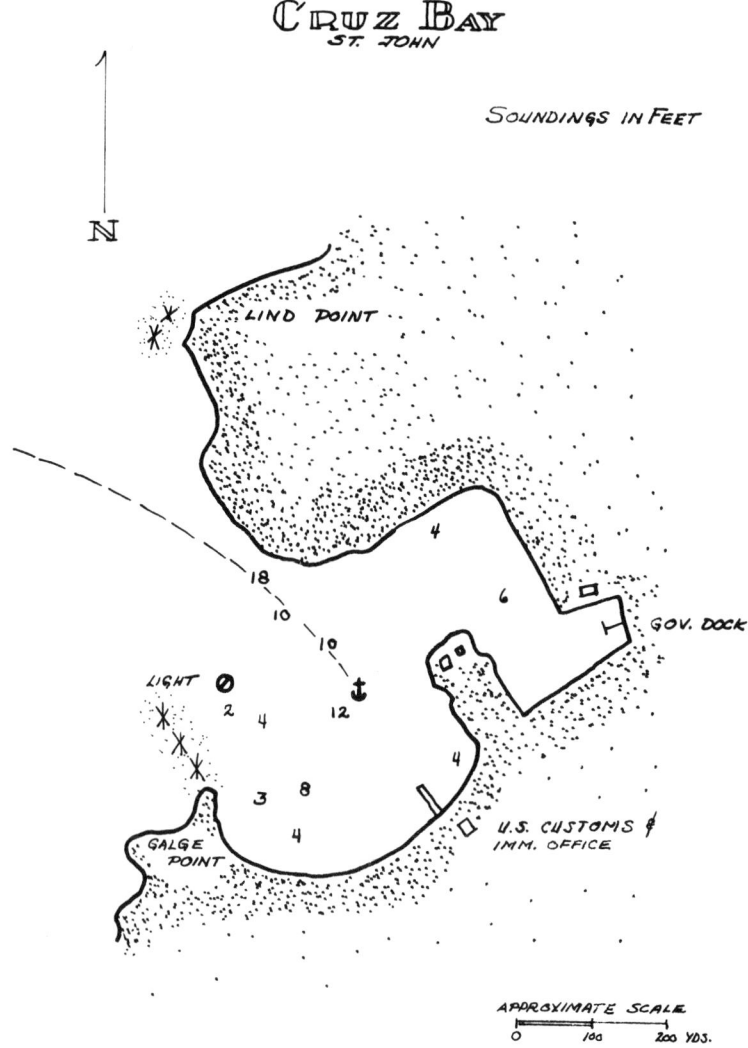

the sugar mill and the Greathouse of what was originally the Durloe Plantation. Durloe must have had a premonition of impending trouble, because he built his home in the manner of a fort, maintained a small arsenal, and even mounted a small cannon on the roof. This house was the one place on St. John where the whites were able to hold out against the maddened slaves during the 1733 revolt.

The approach is open from all directions. The best anchorage is in the NE side of the bay, over a sandy bottom, and outside of the swimming buoys. You may find it crowded, though. The swimming is excellent everywhere, and the little reef on the N side of the bay will interest the snorkelers.

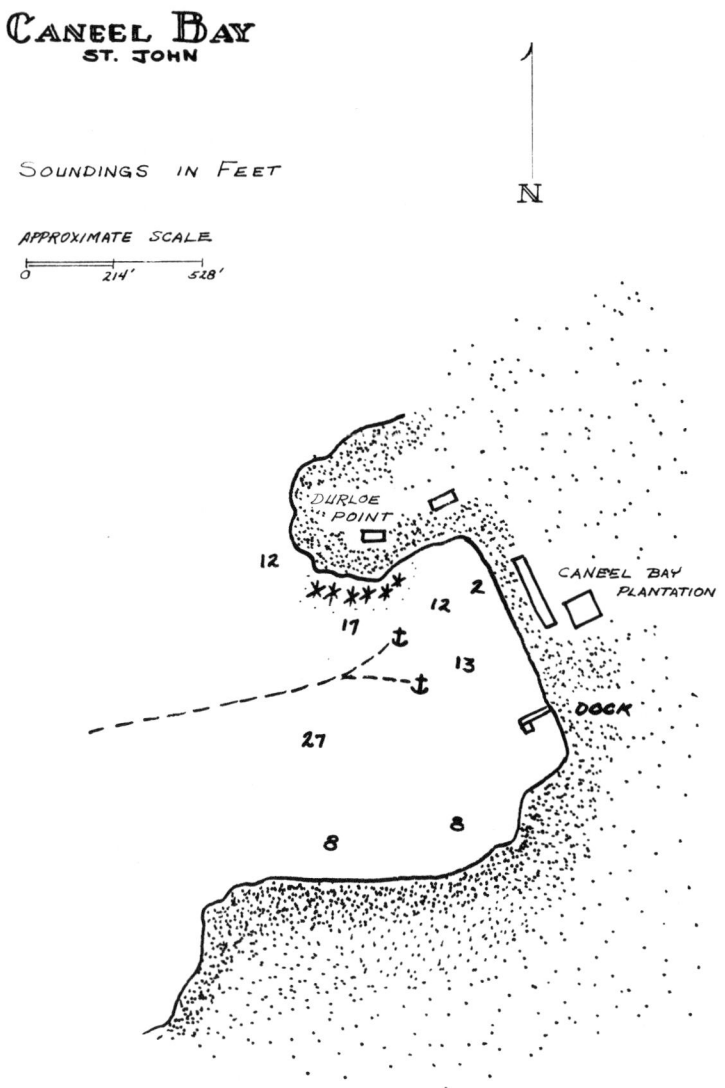

CANEEL BAY
ST. JOHN

SOUNDINGS IN FEET

APPROXIMATE SCALE

Although this anchorage offers excellent protection in easterly winds, it can become quite uncomfortable, even untenable, if the wind moves W of N, or if ground swells come in.

Hawksnest, or Hogsnest Bay (25647), located just around the point from Caneel Bay, boasts three separate, lovely beaches. Unfortunately, this bay is so open to the N that we cannot recommend it as an overnight anchorage during the winter, but it makes a fine lunch or afternoon stop under the right conditions. The center beach is equipped with barbecue pits and tables. The best

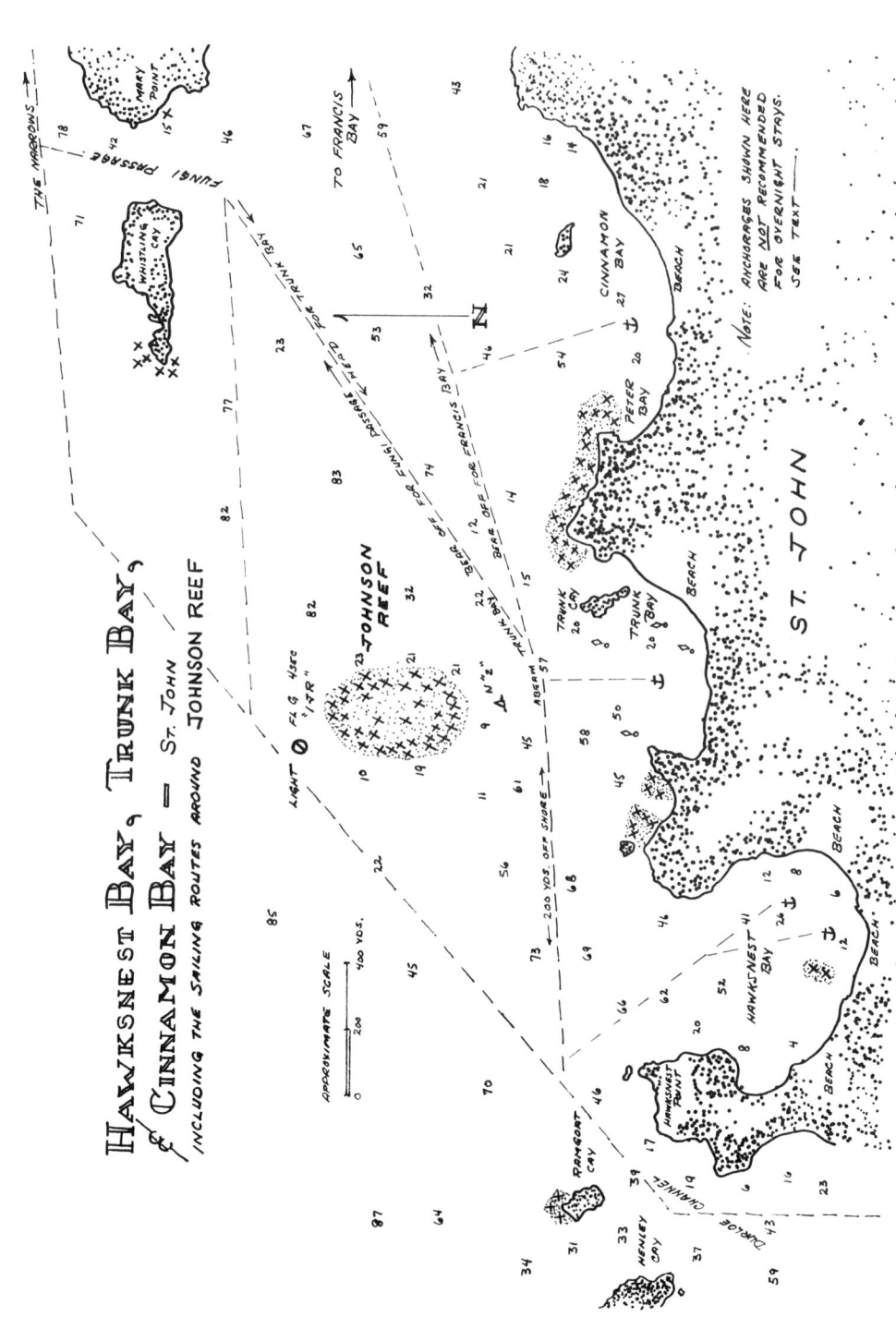

Hawksnest Bay, Trunk Bay, & Cinnamon Bay — St. John

including the sailing routes around Johnson Reef

NOTE: ANCHORAGES SHOWN HERE ARE NOT RECOMMENDED FOR OVERNIGHT STAYS. SEE TEXT.

APPROXIMATE SCALE
0   200   400 YDS.

N

ST. JOHN

anchorage seems to be in the SE corner, 50 to 100 yards off the beach. Stay clear of the reef in the southern part of the bay.

The holding is good in sand, and the swimming excellent. Be prepared for a constant ground swell, caused primarily by the strong tidal stream running across the entrance.

Trunk Bay (25647), just E of Hawksnest Bay, is the most popular swimming and snorkeling spot E of St. Thomas—and with the crowds have come the regulations. An underwater trail, supervised by the Park Service and complete with signs and labels, may appeal to the beginning snorkeler. Ashore is a lunch counter and a bathhouse with showers—nothing primitive here.

You are expected to anchor (without breaking any coral) seaward of the buoys marking the swimming area, and you must land your dinghy (propelled by oars alone) at the western end of the beach.

A slight ground swell is almost always present, and because of the possibility of rollers, this is yet another anchorage that cannot be recommended for an overnight stay during the winter.

Johnson Reef (25647), lying immediately N of Trunk Bay, is now flanked by buoys; it is not the navigational hazard it once was. The western side is steep-to, but the eastern side shoals rather slowly in spots, with isolated outcroppings, and should be approached with caution. A nun buoy marks the southern extremity of this reef, and a black, lighted buoy defines the northern limit.

The reef breaks in all but the calmest conditions, and when the rollers are on the move, seas have been known to break all the way from the reef to the headland of St. John.

The underwater scenery will appeal to the skin diver or snorkeler when the sea is calm. Park Service regulations apply to this reef, so be guided accordingly.

Cinnamon Bay (25647) has a lovely beach under Park Service supervision. Along this strand are complete camping facilities, barbecues, a store, and a cafeteria—for those who like the rough life. Cabins and tent sites are so popular that reservations have to be made far in advance.

The anchorage is comfortable enough under standard conditions, with just a hint of a ground swell. Being exposed to the N, it's not recommended as an overnight anchorage in winter.

Maho Bay (25647), the small area in the S corner of larger Francis Bay, is a lovely overnight anchorage during the summer, but in winter you may find an uncomfortable ground swell. The approach is straightforward, and a good anchorage, in sand and grass, will be found 50 to 100 yards off the beach. Watch your depthfinder as you move in.

The house on the bluff above the bay was built by six donkeys, a couple of natives, and Mrs. Ethel McCully. She wrote an amusing book about it which she originally entitled *I Did It with Donkeys.* When the publisher said no to this title, she changed it to *Grandma Raises the Roof.*

Francis Bay (25647) offers a comfortable anchorage under almost all conditions. Drop the hook 50 to 100 yards off the beach, where there is a picnic area

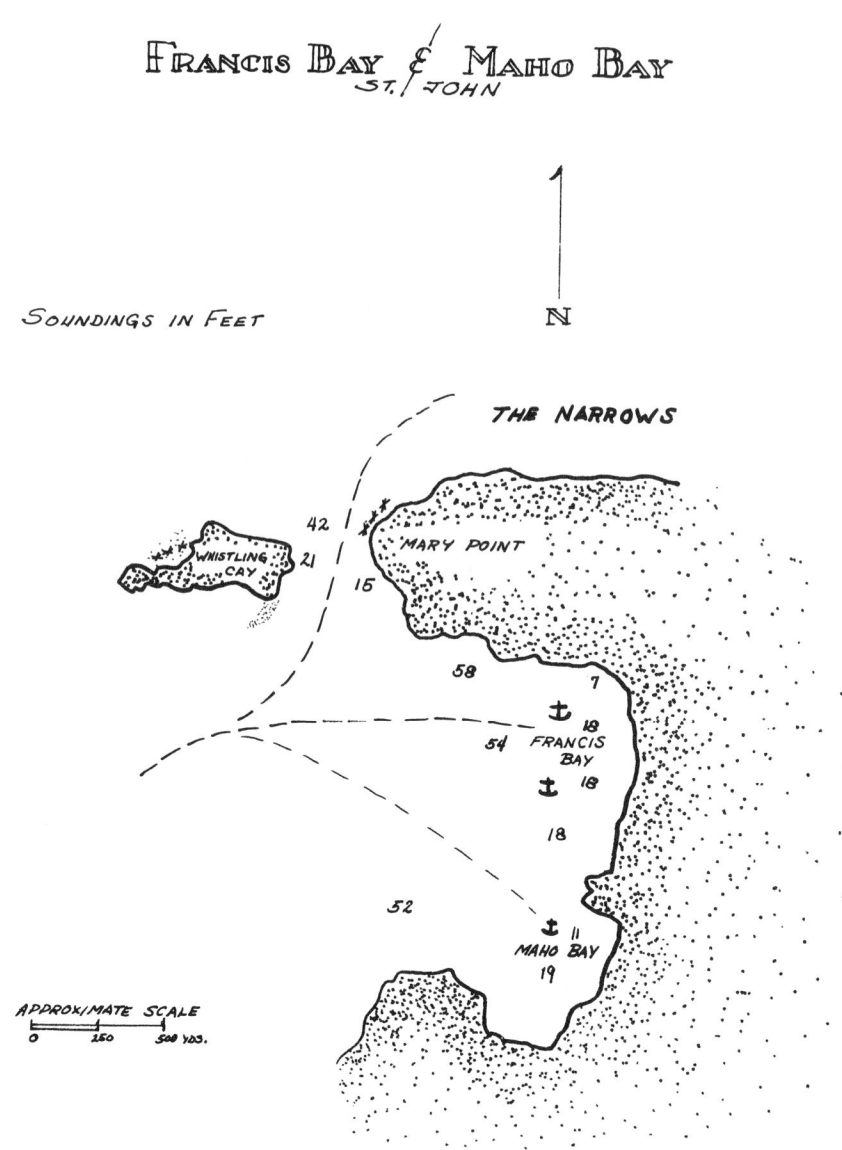

FRANCIS BAY & MAHO BAY
ST. JOHN

SOUNDINGS IN FEET

N

THE NARROWS

WHISTLING CAY

42
21
15

MARY POINT

58
7

54   FRANCIS
BAY

18

18

52

MAHO BAY
19

APPROXIMATE SCALE
0   250   500 YDS.

just N of a post marking the boundary of the National Park. Holding is good in the sand-mud or grass bottom.

From the picnic place, a hiking trail leads to an abandoned plantation house in the col above, whence a new black-topped road runs along the shore of Leinster Bay to the Annaberg sugar mill—but it's a long walk.

At night, in this crystal-clear bay, the beam of a flashlight directed into the water looks like a yellow-white column straight to the bottom. Held still, this column of light will attract a variety of fish. Some will attack it, others come for a look; all are interesting to watch. If you look closely, you may see a small, white sand shark circling quietly just outside the shaft of light.

Fungi Passage (25647) is a deep passage between Whistling Cay and Mary Point, with very little current. A shoal extends a short way S from the SE tip of Whistling Cay.

As you pass through the cut, you will see the ruins of a Customs House or signal post that may have been used to communicate with a similar post on Little Thatch or Frenchman's Cay on the north side of The Narrows. Another conjecture is that the building was manned by armed lookouts stationed there by the Danish planters to intercept slaves attempting to run away to Tortola, where they hoped to find asylum at the British settlement at West End.

Mary Point, on the north side of this passage, is the spot where hundreds of slaves are said to have jumped to their death rather than submit to capture after the great slave uprising of 1733.

The Narrows (BA2452) creates a funnel of wind and current, but the seas seldom exceed 2 or 3 feet. There are no hazards, and yachts may sail to within 50 yards of either shore. To "play" the current most effectively, hold to the St. John side of the passage when eastbound, and to the Tortola side going west.

Leinster Bay (BA2452) gives you a choice of three anchorages, all of them safe in any but the most unusual conditions. The normal approach is W of Water Lemon (or Watermelon) Cay, but you may pass cautiously on the other side of this cay through a 12-foot-deep channel.

The two most popular anchorages are on the eastern side. One just S of Water Lemon Cay offers little protection from the trade winds (which is a happy choice when it's buggy) but the sea is always calm behind the cay. The holding is excellent in sand, but space is limited, since the bottom drops off rapidly. The cay was serving as a landing pad for a large group of pelicans the last time we were there.

The other anchorage in the eastern part of the bay is in Water Lemon Bay (sometimes called Limejuice Bay, sometimes Watermelon Bay). In any case, this anchorage is in the SE corner of Leinster Bay. Depths hold at 20 to 25 feet

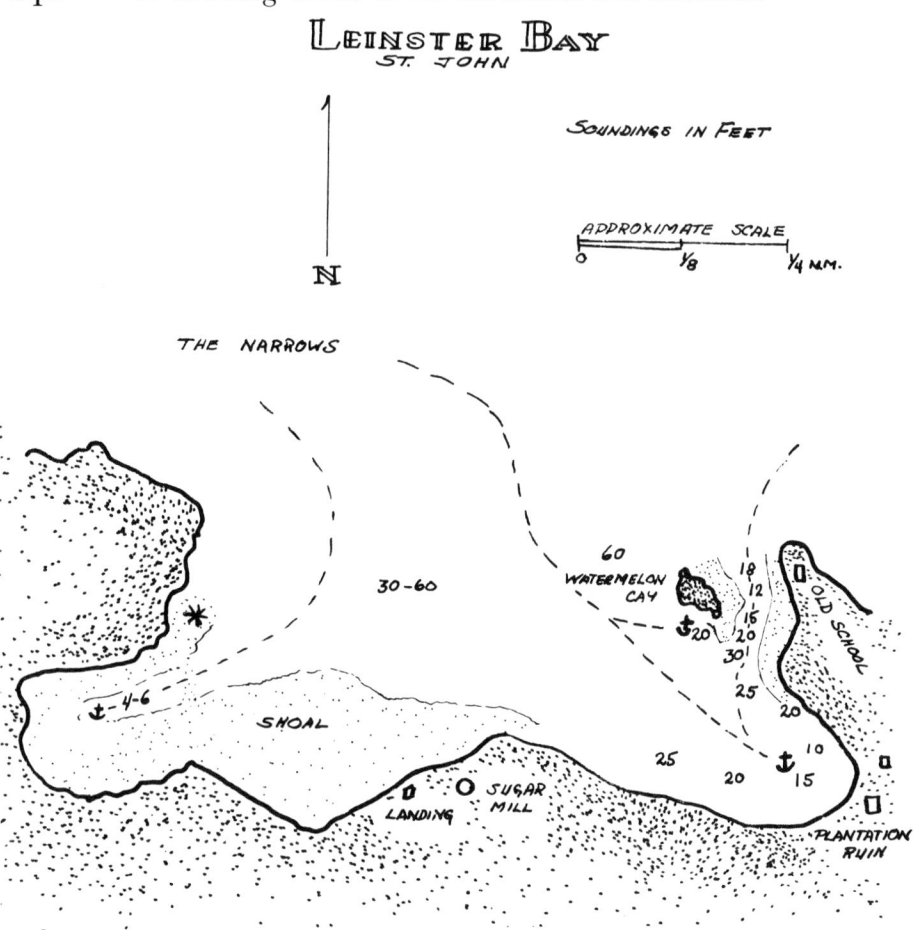

LEINSTER BAY
ST. JOHN

within 50 or 100 feet of this entire shoreline, until you approach the very head of the bay, where it shoals slightly. The holding is good, in sand and grass.

The ruins of Limetree Plantation standing at the head of the bay will interest the explorers in your crew. So will the ruins of a school at the top of the hill on the NE point of Leinster Bay. This building was originally a Masonic Lodge, the first one built in the Western Hemisphere. The view is spectacular and well worth the rugged climb. Take your camera.

The third and least used anchorage is Mary Creek, in the western part of the bay. The sandbank that straddles the entrance to this anchorage limits draft to 4 feet or less, but once over the bar, the creek becomes wider and deepens to about 6 feet. Holding is excellent in sand, and conditions are always calm, despite the exposure to the wind. In fact, this windward situation makes this anchorage relatively bug-free during the damp seasons. Two or three yachts can anchor here comfortably.

On sailing into Leinster Bay, you will notice some ruins on the southern slope overlooking the bay. These are all that remain of the Annaberg Plantation, once one of the largest sugar plantations on St. John. Along the path leading to the mill, you will find a small stand that usually contains pamphlets describing the ruins, which are supervised by the Park Service. There is a dinghy landing W of the ruins, or you can walk along the road from Limetree Plantation.

From Leinster Bay and The Narrows you look across to Great and Little Thatch Islands and to Soper's Hole, which is the first port of entry for the British Virgins after leaving St. John.

Haulover Bay (BA2452), just 2½ miles E of Leinster Bay, is the only other anchorage on the north coast of St. John that holds much interest for visiting yachtsmen. In times gone by, fishermen hauled their boats over this low land into Coral Bay in preference to sailing or rowing around the point.

Shoals encroach slightly from both sides of the entrance, so keep to the center as you come in. The best anchorage is in the SE corner near a small beach. Depths range from 60 to 20 feet, until you come within 10 yards of the beach, where it shoals to 10 feet or less. This is a very constricted anchorage; it would be crowded with two boats, but the protection is good under almost all conditions.

Coral Bay (BA2452), the largest bay on St. John, will be considered in three sections.

The easternmost, and undoubtedly the most beautiful, is Round Bay. Stay well clear of the reef off Moor Point as you enter, and pick an anchorage off any of the beaches on the eastern side. Holding is excellent in sand, and the protection is good under almost all conditions, though there is always a slight ground swell. The two little beaches on the N side of Round Bay are rocky, and anchoring off of them is less comfortable. The western side of the bay should be avoided. A rather nasty reef, always awash and breaking, extends its full length.

If the ground swells become uncomfortable in Round Bay, you can move into one of the four small bays in Hurricane Hole. There is nothing much here but solitude, and the bugs are usually fierce during the rainy season. However, this midsection of Coral Bay is a major haven for yachtsmen during the hurricane season. All four bays are deep and free of hidden dangers, although they shoal rather rapidly close to shore.

Coral Harbor is not as deep as the rest of Coral Bay, and yachts drawing over 6 feet should stay in midchannel and proceed cautiously. There are no dangers in the approach, except shallow water and a rock here and there off the northeastern shore. Nevertheless, deep-draft yachts should favor that shore slightly when entering. The anchorage is well protected and calm under most conditions, and the holding is good in sand and mud.

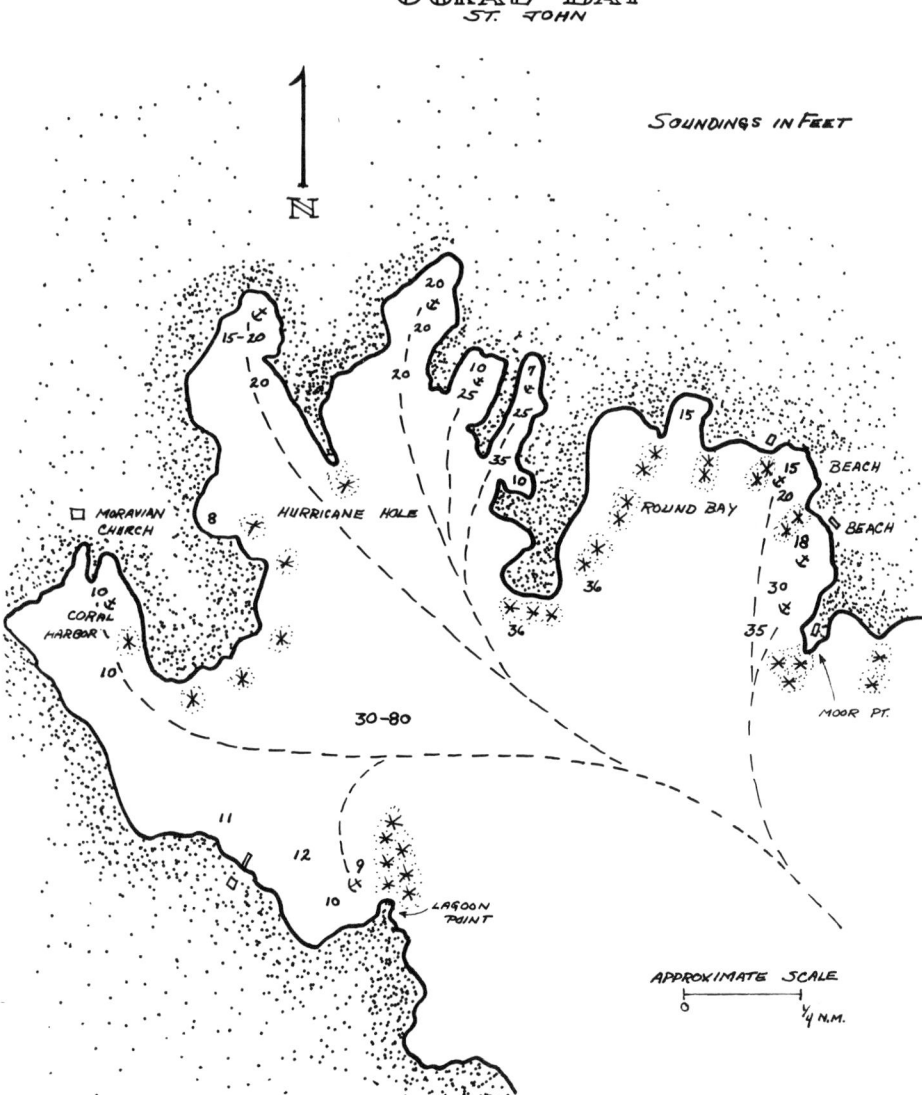

CORAL BAY
ST. JOHN

SOUNDINGS IN FEET

A small native community is clustered around the head of the harbor. Practically nothing can be obtained there except smiles and conversation. In a move to modernize the place, a telephone has been installed next to the school. The Moravian Church has an interesting history, if you can persuade one of the locals to tell you the story. It may seem hard to believe now, but in St. John's sugar-producing days, Coral Harbor was as busy as the harbor at St. Thomas.

There's another anchorage in Coral Bay, just off the southern shore of Lagoon Point, and well protected by a reef that extends N from that point.

When approaching from the E, be sure to stand well clear of the reef. The swimming is excellent here, and the reef affords good snorkeling on calm days.

When approaching Coral Bay from the S, extreme care should be taken to stay clear of the Eagle Shoal ½-mile E of Ram Head. If passing inside this shoal, keep the shore close at hand and continue northward between Sabbat Point and Leduck Island. Once past the island, you will be clear of dangers. When passing outside of Eagle Shoal, keep S of a line between Ram Head and the southern shore of Norman's Island. When Leduck Island bears 359°T, you will be clear of the shoal.

Salt Pond Bay (BA2452), the first cove around the corner of Ram Head, is an excellent anchorage. The big reef in the middle of the entrance has deep water on both sides. Anchor in the NE corner on a sandy bottom. The Park Service maintains a picnic area on the beach and some pleasant hiking trails.

Great Lameshur Bay (BA2452) is a well-sheltered overnight anchorage. In 1970, this was the site of the Tektite Project in long-term undersea living. All that remains of this important undertaking is the stone dock and the headquarters building on the cliff.

Little Lameshur Bay (BA2452) is as well sheltered as its bigger brother. Favor the western shore.

Reef Bay (BA2452, 25647) is an interesting lunch stop or afternoon anchorage, but is not recommended for overnight unless the wind is well to the N and expected to stay there. Being wide open to the S, a ground swell is usually present. This bay is "Genti Bay" on chart 25647.

When approaching, stay clear of the reefs, which are awash or breaking along both sides. The center of the bay is deep and clear. As you approach the anchorage ahead, you'll notice the reefs on both sides dwindle to nothing. Continue slowly past the reefs and into the head of the bay. Anchor in 7-to-10 feet about 200 feet from shore, just E of the old sugar mill (the stack is visible above the treetops).

The area abounds with lime trees. A path leads to a waterfall (it performs during the rainy season) and some ancient Indian petroglyphs.

Fish Bay (25647), immediately W of Reef Bay, is a good anchorage under normal conditions, although a slight ground swell is almost always experienced.

Stay in midchannel; reefs extend a short way from both sides. Proceed cautiously into the bay, as the bottom shoals rather rapidly. Yachts drawing 8 to 10 feet should anchor just outside the mouth of the bay; those of lesser draft

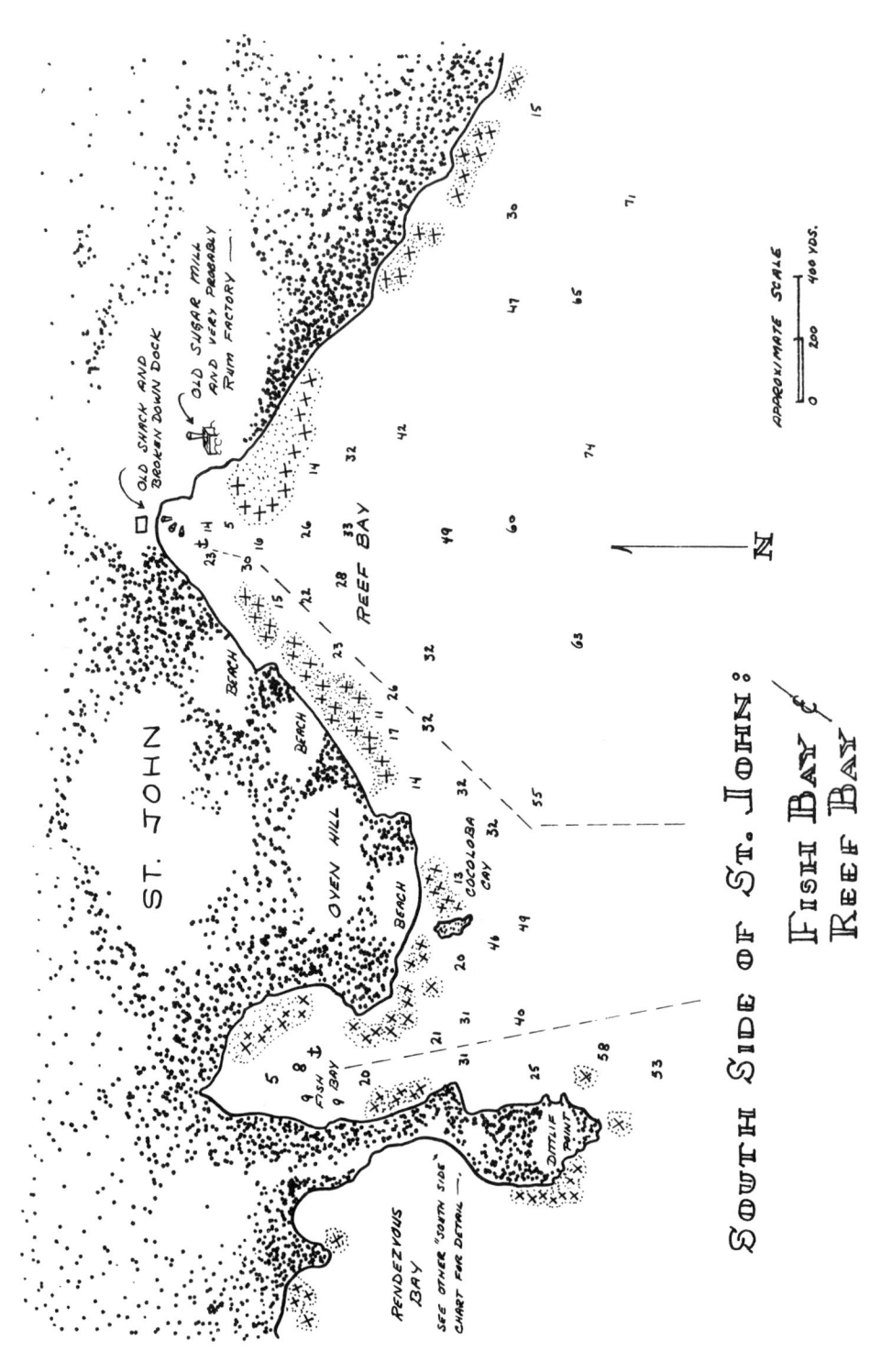

SOUTH SIDE OF ST. JOHN:

FISH BAY &
REEF BAY

may continue well in, where it is generally calm. The holding is good in sand and mud.

A little beach on the eastern side of the entrance is surrounded by reefs but fun to explore. Farther E, just outside the entrance and behind Cocolobo Cay, is a larger beach that can be approached by dinghy through the coral heads, when sea conditions allow.

Fishermen will appreciate the bonefish flats at the head of the bay.

Rendezvous Bay (25647) offers little protection for overnight unless the wind is well N of E. However, one anchorage within this rather open bay is adequate under normal conditions—at least as a lunch or afternoon stop. It's just off the small beach in Ditleff Bay. Holding is good in sand and grass. Expect a slight ground swell at any time of the year.

Chocolate Hole (25647), just W of Rendezvous Bay, is pleasant, quiet, and well sheltered. The approach is straightforward, though you should favor the western side, as a small reef makes out about 15 to 20 yards from Sam Point. Yachts drawing 6 feet or less may approach to within 20 yards of the first line of moorings. From this point to the head of the bay, the bottom shoals rapidly to 4 feet and less. Holding is good in sand and grass.

The little reef on the E side of the entrance will interest snorkelers.

Great Cruz Bay (25647), on the SW corner of St. John, is not particularly scenic but does afford good protection in most conditions. The sea is generally calm, but with a slight ground swell, and holding is good in sand and grass.

The entrance is wide and unobstructed, except for a small reef extending from the N side. The best anchorage is about halfway to the head of the bay and 50 yards or so off the southeastern shore. The bay is shoal near its head.

St. Croix (BA485)

Although the largest of the U.S. Virgins, St. Croix (pronounced "Saint Kroy") is not a cruising ground to compare with the islands that ring Sir Francis Drake Channel. In fact, Christiansted is the only real harbor in St. Croix, and Christiansted depends upon a protecting reef to the north to earn its definition as a harbor. Lacking are the high hills that encircle so many other harbors and anchorages in the main body of the Virgins. But St. Croix has attractions other than the usual cruising amenities. Its Danish heritage is more evident here, and a stronger sense of history seems to pervade the place.

Sugar was always king on St. Croix, and because its terrain was so well suited to the cultivation of cane, the industry died very slowly on this island. The mill towers, the brick stacks, and the crumbling walls of the estate houses still stand

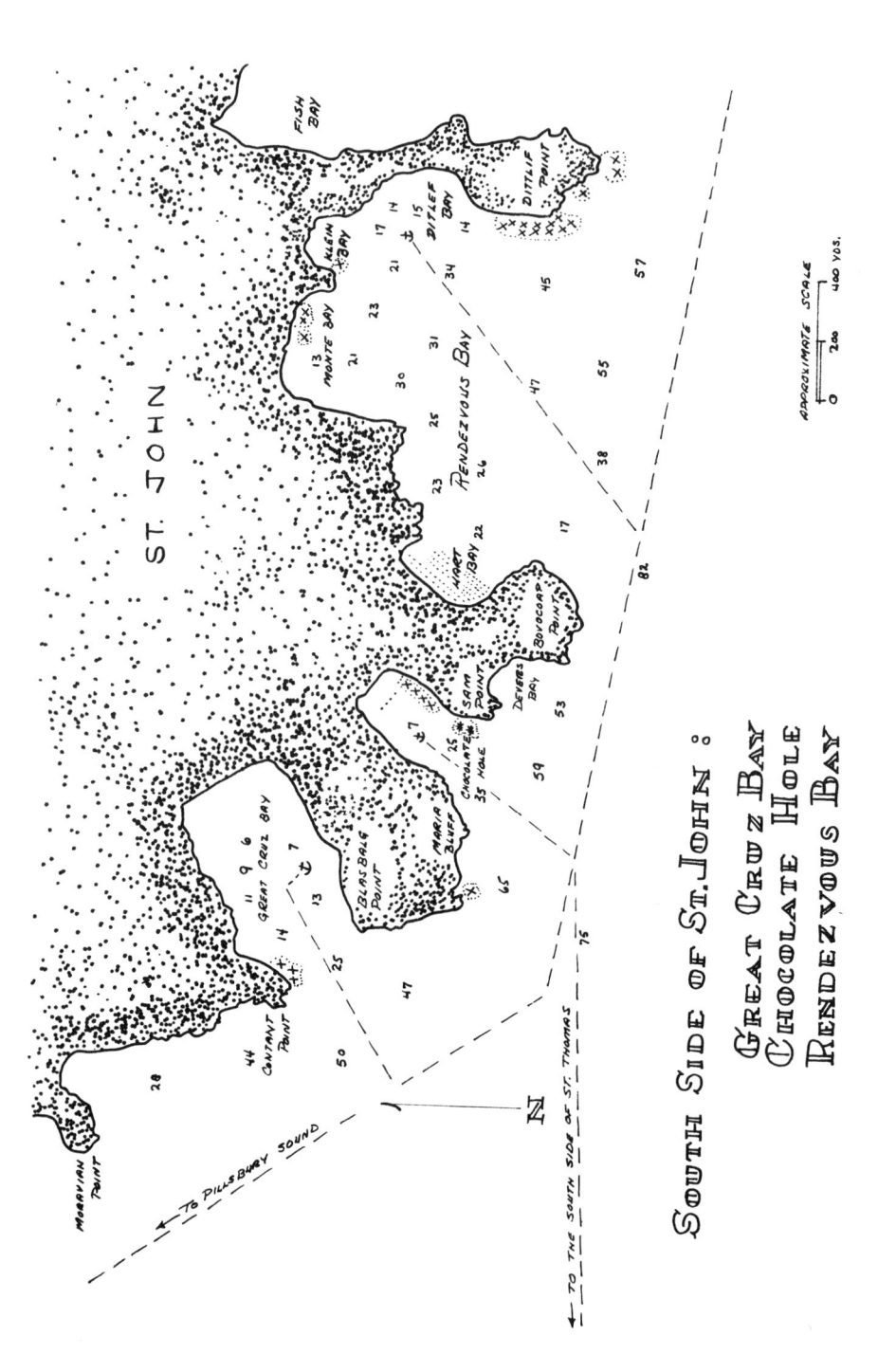

ST. JOHN

MORAVIAN POINT

TO PILLSBURY SOUND →

CANTANT POINT

GREAT CRUZ BAY

BLAS BALG POINT

MARIA BLUFF

CHOCOLATE POINT

35 HOLE

SAM POINT

DEVERS BAY

BOVOCOAP POINT

HART BAY

RENDEZVOUS BAY

MONTE BAY

KLEIN BAY

DITLEF BAY

FISH BAY

DITLEF POINT

28

44

50

47

25

14

13

7

11 9 6

13 ‡ 7

65

59

53

‡ 1

25

22

17

82

38

55

57

45

34

21

17

15 14

14

23

21

13

25

31

30

23

26

47

N

← TO THE SOUTH SIDE OF ST. THOMAS

APPROXIMATE SCALE

0   200   400 YDS.

SOUTH SIDE OF ST. JOHN :

GREAT CRUZ BAY
CHOCOLATE HOLE
RENDEZVOUS BAY

out against the shoreline. To see such sights out of the past is the most persuasive reason for sailing to St. Croix—but isn't that reason enough? Sightseeing is so much of what cruising is all about, anyway. All too often, St. Croix is not included in the brief itinerary of the visiting yachtsman, but if you have time to spare and can afford to choose your days to make the crossings, the sail over and back can be an exhilarating experience in ocean sailing.

If the wind is from the east or southeast, which is usually the case, start your southbound crossing from Flanagan or Salt Island Passage. This will allow a close reach, or at least the cracking of sheets, on the way across, and will certainly be more comfortable and faster than the wet beat to weather that you'll have if you leave from St. Thomas Harbor. Plan to leave by 0900, so you'll have ample time to make your anchorage in Christiansted before dark.

During much of the year, the northbound trip is usually the easier crossing, with a comfortable reach or run all the way. But the wind often blows out of the north during the winter, which makes the trip a dead beat to weather. At such times, it's nice to have a few days in hand so that you can afford to wait for more favorable conditions. This north wind, though, has been known to continue for weeks at a time.

Remember that the current sets west between St. Thomas and St. Croix; the velocity depends on the strength of the trade winds. Generally, you are safe in figuring on 1½ knots of current for the entire passage.

Christiansted (25645) is the major harbor and town, located almost in the middle of the north coast of St. Croix. The circuitous entrance to Christiansted Harbor, though well marked, can prove confusing to strangers. On approaching the entrance, you must locate and positively identify the outer buoy. To be sure to avoid the Scotch Bank, establish a heading of 150°T to this buoy while still a mile or two at sea.

This lighted, black buoy should be left close to port as you head straight down the buoyed channel with the radio tower on Fort Louise Augusta dead ahead. Follow the buoys carefully and turn into the anchorage S of Protestant Cay.

The anchorage off the town is usually crowded, and considering all the moorings with their short scope, and the easterly current which runs through here, you will have to use some rather delicate judgment in placing your anchor. Don't head for the wide open water W of the anchored fleet; that is the landing area for flying boats!

St. Croix Marine and Development lies E of the channel, before you make the swing toward the town docks. This is a full-service marina and a competent shipyard, capable of hauling large yachts. To avoid the congestion in the lee of Protestant Cay, you may well prefer to anchor off here, although it is not convenient for trips into town.

CHRISTIANSTED HARBOR
ST. CROIX

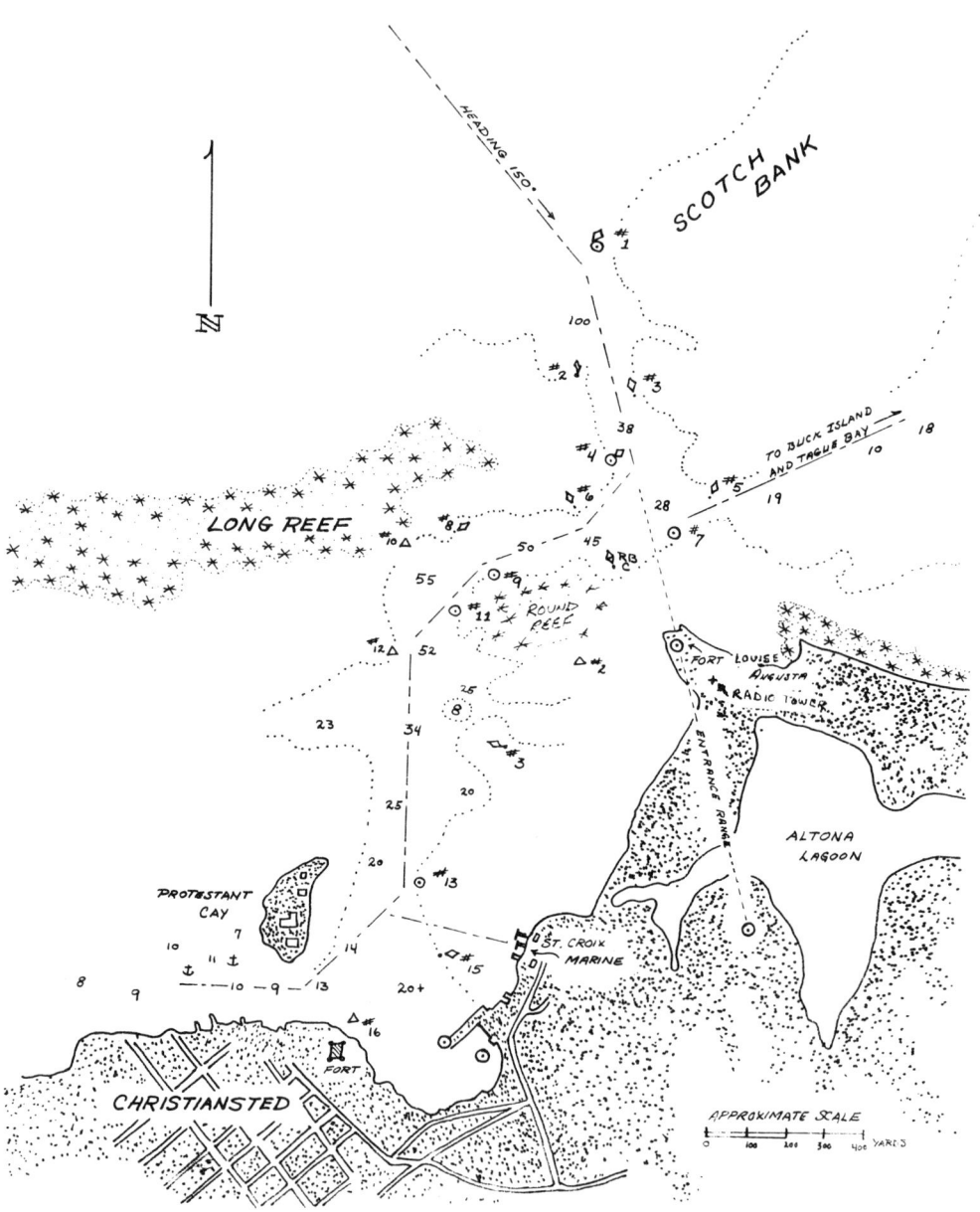

Buck Island (BA485) is a lovely spot for a day's outing from Christiansted, or even an overnight stay. It has the status of a U.S. National Monument.

Follow the main channel out of Christiansted Harbor to Green Flasher "7" and set a course directly for the anchorage on the western end of Buck Island, leaving Can "5" to port and Green Cay at least 50 yards to starboard. Often you'll find the wind directly on the nose, so keep a careful eye on Scotch Bank when short-tacking along this course. This bank is hard to detect under some light conditions.

The best anchorage at Buck Island is just off the lovely sand beach at the western tip of the island. The approach from the SW is clear of hazards and you may anchor very close to the beach. You will have good holding in sand, and the swimming is, of course, excellent.

The famous Buck Island Underwater Park is at the other end of the island, completely enclosed by a barrier reef. On the SE side of the island is a marked opening through this outer reef; yachts drawing slightly over 5 feet can move inside it and anchor. Eyeball your way in, for there are coral heads scattered about, both inside and out. Once inside the lagoon, the holding conditions are good in sand, but the ground swell may make an overnight stay a little uncomfortable.

The National Park Service has installed underwater signs here and there to describe the sea life and to keep you on the trail. Naturally, no spear guns are allowed.

If the prospect of eyeballing your way into the lagoon bothers you, excursion boats leave from Christiansted every day, taking eager snorkelers to the reef.

Tague Bay (BA485) is protected by the reef that stretches along the entire northeastern end of St. Croix. It is the home of the St. Croix Yacht Club, which welcomes visiting yachtsmen and has, in the past, hosted a rendezvous of the Cruising Club of America. It's a busy place on weekends with its fleet of racing dinghies.

Approaching from the W, take up an easterly heading after passing Green Cay, until the old mill tower on the beach at Coakley Bay bears S. Alter course directly toward the tower, and pass through the reef opening, leaving the sandspit to starboard and the breaking reef to port. The pass is approximately 150 yards wide, but keep in midchannel until clear. You will have at least 12 feet in the pass and all the way to Tague Bay. Continue straight along to Tague Bay, staying in midchannel or slightly toward the shore, as there are isolated coral heads, clearly visible, close to the reef.

Upon reaching the westernmost point of Tague Bay, yachts drawing less than 6 feet can continue straight to the club dock. Those with greater draft can go about half the distance to the yacht club. The bottom shoals rapidly once inside the bay itself; the southwestern section is quite shallow and should be

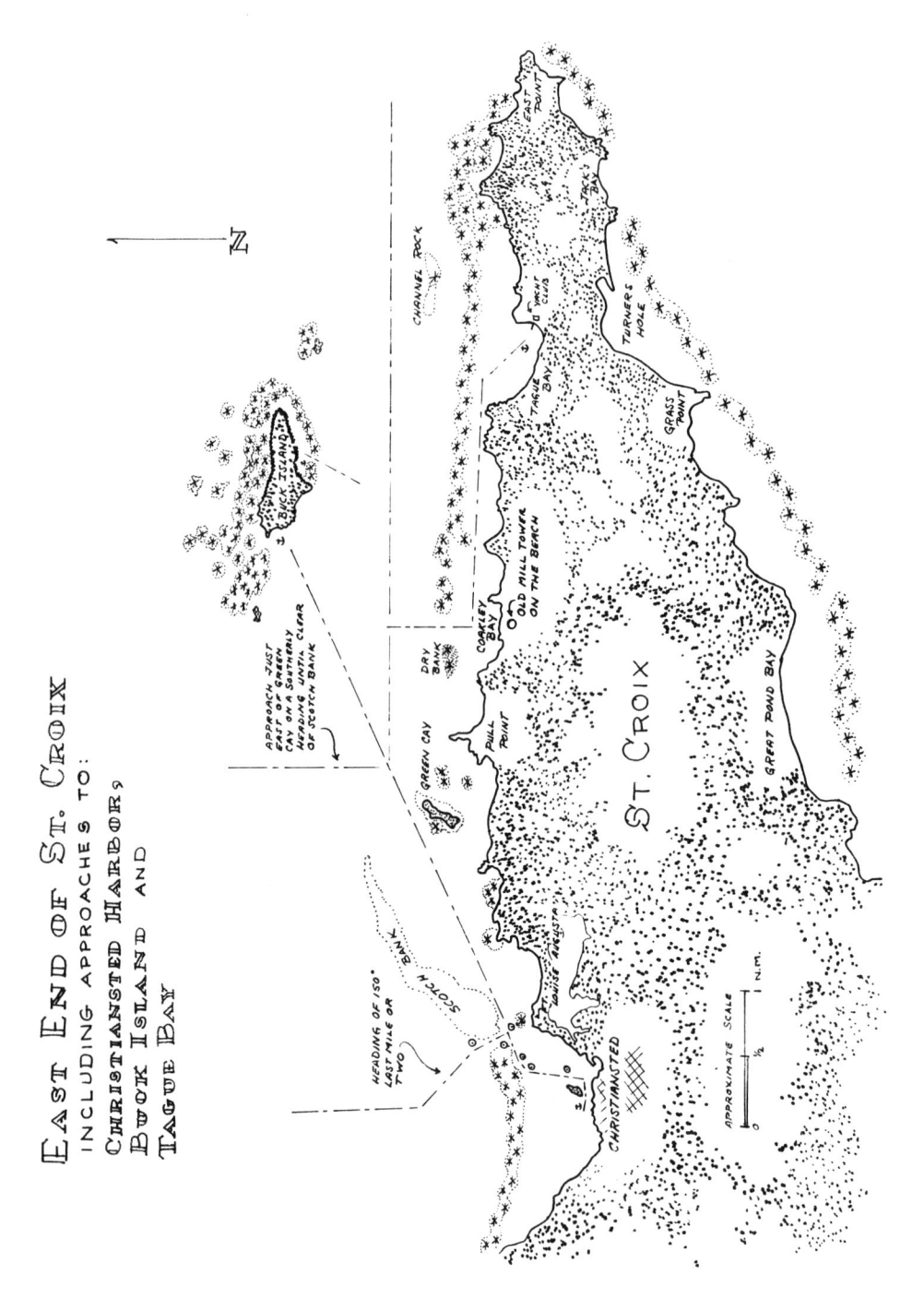

East End of St. Croix

INCLUDING APPROACHES TO:

Christiansted Harbor, Buck Island and Tague Bay

N

CHANNEL ROCK

EAST POINT

ISAAC BAY

YACHT CLUB

TURNERS HOLE

TAGUE BAY

GRASS POINT

OLD MILL TOWER ON THE BEACH

COAKLEY BAY

GREAT POND BAY

ST. CROIX

DRY BAY

PULL POINT

APPROACH JUST EAST OF GREEN CAY ON A SOUTHERLY HEADING UNTIL CLEAR OF SCOTCH BANK

BUCK ISLAND

GREEN CAY

SCOTCH BANK

HEADING OF 150° LAST MILE OR TWO

LOUISE AUGUSTA

CHRISTIANSTED

APPROXIMATE SCALE

0   ½   1   N.M.

FREDERICKSTED
ST. CROIX

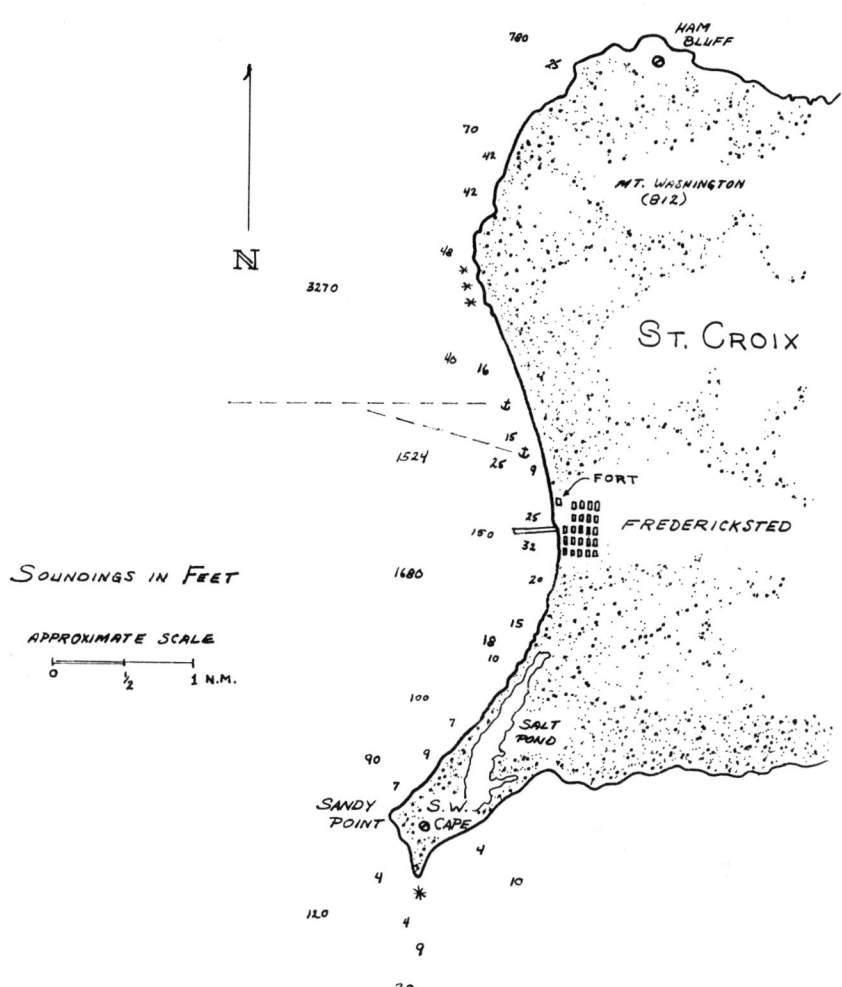

avoided. Holding is good in sand and grass, and sea conditions are always calm. Swimming is excellent.

Frederiksted (25644), on the western end of St. Croix, is the second largest town on the island. Bars, restaurants, and shops do a lively business, catering to passengers from the cruise ships, which use the large commercial wharf.

This anchorage is an open roadstead and cannot offer positive protection except in a period of normal trade winds. The best anchorage is N of the big wharf within 100 yards of shore. The holding is good in sand and the sea is generally calm.

Because of its remoteness and wide open aspect, this anchorage is not very popular. Nevertheless, it is a rather lovely spot, and the town, with its old buildings, has a certain quiet charm.

Salt River (BA485), about 4 miles W of Christiansted, has been the scene of sporadic marina development. We were not particularly impressed with the scenery when we went in there some years ago, but the mangroves and the bugs may have affected our judgment at the time.

When you round Salt River Point, stay outside of White Horse, a detached, breaking reef. The small mouth of Salt River is obstructed by a reef with a pass through it, located about two-thirds the distance W between the two points. Take up a course about due S toward a conspicuous rock, just above the surface, and inside the bar. The reef opening is easy to see on both sides, and there is about 6½ feet over the bar at LW. After crossing the bar, swing ESE and eyeball your way (as best you can in the murky water) to an anchorage as far in as your depthfinder dictates.

This is a scene of early Indian settlements. A little digging may unearth bits of pottery and primitive tools and weapons. Columbus stopped here, seeking to refill his water casks, on November 14th, 1493. He skirmished briefly with some Indians in a canoe, then sailed away to Haiti.

THE BRITISH VIRGIN ISLANDS

Tortola and Adjacent Islands

During the 18th century, the residents of Tortola were quite openly engaged in the business of piracy. Businessmen, planters, doctors, and other respected members of the community apparently owned privateer sloops and cobles, which preyed on shipping throughout the islands. Goods, slaves, and produce were hijacked by these "Tortola Pirates" and either ransomed back to the owners or sold elsewhere.

During a period of overlapping states of war, declared or not, between the major European powers, and lacking any intervention by the local government, such as it was, this grim business flourished for many years. Some historians surmise that the Customs House on Whistling Cay was used as a signaling station to alert the privateers of approaching ships.

Tortola has had periods of wealth and fame, poverty and hurricanes; it has had slave uprisings, warfare, and religious dissension among Quakers, Anglicans, and Methodists. Tortola today is the most populated of the British Virgin Islands and has recently experienced something of a building boom brought on by the burgeoning tourist trade. Roads have been improved, and large hotels and condominiums are going up. New marinas and yacht-chartering enterprises are being established as well.

West End (BA2452) is a small community with meager supplies, located in Soper's Hole at the western end of Tortola. The ferry from St. Thomas stops here, and taxis are available for trips into Roadtown or tours of the island. Decide on the price, however, before you hop in.

Customs and Immigration officials are usually on the dock or in the immediate vicinity during normal hours. West End is the most convenient port of entry when coming from the U.S. islands.

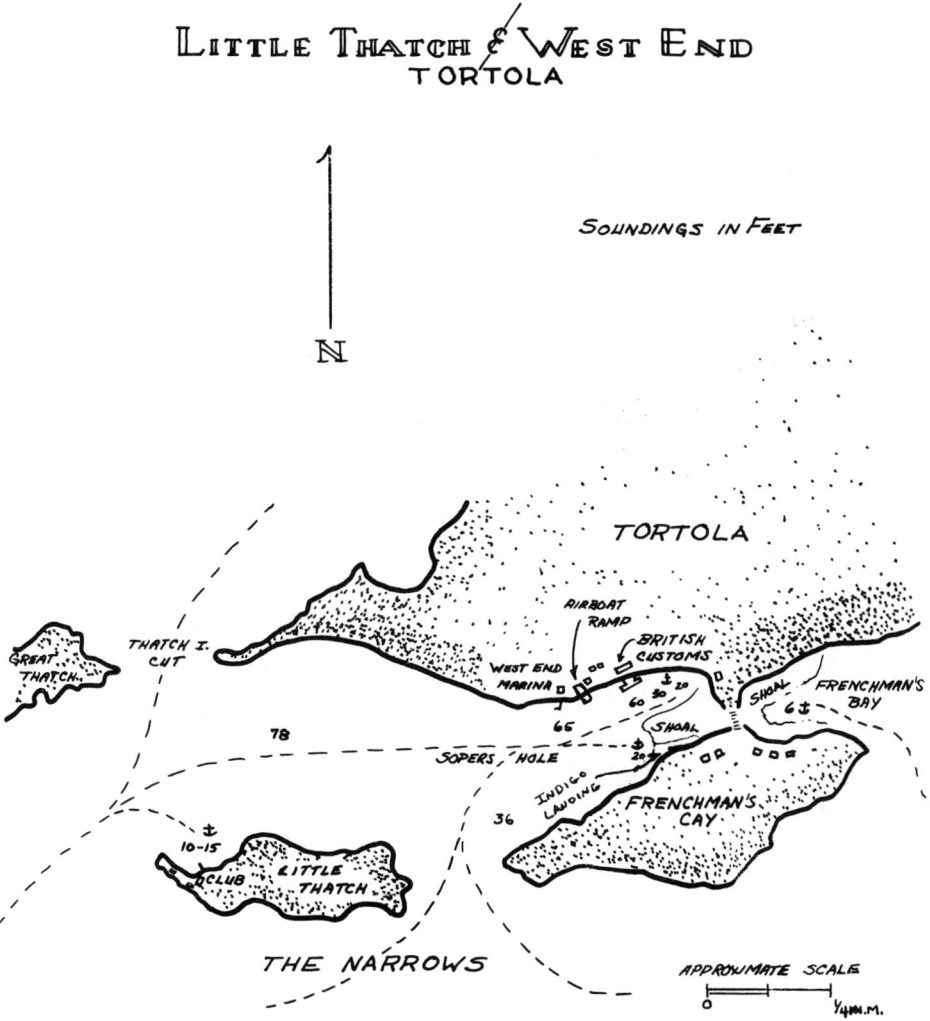

Enter from The Narrows around either side of Little Thatch Island, or from the N through Thatch Island Cut. The best anchorage is in the NE corner in 20 feet of water just 50 yards offshore, with good holding and excellent protection. Another anchorage, but with less protection, is just off the shoal ledge that runs out from Frenchman's Cay.

A new marina W of the Antilles Air Boat ramp offers ice, fuel, electricity, and moorings.

Little Thatch Island (BA2452) has a lovely anchorage off a beautiful little beach on its northwestern corner. An attractive guest house offers meals by reservation. Anchor just outside the moorings, where the holding is good in sand.

Uncomfortable sea conditions caused by the tidal stream that sweeps through Thatch Cut make this a poor overnight anchorage, even during the summer.

Frenchman's Cay (BA2452) is the home of Fleet Indigo, bareboat charterers of Irwin 32½s and 37s. Fuel, water, ice, and evening meals are available here, also supplies from their ship's store. Go alongside the bulkhead, or pick up a mooring outside the sandbar.

On the other side of the bridge (outside of Soper's Hole), Frenchman's Bay is a pleasant anchorage. As you round the eastern point of Frenchman's Cay, you will find a spot close to shore with good overnight protection and little motion. This anchorage is good for 7 feet, and the less you draw, the further in you can squeeze. Approach with caution and leave the cay close at hand; the bottom shoals rapidly to the north at the head of the bay.

Passing along the south shore of Tortola between Frenchman's Cay and Roadtown, stand well offshore to avoid the charted reef about midway between Fort Recovery and Sea Cow Bay.

Nanny Cay (BA2019) now has a dredged harbor and an apartment complex on 25 acres of reclaimed land.

Sea Cow Bay (BA2019) can now be entered by way of a dredged channel deep enough for any yacht. Eyeball your way in and do not approach the shore too closely.

Prospect Reef (BA2019) is about a mile beyond Sea Cow Bay and around Slaney Point, but before you come to Road Harbour. This is a new marine-oriented residential complex with town houses, hotel, two swimming pools, other luxury trappings, and a small but modern marina.

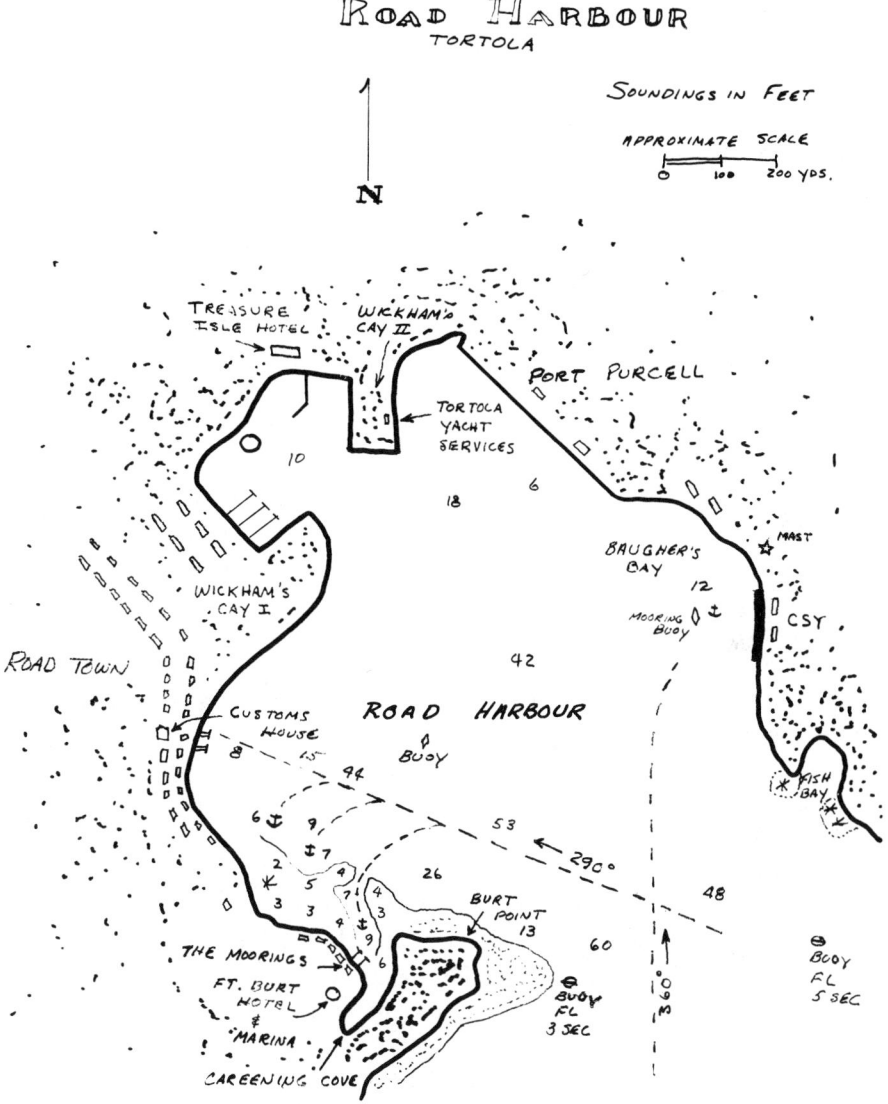

ROAD HARBOUR
TORTOLA

SOUNDINGS IN FEET

APPROXIMATE SCALE

N

TREASURE ISLE HOTEL
WICKHAM'S CAY II
PORT PURCELL
TORTOLA YACHT SERVICES
BAUGHER'S BAY
MAST
MOORING BUOY
CSY
WICKHAM'S CAY I
ROAD TOWN
CUSTOMS HOUSE
BUOY
ROAD HARBOUR
FISH BAY
THE MOORINGS
FT. BURT HOTEL & MARINA
CAREENING COVE
BURT POINT
BUOY FL 3 SEC
BUOY FL 5 SEC

Road Harbour (BA2019, BA2020) is the largest commercial center in the
British Virgins. The last decade has seen many a building project here, with still
more in the offing. Already there is a liberal assortment of hotels and restaurants with lovely views of the harbor and Sir Francis Drake Channel, as well as
food stores, a new ice plant, grog shops, and English-style pubs.

The face-lifting of the harbor has included the development of port facilities
for large ships at Port Purcell, a new area of reclaimed land north of town called
Wickham Cay I and II, and the emergence of The Moorings at the southern

end of the harbor, which encompasses waterside apartments, the Fort Burt Hotel, a large bareboat-charter base, and the marina formerly operated by Tortola Yacht Services.

Road Harbour is exposed for the most part to the prevailing easterly winds and is not a particularly comfortable anchorage unless your draft (and available space) will let you move well up under the shelter of Burt Point.

In making your approach, keep well clear of the rather indistinct shoals about 150 yards NW of Burt Point, and remember that the buoyage is reversed; so that the proper jingle in these British waters becomes: "Red, right, returning is wrong!" We recommend heading toward the town docks on 290°T until you have The Moorings abaft your beam; then round up slowly to port and drop your hook, or continue to the Fort Burt Marina docks. Note in the sketch the 4-foot patch of shoal water projecting into this anchorage area. In the cloudy water, it is difficult to discern. The holding here is excellent in sand.

Very shallow-draft boats can move past Fort Burt Marina into tiny Careening Cove. The swinging room is limited, and you must maneuver around a marine railway that extends about 60 yards from the shore, but if you can get in, it would take a hurricane to bother you.

Docking at the town wharf is not recommended because of the commercial traffic and general activity. It may seem convenient to go in there for entering or clearing; the Customs and Immigration offices are located just across the street, but don't be tempted.

In the artificial basin of Wickham Cay I, the Treasure Isle Hotel invites yachtsmen to use their dock. Much more dock space, and full marina facilities, should be available in 1975 at the new Village Cay Marina in this same basin.

Albie Stewart, a long-time friend of yachtsmen visiting the British Virgins, has moved his Tortola Yacht Services across the harbor to a 2½-acre site on reclaimed land in Wickham Cay II. His expanded services include mechanical and hull repairs, a 37½-ton Tami lift, storage facilities, and electronic, sail, and rigging repairs.

When approaching either Wickham Cay area, do not venture far inside the Harbour Spit buoy E of the main dock.

At times, especially when the wind is N of E, you will find relatively calm conditions for anchoring in Baugher's Bay, although a slight ground swell is always present. The best anchorage is just inside the large mooring buoy, where holding is excellent in sand and the effect of commercial traffic is not bothersome. Caribbean Sailing Yachts (C.S.Y.) now base their large fleet of bareboat charter yachts here, having moved from Maya Cove in 1975.

Eastward from Road Harbour are several bays that are unnamed on the charts. Fish Bay, Brandywine, Half Moon, and Paraquita Bays are either too shallow or are blocked by reefs. However, with the dredging now going on around Tortola, these bays may soon be opened up for yachts.

Maya Cove (BA2019) is W of Buck Island and now the home of West Indies Yachts, a bareboat charter firm that used to headquarter in Benner Bay, St. Thomas. A reef extends nearly across the mouth of the cove, and the entrance is around the red buoy at the NE end of this reef. Anchor in 10 feet, mud bottom. The docks are not open to visitors.

Fat Hog and East End Bays (BA2019), on the southeastern end of Tortola, offer lovely, quiet overnight anchorages. Holding is good in sand and grass, and the sea conditions are usually calm. After passing S of the rocks at the entrance, simply bear off to starboard and drop your hook about 100 yards farther in. Stay well out from the head of the bay, as the bottom shoals rapidly 200–300 yards off the shore. The town of East End is located here, but supplies and facilities are practically nonexistent. Swimming is good.

Beef Island is a small island connected to Tortola by a short bridge, but it is big enough to contain the international airport for the British Virgin Islands, with service from San Juan, St. Thomas, and Antigua. Before the bridge was built, there used to be a quaint ferry manipulated by rope and pulley. Near the new

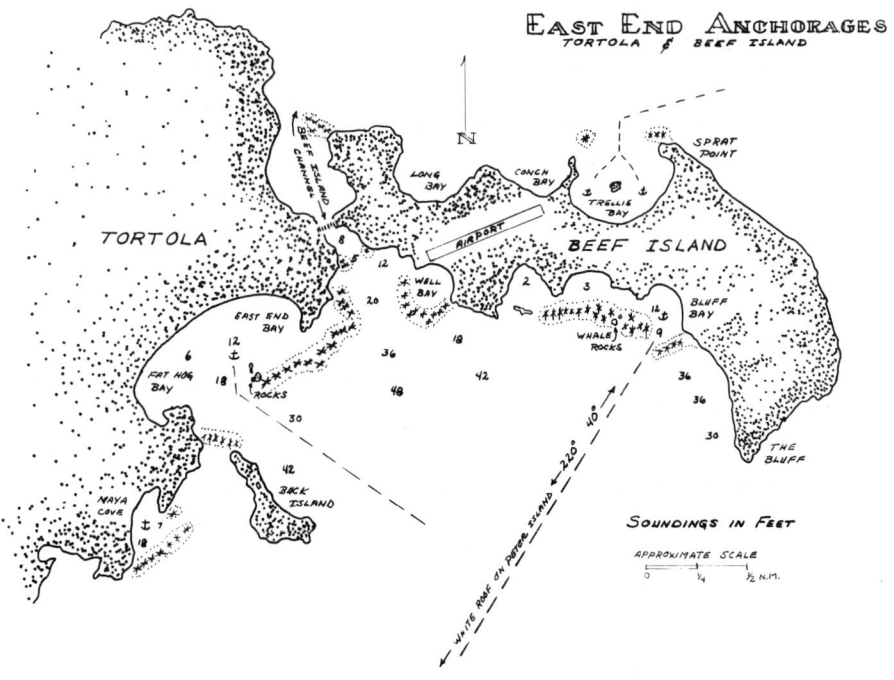

TRELLIS BAY
BEEF ISL. — TORTOLA

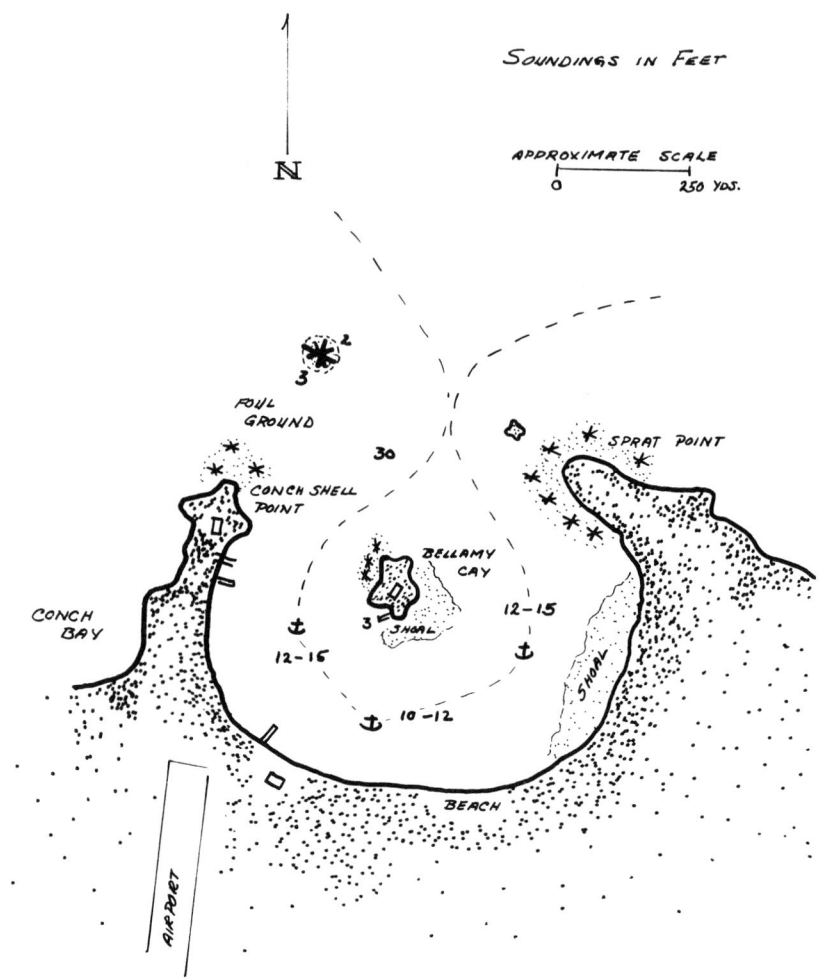

bridge, an Aquatic Center invites visitors to view tropical fish the center has collected for sale and shipment to the States.

Bluff Bay (BA2019), on the S side of Beef Island, is a small, quiet anchorage offering good protection under normal conditions. The entrance is narrow, with dangerous coral heads and reefs on both sides.

First, identify the breaking reef on the E side of the bay, and pass it about 10 to 15 yards off while heading approximately NE. Once inside the reef, alter course about 5° to port and continue slowly toward the sandy beach. Be exceptionally wary of the reef that extends E from Whale Rocks, for there are scattered coral heads at the eastern end. They have 3 to 5 feet of water over them and are difficult to see. Having cleared these hazards, a yacht drawing 7 feet or less can anchor in comfort close to shore. The holding is excellent in sand, and the swimming is good. An old plantation ruin stands in the underbrush just up from the beach.

On leaving the anchorage, favor the eastern side of the channel and head toward the white roof on Peter Island until well clear.

Trellis Bay (BA2019) is the largest and best-known anchorage on Beef Island. Though open to the N, it offers excellent protection and calm water under most conditions. Anchor on either side of Bellamy Cay, or S of it. Holding is good in sand, mud, and grass.

Approaching from the E, keep clear of the rock just above water off the eastern point of the bay. Approaching from the N or W, be careful of the foul ground that extends out from Conch Shell Point. Approximately 200 yards N and slightly E of Conch Shell Point, there is a nasty little reef lying about 3 feet below the surface. You may pass between this reef and the point, if you have positively spotted this outlying reef.

Yachts drawing 9 feet can circumnavigate Bellamy Cay, but note that a shoal extends from the E side of the cay and another from the opposite shore.

Marina Cay (BA2019) is a small island just S of Scrub Island and E of Great Camanoe. Sheltered by these larger islands and by Marina Cay reef itself, the anchorage off the southwestern shore is always smooth. The approach from N and NE is clear of dangers, except for the reef extending E from the NE corner of the cay. The channel between Great Camanoe and Scrub Islands is clear of hazards if you stay in the center.

From the S or SE, take care to identify and pass well clear of the protecting reef that extends about 500 yards SSW from Marina Cay. There is a daymark at its extremity. Your anchor will hold well in the sandy bottom here.

The informal Banyan Tree Bar is open in the evenings, and dinner is available by reservation. The proprietors of Marina Cay have several moorings for the use of visiting yachts; they also sell ice, arrange fishing and snorkeling trips, and rent and refill scuba tanks.

Long before the British Virgins were "discovered" by tourists and bareboat charterers, young Robb White and his wife came to Marina Cay to seek the idyllic, away-from-it-all existence. He wrote an engrossing book called *Our Virgin Island* (now in paperback) about their trials and tribulations in trying to make ends meet. It later became a movie and has been on TV.

The North Shore of Tortola, on a nice day, when no ground swell is running, can be the backdrop for a very pleasant sail. Although there are numerous coves and sandy beaches along here, none can be recommended for overnight anchoring during the winter months. In fact, many of these spots are relatively uncomfortable even in the summer, due to the unsettled conditions caused by current and tides.

The route is generally clear of dangers except for the passage between Beef Island and Little Camanoe. Just N of Conch Bay, Beef Island, there is a reef

Marina Cay

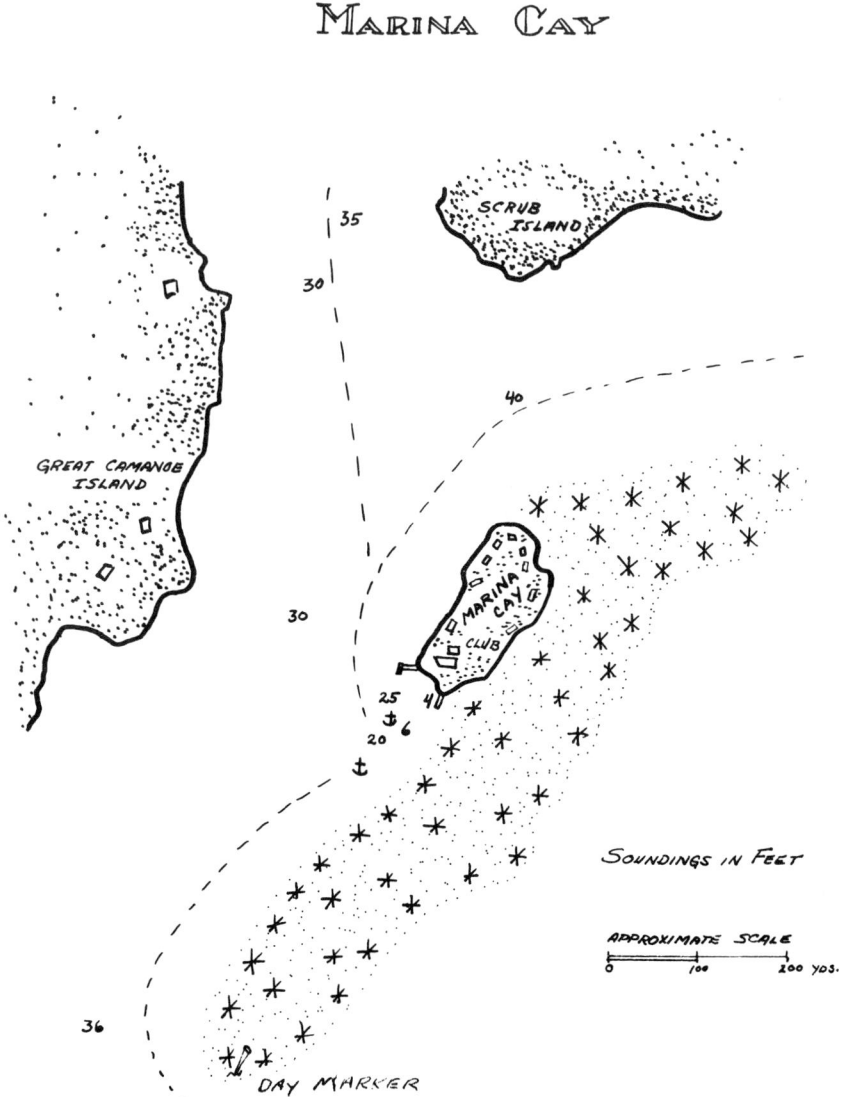

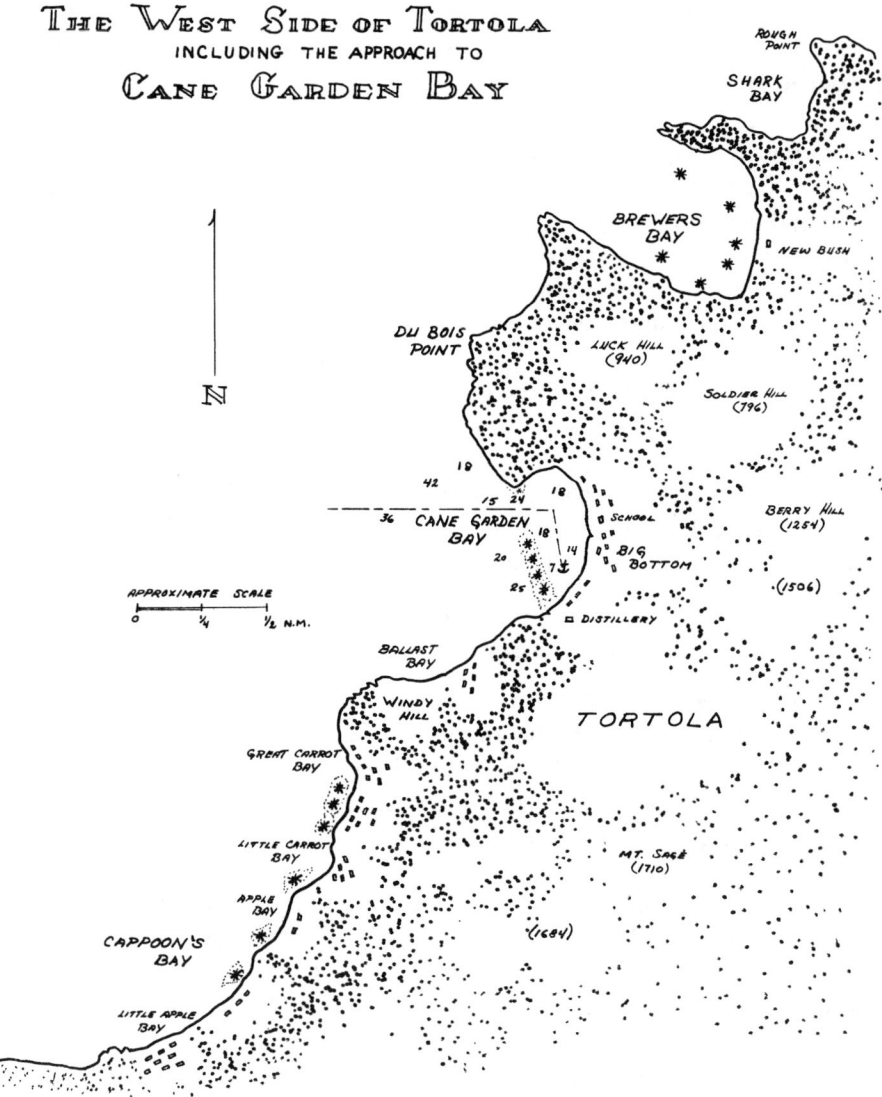

THE WEST SIDE OF TORTOLA
INCLUDING THE APPROACH TO
CANE GARDEN BAY

right in the middle of the passage. It is best to pass N of this one, as another reef extends N from the headland as you pass between Conch and Long Bays.

To wend your way through these obstacles, leave the southernmost points of both Great and Little Camanoe close on your starboard hand, about 20 to 30 yards off. As you come abeam of the tip of Little Camanoe on your westerly heading, adjust your heading toward the nearest high mountain top on Tortola, the 878-foot Lloyds. Hold this heading until you are well past Little Camanoe and the sandbar that extends S from it.

Once clear of this tricky spot, the remainder of the route down Tortola's north coast is uncomplicated. It is usually wise to stay rather well offshore in order to get a clear wind.

Canegarden Bay (BA2452, BA2019) is one of the most beautiful bays in the entire Virgin Islands, but unfortunately it's not a safe overnight anchorage during the winter, because the Atlantic swells can make it dangerous and even untenable within a few short hours. During the late spring and summer, it's an excellent overnight anchorage.

When approaching from the W, favor the northern side of the bay; a reef extends from the southern side almost three-quarters of the way across it. There is also a small reef off the northern point of the bay. The pass between these reefs has 15 to 20 feet of water.

Once inside the reef, the best anchorage is in the southern part of the bay, where the holding is excellent in sand. A lovely crescent beach with a pleasant community, palm trees, a working rum distillery, and lots of friendly children will make your visit one to remember.

Jost Van Dyke and Nearby Islands

Great Harbour (BA2452), whose exposure is to the south, is normally well protected. It is also by far the most pleasant spot in the British Virgins to go through the Customs and Immigration formalities. The official is usually around during regular working hours, but if you can't find him, ask at Foxy's Tamarind Restaurant. There you will find the answer to any and all questions.

The best anchorage is in the SW part of the bay just inside Dog Hole Point. The bay shoals rapidly to 3 or 4 feet, with a narrow channel running through the shallows to the dock. You may go up to the shoal area, but don't drop your hook in the channel; native sloops use it day and night. The bottom is sandy mud and grass, giving good holding.

Foxy's can be a fun place for an evening's entertainment. At the slightest hint of interest, a native scratch band will materialize; ply them with a drink or two and the music goes on and on.

White Bay (BA2452) is located just W of Great Harbour and has a lovely sandy beach that extends the entire length of the bay. There are two approaches through the reefs. The passage on the western side is about 50 yards off the SW corner of the bay. As an alternative, the owners of White Bay Sandcastle have erected range markers that will bring you in through a 15-foot channel between the two large reefs in the center of the bay. Once inside, anchor in 8 feet

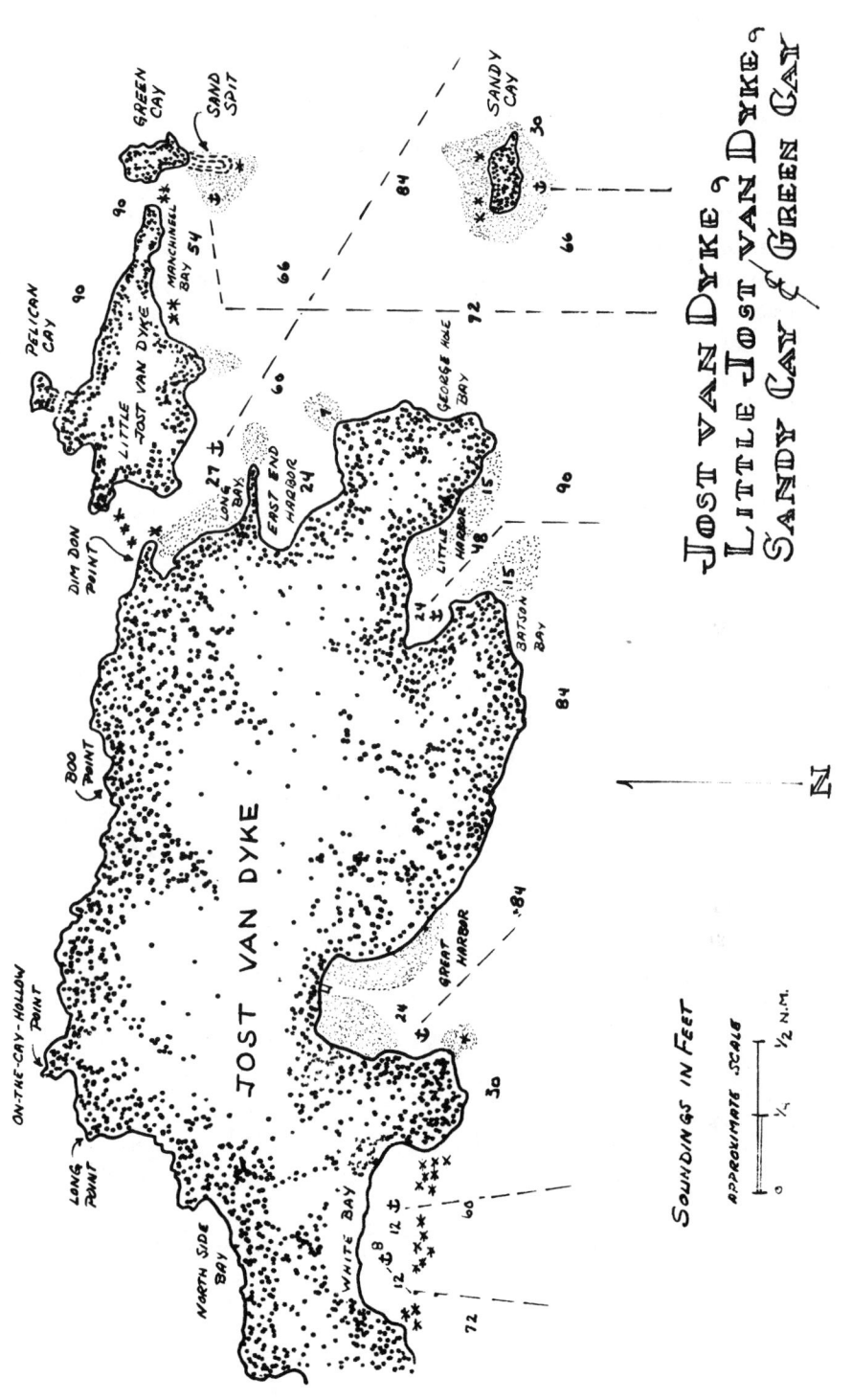

JOST VAN DYKE,
LITTLE JOST VAN DYKE,
SANDY CAY & GREEN CAY

SOUNDINGS IN FEET

APPROXIMATE SCALE

0   ½   ½ N.M.

N

over sand. There's dinner ashore if you wish, and the swimming is perfect. A swell sometimes makes this an uncomfortable overnight anchorage.

Little Harbour (BA2452) is usually a quiet anchorage and not frequently visited by yachts. There is a small settlement ashore, but the general feeling is of being in a remote and isolated corner of the world.

When entering, stay in midchannel, as there are sandbanks on each side of the entrance. Continue to the head of the bay, where you will see on your port hand a tiny beach tucked into the corner. It is called Careening Hole and has 12 feet of water right up to the beach. It's a good idea to set a stern anchor here, because there is little swinging room.

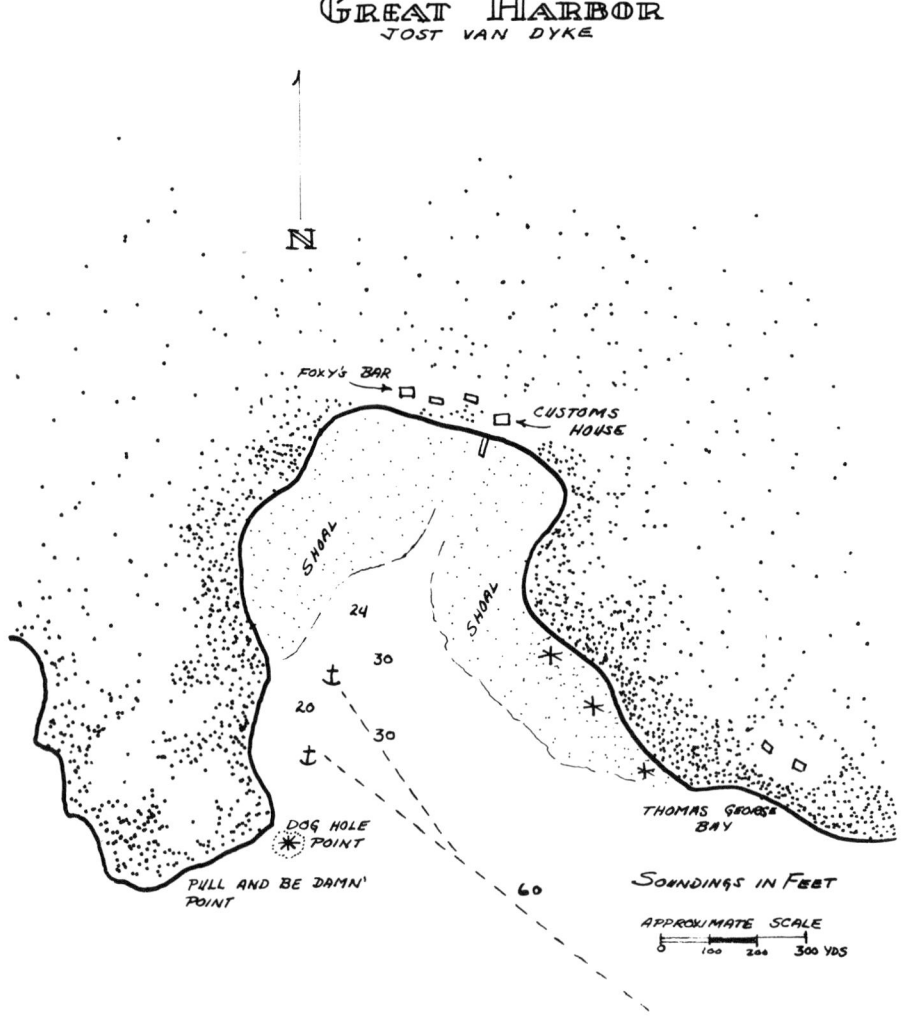

GREAT HARBOR
JOST VAN DYKE

LITTLE HARBOR
JOST VAN DYKE

ALSO KNOWN AS

GARDNER BAY

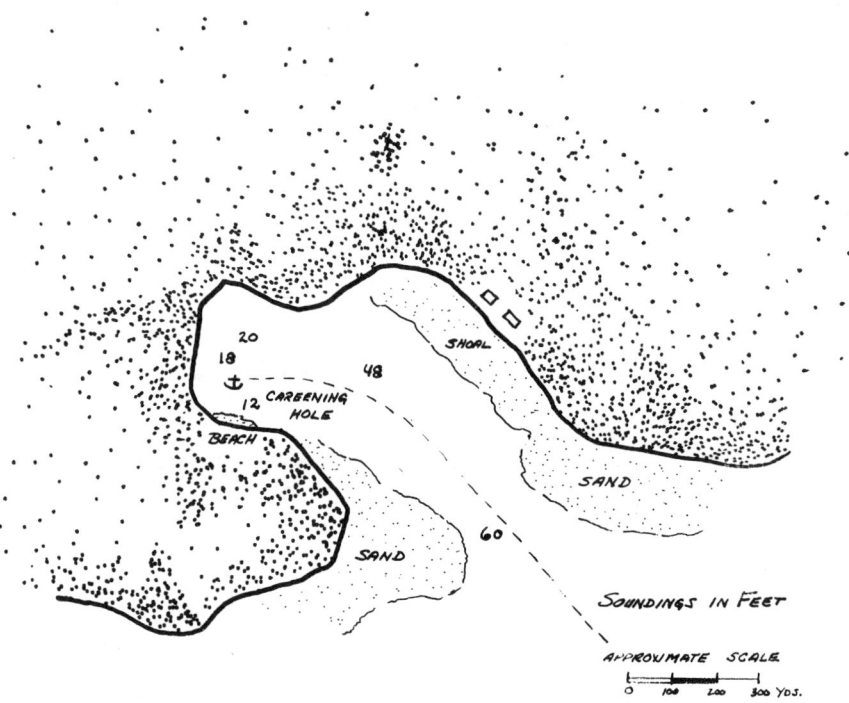

Long Bay (BA2452) should be approached with care to avoid the sandbar extending along the entire head of the bay. Anchor in 20 to 30 feet off this sandbar.

Little Jost Van Dyke (BA2452) has two good swimming beaches on the S shore, some ruins of bygone days scattered about, and a large concrete dock with 6 feet of water at the end.

Dr. William Thornton, who designed the Capitol in Washington, D.C., was born on this tiny island. His plans won a design competition that was advertised in 1792 by the State Department when Thomas Jefferson was Secretary of State.

Green Cay (BA2452), lying just E of Little Jost Van Dyke, is well worth scrambling over, if only to visit the miniature crater on the eastern side. The best anchorage is on the edge of the sandbank that extends westward from the sandspit off the southern tip of the cay. This is not an overnight anchorage.

Sandy Cay (BA2452) is a lovely "desert-island" type of place for lunch or a swim. It is owned by Laurance Rockefeller, who has endeavored to keep it unspoiled and has planted almost every type of vegetation that will grow in the sandy soil. A delightful path runs around the island.

The best anchorage is on the sandbank to the SSW of the cay, about 50 yards from shore. Because it is exposed to the ground swells, it is not a good overnight anchorage.

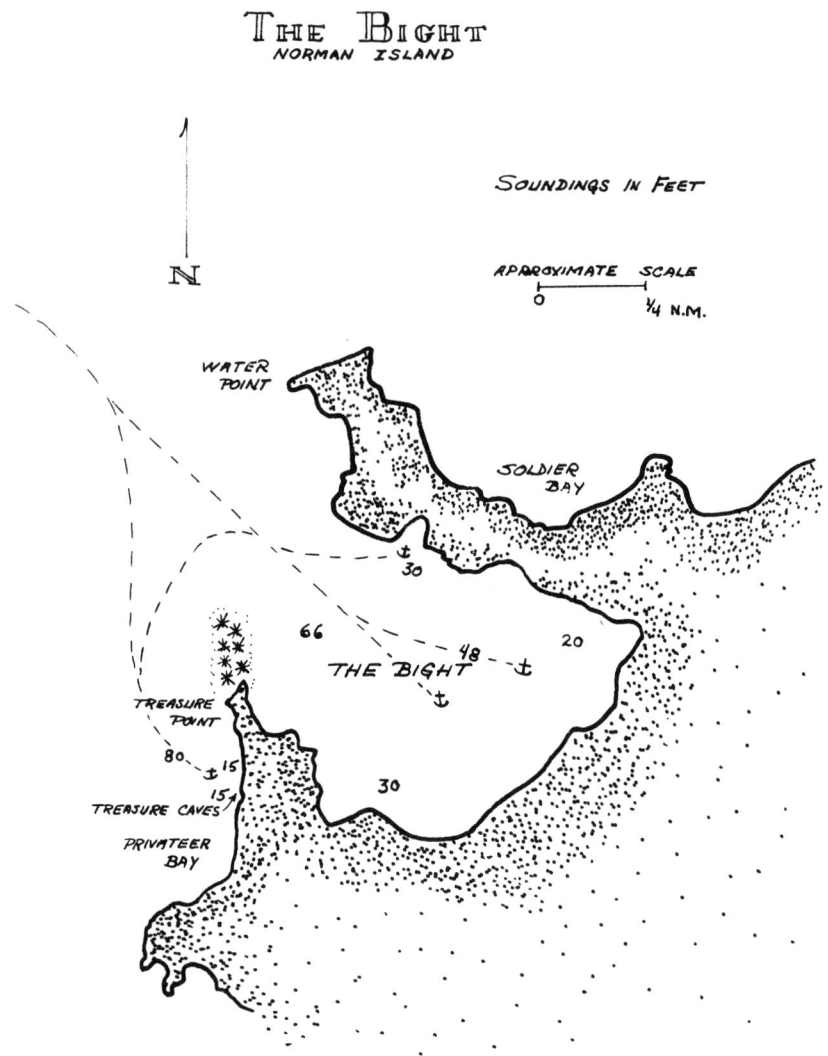

THE BIGHT
NORMAN ISLAND

N

SOUNDINGS IN FEET

APPROXIMATE SCALE
0   ¼ N.M.

WATER POINT

SOLDIER BAY

30

66   48
THE BIGHT   20

TREASURE POINT

80   15
15
TREASURE CAVES   30

PRIVATEER BAY

Sir Francis Drake Channel, as seen from Peter Island

Norman, Peter, Salt, Cooper, and Ginger Islands

The Bight on Norman Island (BA2019) is a large and popular bay offering good protection under almost all conditions. The approach is clear except for a reef that projects N for about 200 yards from Treasure Point. You may anchor almost anywhere in the bay, though we prefer a spot about 50 yards off the beach at the very head of the bay.

Just S of Treasure Point, on the W side of Norman Island, are the three so-called Treasure Caves. Rumor has it that not too many years ago, quite a fortune was found on a ledge in one of them. Norman Island has long been associated with pirates and their treasure, but the substance of this association is elusive. The island is reputed to be the famous *Treasure Island* immortalized in Robert Louis Stevenson's novel. Other islands in other parts of the world have claimed this distinction, but Norman Island probably fits the story as well as any. In fact, Stevenson is said to have written part of the book while living in a camp on the beach at the head of The Bight.

Yachts may anchor on the narrow shelf that runs along this shore, and all three caves can be entered by dinghy under normal conditions. This is a lovely lunch or afternoon stop, but is not recommended for overnight. The swimming is good, though you're likely to see a lot of barracuda about.

Little Harbour on Peter Island (BA2019) is the westernmost and most popular anchorage on this relatively large island. This anchorage is deep and affords

PETER ISLAND

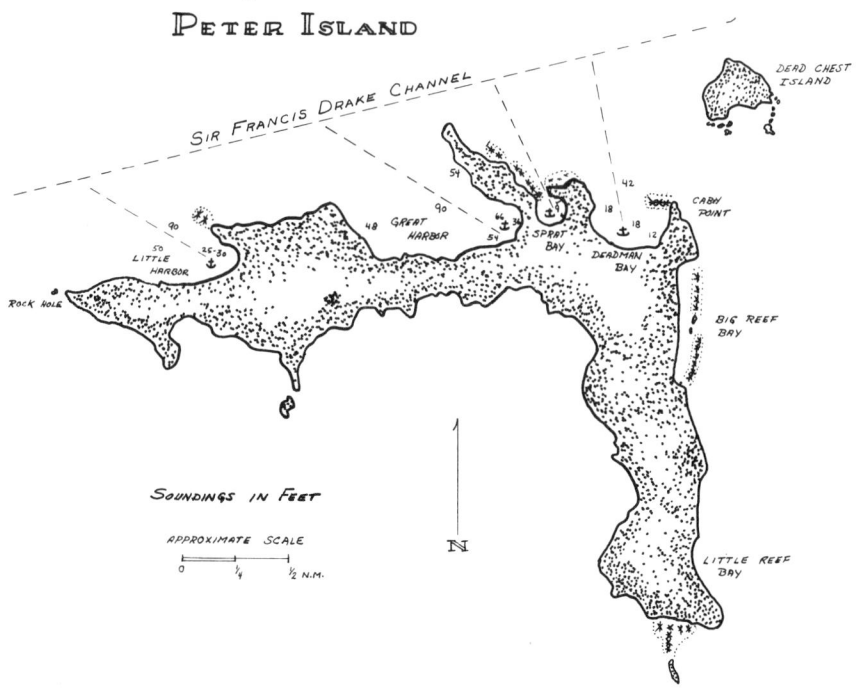

good protection. Because of the topography of the surrounding land, the wind tends to swirl at night, causing yachts to swing and foul their anchors. A stern anchor is advisable.

All the land around Little Harbour is owned by Percy Chubb, of marine-insurance fame. His home overlooks the anchorage from the northeastern bluff. Permission should be requested before going ashore here.

Great Harbour (BA2019), the largest bay on Peter Island's north coast, offers good protection, but the problem is to get your anchor on the bottom—the water is extremely deep. If you have plenty of chain or line, anchor in the SE corner where the holding is good in sand.

Sprat Bay (BA2019) is the site of the popular Peter Island Yacht Club, an elegant facility built and managed by Norwegians, with a 40-room hotel standing on a bulkheaded area over the reef. If it's not too crowded, this is a comfortable overnight anchorage amid luxurious surroundings.

Favor the E side of the opening as you enter, since there are rocks and reefs along the western shore. Anchor S and W of the dock, or moor stern-to on the inside of the bulkhead. A ferry runs between Sprat Bay and The Moorings at Road Harbour, for the convenience of yachtsmen as well as the hotel guests.

Deadman Bay (BA2019), on Peter Island's northeastern end, is generally regarded as one of the most beautiful bays in the Virgin Islands. With its crystal-clear water and lovely beach backed by a grove of palms, it looks like a picture out of a travel brochure. Unfortunately, it is not suitable as an overnight anchorage in winter; it is too vulnerable to large swells that can come in without warning. In fact, a slight ground swell is almost always present here.

A path takes you over to Big Reef Bay, where you can enjoy fine swimming and snorkeling in the shallow water behind the reef.

Salt Island (BA2019) has a small settlement in a shallow bight on the island's north side. At a distance, it appears to have an attractive beach, but on closer examination, both the beach and the village lose their allure. Somehow the

Little Harbor
PETER ISLAND

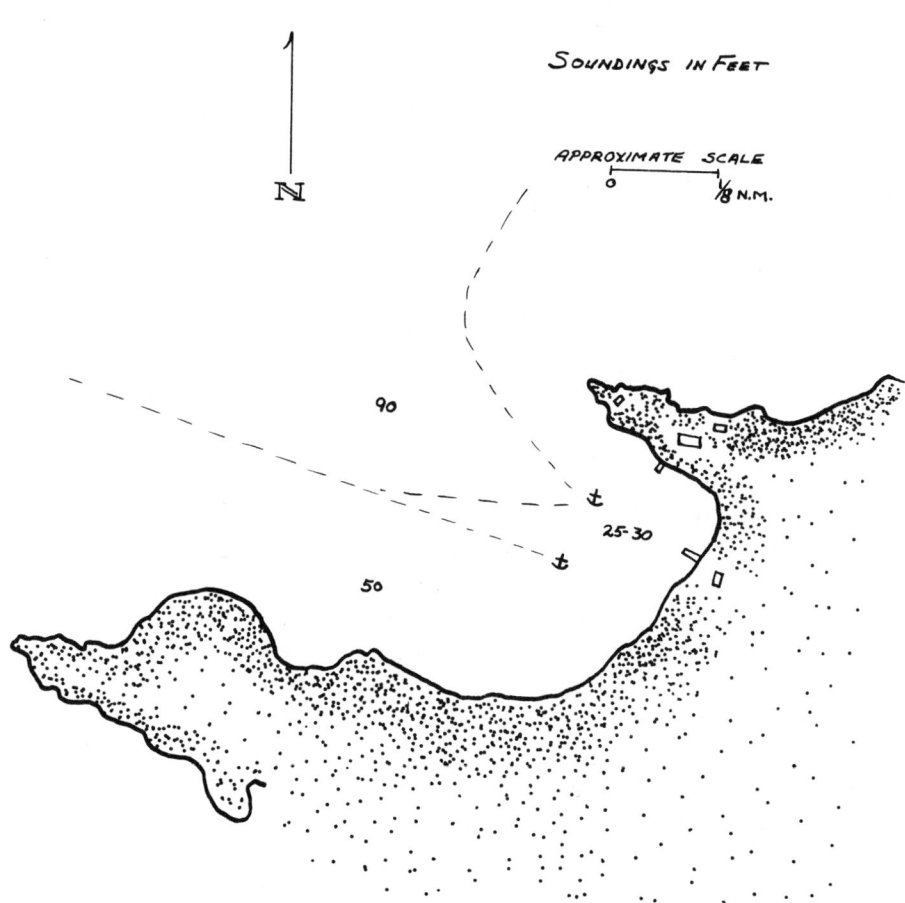

N

SOUNDINGS IN FEET

APPROXIMATE SCALE

0   ⅛ N.M.

90

25-30

50

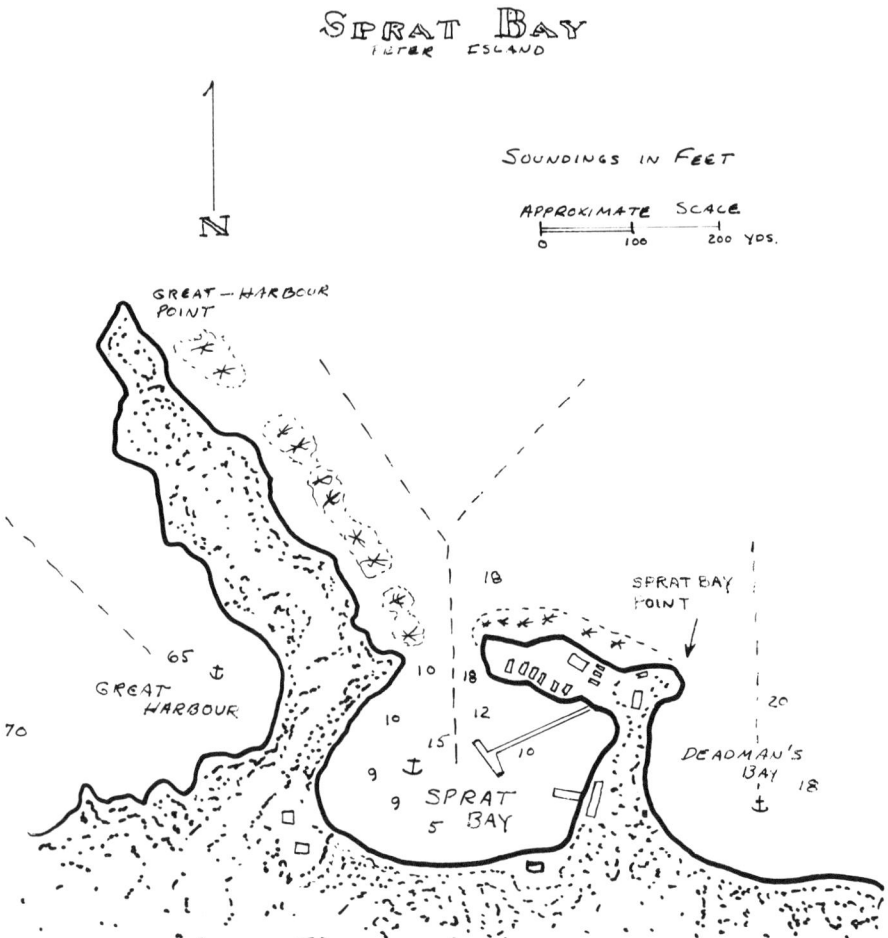

SPRAT BAY
Inter Island

SOUNDINGS IN FEET

APPROXIMATE SCALE

inhabitants eke out a meager living by working the three salt ponds on the island. Although the settlement may be depressing, here is an opportunity to see how salt was produced two centuries ago.

A slight ground swell is incessant. This is strictly a daytime stop.

The passage between Salt and Cooper Islands has rocks and reefs on either hand in the narrowest part of the channel. Favor the eastern side, leaving the exposed rocks on the Cooper Island side about 20 to 30 yards off.

Cooper Island (BA2019) has several vacation homes on its slopes and seems crowded when compared with the adjacent islands. In the lee of Quart-a-Nancy Point, on the island's NW side, is an anchorage of sorts, but it is not recommended for overnight during the winter because of its exposure to the N. The

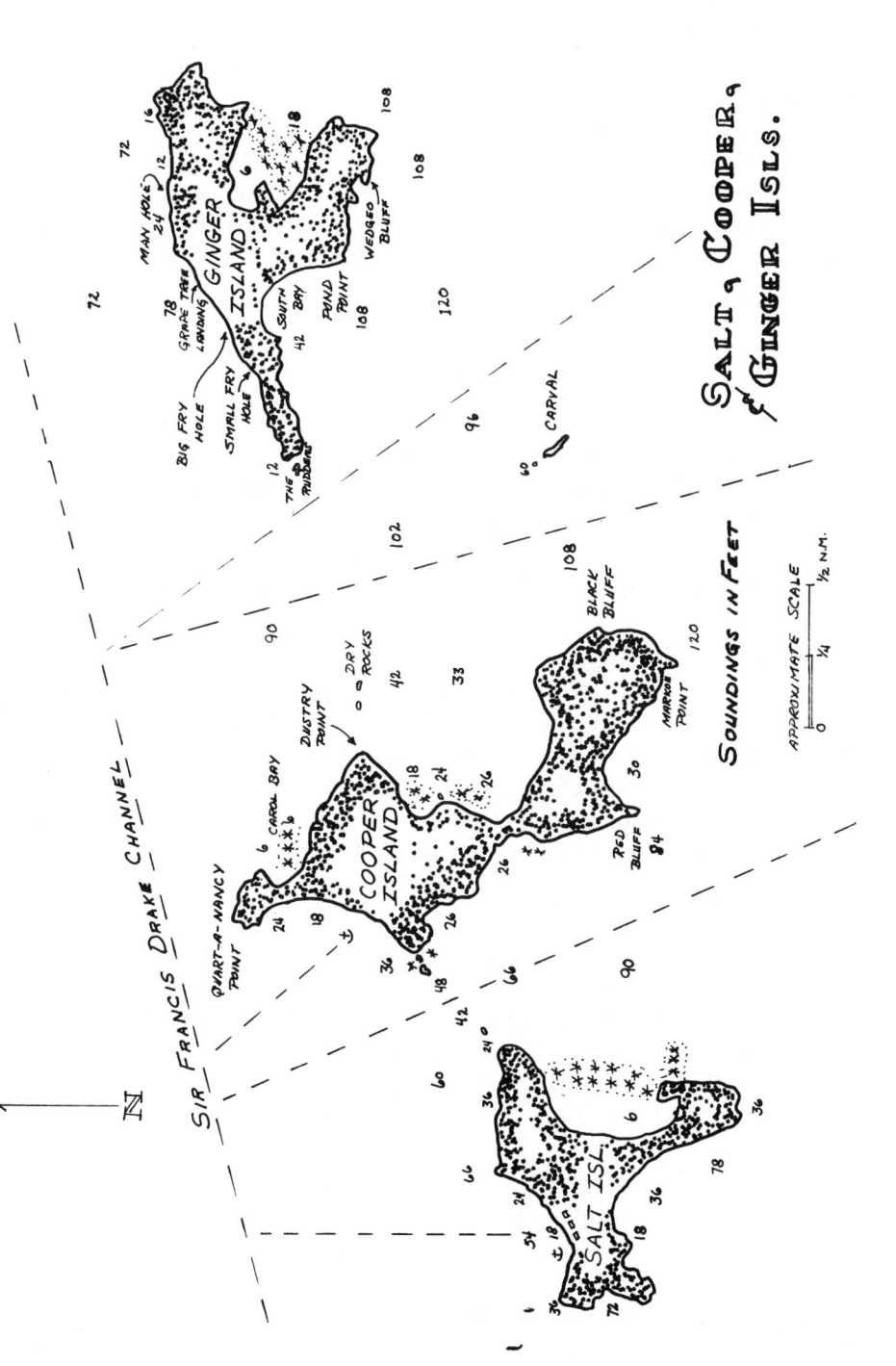

SALT, COOPER,
& GINGER ISLS.

SOUNDINGS IN FEET

APPROXIMATE SCALE

N

SIR FRANCIS DRAKE CHANNEL

GINGER ISLAND

MAN HOLE
GRAPE TREE LANDING
BIG FRY HOLE
SMALL FRY HOLE
THE PYRAMIDS
SOUTH BAY
POND POINT
WEDGEO BLUFF

CARVAL

COOPER ISLAND

QUART-A-NANCY POINT
CARVAL BAY
DUSTRY POINT
DRY ROCKS
RED BLUFF
MARKOE POINT
BLACK BLUFF

SALT ISL.

best spot is in the lower part of this bay. The holding is good, though a slight ground swell is always to be expected.

There are no hidden dangers in the passage between Cooper and Ginger Islands.

Ginger Island (BA2019) is presently uninhabited and offers no safe, all-weather anchorage. There is a bay on the E side of the island, with a 6-foot entrance through the reef, which sometimes offers protection. However, when the wind blows strongly out of the ESE, the entrance becomes dangerous and quite impossible to use.

Virgin Gorda

The Fat Virgin is the second largest of the British Virgins and, to some, the most beautiful. From the grotesque boulders strewn around the southern end to the flat middle area, and on to the high, lovely mountains of the northern section, it is certainly an island of contrasts. Beautiful beaches, some fine anchorages, and ideal snorkeling reefs are to be found around its shores. No wonder it is beginning to feel the hand of the resort developer.

The Baths (BA2019), a phenomenal pile of huge boulders located on a lovely beach in a small bay on the western side of the island, derives its name from the pools of crystal-clear water formed in the sand at the base of the pile. Inside this jumble of monstrous slabs and boulders is a network of caves, archways, paths, and mysterious pools, some in complete blackness, others lit by bright shafts of sunlight bursting through the cracks in this edifice of nature. It is truly one of the wonders of the tight little world of the Virgin Islands.

The bay is easy to spot from seaward. Simply set a course for the southern tip of Virgin Gorda. When you are within 2 miles of the western shoreline, a string of pretty beaches will be clearly seen, stretching northward. The second beach to the N is your destination, and the pile of boulders in the southern corner of this beach is The Baths. Anchor 75 to 100 yards off the beach in 25 to 35 feet of water. Then check your anchor with mask and flippers, as there are numerous coral heads hereabouts that could foul your anchor or sever a nylon line. A ground swell is almost always felt here, sometimes of uncomfortable proportions.

If you run into poor conditions, better postpone your visit until another time, or tie up at Virgin Gorda Yacht Harbour and hire a jeep for a visit by land. But do make the effort.

Virgin Gorda Yacht Harbour (BA2019), in St. Thomas Bay, is in all respects a full-service marina. It has floating slips for perhaps a hundred yachts, along

VIRGIN GORDA

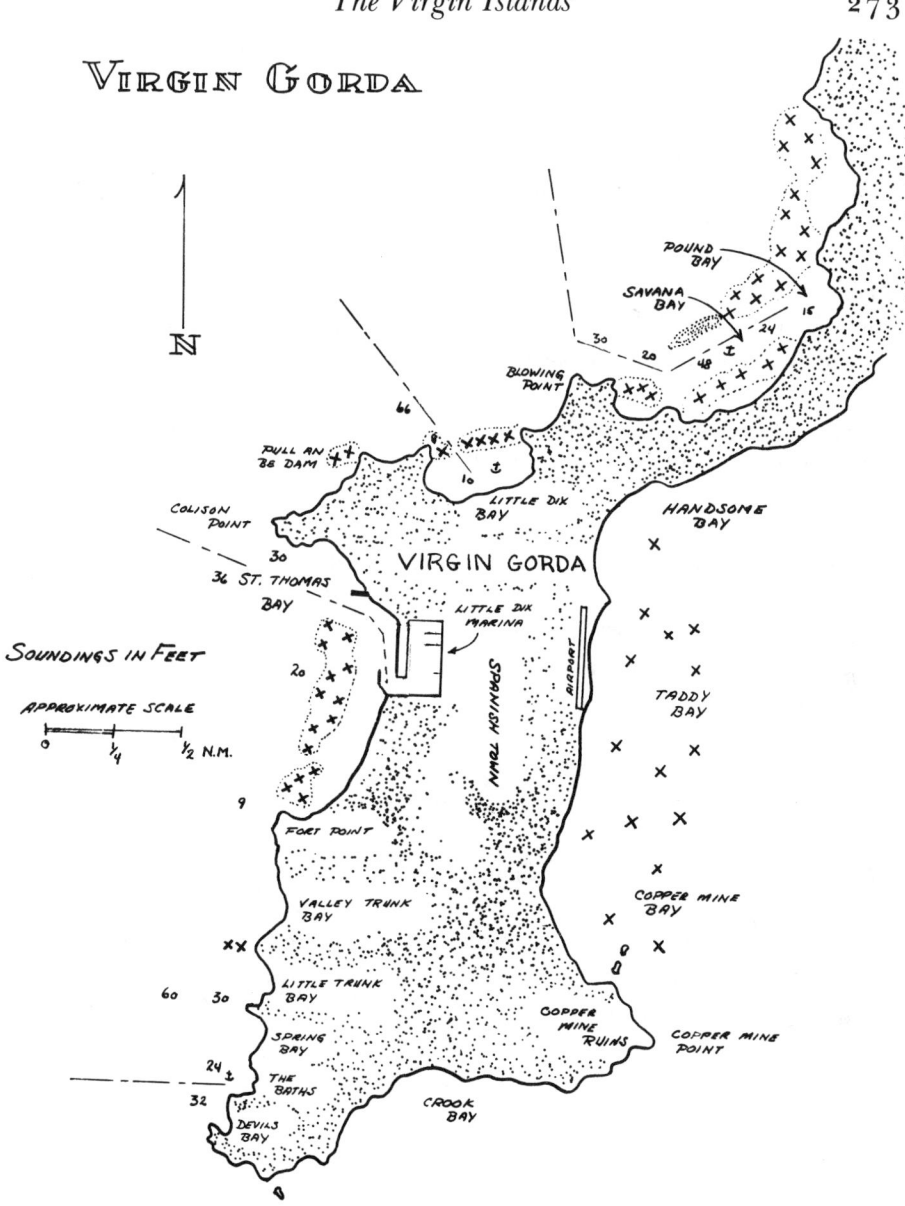

N

POUND BAY

SAVANA BAY

15

30

20

24

48

BLOWING POINT

66

PULL AN BE DAM

LITTLE DIX BAY

HANDSOME BAY

COLISON POINT

VIRGIN GORDA

30

36 ST. THOMAS BAY

LITTLE DIX MARINA

TADDY BAY

SOUNDINGS IN FEET

20

SPANISH TOWN

RAMPART

APPROXIMATE SCALE

0   ¼   ½ N.M.

9

FORT POINT

COPPER MINE BAY

VALLEY TRUNK BAY

XX

60   30

LITTLE TRUNK BAY

SPRING BAY

COPPER MINE RUINS

COPPER MINE POINT

24

32

THE BATHS

CROOK BAY

DEVILS BAY

with such welcome amenities as a food commissary, restaurant, bar, showers, coin laundry, and an ice-making machine. If this is not enough, a shopping center is nearby. You can also clear Customs and Immigration here. Rock-resorts runs this highly civilized place, and also the nearby Little Dix Bay Hotel and Caneel Bay Plantation back on St. John.

Spanish Town is a small and rather sleepy settlement that was the capital of the British Virgins back in the 18th century. A goodly percentage of the native population work for Rockresorts.

A pub called The Lord Nelson Inn, complete with English beer and darts, stands along the road to The Baths.

Across the island from Spanish Town are the ruins of a copper mine and smelter originally worked by British and Welsh miners. A native boy will lead you there, or you can find your own way by crossing to the eastern shore and turning S. After rounding a few boulders, you will spot the stack of the copper works. This is a long hike on foot, but the mine can be reached by rental jeep or mini-moke, available at the Yacht Harbour.

Little Dix Bay (BA2019) is the site of the resort hotel of that name operated by Rockresorts. A beautiful beach runs the full length of the bay, and an outer reef offers some protection for yachts. However, the hotel management prefers that yachts use their marina in St. Thomas Bay, which is quite understandable, since any waste from yachts tends to wash up on the bathing beach. It's not too comfortable here anyway, because of the ground swell.

The approach through the reef is near the western tip of the bay, between a rock located just out from the point and the end of the reef to the E. Once inside, you are in a wide channel, about 12 feet deep, between the reef and the beach. There are no dangers, and the best anchorage is about halfway up the bay. Holding is poor in a shallow layer of sand.

Meals may be obtained ashore by prior reservation.

Savana Bay (BA2019), immediately NE of Little Dix Bay, is a comfortable daytime anchorage under settled conditions. Leave Blowing Point about 20 to 30 yards to starboard, while heading in on an easterly course. Once inside, follow the reef carefully for about 100 yards, staying more or less in midchannel. Don't venture too close to the shore; there are scattered coral heads and reef patches.

A good anchorage may be had either in Savana Bay or Pound Bay. Holding is good in sand. Sea conditions are generally calm, but this anchorage is not recommended for overnight during the winter season.

Gorda Sound (BA2016)

Here is probably the most magnificent piece of protected water in the entire Virgin Islands. Once you have reached this outpost area, treat yourself to several days of exploring, swimming, snorkeling, fishing, and visiting the guest houses and resorts that have cropped up here.

The northern entrance into the sound is used by all vessels drawing over 6 feet. It lies between the NW tip of Prickly Pear Island and Colquhoun Reef.

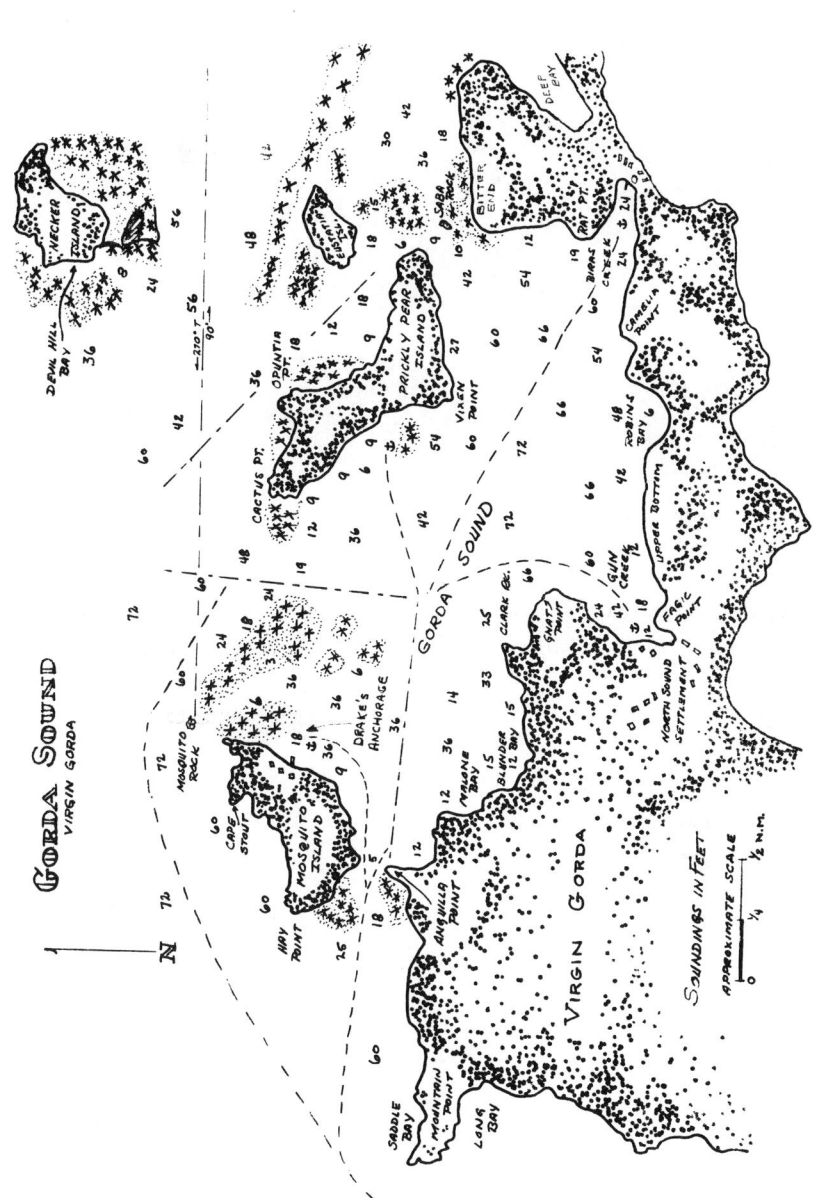

GORDA SOUND
VIRGIN GORDA

N

NECKER ISLAND
DEVIL HILL BAY

VIRGIN GORDA

GORDA SOUND

SOUNDINGS IN FEET

APPROXIMATE SCALE

Gorda Sound looking east

When approaching from the W, keep the reef 30 to 50 yards on your beam until the entrance opens up. The reef is always breaking or awash. Turn into the entrance on 180°T, favoring the western side of the channel, to stay clear of the small reef extending from Cactus Point. Once inside the reef, Gorda Sound is relatively clear of hazards to the S and E.

If you are planning to anchor off Mosquito Island, note the three small reefs that extend southward from Colquhoun Reef. To avoid these reefs, maintain your course of 180°T (and directly toward Gnat Point) until Anguilla Point bears due W, or until Seal Dog Rocks (outside the sound) drop behind the point. Then turn westerly until Drake's Anchorage is approximately N, then continue to the anchorage.

The northern entrance to Gorda Sound has no less than 20 feet of water and is passable even in the heaviest sea conditions.

The western entrance, a narrow passage between Mosquito Island and Anguilla Point, can be used by yachts drawing 6 feet or less. However, heavy ground swells may break across the entire entrance, making it unusable.

The reef extending S from Mosquito Island is always awash and sometimes breaking. Leave this reef approximately 30 yards off the port beam as you approach on a course of 090°T. Stay in midchannel until just inside Anguilla Point. If you draw over 5 feet, you must then bear away NE or SW to avoid a lump of sand in midchannel. This is the shallowest part of a sandbar running across the entrance, but there is a minimum of 6 feet on either side of this lump. Beyond this shallow spot, the sound deepens to 20 feet or more. The southeasterly detour around the shallow spot is the most reliable, because the commercial boats going into Gun Creek tend to keep it open. It can also be easily seen when the sea is calm.

If continuing eastward from this entrance, be careful to stand S of the three reef patches that project S from Colquhoun Reef.

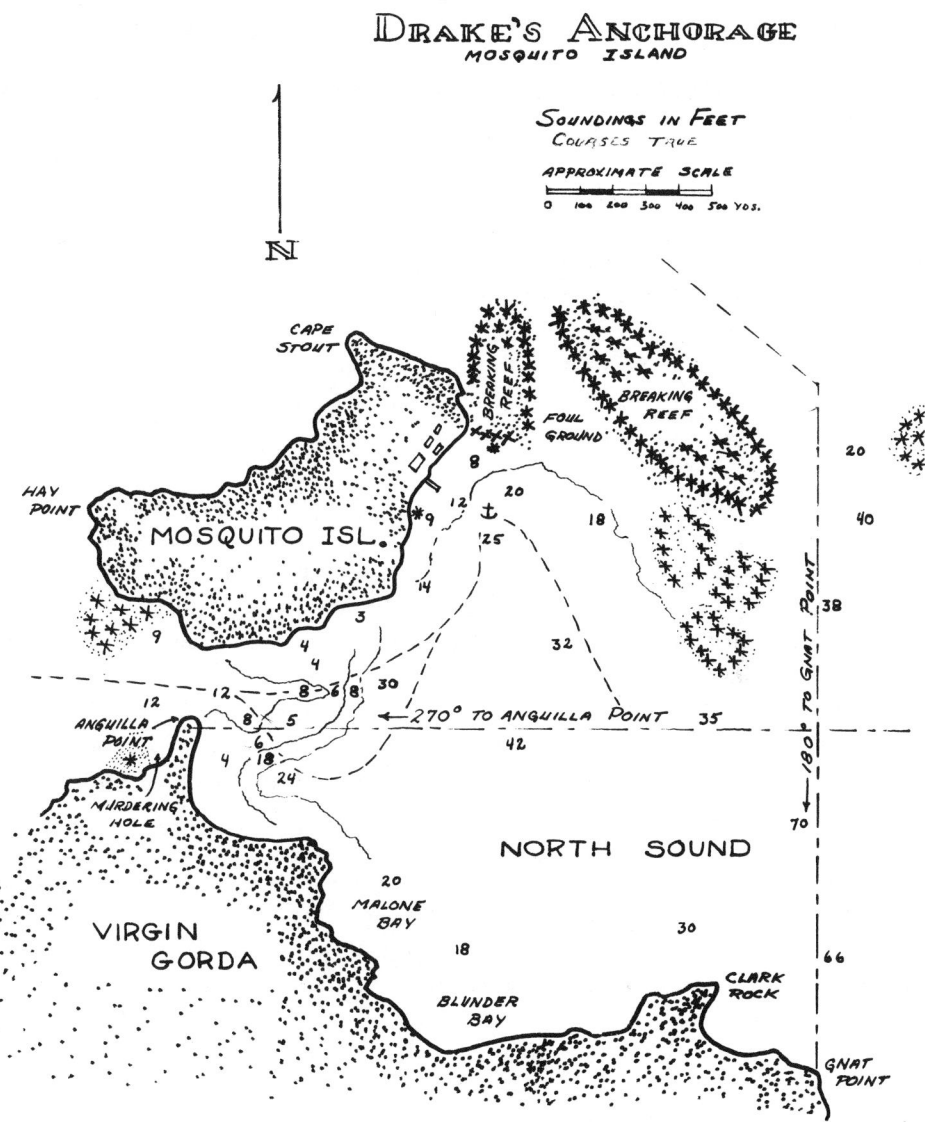

DRAKE'S ANCHORAGE
MOSQUITO ISLAND

SOUNDINGS IN FEET
COURSES TRUE

APPROXIMATE SCALE
0 100 200 300 400 500 YDS.

N

CAPE STOUT

BREAKING REEF

BREAKING REEF

FOUL GROUND

HAY POINT

MOSQUITO ISL.

NORTH SOUND

←270° TO ANGUILLA POINT 35

180° TO GNAT POINT

ANGUILLA POINT

MURDERING HOLE

VIRGIN GORDA

MALONE BAY

BLUNDER BAY

CLARK ROCK

GNAT POINT

Drake's Anchorage (BA2016) is a small guest house, restaurant, and marina facility on the eastern shore of Mosquito Island. The anchorage itself is pleasant and usually quiet, being well protected by Colquhoun Reef. The holding is good in sand. Yachts of any draft can anchor within 50 yards of shore in the vicinity of the dock.

The flagpole here is the mast of Huey Long's first *Ondine*, which went on the reefs of Anegada some years ago. If this can happen to a modern sailing machine, well-equipped with electronic gear, imagine what a hazard the Anegada Reefs were to the lumbering sailing craft of earlier days. The number of wrecks on Anegada is phenomenal, but they make interesting diving.

Gun Creek (BA2016) is the only native settlement in Gorda Sound. Supplies of any kind are very limited. The approach is straightforward. Anchor 30 to 50 yards from the head of the bay, where it is generally calm and the holding is good in sandy mud. The swimming is fair, but there are more attractive places close by.

A climb to the top of the hill will reward you with views of the lovely South Sound, the nearby islands, and Anegada to the N.

Robins Bay (BA2016) is a pleasant and comfortable anchorage when the wind is between E and S. The best spot is along the SE shore, about 30 yards off, in 10 feet with good holding in sand.

Biras Creek (BA2016), in the bottom corner of the sound, affords excellent protection under almost all conditions. The new resort there comprises cottages, pools, and a hotel offering fine meals with a beautiful view amid lovely surroundings. The floating docks are for the hotel's small fleet of boats. You may anchor, or pick up one of the moorings after checking with the dockmaster.

When approaching Biras Creek from the W, keep a sharp eye open for Oyster Rock, about 200 yards offshore, just N of Camelia Point. This menace is just below the surface and cannot always be seen. Otherwise the approach is clear.

Saba Rock (BA2016), which divides the channel between Prickly Pear Island and Virgin Gorda, presents a lovely anchorage off its western side. But be sure to allow ample swinging room, or put out a stern anchor. As the tidal stream changes, it has been known to set the unwary skipper right against the rock. The approach from the W is clear of dangers.

It is usually calm here, and the holding is good in sand. Swimming is excellent, and the place is generally bug-free even under the dampest conditions. Saba Rock is private property, so do not go ashore.

Just S of Saba Rock, you may anchor off the attractive Bitter End Yacht Club, or use their new marina facilities.

Prickly Pear Island (BA2016) offers a pleasant anchorage on a sandy shelf 200–300 feet wide about halfway down its western side. The approach is clear except for one or two coral heads about 400 yards N of Vixen Point and about 150 yards from shore. It is usually calm here, and the holding is good in sand.

Eustatia Sound

The main body of this sound is well protected by an outer reef and provides good swimming and excellent snorkeling right from your boat. The approach should only be made under ideal conditions, that is: a calm sea, unriled water, and the sun overhead and slightly behind you. In such circumstances, all the rocks and reefs along the route can be spotted well ahead of time. Con your way from the rigging if you can. Enter the sound on the S side of Saba Rock on a heading of 060°T until you reach the deeper water.

Start your return trip to Gorda Sound in good afternoon light or you will have a problem picking your way around the hazards while heading into the sun.

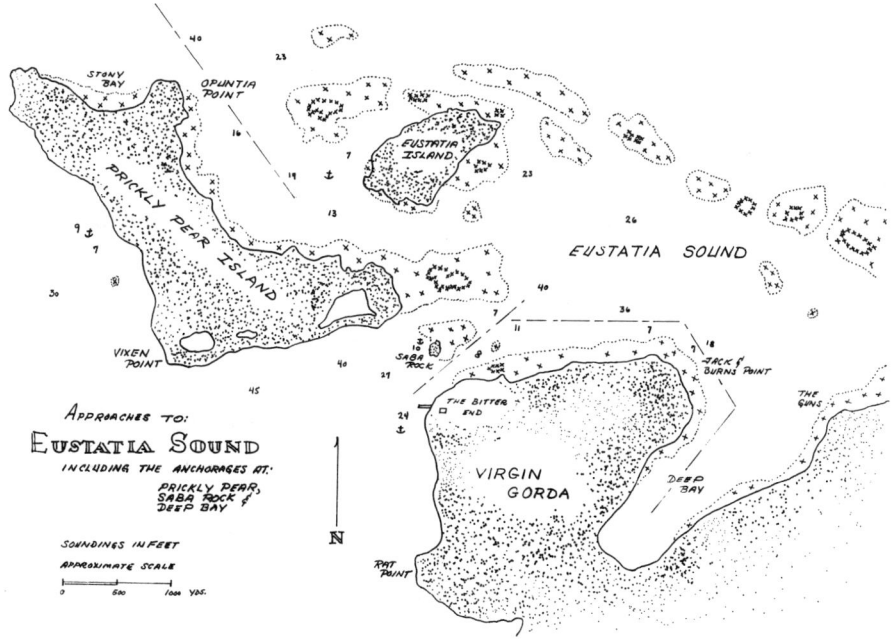

Deep Bay (BA2016), in the southwestern corner of Eustatia Sound, has a clear approach except for some small reefs and rocks close to shore. For a good overnight anchorage, move well up into the bay and drop the hook in 10 feet. Holding is good in sand.

Virgin Sound

Lying between Eustatia and Necker Islands, this small sound is open to the N and E; it is not a really pleasant cruising area except under light sea and wind conditions. The reefs S of Necker Island are quite obvious, but those N of Eustatia Island are not so easily seen, even under ideal conditions. For a safe, midchannel passage through this sound, hold a course or a back bearing 270°T on Mosquito Rock.

Eustatia Island (BA2016) may be easily and safely approached from the NW. Simply pass Opuntia Point (on Prickly Pear Island) about 50 yards off on a heading of 150°T and sail right on in. Anchor off the beach on Prickly Pear or in the lee of Eustatia. You are requested not to go ashore on Eustatia.

On a nice day, under the right conditions, this is a truly delightful spot, but it cannot be recommended as an overnight anchorage in winter because of its exposure to the N.

Necker Island (BA2016) is a lovely, uninhabited spot with beautiful beaches and excellent snorkeling. The approach from Virgin Sound is straightforward. Look for the small rise of land on the island's SW corner; the rise flattens out to the eastward. Approach this rise, which is called Devil Hill, on a northerly heading, with a watchful eye for a small, isolated reef on your port hand.

Anchor about 100 yards off the rocky shore directly below this small rise, or bear off around the point, picking your way through the isolated coral heads, to a good anchorage off the lovely beach in Devil Hill Bay. This is a daytime stop, to be used only under ideal conditions.

Anegada (BA2008)

Loosely translated from the Spanish, Anegada means "inundated"; and that it practically is! Contrasting sharply with the rest of this island group, this northernmost Virgin Island is nowhere more than 30 feet high. It is unapproachable except by eyeballing through a barrier reef that completely surrounds this seagirt patch of land. This combination of low-profile and dangerous fringing reef demands the most exacting dead reckoning, coupled with a healthy respect for the vagaries of the currents in this vicinity. Perhaps it is this last factor that has driven so many fine vessels to their death; perhaps it is the

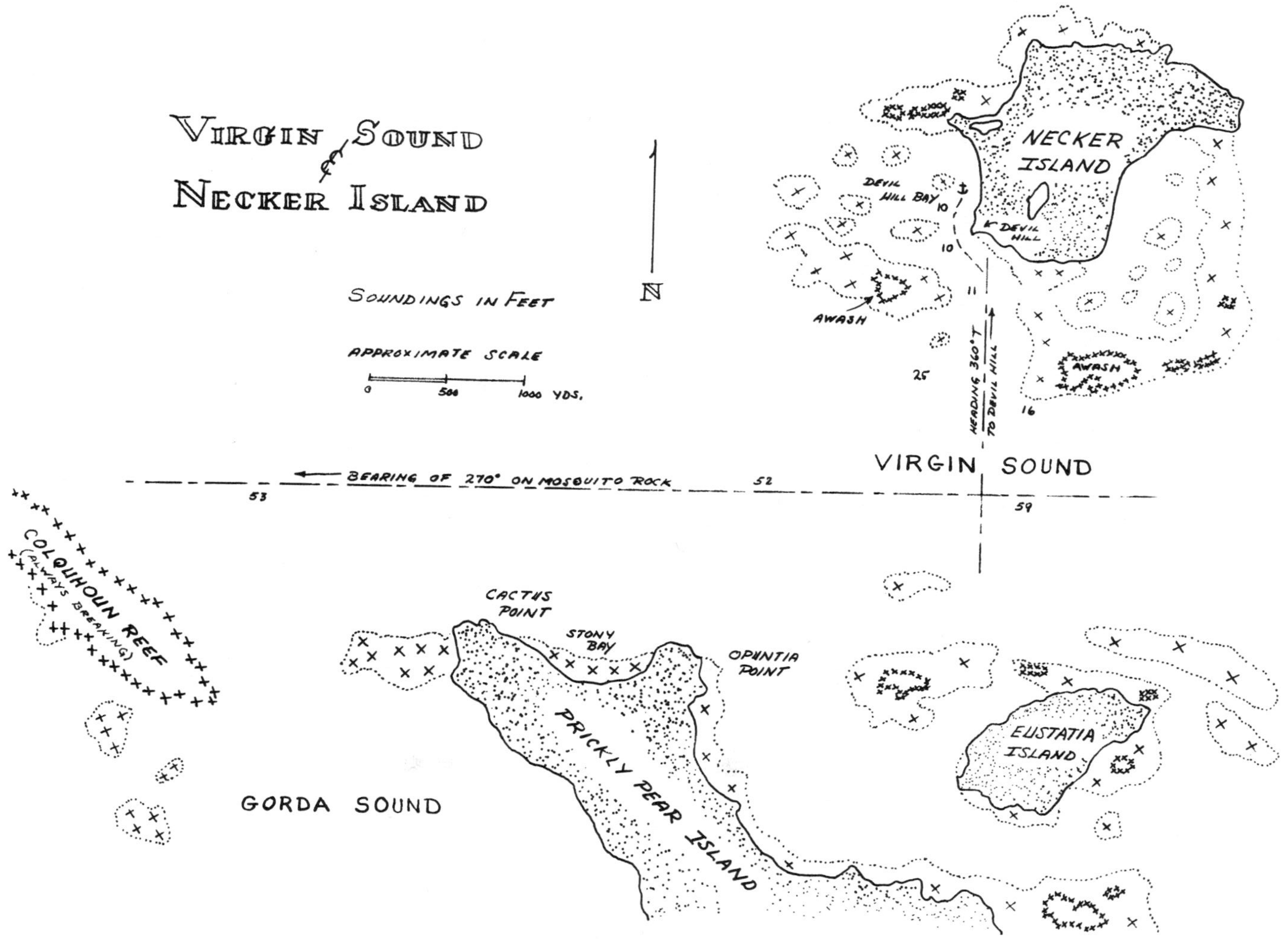

VIRGIN SOUND
&
NECKER ISLAND

SOUNDINGS IN FEET

APPROXIMATE SCALE

0   500   1000 YDS.

N

NECKER ISLAND

DEVIL HILL

DEVIL HILL BAY   10

AWASH

25

16   11

TO DEVIL HILL   HEADING 360° T

VIRGIN SOUND

59

52   BEARING OF 270° ON MOSQUITO ROCK

53

EUSTATIA ISLAND

OPINTIA POINT

CACTUS POINT

STONY BAY

PRICKLY PEAR ISLAND

GORDA SOUND

COLQUHOUN REEF
(ALWAYS BREAKING)

very immensity of the hazard, which stretches in a crescent of 23 unbroken miles, if you include the Horseshoe and Herman Reefs to the south of the island itself.

For years this windswept island had been populated by 300 or so natives, who made their living primarily from the sea. Then, in 1968, the entire island was leased from The Crown to an English land developer, who industriously set about building roads, docks, an airport, a hotel, and a smattering of model homes—in the hopes of generating more interest in Anegada, and more development money. But this bold project ran out of steam, as so many such schemes do, and Anegada is now back to its original population of 300 or so, who make their living primarily from the sea.

No one would dispute the island's potential for resort development. Almost 22 miles of unbroken beach, on an island in the middle of the trade-wind belt, is not an asset to be overlooked. But in the meantime, in a setting about as far from civilization as you can get nowadays, there are unlimited opportunities for the yachtsman (and others who can get there) for snorkeling, diving, and exploring reefs and wrecks.

To make the most of an excursion to Anegada, you might want to engage a local guide, such as Bert Kilbride, who runs the Dive Shop at Virgin Gorda Yacht Harbour. Bert knows Anegada and all its reefs and wrecks in minute detail.

Make your departure for Pomato Point on the western end of Anegada on a course of 020°T from the eastern end of Scrub Island, or 360°T from the western side of Mosquito Island. The distances are 15 and 12 miles respectively, and you will have covered over half the distance before you make your landfall on the "inundated island."

Your first indication of land will be a grove of palms well off the starboard bow; this is the grove at Pearl Point. Maintain your heading. A short time later, a single palm tree will emerge from the horizon almost dead ahead. This palm is on the beach between West End and Pomato Point. Maintain your heading. Almost immediately thereafter, another clump of palms will materialize to the left of the single palm, then another single palm will show itself to the right of the first. This last, most easterly, lone palm is just inland from Pomato Point and is going to be your major piloting reference, so be sure to identify it positively. Maintain your heading.

As the beach begins to appear, adjust your heading (if necessary) so that you are sailing directly toward this palm tree at Pomato Point. You should be then steering no less than 000°T and no greater than 030°T. Continue until the jetty off Setting Point and a white hotel building bears 080°T. Yachts drawing less than 6 feet may then turn to this heading of 080°T and continue cautiously toward the jetty. If you draw more than 6 feet, do not attempt this approach

ANEGADA

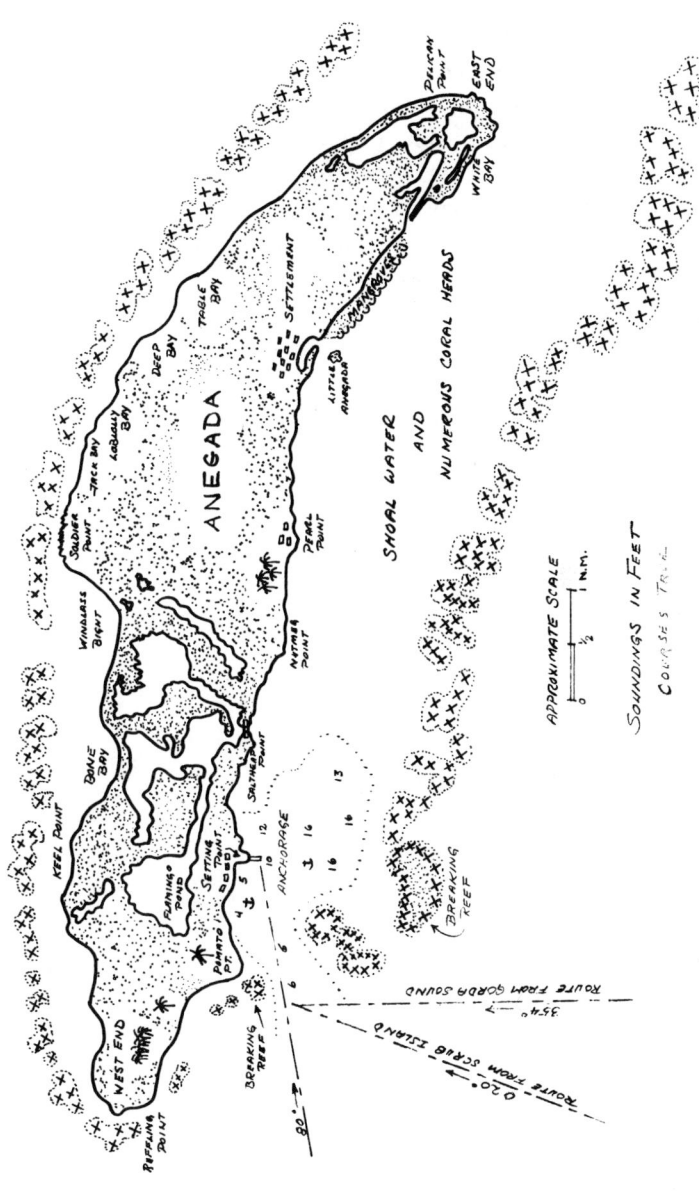

ANEGADA

WEST END · REFINMM POINT · KEEL POINT · BONE BAY · WINDLASS BIGHT · SOLDIER POINT · JACK BAY · LABONIA BAY · DEEP BAY · TABLE BAY · SETTLEMENT · PELICAN POINT · EAST END · WHITE BAY · LITTLE ANEGADA · PEARL POINT · NUTMEG POINT · SALTHEAP POINT · SETTING POINT · POMATO PT · FLAMING POND · BREAKING REEF · ANCHORAGE

SHOAL WATER AND NUMEROUS CORAL HEADS

(BREAKING REEF)

ROUTE FROM GORDA SOUND
ROUTE FROM SCRUB ISLAND
35°·7
0·20°
80·7

APPROXIMATE SCALE
0   ½   1 N.M.

SOUNDINGS IN FEET
COURSES TRUE

N

without more detailed information concerning the channel to the dock. Joe Soares, the owner of the restaurant and bar, can be reached by radio for more information.

A small reef just off Pomato Point must be left to port on your 080°T approach. When you come abeam of this reef, be on the lookout for two coral heads slightly to the E, with only a few feet of water over them. These are the only obstructions in the channel to the jetty, and you may not even see them.

Yachts drawing 5 feet or less may anchor well in the lee of Setting Point. Deeper-draft vessels may anchor S from Setting Point dock, or further E where the water deepens to 16 feet. This anchorage is almost a mile wide and a mile and a half long and provides excellent protection under practically all conditions. The sea is generally calm in the lee of Setting Point. A very light chop sometimes develops in the more open anchorage. Holding is good in sandy mud and grass.

CHAPTER TEN

The Windwards and Leewards

BY JOLYON BYERLEY

When the Caribbean islands burst through into the sunlight, the gods in charge of the area must have had a pretty keen sailor on the board of directors. Admittedly, someone blundered a little in the vicinity of the Anegada Passage, but on the whole, the islands stretch away to the south an amazingly regular 20 miles apart and at a handy right angle to the bustling trade winds. The lee coasts have an abundance of perfect harbors, usually strategically placed at either end of the islands, and most of the loose bits of rock, which in the beginning must have splattered around, fell into deep enough water not to be a nuisance.

The original inhabitants were the Arawaks, a band of cheerful, peace-loving layabouts whose main occupation must have been breaking their cooking pots into a million pieces with a view to occupying the time of present-day archeologists. Nobody is too sure exactly what sort of vessels the Arawaks used for their early exploring of the sometimes rather rough passages. We do know that the Caribs, a group of ferocious gentlemen with prodigious appetites, made long, light canoes from logs of the *gommier* tree: keeping their cooking pots whole, they ate their way northward from Venezuela as far as Haiti and possibly Cuba, much to the consternation of the Arawaks.

Much later, when the British, French, Spanish, and Dutch were squabbling mightily over the islands and blowing each others' heads off with cannonballs the weight and consistency of my Aunt Mabel's Christmas pudding, the Caribs in their almost unsinkable canoes very nearly overcame the might of the European navies pitted against them. Brave and skillful seamen, they easily outstripped the lumbering naval ships, pulling off incredible feats of daring into the bargain.

On one occasion, a war party from Dominica paddled to Antigua and landed just east of English Harbour in a tiny hidden inlet known as Indian Creek. Knocking off a few dozing Redcoats, they kidnapped the Governor's good Lady and a dozen bottles of his favorite port, had dinner, and paddled back to Dominica. They obviously had other attributes, for when Her Ladyship was rescued by all the King's men, she was most reluctant to return, preferring the wild mountain stronghold to the bright lights of Antigua.

Carib canoes are still built in the islands of Dominica, Martinique, and St. Lucia, and are just as popular amongst the fishermen as more conventional boats. Now, mostly propelled by massive government-financed outboards instead of patchwork sails, they are a fabulous sight screaming in rainbows of spray through the tumbling trade-wind seas or lying perilously ahull in mid-channel while their occupants calmly tend their lines.

After the demise of the Caribs, the islands became a focal point in the European struggle for power. Most large vessels of the day, unable to do much more than lumber downwind like runaway haystacks, preferred to take the trade-wind route to the New World. These islands lay like a giant tollgate across their path. Therefore, whoever controlled these little outposts controlled the Americas. With a strange mixture of sadness, awe, and excitement, one can now wander through these old battlefields. Relative to the size of the area, more British and French troops died in combat on the slopes of St. Lucia's Morne Fortune than anywhere else except the trenches of Flanders. Two thousand fathoms down, between the shrouded peaks of Guadeloupe and Dominica and under the hurrying, forgetful waves, lies almost the whole of Admiral de Grasse's battle fleet, outsailed and outmaneuvered by the vengeful tars of Admiral Rodney's West Indian Squadron.

The charm of cruising the islands these days is that, outside of the major cities, things have changed very little through the centuries. Even the most sluggish imagination can leap into the past: anchored in a moondrenched bay, the watcher, already awed by the enormous tropical night, sees close inshore under the shadowy slumbering palms the indistinct image of a six-man Carib canoe slipping stealthily into the darkness. How many times on a similar night had the young Horatio Nelson looked into the depth of the jungle and pondered its secrets?

Yachtsmen were quick to discover the islands: Capt. Slocum, Fritz Fenger, and Eric Hiscock were among those who wrote admiringly of what they saw. Only recently, though, has it become commonplace to sight another yacht crossing the passages, and even now, despite a fairly high density of yachts in English Harbour, Fort-de-France, Castries, Kingstown, and St. George's, one cannot complain of overcrowding. The main reason this yachtsman's paradise is so free of traffic is undoubtedly that few Stateside yachtsmen relish the 1,800 miles or so of slogging to windward. And make no mistake—slog, slog, slog it nearly always is.

In jotting down these notes, I am making no attempt to give sailing directions in intricate detail. The intention is to make life a little easier for the cruising yachtsman. Having found his way to the islands in the first place, he can presumably manage another 400 miles without too much hassle. Finding a

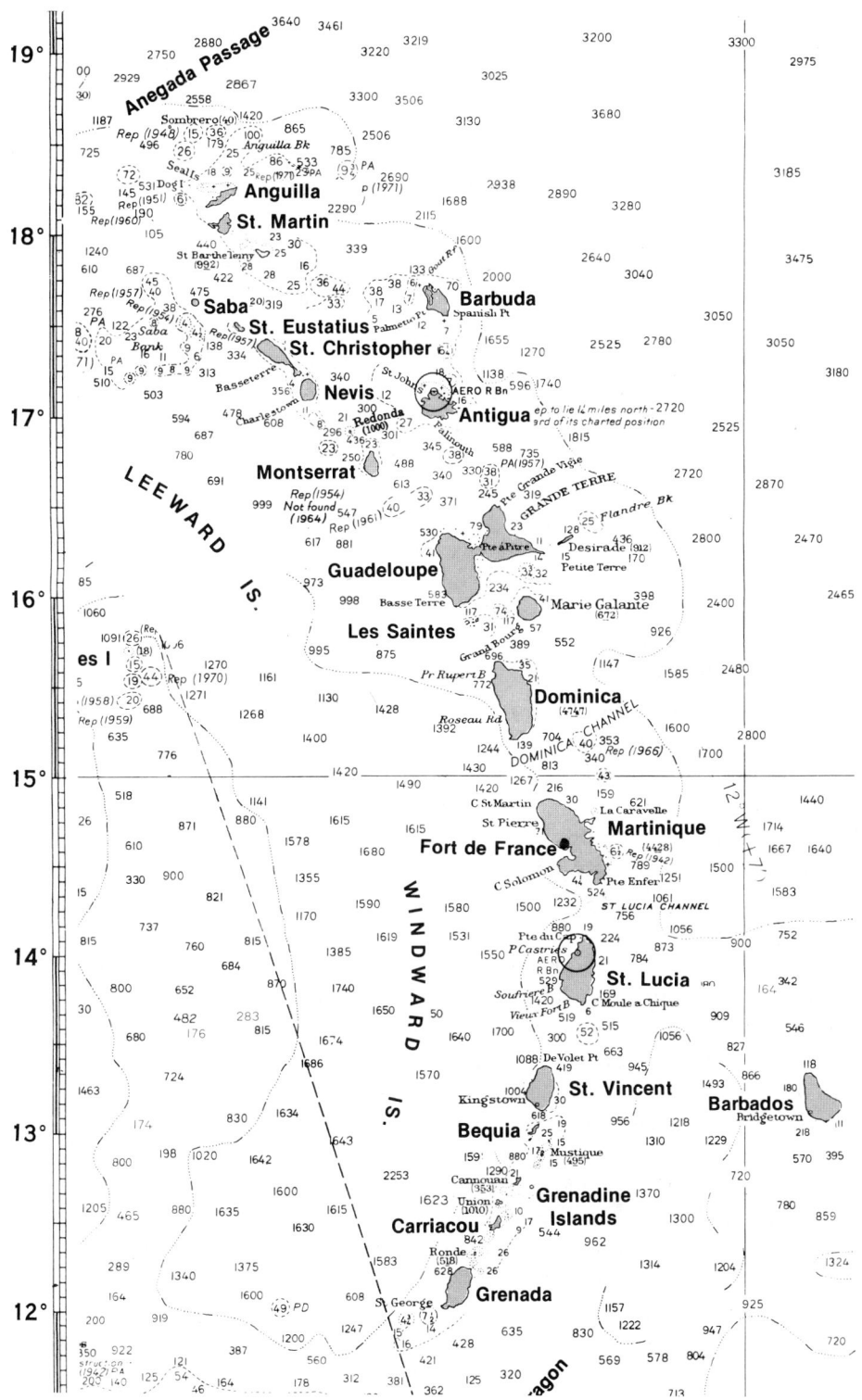

The Windwards and Leewards

reliable taxi driver is generally more of a problem than finding the channel into the next harbor.

Wind, Seas, and Strategy

Weather conditions throughout the islands are fairly predictable. December through April, the trade wind blows at its hardest. I would put the mean at something between 18 and 23 knots from the east. However, I have known weeks at a time when the trades have seldom dropped below 30–35 knots, gusting to 45 at times, and persisting in the ENE or ESE. Conversely, I remember one February so calm that *Lord Jim*'s 2,000-square-foot golleywobbler was constantly in use, more to shade our gently broiling charterers than to catch the fitful puffs. But, luckily, the winter season is almost always a time of superb sailing conditions, when the accent is slightly more on the boisterous than the balmy. The rest of the year generally produces a wind that averages between 12–15 knots and widens its angle to between NE and SE. In August, September, and October, it can get pretty warm ashore at times, although at sea the temperature would compare favorably to that of a summer day off the Chesapeake. In winter, the sea conditions are more of a force to be reckoned with than the wind strength.

For 3,000 miles, the Atlantic has rolled itself along at a fair clip, with the constant trades using plenty of spur to good effect. No wonder, then, that by the time a much-travelled wave is bottlenecked between the islands, it has grown into a rare broth of a boy and eager to make itself felt. On a reach-through, the well-found yacht will find such a sea only exhilarating. To windward it's another matter. Squalls and the higher islands affect local conditions considerably. A West Indian squall, very common in slightly unstable weather, normally increases the wind strength by 10–15 knots.

After many years of shortening sail in such weather, I've eventually settled instead on running off, sheeting everything in hard to keep the speed down, and waiting it out. Five minutes usually does it. There is no hard and fast rule, but if the squall moves fast and you can't see through it, be prepared for a bit of a bashing. As a yacht leaves a high island, she will generally find that the wind will head for 15–20 minutes and blow a good deal harder than in midchannel. Likewise, the wind will both step up and free as the yacht runs under the lee of the next island. If it is a marginal reefing day as you poke your nose from under an island such as Dominica or St. Vincent, hang on for 10 minutes or so, and the chances are you can then have a good full-sail breeze. In the lee, the wind will funnel down the bigger valleys, blow like Stan Kenton's old brass section, and then fan out to the N and S. Under the hills, it will die or even come in from the W. You'll probably do best to stay about ½-mile offshore and play the puffs. At least the seas are flat and the scenery is great.

The traditional point of departure from the British Virgin Islands to the Leewards* is Round Rock Passage, just SE of Virgin Gorda. Many crews, having made it to the Caribbean, become a trifle blasé about the whole thing and are apt to swagger off southward, fully intending "to let the balmy trades waft them gently through the satin-smooth seas of the Indies." That's what it says on the travel posters, anyway, but the first of the slab-sided seas of the Anegada Passage is rather inclined to dampen their enthusiasm.

Between Round Rock and Philipsburg, St. Martin, is 81 miles. The NE trades, which for most of the year can be relied upon to be easterly or even S of E, seldom allow even the most close-winded of vessels to lay St. Martin. From Round Rock it's 82 miles to Saba, a magical, story-book island hardly ever visited before 1973 because it had no safe anchorage whatsoever. Many times we have stood forlornly off, watching the spray hurl itself up the rocks at both of the island's so-called landing places. Now, however, a substantial stone mole has been constructed by the Dutch Government, and provided the wind is not in the N and the limited space not taken up by local trading schooners, a safe night can be spent alongside. Generally, though, a yacht heading S should not rely on finding favorable conditions at Saba, and may find it best to bash on to St. Martin or the nearby islands of Anguilla or St. Barts, where good, comfortable harbors abound.

A word about the Anegada Passage might be in order hereabouts. If you're going south, do not take the Passage lightly. Your vessel should be prepared for steep, confused seas that sometimes bear little relation to the strength or direction of the wind. In February, 1972, the experienced captain of a 130-foot motor yacht reported to English Harbour Radio, Antigua, that he was tangling with conditions as unpleasant as any he had met in 35 years of ocean cruising. Obviously the angle of attack has a lot to do with it, and certain Caribbean yachtsmen advise paying off a fraction, making a proper passage of it, and heading for the first island that can comfortably be reached—Montserrat, Guadeloupe, or Dominica, for example. Only conditions at the time can decide this, but should the wind have a slight northerly slant, jump at the chance to cross this aggravating bit of water.

A very large area of relatively shallow water lies SSW of Saba, with a least depth of 4½ fathoms on its NE corner. In blowy conditions, the local schooner men keep well clear, calling it "a damn vexin' piece of troublesome water."

The current in the Anegada Passage normally sets to the NW or W, but in places seems to have a mind of its own. On one occasion, after a quiet night crossing from the Virgins, we found ourselves so far to the east of our course that the lowlying island of Anguilla came up on the starboard beam instead of the port bow. But if the Anegada is unpredictable and aggravating, remember

* See Appendix A, The Leeward and Windward Islands and Vice Versa.

that once he has crossed it, the sailing man is then in the most perfect sailing conditions in the world.

Radio Communications

Caribbean yachtsmen are a rather individualistic lot, for we are, you see, definitely the only ones in step. Take radio communications, for example. Whatever may be going on in the rest of the world, the AM radio is still the only one worth its crystals and transistors down here in the islands. SSB and VHF, despite their advantages, are hardly used at all. From the Leewards south, the universal ship-to-ship and ship-to-shore frequency is 2527 kHz; 2142 and 2638 are used as occasional alternatives. On the whole, radio conditions are good in the Caribbean, and a well-tuned set of, say, 90–100 watts will usually be heard as far as 300–400 miles, provided the transmitting vessel is not hemmed in by a wall of mountains. Cruising and charter yachts alike are served by several private radio stations, such as Antigua's English Harbour Radio, Martinique's MCS in Fort-de-France, WIT in Bequia (Palm Island), MTV in Carriacou, PSV in Petit St. Vincent, and Stevens' Yachts and GYS in Grenada. All transmit and receive on 2527 kHz and are open for traffic during normal office hours.

The Nicholson family of Antigua pioneered radio communications in the early 1950s, when they realized that their charter clients sometimes found it necessary to keep in touch with their homes and businesses. Cdr. V.E.B. Nicholson bought the second-oldest transmitter in the world, set up schedules at 0900 and 1600 hours, and kept in close contact with his little fleet, a happening that was soon to become a tradition enjoyed by charter crews and guests alike.

"Hello, *Carrina*. Ah, John, old boy," he would boom, "those head parts haven't arrived yet. I can send you down an old bowler hat of mine, or one of Emmie's flower pots. Anyway, old boy, tell Mr. Smith [the charterer] that I hope everything's taking an equal strain. English Harbour clear with *Carrina*, and hello *Freelance*. Bruno, old boy. Good morning, afternoon, and evening to you."

The number of boats and the corresponding traffic density now discourage today's operators from putting on such entertainment, but it can still be amusing. For instance:

"Hello, such-and-such, this is PSV. We have a bikini top and a man's brown headpiece found under the bar after last night's jump-up."

On more than one occasion, these "yachty" radio stations have organized search and rescue operations. Several lives have definitely been saved as a result. It should be pointed out here that a distress call in daylight on 2182 kHz probably stands less chance of being picked up than an appeal on 2527 kHz. If you come unprepared, Desmond Nicholson at Carib Marine, Antigua, stocks a supply of local crystals.

On the subject of distress calls: you must realize that there are no organized coast guard services south of St. Martin and north of Trinidad; yachtsmen are rather on their own.

A full Caribbean weather picture, originating from the government meteorological office in Antigua, is broadcast by English Harbour Radio at 0900 each morning. Cables and messages will be forwarded to yachts by all the above-mentioned stations, and traffic lists are broadcast at regular intervals throughout the day.

Lifesaving Equipment

Most of the islands are steep-to, and even Auntie Mabel, whose watery eyes once mistook a moustachioed Buckingham Palace Guardsman for a red post-box, would become dimly aware of such a land mass before it was too late. The exceptions, such as Antigua, Barbuda, Anguilla, and the Grenadines, have most of their reefs on the windward side, so that a mariner in real trouble, apart from getting scratched up a bit on the way in, would soon drift ashore, perhaps in the middle of the local hostelry's lobster barbecue. More of a problem would be the yacht that foundered because of fire, explosion, or tired caulking and happened to be in the middle of an island passage at the time.

An inflatable life raft, especially the type with a canopy, takes off to leeward at the very dickens of a rate in the usual trade-wind conditions, so the important thing (if it is impossible to work north or south across the trades to the nearest island) is to endeavor not to drift too fast to the west. Once through the island chain, it's a long haul to Central America; therefore, a larger-than-usual sea anchor should be carried, along with a good set of rockets for nighttime and a mirror and smoke for daylight.

Personally, my choice would every time be a good, nonsinkable sailing dinghy. Even a small one would stand a chance of towing a medium-sized life raft on a reach and into the lee of the nearest island.

Sunburn

For as long as I remember, I've had a horror of pajamas. At a very early age, I was given a pair by Auntie Mabel. They were bedecked with a ghastly maroon-and-blue stripe and had a weight and bristliness similar to the coat of an old Highland bull. I distinctly remember that you could stand them alone on the floor and crawl through their hairy interior; it was like entering an empty suit of armor. Regulation boarding-school and army pajamas did little to change my attitude. Anyway, I haven't owned a pair for 22 years. This fact, I am told, should stop me from ever emerging into the West Indian sunlight. Pajamas are the only way to avoid being frizzled to death, say the experts, and bound by this advice, there seems to be a never-ending parade of the nasty, floppy things.

The great pajama game has been going on for all my time in the islands, but unless you are one of those unfortunates who immediately becomes burnt to a crisp and never tans, common-sense exposure—with the help of one of the excellent, nongreasy liquid sun creams—will suffice. Make no mistake, however: the sun can be wickedly hot and damaging to an unbronzed northern skin; therefore I suggest you give serious thought to equipping your boat with a small sailing awning or even a collapsible Bimini top.

A strong trade wind blowing against a salt-encrusted face can do just as much damage as the sun, so it's not a bad idea to rinse off with fresh water every so often, then apply a fresh load of gunk. A barrier cream such as "Shade," applied between 1100 and 1400, is very good protection.

In harbor, an awning is a must. It should be easy to rig, preferably of dark-colored material like blue Vivetex, and fitted with roll-down side curtains as a protection against driving rain and the late-afternoon sun. A roll-down curtain on the rear of the awning is a good thing if, as on most medium-sized yachts, the relaxing-place is in the cockpit. One always lies at anchor facing east or thereabouts, and from 1600 until dusk the only shade is up at the pointed end! Whatever you do, make your awning simple and taut. The pretty, scalloped affair so carefully arranged with battens and myriad pieces of string may have looked shipshape in Force 0 up a quiet Florida creek, but during a squall in the Tobago Cays it will become a passable imitation of Aunt Mabel's washing in a wind tunnel.

The Northern Leewards—St. Martin (25606)

Anguilla, St. Martin, and St. Barts offer as much variety as one can expect to find in the West Indies. The only feature lacking on these three islands is the dense mountain foliage found on the higher, more tropical islands to the south. St. Martin, very small, half French and half Dutch (the Dutch call their half Sint Maarten), is both bustling with commercial enterprise and lazing in the warm peace of the tropics. It is ringed with bays and beaches, and a yacht of moderate draft, say up to 8 feet, can find many empty anchorages around the coast.

Philipsburg (25608) is the capital of the Dutch section. By comparison, it makes the French capital of Marigot seem quaint, forgotten, and forlorn. However, after one has sampled the pleasure of free-port shopping in Philipsburg (cameras, watches, tape recorders, binoculars, and booze), I personally prefer the rural French side.

On entering Philipsburg, fly the yellow flag and as a courtesy, the Dutch

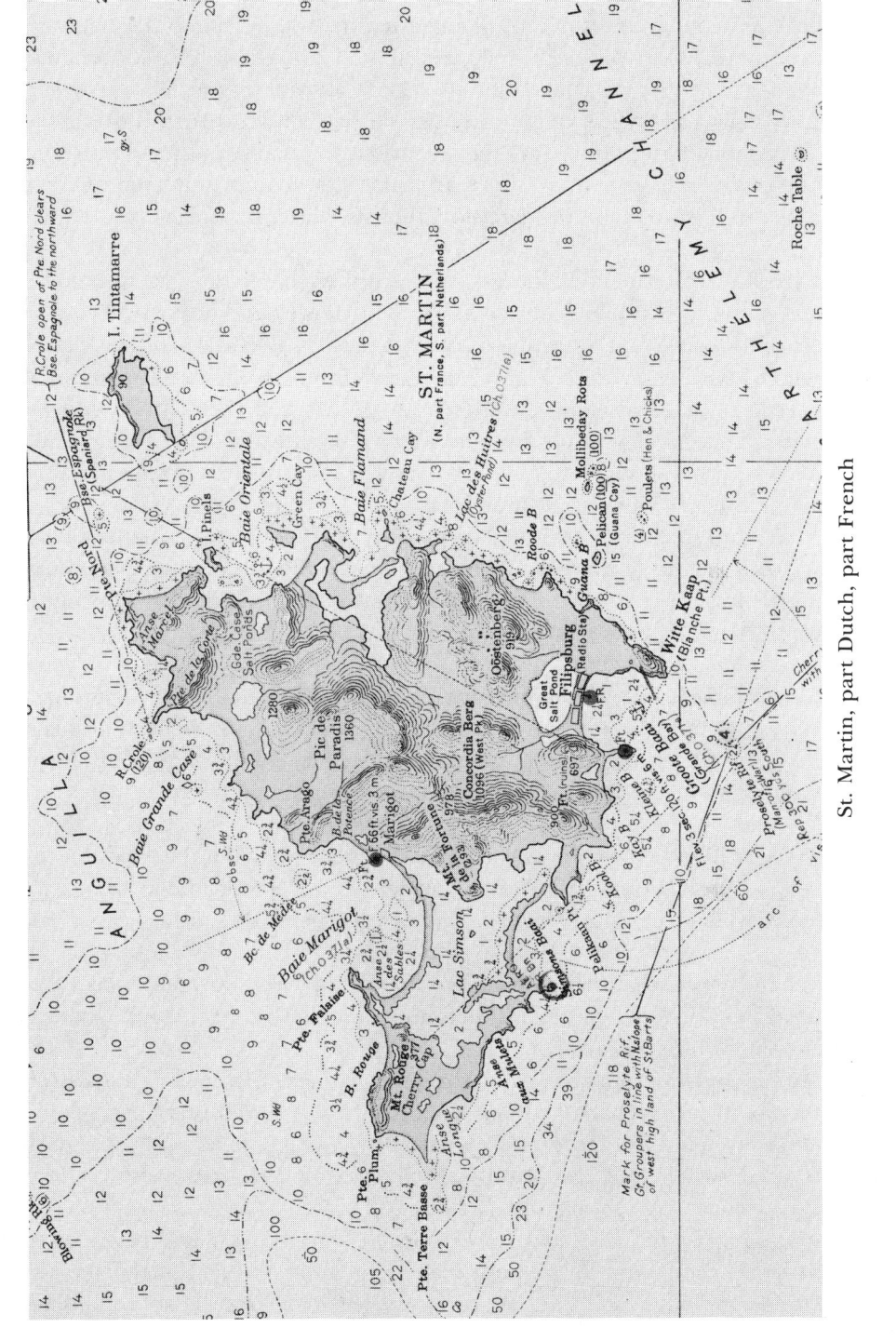

St. Martin, part Dutch, part French

national flag (if you have forgotten to get one, then fly the French flag with the stripes horizontal, but don't say I suggested it). You will find that nobody is much interested in you, so the skipper should proceed ashore to the Police Station, just behind the church at the back of the main square. Three copies of your crew list will suffice, and the officials will give you a form to fill out. Neither customs nor immigration worry as much on this island as they do on some others—at Marigot, in fact, there appears to be completely free access to the island. Best to be on the safe side, though, and enter formally at Philipsburg.

Favor the western end of the bay for the approach. Philipsburg, like most of the bays on the S and W coasts, occasionally suffers from a heavy swell, but the most comfortable and untroubled part of the bay is the NE corner, as close to Bobbie's Landing as draft allows. Capt. Tony's Lifeboat Bar and Restaurant is a good spot both to leave one's dinghy and to cool off, and Tony is building a jetty at which he hopes to supply fuel and water to yachts of 7-foot draft. The bay shallows quickly about ½- to ¾-mile from shore, and 7–8 foot draft is just about maximum to get close up to the beach.

Water and fuel can be obtained from the government jetty at Blanche Point, but a constant surge thereabouts makes the wooden piles rather frightening. Nevertheless, on a couple of occasions I have anchored *Lord Jim* facing the town and made fast stern-to.

Simson Lake (25606, 25608) may now be entered through the swing bridge at Simson Bay, but you will have to phone Zinche Smith & Co. well in advance to arrange for the bridge to open. There is no fee. The holding is good inside, but the milky water and a number of shallows make it a bit tricky.

Marigot (25608), on the French side, has recently been dredged and is a reasonable anchorage provided a northerly swell doesn't build up. If it is uncomfortable in Marigot, it's usually good in Philipsburg, and vice versa.

When I asked what the dredged depth was supposed to be, there was a great deal of shoulder-shrugging, but we found 9 feet in the vicinity of the moored boats close under the town.

At midday, a Grumman Goose amphibian comes in from St. Thomas. The pilots are of the old barnstorming school and come to rest in a cloud of spray and obscenities a few feet from one's stern. They then power up through the anchored vessels and shovel out passengers, luggage, and livestock into a waiting dinghy. All great fun to watch.

Don't rely on buying a lot of provisions in Marigot; you'll do better on the Dutch side. However, if you appreciate good food, toddle down to Le Mini Club, a waterside restaurant run by ex-yachtsman Pierre Plessis and his wife

Claude. Both speak English as it was spoken by Maurice Chevalier, are delightful hosts—and their food is the best on the island.

In their chartering days, Pierre and Claude had on their yacht a tame ocelot named Pompidou. It slept on Claude's bed in the master cabin, a situation obviously not possible when the cabin was given over to guests or on charter. At such times, Pompidou was banished to the fo'c'sle and exercised ashore in the dead of night—the charterers, of course, had no idea he was aboard. One night, by means of an open cupboard, the big cat found his way into the bilge and was able to creep aft and into the master cabin. The charterers were a hard-drinking elderly couple from Rhode Island. Pompidou padded onto his accustomed bed, put his paws on the good lady's shoulders, and with his big whiskery face inches from hers, began purring in loud contentment. The resulting scene hardly needs enlarging upon.

Orient Bay (25606), on the E coast of the island, can be entered in good light. An especially pleasant anchorage for small yachts can be taken behind Pinel Island.

Oyster Pond (25608) is a great place for the adventurous when a strong trade is blowing. There is a narrow entrance between the reefs, and since this anchorage is on the exposed eastern side of the island, a large, breaking sea can really enliven the proceedings.

I've entered Oyster Pond many times without incident, but once I nearly put *Mirage*, a single-screw, deep-draft trawler, halfway up a cactus bush on the nearest hill. Caught by a breaker, we were suddenly going sideways at an angle of 45° and at about 15 knots, with white water foaming angrily around the deckhouse. After the breaker had gone through, we clawed round again (thanks to a big rudder) and slipped inside before the next one grabbed us.

The channel, which is privately marked, has a red-and-white vertically striped can buoy at its entrance, which can be left to either side. Small red cans mark the starboard side of the channel, which should be favored. Once around the dogleg to starboard, halfway along the channel, your problems are over.

Fuel, water, and electricity can be obtained inside the lagoon, where 10-foot draft is maximum. The hotel is delightful (if slightly stuffy), and the staff is most anxious to please.

On another occasion, in January, 1975, we were in Oyster Pond during a period when the trades had been blowing at 30 knots for nearly three weeks. We had gone in with *Étoile de Mer* just as it started to blow, and getting out over the bar a week later was a hair-raising experience we won't soon forget. Mike Beal, the very experienced skipper of the Bill Tripp-designed *Katrinka*, watched us negotiate the channel from a vantage point about 12 feet above sea level and told us later that our 73-foot, heavy-displacement trawler completely disappeared in the troughs and looked like an exploding soufflé amongst the breaking crests. Obviously some of these waves must have been over 14 feet high.

I mention this as a reminder that the E side of any of the islands is no place to be during blustery winter weather. Save your exploring of the exposed coasts for another season.

Tintamarre Island (25606), once a secret airfield, was much used by a former mayor of St. Barts. He assembled a veritable squadron of antiquated aircraft on the tiny strip. Quite what he did with them no one knows, but the remains are still there, littered over the tiny island. Anchor off the western tip in 3 fathoms.

Spaniard Rock, a real hazard situated bang in the middle of the channel between Tintamarre and St. Martin, is accurately charted and breaks in most weathers.

Anguilla (25606)

You'll probably remember this little island's sudden climb to fame a few years ago. It went through a series of real-life events that would outdo a better-than-usual Hollywood farce. The scenario was written by Her Majesty's Britannic Government and was well up to their usual standard. The only snag was that someone forgot to invite the cameraman, which was indeed a great pity. Anyway, sandy little Anguilla used to be part of a group that also comprised St. Kitts and Nevis, both relatively large and prosperous islands. The good people of Anguilla developed a "thing" about being poor relations, and one sultry day, in the best Gilbert and Sullivan tradition, armed with sticks and stones and the odd coconut, they packed their half-dozen Kittian policemen into a local schooner and sent them back to St. Kitts with strict instructions for that island's leader. According to well-informed sources, the instructions had something to do with the bristly end of a pineapple.

Here the plot thickens. The government of St. Kitts became convinced that nasty Sicilian-type gentlemen in wide-brimmed hats and sinister dark suits were behind it all and were planning to take over the island to build a private kingdom of naughtiness. St. Kitts sent an impassioned appeal for assistance against the forces of evil to Her Majesty's Government, who, lacking a gunboat but dying to do something exciting for a change, promptly dispatched a relief force of two battalions of paratroopers, a squadron of helicopters, an anti-submarine frigate, six turboprop aircraft, and half the City of London police force, complete with blue serge jackets and pointed helmets.

Meanwhile, back at Anguilla, the citizens were employed in revolutionary activities like lobstering, boatbuilding, and lying in the sun. It obviously had to

Anguilla

stop. At dawn one morning, the paratroopers, the helicopters, the antisubmarine frigate, and the London police force, backed by the six aircraft, stormed the beaches!

The opposing force—two small boys, one old lady, and six nanny goats—were soon in full flight back to the village, where the inhabitants were beginning another revolutionary day. Told of the landing, they rushed to the beaches. Soon the London police force was heavily engaged in solving two cases of poultry theft and a drunk-and-disorderly charge. The paratroopers, finding very few roads for their vehicles, proceeded to build some, plus a couple of schools, a clinic, and improvements to the airstrip. Never have an invading force and a crushed nation been so happy with each other. However, now that the actors have all gone home, Anguilla still does not know whether it is a part of St. Kitts, a Crown Colony, or an independent nation.

In any case, the cruising yachtsman will find it delightful. The people are very courteous and well-disposed toward visitors. For years they have held the position of being amongst the best seamen and shipbuilders in the West Indies. Now that the schooners are being superceded by small modern coasters, the shipwrights will be hard put to keep going.

Sandy Ground, or Road Bay (25608), as the principal settlement is called, looks like a good, sheltered anchorage on the chart, but for much of the year it is plagued by an unpleasant swell.

Since the Bobbies went back to beer and blighty, a new police force has been trained. The skipper should visit these worthy gentlemen with 3 crew lists. There are really no provisions to be bought anywhere on the island, except local vegetables and canned goods, but do go there before the supermarkets and hotels go up.

Rendezvous Bay (25608) is one of several around on the S coast opposite Marigot. At their extreme eastern ends, they usually give good shelter. The local sloops and schooners use 2 or 3 reef-fringed anchorages that are inclined to become rather crowded.

The island's beaches are the color and consistency of freshly fallen snow, and swimming off them is a sheer delight. Snorkeling is excellent all around the island.

Prickly Pear Cays (25608) will appeal particularly to the snorkeling enthusiast. Sneak just to windward of the easternmost island, between the reef and the little beach. Maximum draft is about 8 feet, but the fine sand bottom is subject to shoaling after heavy swells from the N.

All the reefs to the N of Anguilla offer some of the best diving in the Caribbean.

Dog Island (25606) is uninhabited, and is intriguing because of an unexplained, unused airstrip, but to find a good anchorage here is difficult indeed. Slip in through the coral heads on the western tip in good, calm weather only.

Sandy Island (25606) qualifies as a daytime anchorage and gives the crew a chance to explore everyone's dream island. Watch out for Long John Silver, though.

I would rather keep this last place a secret; as a compromise, it shall remain nameless.

A little way to the NE of Crocus Bay there is a long rocky point with a tiny sand beach at the eastern end. Anchor stern to the beach and make fast to a boulder. Jagged white cliffs fall into crystal-clear water, long-tailed bosun birds swoop through the masthead, and not a soul will you see. Absolutely idyllic.

St. Barthélemy (St. Barts) (25606)

I suppose that St. Barts is pretty close to being my favorite island, yet it's hard to say exactly why. It's a French island. Ever since I tacked the old schooner *Mollihawk* into Gustavia, way back in 1958, this tiny little fragment of Brittany has captivated me. The Swedes at one time owned the island, and maybe a little of their neatness has rubbed off on the more happy-go-lucky Breton fishermen who have lived here since the late 1800s.

Gustavia (25608), the island's minute capital, rings the harbor. Until a short time ago it was the base of smuggling operations for the entire Caribbean. Even now, battered old sloops from as far away as Trinidad and Venezuela can be seen alongside the dock loading up to the point of absurdity with case after case of Scotch whiskey. Prior to 1973, only a quarter of the harbor was deep enough for anything but a short-legged seagull. Now just about all the space can be used, but so much mud and sand was removed from the bottom that some of the houses close to the water are leaning inwards a little more than usual. Ten feet can go nearly anywhere, and it's quite normal to pick a spot and tie stern to the old walls.

Although customs and immigration formalities are minimal, the gendarmes sometimes feel a little neglected, and it's a good plan to nip along to their office (3 minutes from the dock) and ask if they require anything. They will usually hand you a printed leaflet which, amongst other things, tells you how to get to the *abattoir* and that riding a bicycle in the nude is prohibited. This apparently does not apply to motor scooters; recently, by the Eden Roc Hotel, two tanned and topless young things put the law regularly to the test.

Very good marine supplies are available from the family business of Magras

& Sons. Nearly everyone speaks fluent English, and just about any of the world's major currencies seem acceptable. Although St. Barts is a free port, some things are not quite as cheap as St. Martin, but with a little bargaining you can do pretty well.

Depending on the wind direction, it's fun to spend some time in the bays around the island.

There is talk of a big marina complex to be built on the SE side of the island; I have seen the plans, in fact, and work was scheduled to start in 1974. But one wonders why the French can't take a leaf out of their own book and build more in the style of lovely Port Grimaud in the south of France than in the style of south Florida's monumental concrete and glass.

Baie de Colombier (25606) on the island's NW corner is quite free of dangers right up to the beach.

Baie St. Jean (25606), good in calm weather, is adjacent to the small and delightful Eden Roc Hotel. The wealthy young French jet-setters congregate here, and there is a little of the sparkle of St. Tropez about the place. Nip along by taxi and have a look at the entrance before going in, or ask advice from Dominique, owner of l'Entrepont restaurant on the Gustavia waterfront. On the way, if you are a light-plane enthusiast, pause for a few moments of thoughtful study of the airstrip.

High in the mountains overlooking this bay is a tastefully built and delightfully decorated hotel called Les Castelets. Managed by delectable Madame Geneviève Jouney, this little place is a real surprise and as different from the average Caribbean hotel as you could imagine. The rooms are palatial, the view superb, and the restaurant excellent. Try to make it before sunset.

Isle de Fourche (25606) is a tiny but spectacular spot just to the NW of St. Barts. Completely barren and deserted, but boasting an imposing skyline of humps and pinnacles, it offers a fairly good but blowy anchorage. Keep a good lookout on entering the bay; the odd rock is littered about.

For some reason, people always take their clothes off here. Maybe it's the solitude, but the dear old inhibited and morally constipated human being can be seen gamboling about, doing what he's always wanted to do, white rumps flashing like a herd of startled deer.

Saba (25606)

This spectacular Dutch island, and nearby Statia (St. Eustatius), are drifting along about 20 years behind the times. Particularly in Saba's case, that makes a stop quite delightful. The problem is finding a secure spot. On rare occasions, it is possible to anchor off or make fast to the large steel buoy off the Customs House landing. Before the stone mole was built in 1973, a surf boat would come out to ferry one ashore, and yachts would most likely stand off while shore parties explored this mountainous paradise. Now, with luck, you may be able to make fast alongside for a night.

The wind howls and moans fitfully around the great grey cliffs, and the sea does its best to reach over the stonework of the new wall. One becomes more aware than ever how fragile a creation a yacht really is. In spring, summer, and fall, long periods of really calm weather would make Saba a really attractive proposition, for with your yacht safely alongside, you could spend days ashore absorbing the marvelous beauty of this unique island.

The main town, Bottom, is about a quarter of the way up the steep-sided island, snugly nestled in the bowl of a long-dead volcano. After an awe-inspiring ride up the unbelievable switchbacked road, the little town pops into view like something from a Hans Christian Andersen fairy tale: neatly painted dollhouses are surrounded by a riotous explosion of flowers. Much higher still are the villages of Windwardside and Hell's Gate, where the little white houses cling to the cloud-shrouded side of the great green mountain.

Nearly two out of three Sabans are of pure white origin. The rest are of varying hues—and everyone is either very young or very old. The men and women of working age are all earning a living in St. Martin, Curaçao, or Aruba. Considered to be amongst the best bluewater seamen in the world, Sabans will be found as deck officers and crew aboard freighters, coasters, and supertankers. But somehow, when you meet them in a far-off port, you get the impression that they are only waiting for the moment when they can step back into yesterday and sit with their blue-eyed, stubbly-chinned old uncles, high in their windy eyries, watching the sea below, which from 2,000 feet up looks almost benign.

English is spoken as much as Dutch, and dollars seem to outnumber the official guilders.

Tourists are beginning to find their way to Saba, so go quickly while the magic remains. If necessary, leave your yacht in St. Martin and fly across (which is an experience in itself). There is a superb little hotel in Bottom called the Captain's Quarters. You won't believe it.

St. Eustatius (25601)

Statia, as it's called locally, is also living in the past. Unlike Saba, though, the island has a slightly sad atmosphere; it has probably never recovered from the sacking administered in 1780 by Admiral Rodney because the Dutch were supplying provisions to American warships. The ruins of the demolished town of Oranjestad are still partially visible, but one finds it hard to believe that this tiny forgotten island was once the principal trading port in the West Indies.

The anchorage at Oranjestad shown on the chart is inclined to roll badly, but if you have a taste for out-of-the-way places it's certainly worth it.

St. Christopher (St. Kitts) and Nevis (25601)

From Statia, the great bulk of Mt. Misery on the northern end of St. Kitts dominates the southeastern horizon. Along with its little sister Nevis, St. Kitts was, in the early days of colonization, the most important island in the British West Indies. For some reason, the two islands lacked the density of mosquitos which, unbeknown to the settlers, were the principal carriers of the killing

The waterfront, Basseterre, St. Kitts

Statia and Saba (far distance) seen from the fort on Brimstone Hill, St. Kitts

diseases on islands such as Antigua, St. Lucia, and Martinique. Initially, the purity of the drinking water was thought to be responsible for this healthy situation, and Nelson, then a young captain, watered his squadron regularly at St. Kitts.

Today, owing to a lack of good anchorages, these islands are not too popular with yachtsmen. However, with a little care, a comfortable night can be spent in one or the other of the islands without Auntie Mabel ending up with her head in the vegetable locker.

Neither island has any facilities for yachtsmen, but they are handy stopovers on the way north or south.

Basseterre (25601) is a tolerable roadstead when the wind and swell have a northerly slant to them, a quiet spot being as far to the NW as depth allows. A tripline on the anchor is a good idea here, since there is a maze of old moorings and odd bits and pieces on the bottom.

In a strong easterly, it is pleasant enough in one of the little bays on the hook of land known as Salt Pond, about 4 miles SE of Basseterre. With the wind further in the S, Nevis offers fairly good shelter, either off the beautiful beach that faces the Narrows or tucked up as close as possible to Charlestown.

Customs and immigration take themselves very seriously here (as they do, in fact, in all the islands south of St. Barts). The skipper should report immediately on arrival to the police, with 3 crew lists. Since St. Kitts and Nevis are under the same jurisdiction, you may enter at either Basseterre or Charlestown.

Brimstone Hill on St. Kitts, dubbed the Gibraltar of the West Indies, is truly worth a visit, especially for the view up and down the island chain from the old ramparts.

St. Kitts remains one of the few large islands virtually untouched by the tourist trade. Thousands of acres of gently ascending sugarcane fields give the island a cool, green, garden look.

The Narrows (25601) is the 2-mile-wide channel between St. Kitts and Nevis. There are several rather dangerous shoals in the E and NE section of this passage, and it is no place to be fooling about with a deep-drafted, unhandy sailing vessel in failing light. With a clear sky and midday sun, however, there is no problem. Keep within ¾-mile of the St. Kitts shore and all will be well.

On approaching a place such as this from, say, the NE, there are several complicated ranges published to lead you through the dangers, but in my view it is just too easy to make a mistake unless you have done it first under ideal conditions. "Is it a church or a windmill we want?" croaks Dad as his knuckles gleam white on the tiller and the wind blows the pages from Mother's nervous fingers. Remember, there is always a hefty sea running in exposed parts of the Caribbean, and you just don't go aground, you explode like a kamikaze bomber!

Charlestown (25601) is the port for Nevis, a quiet and beautiful island, surprisingly full of historic interest. The town itself is attractive and has plenty of fresh fruit and local vegetables in the market. High on the southwestern slopes of the island, the Golden Rock Hotel is a wonderful place for a sundowner.

The shoal off Fort Charles should be given a wide berth—at least ¾ of a mile.

Not too long ago, all the traffic between St. Kitts and Nevis was conducted by sailing lighters—huge, high-sided, straight-stemmed antiquities with booms extending 15 feet or more over their transoms. On the rare windless days, their 2-man crews would labor at 30-feet sweeps propelling their 25 tons of cargo at a pace similar to Uncle Albert's on his way to the dentist. One or two are still soldiering on, and given the present price of fuel, they might all be back before long.

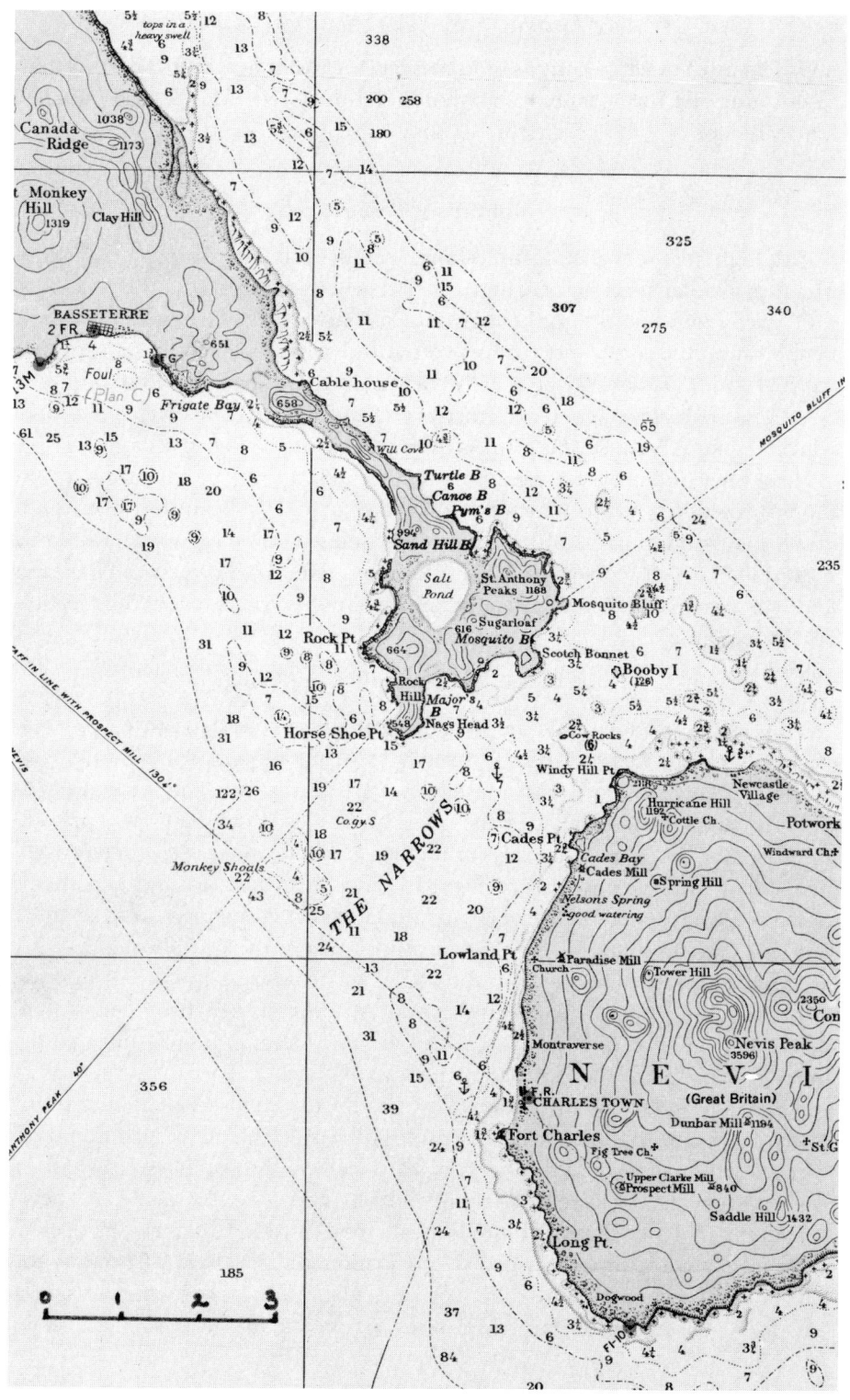

The Narrows between St. Kitts and Nevis

On leaving Nevis for Antigua or Montserrat, a rather uncomfortable sea may be encountered for 5–10 miles offshore, and the Golden Rock rum punches are really not as good coming up as they were going down.

Montserrat (25601)

Although it's very beautiful ashore, Montserrat has little to offer the yachtsman other than an overnight shelter when on passage.

Officially, one should go through the customs-and-immigration routine at Plymouth on the southwest corner. Here, under the usual conditions, even a half-mile-wide trimaran will usually turn itself into a passable imitation of a berserk windshield wiper. It's distinctly not Auntie Mabel's favorite anchorage, which is a pity, because the town is as pretty as any in the islands.

However, a little bird once told me that there is a roll-free cove right up on the northwest tip, called Carr's Bay on the charts. It's a beautiful spot, and a yacht that through stress of weather might find its way into the bay, would be most unlucky if disturbed. Another alternative would be to clear at Plymouth and pop back to Old Road Bay about halfway up the coast. Most of the time it is reasonably quiet.

Antigua, the Yachtsman's Isle (25602)

Southwards from Antigua the voyage becomes a joyous sleighride. A succession of cracking reaches, which invariably leave all skippers in a delirious state of Walter Mittyism ("and with a last gallant effort, the little ketch eased across the line, just seconds ahead of the giant *Ondine*" is usually how it goes). No wonder then that after a few days in English Harbour, most crews, having had their fill of windward work, are eager to put to sea again, easing their sheets towards the hazy blue outline of Guadeloupe. It's actually a pity, for in so doing they are missing some of the most pleasant spots in the Caribbean.

Antigua's 60 miles of coastline abound in anchorages that match even those of the Grenadines and the Virgin Islands. And for the beachcomber or skin-diver, the island of Barbuda (a dependency of Antigua) just 24 miles to the north is probably without equal in the islands.

Nevertheless, to most yachtsmen Antigua means English Harbour, and for many years cruising men from both sides of the Atlantic have planned their voyages around a visit to this lovely old port. Indeed, the popularity of Nelson's Dockyard—"the Dockyard," as it's universally known—increases every year.

Everyone knows that Horatio Nelson, then a young and rather acerbic captain, based his squadron here. And Prince William, later to become the Duke of Clarence and King William IV of England (he was known in Europe as "the Sailor King"), built Clarence House overlooking the harbor. It still stands

Dockyard, English Harbour

today. Older yachtsmen will probably know that the pioneers of postwar cruising—Allcard, Hiscock, Pye, Johnson, and many others—regularly met up in English Harbour for Christmas and were, in those days, the only boats in that quiet and lovely place.

And of course everybody knows that English Harbour is the home of Cdr. V.E.B. Nicholson and his family.

English Harbour (25603) can hardly fail to impress one deeply, as, out of the tumble and jumble of the seas normally encountered at the foot of Shirley Heights, the yacht slips for the first time between the battlements of Fort Barclay on the port hand and Charlotte Reef to starboard. This description, written in 1800, tells us:

> The entrance to English Harbour is difficult and narrow, and resembles that of Malta. You give the ship good way through the water clue all up, and shoot her in to an anchorage; from which she is afterwards warped to that part of the Harbour she is destined for.*

* From: *The Romance of English Harbour,* obtainable at the Dockyard.

Today, even with far more nimble craft, we prefer to give you more complete directions. The westernmost rocks of Charlotte Reef should be given a berth of about 50 yards. The old Admiralty entrance range has become rather lost amongst the new hotel buildings, so stick to the middle of the channel all the way in, and the Dockyard buildings will spring into sight, looking perhaps more like a film set than the real thing.

If under sail, a perfectly safe entrance can be made under easterly conditions, when at the worst the vessel may have to pinch a little as the wind heads in the narrowest part of the channel. Fifty yards further on, it will usually free again, and the problem then becomes one of easing sheets in time for the 80° turn to port and the run down to the Dockyard.

If the wind has a slight northerly slant, hug the eastern side, under the Pillars of Hercules, keeping an eye on the quite rapidly shelving reef. The water is normally crystal clear here, and the reef very easily seen.

Under the Pillars, the wind will die, but the yacht will have enough way to shoot through the calm until fairly heavy puffs are met coming out of the NE. After paying off to meet this new wind, the yacht will be heading straight for Barclay Point, which has a rock with 4 feet of water over it, 12 feet off its eastern extremity.

Come about in good time, whereupon the wind will invariably head and follow you around. Sail half the distance back towards Charlotte Reef, tack again, and you should weather Barclay Point without trouble. If you keep in mind that 60–70 yachts use this same entrance for a starting line during Antigua's annual Race Week, it will not seem so bad.

Immediately inside the entrance and slightly to starboard is Freeman's Bay, a beautiful calm-water anchorage 5 minutes away from the bustle of the Dockyard. Don't anchor in Freeman's Bay until you've cleared at English Harbour.

Customs and immigration formalities are strict but simple in English Harbour, and the normal procedure should be carefully followed. Therefore, run quietly down towards the yachts anchored stern-to at the old walls. If you think you're up to maneuvering stern-first into a slot that may be just big enough, round up under Pt. Helena (on which stand the buildings of Antigua Slipway Ltd.) and drop back onto the wall. If you'd prefer to anchor out in the stream, carry on round to Ordnance Bay on the northern side of the harbor. This is the traditional anchorage, where cruising yachts drop their mud-stained hooks and pause to regard the Dockyard's frantic charter activity with an air of bewildered amusement.

For those who may be attempting the stern-to or Med-moor for the first time, these notes may help avoid a few embarrassing moments.

The first and foremost rule is: Whenever possible, always plan to let out as much chain as you have in the chain locker. You'll see why later. Having dropped the hook in line with the chosen spot, be sure the foredeck hand lets go enough scope to begin with for the anchor to hold, even if the bow begins to swing alarmingly off the wind and the yacht appears to be going at right angles to the dock. With the engine still going gently astern, the chain should then be held so that the vessel is hauled around onto the right approach again. The foredeck man should then work closely with the skipper, easing and holding the chain when necessary and steering the yacht into the berth more with the help of the anchor than anything else.

Try to avoid going ahead on the engine to kick the stern in the right direction; that will only result in slacking the tension on the chain and allowing the bow to fall off even more.

Meanwhile, fenders should be arranged along the topsides at the right height for the vessels on either side, and mooring warps should be led through the fairleads and coiled for heaving. If the wind is more off one side of the vessel than the other, the windward line should of course be the first ashore.

When the yacht is secured close enough for the crew to step ashore, the chain should be taken up until it can be brought in no further. In the event of a sudden squall (far from unknown in the islands), the yacht should be unable to fall back more than a few inches towards the stone wall. Obviously, the anchor should hold at all costs, hence the maximum amount of scope. Unfortunately, there are a few isolated patches of rather bad holding ground scattered around the bottom, and to add to the problem, a heavy hurricane chain lies halfway across to Pt. Helena and parallel to the walls.

Uncle Albert particularly enjoys this whole maneuver. With the aid of several stiff gins, and much to the horror of the already established fleet, he drops his hook halfway to Guadeloupe and steers his hoary old Colin Archer full ahead at a minute gap in the gleaming ranks. With his bowsprit just about to shatter the plate-glass deckhouse of some petrified Panamanian, Uncle Albert is seen to collapse on his windlass brake, and his 30 tons of pitch, oakum, and rust is spun ponderously around in a mad pirouette, sending Auntie Mabel head first across the saloon table into a foc's'le drawer marked "Odds and Ends." Luckily for us all, he doesn't go out very much.

Be sure to fly the Q flag and Antigua courtesy flag, and definitely do not allow your crew ashore until formalities have been completed. If you are anchored out, take the dinghy ashore and go straight to the Police Station, inside the Dockyard walls. Three crew lists will be required, and occasionally you may be asked to furnish a liquor list. On departure, the master of a foreign-going vessel must fill out an official certificate of clearance.

Compared with most modern marinas, the Dockyard lacks many facilities that yachtsmen have come to expect. However, therein lies its charm. As of 1975, the waterfront was administered by a strangely invisible, perhaps even headless body known as the English Harbour Authority, which we are told is an amalgamation of the Friends of English Harbour (the society responsible for the renovation of the old buildings) and Antigua Slipway Ltd. All this is very fine, but it is to be hoped that the new management will realize that many yachtsmen just might prefer to pay a nominal docking fee and do without electrical facilities than to pay an arm and a leg for the dubious benefits of modernization.

In recent years, Chris Blackstone, the Dockyard supervisor, has done wonderful things with flowers and pots of paint, and the old place looks as if it were preparing for a visit from Horatio himself.

Governing bodies may come and go, but the Nicholson family is, after Nelson, the name most closely associated with English Harbour. Others may claim to be mainly responsible for the rebirth of Nelson's Dockyard, but without doubt this fascinating Irish family has done more to mold the character of the place than any other group or body combined.

In 1948, Cdr. V.E.B. Nicholson, his wife, and two sons sailed from England in their old schooner *Mollihawk*, en route to Australia. Falling in love with a deserted English Harbour, then a place of crumbling buildings, creaking shutters, and magical lonely beauty, the family decided to refit the yacht and stay the winter in the Caribbean. Then an American acquaintance asked if they would sail him south through the islands; *Mollihawk* thus became the first charter yacht in the lower part of the Lesser Antilles.

For many years the Nicholsons lived an idyllic tropical life, cruising in the winters and making homes out of the ruins of the Dockyard in the summers. They survived hurricanes, droughts, and the hard times of the early years of charter. The occasional wanderer who sailed into the Dockyard was made royally welcome; several whose boats were large enough stayed to join the Nicholson fleet. Nowadays, as 80 or so yachts jostle for mooring space and their hundreds of crewmen turn the place into a facsimile of what it once was, the old Commander can be excused if he pauses once in a while and smiles in deep satisfaction.

Just about everything the yachtsman may want is available here. Desmond Nicholson's Carib Marine is chock full of both English and American gear; there is an excellent sail-repair and awning-making establishment, a well-stocked provision store, a snack bar, a boutique, and a very pleasant waterside bar and restaurant at the Admiral's Inn.

On the opposite side of the harbor, Antigua Slipway Ltd., under the capable and enthusiastic management of David Simmonds, is well equipped to handle most repairs and can haul vessels up to 160 tons. Unlimited supplies of diesel oil are available alongside a clean but very small fuel dock. David, a master boatbuilder previously with the Lymington Slipway Company in England, is a qualified surveyor and undoubtedly one of the most knowledgeable men in the entire area.

Reliable women from English Harbour Village will do one's laundry, and there is no shortage of casual labor if it's required. Mail will be held by the Nicholson charter office in English Harbour and should be addressed c/o V.E.B. Nicholson & Sons, Box 103, St. John's, Antigua. Cables addressed to "Yachts, Antigua" will be read out over English Harbour Radio if so requested. Airline arrangements can also be made through this office. Taxi driver Oliver Bailey has been catering to yachtsmen's needs for many years and also happens to be one of the most pleasant and charming people around.

If you intend to see more of Antigua (and we thoroughly recommend that you do), your circumnavigation should be clockwise, and you should allow at least 5 days for the full trip.

Falmouth Harbour (25603) lies less than a mile W of English Harbour. A very large, cool bay, it provides a pleasant alternative to anchoring out in Freeman's Bay, and since the road from St. John's to English Harbour runs past its eastern shore, Nelson's Dockyard is less than a 5-minute walk away. The most pleasant anchorage is just off St. Ann's Pt. at the northern end of Pigeon Pt. Beach.

Care should be taken entering this harbor, as there are several shoal patches, the most dangerous being Bishop Reef, which lies just inside Black Pt., the eastern entrance of the bay.

The Antigua Yacht Club is located in Falmouth Bay and holds races for 420s and Sunfish each Sunday throughout the year. Visiting yachtsmen can become temporary members, and the club is a very pleasant place to spend a Sunday afternoon.

Carlisle Bay (25602) is only 4 miles further W along the coast, just to windward of Curtain Bluff, on which stands Antigua's premier hotel of the same name.

This bay has a beautiful palm grove at its head and is particularly lovely in the early evening, when the sun paints the mountains and the village of Old Road in pure gold. Sometimes there is an uncomfortable roll, but a shallow-draft vessel can usually escape it by tucking right up into the NE corner.

Curtain Bluff Bay (25602) is also inclined to be rolly, but the hospitality of the hotel makes up for a lot.

Half a mile offshore here is the eastern end of Cades Reef. This large and dangerous obstruction has claimed many vessels, and why its eastern and western ends remain unmarked is a mystery to me. Luckily, however, the seaward side breaks in all but the calmest weather, and an alert crew will have no difficulty spotting it.

If you approach Antigua at night from the NW, be sure to give the SW corner of the island a berth of at least 2 miles. Once inside the reef, assuming the light is good—that is, the sun high and the sky clear—a straight course can be held until one is clear of Johnson's Island. The water is calm, and an anchorage can be made anywhere along the edge of the reef and along the shore. The deep-water passage between Cade's Reef and the mainland is never less than ¼-mile wide, and this channel offers a perfect chance for the neophyte reef-hopper to practice eyeball navigation. I would even suggest that the skipper purposely veer back and forth across the channel so that the brilliant blues, greens, and browns begin to mean something to him.

Once past Johnson's Island, stand on 200 yards before turning to the N. Ten feet can safely be carried 200 yards off the shore as far as Ffrye's Point, a distance of 1¾ miles.

Ffrye's Mill Beach (25602) is the most northerly of a succession of palm-fringed beaches that vie with each other in beauty. Ten feet can be carried close inshore here. A rocky patch, accurately positioned on the chart off Ffrye's Mill, covers an area as big as a pair of tennis courts and should be given a wide berth.

Mosquito Cove and Morris Bay (25602) unfortunately are very shallow and 5 feet should proceed with caution.

An 8-foot draft can proceed in a straight line from Ffrye's Point to the easternmost of the Five Islands, but shoaling may occur in this area after heavy swells.

Five Islands Bay (25603), identified by 5 rocky islets off its southern arm, offers a whole slew of possibilities. Seven feet can proceed between the eas-ternmost islet and the shore, and the vessel may then turn to the E in deep water close to the beach. This bay boasts some of the most beautiful and secluded beaches on the island—there are at least 5 to choose from.

Up at the head of the bay, leaving Maiden Island to port, a beach that fronts gently rolling meadowland offers perfect solitude (except for the odd local smuggler), but the draft is limited to 6 feet. Head for the rocks at the northern end of the beach, but proceed slowly, since the bottom can change as a result of swells that sometimes plague the whole of the western side of the island.

Deep Bay (25603) is situated immediately W of St. John's Harbour and is the most secure anchorage under any conditions on this western coast. Eight feet can practically sit on the beach, and the holding is excellent.

The wreck of a large three-masted sailing vessel is breaking water right in the middle of the entrance, but there is oodles of water on either side of it. The twisted, cavernous old hull offers some exciting snorkeling.

St. John's Harbour (25603) is commercial, but it offers good shelter, if necessary, from N through E to S. Warrington Bank is marked by a red spar buoy to the N and a black can flasher to the S. Just NE of the bank is a large mooring complex belonging to the West Indies Oil Refinery. Large vessels frequently refuel at this berth, and the whole thing is surrounded by large mooring buoys.

Antigua's only light stands on Sandy Island, and in calm weather a landing can sometimes be made on the southern tip. Diving around the island is very good.

Dickinson Bay (25603) should be approached from outside the Sisters Rocks by vessels drawing more than 7 feet. The bay itself, although very popular with local yachts, is quite shallow, but the bottom shelves gently and a controlled approach under Wetherill Point is perfectly safe. Two or three excellent hotels are situated along here, and the area is only 15 minutes away from St. John's by taxi.

The North Coast (25603, 25604)

The stretch from Dickinson Bay to Parham Sound is a flat-water windward sail protected by an outlying reef that in good light is clearly visible. Salt Tail and Diamond Banks, at the western end of the reefs, are a real hazard for vessels approaching the island in bad light from the N and NW. A yacht should approach no closer than 4 miles until the West Indies Oil Refinery flame bears 100°T.

For coast-hopping yachts, however, the whole chain of coral heads forms an excellent breakwater and a really delightful 2–3 hours can be spent working one's way to windward along this coast. A good point of reference along here is Prickly Pear Island, which lies approximately halfway between Dickinson Bay and Parham Harbour. Between the island and the shore 11 feet can just scrape through, provided one favors the island side of the passage.

From Prickly Pear to Maid Island, the preferred course takes one to the NW corner of Maid, which is rather hard to see against the background of Crabb's Peninsula with its many radio antennas. The channel past Maid is marked by red cans to starboard and black to port, and was dredged during the war by the U.S. Government. It is maintained now by the Antigua Cement Company.

A pleasant anchorage can be had anywhere under Maid Island, but don't drop back into the deep channel—a 2,000-ton cement carrier from Puerto Rico is a regular visitor.

Every reef along this N coast offers good snorkeling, and since reefs are littered about like mushrooms in a cow field, the enthusiast can just take his pick.

Long Island (25604), to the N of Maid Island, is a park-like place that is slowly being developed as an exclusive resort. However, things seem to have slowed down a bit over the past 4–5 years, and one can wander through pleasant meadowland and seldom see a soul.

The anchorage in Jumby Bay is cool and beautiful but definitely limited to 6 feet.

Once through into Parham Sound, there are many little sheltered spots, but out to the E we particularly like this next place.

GREAT BIRD ISLAND
ANTIGUA

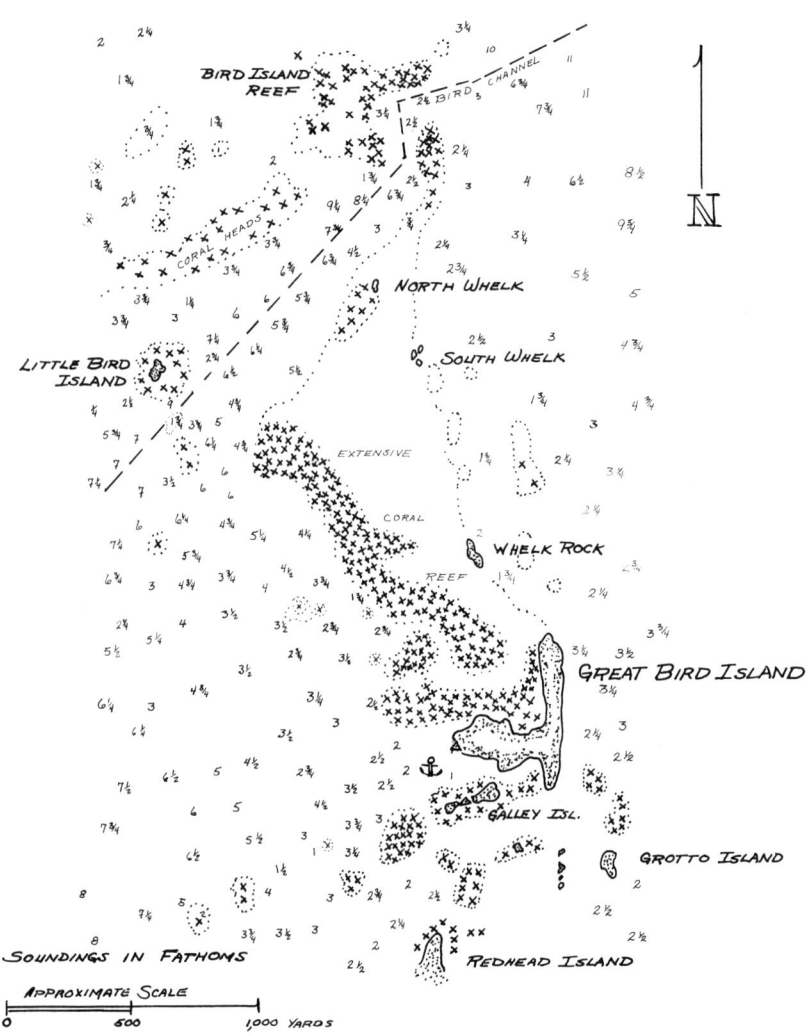

Great Bird Island (25604) lies snuggled up under the windward reef. Uninhabited, windswept, and beautiful, rising to a height of 150 feet and standing in crystal-clear water and white sand, it offers the yachtsman a calm and secure anchorage, with only a colony of long-tailed bosun birds for neighbors.

A yacht should anchor under the 2 protruding arms of the island, whence you can take your dinghy through the small boat pass at the head of the cove into what must be one of the most beautiful little bays in existence. Lumps of red coral are dotted about like flowers in a carefully planned garden, and the reef fishes gambol about in the shallow, satin-like water off the beach. A path leads up to the weather-blasted cliff, and the view from the top is breathtaking.

Many small islets can be visited by dinghy, and days could be spent exploring. It's actually possible to swim under a little, grotto-like islet immediately SE of Bird Island—as long as one isn't panicked by strange, glinting eyes and rather sinister shapes met along the way.

The only problem with Bird Island is that having found your way in, it's a bit tricky getting your vessel out.

Bird Island Channel (25604) is for the adventurous who have confidence in their motors, for it's a narrow and rather nerve-wracking passage out into open water. I really hesitate to recommend this route: only one mistake is necessary for the yacht to be badly trapped and possibly lost. We have done it in a variety of large vessels drawing up to 11 feet and now think nothing of the channel, but admittedly the first time was decidedly hairy.

The channel actually has over 20 feet of water throughout its length, but is no more than 60 feet wide in places and has a couple of abrupt 90° turns. Nevertheless, viewed from the rigging on a clear West Indian day, the blue-water channel is as well defined as the Connecticut Turnpike.

From the western end of Great Bird, the yacht should pick her way across the shallows heading for the SE end of Long Island. The channel will soon be seen stretching away to the NE, with Little Bird to port and North and South Whelk to starboard. Two right-angle turns, one to port and the other to starboard, follow in quick succession. The yacht will now be feeling the effects of the open sea and should be driven ahead with conviction into clear water. The chart is none too accurate here, and it's definitely up to the watery old eyeballs to keep you in deep water.

The alternative is to return to Prickly Pear, and using this little island in line with Hodges' Point as a range, to proceed out to sea through a 150-yard gap in the coral. A good lookout should nevertheless be maintained until well clear, and neither route should be attempted unless the sky is clear and the sun overhead.

Although the E coast of Antigua between Great Bird and Nonsuch Bay appears to offer an abundance of gunkholes, the prevailing easterlies make any of the approaches decidedly dicey except in the calmest of weather.

Nonsuch Bay and Green Island (25602) are, on the other hand, simple to enter and utterly beautiful. Approaching from the N, Green Island should be left to starboard and the yacht should run down into calm water towards Fort Hasman and Submarine Rocks on a heading of 300°T. Take great care to avoid the reef that extends outwards from the SW point of Green Island. It is usually clearly visible, white water breaking over brown coral.

Both Green Island and the adjacent mainland are the property of the Mill Reef Club, an extremely elegant retreat frequented only by those whose blood is as blue as the sea at their gilt-edged doorsteps. Nevertheless, despite an insane and idiotic desire to scribble revolutionary rhetoric over their rock gardens, I deeply respect their attempts to keep lovely little Green Island uninhabited.

Under a mutual agreement between local yachtsmen and the Mill Reefers, yachts use the N and NW sides of the island, leaving the entire S and SW sides to the club members. It goes without saying that you will not dump garbage in the landlocked Nonsuch Bay, and that the delightful little sandy beach of the NW corner be composed only of clean white sand and not half-eaten hamburgers and buckled beer cans.

Anchorages in Nonsuch can be found almost anywhere. The fabulous windward reef offers complete protection from the seas, and in places 15–20 feet of water can be found right up to the outlying coral heads. A very sheltered little bay just behind the aforementioned beach is calm and secure in any conditions. Large patches of coral, clearly seen even on an overcast day, are liberally sprinkled all over the bay, so a good watch should be kept.

The Spithead Channel, a narrow opening through the barrier reef, is fairly easy when used as an exit, but a bit on the teeth-grinding, lip-sucking side if going the other way. Going out, the secret is to hug the western or leeward side of the channel until there is no sign whatever of discolored water to windward. Then, and only then, claw out to the deep, me lads! Trying to make an entrance would, in my opinion, be inadvisable until the skipper had come in another way and made a successful exit once or twice.

Anyway, for those who see beauty in the wonders of the Caribbean—the diamond sparkle of early morning over the reef, the soft pastels of the shallowing water, and the constant murmur of the velvet night—Green Island and Nonsuch Bay will never be forgotten.

Willoughby Bay (25602) is a large, reef-sheltered but windswept anchorage seldom used by yachts because of what appears to be a strictly nail-biting entrance. In actual fact, it really presents no problem to the now-expert eye-

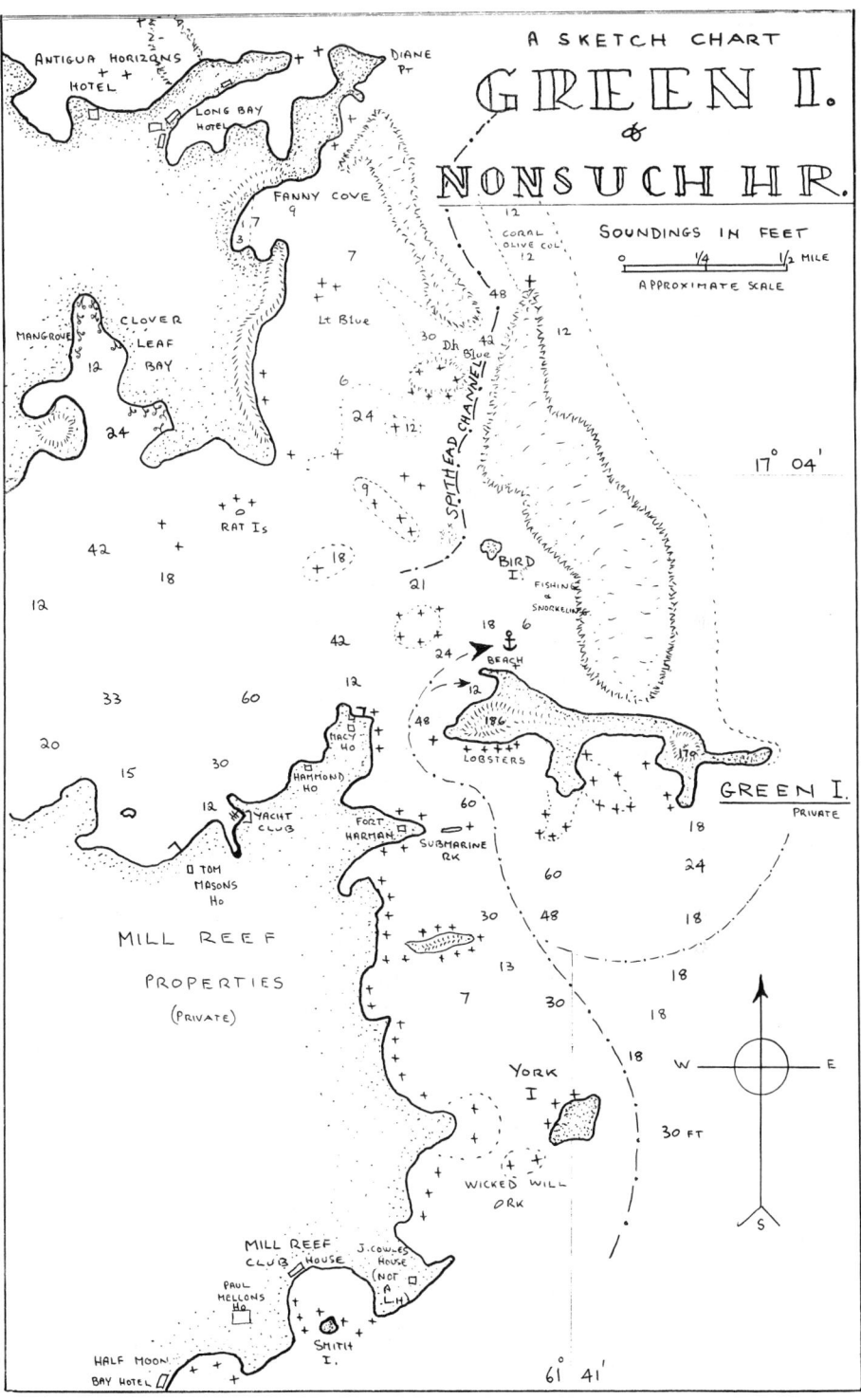

A SKETCH CHART

GREEN I.
&
NONSUCH HR.

SOUNDINGS IN FEET

0   1/4   1/2 MILE

APPROXIMATE SCALE

ANTIGUA HORIZONS
HOTEL

DIANE Pt

LONG BAY HOTEL

FANNY COVE
9
1.7
3
7

CORAL
OLIVE COL
12

48

12

MANGROVE
CLOVER
LEAF
BAY
12
24

Lt Blue
30   Dh
Blue
42
12

6

24   12

17° 04'

9

RAT Is

42
18

12

18

21

BIRD
I.
FISHING
&
SNORKELING

18   6

24   BEACH

12

42

33   60

186

20

30

15

MACY
Ho

HAMMOND
Ho

12   YACHT
CLUB

LOBSTERS

GREEN I.
PRIVATE

17ª

18

FORT
HARMAN

60

24

SUBMARINE
RK

TOM
MASONS
Ho

60

48

18

MILL   REEF

30

18

PROPERTIES

13

18

(PRIVATE)

7   30

18

N

W   E

YORK
I.

30 FT

S

WICKED WILL
ORK

MILL REEF
CLUB HOUSE

J.COWLES
HOUSE
(NOT
A
.L.H.)

PAUL
MELLONS
Ho

SMITH
I.

HALF MOON
BAY HOTEL

61° 41'

baller, and once you're inside and tucked up under the reef, the world is indeed a wonderful place.

The best practice is to put a man in the rigging and stand bravely in for the corner of the reef on the eastern side of the very obvious channel, which is at least ¼-mile wide. Run close down the side of the reef on a heading of 300°T until all dangers are on the starboard quarter, then turn upwind into the light-blue and turquoise water, and pick a spot behind the reef according to your draft. At certain times of the year, large rollers in the entrance could make entering inadvisable.

At the head of this very large bay, below the village of Bethesda, there are some really excellent clam beds, and you can spend a pleasant morning groveling in the mud up to your nostrils.

Marmora Bay (25602) is distinguished by a large white building that stands on the spit of land to the E. It is not, as you might suspect, an experimental germ-warfare station but the hallowed halls of Antigua's Holiday Inn and Casino, and a very pleasant evening can be spent here in air-conditioned comfort. A draft of 7 feet can be squeezed into the bay itself, enabling the whole crew to lose everything at the tables at one fell swoop.

Indian Creek (25602), scene of the kidnapping of the Governor's Lady, is a miniature version of English Harbour, but unfortunately it shallows abruptly halfway in. Nevertheless, it is well worth a visit: it is chock full of fish (tarpon, snook, jack, and the like), and the nesting ground of several kinds of exotic tropical birds.

Watch out for Sunken Rock, a tall pinnacle standing in 6 fathoms less than 100 yards off Indian Point. This dangerous obstacle breaks in nearly all weathers and can be easily seen. There is excellent diving around its craggy sides.

Once inside, stay slap in the middle of the channel. Seven feet can just scrape through the narrows, and once inside the inner basin, the yacht should quickly round up and let go, allowing swinging room for a sometimes flukey wind.

Very still and lonely, and in complete contrast to anything else in Antigua, Indian Creek makes an interesting finish to a round-the-island cruise.

Barbuda (25605)

Below the horizon, but just 25 miles N of Antigua, sleeps the flat and sundrenched island of Barbuda. In the days of sail, it was considered the greatest menace to navigation in the Indies. On moonless nights it lay crouched behind its coral teeth, hungry for the taste of oak, and more than 360 vessels, their lookouts screaming a belated warning, met their fate along its shores. Only the area immediately to windward of Barbuda's 200-foot hill is relatively

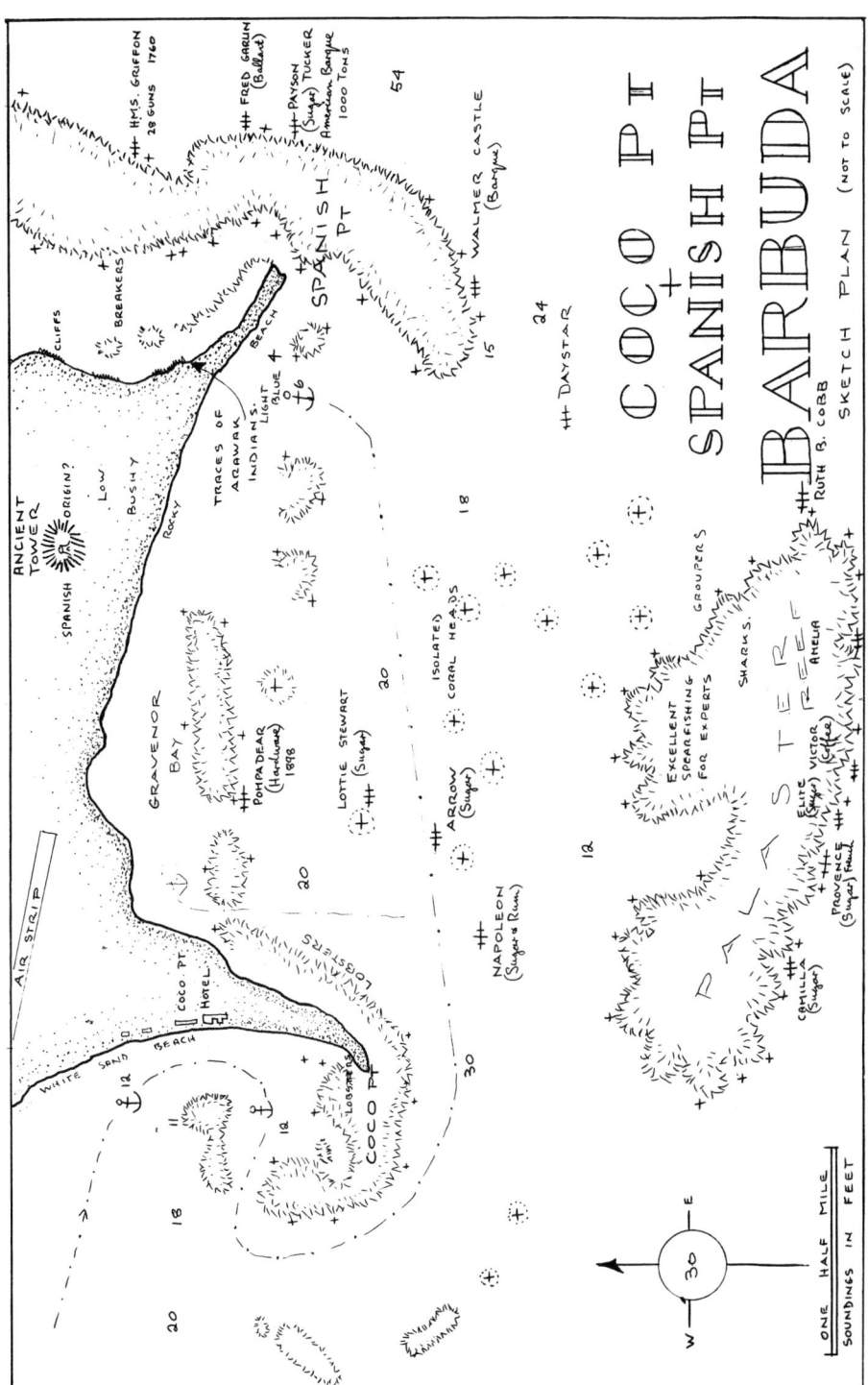

COCO PT
+
SPANISH PT
+
BARBUDA

RUTH B. COBB

SKETCH PLAN (NOT TO SCALE)

ONE HALF MILE

SOUNDINGS IN FEET

AIR STRIP

ANCIENT TOWER
SPANISH ORIGIN?

SPANISH PT

HMS. GRIFFON 28 GUNS 1760

FRED GARLIN (Ballast)

PAYSON (Sugar) TUCKER American Barque 1000 Tons

WALMER CASTLE (Barque)

54

24

DAYSTAR

15

18

CLIFFS

BREAKERS

BEACH

TRACES OF ARAWAK INDIANS.
LIGHT BLUE

LOW BUSHY ROCKY

GRAVENOR BAY

POMPADEAR (Hardware) 1898

LOTTIE STEWART (Sugar)

ISOLATED CORAL HEADS

ARROW (Sugar)

NAPOLEON (Sugar & Rum)

18

20

20

20

18

EXCELLENT SPEARFISHING FOR EXPERTS

GROUPERS

SHARKS

PALASTER REEF

ELITE (Sugar) VICTOR AMELIA

PROVENCE (Sugar) FANAL

MAIN (Coffee)

CAMILLA (Sugar)

COCO PT HOTEL

WHITE SAND BEACH

LOBSTERS

COCO PT

LOBSTERS

30

18

20

11

12

W — E
30

free of wrecks. The rest of the island, just a few feet above sea level and virtually treeless, is not seen until the navigator finds himself but a few miles offshore.

It's hardly surprising, therefore, that yachtsmen unfamiliar with the area are inclined to give the island a miss. Uncle Albert talks about it in the same hushed tones he uses for the dreaded Skeleton Coast and the Potter Heigham Mothers' Institute. Actually, although not a place to be stumbled upon, Barbuda is not all that difficult to approach, and once you're there, the island offers at least a couple of really secure anchorages.

The ideal time to visit the island is during peaceful conditions in spring, summer, or fall, for sometimes in winter a heavy northwesterly swell turns the shallow but normally calm western side into a very harrowing place indeed, no place to be in a sizeable vessel. However, for the greater part of the year a yacht of less than 8-foot draft can be quite secure in the Coco Point area.

Approaching Barbuda from the S, the first little problem to be encountered is Codrington Shoal. In normal weather, the sea bottom can be glimpsed all the way from Antigua, the deepest part of the channel being less than 17 fathoms. Wave action, therefore, is pretty short and sharp, and the shoal with less than 1½ fathoms on it seldom seems to break as it most certainly would in deeper water. We have usually been able to spot it because of its lighter color or, in brisk conditions, the amount of sand that has been stirred up.

Anyway, once outside Antigua's Diamond Bank, you can steer a course of due N, putting the nasty thing safely to windward. On no account should a yacht try to sneak to windward between the shoal and Palaster Reef off Barbuda's S coast. Rather conveniently, however, the old Martello Tower on the SW coast crawls up over the horizon and into view before you reach the shoals, and you should never allow this handy landmark to bear westward of 011°T.

From here on in, it's the old eyeball stuff again, and the intrepid mariner, fresh from his death-defying feats around Antigua, should have no trouble.

Before leaving Antigua for Barbuda, the skipper must make sure to contact the Warden of Barbuda by telephone and advise him of the yacht's visit. This is easily done in English Harbour and should not be forgotten.

Coco Point Hotel (25605), a lone white building, should be approached carefully on a heading of 105°T until a clear path through the reefs becomes obvious. Seven or 8 feet can get very close to the beautiful white beach just N of the hotel. This same beach stretches away out of sight—miles and miles of virgin sand, pastel water, and probably not a soul in sight.

Coco Point Hotel now welcomes yachtsmen, which is a pleasant change; the management was decidedly frosty a few years back. Another small establishment is being constructed in the region of the Martello Tower. Otherwise this island is as close to true isolation as you will probably ever get.

Gravenor Bay (25605) is a reef-fringed anchorage on the eastern side of Coco Point. It affords the best protection on the island, especially if a westerly swell should build up. Eight feet is the absolute maximum draft, but the holding is good and a vessel may safely be left unattended.

The entrance will be clearly seen very close to the hotel boat dock, normally the home of a white sportfisherman and a small motorsailer. Light-tackle fishing is really excellent here, and you can have loads of fun with the dinghy in and around the reefs.

Spanish Point (25605), which lies 1¾ miles E of Coco Point, is yet another long, sandy spit behind which a yacht of no more than 7-foot draft may shelter. The approach should be made only in good light, as there are several isolated coral heads between the two points. Also, the weather should be settled, because it is impossible to leave in bad light. But what a truly wonderful place it is!

If the crew tires of fishing, snorkeling, or just plain gawking at the view, take a walk across the point and then up the island's wildly windswept eastern coast. If you are a bit of a romantic (and what sailor isn't?), there will be sheer childhood magic in the excitement of exploring a seldom-visited shore, of turning over with sandy feet a battered box inscribed with strange, unreadable letters, and of sharing with the sandpipers the sounds of solitude.

Take a mask and snorkel with you, for the windward reef is only a few feet away from some of the little coves, and here bones of a long-gone fleet, reaching helplessly for the surface, are waiting to be found.

Palaster Reef (25605) has become a National Park, administered by the government of Antigua and Barbuda, and fishing with rod or gun is of course strictly *verboten*. A beautiful anchorage can be found right in amongst the coral in 5–10 fathoms.

The reef, which is only just below the surface, breaks up any sea, and even a large yacht can easily find a spot with room enough to swing. It's quite a sensation to be several miles from land but in calm water and surrounded by some of the most beautiful coral in the world.

West coast of Barbuda (25605) is shoal-infested and inclined to suffer from both the murky water and a northwesterly swell. If neither of these conditions exists, however, give it a try, for it's fun to anchor opposite the town of Codrington and portage the dinghy over the sand into the lagoon. You can then reach the town, and arrange expeditions into the interior of the island where, according to fancy, one may descend into ancient Darby's Cave, hunt for Arawak and Carib relics, or, rather pointlessly to my mind, hire several antiquated blunderbusses and attempt to blast the few remaining game specimens into Kingdom Come. The latter requires special permission from the Warden of Barbuda; having examined some of the guns, I would feel a good deal safer in front of the barrels than behind them.

There are virtually no staple provisions to be had anywhere in Barbuda, but you can buy lobster and fish from almost any fisherman. You can also get fresh local vegetables, yams, sweet potatoes, and pigeon peas.

Guadeloupe (25563)

As I started this sub-chapter, I suddenly realized that from a yachting standpoint Guadeloupe is the poor relation of the Caribbean. For years I have regarded it as one hell of a big island with a long and dreary west coast and very little else. It's all because the French Government is moving at less than a snail's pace in rebuilding a canal.

Guadeloupe is actually two islands in the shape of a flattened butterfly. The wing to the east, Grande Terre, is low, whilst the western wing, Basse Terre, is high, slightly mysterious, and steep-to along its entire leeward coast. The two halves are joined by a narrow neck of land, and through this neck runs the River Salée.

Fifteen years ago I took *Ron of Argyle*, drawing 8½ feet, through the river, and about the same time Carleton Mitchell went through with *Finisterre*. It was a delightful experience, and in addition to giving a better sailing angle to Antigua, the two great bays of Grand and Petit Cul de Sac Marin have dozens of excellent reef-fringed anchorages seldom if ever visited by yachts. Then the swing bridge at the river's southern end ceased to swing, the river silted up, and that, *mes amis*, was the end of that.

Since then there has been much muttering by the authorities on the subject of reopening, but as of December, 1974, no fixed date could be given. A new swing bridge has been completed, however; the channel is to be dredged to a depth of 4 meters, and no less a personage than the chief of civil engineering believes that the channel will be navigable early in 1976. When these plans materialize, a whole new area will be ready for exploration. As it is now, we are relegated to the western coast, since not many crews relish the idea of bashing to windward, however shiny the gold is at the end of the rainbow.

Deshaies Bay (French 3418; 25563) is a well-protected and safe anchorage on the NW tip of the island, much used by yachts going to or coming from Antigua. A fairly sizable swell sometimes finds its way into the bay, but owing to the prevailing wind, one normally lies stern-on to it, so that it is seldom uncomfortable.

There are no natural dangers, but when approaching the bay keep a good lookout, as the waters of the W coast of Guadeloupe are absolutely littered with fishpot floats. Usually these are large chunks of bamboo up to 6 feet long, very difficult to spot, and connected by rope to chicken-wire traps on the bottom. As there is sometimes a strong current running up and down the coast, the lines trail a long way and are absolute murder on skeg rudders and propellers. They are a nuisance up to 5 miles off the coast.

On arrival, take 3 crew lists ashore and hand them to Madame Racine, a splendid lady who runs the little café at the head of the jetty. This delightfully casual arrangement has been accepted by the gendarmes for years, so don't rock the boat and long may it last. Incidentally, the "nosh" at Madame Racine's is *pas mal de tout*, but the garlic can sometimes be detected as far away as Antigua!

A small stream runs into the southern end of the bay, and it's fun to wander up along its course and wash away the day's accumulation of salt in one of the small pools.*

West Coast of Basse Terre (French 3418; 25563)

This stretch is a little barren compared to most parts of the other islands. Perhaps it's the fitful winds that wander gloomily along the shore here, sometimes whispering in from the west, sometimes blasting out from the valleys. Or perhaps it's the deep, still waters and the silent towns. Anyway, to my mind, something is rather sad about this long stretch of coast, especially in contrast with the southwest coast of Guadeloupe's other half, Grande Terre, where all is action, color, and movement.

I usually plan to leave Deshaies in time to have lunch just before plunging out into the passage to Îles des Saintes ("the Saintes," as they're called). However, there's a pleasant place to anchor for lunch in a small bay on the SW side of Île des Ramiers, or Pigeon Island, which lies just about halfway down the coast. On such a schedule, the crew with a little time to spare may want to spend the night in Anse-à-la-Barque, a very deep but protected bay 5 miles S of Pigeon Island, marked by a red-and-white concrete tower which at night displays a flashing red light. The main coast road runs round this bay, and one may rather get the impression of being in the middle of the Indianapolis 500.

Basse Terre (25567), although a smaller city than Pointe-à-Pitre, is the seat of government for Guadeloupe and its dependencies. It has little to offer the cruising yachtsman except a chance to stock up on some superb French goodies and excellent fresh vegetables in the market.

---

* Authors' note: See page 23, on which we warn against the very real danger of contracting schistosomiasis from bathing in such pools.

A good place to anchor is in line with the northern end of the banana dock, but the bottom is foul here and a tripline should be used. Perhaps a better place would be amongst the moored yachts off the Club de Voile just S of the town. If there is no swell, you may be able to lie stern-to at the sailing-club dock, where fuel and water are usually available. The trouble is that there is seldom anyone around to authorize this.

The harbor authorities and the gendarmes will want to see you, and quite a large amount of paperwork is involved. Both offices are immediately behind the dock.

The coast between Basse Terre and Vieux Fort at the southern end is rugged and hilly, and 90 percent of the time the wind will blow hard here, usually from the S. This means that a yacht under sail, when the point is abeam, will be several miles to leeward. In the channel, of course, the prevailing easterlies will return, and a lengthy beat against wind and current will be required to reach the Saintes.

After many years of being a terribly gung-ho purist, I eventually took to motorsailing along this coast in the permanent calm patch that extends about 200 yards offshore all the way from Basse Terre to the southern point. At the lighthouse, the wind almost immediately frees, and the Saintes can normally be laid in one.

Îles des Saintes (25564) have become a showpiece in recent years, and the locals have suddenly realized the importance of tourism. Already many substantial holiday homes have appeared, most of them built by wealthy Guadeloupeans. The atmosphere ashore is delightful and very French.

As a quick insight into the history of the Saintes, here is a story I once heard from an old priest who had lived there all his life.

It seems that there were some islands which lay a short distance off a much larger island (just like Guadeloupe, in fact), and the inhabitants, being mainly descendants of Breton fishermen, had stuck together rather than intermarry with their darker brothers across the water. Inevitably the stock had weakened, resulting in an illiterate, unhealthy, and slightly barmy population with a future that could only go from bad to worse.

A highly concerned government stepped in, and a team of military doctors was given the unenviable task of cleaning up. Many of the ailing were sent to another small island, where in isolation they ended their days behind the ruined wall of an old leper colony. But what to do with the remaining population? How could new blood be introduced? Then someone came up with a brilliant solution.

The government had a large training fleet that called regularly at other West Indian ports; why not base the fleet (and its sailors of course) in the little archipelago for a couple of weeks each year?

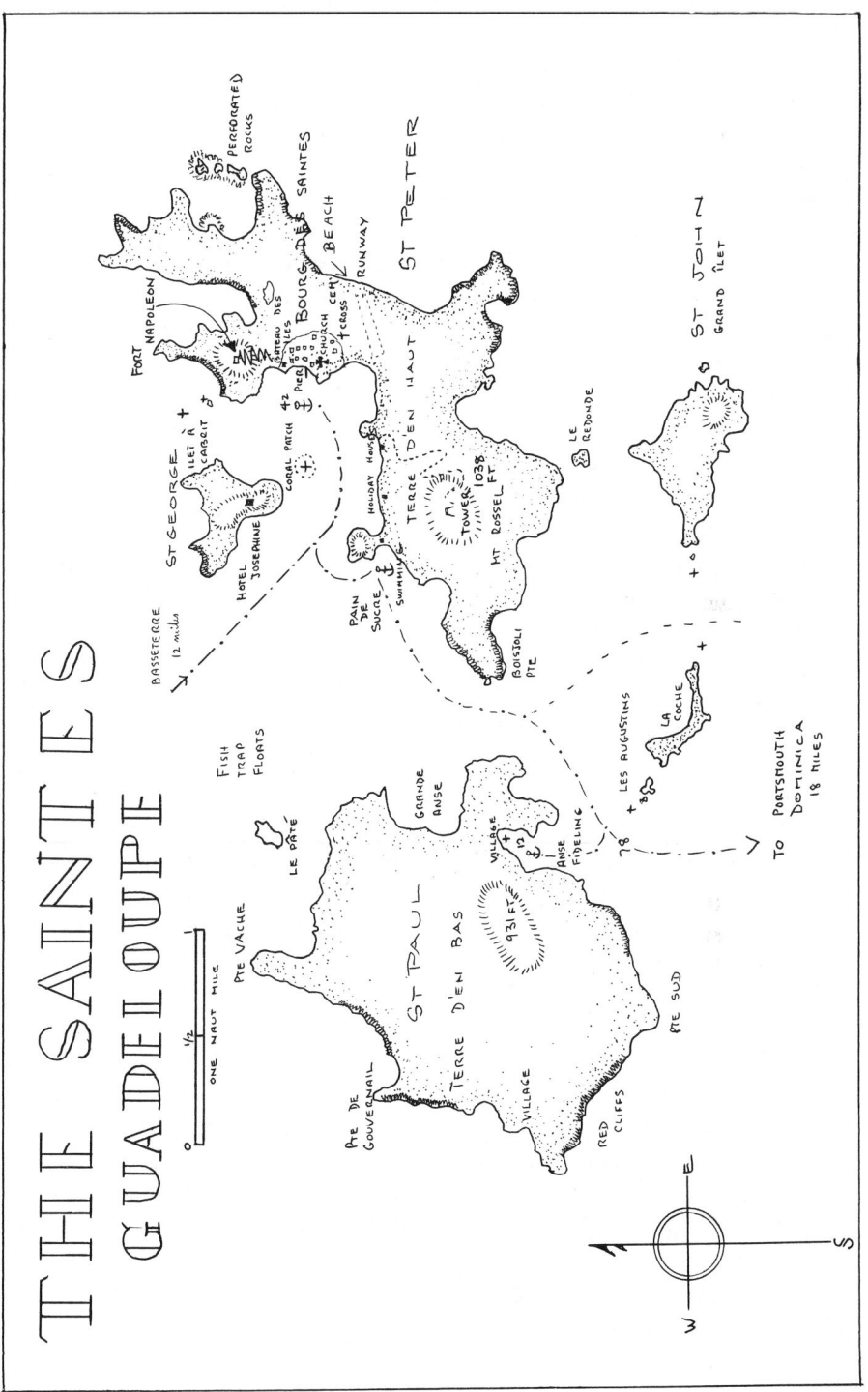

THE SAINTES
GUADELOUPE

ONE NAUT MILE
0   ½

BASSETERRE
12 miles

ST GEORGE
ÎLET À
CABRIT

Fort
NAPOLÉON

CHATEAU DES
... Pier ...

CORAL PATCH
42

HOTEL
JOSÉPHINE

PERFORATED
ROCKS

BOURG DES SAINTES

CHURCH
CROSS
BEACH
RUNWAY

ST PETER

TERRE D'EN HAUT

HOLIDAY House

SWIMMING
PAIN DE
SUCRE

TOWER
1038 FT
Mt ROSSEL

LE
REDOUDE

BOISJOLI
PTE

ST JOHN
GRAND ÎLET

LA
COCHE

LES AUGUSTINS

To PORTSMOUTH
DOMINICA
18 MILES

78

FISH
TRAP
FLOATS

LE PÂTE

PTE VACHE

GRANDE
ANSE

VILLAGE
ANSE
FIDELING

ST PAUL

TERRE D'EN BAS

931 FT

PTE DE
GOUVERNAIL

VILLAGE

RED
CLIFFS

PTE SUD

N
W   E
S

And so it came to pass that healthy children with blond hair and blue eyes once more appeared in the islands, and everyone lived happily ever after, except possibly my friend the priest.

Other things are changing, too. The dozens of graceful fishing boats based in the Saintes were only a few years ago powered by sail alone. Now government-financed outboards are changing the design, and ugly square transoms are appearing.

Both northern entrances are straightforward, and the charts are accurate; however, watch out for Baleine Shoal. On the southern side of the islands, most yachts favor the western passage. The middle passage, between Grand Îlet and La Coche, is perfectly safe in good light. Slightly favor the western side and be aware that rocky outcrops extend further out than shown on the chart.

My favorite anchorage is under the Pain de Sucre at the western end of Terre d'en Haut. During a northerly spell, Anse Fideling on Terre d'en Basse can be very comfortable, although there is not a great deal of swinging room.

The anchorage off Bourg des Saintes, the main town of the group, is deep, but the holding is excellent. Give the local ferry boats from Guadeloupe enough room to use the pier. They are highly powered and make a large wake. A small slipway has been established adjacent to the town, and several yachts report that the standard of woodwork is excellent but not cheap.

Walking is the great thing in the Saintes. Some of the best strolls are: Across to the beautiful windward beach on Terre d'en Haut for body surfing (sometimes there is a very strong undertow, so be careful); up to Fort Napoleon (used to imprison Free French supporters by the island's Vichy Government during World War II and still in excellent repair); a short stroll to the cross overlooking the harbor, and a long one up to the Napoleonic tower just visible atop the highest point on the island. Then sip a local *ponche* on the balcony of the Coq d'Or and maybe buy one of the coolie hats worn by the local fishermen. But please don't just sit on the yacht; the Saintes are too attractive for that.

From Terre d'en Haut it is sometimes possible to lay Pointe-à-Pitre and the southwestern side of Grande Terre, and if you've got time it's certainly worth it.

Pointe-à-Pitre (25566) is very big, surprisingly modern as well as ramshackle, and full of bustle. Not the best place for a yacht, though, so either nip in behind Gosier Island off the pleasant little town of that name, or find your way into one of the new marinas between Gosier and Pointe-à-Pitre.

In February, 1975, the main marina project in Baie du Fort was navigable although not completed, and the site looked great. A completed marina 1 mile S of Pointe-à-Pitre on the old sugar wharf seems to lack a name, although the locals refer to it as the Carènage. Fuel, water, ice, and repairs are available here, but no one was too sure what the depth was alongside, and most of the space was taken up by local boats. I have seen several large yachts stern to the docks and assume there has to be around 15 feet of water.

South Coast of Grande Terre (French 3419; 25563)

This coast deserves your attention before leaving for Dominica, for there are scads of really beautiful reef-protected anchorages, some a little rolly, some not; some buoyed, some just a narrow hole in the coral. If you can stand the pace, become a temporary member of the Club Méditerranée and spend a day romping with the monokinis in the surf (quite a refreshing change from the blazers of Marblehead and points north). The anchorage off the club is safe but inclined to be rolly. Casual visitors are not allowed, so call up from Pointe-à-Pitre and ask for a temporary membership.

St. François Harbour (French 3419; 25563), towards the eastern end of Grande Terre, is the site of the new Meridian Hotel and Casino. The entrance is buoyed and the swimming and snorkeling great.

Marie Galante (25565) makes a convenient lunch stop in good weather off the lovely southwestern beach. Columbus stopped here on his second voyage, but whether or not for lunch we do not know.

Petite Terre (French 3419; 25563) is fascinating but seldom visited. Seven feet can just make it across the bar here, and a tolerable anchorage can be found off the little beach on the northern island. If the swell builds up, though, you may get trapped until it goes down again.

The entrance is from the NW and should only be attempted in really good light, since the coral heads are very dangerous although quite obvious to the experienced eyeballer. If there is any sort of swell on the bar, I should forget it.

La Moule (BA 491; 25567), on the windward side of Grand Terre, is for the really adventurous. Maybe one yacht a year visits this place, because the entrance through the reef looks very hairy. Actually it is not too bad, and by the look of the many fine old buildings ashore, it was once a port of some significance.

Sand resolutely on, rather like Lord Cardigan at the head of the Light Brigade. Approach the old battery at the NW end of the town on a SSW heading until the reefs close ashore are nearly under your bowsprit. Turn hard aport and run along the shore into the calm water.

The weathered flukes of old anchors mark the windward reef, and in the old days large vessels would make fast to these and run stern lines to the walls.

Dominica (25561)

If there is one island in the West Indies that has hardly changed over the years, it's the great, green jungle wilderness of Dominica. Admittedly, a few freshly hewn roads have appeared, and the odd new hotel waits patiently under the trees for clients, but in truth the sheer ruggedness of the island barely tolerates any attempt to keep pace with the times.

High in the hills, village headmen no doubt still sit in a circle of elders just as they did when their forefathers licked their chops over the occasional exploring European. Red clay paths, made hard and smooth by the tramping of generations of bare feet, wind through the valleys and up to the cool heights. Rivers of pure, rushing water explode from every hillside, their sources in some cases still undiscovered somewhere beneath the island's cloudy cap. Dominica is an island to explore: an island, dare I say, to be almost protected from progress, and to be savored while the taste of purity remains.

For the cruising yachtsman, however, there are some snags, for Dominica is unfortunately rather badly off for anchorages. Recently, too, civil disorders have wrecked the tranquility, and especially around Roseau, the visitor is apt to be abused. When this all blows over, as it undoubtedly will, give the sea a rest for a couple of days and take a trip to the Dominican hills.

Prince Rupert Bay (25562) offers the only really good anchorage on the island. Easily recognized by the high, round bulk of Barbers Block to the S and Prince Rupert Bluff to the N, the bay is without doubt one of the most beautiful in the islands.

If the trades are on the move, a real bagful of wind can be encountered at the entrance. Gusts up to 35 knots are ridiculously common, but the water is flat and there is tons of sea room. A really tremendous sail can be enjoyed, and the bay one of the best places I know to get some good action shots of the boat. Hang on to Grannie, though!

I love to anchor in 3 fathoms under the palms at the NE corner of the bay with the Spot Light Restaurant (don't worry, it's just a little thatched hut) on the bow. Then take the dinghy down to the town and go directly to the Police Station, a large building standing on the water's edge about 100 yards N of the old wooden jetty, climb the back stairs and ask for the Harbor Master. He will usually require 3 crew lists and a selection of old paperbacks.

A pleasant walk from the anchorage will take you to the ruined fortifications on Prince Rupert Bluff. Just follow the shoreline and the path will soon appear.

The Spot Light can be a lot of fun, too. The management is only too delighted to supply anything from limbo dancers (a rather spicy rendition, so be warned) to crab racing. Lobster is the thing to have, but if you are expecting the Hilton, forget it!

If the swell finds its way to the northern part of the bay, a quiet spot can usually be found somewhere along the beautiful southern shore. An old plantation house standing in a palm grove marks the best place.

The anchorage off the town dock is secure, but the local small boys become a little insistent at times. Just to the S of the town, between two stone breakwaters, is the mouth of the Indian River. Take the dinghy up as far as you can go—until the water shallows and becomes clear. The jungle around you is almost too wonderful to be true. The whole thing seems like a Walt Disney creation, but the sights and sounds are real enough. Don't forget the shampoo, towels, and a pitcher of punch.*

The Carib Indian Reservation is within easy reach of Portsmouth. Allow the best part of a day and arrange the trip with Dominica Safaris, a company specializing in trips into the interior.

West coast of Dominica (25561) is steep-to and offers little in the way of protection. You can make a lunch stop, however, at the Layou River, and use the dinghy for an expedition to some of the really beautiful pools less than ¼-mile upriver.*

There is also a reasonable anchorage off the Castaways Hotel halfway down the coast.

Roseau (25562) is the island's dilapidated but strangely attractive capital. Yachts may clear customs and immigration here, but compared to the simple formalities at Portsmouth, it's a bit of a hassle.

Your best bet is to pick up one of the moorings laid down by the Anchorage Hotel, which is situated on the bay just S of town. The hotel is inside the harbor limits, and it is quite legal (or it was in 1974) for the skipper to take a taxi to clear with the authorities.

Carl and Janice Amour, a delightful Dominican couple who own and operate the Anchorage Hotel, are two of the most hospitable people I know. They are only too pleased to have yachtsmen use their pool, tennis courts, and showers. For the gourmet, one of the great taste treats in the Caribbean is Janice's mountain chicken and Écrevisse. The former, you should know, is a large and distinctly gormless frog.

In Portsmouth, we arranged for a boat boy to deliver us a load of these succulent little chaps. We assumed they would be prepared for cooking. A large sack was duly dumped on deck, and before an aghast crew and charter party, 20 or so large, leaping creatures transferred the cocktail hour into a scene from a Marx Brothers' movie. At least half the idiot things leapt through the galley hatch!

---

* Don't forget the snails, either: See page 23.

Dominica is the main supplier of citrus produce to the Rose's Lime Juice Company, and the island's oranges, grapefruit, and limes are beyond compare.

An hour's trip up the Roseau Valley to either Trafalgar Falls or Peter and Margery Brandt's beautiful little Island House Hotel is well worth while. Also in Roseau is a very beautiful botanical garden and a world-famous little convent school that produces exquisite straw and basket work.

Soufrière Bay (25561), at the S end of the island under Scott's Head, looks excellent on the chart, but on the whole is too deep for secure holding. It is possible, however, to drop a hook in about 7 fathoms immediately off the Rose's Lime Juice factory and go stern to the old dock. This may result in the whole shebang collapsing around your ears—in which case, I certainly didn't suggest it.

This large and beautiful bay produces a distinctly moving phenomenon known as a white squall: the high mountains to windward play havoc with the trade winds, and once in a while a gust will come tearing down the hillsides and hit the water at about 45°. A curtain of spray rushes off to leeward with the speed and authority of a runaway bus. You can usually see them coming well enough, and the best thing to do is run off for a moment. Uncle Fred steadfastly refused to believe it until one day, while he was suspiciously peering into his leaky lazarette, his whole gaff-topsail disappeared over the leeward horizon, no doubt throwing the radar operators at the Panama Canal into a bit of a dither.

Watch out for the large rocky shoal just to seaward of Scott's Head; it's further out than indicated.

Martinique (25524)

Make no mistake, this is a wonderful island. Apart from its well-known natural beauty, it is brimming over with splendid things such as *boudin creole*, a slightly explosive but delicious pig's-blood-and-spice sausage, *crabes farcis*, made from a large and voracious land crab which, when alive, is treated with the respect usually shown to a Bengal tiger, and 50,000 characterful and friendly Frenchmen of a rather darker hue than those normally found tottering about the Eiffel Tower.

Many happenings, some tragic, some joyful, have occurred in the history of the island—none was so shattering, though, as the fearsome eruption of the volcano Mont Pelée at the beginning of this century.

It was a morning in May, 1902, and the mayor of the city of St. Pierre returned from a meeting of the council, feeling relieved. He had just heard a well-known seismologist confirm that Mont Pelée would not erupt. Despite the heavy cloud of volcanic ash that had settled around the town in recent days, he issued instructions that would cancel the evacuation. After all, the volcano had threatened the town many times before, and besides, the next day's elections, which would no doubt assure him of a further term in office, should not be delayed.

In the anchorage off the town, 30 or so vessels lay stern to the walls. One of them, her loading completed, was slowly getting under way. The time on her wheelhouse clock, the captain noted, was 0750.

Six minutes later St. Pierre, known as "the Paris of the West Indies," and all its 30,000 proud inhabitants ceased to exist. In a gigantic explosion, the southwestern side of the volcano split open and a huge quivering mass of flaming gases began to roll down on the town.

In the harbor, as the paint blistered off the hull, the ship's captain watched with horrified fascination as the center of European culture in the Antilles was engulfed in the holocaust. Then, suffering terribly himself, his deck crew already dead from suffocation, the captain managed to maneuver his ship away from the inferno and take the terrible news to the outside world, the only eyewitness to the worst disaster in Caribbean history.

In actual fact, there was one more survivor, a condemned man in an underground cell many feet below the city, but he knew nothing of the death and destruction going on above him. Later he was to become a popular exhibit in a world-famous circus.

St. Pierre (25524) has, after a fashion, been rebuilt, but it has never regained its former glory, and an aura of sadness hangs over the place even today.

Although St. Pierre is not an official port of entry, the gendarmes who lurk about amongst the ruins seem happy enough to accept crew lists. I have found the best anchorage to be just N of the town jetty, but not only is the bay very deep, its bottom is littered with wreckage.

The west coast of Martinique (25524) is greatly influenced at its northern end by the massive bulk of Pelée. Heavy rains fall around and about the mountain when it is completely dry elsewhere, and cloud, which is seldom absent from the summit, nearly always shades the surrounding countryside. To leeward, a calm extends up to 12 miles from the coast, and I have sometimes barreled out of a steady Force 5 or 6 into a complete hole in the wind that has left the sea leaping drunkenly about like Uncle Albert at the Christmas office party.

For this reason, yachts approaching from Dominica should hold high and attempt to run up on the island close under the small islet of La Perle. This is one spot where it may really be necessary to exercise the iron topsail. The bay of St. Pierre is a perfect example of the workings of an island wind pattern: it blows hard down the valley and then fans out to the N and S.

Once S of the bay, the wind will again disappear under the lee of the Pitons du Carbet, a ridge of high, green peaks in the center of the island. From here a yacht under sail alone will have a frustrating time, as the wind will gust fitfully from the SE or S. It might be best to stand offshore and head for Cap Solomon on the southern side of Fort-de-France Bay, where the breeze will be back in the E and strong and steady.

Fort-de-France (25527) lies in the large bay of that name, which has more than its fair share of shallows. The approach to the town anchorage is straightforward, however. Once Pointe à Negres is rounded, the sheer size and sophistication of the town will be very obvious.

When anchoring under Fort St. Louis, try to leave the eastern side of the harbor clear, as ferries and cruise ship launches load and unload passengers at the two jetties that extend from the Savannah.

If you want a good giggle, mingle with the crowds when a large ship such as the *France* sends her packed launches ashore. Where they find such an incredible lot I'll never know, for they are certainly not evident on the streets any place I've ever been. One can only assume that, deep in the heart of some Never-Never Land, there are cavernous storehouses of luridly dressed little people, all stamped Cruise Ship Only.

On the northern side of the anchorage, a small, brown office at the head of a wooden jetty is the former headquarters of Daniel Valin's Martinique Charter Service, now located in town. Yachtsmen owe a lot to Daniel, for not so long ago it was the very devil of a job to find fuel and water in Martinique, and clearance formalities took literally forever. Now, however, thanks to his efforts, things couldn't be easier. Fuel, water, and ice are available on the dock, M. Roger Le Breton and his customs and immigration men are located in the office, and whatever else you may want, Daniel or Roger can usually take care of it.

Once upon a time I complained in my monthly column in *Yachting* that the red tape in Martinique was ridiculous, but owing to the touchiness of the officials, I advised yachtsmen to "grin and bear it." Somewhere along the way the translation from English to French became a little fouled up, and the Chief of Customs was told by his interpreter that I had warned yachtsmen to "beware the grinning bear." When we see each other now, I grin, but he still looks a little strained.

Then of course there was the matter of Diamond Rock.

In 1804, a party of British sailors garrisoned this almost sheer pinnacle situated just a mile off Martinique's south coast, and by lugging whacking great cannons to the secure heights, completely disrupted French supplies. The gallant party was eventually starved out, and surrendered with full military honors after 18 months.

One evening, when we were young and stupid, John Guthrie, Steph Traptnar, and myself, after partaking of the culinary wonders of the Hotel Europe, decided to honor the Royal Navy on the occasion of the annual visit of the

French Training Squadron. We would fly a giant white British ensign from the very top of The Rock. What a splendid idea! Just one more brandy and then to work!

Back on John's lovely old sailing trawler *Pas de Loup*, we fabricated a flag out of a bedsheet and a broken spar and, with piratical cunning, slipped quietly out of the anchorage under cover of night. As John had lightened his ship many years previously by dumping his huge old diesel over the side, it took several hours to work the elderly 100-tonner around the corner, but we pressed on and dropped the hook in the shadow of The Rock about midnight. One hour later we were at the top, which is covered with cactus. We were cut to bits and stone cold sober, but our makeshift flag fluttered proudly at the summit. What was disturbing, however, was that the moon had fallen behind The Rock, it had started raining, the only way down had completely disappeared from view, and it rather looked as if *Pas de Loup*, 600 feet below, was dragging off the bank and also in danger of disappearing. In desperation we plunged downwards, and an hour before dawn were back on the yacht.

With the daylight, the sparks began to fly. A fisherman reported the great flag to the gendarmes. "*Mon Dieu*," said the gendarmes, "*c'est terrible*," and they sent a detachment off to The Rock. After much groveling about, they couldn't find the way up. So they sent for a mountain rescue squad, complete with rope ladders, grappling hooks, and antisnakebite serum. They did manage to find the way but were robbed of the prize by a flight of police helicopters that swooped on the flag at the last minute.

Meanwhile, between Fort-de-France, Paris, and London, cables flew at the highest diplomatic levels. Most unsportingly, the French fleet was diverted around the northern end of the island, while back at the anchorage, gentlemen in soft hats and rimless glasses began stalking around the yachts with nasty black notebooks.

It all blew over eventually.

In Fort-de-France, you should leave dinghies at the MCS dock, not at the town jetty. The shopping in town is superb, but do it early in the morning or late in the afternoon. The huge covered vegetable market is the finest in the West Indies and a sight never to be forgotten.

Fort-de-France has always been proud of its women, and no wonder. Some of them are absolutely gorgeous. They walk well, sit well, drive well, and at the weekends when they flock to the beaches, dress and undress very well. Martinique, and not Arthur Murray, began the Béguine, and the motions of a Martiniquan dolly bird make a modern go-go girl look like a spastic giraffe.

Food, however, is the island's *pièce de résistance*. Allow twice the time you would think necessary anywhere else in the world, and be adventurous in your choice. The restaurant above the Club de Voile is one of the best. Also first class are La Foularde at the village of Schoelcher, Le Gommier in town, and sometimes, when maestro Robert Provost is in form, Le Foyal isn't easy to beat. Quite a character he is, too. Once he made a huge baked Alaska (called a Norwegian omelet in Martinique) for a group of yachtsmen and then proceeded to throw it at everyone in sight. Chunks of it were still dripping off the ceiling a week later.

Anse Mitan (25527) lies immediately across the bay from Fort-de-France and is marked on most charts as Anse de Cocotiers. From the spit buoy off Fort St. Louis, head straight for Pointe de Bout, on which stands the distinctive red-roofed Hotel Bakoua and the brand new Méridien Hotel. The latter is completing a small landlocked marina, which should be a blessing to Martinique-based yachts during the hurricane season. A black, unlit buoy off Pointe de Bout should be left close to port, as should the ferry docks at the Bakoua Hotel. A dangerous unmarked reef lies not more than 130 yards W of the Bakoua dock. An old submerged wreck once lay close to the beach in the middle of the bay, but I have looked for it recently and been able to find nothing.

Anse Mitan is a very popular place with the locals, has excellent beach restaurants, and is altogether a lot of fun.

Trois Îlets Bay (25527) and village (supposedly the birthplace of Empress Josephine) is fun to explore by dinghy. The holding off the little town is not too good, though.

Îlet des Ramiers (25527) makes a good dinghy trip too, although the military sometimes closes up the old fort while they play soldiers.

Halfway along the coast between Îlet des Ramiers and Cap Solomon are two little bays right next to each other. One has a very black beach and the other a very white one. The two tiny villages are primitive and the people delightful.

Grande Anse d'Arlet (French 385), just S of Cap Solomon, is one of the most beautiful anchorages on Martinique. Go to either end of the bay, depending on where the swell is coming from.

Petit Anse d'Arlet (French 385), further to the S, is pretty, with its small village, but more rolly than its larger neighbor.

For the cruising man with a little time to spare, a trip to windward up the island's south coast is very productive.

Diamond Rock (French 385) beckons any and all who fancy themselves as mountain-climbing types, and indeed it's fun to clamber around the old fortifications and to wonder at the fortitude of the men who manned this towering monolith; it was known in 1804 as H.M.S. *Diamond Rock*.

Anchorage is in 5 fathoms off the NE corner, and the landing place faces N.

The only way up is on the eastern side, behind the sole flat piece of land. Many old cannon are in the water at the base of The Rock, and there are some interesting ruins in the caves.

Cul de Sac Marin (French 391) is a deep bay, but rather spoilt by an over-abundance of mangroves. Super fishing though. A beautiful anchorage can be found in 2 fathoms ½-mile S of Pointe du Marin. Take the dinghy in first and look for the deep-water channel right up to the beach. A yacht may actually lie alongside beautiful white sand in clear, still water.

Further along still is the Club Méditerranée and the town of St. Anne.

The east coast of Martinique (French 384, 391) has several really beautiful anchorages, but on the whole I have found it to be rather too bumpy and harrowing in the blustery winter months to be pleasant. In the summer it's another story, though, and for the experienced eyeball navigator a whole new Caribbean cruising world is waiting to be discovered.

Don't forget that you must clear with the authorities before leaving Martinique. They have unusually long memories.

One more thing. If you are fit and healthy, a great day can be spent in the interior of Martinique. Get a taxi driver like Joe Ratin or Johnny Robbins to drive you to the N end of the island and drop you off at the entrance of Gorge Falaise, which is halfway up the slopes of Mont Pelée. Climb down through the jungle to the riverbed and follow the stream along to the magical waterfall and pool at the head of the gorge. Afterwards, drive on to the Plantation Leyritz for a vintage *Ponche Planter* and a late lunch. I won't attempt to describe it; just go and enjoy it.

St. Lucia (25521)

Once upon a time there was a wonderful laughing lady called Josette Snowball. She was the queen of a beautiful, flower-filled place called Pigeon Island, just a hop, skip, and a jump off the northwestern coast of St. Lucia. Around her, in a state of joyous confusion, lived her children, grandchildren, and many friends, as well as an assortment of loquacious birds and animals, and for good measure a host of gnomes, pixies, and jumbies. She had a palm-thatched beach bar, its open front just inches from the velvet warm waters of the bay, and for the handful of yachtsmen who in those days led the carefree but hard-working charter life, Pigeon Island days and nights were sheer magic. Maugham, Hemingway, Conrad, or Gauguin couldn't have created a place of equal enchantment.

Then the government in its farseeing wisdom decided to develop and improve the spot. They pronounced it a national park, and up went signs and picnic tables. A huge causeway was bulldozed out across the bay to connect the island with St. Lucia. Empty cans and plastic bags soon replaced the children and the birds and animals, and of course no self-respecting jumbie likes transistor radios and rock-and-roll. Then down came Mrs. Snowball's beach bar, and Josette herself fled to a rocky corner of the island, where she now lives, a prisoner of progress.

St. Lucia for some reason has always attracted people like Josette, and even now it is probably the last island outpost of the charming, eccentric British colonial who lives in a world of baggy khaki shorts, China tea, and those slow-moving, grimy fans that hang precariously from ceilings like capsized helicopters.

Nevertheless, for the present-day yachtsman, St. Lucia is still a great place to explore.

Castries (25528), named after a singularly unsuccessful Frenchman, is the capital and main port of entry, although vessels may also enter at Vieux Fort on the island's SE tip.

The harbor is rather deep and has a soft, muddy bottom. Since it usually blows pretty hard from the E, use plenty of scope. For customs and immigration, anchor close to the large black warping buoy opposite the center of the town docks or, if there is space, go alongside—although you may regret this, because the yacht will soon be covered with dust and a multitude of small boys.

Customs and immigration officials share the same office and will require quite a large amount of paperwork—including, probably, a stores and liquor list. A 48-to-72-hour cruising permit will also be issued, enabling the yacht to depart without having to return to Castries for her final clearance. The government apparently considers all yachtsmen to be rolling in money, and if they don't get you to cough up for one thing, they will for another. I once sat for 45 minutes watching a customs officer scribble on a dirty piece of paper only to be finally told that since it was two minutes past 4 o'clock, I would be subject to overtime charges.

On the N side of Castries Harbour is Vigie Cove, home of St. Lucia Yacht Services, a project started some 20 years ago by Bert and Gracie Ganter. Bert of the booming voice was a master Mr. Fix-it, and in the days when his work shops were the only ones between Trinidad and St. Thomas, we would all rush in with our sick and stuttering Stuart Turners and bulging and bunged-up Blakes. But "Wiskey Hollow," as it was known among Caribbean yachtsmen, eventually became too much for Bert, and he was forced to move to cooler, calmer climes. Gracie, bless her heart, stuck it out until quite recently, when she sold out to two young American brothers (both positively glowing with enthusiasm) and retired to peace and quietness in England.

Fuel and water can be obtained in Vigie Cove, and when you enter, don't pass

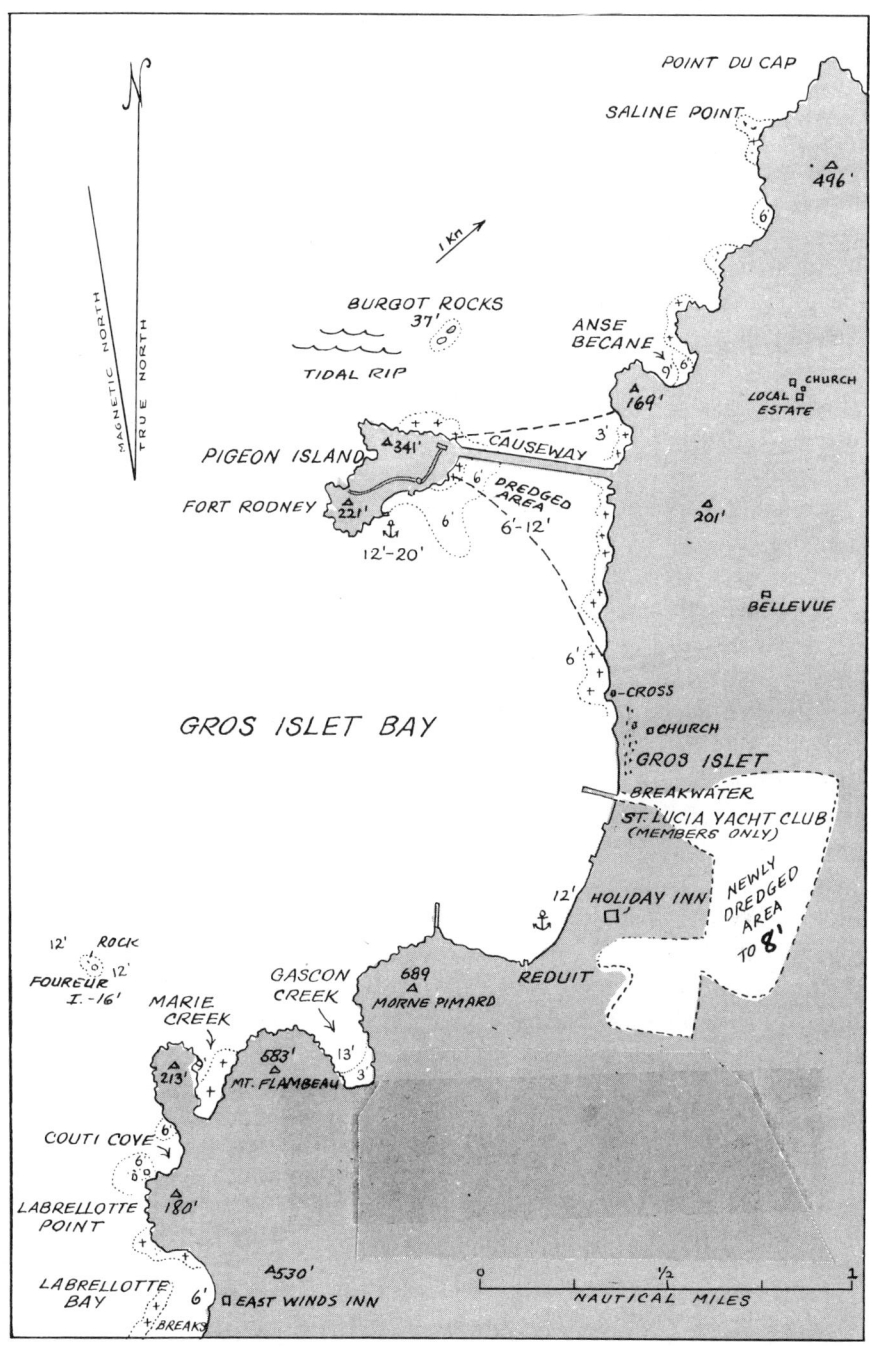

MAGNETIC NORTH
TRUE NORTH

POINT DU CAP

SALINE POINT

△ 496'

1 Kn

BURGOT ROCKS
37'

ANSE
BECANE
9'6

TIDAL RIP

CHURCH
LOCAL
ESTATE

PIGEON ISLAND
△ 341'

CAUSEWAY
3'

△ 169'

DREDGED
AREA

FORT RODNEY
△ 221'

6

6'-12'

△ 201'

12'-20'

6

BELLEVUE

GROS ISLET BAY

6

CROSS

CHURCH

GROS ISLET

BREAKWATER

ST. LUCIA YACHT CLUB
(MEMBERS ONLY)

NEWLY
DREDGED
AREA
TO 8'

12'
ROCK

12'
12'

FOUREUR
I. -16'

GASCON
CREEK

HOLIDAY INN

REDUIT

MARIE
CREEK

689
△
MORNE PIMARD

583'
△
MT. FLAMBEAU
13'

△
213'
3

COUTI COVE
6

6

LABRELLOTTE
POINT
△ 180'

△ 530'

LABRELLOTTE
BAY
6'

EAST WINDS INN

BREAKS

0   ½   1
NAUTICAL MILES

Pigeon Island area, St. Lucia

to the NE of the stake marker at the entrance. You won't make it that way, whatever the charts say. Large vessels should drop a hook and go stern to the rather small dock.

Bob Elliot's attractive little restaurant, The Coal Pot, is opposite the marina and is to my mind the best place to eat on the island.

Castries has had a habit of burning down in the past and as a result is horridly modern in appearance. There is good shopping, however, and the huge store of Minerval and Chasternets has to be one of the best in the islands. Leave the dinghy in the tiny carenage, and don't be put off by the many helpful types who will insist that they look after it for you, carry your bags, fetch ice, do the washing, and sell you their sister. A joke goes a long way in St. Lucia.

Pigeon Island and Gros Islet Bay (25521) are still very much worth a visit despite the absence of Mrs. Snowball. Anchor off the island itself so that you will clear the SW end of it should you drag during the night. The holding here is rather dodgy. On the mainland side, an optimistic developer has dredged out a massive Florida-type site for a marina, but, characteristically, has allowed for no more than 8-foot draft.

Sometimes a pleasant anchorage can be had off Gros Islet Beach, but a big swell often makes it a roll hole.

This bay was used as a fleet anchorage by Admiral Rodney during his relentless pursuit of de Grasse, which was to end so disastrously for the French in the Saintes Passage. Later, from the fort on top of Pigeon's southern hill, Admiral Hood's men would signal with mirrors to a small sloop on station in the channel between St. Lucia and Martinique. The sloop would similarly relay the message to the tiny garrison clinging to Diamond Rock. When the French fleet hoisted their yards, spies in Fort-de-France reported to Diamond Rock, and the Royal Navy, a slightly more spirited bunch then than now, were ready to pounce.

The W coast of St. Lucia has many beautiful and protected anchorages, and I suppose that of all the islands, St. Lucia best epitomizes the tropical image of the West Indies.

Grande Cul de Sac (BA197) is a large, cool and usually calm bay 2 miles S of Castries, but it unfortunately suffers from very cloudy water caused by the fast-flowing Cul de Sac River. Tuck right up in the NE corner to avoid the worst of the swell that normally runs down the coast.

Marigot Lagoon (BA197) is only a mile S of Grande Cul de Sac, and here a yacht would be quite secure even if a hurricane passed overhead. I was in Marigot once when just that happened. The only danger was the threat of

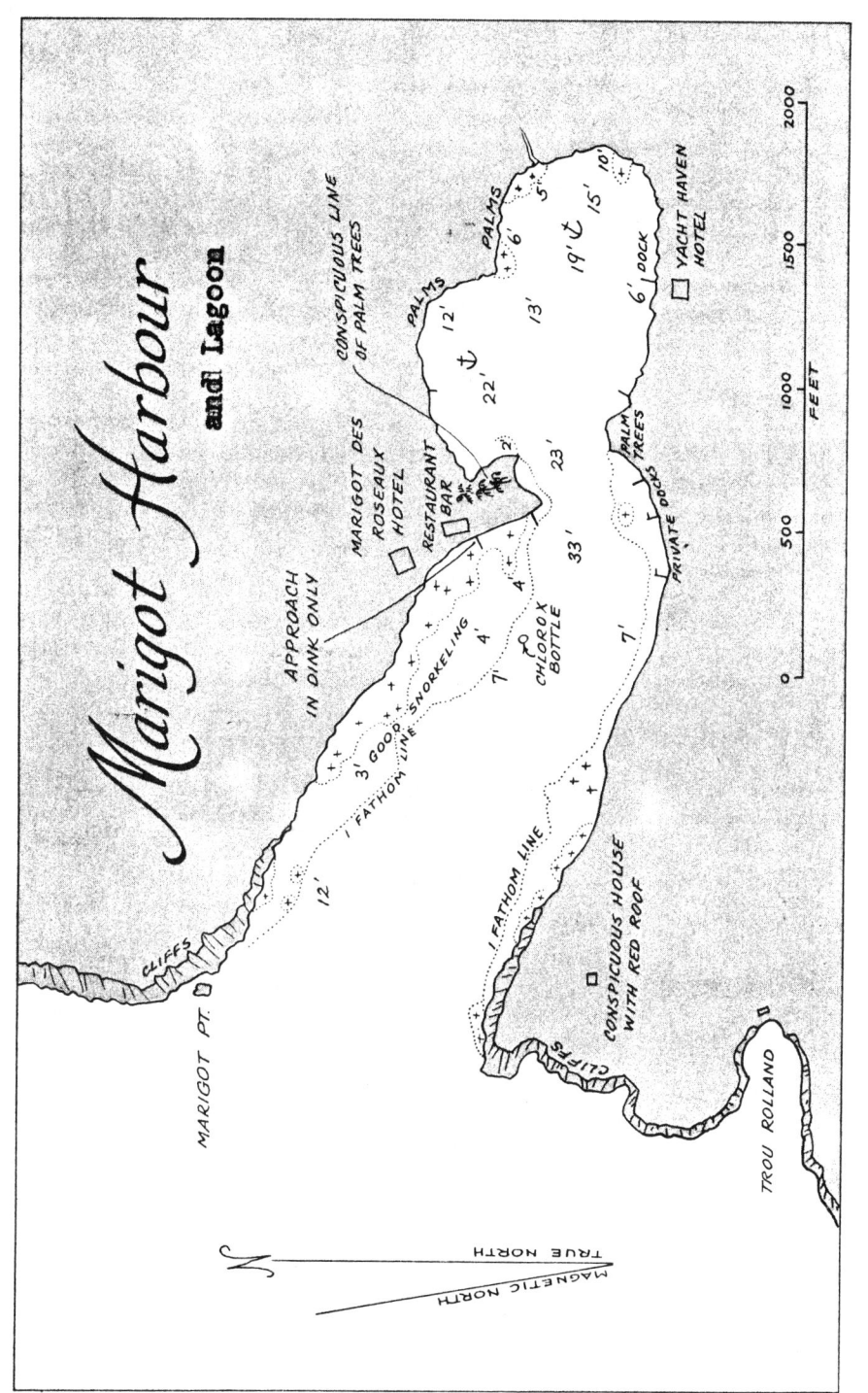

Marigot Harbour
and Lagoon

CONSPICUOUS LINE OF PALM TREES

PALMS

PALMS

PALMS

12'

13'

6'

5'

15'

10'

19' ⚓

6' DOCK

YACHT HAVEN HOTEL

22'

⚓

23'

2'

MARIGOT DES ROSEAUX HOTEL

RESTAURANT
BAR

APPROACH IN DINK ONLY

33'

PALM TREES

PRIVATE DOCKS

7'

CHLOROX BOTTLE

4'

4'

7'

3' GOOD SNORKELING

1 FATHOM LINE

12'

1 FATHOM LINE

CONSPICUOUS HOUSE WITH RED ROOF

CLIFFS

CLIFFS

MARIGOT PT.

TROU ROLLAND

0   500   1000   1500   2000

FEET

MAGNETIC NORTH

TRUE NORTH

flying coconuts, and if you've ever seen an 80-mile-an-hour coconut you'll know it wasn't funny.

Not long ago the lagoon was deserted. At night the beat of drums could be heard coming from the village on the hill, and the only lights to be seen were the fireflies amongst the palms. It was exciting and somehow all very African.

Then along came our friendly developer and in came suburbia, St. Lucia style. The tragedy of it all is that despite the hotels and houses, hardly anyone seems to stick to living there. The little Marigot des Roseaux Hotel soldiers on, however, and is a great place to have a party.

The sandspit that divides the inner and outer harbors is steep-to, and if you don't mind losing a bit of bottom paint, it's possible to lie alongside and step off the yacht into a couple of feet of water. The best way is to drop the hook well to windward and fall back to lie opposite the end of the spit. Then run a line from the bow to a palm tree and warp in. On windless nights, there is, however, a species of no-see-um that penetrates even Uncle Albert's pipe smoke.

Our old friend Admiral Rodney, when he in his turn was being hounded around the islands by the unsporting French, hid a small squadron behind the palms by lashing fronds to his mastheads.

On entering Marigot, favor the southern side of the channel until abeam of the Marigot des Roseaux Hotel. Very shallow water runs out from the northern shore, almost to midchannel. The inner harbor is deep with a muddy bottom. There appear to be a few pieces of coral and rock on the bottom, and the holding in places is indifferent.

L'Anse le Raye (25521) is a pleasant enough little spot and a great place to study the local fishing boats, of which about 75 percent are Carib canoes. They still use sail around these parts, too.

Beware, inshore mariner, of a devilish rock off Grand Caille Point. The water is very still, and you won't see it break.

Soufrière (25521) is worth a stop if only so that the crew can visit St. Lucia's drive-in volcano. If you are lucky and the thing is feeling bilious, it's a really worthwhile experience. A bit like a Fellini film: a moonlike landscape wreathed in swirling yellow mists, huge chunks of mud hurtling upwards from fiendishly bubbling pools, and a constant rumbling that makes Auntie Mabel's indigestion seem like whispers in a summer's night. At other times, though, these fabled sulphur springs can be about as exciting as a bowl of cold porridge.

Anse de Piton (25521) lies around the corner from Soufrière, and if you fail to be thrilled by this gorgeous place, which has become almost a symbol of the West Indies, you really should have stayed at home. Like Soufrière, it is very deep, but the Pitons' Bay produces some vicious squalls from time to time, and a

Soufrière, St. Lucia

yacht must be securely moored. The best method is to approach the beach slowly, having let out 15 fathoms of chain. When the anchor touches bottom, swing round and go stern to the beach. Have a line ready and secure it to a palm tree, then back up to within 30 feet of the beach and take up on the anchor.

The Pitons are magnificent. Nearly 2,700 feet high, they appear to rise almost vertically when you are close under them. Guarded by legions of tall, silent palms and occupied only by the ruins of an old estate house, the area has an atmosphere like nowhere else in the islands. Try to be there on or near the night of the full moon, and watch the shadows inch their way down the mountain.

Laborie (25521) offers a pleasant overnight anchorage for eyeball experts. I have been inside the reef several times and only once found the conditions too rolly to stay.

Don't rely too much on the charts here, and make sure the sky is clear before entering. The village is primitive and the locals very friendly. Plenty of fish and fresh vegetables can be had ashore.

Landmark of the Windwards, the Pitons on St. Lucia

Vieux Fort Bay (25528), on the extreme southern tip of the island, is a seldom-visited but calm enough anchorage. It would make a good jumping-off spot for a yacht heading for Barbados. Customs and immigration clearance is available here, although the officials are far from happy dealing with a yacht instead of a 7,000-ton banana boat.

The old American wartime airfield has now become St. Lucia's international airport, and the island's biggest hotel is within a stone's throw of the anchorage. Don't anchor too close to the power station; it makes a noise like a 747 at full chat.

For a real West Indian meal in old colonial surroundings, try the Clouds Nest Hotel.

St. Lucia–St. Vincent Passage (24032)

As spectacular as the Pitons are, I sometimes wish they were not there, for they play absolute havoc with the wind off the southern end of St. Lucia. Once we tried to work *Lord Jim* up against a blustery northeaster on passage from St. Vincent to St. Lucia, and I'll never forget the wracking strain on the gear as the schooner reared and plunged through the confused and tumbling seas with hardly a breath of wind to ease her pain.

Going S, head high after leaving St. Lucia's Beaumont Point, and keep going high until the true wind fills in. Going N, especially if there is any weight in the wind, do everything in your power to lay the Pitons rather than being swept down to leeward with the 1-knot westerly current.

St. Vincent (25484)

Perhaps the most beautiful island of them all, St. Vincent is a mass of jagged green peaks and steep-sided, verdant valleys, many of which are partly cultivated. The people of St. Vincent are industrious both on land and sea, and if it were not for the limitations imposed on air traffic by the very inadequate runway, the island would surely have made great strides. As it is, however, a country-village atmosphere still prevails, and St. Vincent is utterly delightful.

Unfortunately, the port of Kingstown has some of the worst two-legged wharf rats in the Caribbean. They can ruin a visit to the otherwise attractive old town, and why the authorities remain indifferent to the problem is beyond me. I must also criticize some of the taxi drivers who congregate in the area of the Aquatic Club, opposite lovely Young Island. No doubt there are plenty of honest and polite souls amongst them, but alas, they are in the main a rude, surly, and greedy bunch.

Apart from being staggeringly beautiful, the northern end of the island beats even Dominica for sheer ruggedness. The lightly slumbering volcano Soufrière (if you have been counting, this is the fifth with that name) dominates the area, and from its 3,600 foot summit one can look down into the dark-green depths of a crater lake that itself is 2,000 feet high.

Although there is no anchorage under even the most perfect conditions, the yachtsman should try to land a party to visit the Falls of Baleine on the northwestern extremity of the island. Get in as close to the little beach as possible and send the dinghy in through the surf. The yacht should then stand well offshore, for there can be some really violent squalls close in under the cliffs.

The tiny village of Wallibu is situated just north of Chateaubelair Bay. When we first went there with *Ron of Argyle*, the inhabitants disappeared from sight, and we were aware only of furtive movements in the surrounding jungle. Later the locals overcame their shyness, and whenever we appeared they would flock out to the yacht in their canoes. The village headman told me that up to the time of our first visit, some of his people had never seen a white woman! The mud and thatch huts are straight from Africa. Take some old clothes ashore and your kindness will really be appreciated. Here again, the yacht should stand well off rather than attempt to anchor close ashore.

Chateaubelair Bay itself is deep and usually too rolly for anything longer than a lunch stop.

Cumberland Bay (25484) was once a favorite with everyone. Very deep, it is a calm, well protected and beautiful spot. Unfortunately the locals have become a little light-fingered, and apparently believe they should be showered with gifts whenever a yacht appears. They have also perfected (after no small amount of effort) the worst steel band in the world, for which they charge astronomical sums whether you have requested it or not.

Stay in the middle of the bay when you enter, there are rocks off both sides. Anchor by dropping in 7–8 fathoms and running a line over the stern to a palm tree or to the remains of the old jetty.

Wallilabo Bay (25484) is a better bet if the situation in Cumberland does not improve. Only 1½ miles S, the surroundings are just as attractive as Cumberland, and you find here the Stevensons, a hard-working English couple, who, in addition to making interesting pottery and suchlike, have established a beach bar and laid moorings for visiting yachts.

Layou Bay and Buccament Bay (25484) can, with careful soundings, sometimes be used, but if the anchor ever dragged off the 5-fathom shelf, it would plunge to 30–40 fathoms.

Kingstown (25483) is the capital and port of entry. A new deep-water dock, paid for to a large degree by the Canadian government, has helped the island no end. Yachts, unfortunately, are still not catered to. Considering the amount of business they bring to the island, that is quite surprising.

The only surge-free small-boat anchorage in the harbor is at the extreme ESE end of the bay, in line with the end of the dock. Here it is deep, and the wind can blast in anywhere from the N to the S. The holding is good, though, and as long as there is swinging room, the crew can sleep easy.

In 1970, I wrote in *Yachting* that the St. Vincent's customs and immigration people were the most efficient in the West Indies. Always smartly dressed, they would come out to the ship within minutes of getting the hook down. Unhappily, things have deteriorated. Like a traveling salesman on a Sunday afternoon, one wanders rather forlornly around town from office to office, and if you arrive late or on a weekend, it's the devil of a job to find anyone at all. Try calling St. Vincent Signal Station on 2182 kHz, and get them to contact the officials at least half an hour before you arrive.

There is nearly always a surge at the dinghy landing. To be on the safe side, always return your dinghy to the ship. Good drinking water is available at the dock, but with the ever-present surge I have found it necessary to anchor off and come in stern-to. Fuel can also be loaded from a truck if prior arrangements are made. Once away from the dock area, Kingstown is a rather splendid old town, in its way almost as attractive as St. George's in Grenada. Shopping is reasonable; the major stores are Hazell's, Corea's, and Greaves, which will supply almost anything, including fuel. Kingstown ice is particularly good; the proprietor of the local ice-house explains that his ice is colder than anyone else's. So there you have it!

To avoid problems with taxis, I strongly suggest you contact either Alfred McClean, Sidney Agard, or Kim's Rental Car and Taxi Service. Any hotel will know how to reach them.

Young Island (25443) is the place to move to after you've cleared at Kingstown. It's a very pretty place, but the current, which runs both ways at anything up to 3 knots, can cause no end of confusion. The least troublesome spot is to the NW of the channel that runs between Young Island and the mainland, but a swell sometimes makes it rolly here. Then there is no choice but to push further in. A light Danforth or a CQR will seldom hold in the deepest part of the channel, so if there is room, try to drop in the shallower water opposite the Mariner's Inn. A submerged power cable is clearly marked and should not be used as an aid to anchoring.

When the stream is running to the NW, there is really no problem. The fun begins when it's going the other way against the wind. I remember one night when, at about two in the morning, a whole mass of boats became hopelessly snarled up. *Lord Jim, Redonda, Ticonderoga, Eudroma, Spearhead,* and *Lunaquest* were, I think, the main participants. We eventually gave up the unequal

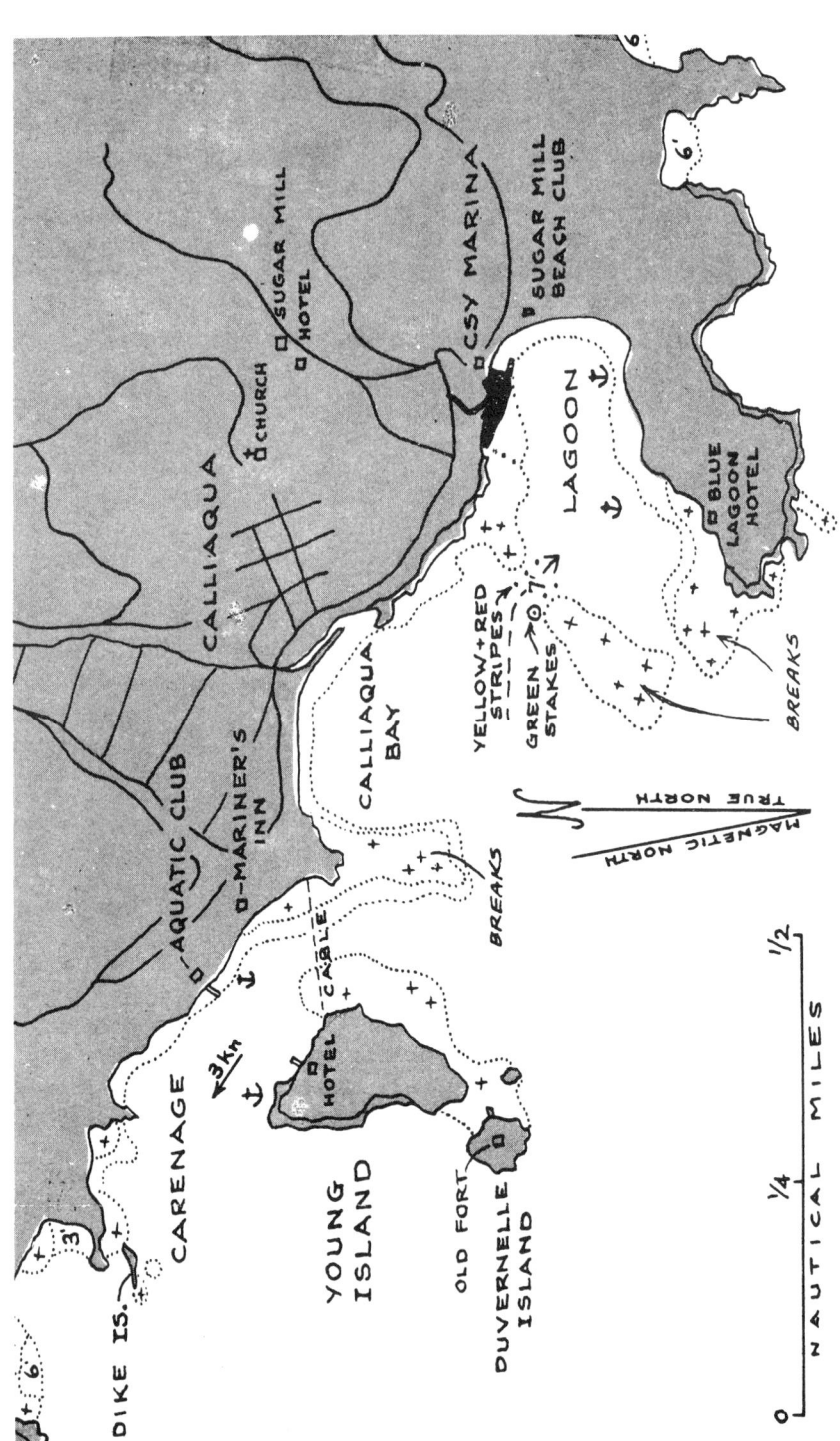

Young Island vicinity of St. Vincent

struggle and rafted alongside each other until the tide changed. A yacht lying to a nylon rode will dart about like a tethered stallion, and it doesn't really help to moor fore-and-aft unless everyone else does so too. Despite the problems, though, we have been anchoring there for years and will, I guess, carry on crashing and banging around like jousting juggernauts for a few more years.

Young Island Hotel is the work of John Hauser, a one-time American Express executive. He has created one of the most beautiful tropical retreats in the Caribbean and, quite rightly, has strong feelings about the behavior of visitors to his island. What a pity that some of the concrete-block and tin-roof type of hoteliers could not have shown John Hauser's imagination.

On the mainland side is the Mariner's Inn, operated by Dave and Jo Corrigan. It's a simple but very pleasant little place, and a great favorite with yachtsmen. Dave has been around the islands for quite a while, and I can think of no better person to seek out should you require information on anything from booby birds to banana daiquiris.

A fun thing to do is to take the dinghy around to the landing at Fort Duvernelle and scramble up the old stone steps to the battery at the top. A craftily placed mortar is still in the position that enabled it to lob a damned great ball over the top of Young Island and into the channel, where even a large vessel would be sheltered from ordinary cannon.

The Blue Lagoon (25483) is ½-mile to the SE of Young Island and for smallish craft offers good shelter, although both entrances are narrow and none too easy. Right now, it is the home base of Caribbean Sailing Yachts' Grenadine bareboat fleet, and their marina does not really encourage visiting yachts.

The best entrance is through the marked break in the reef on the southwestern side, utilizing a 9-foot channel. Once inside, there are no dangers, but the water is deep and I have sometimes seen a roll even here. The northern entrance has little more than 5 feet of water, but it is normally quite calm and the water is clear. Anchor as close to the Sugar Mill Hotel beach bar as possible.

Whales, and the Northbound Passage

Cruising the western coast of St. Vincent, keep a good eye open for the last of a dying breed, the hunters of blackfish. For some reason the blackfish, or pilot whale, is more numerous in the vicinity of St. Vincent than around the other islands. Their rounded heads and porpoise-like dorsal fins are quite a common sight. Since whaling first began in the island, Vincentian fishermen have hunted the blackfish, and even now the men can be seen in their long, grey whaleboats, quietly waiting for the telltale spouts of spray as the little whales break water to breathe. Although most boats still use a hand-thrown harpoon, some have developed a highly lethal-looking device fashioned out of an old

12-bore shotgun supported on a tripod up in the eyes of the whaleboat. Before the conservationists roar too loudly, let me just say that the St. Vincent fishermen exist on a pittance and, like the creatures they hunt, are fighting pretty hard to survive.

One last word of advice. If you're headed north from St. Vincent, there are two paths open. Either press on under sail past Dark Head, in which case you will probably not be able to sail high enough to lay the Pitons without tacking, or motorsail really close under the cliffs until De Volet Point is abeam. The problem with the latter is that in blowy conditions, squalls of really ferocious intensity can be encountered as you leave the lee, added to which there is sometimes a healthy tide rip about 4 miles N of the island. Of the two, I prefer motorsailing to De Volet Point unless the wind has a good deal of S in it.

The Grenadines—The Yesterday Islands (25482)

Over the past ten years, quite a change has taken place in this wonderful 50-mile chain of islands. Hotels and other developments have sprung up, and airstrips have appeared where previously even the seagulls had a hard time taking off. However, to be honest, I don't think anyone could say that the Grenadines have lost much of their charm because of all this. There are still scads of places to hide away from the crowd; still beaches where nary a soul will be seen, and still water as clear and as pure as it was when the first Arawaks paddled their way north from the vastness of South America.

Some of the following anchorages will not appeal to everyone. They may be too lonely and exposed for the average taste, but to me solitude is a great luxury, becoming rarer as the world gets smaller. I am always amazed at the way most yachtsmen tend to huddle together in a wide-open anchorage. Nothing is more galling, after having pointedly left the pack for a more isolated spot, than to have some cheerful character, with all the water in the world to choose from, let go within a few yards of me, grimy pajamas flapping hideously in the breeze.

Bequia (BA791; 25483) is the northernmost of the Grenadines, strictly speaking, but somehow the island is a little too grown up to think of in the same terms as Union or Mayero. Admiralty Bay on Bequia is a port of entry for St. Vincent, and the formalities are simple and easy. Just pop into the Police Station behind the jetty and see what they require.

Bequia is only 5 miles S of St. Vincent and is subject to its large sister's weather; Bequia gets a good deal more rain than the rest of the Grenadines.

Its people, many of whom are descendants of Scots engineers who originally came to Barbados and St. Vincent to operate the sugar estates, are the most able shipwrights, carpenters, seamen, and general handymen to be found anywhere in the Lesser Antilles. They truly love the sea and are steeped in the tradition of working sail, thanks to the influence of the New England whaling crews who once were based on the island. There are no keener critics of a sailboat's performance than the old schooner men who sit ashore 'neath the shade of the flamboyant trees watching with knowledgeable eyes all that goes on in the harbor.

Whaling is, in fact, still carried on in Bequia. High up on Mount Pleasant, impatient small boys and philosophical old men scan the seas to windward for signs of the migrating humpback whale. Great excitement follows a sighting. The small boys pelt down the hill to the villages of Friendship and Paget Farm, where the 18-foot, 6-oared whaleboats are drawn up on the beach. Once at sea, the whaleboats are guided to the right spot by the old men on the hill, who flash signals by mirror. Should a humpback be sighted to leeward, there is no way that, if killed, its huge bulk can be towed back against the trade winds.

One day we were asked to take *Lord Jim* to sea to stand by three of the more determined whaleboats, which refused to give up the chase even when they were well downwind and in heavy seas. It had been a lean year for the whalers (they had killed only once instead of the average six times, and the whole island would suffer as a result), and so we steamed off, preparing a bridle and a long warp for a possible heavy tow. There were mixed emotions as we watched the tired men row all over the ocean while the whale surfaced and sounded around them. Then there was an unbelievable commotion alongside the lead boat. The harpooner stood poised and for a split second of time we were with Ahab and the *Pequod*. But it was not to be. The great creature shrugged off the harpoon and sounded, to disappear for good. We towed the exhausted men back to Bequia, feeling strangely sad.

When you have anchored in Admiralty Bay, take time to observe and absorb some small part of the island's atmosphere. On the beach, shipwrights and sailmakers are at work, and fishermen fiddle with their nets and fishtraps. Local schooners, most of which were built right on the beach here, come and go. Small boys swim alongside their beautifully made models, some of which are perfect replicas of the charter yachts anchored in the bay. Ashore, the church bell rings, Estelle Fredericks bakes her delicious bread, and across the way in Elizabeth Town a steel band tunes its pans.

For a more active absorption of the island's spell, take the dinghy to Princess Margaret Beach and walk up the hill to Lulley's Fishing and Chandlery Shop. Have a sundowner at the Frangipani or the Sunny Caribee. Nip over to Spring Bay and see if my old friend Sidney McIntosh has some eggs or fruit to sell. Or just walk through the little town in the quietness of early evening.

If the Bequia slipway is operating, fuel and water can be had from its small dock on the N side of the harbor.

Leaving the island, sail close to the coast on the way to West Cay and take a look at Moon Hole, the house in a cave that Tom Johnson built.

On the other side of the island, Friendship Bay is a pretty anchorage, but it usually rolls badly during the winter months. Petit Nevis has a very pleasant anchorage under its lee, but if a whale has been caught, give it a wide berth, as the smell is horrendous. This is where the unfortunate creatures are cut up, processed, and shared out.

Balliceaux, Battowia, and Île de Quatre (25482) have no really comfortable winter anchorages, which is a pity, because the first two are interesting ashore. In summer, Balliceaux has a lovely hideaway in the bay on the SW side.

Mustique (25482) is a sort of European equivalent of Antigua's Mill Reef Club, having been quite beautifully developed by Colin Tennant, who counts Lord Snowden and Princess Margaret amongst his regulars. As you may well imagine, things are therefore done with a certain style.

Off the N coast of the island is the spectacular wreck of the 20,000-ton French liner *Antilles*, a rather striking example of aberrant piloting.

Close to the small dock in Grand Bay is the best place to anchor, and it is sometimes best to hang a stern line onto the dock in order to keep your bows into the swell.

Half a mile off the dock, on a bearing of 300°T, lies the Montezuma Shoal, where my beloved *Lord Jim*, a year after I sold her, very nearly ended her days. Her Bostonian pride would not allow it, though, and she survived 24 hours of pounding on this treacherous bank with only a damaged rudder to show for it. Old Mr. Lawley apparently knew a thing or two!

There is talk that one day a channel will be dredged into the south pond and a marina constructed.

A truly delightful clubhouse in the center of the island serves excellent meals, but reservations must be made in advance. Don't rely on buying any provisions, although I'm told this situation will improve shortly. Off the S end of the island there is excellent trolling.

Savan Island (25482) is a possible overnight anchorage under summer conditions, and a good lunch stop. The snorkeling is good, and apart from a few fishermen camping in some primitive huts ashore, this little island is deserted and seldom visited. Tuck up into the bight and set a stern anchor.

Cannouan Island (25482) has a variety of anchorages to suit nearly all wind and sea conditions, but few yachts seem to use the island. In summer only, push right into the SE corner of Maho Bay.

On the west coast, two delightful spots are the minute cove of Corbay or, if the northerly swell is being a pain, behind the point immediately S of Corbay. The latter is nearly always calm, has beautifully clear water, and is seldom used.

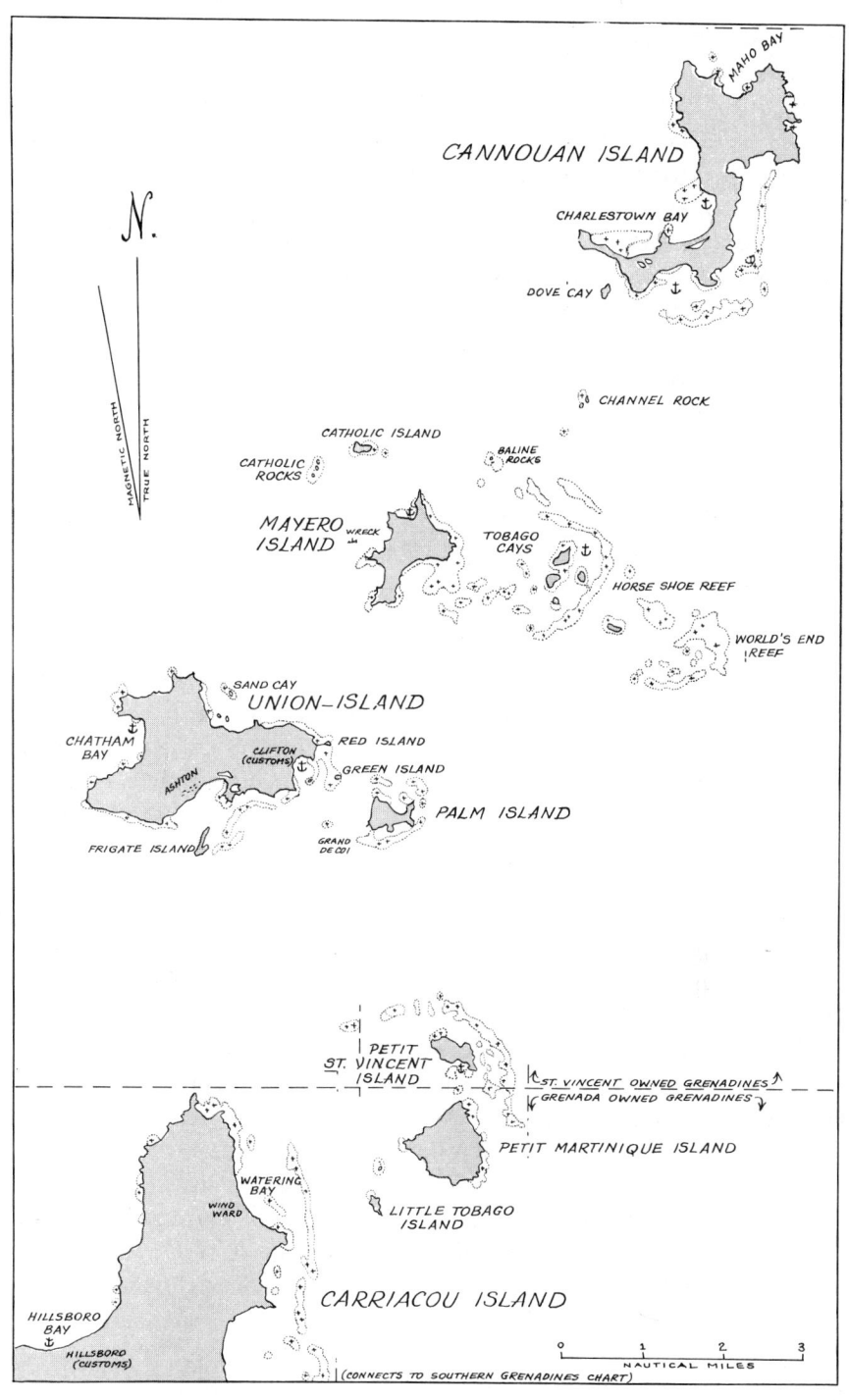

The heart of the Grenadines

Charlestown Bay looks good but is a roll hole except in the NE corner close to the fish dock.

A beautiful anchorage can sometimes be found between Glass Hill and Taffia Hill. An eyeball expert will be required for the anchorage behind Friendship Point, which is good in a northerly breeze, and for the superb hideaway behind the windward reef on the eastern side of the island. Although it will frighten the daylights out of Auntie Mabel, this is one of the best anywhere.

Push on close inshore past Friendship Point until you are behind the barrier reef. Carry on as far as your draft allows and drop back close to one of the beaches. Lay out a second anchor if there is any wind in the offing. Sometimes a strong current runs here, but it slacks off in the shallows close to the reef, and the snorkeling is fabulous. There is great walking ashore, and unless too many people read this, you will have the place to yourself.

Between Cannouan and Carriacou there are so many beautiful and secure anchorages a yachtsman could go bananas worrying about which ones to use. This is the very heart of the Grenadines, and it is safe to say that once you've sailed here, Montauk Point and the Isle of Wight will never seem the same again.

It's a world where wind and sea and land have combined to make a kaleidoscope of color and beauty: a world where even the most hardened *homo sapiens* may realize that there is more to life than highways and hamburgers and movies and goggle boxes. Even the place names ring with excitement. Roll them around your tongue for a moment: Saltwhistle Bay, World's End Reef, Petit Bateau, and Bloody Bay. You will remember them, all right, as the first snows of the long winter freshen your memory.

The Tobago Cays (25482) lie behind the sheltering barrier of World's End and Horseshoe Reefs. Most famous of all the anchorages in the Grenadines, the Cays (provided the weather is its usual benign self) are the epitome of tropical cruising. Uninhabited, ringed with beaches, and with deep-water channels winding through the pastel shallows, the yachtsman can spend days living in the midst of their beauty. They are inclined to become a little crowded in the height of the winter season, but even then the canny skipper can escape the mob by picking a spot out to windward under the lee of the reef.

The northern approach to the Cays is simple enough. Once past Glass Hill on Cannouan, head a little higher than the easternmost of Mayero. Soon the wicked-looking Baline Rocks will be clearly seen. Pass between these rocks and the end of Horseshoe Reef. Slowly head up until the western end of the reef can be seen, and then head for the middle of the northern Cay. I have purposely not given ranges or compass headings, because in this world of reefs the skipper must simply get used to eyeballing his way around.

Tobago Cays in the Grenadines

The southern entrance is more complex and should only be attempted for the first time in good light. In 18 years I have only once seen one of the two sand cays which are supposed to mark this entrance. From the rigging, though, the dark-blue water of the channel is very obvious.

The most popular anchorage is in the gut between the two islands. A strong current sometimes rushes through the channel, and yachts should lie to a mooring with two anchors off the bow, one to the E and the other to the W. Stern anchors for heavy, deep-drafted vessels seldom hold well, for the strains are enormous.

In summer conditions, my favorite place is just to windward of the little beach on Jamesby, the southernmost of the group, or as far to the SE of Baradal as draft allows. In *Mirage* and *Etoile de Mer*, both trawler types drawing 6 feet, we could roam all over the banks inside the reef.

It was a little different with *Lord Jim*'s 10½ feet, however, as we once found out. For years I had been thoroughly disgusted with the so-called sportsmen (generally from the French islands) who would dash down to the cays in fast motorboats and blast away at every animal and bird in sight. Expended shotgun shells were everywhere, and the iguana and dove population had been decimated.

One day, following our normal practice, which was to give the charter party a bit of a thrill, we executed a quick circumnavigation of the two larger islands under full sail—topsails and the lot aloft. We normally would conclude the tour by strapping everything in tight while running downwind through the narrow gut, then dropping headsails and foresail simultaneously. The 70-ton schooner, under main alone and full helm, would spin round on her heel to drop anchor and fall back alongside the beach. All rather hairy, but a lot of fun.

On this occasion, a fusillade of gunfire from Jamesby attracted our attention to a flotilla of cabin cruisers anchored in the lee of the cay, their crews merrily banging away. Full of righteous fury, I decided to stop this nonsense, and down went *Lord Jim*'s helm. Straight at them we thundered.

Quite what I really intended escapes me now but, with a few feet to go, we ran up the gently sloping sand and stopped dead. Why that long-suffering rig didn't carry on going beats me. Anyway, with gunmen and crew all frozen to the spot in stupefied amazement, I stood up and with imbecilic pomposity shouted, "*Vous êtes une vache, alors!*" With that brilliant rapier thrust, *Lord Jim* jibed all-standing, heeled over, and trundled off into deep water, and I sat down feeling more stupid than usual. One of the charter party, new to the game, commented seriously, "Hey, how about that? I never thought a sailboat had brakes."

Snorkeling is of course superb out on the Horseshoe Reef, especially due E of the northern tip of Baradal, where there is a break in the reef. A good place for beginners to practice is off the beach on the SE side of Petit Bateau, the southernmost of the two main islands.

Outside the Horseshoe in Petit Tabac, in settled or summer weather, an anchorage can sometimes be found in the Horseshoe's lee. If not, take the dinghy through the small-boat pass up by Baradal and play Robinson Crusoe for a bit. Also in settled weather, eyeball it out to the sprawling World's End Reef, where you will be absolutely alone, seemingly in the middle of the ocean. The holding is good and there's no reason why you shouldn't overnight there in a calm spell. It's a funny feeling, though—there's not a scrap of land between you and central Africa.

Mayero Island (25482) lies just to the W of the Tobago Cays and has four anchorages, beautiful beaches, wonderful walks, a very interesting wreck, and a population of under a hundred souls. Saltwhistle Bay is tiny, and more than 9 feet can't really escape the swell. Saline Bay is the better of the other two coves on the W side of the island if there is a northerly swell running.

The reef which runs out SW from Grand Col Point extends a good deal further than the chart shows, as the captain of the World War I gunboat *Purina* found out to his cost. She lies about 400 yards NNW of the point, and her shadowy form 35 feet down is an almost irresistible lure for experienced skin divers. Line up the end of the point with the dock in Saline Bay and search with the dinghy.

A beautiful, seldom-used anchorage is on the eastern side of Mayero behind the reefs. Tuck up to the NE as far as you can go.

The island was once ruled with an iron fist by two West Indian fishermen named the St. Hilaire brothers. On certain nights of the week, the brothers preferred there to be no yachts around. "Why?" asked one of my charterers. "Because de debil come to talk wid us and you folks might frighten him," replied the St. Hilaires, leering horribly. "De debil," it seemed, travels in an unlit sloop.

Union Island (25482), with its spectacular skyline of soaring peaks, always looks bigger than it actually is. Viewed at sundown from the Tobago Cays, it is sensational. Apart from being a port of entry for St. Vincent, it is the administrative center for the northern Grenadines and enjoys a greater degree of prosperity than its immediate neighbors.

The township of Clifton looks from the harbor to be a badly executed backdrop for Sadie Thompson. On my first trip through, in 1958, I was trying to pretend to the charter party that I had been there before. A rather imposing building displayed a sign which said "Hotel," and with great confidence I suggested a meal ashore. When we arrived, the "hotel" had chickens in the lobby, goats in the dining room, and a load of saltfish in the bedroom. Now, of course, it's a smart place, with curtains and plants and things in conch shells. The island is still very primitive, but the people are healthy and their laughter is one of the loudest noises to be heard.

A Union Islander, who for purposes of this tale had better remain nameless, once quite literally saved my life. We were in the Martinique drydock, and he was the crew on a friend's boat. One night a young Spanish gent, crew on another boat, went completely off his little rocker and began trying to stick a large rusty chisel into all and sundry. I believe I was relieving myself at the time El Nutcase roared onto the scene waving his trusty chisel. All was very nearly lost, when my Union Island friend leapt out of the rigging and with great dexterity disarmed and disabled the noble Spaniard.

Many years later, my rescuer turned up in Clifton with a huge boatload of lobsters for sale at a most reasonable price. We stacked our deepfreeze, and he went off to the other yachts. Later, an acquaintance who had a beach bar in Clifton called me on the ship-to-shore from Grenada to say that his lobster pound had been robbed and would I go ashore and investigate. Being a man of honor, I thoroughly enjoyed the lobster.

Clifton Harbour is simple to enter and very secure, and the outer harbor just behind the reef is beautiful. To clear customs, which is only necessary when coming from Grenada, don't forget the Q and courtesy flags, and go ashore to the Post Office with 3 crew lists.

The previously mentioned beach club has been taken over and enlarged upon by André and Simone Beaufraund of Martinique. They have also constructed a slipway for yachts up to 60 feet, and crews are allowed to do their own work. Anything that André and Simone do, they do well. When this enterprising project is completed, not only will there be a first-class place to eat in the Grenadines, but hauling out will be a pleasure, too.

Leaving Clifton Harbour, beware the Grand de Coi Reef, a very real and unmarked danger. Best leave it to port when going S.

A lovely and secluded anchorage can be had behind Frigate Island. Trolling off the point is very good.

Even more beautiful is Chatham Bay on the W coast of Union. Favor the NE corner and, if there is a fresh trade blowing outside, drop two anchors, for, my goodness, it can squall in there!

Prune Island (25482) is just across from Clifton. Perhaps I should say it *was*, for it is now called Palm Island and, for that matter, doesn't even look like a prune any more. The people responsible for the change are John and Mary Caldwell, and whatever your feelings on development in the Grenadines may be, you have to give these two credit for completing a seemingly impossible task. You may remember that John wrote a best-selling book called *Desperate Voyage*, in which he fought against incredible odds, including wrestling with a shark in the cockpit of his tiny boat. More incredible to me is that he has done away with the mosquito on Palm by personally tracking down and killing every land crab on the place, and then filling in thousands of their dank, larvae-infested holes. For that sort of dedication a man has a right to change an island's name, don't you think?

In the days when John chartered *Outward Bound*, the yacht he and Mary built for a world voyage, he amused himself by planting palm trees on every little barren islet and cay he found. In fact, the yacht sometimes looked like a floating coconut grove. But nearly all the palms you now see in the Grenadines were planted by John during his charter years.

The island has one of the most beautiful beaches in the Caribbean, but is plagued with a surging anchorage. The best answer is to stop for lunch and a swim and then pop over to Clifton for the night. Anchor close to the beach, anywhere between the point of sand opposite the beach club and the southwestern corner of the island.

LIAT has regular flights going into Palm Island, so that being in the middle of nowhere is now actually quite close to everywhere. Yachts with tall spars should not anchor between the two red flags; they mark the approach to the runway, and LIAT has enough problems without having to mast-hop.

Petit St. Vincent (25482) is the one of the three "Petit" islands that has made the big time. It has become a justifiably favorite overnight stop for charter yachts. The others, apparently named while someone was in a state of frustration, are Petit Martinique and Petit Tobago.

"P.S.V.," as it is affectionately called, was once the property and lonely abode of a splendid West Indian lady named Lily Bethel, who came from neighboring Petit Martinique. Her many sons ran a fleet of schooners engaged in interisland trading. With increasing age, Lily was forced to spend a considerable amount of time in bed. One day a hurricane blew her house off the top of the hill. Lily sat up in bed and peered indignantly out the window while her house took off down the slopes to execute a reasonable landing at the bottom. Apart from breaking her leg when she fell out of bed, Lily enjoyed the flight, or so the story goes, and next day the house was carried back up the hill, where it stands to this day.

In the early 1960s, a charter party from the States fell in love with P.S.V. and persuaded Lily to sell. Under the direction of Doug Terman and Haze Richardson, a very tasteful resort has since come into being. Former charter skippers themselves, they realized that yachts would not only bring business but would supply life and interest to the place. Doug and Haze set out from the beginning to encourage yachtsmen in every way possible. An interesting solar-powered watermaker provides enough fresh water for the club to offer showers, which are of course a real Godsend to the salt-encrusted mariner in an otherwise arid region. Ice and bread are also available here. The Wednesday evening steel-band jump-up has become an event not to be missed, and the annual P.S.V. Regatta is one of the major West Indian racing fixtures. All in all, we should be thankful that if the island had to be developed in the first place, such an excellent team was there to do it.

Petit St. Vincent is sheltered from the seas by a crescent-shaped reef, and except in real blowy conditions, an anchorage can be found under its lee on the seldom-visited northern side of the island. In general, however, most people use the southern anchorage, but care should be taken to avoid an 8-foot shoal rather inconsiderately placed off the SW corner of the island. It can clearly be seen, since it is a lot lighter in color than the surrounding water.

If there's room, anchor between the shore and the isolated reef almost directly opposite the clubhouse. On jump-up night the anchorage is crowded, and I usually find it necessary to go right up to the head of the bay and tie stern to the little dock. This procedure not only prevents us from becoming entangled with anyone else but also enables me to go straight home rather than bumbling about in the anchorage at two in the morning.

Although the holding is poor, it's really great to anchor off the southern side of Mopion, the easternmost of the two tiny sand cays marking the end of the reef to the WNW of P.S.V. There's wonderful swimming and snorkeling here, and it's a great place to lie in the sun with a pitcher of rum punch.

Petit Martinique (25482) is interesting because you may still be able to buy here a variety of strange liqueurs such as I have never seen, or even heard of, anywhere else in the world. There are no real shops; just ask around. But if you've ever been told that you look even vaguely like a customs man, best forget the whole thing.

They still build the traditional schooner on the beach here, and the shipwrights are a delight to talk with.

Carriacou (25482) is the first port of the Grenadines under Grenada's jurisdiction. If you plan to stop there, don't forget to fly the Grenada courtesy flag, the Q flag, and to go ashore and clear at Hillsborough. A northbound yacht leaving Carriacou and heading for P.S.V. should very definitely remember to clear in Union Island first.

Carriacou is an island worth more attention than cruising or charter yachtsmen normally give it. Most people, I suppose, are in too much of a hurry to get to the Tobago Cays area, and probably spend only a night in Tyrell Bay before rushing on. However, both the E and S coasts have a variety of good anchorages, and you are almost certain to be alone.

Hillsborough Bay during the winter months can produce a really nasty roll, which reminds me that one of the funniest but most tragic sights I have seen in the islands was watching the Grenada mailboat try to load her cargo alongside the dock there. Cattle and motor cars, cardboard cartons and cooking stoves—all were dropped in the sea or onto the heads of gawking passengers. Anywhere, in fact, except into the hold of the schooner as she plunged and rolled to the swell.

After clearing, provided it is not blowing too hard, you can spend a good night at the south side of Sandy Island. Drop in about 4 fathoms and fall back so that the vessel is in relatively shallow water about 150 yards from shore. The island will break up the northerly swell and the short easterly chop will hardly be felt. The reef that extends to the E off Sandy Island offers perhaps the most beautiful snorkeling in the Grenadines. Spearfishing is strictly *verboten*, since the island is a Grenadian national park. As if to confirm the island's new status, the department of something or other has erected a hideous pillbox-looking structure slap in the middle of the tiny place. Now, who on earth needs a changing room on an uninhabited island?

Tyrell Bay is almost always snug and naturally popular with yachts. Surpris-

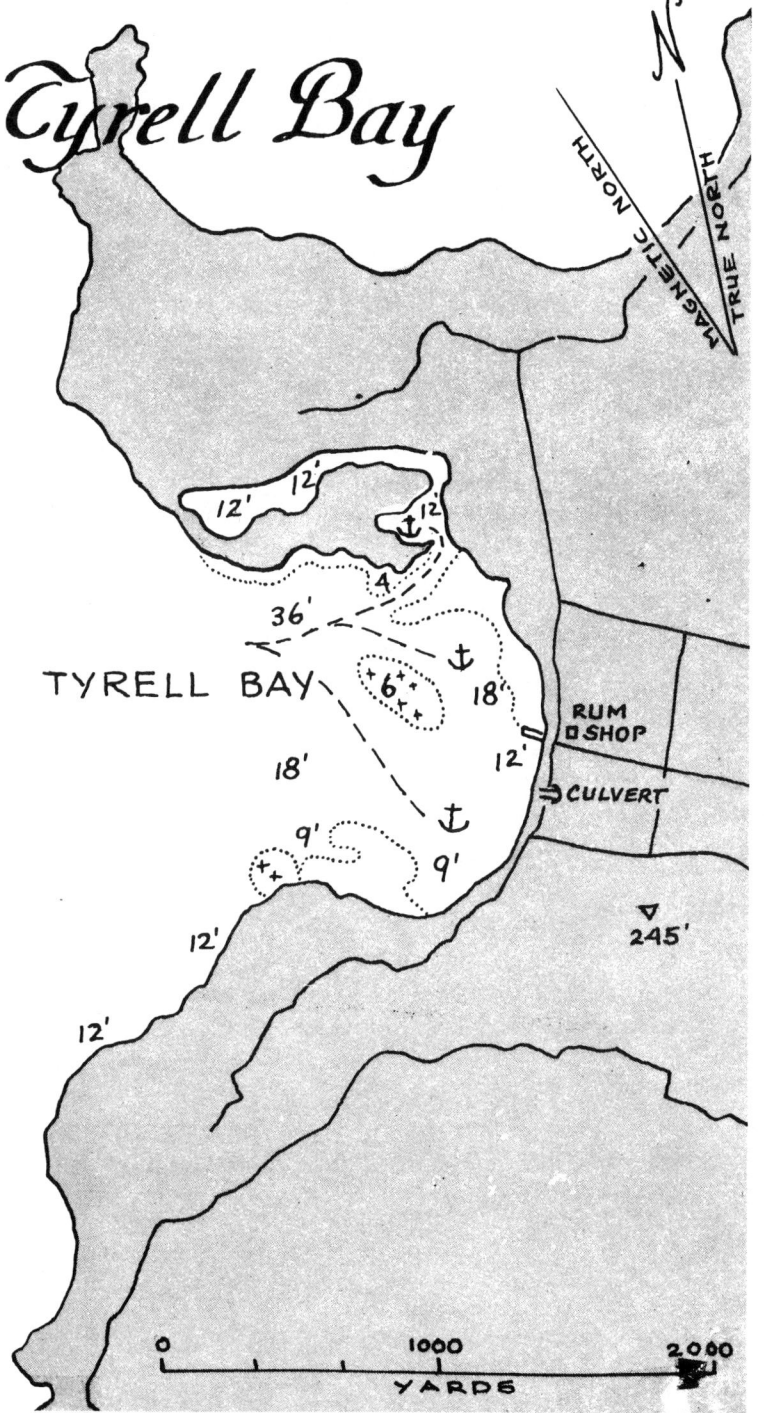

ingly, however, loads of people run happily up onto the shoal opposite the jetty, despite its being accurately marked on the charts. Sometimes, for a change, I drop the hook almost on top of the little island that lies at the entrance to the lagoon, or *carenage*. This is preferable to going all the way inside, as the mosquitos can be bad on windless nights. Take the dinghy in there and try for tarpon. They are there, all right. For a yacht drawing no more than 7 feet, the *carenage* would make an excellent hurricane hole.

On the S coast, eyeball in anywhere that looks good under the prevailing conditions. Saline Island is excellent, although a quiet night cannot be assured because of the occasional strong current. More interesting is the area behind the windward reef on the E side of Carriacou, where 6 feet can, with care, go all the way from one end to the other.

Ashore, the island is attractive except for the unfortunate little capital which has all the beauty and charm of the public convenience at Liverpool Street Station. That is a great pity, considering the excellent job the original French settlers did with the town of St. George's and, come to that, with the first-class little roads of Carriacou.

A few provisions can be obtained, and I would suggest that for current information you pop along and chat with the people at the Mermaid Tavern, the pub originally operated by the well-known yachtsman and author Linton Rigg. Linton was a guiding light in organizing the Bahamian Out Island Regatta, and then moved to Carriacou and set up a similar event, which has become extremely popular with the locals.

Île de Ronde (25481) is one of a small group of lonely islands between Carriacou and the north end of Grenada, on which a handful of people exist in very much the same manner as the original settlers. It's most unlikely that things will change much in the near future, and if only to observe a minute part of this globe where the clock has stopped, Île de Ronde is worth a stop.

Although Cornstone Bay on the NW side is supposed to be the best anchorage, I have always found it more comfortable off the small village on the SW side. Go ashore and, like Alice, step through the looking glass into yesterday.

Kick'em Jenny, around which flow some of the strongest currents in the West Indies, is uninhabited, has no place to anchor, and is quite literally for the birds.

Grenada (25481)

In the days of wine and roses, when crewed chartering was the height of fashion, Grenada was our southern terminal: the end of the line and the place to offload one "lot" and take on another. With practiced ease we would wash down, clean up, send out laundry, reprovision, refuel, revarnish, change filters, take a shower, grab a beer, meet the new people, and dash off again. A constant stream of charter yachts followed one another out of St. George's, and there is no doubt that in a modest way we contributed quite a bit to Grenada's prosperity during the 1960s. However, certain elements, both political and commercial, became perhaps a little too greedy, and from a yacht skipper's point of view, a stay in the island began to be something of a hassle.

The civil disorders of 1974 temporarily put an end to most tourist-oriented activities in the island, and the yachts mostly took off for new pastures. However, as my Auntie Mabel is often heard to say, "Nothing beats a nice good cleanout," and now, with everyone a little wiser, things are looking up once more. The government is actively encouraging yachtsmen again, and there is a good chance that Grenada will soon return to its rightful position as the lower Caribbean's foremost yachting center. After all, there is certainly no more attractive town or harbor than St. George's, and the Lagoon, home of Grenada Yacht Services, is the ideal place to rest up and refit before either carrying on westward or returning to the frozen north.

The sail from Tyrell Bay on Carriacou to St. George's is one of the most wonderful you can have. On a broad reach, the yacht slips along before the trades while flying fish burst away from the lee bow and frigate and bosun birds come out from the scarred cliffs of Kick'em Jenny to wheel lazily over the masthead. Grenada, cool and green after the sun-bleached Grenadines, calms the seas as you run into her lee. A good breeze, normally from the northeast, will stay with the yacht until the town of Gouyave is abeam, and from then on one flirts with calms and capricious puffs along a coast that is as beautiful as any in the entire island chain.

Halifax Harbour (25481), just S of Black Bay Point, is the only anchorage of note on the W coast N of St. George's, and here the wind is so flukey that a yacht will swing around and around all night long.

Shallow-draft vessels should anchor in the southern bay, but yachts drawing more than 9 feet will do best to find a 5-fathom patch just to the N of the point that separates the two beaches and run a stern line out to any suitable tree. The lack of a steady breeze can at times make this pretty little spot rather warm, and once in a while an aggravating short swell finds its way in. Charter yachts on the way north find it useful as an overnight anchorage; it gives their guests time to settle down before the fairly hard windward sail up the Grenadines.

Halifax can only be used if a southbound yacht has first cleared customs in Carriacou.

Dragon Bay (25481) is a tiny cove S of Halifax; at a pinch it might accommodate 3 or 4 yachts. It is popular with local yachtsmen and day-sailers from the hotels.

During the day, between Molinière Point and Grand Anse there is always a splendid breeze to guarantee an exhilarating final sail as the yacht tramps up to St. George's with the late afternoon sun painting the little town in gold.

St. George's (25481) has plenty of water inside the channel-marker buoys off the harbor, but don't wander too far to the S of the clearly seen range situated on the hills behind the main docks. The channel into the Lagoon is well marked and is supposed to have 12 feet of water, although with *Lord Jim*, drawing 10 feet 3 inches, we twice came to a grinding halt right in the middle.

Customs and immigration clearance are available at the G.Y.S. docks, but it is best to contact G.Y.S., Stevens Yachts, or Langley Yachts on 2527 kHz and ask them to inform the authorities of your ETA. The authorities at Grenada take life very seriously, and no amount of jocular backslapping or overloud laughter will prevent the bond locker from being firmly sealed. It's all done very correctly, though, and with that vaguely indifferent air that seems to be the specialty of customs-men the world over.

The commercial harbor at St. George's, Grenada

From the Lagoon to the main part of town is just 5 minutes by dinghy, and it's perfectly safe to leave it outside the Portofino or Nutmeg restaurants. The Food Fair, an excellent supermarket, is located right on the waterfront, and in general the shopping here is first class. Surely one of the most colorful sights in the Caribbean is the market place, situated in the main square opposite Everybody's Store. It's a 10-minute walk from the Careenage. The collection of fruits, vegetables, and fresh spices here will boggle the mind.

Grenadians are, on the whole, a hardworking and intelligent people, and almost any job can be taken care of, provided there's not too much of a rush. To get the most current picture, toddle over to the Grenada Yacht Club and chat with the members.

St. George's is still the one harbor in the West Indies in which it is possible to get a close look at a large trading schooner. Although most have had their mainmasts chopped off and garage-like affairs built on their afterdecks, you might be lucky enough to see an original. The schooner men are a proud breed, and some are determined enough to keep on going with only the necessary addition of an engine, making their vessels little different in concept from the Canadian Bluenose fishermen that carried on into the early part of this century.

Grand Anse (25481) is a convenient anchorage off the beach just S of St. George's, but, unfortunately, a very large swell can ruin this otherwise idyllic spot. The best anchorage is at the NE end of the beach, close to the Silver Sands Hotel. There are two reefs to be avoided, both of them close inshore and clearly visible, so go in when the sun is high.

Long Point Shoal, directly between St. George's and Point Saline, is dangerous and unmarked.

Port Egmont and Calivigny (25481) are the best of the many excellent harbors along the S coast. Both are in the category of safe hurricane holes. Port Egmont is relatively simple to enter for the confident eyeballer.

These south-coast harbors are seldom visited by yachtsmen, perhaps because they generally lack the beaches and crystal waters that are so much a part of tropical cruising.

Prickly Bay (l'Anse aux Épines) (25481) is a very pleasant bay in which is situated the boatyard operated by Spice Island Charters. One may receive customs and immigration clearance here and avoid having to pop into St. George's; this also allows the gung-ho types to sail from Carriacou down the eastern side of Grenada.

Very close to Prickly Bay is the Red Crab Pub. I suppose it's why everyone anchors there in the first place.

Grenville Harbour (25481) is mainly used by fishermen at present, and since it's on the way to nowhere, I really can't see that the situation will change much.

The northeast coast (25481) offers three delightful little islands—Levera, Green, and Sandy—definitely worth visiting, but only in pleasant summer weather. The most pleasant anchorage is off the W coast of Sandy Island.

CHAPTER ELEVEN

Barbados

If Carlisle Bay looks like the headquarters of the international yacht set from late November through February, it's only because Barbados (25485) is the easternmost and thus the most logical target for the transatlantic sailors who annually scoot across from the Canaries at the end of each hurricane season. Some say that eight out of ten such sailors make for Barbados, and it's not uncommon to find 20 or more of them in the bay at one time. During the rest of the year, visiting yachts are few and far between, for Barbados really has little to offer in contrast to the cruising attractions of the Windward chain—and Barbados lies a hundred miles dead into the wind. Indeed, the best way to reach this island outpost is downwind from Europe—or south from Martinique, hopefully on one tack.

Perhaps because Barbados is less than 20 miles long and its highest hill only 1,100 feet, Columbus never sighted it on any of his four voyages. While the quest for gold drew sailors further to the west, this small island to windward lay virtually undiscovered until the British established a colony in 1627. They continued to hold it until 1966, when colonial possessions had become taboo. In the course of those 339 years of uninterrupted British rule, Barbados has, in spite of its climate, absorbed the look and feel of the British countryside, Devon and Cornwall in particular. Ancient stone parish churches, cricket on the green, schoolboys in caps, and girls in starched uniforms and straw boaters are common sights around the island.

Making his landfall after a fast passage from the Canaries with his 47-foot ketch, *Xanadu II*, E. Bates McKee, a member of CCA, reports:

> Approaching from the east at night, the light on South Point can be seen 15 miles at sea but the island actually becomes visible far beyond that range because of the loom of the lights of the airport and the metropolis of Bridgetown.

Not only is Barbados so far to windward of her neighbor islands, she lacks any natural harbors for yachts. And so she is even less attractive. Of course, the

The Careenage, Barbados

wind never blows from the west, so anchorage may be taken anywhere along the west shore, but there is a persistent surge, and during the summer and fall there is always that worrisome feeling that a tropical storm just might come through to upset the trade wind's steady pattern. If one comes, there's no place to go.

Actually, the Careenage, right in the center of Bridgetown is a natural harbor, but it is too small and too commercially oriented to be suitable for a yacht. The approach channel carries 12 feet through a restricted entrance that *Xanadu II* found most uncomfortable at 0200 on Christmas morning in 1973.

Frankly admitting that attempting the entrance at night proved to be a mistake in more ways than one, McKee continued:

In the first place, we were without use of our engine and were almost carried up on the rocks by the surge in the narrow entrance. In the second place, it turned out that one is supposed to anchor off until cleared by customs. However, these gentlemen were most understanding and cleared us next morning at the dock. Once cleared, it soon became apparent that the Careenage was no place to lie alongside for, when the trade wind made up in the morning, the dust of the town completely covered our decks 'til we looked like a sand barge. As soon as it was possible to move we sailed out and joined the other yachts at anchor off the yacht club in Carlisle Bay.

Carlisle Bay (25486) is the deepest indentation on the lee side of the island and thus the principal anchorage. There are no special facilities for yachts, no moorings, and no convenient dinghy landings. Just bring your dinghy through the slight surf and up on the beach, where, we are told, there is no problem with thievery or vandalism. Some yachtsmen use the rather awkward landing platform on the Holiday Inn's pier, which gives the guests some action to watch while they dine.

The swell becomes progressively less toward the northern end of the bay, the best anchorage being between the fish market and the Esplanade, or even as far N as the public pier, where there is very little swell. In this general area, and immediately N of the Barbados gas plant, is a refreshment and ice-cream stand called Bico, where bag ice may be picked up as you come and go ashore. Just S of the gas plant is a water tap for filling jerricans.

For water in volume, and for fuel, prior arrangements must be made with the Berthing Master on the N side of the Careenage.

Haulouts up to about 7½ tons can be handled by a crane located in the corner of the Careenage just before the first bridge. Otherwise the ancient screw-lift at Central Foundry's shipyard, also in the Careenage, is the only answer. This museum-piece of equipment has been in use at least since the turn of the century and has only recently been converted from steam to electric power. As a rule, the waiting time extends into several weeks, and the scheduling is further complicated because the lift is designed for three medium-sized boats, end to end, which means that haulings and launchings cannot be handled independently.

The new Holiday Inn and its old concrete pier stand out like a sore thumb directly on the beach, flanked by the Barbados Cruising Club to the S and the Royal Barbados Yacht Club on the other side.

The Barbados Cruising Club has about 200 members; it's basically a small sailing-boat operation, although it boasts a core of hardy long-distance cruisers. Nothing is fancy here, but the bar on the second story is an ideal place to sit and scan the scene of anchored boats in the background and the bathing types from the inn strewn along the delightful beach below. Visiting yachtsmen are cordially received here, and the shower rooms on the beach level are yours for the asking. If you wish to anchor off this club, stay N of the tanker mooring buoy that lies off the Hilton Hotel pier. Since this pier (now condemned) was built, the water has shoaled up in its lee.

The Royal Barbados Yacht Club is far more pretentious, and is an important part of the island's social scene, but here too you will find the welcome mat out if you have a yacht-club affiliation at home. Upon application, an honorary membership will probably be issued for a 10-day period, with an opportunity to renew it if desired. The clubhouse is comfortable, and the premises include a nice beach, showers, and tennis courts. Anchor about 200 yards off over a good holding sand bottom in 20–30 feet. Since there is some coral on the bottom, chain is advised.

Near the innermost of three black can buoys in a line toward the city, snorkeling enthusiasts will find an interesting wreck with about 4 feet of water over it.

R. Landry & Co. Ltd., 12 Borde Street. Hub Travel at 44 New Street,
old Queen's Park Hotel, is helpful if you have any such business.

Port-of-Spain to Dragon's Mouths (BA 483, 24405)

have said, this northern pincer of the island is where the yachts are, but
r is uninviting for swimming and the coast is exposed. We are now
ing west from Port-of-Spain.

ad *Yacht Club (24406)*, which lies in 61°34.2′ W, takes a merciless chop
ernoon. The anchorage is practically untenable for live-aboards. The
will accomodate 9-foot draft, but no regular dock facilities exist and
ouse burned down, with its pier, in 1973. Most club members own fast,
verboats that are hauled out after each use and stored in sheds on the
. The club's lift will take 10 tons and 6-foot draft.
s plans are afoot to build a breakwater with a pier for stern-to mooring,
urse a new clubhouse. The members are a congenial lot, and some of
d to congregate every afternoon after work for a beer and a gam at the
ry bar and beach terrace.

ad *Yachting Association (24406)* is based in the cove on the NE side of
le. Unfortunately, it is also quite open to the prevailing swell. This club
imarily to the sailing population hereabouts.

aramas *Bay (24405)*, formerly the U.S. Navy's lend-lease base, pro-
e of the snuggest anchorages in the area up in its NE corner, but it's
with permanent moorings. Dockage may be taken at the Alcan pier,
naintained for the transshipment of bauxite. A half-mile further W in
the Swan–Hunter Shipyard, which caters to big ships but will handle
blems. They are said to be resourceful in making up things in their
shop that would be otherwise quite unobtainable in these parts.

s *Bay (24405)* is the local name of the next bight to the W. Here you
good shelter, fuel, groceries, and a coast-guard station that is an
source of "local knowledge" about this area.

d *Bay (24405)* is attractive, very snug, and so popular that it is usually
on weekends. Contrary to the chart, the deep water runs way up to the
one can, in places, tie to a tree.

Island (24405) gives you Morris Bay, also the bay on the SE side of the

CHAPTER TWELVE

Trinidad and Tobago

TRINIDAD (24401, 24405, 24406, BA483)

Back in 1498, the ubiquitous Columbus came again with his fleet to the New
World, this time from the southwest after being becalmed for more than a week
in the sweltering doldrums. When finally the southeast trades filled their sails,
and, a little later, they made their landfall on three small peaks, the devout
Admiral named the land for the Holy Trinity. The hills he saw, reportedly
from 40 miles out, are still called the Trinity Hills.

Thereafter, Trinidad remained rather removed from the action in the rest of
the Caribbean, except for a flurry of activity when a city of gold known as El
Dorado was rumored to exist far up the nearby Orinoco River, a rumor that led
Sir Walter Raleigh to mount an expedition there. While he never found a trace
of gold, his imagination went wild: he wrote luridly of a country "that hath yet
her maidenhead; the graves have not been opened for gold, the mines not
broken with sledges nor their images pulled down out of their temples," in fact,
a place that was "the very magazine of all rich metals."

Unlike Columbus, most yachtsmen approach Trinidad from the north, often
on a close reach from Grenada and usually with some bewilderment as they
discover how far the west-going current has set them off course. In fact, a
landfall during the last hours of darkness makes sense, in order to take advantage of the powerful Chacachare Light. But plan, by all means, to come through
the Bocas in daylight!

The usual choice among the Dragon's Mouths is the Boca de Monas, where
the current, if you hit it at the wrong time, may be running as much as 5 knots.
In this case you will find less current in Boca de Huevos. The current sets north
except for about 2 hours at each change, when, in effect, it is only neutralized.
The current almost never sets south. Sea conditions are generally rough as a
result of the confluence of winds and currents coming out of the Gulf of Paria
and around the north coast of Trinidad.

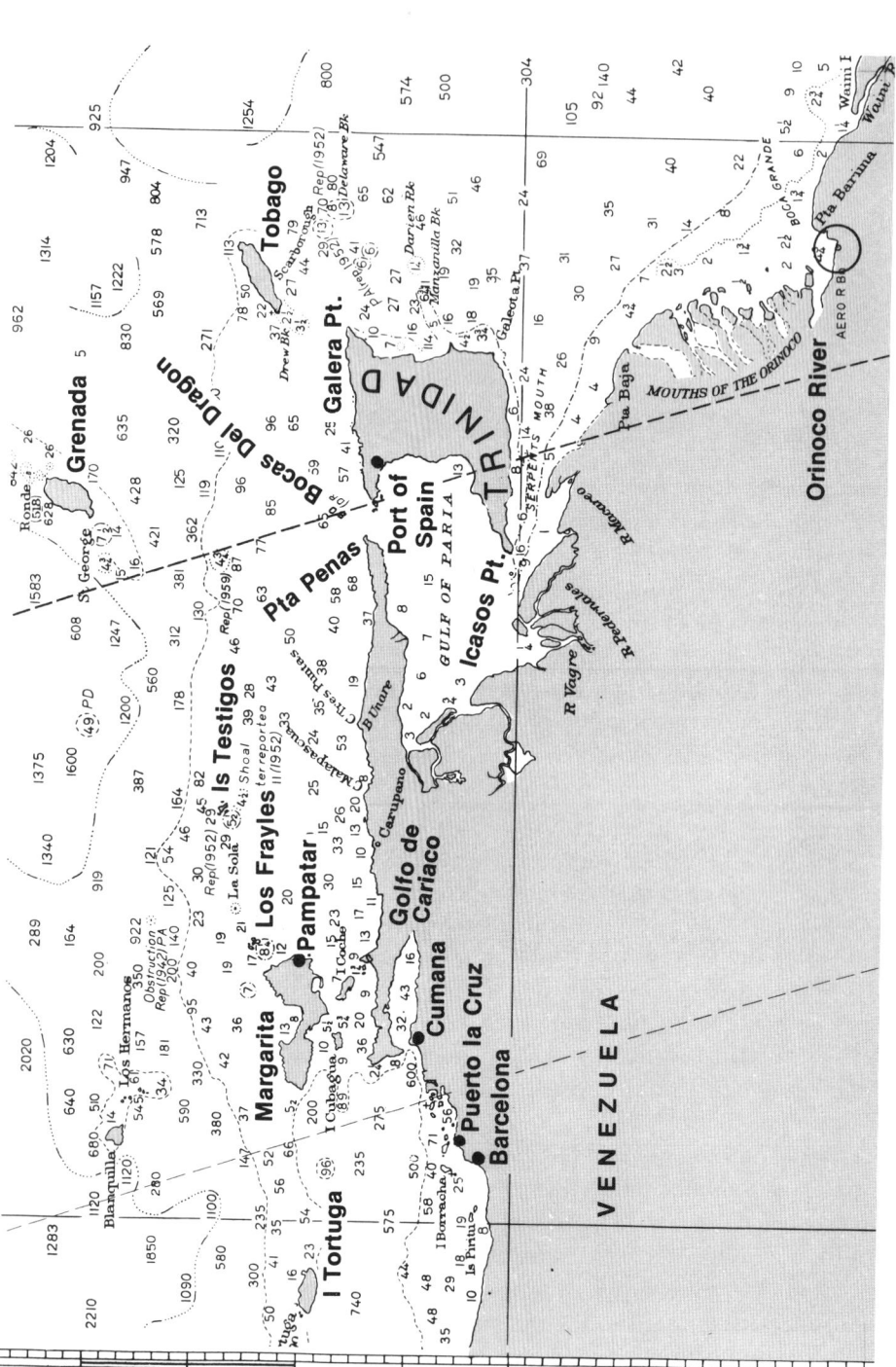

Grenada to the Venezuelan coast and islands

The people of Trinidad are cordial and efficient,
impressed with the East Indians, who are as prevale
whole island is a fascinating mixture of races, inclu
Syrians, Jews, and various Latin Americans. No otl
racially diverse. Here, too, are the people who in
itiated the sly and beguiling calypso, and who stage
carnivals.

We cannot give Trinidad high marks as a cruisi
many more beautiful spots a few hundred miles i
Paria is big, and its waters are muddied by the Oi
wind sweeps across the low plains that border the
builds up every afternoon to belabor the only popu
extends from Port-of-Spain out to the islands in the
the southern part of the gulf is taken up with oil rig
least they're interesting if you want a glimpse of t

The rainy season comes in June, July, and Au;
March and April. A big plus is that Trinidad lies so
in fact, on only two or three occasions in the island'
been storm damage to crops.

Port-of-Spain (24406) is strictly a commercial por
tive for a yacht, but it is possible to tie up at the S enc
cargo and cruise ships lie. A finger dock juts out he
small basin behind it and be right next to the quara
away from immigration. Expect a quarantine offi
will then be directed to immigration and finally to
cat aboard may have trouble here; there is a regul
ashore. This dock area is semi-secured, there is
nearby, and 110V AC (60-cycle) is only in the pl;

On the other hand, you can arrange the entry for
yacht club, at the coast-guard pier in Staubles B
Chaguaramas Bay. Directions for these places fc
ahead on VHF-FM to give your ETA so the offic

Across Wrightson Road from the quarantine sta
clean, well-run establishment supported by a chui
the benefit of all seamen, including yachtsmen. Gii
reports that the amenities include free showers,
week, a bar serving beer and soft drinks, a clean sv
fee), and a small restaurant producing good, l
reasonable prices.

Admiralty and U.S. charts and a limited stocl

found a
near the

As we
the wate
progress

Trinid
every af
fuel doc
the clubl
open po
property

Seriou
and of cc
them ten
tempora

Trinid
Pt. Gour
caters pi

Chague
vides one
crowded
which is i
the bay is
yacht pr
machine

Stauble
will find
excellent

Scotlan
crowded
end, and

Monos

island called Copper Hole by the locals. Though it would not appear so from the chart, this latter bay is quiet at almost all times.

Chacachare Island (24405) houses a leper colony along the N shore of the bay of that name. Good anchorage will be found deep in the western portion of this bay. When rounding the SW point of the island, there is safe water for passing inside of Diamond Rock to an excellent anchorage called Tinta Bay. Drop the hook anywhere off this reef-strewn shore.

Lower Gulf of Paria (BA 483)

Running down the W coast of Trinidad (in case you want to have a look at the forest of drilling platforms and maybe a 200,000-ton tanker or two), stay well off the shallow mud flats all along this shore. On the sail down, the oil rig in about 10°28′ N, 61°33′ W makes a conspicuous mark along an otherwise nondescript shore.

Pointe-à-Pierre (BA 483) offers a safe and comfortable anchorage just off the Texaco pier about a cable N of the light near the church. This is the locale of the Pointe-à-Pierre Yacht Club, whose members are employees of Texaco-Trinidad, Inc. The whole area is under Texaco security control.

From here a circular cruise might be made to the fishing port of Guiria, an artificial harbor on the Venezuelan shore, thence back to the island in the Dragon's Mouths.

The North Coast of Trinidad (24401)

All the bays along this shore are subject to big swells, but Las Cuevas Bay is said to be tenable.

TOBAGO (24402)

Stepchild of Trinidad, to which she has been politically and economically tied ever since the final collapse of her sugar industry in 1888, poor little Tobago languishes in the sun, wearing the wistful smile of an island that once was prosperous and much desired by several of Europe's big powers. In many ways, Tobago (named through some obscure reference to the pipe with which the natives smoked their tobacco) is an example of the West Indian Islands-that-were. The tourist hotels are there, to be sure, but so far they are the low-key type and rather few and far between.

Many yachtsmen, lulled by the steady breezes that have let them sail down the island chain in comfortable reaches, think twice before heading out to still another island that actually requires tacking to reach—and against a substantial current too. Consequently, Tobago remains a neglected island so far as yachts are concerned, and more's the pity, to use a British expression, for in its 26-by-7-mile compass, Tobago offers sandy beaches (albeit dark sand on the windward side) with graceful stands of coconut palms, clear waters, a diving reef to remember, some spectacular rockbound coastal scenery, and a handful of secure anchorages, each picturesque enough to hold a yachtsman for a couple of days or so.

Ginnie Higman and her husband, Bob, spent two months in Tobago aboard their motor-sailer, *Tormentor III*, a 40-foot "Newporter." Ginnie had this to say about getting there:

> This island is easier to reach from Grenada, about 70 miles northwestward, than from Trinidad. However, we left Port-of-Spain, Trinidad, at noon and power-sailed to Las Cuevas Bay, a rolly but protected roadstead midway along Trinidad's north coast. The next day it took us from 0545 to 1830 to power-sail the 35 miles against wind and current to Milford Bay on the southwest corner of Tobago.

When approaching from the southwest the Drew Shoal, 3–4 fathoms, is so clear that the bottom can be seen, a welcome relief from the Orinoco mud that taints the waters all around Trinidad. Only the north shore of Tobago is a practical cruising area, since the windward side, even when the wind is down, is subject to an incessant ocean swell, except for King's Bay, near the east end of the island, which is sufficiently indented to dissipate most of this swell. The beaches on the windward shore are a dark and unappealing sand, whereas much whiter sand and clearer water will be found on the northern coast.

The northeastern end of Tobago is mountainous and sparsely settled, and most of the activity and the resort operations are at the westerly end, which tapers to a flat plain.

Scarborough (24403) is the principal town and a rolly anchorage, in addition to being untidy and generally unattractive for a yacht. However, there is a government dock where one may lie alongside or moor in Mediterranean fashion. Ginnie Higman of *Tormentor III* said of the perils of Scarborough:

> Try to tie on the E side of the U-shaped dock because of the havoc created by the passenger-freight boats, *Scarlet Ibis* and *Bird of Paradise*, when they arrive early in the morning thrice weekly from Port-of-Spain. If you are Med-moored they're liable to set their breast anchor on top of yours and

Scarborough, Tobago

when they weigh it for their 2200 departure, you may be hauled along too! Furthermore, if you are anchored too close, their propeller wash may push your boat right onto the cement quay. Our dinghy, which hangs in stern davits, was crushed this way when we were there.

While in Scarborough, visit the Botanical Gardens and also climb the 430-foot heights to Fort George for a panoramic view of town and countryside, and Trinidad on a clear day. Look for the old water tank shaped like a bell and shout into it: "Bell, tank wants more water," then listen for the results. . . .

In 1801, the old fort was the scene of an interesting subterfuge by a clever officer of the garrison, who, hearing of a planned revolt by the slaves, arrested thirty of the leaders and, to the horror of the townspeople watching from below the walls, summarily hanged them one by one from a conspicuous gallows. Later, to the immense relief of the owners of these valuable slaves, it developed that the same man had been hoisted thirty times to the peak of the gallows.

Milford Bay (24402) is the popular initial anchorage upon arrival at Tobago. Anchor anywhere, according to draft, off the white sand beach between Sandy and Pigeon Points. Even though you have been duly entered in Trinidad, you are expected also to present your papers to the officials at the nearby airport; the Tobagonians are fussy about this.

For provisions a taxi may be hired at the airport for the short trip to Scarborough.

The peninsula of Pigeon Point is a private "aquatic park" with thatched cabanas and tables surrounded by beautiful coconut palms. The vivid colors of the water inside Bucco Reef add to the uncontrived beauty of the place. The well-defined reef is constantly breaking, and with some advance soundings from the dinghy, it should be possible to gain the shelter of this pretty body of water through the more northerly of the two obvious reef openings.

Mt. Irvine Bay (24403) provides anchorage anywhere along the reasonably white sand beach. This bay is readily identified by the conspicuous jagged rock off Booby Point and by the hotel of the same name as the bay at the place marked "Chy" on the chart. Expect a low, lazy swell here.

Courland Bay (24403) affords excellent shelter under the high bluffs toward Plymouth town, and a pleasant anchorage will be found off the Turtle Beach Hotel. The bay gets its name from the Earl of Pembroke, who was also the Duke of Courland and ruled the Baltic principality of that name, now Latvia and part of the USSR. Charles I of England gave Tobago to the Earl in 1628, as a birthday present.

On the bluff overlooking the bay are the ruins of Fort James, finished in 1666 and the island's oldest fortification. Not far away is a famous gravestone with the baffling epitaph:

> Within these Walls are Deposited the Bodies of Betty Stiven and child. She was the beloved wife of Alex B. Stiven who to the end of his days will deplore her Death which happened upon the 25th day of November, 1783, in the 23rd year of her Age. What was remarkable of her, she was a mother without knowing it and a wife without letting her husband know it, except by her kind indulgences to him.

A household slave and planter's mistress with unborn child? The conjectures go on and on, but no one really knows.

Man of War Bay (24403) at the NE corner of the island is enclosed by precipitous hills and a curving beach. It is an exceptionally delightful anchorage. Ginnie Higman of *Tormentor III* found the people of Charlotteville here not as friendly as elsewhere in Tobago and some of the officials rather rude. She also advises not to put in here without first having cleared immigration and customs at the airport or in Scarborough.

Man of War Bay, northeast end of Tobago

Rounding the corner of the island amidst the tide rips, it is best to stay outside the St. Giles and Marble Islands and avoid the awash rocks and swift current that sluices between St. Giles and the mainland. Though the anchoring possibilities in the vicinity of Tyrell's Bay look promising on the chart, local sailors have termed the area "impossible" because of wind, sea, and currents. If you want to visit the wild-life refuge on Little Tobago Island, home of the Birds of Paradise introduced from the Aru Islands of Indonesia in 1909, the Higmans suggest anchoring in King's Bay and coming back 3½ miles by dinghy.

King's Bay (24403) is surrounded by high hills, and a brook of clear water spills into the cove through a coconut grove. Lieutenant-Governor Alexander Brown, the first British Governor of Tobago, landed on the beach here in 1764 and reviewed a guard of honor.

Picture that ceremonial event as you stand into this uninhabited anchorage in the NE corner of the bay off the ruins of a concrete dock. There will be some motion here, but it is cool and perfectly safe.

Prince's Bay (24402) offers reasonable shelter from the wind up in the NE corner, but the swell makes it uncomfortable and the rather squalid village of Roxborough doesn't enhance the surroundings. Nearby King's Bay is a much better choice.

CHAPTER THIRTEEN

The Venezuelan Coast and Islands

BY KIT S. KAPP

Sailing westward from Grenada or Trinidad, the yachtsman will join and follow the routes sailed by the earliest Spanish explorers, Columbus and Alonso de Ojeda, and later by the Elizabethan opportunists, John Hawkins and his nephew Francis Drake. Voyage accounts are sometimes confusing, because many place names have been lost in the fog of history or are seldom used today. "The Spanish Main," for instance, was coined by the English as a contraction of the Spanish-controlled mainland that included the Caribbean coastlines of South and Central America as far as the Miskito Coast of present-day Nicaragua. Today, Spanish Main has mostly a romantic meaning, but it applies to the same general area.

The Spaniards had other names for this part of the New World, the most common being *Tierra Firma*, to denote the first significant body of firm land that Columbus discovered in the course of his third voyage. This time he had sailed westward from Trinidad to touch upon the coast of present-day Venezuela; his previous discoveries had all turned out to be islands.

Shortly afterwards, an expedition led by Alonso de Ojeda continued along this coast (Ojeda named it "Maracapana") as far as Cabo de la Vela in modern Colombia. Before leaving Tierra Firma, Ojeda discovered the great lake of Maracaibo. The villages there, built out upon the lake itself, so reminded him of Venice that he named the locale Venezuela, or Little Venice, later applied to the whole province and carried down to this day.

By 1525, the limits of the Caribbean had been well defined by the Council of the Indies, the august body in Seville that oversaw for Spain the colonizing and exploiting of this vast, rich New World. First came the large northern islands, the smaller Caribbees in the east, the Antilles, and Tierra Firma, most of them the discoveries of Columbus and his captains. Then, in 1512, Ponce de Leon, the roving governor of Puerto Rico, discovered *Las Floridas*. In 1519, Hernan Cortéz found a new land mass even farther west than Tierra Firma. He named it *Reino de Nueva España*: it embraced mainland Mexico and the Yucatan peninsula. Then the Council reshuffled its deck: it gave the name *Reino de Tierra Firma* to present-day Panama and called the eastern part of the mainland, present-day Venezuela, *Nueva Andalusia*.

Weather Along the Spanish Main

The trade winds blow steadily along the lower Caribbean from the northeast. However, there are seasonal and local variations close in along the shore, which occasionally provides better shelter than you might expect.

Hurricanes are practically unknown. Only one was recorded in the Gulf of Venezuela prior to 1923, and another raged through the Gulf of Cariaco to Bonaire in July, 1933. Northers, which are the bane of the upper Caribbean, seem to tucker out by the time they reach the Main. However, the ground swells that they generate do not dissipate so easily; they cause tremendous breakers along the coast. Sometimes, for instance, these swells send spume as high as 120 feet into the air at the La Guaira seawall, on the coast near Caracas.

The trades blow strongest from January to May. From July to October, they are more variable in direction, and you may expect calms and even mild westerlies. In autumn, look out for *calderetas*, hot, sharp blasts from mountain gorges that are strong enough to take the roofs off houses.

May to November is the season for *chubascos*, local afternoon squalls in the Maracaibo area that blow up to 50 knots from the south to southwest. Fortunately, they are of short duration and are similar to the *chocosanas* in Colombia. Elsewhere along the coast, May to November is a time to expect strong southerly squalls that lose intensity as they blow off the shore.

Close to shore, land breezes, if any, commence toward evening and ease up about dawn. The trades start to pick up in midmorning and tend to drop off after sunset.

West of Aruba, particularly near the Guajira Peninsula, and from the Magdalena River to the Rosario Islands, the winter trades reach gale force. Winter winds along the Paria and Araya Peninsulas of eastern Venezuela are not quite as strong, and moderate considerably during the summer. Northeasterly winds prevail in the long coastal indentation from Puerto La Cruz west to Carenero. They seldom blow much over 6 knots, and conditions are usually dead calm at sunrise from June to December.

The regular trades produce moderate seas. However, from December to March, the seas seem to break more heavily and are often dangerous following strong gales in the Atlantic.

The prevailing westerly current is generally weaker near shore, averaging about ½-knot, but sometimes the reinforced trades will increase the rate to 3 knots. Near the coast, counter-currents are sometimes experienced in the summer. Tidal currents are usually weak, since the tidal range is only about a foot. However, spring tides may range to 2¼ feet. When they do, they may speed up surface currents substantially in bottleneck areas such as the lower Gulf of Venezuela. Among the offshore islands, currents set west to west-northwest at ½-to-1½ knots, and even more under reinforced trade-wind conditions.

Rainfall on the coasts of Venezuela and Colombia ranges from moderate to extremely light (on the Paraguana and Guajira Peninsulas). In general, the wet season is from May to December in eastern Venezuela. In the Puerto Cabello area the rainfall is light from October to May and moderate during the rest of the year. In the Maracaibo area, expect light rain during May and June and downpours from September to December.

Rollers may become heavy when the trades veer northward during November and December.

Entry Procedures, Venezuela and Colombia

Yachtsmen have long been aware of the reputation of the Venezuelan and Colombian coasts for insurrection, piracy, and smuggling, and for overzealous and trigger-happy patrol-boat crews eager to impound foreign boats on the slightest provocation. We are now happy to report that (except for some smuggling) these are legends of the past. A new attitude prevails; it involves just and rigid enforcement of laws and regulations by the Guardia de Costa and port officials, coupled with a sincere desire to encourage the growth of commerce and tourism. This means friendly relations with yachtsmen.

Here are a few rules that will foster mutual respect and make your cruise on the Spanish Main less difficult and more enjoyable:

1. Always fly (right side up) the national courtesy flag from 0600 to 1800 (never after sunset) from a prominent, high position; also display your vessel's national flag.

2. Respect and cooperate with all officials. Don't be in a hurry, and don't expect to be cleared outside of regular hours or on holidays. If you treat those in authority politely, assist them in inspecting your boat, and offer them refreshments and congenial conversation, then, more than likely, they'll go out of their way to assist you.

3. At all ports where there is a Port Captain's office or Customs House, present your clearance upon request and graciously comply with all paperwork required.

4. Immediately upon entering Venezuelan or Colombian waters, go directly

to a port of entry. In Venezuela these are: Carúpano, Pampatar, Puerto Sucre (Cumaná), Puerto La Cruz, La Guaira, Puerto Cabello, Las Piedras, and Maracaibo. Colombian ports of entry are: Ríohacha, Santa Marta, Barranquilla, Cartagena, Turbo, and Zapzurro.

The initial clearance fee will cost about $10. Extra paperwork, such as crew-passenger, cargo, arms, and food lists may be essential if you are to obtain your sailing permit for Venezuela. However, we recommend writing in advance to the Minister of Communications, Director of Marina Mercante, Caracas, to apply for a Venezuelan cruising permit. Include a detailed list of all the ports you wish to visit. It is said that a pre-clearance from the Venezuelan Consul in Grenada or Martinique may be obtained for a fee of about $10. However, with this type of entry permit, it may be necessary to clear from one customs district to another.

Passports are essential, and visas are desirable, especially for any crew members expecting to sign off the vessel or desiring to travel to the interior.

When sailing at night along the coast, it is advisable to keep your vessel brightly lit, in addition to the running-lights prescribed by international rules. Patrol boats are on the alert for smuggling operations in this area, and a brightly lit boat is unlikely to arouse suspicions.

Try to speak Spanish, which is one of the simplest languages. If you cannot, at least present a happy disposition, even in the face of disappointments. In a decade of cruising the Caribbean, we have found nothing to compare with the friendly hospitality accorded to us in Venezuelan and Colombian waters.

Isla de Margarita and Isla La Tortuga (24430)

Venezuela's largest island, Margarita, was settled early in the Spanish conquest, as a direct result of the flourishing pearl fisheries found there. It is an island of high, serrated hills and fertile valleys, contrasted with areas of barren, desert scenery dotted with divi-divi trees, their foliage curiously shaped to flow with the sweep of the trade winds. The beaches are magnificent. Margarita's towns are very Spanish, and there are ruins here and there to conjure up a feeling for this island's past.

Little industrial activity is evident, although 125,000 people live here. Only a 35-mile ferry trip from Cumaná, Margarita has become a popular resort for Venezuelans, which in turn creates an atmosphere to be appreciated by most yachtsmen.

Pampatar (24432), on the eastern end of Isla Margarita, was founded early in the 16th century and is the principal port of entry for the state of Nueva Esparta, which is comprised of Islas Cubagua, Coche, and Margarita. It may well be your first clearing point in Venezuelan waters, particularly if you are coming from Grenada.

The castle of San Carlos Borromento, built of cut-coral masonry by the engineer Bedin in 1665, is a striking landmark for your approach to the town and is well worth a visit when the hook is down. An older fort, La Caranta, lies in ruins across the bay.

Pampatar appears to be exposed to the prevailing winds, and occasionally high seas do indeed make it too rough to land at the public pier. However, we have anchored in 3 fathoms off the dock and found it to be a quiet place, even though there was wind enough to sail.

The Port Captain, whose office is near the dock, will expect to review your ship's papers and endorse your Venezuelan sailing permit, but you may have to have your passports stamped by the Immigration Authorities at the airport.

July is the time of a gala fiesta. It includes a water procession of decorated vessels, fireworks, music and a grandiose parade in honor of St. Carmen, the Patron Saint of Margarita.

This town of only 4,000 inhabitants offers little in the way of supplies, but the principal shopping center at Porlamar is only 5 miles away by taxi or motor coach and about the same distance by sea.

We suggest an excursion by public bus to the island's capital, La Asunción. This beautiful town, with its ornate cathedral facing a typical square, was founded in 1565 and has been slumbering ever since. Even today, its population is only 6,000. For a look into the history of the place, see the castle of Santa Rosa and its dungeon, and the Capitular House, now a museum.

Porlamar (24432) is Margarita's principal resort center and the best place for supplies. The original settlement was called Pueblo de la Mar and was founded in 1536 by Father Francisco de Villacorta. Although there are "free port" shops, you must have been on the island for three days to become eligible to buy the duty-free goods.

The anchorage off the municipal jetty in 2 fathoms is rather open, although there is some protection behind the jetty for drafts up to 6 feet. There is talk of a marina off the beach hotel, but there were no signs of such a development in 1974.

The public market is convenient to the jetty and offers a wide selection of vegetables, fruit, and fish at reasonable prices.

Bahía Guamache (24432) provides refuge anywhere along its shores from the prevailing winds, which may range up to 30 knots by mid-afternoon. Several small fishing villages dot the shoreline.

Punta de Piedras (24432) is a fishing town of 6,000 inhabitants, the terminal

Beach near Porlamar, Margarita Island

for the ferry from Cumaná, and a source of fuel by the drum. Nearby is an oceanographic experimental station.

Boca del Rio (24431) lies at the mouth of the Laguna La Arestinga, which almost splits Margarita into two islands. The shallow lagoon, accessible only to dinghies, is thick with mangroves and is a rookery for the rare *Ibis Escarlata*, a beautiful red-plumed heron.

San Juan Griego (24432) is a picturesque bay on the N coast of Isla Margarita. Though we have not tried the anchorage here, it is a haven for fishing boats and is considered secure except in a strong northwester, which would be an exceptional occurrence.

Food supplies, ice, and water are available. Fort Galera offers a splendid panoramic view.

Isla Coche (24431, KSK-1) appears, on first approach, to be a desolate, windswept island with scarcely a tree in sight. However, upon sailing into the anchorage off San Pedro village, a charming view unfolds of adobe houses with old tiled roofs and wide dirt streets, like a bit of old Mexico.

Anchor 300 yards off the small village dock in 9 feet, free from roll. At the head of the dock there is only 4 feet. Show your papers at the office of the Guardia Nacional, east of the dock, in order to avoid arousing any suspicions over your activities in this seldom-visited place. You will find a rewarding view from the hill east of the village, where a curiously shaped rock overhangs a shrine.

The bronze-skinned, square-jawed people appear to be of Indian stock. They are, in fact, specialists in farming the famous Margarita pearl beds. These, for the most part, occupy the shallow water of Bahía San Pedro and the coast of Isla Coche. These friendly people engage in sardine fishing as well as pearling. Furthermore, the island has one of the richest salt mines in the country.

Isla Cubagua (24431) is practically deserted today, yet it was the site of the first settlement in Venezuela. Nueva Cadiz, founded about 1522 on the eastern tip of the island, flourished in the early days when pearls were abundant and valued highly among the other riches of the newly found Indies. But the oyster beds were soon depleted, and in 1541 the place was devastated by a tidal wave. All that remain today are ruined foundations and heaps of pearl shells. Visitors are welcome to look around, but a caretaker quite rightfully discourages souvenir hunters.

Temporary anchorage may be made in 2 fathoms S of a dock situated SE of Punta Las Cabeceras (Nueva Cadiz). However, the best anchorage for overnight is in the northeasterly bay, Ensenada de Charagato, where you should drop the hook deep in the bight, in 2 fathoms, abreast several fishing huts. From here a path crosses a dry salt flat to the Nueva Cadiz archeological site, a mile away.

Isla La Tortuga (24441) is low, arid, and apparently uninhabited, except for an occasional fishing camp on the western shore. In colonial times, this desolate island was known as Tortuga Salada and was the scene of a salt-panning industry.

On the southeastern shore, a sandspit encloses a shallow lagoon called El Carenero. As its name implies, it was used for careening ships. Vessels drawing over 5½ feet cannot enter the lagoon but will find anchorage at the entrance in 9 feet. The water is exceptionally clear here.

We have not explored the N coast, but an ancient chart indicates there was an anchorage called Puerto del Rey, just W of Punta Delgada.

On the NW side of the island, the islets of Las Tortuguillas may be approached from the SW to a comfortable and secluded anchorage, in 2 fathoms, just S of the islets and in the lee of a reef to the E.

The Northeast Coast, Including Golfo de Cariaco (24420, 24431)

Puerto Santo (24420) is a charming anchorage, mentioned by the Conquistadores, located 6 miles E of the much larger port of Carúpano. This beautiful bay is formed by a slender sandspit that connects the shore to a lofty rock, El Morro de Puerto Santo.

La Restinga, a fishing village of a hundred homes or so, sprawls along a beach lined with tall palms. In Bahía del Oeste (West Bay) is a quiet anchorage, SSE of El Islote, in 3 fathoms, mud. A paved road runs to Carúpano.

Carúpano (24420) may well be the entry port to start your cruise of the Spanish Main. In your approach, allow for a substantial current setting W. The high peaks along this coast can be seen for many miles at sea.

Proceed to the dock behind the breakwater, where you will be reasonably free of swells. You may prefer to anchor bow out, and warp your stern into the dock. In any case, avoid the water dock, where the fishing fleet congregates at dawn. When we were there, we found the Port Captain, Customs Officers, and Guardia efficient and courteous. Ice, water, fuel, fresh food, and staples are all available here.

Carúpano was founded in 1647 by Spanish settlers and the Bishop of Puerto Rico, Damian Lopez de Haro, although little evidence now remains of the old dwellings. It is a fishing port and a casual town of tiled roofs, many with air plants or cactus growing out of the eaves and decorative spoutings. The walls of adobe and wattle are occasionally interspersed with cement block in bright pastel colors, and, as further signs of modernization, the cobbled streets are gradually being paved.

At the end of September each year, this small port springs to life with an international carnival, the Feria Exposición Agropecuaria, said to be the most important fair of its kind in Venezuela.

Near town are several splendid beaches for swimming: El Copey, Playa de Oro, Los Uveros, and Playa Caribe.

Esmeralda Bay (24431) is an open but reasonably protected anchorage in normal weather. We have entered in the dark and found the muddy water extremely phosphorescent. Anchor in 2 fathoms in the lee of Esmeralda Point. This peaceful bay, disturbed only by the putt-putting of fishing smacks, is a handy departure point for Isla Margarita.

Puerto Sucre (24433) is a port of entry and the seaport for Cumaná, the oldest city in Venezuela. Although the anchorage appears open, it is well protected from both swells and the prevailing winds by the Peninsula de Araya.

Find a place, if you can, at the municipal pier between the naval ships and the local fishing vessels. Fuel may be ordered for delivery by the drum or by tank truck, and there is plenty of drinking water available on the pier; big ships take it from a 2½-inch pipe at the rate of 20 tons per hour. Carry identification when you leave the dock area, or, better still, obtain a gate pass; otherwise you may have trouble reentering. Incidentally, this advice applies to any guarded dock in Latin America.

We have a report of a marine railway with a capacity of 200 tons, located about 700 yards N of the municipal pier.

Cumaná is a mile away from the port by bus or taxi. Founded by the Spaniards under Gonzalo de Ocampo in 1521 and named Nuevo Toledo, the settlement was rebuilt in 1569 and given its present name after the Cumanágoto Indians who occupied the land. The old colonial part of the town is centered around the plaza. Nearby, on a small hill, is a dramatic citadel, the Castillo de San Antonio. The view from the ramparts is splendid and the fortress itself is a 17th-century classic, complete with moat, tunnels, and dungeons.

Several restaurants near the plaza feature typical dishes, including such specialities of the state of Sucre as Carúpano mussels (*mejillones carúpaneros*), Cumanese box turtle in garlic and pepper sauce (*olleta cumanesa*), small shark pies (*empanadas de cazon*), Rio Manzanares fish eggs (*huevos de lisa*), and salt-water appetizers such as dried octopus with cassava bread or anchovy loaf.

Golfo de Cariaco (24431) is an inland arm of the sea about 30 miles long and 8 miles wide. Protected from the Caribbean by the Araya Peninsula, it offers some remarkable sailing waters, ruffled only by a small chop produced by the afternoon trades, which may pick up to Force 7 before dropping at sundown. One visitor likened it to an oversized Buzzard's Bay (without all the boats and people), and another to Baja California—perhaps a bit of both. In any case, this gulf is seldom visited by commercial craft and is truly a yachtsman's hideaway.

Although much of the surrounding land is semiarid, some of the coves are gracefully fringed with towering coco palms—the anchorage off the sand beach at Punta Guacaparo at the eastern end of the gulf, for instance. There you will find shelter from the afternoon trades, which are strongest from January to July, and good holding in the sand and mud bottom.

The southern shore, which has no anchorages of consequence, is a low, green plain that gradually slopes to a ridge of mountains, the Cerro de Bergantin. The north shore, with its lofty, arid hills, boasts several anchorages. Laguna Chica, where there is a quaint fishing village, is one; but the best is Laguna Grande del Obispo (Bishop's Lagoon), a tranquil bay with a half dozen or more coves to tempt the gunkholer. Take your choice, for there is good holding almost everywhere on a sand and mud bottom. There are no roads, no houses, only an occasional fishing camp to break the wilderness. For detail, you will need chart 24421, Plan B.

The rise and fall of the tide is only about 3 inches in the gulf, and the weak current sets generally to the W.

Puerto Mochima (24421, Plan A) is a deep and secure haven with several sandy beaches, surrounded by arid hills, and practically devoid of habitation, except at Mochima settlement. The solitude and serenity of this maze of coves is overwhelming. Anchor anywhere out of the fairway.

Bahía Varadero Oeste (24433) is on the W side of the Manaure Peninsula and about a mile SE of Isla Los Venados. With its sand beach and several attractive shade trees, this is a more scenic anchorage than Puerto Mochima.

The nearby Islas Caracas also offer a number of small-craft anchorages, adjacent to a score or more of fishing camps.

The Coast from Puerto La Cruz to La Guaira (24430, 24440)

Puerto La Cruz (24434) faces Bahía de Pozuelos, a large, open bay somewhat protected from wind and swell by the Chimanas Islands to the N. Along this low coast, the beautiful white beaches are, alas, being developed into inelegant seaside resorts.

Puerto La Cruz is a gaudy, mushrooming town with a new refinery and facilities for shipping oil. Despite the industrial aspect, the beaches remain clean and the water reasonably clear, because the commercial docks are relegated to Bahía Guanta and Bahía de Pertigalete.

Fishing and pleasure boats anchor in 2 fathoms off the shaded beach, where the waterfront drive, Paseo de Colón, fringes Pozuelos Bay. The Port Captain's office faces this beach. Bring your dinghy in and tie to a handy tree. All sorts of food supplies may be purchased here. For greater variety, the larger city of Barcelona is only 8 miles away. With some difficulty, you may be able to arrange to have ice delivered to the beachfront.

Bahía de Barcelona (24434, KSK-1), also called Old Spanish Port, provides an interesting anchorage in the SW cove of Morro de Barcelona, in 2 fathoms. On the heights of Punta Castilla are the ruins of an old fort, only a short climb from the anchorage. A mile to the ESE is La Lecheria, a beach resort along the causeway that links the sugarloaf-shaped promontory of El Morro to the mainland. A road leads 4 miles S to the old city of Barcelona.

Carenero (24442, KSK-1) is a small, secure port in Bahía Guayacan, a mangrove-lined bay with a maze of small cays and boat passages. Lately, the bay has come to be known as Bahía de las Piratas.

Carenero was founded in the 1890s as a narrow-gauge-railroad town, but has recently become very much down-at-the-heel—except for the enterprising yacht club, which faces the inner bay. We suggest anchoring about 600 yards NE of the club, in 2 fathoms. Otherwise, you may tie to one of the derelict piers or scuttled vessels. The club, and boating activity in general, springs to life during the weekends; otherwise life in this old careenage is rather quiet.

Puerto Azul (24440, KSK-1), at Punta Naiguata, is the artificial harbor of the Club Puerto Azul, which is no doubt the most spectacular yacht club in the Caribbean.

The harbor, the recreational facilities, and the clubhouse itself were tastefully designed and built, seemingly without regard to cost, by the commodore, Dr. Daniel Camejo. The whole complex seems to blend comfortably into the natural environment of trees and beach terrain to create a restful, luxurious

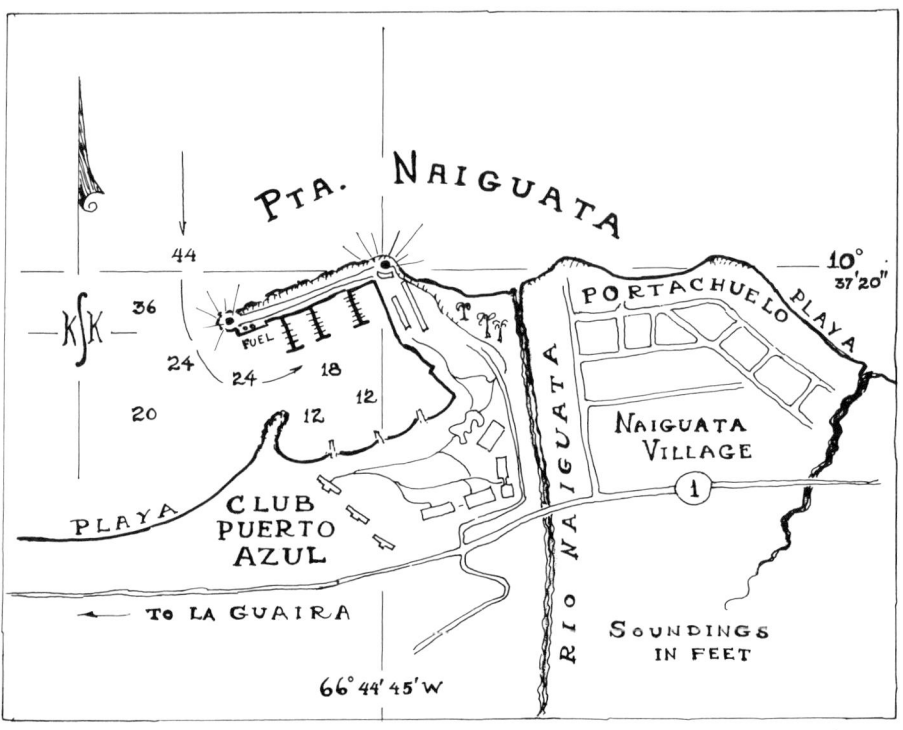

Puerto Azul

atmosphere. An informal cafeteria serves snacks and meals, or you may repair to the exotic, formal dining room with its suspended floor and 90-foot-high ceiling, eminently suitable for the most fashionable of state events. As you would expect in such surroundings, the food is superb.

Visiting yachts are accorded reciprocal yacht club privileges. There is seldom space available at the docks for transients, and even anchoring space (for which there is no charge) is limited; but you should try to visit this place.

Fuel, water, and ice are, of course, available at the modern fuel dock just inside the entrance.

La Guaira is 20 minutes away by public bus, and downtown Caracas is 35 miles by rapid motorway.

Punta Carabelleda (24440), 5 miles W of Puerto Azul, has a huge breakwater with two marinas in its lee: the Carabelleda Yacht Club, which is affiliated with Caracas's posh Carabelleda Golf and Country Club, and a marina attached to the Macuto-Sheraton Hotel. The prominent sign atop the Macuto-Sheraton high-rise is a landmark for your approach.

The Carabelleda Yacht Club occupies a lagoon to starboard after you've passed the breakwater. Visiting yachts are accorded reciprocal yacht-club privileges. If there is room, you will be assigned dock space at the cement guest quay, where you will moor in Mediterranean fashion. All the usual marina facilities are here, including a marine-hardware store.

Slips at the Macuto-Sheraton are permanently leased to local yacht owners, but the management is empowered to rent the slips of local yachts that are out cruising.

There is room to anchor at both establishments.

A large and complete shopping district is within walking distance of both marinas.

La Guaira (24451) is a port for naval and commercial ships, has no small boat facilities, and should be avoided unless you must go in for clearance purposes. If you do, turn to starboard after entering the port and try to find a space in the western dock area. All the port regulations and security requirements are administered to the letter here, and every detail of clearance, such as a change in your crew list, will be handled as though you were an ocean liner.

While you are in this vicinity, you should take a day off to see the sights, both colonial and contemporary, of Caracas, Venezuela's majestic capital city. It is only a half hour ride on the expressway from La Guaira, but the cable car provides a much more thrilling (and cooling) way to go. Departing from Macuto, it rises to the heights of Mount Ávila before descending into downtown Caracas, which is itself at 3,100 feet. The trip by cable car affords spectacular views of the valley and of this ultra-modern city during the hour or so in transit.

Western Venezuela and the A-B-C-Islands

The Offshore Islands: Orchila, Los Roques, and Aves

Isla La Orchila (24443) is low and arid on its western end, with some 450-foot radio towers that are lighted at night. Although we have anchored in a cove on the SW side near a large dock, there is a military prison here and the waters for 12 miles around are restricted. Yachts may be fired upon at night, or taken into custody by day. Stay away from Orchila!

Islas Los Roques (24444) consist of some 60 attractive, low, sandy cays. They resemble atolls and are spread over about 350 square miles. Only about 25 are named. The majority are less than 30 feet high, with sand dunes, beaches, and a few mangroves. On the principal island, El Gran Roque, the limestone hills rise to 386 feet. A yacht could spend weeks exploring the waterways and protected anchorages, observing the marine and bird life.

Cayo de Agua, the westernmost of the group, and a rookery for brown boobies, offers an easily reached anchorage 150 yards off its beautiful sandy beach, not far from a clump of coconut palms. A passage to the NE leads to the sandy, southern shore of Cayo Bequeve. There, fading into the distance, you will see a profusion of sandy islets with scarcely any vegetation.

The channel continues eastward along the S side of Cayo Landquí de Carenero to its eastern end, where you will see a group of 10 huge, thatched buildings; thence eastward of the rockpile of Yanquí to Sarqui Island, where there is a pretty anchorage.

A safe channel passes through the unsurveyed area along the S side of Isla Espenquí to the lee of Crasquí, which has a cluster of drab, wooden houses, then N around Crasquí and across the open water to Cayo Pirata.

From the SW, we suggest you approach Cayo Pirata through the narrow but deep channel between it and Cayo Namans. Here you will come upon an interesting miniature port, busily engaged with boat building. True to its name, it somehow seems reminiscent of a pirate hangout.

Within the spacious haven of Puerto El Roque, the most interesting anchorage is off the town of about 60 adobe buildings on El Gran Roque. Fresh fish, bread, canned goods, and diesel fuel are available in limited supply. Anchored here is a fleet of typical Venezuelan fishing smacks, neatly painted white and proudly maintained, each as bright as a new penny. The characteristic features of these powerboats (which carry a steadying sail in rough weather) are a small wheelhouse, a high bow, gunwales that taper to a tumble-home stern, and a symbolic eye, the seaman's protector, carved on the bow.

Aves de Barlovento (24441), easternmost of the Islas de Aves group, offers a quiet anchorage behind the hook of the southern point. By all means, approach

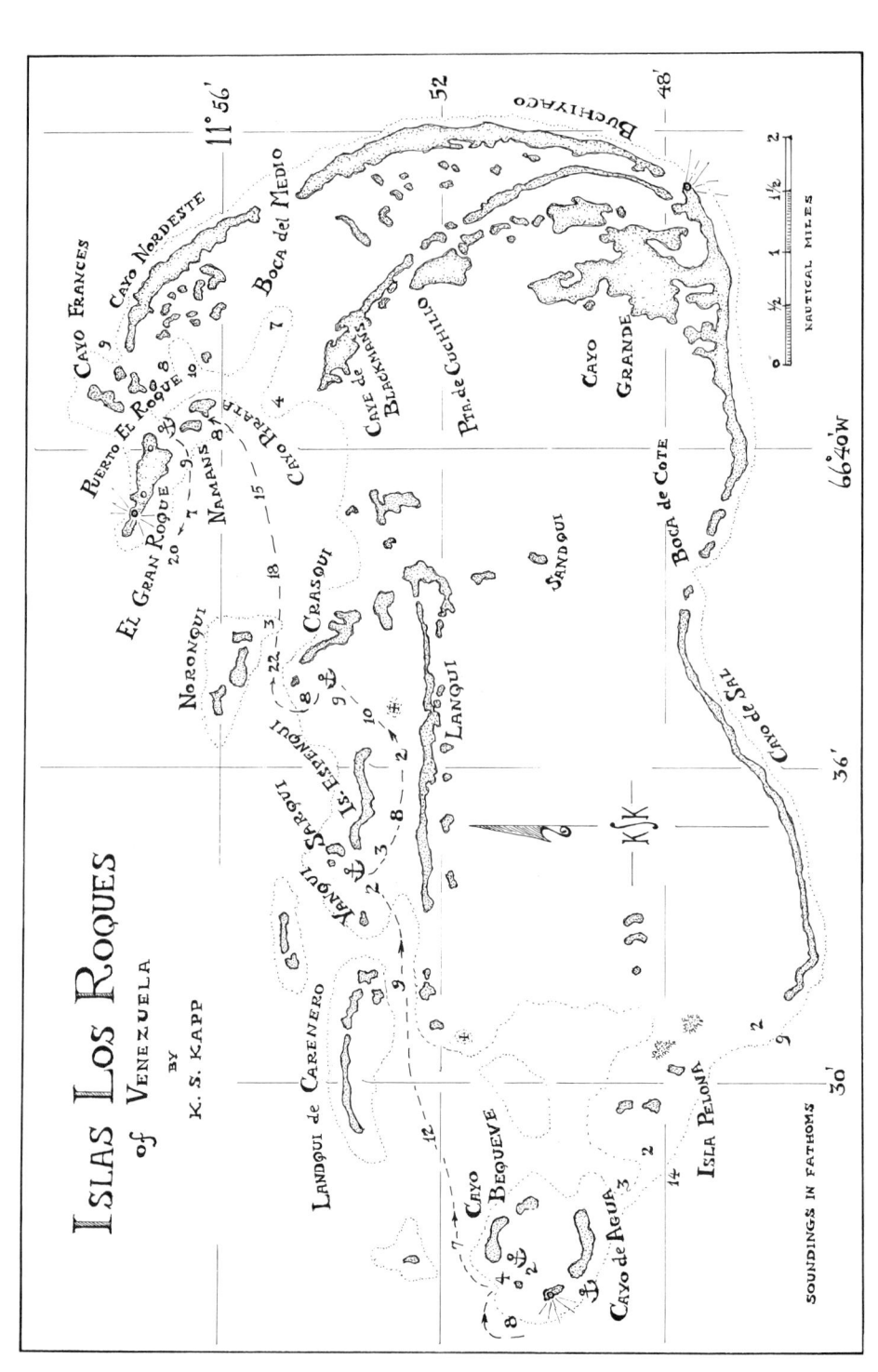

ISLAS LOS ROQUES
of VENEZUELA
BY
K. S. KAPP

SOUNDINGS IN FATHOMS

these dangerous coral banks, covered with sand and deposits of phosphate, from the S and in sufficient daylight.

Fishermen occasionally camp out on these forlorn cays; according to Bob and Ginnie Higman of the ketch *Tormentor III*, "the solitude is great, but the fishing poor." They also reported (1974) that the light was not operating for lack of batteries.

The Coast from Puerto Cabello to the Paraguaná Peninsula (24450, 24460)

Isla Larga (24453, KSK-2) lies 6 miles east of Puerto Cabello and, though only 10 feet high, offers a secluded and well-protected anchorage, free from swell. Approach from E or W to the anchorage in the SE cove, opposite a sandy beach.

On the NE point is a curious blowhole, which usually spouts surf high into the air. Near the SW point of the island lies a mysteriously scuttled German freighter, its hull and 60-foot mast still intact. Good spear fishing is reported in this area, and there is a reef, which may uncover at low water, about 200 yards SW of the wreck.

Puerto Cabello (24454) has a nearly landlocked inner basin with docking facilities for big ships. If approaching after dark, anchor in 4 fathoms in the roadstead of Bahía San Esteban, about 300 yards SW of the fairway, where it is reasonably quiet. Otherwise, pass into the Darsina Canal to the Custom's bulkhead on the town side for clearance. A pilot will direct you to a dock in the commercial inner basin. Water, ice, and fuel are available if you persevere.

Across the canal to the north is the naval dockyard (*Base Naval*) with heavy-repair facilities, including an 80-ton sheer-leg derrick, a foundry, and a drydock where yachts may be hauled. Naval and civilian craftsmen under government management will take commercial work when time and space are available. In this compound is the impressive Castillo St. Philip, built in 1731. It was a penitentiary for two centuries—until 1949—and was ironically called Liberator's Castle.

The slips at the Club Nautico Nubarron are so overcrowded with members' powerboats that you are not likely to find accommodation there. Perhaps that's just as well, for the club is unfortunately situated in the stevedoring part of the port. The *Darsina*, or Great Bay, has a maze of deep passages and coves, but extensive mangrove islands make anchoring unattractive for yachts.

In town, there are a few colonial buildings and several old cannon mounted near the western shore at Plaza Flores. You may enjoy a stroll along the promenade or a rest in the pleasant Plaza Bolivar. Or you might take a humorous photo of your companion hugging the stone mermaid. San José church is an outstanding landmark, built of coral and limestone laid in an unusual pattern. Calle Lanceros is a narrow, cobblestoned alley reminiscent of old Andalusia. Fortín Solana, a small fort on a hill SW of the bay, constructed in 1750, offers a splendid view of this historic port.

Tucacas (24455, KSK-2), formerly a railhead for the Aroa copper mines, is now a pleasant little fishing town of unpaved streets. It has obviously seen better times; yet, in a country of rapid industrial development, the place has a certain run-down charm.

You will find up to 10 feet alongside the old railway pier, and no crowded docking conditions. The channel in the approach to the dock is narrow, however, and shoals to 8 feet, so proceed with caution. Fuel and ice are not to be had, and only limited supplies of bread and other food.

Boca de Suanchez (24455, KSK-2), located 3 miles ENE of Tucacas, is a secluded inlet, easy of access. Enter this narrow channel on the NE side of Isla Brava and anchor in 40 feet near the beach on the W side of Cayo Suanchez. A deep-water channel continues around the mangroves on the N side of Cayo Suanchez and out through Boca Animas.

Boca Animas (24455, KSK-2), called Boca Pailas on 24455, on the E side of Cayo Suanchez presents a beautiful, remote anchorage just N of Punta Animas. Head for the tall tree on the sandy point N of the mangroves. Anchor in 40 feet not far from the tree.

Among the subtle beauties of nature in this lagoon so far off the beaten track are the rookeries of the scarlet ibis and several varieties of herons.

Chichiriviche (24455, KSK-2) is an unattractive commercial port, and there are more suitable anchorages in the vicinity. Even if you do not stay there, it is best to anchor in 3 fathoms just S of the town docks in order to show your papers to the Port Captain, who has a boarding launch, before proceeding elsewhere.

You will find a more picturesque anchorage ½-mile NE, in the lee of Cayo Los Muertos, a minature resort with beach cottages. Anchor off the beach in 12 feet. A half mile further N is a less frequented anchorage in 3 fathoms, off the beautiful beach on the W side of Cayo Sal.

An exceptionally secure refuge will be found in Chichiriviche's grand lagoon, Golfete de Guare, near the wreck of the *Gaviota*, an old sailing vessel whose clipper bow and helm are still intact. Proceed 1 mile S of Puerto Chichirivichc, past the commercial complex, and make a semicircular turn W around the mangrove point. This channel runs from 2 to 4 fathoms in depth. Continue another mile W, then turn NW past two small islets and drop the hook in the vicinity of the wreck, in 2 fathoms, sand and mud.

From here, by outboard, you may explore the lagoon that extends for several miles beyond Cayo Villalba. In this area, we found an abundance of tasty mangrove oysters ranging up to 4 inches long. But because they are so thin, it took a 10-quart bucketful to make a proper treat.

Preparing mangrove oysters isn't all that different from preparing steamed clams or mussels in northern waters. First brush off the mud film with several salt-water rinses; then steam (do not boil) the bivalves for 10 minutes, or until the shells open easily. Try dipping the pea-sized morsels into a seasoned, warm, butter-lemon sauce. Delicious!

Puerto Cumarebo (24443) is an open roadstead, sheltered somewhat from the prevailing wind and current. Anchor in 2 fathoms off the new dock.

This pleasant little town has an attractive plaza and two nearby beach resorts, Santa Rosa and Bella Vista, and the small Balneario Hotel for that meal ashore.

For a speciality of the region, try *talkary*, a tasty curry dish made of goat meat and coconut. Incidentally, the goat is the prized animal of this state of Falcon, and is the source of leathercraft and numerous other local items, including a unique preserve made from goat's milk.

We visited Cumarebo on a Sunday morning when church services were being held. At the same time, four *cantinas* surrounding the square were doing a land-office business. People were enjoying billiards and dominoes, *cerveza* and *música*—and the genial Port Captain waived all formalities for us.

A climb to the top of the lighthouse will provide a fine panorama of the port. We found weeds growing inside the light lens, which probably hadn't functioned for years. The Customs House, very grandiose in design and apparently of a different era, also had weeds and cacti growing, quite artistically, out of the roof tiles!

This again brings to mind the unreliability of lighthouses and buoys in the Caribbean. For instance, in one cruising season alone, we found the following lights not operating, although they were supposed to be in service according to the charts and light lists: Pta. Hermano (Colombia), Isla Tesoro, (Colombia), Half Moon Bay (Belize), Little Corn Island (Nicaragua), and Isla Providencia (Colombia).

La Vela de Coro (24460) offers only limited shelter. We recommend anchoring NW of the town in 2 fathoms. Since the bottom is hard clay, it is advisable to set two anchors.

The port serves the city of Coro, 10 miles away. It was founded in 1527, which makes it one of the oldest cities in Venezuela. On the shore is a flag monument to Francisco de Miranda, who landed here in 1806 and hoisted the national liberation flag for the first time.

The small city of Coro (population about 70,000) is well worth a visit by bus, since it has some of the best examples of colonial architecture in the Republic.

Not to be missed are the cathedral, built in 1583, the José Garces House with its iron windows, and the Diocese Museum, where you may learn more of the history of Nueva Andalusia. Elsewhere, the cobbled streets and the houses of whitewashed adobe with tiled, terra-cotta roofs help to frame the city within its colonial past.

We also recommend a visit further afield to Los Medanos, a miniature desert of remarkable sand dunes facing the shallow Golfete de Coro. Prey to the vagaries of the winds, the dunes constantly change their delightful, capricious forms.

The Gulf of Venezuela and Lake Maracaibo (24470, 24481)

Most of the Paraguaná Peninsula is a low, dry, windblown area surrounded by beaches, relieved only by a ridge of hills in the central area culminating in the 2,800-foot peak of Pan de Santa Ana. An outstanding landmark resembling a miniature Matterhorn, it often rises into the clouds and may be seen up to 40 miles at sea. At night, the sky glows from the huge refineries at Amuay and Punta Cardón on the west coast of the peninsula. (Similar glows illuminate the sky over Curaçao and Aruba, and all of them make useful navigational aids when cruising this area.)·

The northeast shore, from Punta Braya to Punta Tumatey, is a veritable graveyard of ships that have unsuspectingly grounded because of the strong current which sets directly onto this very low coast.

Las Piedras (24471, KSK-2) is the port of entry for the west coast of the Paraguaná Peninsula. The authorities prefer that a yacht entering from a foreign port dock at the Custom House pier in Ensenada Caleta Guarano (south of Bahía Boca de Las Piedras), where all formalities may be completed before moving to other anchorages. Water is piped to the dock; ice and fuel by truck or drum may be ordered for delivery here. We have anchored off the nearby Club Náutico Shell dock, where there is 6 feet alongside. The president of the club and other members were most hospitable.

This area of the southwestern Paraguaná, from Los Toques to Punta Cardón, is the fastest-growing development on the Spanish Main. The mammoth oil refineries at Amuay and Cardón provide the principal employment, but there is also a shrimp-fishing industry.

The daily weather here is phenomenal. Almost without fail, the wind starts to blow off the land at midmorning and picks up to about 35 knots before dying down after dark. Out in the Gulf of Venezuela, from December until March, the winds blow almost constantly at Force 5 to 7. Only occasionally, during the summer, will the wind blow from west of north.

Canal-Barra de Maracaibo (24481) is the dredged entrance channel to the city and lake of Maracaibo. We suggest you plan to arrive at Isla San Carlos at about low water, so that the flood current will carry you through the well-marked and well-lighted channel with less swell and current eddies. Conversely, plan your exit to pick up an ebbing current. The current here may run up to 5 knots, and when opposed by the wind, will produce some frightening, steep waves.

The ship traffic in the channel and its approaches is considerable, so remember the ditty about Michael O'Day and his fight for the right-of-way, and be warned! Stay out of the way of large tankers; they certainly will not alter their course or speed.

Windwise, the best time to pass through the outer bar, N of Isla San Carlos, is between 0700 and 1000, when the wind is usually moderate.

Your first sight of land will probably be the 400-foot hills of Isla de Toas; all of the rest of the surrounding shore is very low. A pilot from the station at San Carlos Point will board your vessel for the passage down the channel and will possibly remain aboard all the way to the Port Captain's dock at Maracaibo. You must present your papers at Maracaibo, and chances are you may be able to stay at the dock for a day or two, *gratis*. Water is available, but fuel and ice must be ordered.

Maracaibo (24481) is, understandably, rather congested at the dock. After clearing, you may wish to anchor SW of the wharf, or perhaps berth at one of the two pleasant yacht clubs, which have breakwaters protecting their docks. You must telephone these clubs—better still, visit them by taxi—to obtain permission and instructions on where to tie up.

Club Náutico de Maracaibo is a handsome, modern club with attractive landscaping and all sorts of sports facilities. The dining room is especially recommended. The club membership is about 300, and there are some 30 powerboats and a few sailboats to be seen.

The Caribbean Yacht Club of Maracaibo, founded by Shell Oil employees has a two-deck ferryboat for a clubhouse, and this vessel forms a part of the shelter for their mooring basin. This organization, less formal than the Club Náutico, places more emphasis on small class-sailing designs.

Both clubs extend reciprocal yacht club privileges, but their docking basins are limited to about 5-foot draft.

In general, yachting on Lake Maracaibo is confined to the western shore because unattractive oil rigs, dangerous high voltage wires, submerged pilings, and oil slicks mar the eastern side. We also noticed a number of fast-moving hydrofoil vessels, undoubtedly used for servicing the oil rigs.

The old part of the city of Maracaibo, which was founded in 1570, is within walking distance of the steamer docks and centers on the tiled walks of the Plaza Bolivar. Here you may hear a lively concert played by *La Banda Bolivar*, watch the vendors with their fold-away stands offering all sorts of tidbits, sip a demitasse of coffee served from a large thermos, sometimes mounted on the vendor's head, or puff on one of the hand-rolled, mild, savory cigars offered for sale. Then visit the *Mercado Central* for a wide variety of fresh foods and assorted handcrafts made and sold by Indians dressed in colorful traditional costume.

For a full day's excursion, take a bus to Sinamaica Lagoon, 45 miles NNE of the city, where the Goaro Indians live in primitive dwellings built on pilings in the lake. The bird life, cultivations, and natural surroundings are most interesting.

This Maracaibo region is not the oil-polluted sump you might think it is. In fact, if you are not pressed for time, it may prove to be a rewarding detour.

CHAPTER FOURTEEN

The Dutch A-B-C Islands

Sailing into the Dutch Leeward Islands from the generally somnolent and happy-go-lucky mainland is like sailing into another world: a vibrant one, in which efficiency is a habit, cleanliness a trait, and courtesy a custom. Here live the people who built the dikes of Holland to hold back the sea and make land where there had been only water. These are descendants of the same people, intermixed with other European stocks, transplanted to a balmy climate. They have thrived on adversity, and to them, almost any project is a challenging possibility.

Nobody really wanted these low, rocky, barren islands at first, although they had been discovered for Spain in 1499 by one of Columbus's roving captains, Alonzo de Ojeda. Since the Dutch were at war with Spain anyway, and needed a base in the fast-developing Caribbean for their traditionally mercantile aspirations, it was only natural that the Dutch should take over. This they did in proper fashion, in 1634, by establishing the Dutch West India Company, whose purpose was to trade along the Spanish Main, pan salt, and market slaves from Africa. Except for two brief periods of British sovereignty, the islands have been Dutch ever since. In 1954, they became self-governing.

Of those original industries, the slave trade especially boomed—and then went bust in 1863, when the trade was outlawed. After a period of economic doldrums came the discovery of oil in Lake Maracaibo in 1915. Quick to capitalize on their location only 180 miles from the source of this "black gold," the Dutch set about to build a huge refinery on Curaçao to process the crude into usable products.

Refining oil is still the mainstay of the islands' economy. In fact, your landmarks approaching Curaçao and Aruba are the smoking refinery stacks by day and their flickering reflected torchlight by night. Another smelly industrial jungle, no place for a yacht,you might think—but not so. Even within the commercial harbors there are attractive yacht anchorages, upwind or otherwise separated from the refinery ports. As a matter of fact, the first of these islands, if you're coming from the east, is Bonaire, which has no refineries at all.

Language problems seldom arise in the Dutch islands. In contrast with the average American, who tends only to talk louder and louder in English when his English is not understood, the Dutch are usually fluent in several languages, most commonly in English, Spanish, and French. And so it is in these islands. They even have a working language of their own, *Papiamento*, a fascinating mixture of Portuguese, Spanish, some Dutch, and a little English, an appropriate reflection of these islands' history. It is more than a dialect or *patois*; newspapers and books are published in this unique language. Some say that if there is ever to be an international language, it should be Papiamento. In any case, it is a living, growing language, which Esperanto is not.

We have never heard anything but praise for the attitude of officialdom in the Dutch Leewards. This is what Alma and Maury Gladson of *Dubloon* had to say of their reception in Curaçao:

> We were directed to dock in front of the officials' offices, where men were waiting to take our lines. Now, we'd feel smug about how well we were treated, except that we know too many others who got the same treatment. Every official ready to help us with anything, and *Dubloon* just a little boat among the 30 to 40 tankers and freighters that come and go every day.

Ginnie Higman of *Tormentor III* had these glowing words:

> There's a dreamlike quality in the ease with which Dutch officials treat yachtsmen. If you're tied to the government pier in Bonaire, they may or may not come in person to check you in. They are efficient and courteous and don't seem to care whether or not you have papers from your last port. They love to sit and have a cup of coffee and tell you all about their nontouristy island, of which they are very proud.
>
> If they don't come out, you are simply supposed to check in at their offices before going sightseeing.

Going many steps further, the port authorities in Curaçao will treat you like a mother hen clucking over her chicks. They have appointed themselves to look after the welfare of small craft all over the Caribbean; they do their utmost, in cooperation with the U.S. Coast Guard, Interpol, and other such organizations, to track down reports of missing yachts. They will mount search and rescue operations by helicopter, airplane, and patrol boat anywhere within range of their equipment. In 1973, they conducted 22 major search-and-rescue operations that involved the use of aircraft, and 14 in 1974.

A major cog in this machinery is the insistence by the officials in Curaçao that you fill out a detailed "Floatplan." It includes, besides your cruising plans after departing Curaçao, every item of information you can imagine about your vessel and its electronic and safety equipment. They even ask for a sketch or photograph of your boat to help them to help you in case of trouble at sea. The

U.S. Coast Guard has such a plan for the benefit of long-distance cruising yachtsmen, if they care to use it, but in Curaçao the plan is mandatory. It all seems to add to the warm feeling that yachtsmen have for the A-B-C Islands. Somebody cares.

You can count on assistance through channel 16 on VHF radio within 20 miles or so of the islands, although their working channels—12 and 14 in Curaçao, 11 in Aruba—are unusual for yachts. The working AM frequency, 2760 kHz, is also an odd one for yachts.

Bonaire (24461)

Approaching from the southeast around Lacre Punt, you can expect a smooth, soul-satisfying reach up to the island's only port, Kralendijk (meaning coral dike). Though you will have no sea in the lee of the island, this low land of salt flats hardly disturbs the trade wind. In the *salinas* you will see flight after flight of pink flamingos enjoying their sanctuary (their droppings actually contribute to the salt-making process). Also, you will see along this coast obelisks that were used to guide ships calling for cargoes of salt in earlier days.

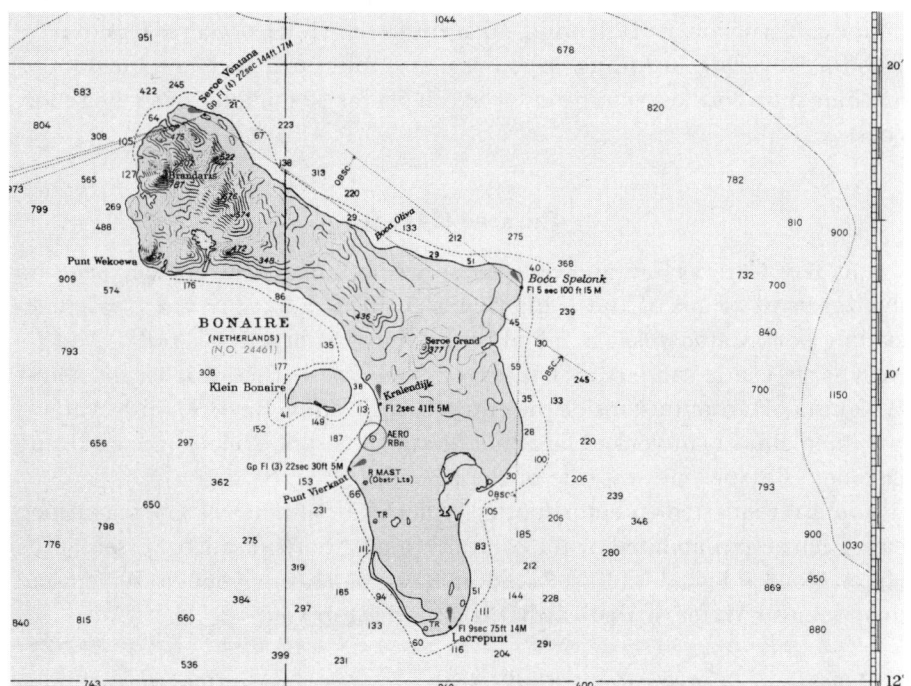

Bonaire, most easterly of the A-B-Cs

Kralendijk (24461, Plan) is an almost open roadstead, protected only by a low and reef-fringed island, Kleine Bonaire, but you're likely to be in dangerous trouble here only if you get caught in southwesterly winds. According to the *Sailing Directions*, these may occur from August through the first part of November.

Anchor off the Flamingo Beach Club, which is about 300 yards S of the new steamer dock. You will have 15 to 20 feet here and a sand and coral bottom. Use the small club dock when you dinghy ashore. Bring your papers to the Customs and Immigration offices at Fort Kralendijk. In town is a fine supermarket, one of the Henderson chain found throughout the A-B-Cs. Ice is available in cubes from a nearby shop that also dispenses coke and beer; pure distilled water is available on the town dock for a small fee, but you must arrange with the dock guard to unlock the tap.

To regain your land legs briefly, take an excursion out to Washington National Park, a wild-life sanctuary in the "mountainous" NW end of the island. This is desert country, with forests of cactus; iguanas scurry across the road, and you'll see, perhaps for the first time in your life, uncaged parrots roosting in the trees.

We are usually skeptical of projected marina plans, but we have it from reliable governmental authority in Curaçao that a marina with a slipway is under construction at Kralendijk, adjacent to the Hotel Bonaire. It is to have slips for 50 yachts, including large ones; also full repair facilities, including a machine shop and "everything else you can get for $2 million," or so the report goes.

Curaçao (24462)

Fuik Bay, Caracas Bay, and Bullen Bay are not suitable havens for yachts on this foremost island of the Netherlands Antilles. Fuik Bay is a phosphate-loading port; Caracas Bay is full of cruise ships; Bullen Bay is full of VLCCs (very large crude carriers). That leaves three good places for yachtsmen— Willemstad Harbor (just inside the entrance in St. Anna Bay); Spanish Water, a large and almost landlocked lagoon a few miles east of Willemstad; and snug Piscadera Bay on the west side of the big city.

You are requested to enter first at Willemstad, although some yachtsmen have been accommodated by the officials' coming out, on call, to vessels at the Hilton Hotel at Piscadera Bay. Piscadera Bay is more convenient to Willemstad than Spanish Water, if that is what is important to you.

Willemstad, St. Anna Bay (24465) dockage is just inside the Queen Emma Pontoon Bridge which, since 1888, has been handling street traffic from Punda, the main part of town, to Otrabanda (meaning, of course, "the other

Entrance to St. Anna Bay, Willemstad

side"). The pontoon bridge hinges on the western side of the bay and swings inward. A good deal of ship traffic is usually waiting to get through, so just stand by patiently and await developments. If you seem to be unnoticed after a long wait, call Curaçao Radio on 2182 kHz for advice; their operators speak English. The wait through the bridge can be long, but it used to be worse: much of the vehicular traffic has been diverted over the new, high Queen Juliana Bridge.

Once past the pontoon bridge, proceed to the commercial docks on your starboard hand, where you will receive berthing instructions from the port authorities. Under the bridge abutments on the other side of the channel is a dock where fuel and delicious distilled water may be taken on.

Whether or not you stay here after clearing Customs and Immigration depends on whether you prefer activity or peace. You and your yacht will be perfectly safe here, and the procession of big ships in and out of the huge Schottegat Bay is a sight to see; among Dutch ports, Willemstad is second in importance only to Rotterdam. The city itself is a shopper's paradise, even if you only look through the store windows. Then, too, you will be only a few steps from the bustling Waaigat, where, awnings rigged, sailing coasters have come from Aruba, Bonaire, and Venezuela to sell their produce right off their decks.

Of course, you can make excursions from Spanish Water or Piscadera Bay to see all this, and you'll keep your topsides clean if you don't stay in St. Anna Bay. It is, after all, a refinery port.

The American Express office here is run by the Maduro Travel Agency; it is prepared to do an efficient job for you in receiving and forwarding your mail.

Complete repairs to large and small yachts can be handled by Small Craft Yard Antilles, Inc., on the west side of the Schottegat, at Batipanja, close to the Otrabanda ramp of the Queen Juliana Bridge. Of the two slipways, the smaller one will handle craft up to 50 tons. This yard has been in operation since 1968 and is engaged mostly in the construction and repair of tugs, pilot launches, and similar commercial vessels.

Spanish Water (24464) is about halfway between Curaçao's easternmost point and Willemstad. Coming from the SE, you will see the phosphate port of Newport, distinguished by a white mountain of phosphate and a high stack, just N of the entrance to Newport. Continuing W another mile, you will come to the rather obscure entrance to Spanish Water. A cluster of oil storage tanks jut up

Spanish Water, Curaçao

on the top and sides of the hill that forms the left bank of the entrance into this lagoon.

The entrance channel is narrow and buoyed, although the water is clear enough to eyeball your way in anyway. This is not a place to enter at night. You will be well received at the Curaçao Yacht Club, but will probably have to anchor off. Their dock space, even after a recent expansion, is still limited. The club has about 350 members and slips for 40 to 50 yachts. Many are sportfishing boats, evidence of the good fishing in these waters. The club holds a fishing tournament each April. C.Y.C. maintains a marine railway capable of handling 40 feet and 6-foot draft.

Club Asiento, also called the Shell Club (because Shell Oil helps to support it and many of its members are Shell employees), is located in the NE corner of the NW arm of the bay. This is primarily a small-boat sailing club with a special affinity for cruising people who come by sail. You may be able to dock here for a small fee. There is a small railway here, too, said to accommodate 12 to 15 tons.

Spanish Water is a delightful and secure spot to stay for a while, and many cruising people do just that. The exorbitant taxi fare to Willemstad is perhaps the only detraction.

Hilton Hotel Marina, Piscadera Bay, near Willemstad

Piscadera Bay (24462) is about 2 miles W of Willemstad. The government seems to have every intention of developing this bay as a full-service marina. In the last few years, they have dredged the entrance to 20 feet and deepened a basin for anchoring just inside. Further funding seems to be the stumbling block, however. As it stands now, you can drop your anchor in this basin and run a stern line ashore, all in perfect shelter. The hotels provide frequent free bus service to Otrabanda.

At the entrance to this bay, the Hilton Hotel operates a marina that makes use of a government dock (completely repaired in 1974), where you can lie alongside with electricity, water, showers, all the recreational facilities of this resort hotel at your disposal—and a 25-pound bag of ice cubes delivered daily at cocktail time! In 1972, they charged $10 per day for any size yacht for all these benefits.

West Punt Bay (24462) is an open roadstead about 1½ miles S of the NW tip of Curaçao. An attractive beach and a well-known native fish restaurant called Janchie's are there. You will have to move close in to the beach before letting go; the bottom shelves steeply.

This might be a useful temporary stop to break the usually tempestuous passage between Curaçao and Aruba.

Aruba (24463)

Of the three harbors on Aruba, only Oranjestad is suitable for yachts. San Nicolas Harbor at the eastern end of the island is the huge refinery port of Lago Oil and Transport, an Exxon affiliate; the barren, windswept quay and dredged basin inside the reef at Barcadera is strictly an industrial development project of the government.

Approaching from the east, lay a course that you feel is a safe distance south of Point Basora, to avoid being unexpectedly set toward the dangerous windward coast of Aruba. The currents in this strait are capricious, although they set generally to the west. The land is very low, and made hazy by the smoke from the refinery stacks, so you may not have much time on an adjusted course after you sight the island. Approaching by night is almost easier than by daylight. By night you will see the torchlike glow of the Lago refinery shortly after you lose sight of the fiery stacks of Curaçao.

Oranjestad (24463, Plan A) lies completely sheltered behind an outlying reef, with a straightforward, buoyed channel at each end of this reef. We would not hesitate to enter at night. Big ships enter through the western channel and exit through the eastern, but small craft are free to enter and leave from either direction. Coming from Curaçao, your clue to the eastern entrance will be the airport control tower 1½ miles SE.

The yacht anchorage is in the lagoon near the floating Bali Restaurant, which is an extension of a pier making out from the city's waterfront. The restaurant usually encourages yachts to moor Med-fashion to their establishment. The masts and spars and gleaming white superstructures of yachts from faraway places like New Jersey and Hamble, England, apparently provide an exciting backdrop for the Bali's patrons as they munch their way through a mountain of rice and 20 or more delicate side dishes.

The Bali dock is within a block of the Customs and Immigration office and very convenient to a well-stocked supermarket.

Though we have not checked it out, we understand there is a slipway ready to handle yachts in the vicinity of the Harbor Master's office at the W end of the dock complex.

A full-service marina is in the planning-and-funding stage, to be located along the wooded peninsula which juts out from the waterfront boulevard near the Bali Restaurant.

As a nostalgic reminder of our own Prohibition days, Dick Steele of the ketch *Bonhomme Richard,* who cruised in 1972 from California through the Caribbean to Maine and back home again, told us this tale about some almost unbelievable craft engaged in what seems to have been a rather regular trade in these parts:

> While sitting in Aruba, we noticed a fleet of outboard-driven speedboats about 30 feet long, packing as many as six 150-horsepower Mercuries on the transom, with some kind of cargo covered with tarps. We watched one or two of them depart, and once clear of the harbor entrance, they disappeared in a cloud of spray in the 12-to-15-foot seas that roll down between Aruba and the north coast of Venezuela. The channel is only 15 to 18 miles wide here, but the seas generated by the never-ending trade winds are sometimes a fright.
>
> We asked some questions of the customs people and others, including the crews of several boats waiting to leave, and they were all very frank and open about it and most willing to describe the operation.
>
> It seems that while liquor is very inexpensive in Aruba, taxes and duties in Venezuela make liquor twice even the U.S. price. Consequently, everybody "in the know" in Venezuela buys bootlegged liquor.
>
> These boats, which I assume can make 30 knots plus, load up with 100 or more cases of liquor and cigarettes and, by prearranged radio messages from the coconspirators in Venezuela, depart when advised that the port officials will not be present, and then make a three-hour dash to some remote port or beach on the Venezuelan coast. The Venezuelan navy frequently intercepts them, but they're very careful simply to confiscate the cargo and let the crew

and boat return for more, since the boats are in international waters. Sometimes the smugglers simply contribute a few cases to the crew of the Venezuelan vessel and are then allowed to proceed on their mission. This is rum-running in the best tradition, and nobody seems to get hurt.

Adjacent to the loading dock for the rum-runners is a well-equipped repair shop with perhaps 10 or 15 spare monster outboards on racks, with a crew of mechanics constantly working them over. The crews are rollicking, rough-and-tumble Arubans, who are undoubtedly very well paid for their work.

When the boats leave Oranjestad, everything is in order from the standpoint of customs there. They take out papers for some odd-ball port like Port-of-Spain, Trinidad, and return; but no one seems to ask any questions about how they make that 1,020-mile round trip in less than ten hours!

CHAPTER FIFTEEN

The Coast of Colombia

BY KIT S. KAPP

The Colombian coast offers the greatest contrasts in natural scenery to be found in the Caribbean. From the sand dunes and flat, arid cactus country of the Guajira Peninsula, almost devoid of vegetation, the landscape gradually changes. As you sail west, pine-clad slopes and lofty peaks begin to appear, including the magnificent, snow-capped Mount Cristóbal Colón of the Sierra Nevada de Santa Marta, often visible 100 miles at sea. The land breeze becomes refreshingly cool, for the descending air is chilled by the perpetual snow that caps this 18,900-foot peak only 22 miles from your Caribbean anchorage.

The coast continues southwestward past Cartagena, clothed in semitropical forests and rolling green savannahs with cattle ranches, fringed by mile after mile of sand beaches. Farther west, the lush, primeval forests of Darien reach down to the water's edge. From an anchorage here, one can hear the roar of a cougar and the chatter of howler monkeys.

Part of the delight of cruising this western half of the Spanish Main is the pervading atmosphere of yesteryear. Everywhere is the awareness of the Spanish Conquest, of the wars seeking to unseat the Spaniards, and of daring adventures in piracy. Defenses all along the coast of Nueva Andalusia, old cannon on the beach at Ríohacha, forts in ruins since the War of Jenkins' Ear, and the skeletons of galleons on Salmedina Reef, are all there today for the skin diver and beachcomber to explore.

Colombia produces 95 percent of the world's emeralds. These precious stones, a worthy souvenir of your cruise, were being mined here more than 300 years before the Spanish Conquest. The Conquistadores were quick to take possession of the fabulously wealthy mines and to enslave the Indians to work them. Mostly for humanitarian reasons, the mines were closed by order of King Charles II in 1675. Dense jungle vegetation gradually obliterated all traces of them, especially of the famed Chivor excavation of Boyaca, the location of which was lost for over two centuries. Then, in 1899, in a stirring tale of adventure, Dr. Francisco Restrepo rediscovered the lost mine after a three-year search.

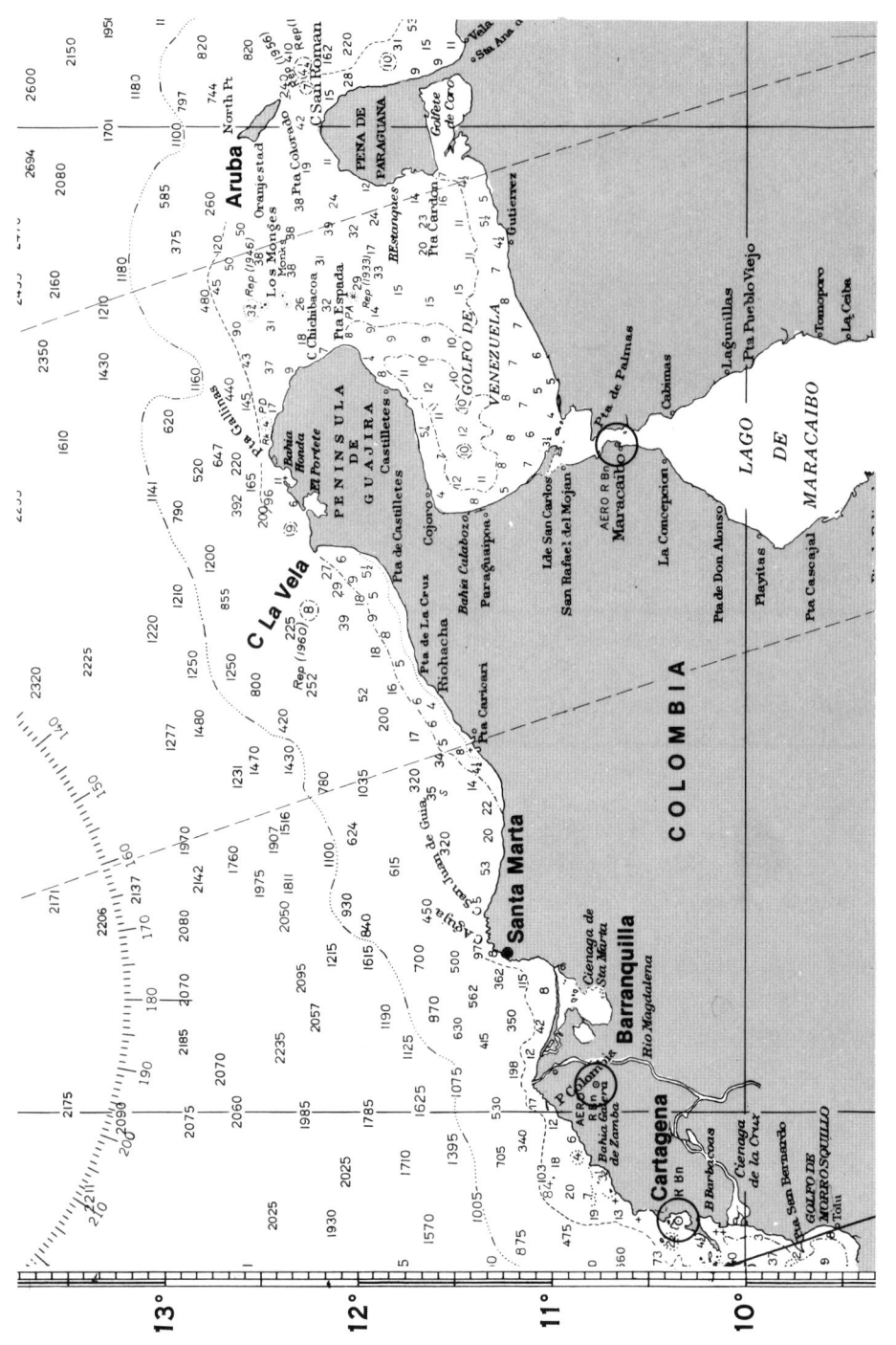

Aruba to Cartagena

Today, the emerald mines are again in operation, and splendid stones may be purchased in Bogotá, Barranquilla, and Cartagena. When buying an emerald, keep in mind that stones of deep green are more esteemed than the paler ones; that all emeralds are flawed to some extent; and that the clearer the stone and the greater the sparkle, the more valuable it is. Resist buying emeralds from street vendors, who tempt the novice with low prices and questionable quality. Always buy from a reputable dealer in an established shop.

La Guajira Peninsula to Cartagena

Islas Las Monjes (24470) are sugarloaf-like rocks which, although possessions of Venezuela, serve as distinguishing landmarks for the approach to the low, barren Guajira Peninsula. In this area, the current may set as much as 3 knots to the W, so keep close track of your position by identifying such unmistakable landmarks as the 2,800-foot peaks of the Sierra de Chimare. Point Cañón, a 120-foot-high rock, half a mile off the point, is also easy to distinguish.

Vessels carrying contraband navigate these waters at night without lights. Colombian gunboats also patrol without lights and may take aggressive action towards unidentifiable vessels. While the patrol boats usually base at Puerto de Chimare and do not bother yachts, it is best to keep your vessel well lit in addition to your usual running lights, and to display your flag prominently, even during darkness.

Bahía Honda (24473) offers the first comfortable anchorage along the arid, desert-like Guajira Peninsula.

It is difficult to understand why, in 1502, the Conquistadores under Alonso de Ojeda chose this low, windswept spot for the first settlement on the Spanish Main. The colony, unable to eke out an existence in this sterile land, proved to be short-lived, but beachcombers today will be intrigued with the assortment of ruins that abound in the vicinity.

Anchor in 2 fathoms S of Punta Soldado, where the water is usually calm. The point has been abandoned for the past 15 years. The white Customs House has been destroyed, perhaps bombed, and a few other ruins are to be seen, among them a curious concrete block inscribed: "*U.S.S. Niagara*, June 18, 1927." Along the shore are numerous mounds of sea shells that resemble white roofs on a moonlit night. These old shell heaps are probably pre-Columbian. Many bricks lie about on the ridge; several cisterns and two water holes, usually dry, are nearby.

Incidentally, the large Bahía de Portete appears at first glance to provide small-craft protection. However, the entrance is too tricky to be recommended.

Cabo de la Vela (24470) was an anchorage recommended by Ojeda and other early sea rovers because of its wide-open approach and splendid protection. With a fresh N wind, seas can be steep off the cape, so round the small island, Isla Farallon, into the lee of the cape, and anchor in 2 fathoms of quiet water. Here the wind will sing in your rigging while tumbleweeds roll along the barren shore, which seems to resemble a moonscape.

When eastbound, one may choose to pass between Isla Farallon and the cape. Favor the island side, where a 3-fathom channel will be found; a shoal patch extends 400 yards N of Cabo de la Vela.

Ríohacha (KSK-2) was founded by the German Conquistador, Nicholas Feldman, for whom the town's main plaza is named. Sir Francis Drake raided this village on several occasions (first in 1565) to revictual his vessels with corn and fresh meat. Since then, this old port has mercifully suffered no growth pains. The avenues are still unpaved; the adobe buildings are mostly one-story with tiled roofs. Several ancient cannon still lie in the streets, too heavy and too much trouble to mount in the plaza near the statue of Feldman.

When sailing westward, Ríohacha is the first Colombian port of entry. From seaward, only the high water tower and white church are landmarks on this low coast. Anchor anywhere off the pier in 12 feet of water, where there is good holding ground. If the port authorities do not come out within a reasonable time, take your papers to the Customs Office at the far end of the dock.

The open roadstead is subject to swells in fresh winds, but if the sea is calm enough, you may prefer to use the dock, providing lighters are not loading an anchored ship at the time.

This dusty little town has an air of intrigue, resembling in some aspects a frontier settlement west of the Pecos. Adobe houses are built of knitted sticks, wattle-plastered with red clay; some are topped with thatched roofs. Guajira Indians come into town to sell their handcraft and produce. Outstanding is the *chinchorro*, a beautifully woven and extremely large hammock.

Guajira men have a stately bearing and a disconcerting, icy stare; their cheek bones are high beneath a drum-tight, dark-brown skin. They wear mustaches and their jet black hair long. Their costume includes a felt sombrero and, for city wear, a towel wrapped around their middle to cover the traditional loin cloth. In modest contrast, the tall women dress in a commodious, toe-length, Arab-like smock, a drab bandana around the head, and sandals with large, brilliantly colored pompons.

To the E of town, the Rancheria River empties swiftly into the sea, and there a number of flat-bottomed *piraguas*, dugout canoes, will probably be engaged in river fishing. Nearby is a thatched-roof turtle store, where often a score of gigantic, whimpering sea turtles will be seen, turned helplessly on their backs awaiting coastal transport to Barranquilla.

Bahía Cinto (KSK-3) is the first of numerous snug anchorages to be found along the northern coast of Colombia. Although open to the NW, the anchorage is well protected from the prevailing weather, and the same can be said of the neighboring bays of Ancon Nenguange and Bahía Guayraca further to the W.

A sand-and-silt bottom at 5 fathoms provides a good holding with few swells. Opposite the hacienda at the head of the bay is an attractive mountain stream, which may be explored in the dinghy and is a source of good drinking water. This bay, with its sandy Caribbean beach, seems, however, more like a Scandinavian fjord: steep slopes and the fleeting scent of pine in the air. To counter the "willywaws" that swirl down unexpectedly from the surrounding heights, we suggest mooring with two anchors on a bridle to avoid doubling over the hook.

Ancon Concha (KSK-3) has an anchorage bold to the beach, in 8 fathoms and good holding in sand, where there are several small docks and cabanas. A primitive road connects with Santa Marta, and on weekends this is a favorite rendezvous for local yachtsmen.

With snowcapped Mount Cristóbal Colón scarcely 25 miles away, you can expect land breezes and downright cool evenings. The northers that are seasonally common to this coast of South America are seldom experienced here. The SE section of this bay is generally free from swells.

Isla de la Aguja (24491, KSK-3) is a barren, windswept island 3 miles W of Ancon Concha, inhabited only by wild goats. It resembles a mesa on the Arizona desert. A landing may be made on the small beach on the NW (lee) side, a spot that is also frequented by the *contrabandistos*.

This island is mentioned not for its anchorage, however, but for the Pasaje La Mesa (Table Passage) on its S side. Many a small eastbound vessel has pounded its caulking loose trying to fight the strong current and rips in order to round the N end of this island, only because they did not have a chart of the convenient passage. Even if the passage looks rough, don't change your mind at the last moment. There is sufficient depth—18 feet on the S side of Mesa Rock, which lies in the center of this channel, and more on the N side of that rock. The current may be running in either direction, so approach under power at 5 knots or more on a due E or due W heading through the center of either channel. Although the surf on the cliffy W side of Isla Aguja may be disconcerting, have faith in those who have sailed through here before you; this passage is safe even in rough weather.

Santa Marta (24492), a large banana port and tourist resort, still retains its colonial charm despite the recent high-rise and cement-jungle invasion. In any

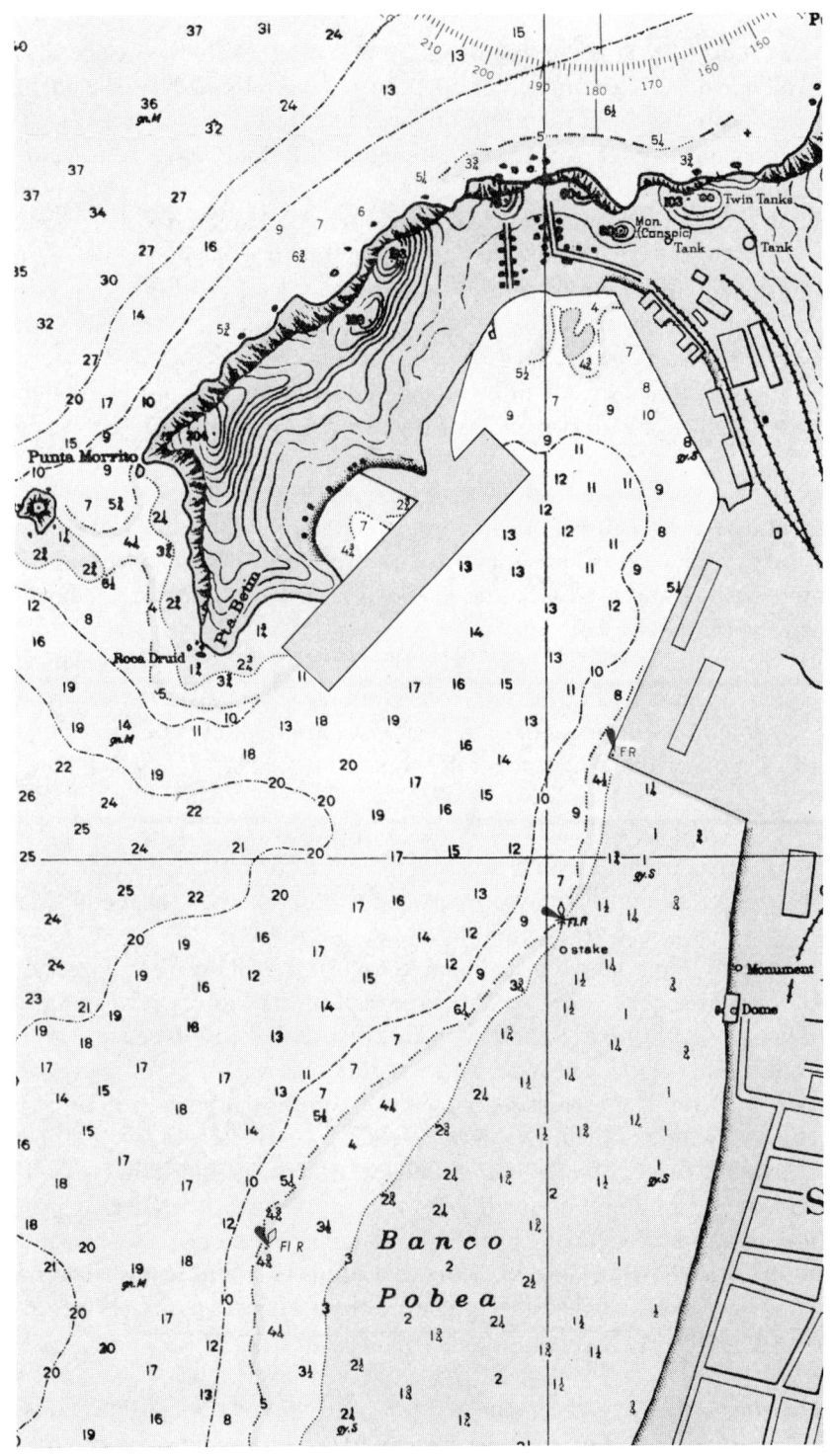

Santa Marta, Colombia (soundings in fathoms)

conditions, this port is easily accessible, even at night, and is well protected from the weather at all times.

Upon entry, proceed to a berth along the westernmost dock directly N of the Customs and Port Captain's building; if no space is available, anchor 100 yards W of this bulkhead. Even though you may have cleared the yacht at Ríohacha, you must show all your papers and obtain a fresh clearance if you come in here. There is usually no charge during normal office hours, but the officials prefer to board at the dock.

Water is available, but fuel must be ordered for delivery to the dock in drums or by tank truck. The ice-delivery truck will only be found after diligent inquiry. About 10 blocks S of the beach is a large city market that offers a variety of tropical fruits, vegetables, and meats. The old cathedral, downtown plaza, and balconied colonial homes are all within strolling distance of the scenic beach boulevard.

Caution: this place has an almost universal reputation for burglary, especially the "swim-aboard" type. Be extremely vigilant after dark and secure all deck gear, particularly outboard motors.

Crossing the Mouth of the Rio Magdalena (24491) presents an obstacle to all who pass along this coast. Having traversed this bumpy and sometimes treacherous piece of water at least a score of times, in all seasons and in good and bad weather, we advise staying offshore at least 4 miles in daylight and 8 miles at night. Why be uncomfortably wet, or needlessly slat about in the usually steep rollers closer in? The possibility of haze, which rises off the marshes; the lowness of the terrain; the unreliability of the navigational lights—all combine to make your piloting more difficult than might appear from the charts. Waterlogged debris, including huge trees barely awash, represent the greatest hazard during the rainy season, or during the night at any time. If you have a choice, we recommend crossing just after daylight, when it tends to be calm and you can see and avoid these floating menaces.

Barranquilla (24502) is visited by yachts not for its charm but for the convenience of its facilities as a port along a difficult coast. We would normally avoid this haven; it is a detour, and there are complications in entering the mouth of the Magdalena (it is very fast-flowing). But on the other hand, there are the advantages of cranes for lifting smaller vessels onto the pier for hull repairs, drive-on pier service for speedy removal of an engine directly to a repair shop, international agencies with stocks of repair parts, and generally good facilities for hull and machinery repairs. In these respects, Barranquilla would be a better choice than Cartagena, although Cartagena is a bigger shipping port.

The city is large, dusty, relatively new, and devoid of character. The two yacht clubs, Club Náutico Barranquilla and Club de Pesca, are cordial to visitors, but docking facilities are limited, and then only for 5-foot draft or less. Yachts usually have no alternative but to use the high-walled and dirty commercial docks. Anchorage in the river is dangerous and strictly not recommended. The river traffic is heavy and hectic, since the "bongo" boat helmsmen do not always observe the rules of the road. Beware of bumboats and pilferage, and never leave your yacht unguarded.

Do not be tempted by the chart to take overnight shelter outside the breakwaters—to leeward of the western breakwater, for instance, which appears to offer shelter. The soundings are very unreliable.

Entering the mouth of the Magdalena should be attempted only when you know you have sufficient daylight to see you all the way to the city. This mightiest of rivers on the Spanish Main is compressed at the entrance to less than half a mile from seawall to breakwater, so the convulsions of the water at this point are understandable. Close all ports and hatches and secure loose gear. You can expect waves to break completely over the deck when you enter the breakwater, depending on river height, current, sea temperature, and the phase of the tide. Small craft should favor the east seawall on a straight, speedy approach—and never, never try to turn in the steep troughs. Do not depend on the range lights.

Once inside the breakwaters, be prepared for a current of 3 to 5 knots. The flow of water is tremendous, although the wave action is reduced. In any case, the 10-mile run upriver to Barranquilla will be a memorable experience of dodging driftwood, trees, floating hyacinth "islands," and other assorted debris.

Enter Barranquilla flying the Q flag, dock where you can, and then ask for a berthing assignment. Expect to show your papers in the Port Captain's office.

Taxi service from the docks to downtown should be reasonably priced, especially if you speak Spanish. There are several nice restaurants: the Yacht Club and the fashionable Del Prado Hotel are among them.

Puerto Colombia (24503) formerly bustled with steamer traffic, before the mouth of the Rio Magdalena was dredged to enable big ships to reach Barranquilla. The majestic four-track railway pier still dominates the port, although it's now ravaged by time. Puerto Colombia has become a resort town; vacationers stroll along this pier, which strangely seems to move further and further inland each year. In fact, the entire shoreline has silted in considerably. Even the large, charted island of Isla Verde has completely vanished since we first anchored here 14 years ago. Punta Velilla and its light tower have also disappeared, and only the curling, white breakers in rough weather indicate where they once were.

At best, this is a rolly anchorage, but in moderate weather, temporary anchorage may be taken in 3 fathoms, 50 yards S of former Punta Velilla. A steamer wreck, barely awash, lies 1,700 yards WSW of the pier head.

Punta Las Canoas (24504) is mentioned only as a refuge from the ferocious afternoon winds and steep chop or, at most, as an emergency overnight stop. The open roadstead is subject to swells but does offer some shelter from the prevailing weather. We have anchored here many a time for a few hours' pause when beating up the coast from Cartagena to Santa Marta. Take great care in approaching Pta. Canoas in poor visibility, because the water N of the point has shoaled considerably since the last hydrographic survey. The light here, as well as Pta. Hermano light, are occasionally not operating.

Boca Chica (24505) is the only entrance to Cartagena Bay safe for strangers. Guarding the narrows are the formidable strongholds of Castilla San José and Fortaleza San Fernando, which are visited daily by excursion boats from Cartagena, 9 miles away. Adjacent to Fortaleza San Fernando, on Isla Tierra Bomba, is a beach and refreshment area. Still another fort, Castel Angelo, in poor repair, is located on the hill 500 yards to the north.

Anchor in 4 fathoms 100 yards SW of the pilot-boat dock at Boca Chica village. Since the sand and mud bottom provides only fair holding, you had best put out a second hook if the wind is strong. There is no objection to anchoring for a short time closer to Fort San Fernando, but the greater depth involves a lot more scope.

Boca Chica village is perhaps best known for the *canoas* built here with adze and cross-saw; they are widely used in river and coast-wise trade. This double-ended, distinctly Colombian vessel is beamy and of shallow draft. Some are large enough to carry 150,000 coconuts and a crew of ten. Many schooner-rigged *canoas* line the picturesque inner harbor of Cartagena.

Cartagena (24505) "of the Indies" was for several centuries the most important Spanish port in the New World, and certainly the most heavily fortified city. The spacious, thoroughly protected anchorages within the bay could comfortably accommodate the largest sailing vessels. Moreover, its strategic location made it the ideal western base for the Plate Fleet sent from Spain every other year to gather the riches of the Indies. Here the galleons could be careened for repairs in perfect safety; here the fleet could be regrouped after taking delivery of its precious cargo at Porto Bello. Here, too, the fleet could establish a suitable windward position for the close-hauled passage to the Yucatán Straits.

Cartagena must be entered through the Boca Chica Channel. The wider Boca Grande entrance is shallow and studded with submerged rocks, the remnants of a seawall built for defense purposes two centuries ago. Actually, there is an obscure, 10-feet-deep channel through here, but it is too risky to describe.

Proceed to Cartagena's inner harbor, favoring a route close to the naval base on Boca Grande peninsula, then turn right when the yacht club bears due E. This "L" turn will avoid a 6-foot shoal SW of old Fort Pastilello (now the attractive dining terrace of the Club de Pesca).

Most yachts prefer to dock at the club. However, if no berth is available, anchor W of the club, where the bottom is mud and debris, with only fair holding. Use two anchors for the heavy blows that may be expected January through March, or the occasional *chocosana* in the summer months. Fly your Q flag and request the *jefe de muelle*, dockmaster at the Club de Pesca, to telephone

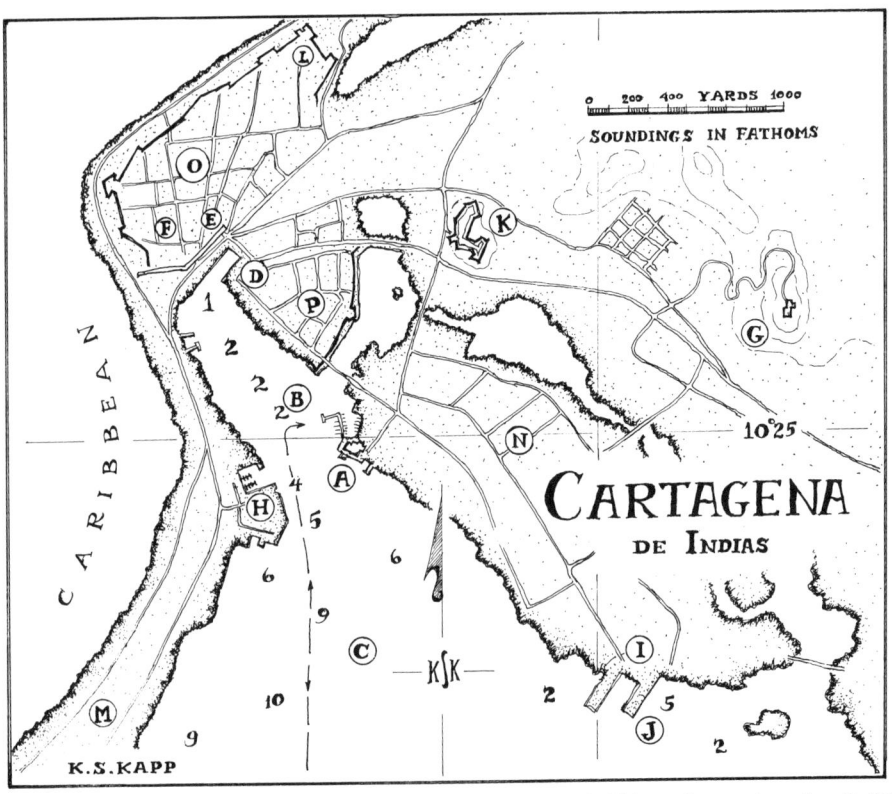

Key to city of Cartagena: (A) Club de Pesca; (B) Yacht anchorage; (C) Ship anchorage [restricted]; (D) Public market; (E) Old Clock Gate; (F) San Pedro Claver church; (G) La Popa convent; (H) Base Naval; (I) Aduana—customs building; (J) Commercial docks; (K) Fort San Felipe; (L) Fort Tenaza; (M) Boca Grande [residential suburb]; (N) Manga [residential suburb]; (O) Old city; (P) Gethsemane.

for the clearance officials.

The Club de Pesca and its Grandee Board of Governors are particularly hospitable to yachtsmen. Diesel, gasoline, water, ice, and shallow-draft haul-out facilities are all here. Other supplies, including bottled gas, can be ordered for delivery to the dock. For major repairs, the Colombian naval base has machine and electric shops (for balancing propellers and regrinding armatures, for instance) and also a huge marine railway that we have used for years.

The walled city of Cartagena, 15 minutes walk from the Club de Pesca, has preserved much of its colonial charm. In particular, don't miss the cathedral, the Clock Gate, the church of San Pedro Claver, the Plaza de la Aduana, and the Palace of the Inquisition, now a museum.

This heroic city endured many a battle for its survival. In 1543, it was sacked by the Frenchman Robert Baal's corsairs while the treasure fleet was assembling to sail for Spain. Then came Martin Cote, followed in 1586 by the much feared Sir Francis Drake, who started to burn the city block by block until the ransom he demanded was paid. Eleven years later, the French Baron de Pointis looted the city with 9,000 buccaneers. Thus many a good ship has gone to the bottom of this harbor.

The dungeons and high ramparts of the majestic fortress of San Felipe, which so courageously withstood Admiral Vernon's three-month siege in 1741, are within walking distance of the Club de Pesca. La Popa monastery, a fascinating place to visit, dominates the skyline 1½ miles to the E and is a conspicuous landmark for many miles at sea.

Cartagena has a number of fashionable restaurants, featuring *de la costa* cuisine. Most notable are La Capilla del Mar at Boca Grande, and the restaurant at the Club de Pesca. This small but cosmopolitan city stages numerous colorful events, such as the annual film festival.

Cartagena to Zapzurro

El Dique Canal (24511, KSK-4) connects Cartagena with Colombia's mighty Rio Magdalena at Calamar. This waterway, 62 nautical miles long, begins at the bottom of the bay, at Pta. Pascaballo, and was first opened to navigation in 1650 by Don Pedro Zapata. By 1726, it had silted so badly that traffic was restricted to canoes. After a long history of widening and dredging, El Dique was opened to 500-ton vessels in 1903, although the channel, lined with mangroves and interlocking lagoons, shallowed to 8½ feet in some sections.

Today, with ever increasing commercial traffic, project dimensions call for a width of 260 feet and a depth of 8—but from time to time, when the water is low in the Magdalena, the "guaranteed" depth is only 6 feet. In 1970 we found only 6 feet on the sand bar at Pasa Cabellos, where one enters the canal at the Cartagena end. There are two bridges, one near Pasa Cabellos and the other about midway, each having a vertical clearance of 49 feet.

Cartagena to the Canal Zone

If you're passaging against the trades, this bypass from Cartagena can save a yacht a nasty dusting while working some 70 miles to windward to the mouth of Rio Magdalena.

Islas del Rosario (24511, KSK-4) are an attractive group of islands only a few hours by boat from the metropolis of Cartagena, where a yachtsman could spend an enjoyable week or more fishing, skindiving, and exploring the lovely coves of these enchanting, palm-fringed islands. From time to time for over a decade, we've enjoyed gunkholing and hydrographic surveying in these sparkling, clear waters. Another cruising man, Dick Johnson of the schooner *Migrant*, sums it up neatly: "The Rosarios offer the visiting yachtsman a mini-South Sea experience without having to leave the Caribbean."

The Rosarios are a popular weekend retreat for businessmen from Bogotá and are also renowned as a sportfishing ground, particularly for marlin and sailfish. J.V. ("Pepino") Mogollon, Jr., has written an account of his technique in these waters entitled *Sailfishing in Cartagena*, published (in English) by the Corporación Nacional de Turismo, Bogotá, 1972.

From Cartagena, approach these low-profile islands with sufficient daylight to navigate the Canal Rosario, which separates Isla Grande from the mainland area of Punta Baru. The reef, Arrecife Cebolleta, which extends 1½ miles E of Isla Grande, is not so easily defined as might appear from chart 24511. However, proceed on a SW course for Isla Arena, and when Isla Tesora light tower comes in line with the W tip of Isla Cebolleta, turn to starboard and proceed on that range toward Isla Cebolleta, keeping a watch for the few isolated coral heads along this track. Anchor over the sandy bottom about 100 yards S of Isla Cebolleta, or continue to the S side of Isla Pirata.

Several secure and reasonably deep anchorages will be found in the lee of Isla Fiesta, which lies between the N shore of Isla Grande and the barrier reef to seaward. Enter from the S through Pirata Channel, which is limited to 6-foot draft, or from the N through Canal Seco, which will carry 7½ feet.

Approaching the Rosarios from the SW, the W coast of Isla Rosario presents a convenient anchorage, although there may be a little roll during the December-to-April dry season. Isla Rosario has some lovely beaches, but to move close in for secure anchorages, you'll need chart KSK-4. This is especially true for entering Puerto Antonio on the W side of Isla Rosario, or for reaching Puerto Escondido, a delightful and thoroughly protected port on the N shore of the island.

Isla Caribaru is dotted with picturesque cottages and provides attractive anchorages in Bahía Macabi, where the quiet is broken only by the putt-putt of generators on the weekends. In good light, this area is easily reached via Canal Marmoleto from the S. Approach on course 010°T, then turn to starboard when Pta. Obregon, the N tip of Isla Caribaru, bears E. Bahía Macabi is

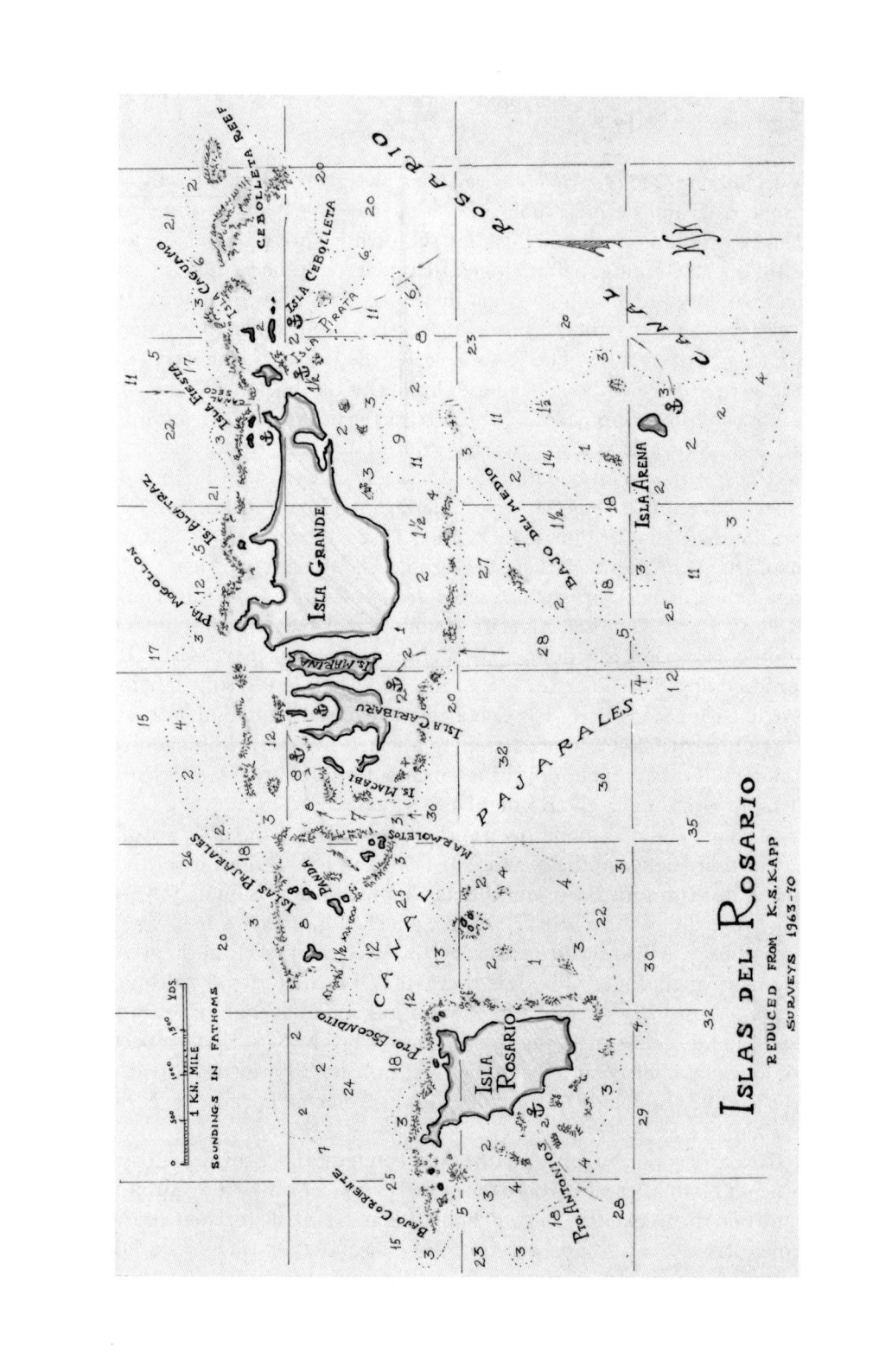

ISLAS DEL ROSARIO

REDUCED FROM K.S.KAPP
SURVEYS 1965-70

spacious, with depths to 90 feet. Anchorages of the gunkhole variety will be found SE of Isla Macabi and in Puerto Caribaru.

Islas San Bernadinos (24512) offer several comfortable, roll-free anchorages. A bay on the lee side of Isla Tintipan is the most popular and could even be entered by moonlight. Anchor here about 200 yards S of the eastern beach in 15 feet, where there is good holding in white sand. Moor too close to shore, however, and you will become victims of carnivorous sandflies!

To the W, and within view of this anchorage, is Islote, a village island of 250 souls, scarcely an acre in size and crammed full of chickens, dogs, pigs, and thatched huts. How strange it is that these natives from a primitive culture prefer to crowd together when there is so much unoccupied land all around. Their chief occupations are fishing, mostly for conch, and hollowing out log canoes by adze.

The San Bernadino Islands, now so pleasantly quiet and insignificant, were featured on a 1681 Dutch chart by Johan van Keulen as a haven for the corsairs who lay in wait for the treasure fleets sailing from Cartagena.

Isla Fuerte (24512, 24514) is frequently used as a rest stop, until the wind abates, by the large *canoas*, schooner-rigged and double-ended, making their passage from the San Blas coast laden with coconuts. Unlike the rather dry San Bernadino cays with their mangroves, this island evidently enjoys heavier rainfall and is correspondingly lush, green, and typically tropical. In a short stroll ashore, you will see trees of guava, sugar apple, Spanish plum (*Spondias Purpurea*), coco sea plum, papaya, almond, and seagrape.

If you are approaching by night, head NW toward the light tower and anchor in 15 feet about 300 yards from shore. There is a light swell and a current that sets NE, but you can expect considerable protection from the winter winds.

Puerto Limón is a settlement of some 300 persons living in thatch-roofed houses, many with wattle walls and portways with swinging half-doors. The village supports a small boat-repair industry, and occasionally a large vessel is built on the beach. A limited variety of fruit may be purchased.

Tortuguilla (24514) is a tiny island like Robinson Crusoe's, but is a distinctive landmark along an otherwise nondescript coast; that is undoubtedly why it was noted on the early charts. Only a stone's throw wide, the island is flat and studded with towering coco palms, but there are no sandy beaches. We have anchored here several times, 100 yards off the E shore, and found current eddies that make the water confused at times. Otherwise the current sets steadily NW.

Laguna Aguila (24515, KSK-5) offers a landlocked, uninhabited anchorage amongst a maze of mangroves. This place is a paradise for bird lovers. Strangely enough, the "bug menace," which usually applies to mangrove swamps, does not seem to be too troublesome here.

Access is limited, since the channel into the lagoon shallows to 6 feet just off Pta. Negro, a sandspit.

Note that Pta. Aguila and the dangerous shoals that extend 5 miles off this point have sent many a vessel to a watery grave. We recommend circumventing this reef. Even in light weather, a misty haze may obscure the hills of Cerro de Aguila, which are your best landmarks for determining your distance off.

There is a rather shallow passage inside the reef close to Pta. Aguila, but we do not recommend it, due to the vagaries of wind, current, and tide—and especially the murky water all about this coast. If you must try this channel, the easiest entrance is from the SW.

Bahía de Turbo (24515, KSK-5) is shallow, although a narrow channel has been dredged partway to the town. The recommended anchorage is in a small cove 600 yards NE of Pta. Las Vacas, where diesel, gasoline, and water are dispensed at a dock. The water is so murky that a submerged wreck bordering the E side of the channel is difficult to detect. If your vessel draws over 5 feet, proceed to the basin very slowly, sounding as you go. This is a port of entry; the Port Captain's launch usually comes alongside to check your papers.

To visit the town of Turbo, take the dinghy N about 1½ miles to the town canal's honkytonk, water-rat setting, the like of which you have never seen before. Dock at the foot of Main Street, where there is a large public market selling fresh meat, vegetables, and ice. Turbo is a rugged frontier town, with unpaved streets shared by transport trucks and horsemen alike. In the commercial bustle, you will see Indians, barefoot *campesinos*, Choco bushmen, wranglers, and ranchers. Meantime, keep an eye on your dinghy!

Bahía Pinololo (24515, KSK-5) is a picturesque, secluded anchorage, flanked all around by a sandy beach and towering coco palms. On the western side, at the base of a steeply sloping, dense jungle, is an unubtrusive hamlet called Pino Roja.

Isla Los Deseos has a small cottage, the retreat of a Colombian; it is seldom occupied. Around the island reef there is good spearfishing and lobstering. This is a lovely anchorage except from January through March, when a swell usually creeps in. It is untenable, however, in the event of a winter norther.

In this pretty anchorage, we once experienced a *chocosana* that sent our Alden ketch onto the beach. A *chocosana* (also known as a *chubasco*) is the local term for a regional hurricane. We have personally experienced them as far E as Punta Las Canoas and as far W as the Gulf of San Blas. These miniature tropical disturbances, which occur from June through November, give distinct warning of their approach. The *chocosana* usually originates in Choco Province in the early hours of the morning, but in other areas later in the day. The telltales are a deathly quiet atmosphere and noiseless lightning flashes in the S. When you observe these signs, set out two or more anchors, expecting to be blown in any direction, and ready a larger hook on deck as a standby. Keep a watch for a sound like Niagara Falls approaching. When it hits, with winds of hurricane force, use the engine to ease the strain on any one of the anchors. The rain will be blinding. The duration is about 15 minutes, usually not long enough to build up a large sea—but it seems like an age.

Incidentally, if a *chocosana* catches you at sea, take down *every* sail, or they'll be blown to shreds. The vessel will heel right over, even under bare sticks. Maintaining steerageway is not really important, as the front will pass through very quickly.

Zapzurro (24515, KSK-5) is an obscure little keyhole-shaped harbor and, like the Z in its name, is the last anchorage in Colombia when going westward. Quite naturally, it is a port of entry, and the Customs Office here handles a considerable amount of paper in clearing the coastwise coconut carriers.

The harbor entrance is deep, but frequently subjected to huge swells. Keep to the center when entering and turn N to anchor in 3 fathoms, sandy bottom, E of the dock. If you already have a Republic of Colombia *zarpe*, don't fly the Q flag. Present your papers ashore to the Port Captain, explaining you just stopped in Zapzurro to enjoy a rest, and they will probably not bother to issue new papers.

A pleasant walk N of the Customs Office will bring you to a saddle on the ridge with a good view of the Caribbean. A plinth there marks the frontier with Panama, agreed to in 1921.

Back in town is a charming *cantina* serving cold beer to barefoot *campesinos*, and a general store with a genuine Butch Cassidy atmosphere of the Old West. This is truly the Republic of Colombia's *frontera*.

CHAPTER SIXTEEN

Panama and the San Blas Coast

BY KIT S. KAPP

Roderigo de Bastidas, in 1501, was the first of the busy Conquistadores to discover the San Blas Coast, during the feverish search for a water route to the East Indies. Christopher Columbus, who arrived the following year, noted in his log that the islands, which he named Las Cativas, were more numerous than the days of the year, which proved to be a nearly accurate appraisal.

Panama, a mystical-sounding name derived from an Indian word meaning "abundance of fish," with which the waters on the Pacific side still abound, is a land of lofty, verdant mountains, rolling savannahs, and luxuriant rain forests. Much of that can be seen while cruising along the shores of the Isthmus. Nowhere else along the coasts of the Americas, in the Atlantic or Pacific, can a yachtsman see at such close range the high summits of the Continental Divide. In fact, two characteristic peaks in the Darien Cordillera—Obo Yala, rising to 5,000 feet, and Ella Popa, slightly lower—are imposing landmarks for the coastwise navigator.

Panama has maintained a strategic position ever since Vasco Nuñez de Balboa crossed the Isthmus from San Blas in 1513 to discover what was then called the great South Sea. Verbally he took formal possession of "all the lands and islands bordering upon the sea . . . for our Sovereign of Castile and Léon till the day of judgement." Rather an ambitious claim even in those days of speculative imperialism! However, Spanish sovereignty over Darien proved to be a futile claim, for nowhere else in North or Central America have the indigenous people held more continuous control of their land. The fact is that the Kuna Indians, who have inhabited this country ever since history began here, have never been conquered and are today unique in having maintained tribal customs by openly opposing the inroads of civilization.

All who have seen the San Blas Islands have been captivated by the profusion of coconut palms, white-sand beaches, unexplored coral reefs, and luxuriant jungle spreading to the water's edge. The cruising yachtsman will appreciate the lack of commercialism, the clarity of the water, and the many opportunities

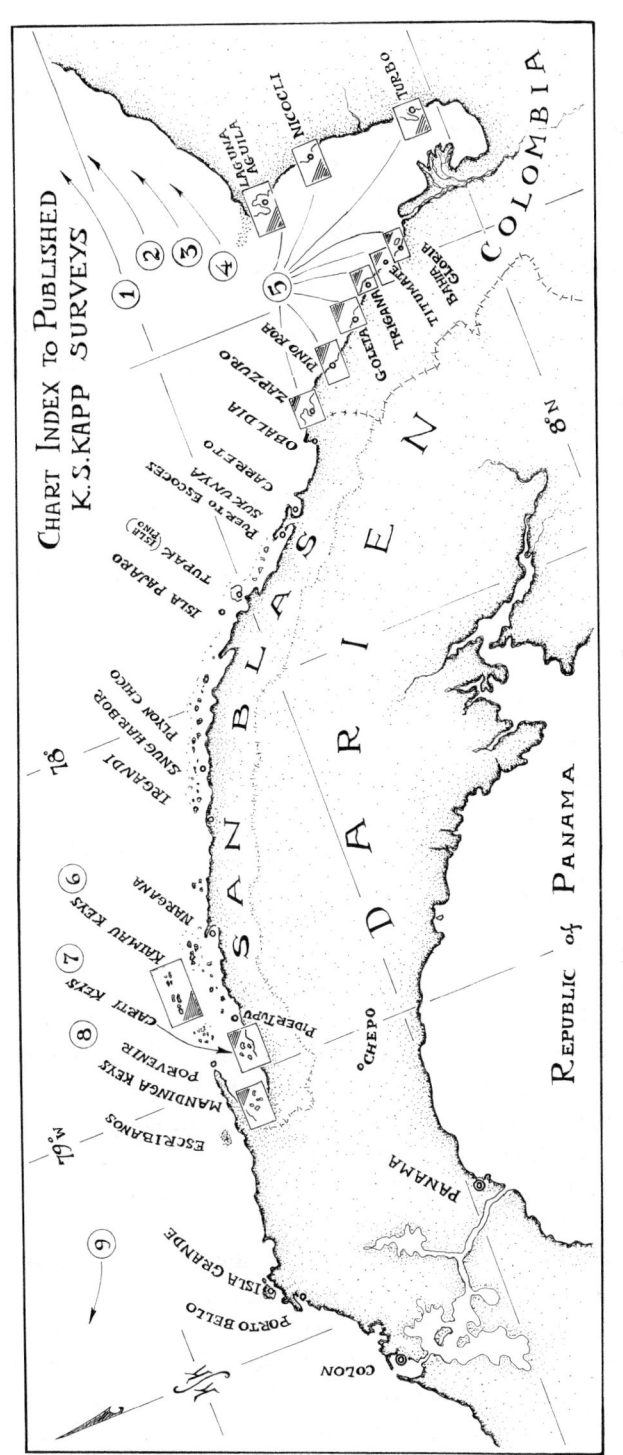

The San Blas coast (see Appendix B for Kapp charts indicated here)

for deep-water gunkholing. (Note that anything over 15 feet is deep in our book!)

The Kuna Indians are thought to be the last of the full-blooded Carib strain that inhabited the Caribbean before the Spanish conquest. The women are spectacularly attired in gold jewelry, red-and-yellow cotton headdresses, sarong-type skirts, and the multicolored *mola* blouses. The front and back panels of the *molas* have become a popular souvenir of primitive art, used for home decor in the United States and Europe, and most visitors to the San Blas Islands are tempted to purchase a *mola* or two. The Kunas consider a bright, new *mola* to be more valuable than a worn and faded one, although from an aesthetic point of view an older *mola* may be superior in both design and workmanship. Today the more modern, acculturated designs are growing in popularity with the Kuna women, although traditional motifs featuring flora, fauna, and geometric designs are still prevalent. In making your choice, a rule of thumb for judging the quality of a *mola* is to compare these basic points: (1) design, (2) color with balance and harmony, and (3) workmanship. A detailed treatise of this subject will be found in the publication *Mola Art*, by this writer, available at bookstores in Panama and the U.S.

San Blas Etiquette

The San Blas people have been accustomed to sailing and trading vessels visiting their islands for many years and are quite friendly towards strangers, providing the strangers follow the unwritten rules of the territory. However, don't feel slighted if some Kunas seem to show a studied indifference to you; it is part of their impassive nature. Others may appear to you to be too "pushy," especially the women who often approach visiting vessels in dugout canoes and will clamber aboard, without invitation, to try to sell their *molas* and trinkets. Be patient, be firm, and laugh in face of argument, for you will find they respond well to a sense of humor.

Upon entering a village, strangers should go first to the Congress House and introduce themselves to the *saila*, the chief, or to one of the secondary chiefs, for the traditional approval to visit the village. Just speak up—there is bound to be someone about who knows some English or Spanish, even though the local language is, of course, Kuna. Additional permission should be obtained if you intend to remain ashore after dark.

The San Blas islanders lead an idyllic life. They divide work equally between men and women, which affords ample time for handicrafts, for relaxation at the end of the day, and for talking over village affairs. The crime rate is unbelievably low, due to religious and traditional beliefs, so there are no jails. Furthermore, the islanders live so close to one another that they take a keen interest in watching everyone else and their movements about the village,

Molas, stock-in-trade of the Kuna women

especially those of the *wakas*, or strangers. The *suaribeti* are plainclothes police-men who will not hesitate to snatch an offender off to the Congress Hall for swift but democratic justice. For minor offenses, this usually involves only a stiff fine, but for more serious cases, such as smuggling marijuana, the culprit is turned over to the *Guardia Nacionál* for a second trial in Panamanian courts.

Life in the islands for the most part is easygoing and relaxing, as we have said, but there are a few rules of the territory to bear in mind. For instance: never, but *never*, help yourself to coconuts, even though you may see some lying on the ground on an uninhabited island. Coconuts are the mainstay of economic life in the San Blas, and *all* of them should be purchased. Coconut thievery in these islands is considered nearly as bad as horse thievery was in the Old West. Another point: if a village has red flags flying or posted at the dock, it strictly means do not enter, or you will be subject to a heavy fine. In such cases the village is undergoing a *nia*-exorcising ritual (*nia* means devil), which may last up to 10 days.

Photographing an Indian or his village may require special permission, which usually involves a fee. The Kuna have a traditionally negative superstition about the photographing of their persons, so be discreet with your camera. Usually an offer of 10c or so per person will remove the shy hesitation of photogenic subjects!

One can hardly fail to enjoy cruising in tropical waters of such exceptional beauty. In addition, there is an unusual opportunity to observe at close hand a life-style entirely different from your own, one that contains much to be admired and respected.

Entry Procedures

Procedures for entering the Republic of Panama are rather cumbersome, and the distinction must be recognized between the Republic itself and the Comarca de San Blas, which is the semiautonomous Kuna Indian territory. As explained later (see Porvenir, page 435), separate permission is required to cruise the San Blas Islands.

When entering Panama, you are expected to produce the following papers:

1. *Zarpe*, or clearance document, from your last foreign port, designating your port of entry in Panama, which should be Obaldía or Colón.

2. *Lista de trabajandos*, or crew list.

3. *Lista de ranchos*, or inventory of food stores.

4. *Lista de pasajeros*, a passenger list—but all persons aboard a yacht are normally listed in some crew capacity.

5. Other particulars concern the vessel itself and should include its official number, flag, radio call sign, captain's name, tonnage, where from and where bound, and a statement, *"No lleva carga,"* which means "carrying no cargo."

These documents should be typed in Spanish and in triplicate, and signed and dated by the Master. If this all seems too complicated, then hire an agent upon the Port Captain's advice.

Cruising permits are $5 per month, when issued during working hours; they cost more after normal hours and on holidays or weekends—if the officials are willing to open the office at all. Special clearance to cruise the San Blas Islands, obtained from the *intendencia* at Porvenir, should be issued without charge during office hours.

Charts

The San Blas Coast E of 78°W is inadequately charted both as to scale and coverage. The coastline E of 78°09′W is taken from a small-scale Spanish chart of 1817, and BA1278 is needed to fill most of the gap in the small-scale coverage of this area by U.S. charts. This British chart, albeit on a scale of 1:200,000, substantially covers the coastal section between charts 24514 and 26061. A folio of four KSK charts of this coastal segment is planned for publication in 1976.

Obaldía to Tup-Pak (Isla Pino) (BA1278)

Obaldía (24514) is a miserable anchorage at best, but an unavoidable one because it is a port of entry.

After spotting the few roofs camouflaged among the palms, approach the anchorage in range SE towards the beach S of the town in order to avoid the reef that juts out westerly from the offices of the Port Captain and the Guardia. Feel your way in among the several schooner-rigged *goletas* that are usually anchored in the best spots. The sand-mud bottom at 4 fathoms provides reasonable holding, but it is advisable to use two anchors to reduce the risk of dragging on a short scope in the heavy swells.

The ideal mooring position is closer to the beach in 3 fathoms, just S of the town-creek mouth, where the roll is less. The cove appears wide open, but is used throughout the winter by local coasters, which must come here for clearance. The winter rollers are tremendous and would make anchoring impossible, except for the fact that the wind is generally light in the roadstead.

Put up your Q and Panamanian courtesy flags, and wait to be boarded by the port officials—but don't expect any action on Sundays or holidays.

The territory of San Blas begins 1 mile W of Obaldía and extends through to Porvenir, about 110 miles away.

Carreto (BA1278) is a commodious bay where, in 1510, Nuñez de Balboa befriended the Indian chief, Carreta, and took his daughter for a wife. Today, descendants of the same Kuna live in Carreto village, which is nestled among giant palm trees.

Do not enter the village or the river unless you are invited. The Indians in this part of the San Blas shun strangers and have been known to shoot at anyone "toting" coconuts. Be sure to read our previous section on Kuna etiquette before attempting to trespass onto San Blas cultivations, rivers, or villages.

The bay has a wide mouth and is easy to enter despite the caution in the U.S. chart about the Carreto Shoals. The writer has extensively surveyed this coast and found a least depth of 3 fathoms on the shoals, which break in rough weather. Upon entry, select an anchorage well up into the lee of the NW point, where there is good holding in sand and silt in 3 fathoms 100 yards from shore. A slight swell may enter the anchorage even during the quiet summer and fall.

Puerto Escocés (26041) is entered by bearing SE around Patterson Hill and Point, which stand out distinctly against the distant hills of the inner bay. A reasonably quiet anchorage will be found immediately ESE of Fort St. Andrew Point in 4 fathoms.

You will see the Kuna village of Sukunya bearing ENE, where remnants have been found of the moat built by Scottish colonials in 1699 under the direction of William Patterson, financial wizard and cofounder of the Bank of England. A score of books have been written about this fantastic two-year venture; one title, *The Disaster of Darien*, by Russel Hart, best sums up the only attempt the Scots ever made to colonize in America.

A quiet, down-to-nature anchorage can be found deep in the bay in the lee of Cullen's Islands, but unless there is a breeze, the sand fleas may disturb your sleep. Also, the wild-animal calls that come out of the darkness add to the drama of the jungle surroundings. Beware—don't swim here; the writer has been chased on two different occasions by "Charlie," a charming crocodile 18 feet long. Special behavior in the Camarca de San Blas dictates that you pay respect to nature and don't try to hunt Charlie down. The people of Sukunya won't like it, and besides, their *tiolele* (god) will get you for it. And where else in the Caribbean does a yachtsman have the chance to see a granddaddy crocodile in the wild?

Tup-Pak or Isla Pino (BA1278) is an anchorage used by none other than Sir Francis Drake, in 1572, when he lay here to stage his surprise attack on the Spanish gold port of Nombre de Dios. He called the anchorage "Port Plentie" and noted that it was a fine watering place with an abundance of pines for making ship repairs. Later, privateers Basil Ringrose and John Esquemeling (see Esquemeling's *Buccaneers of America*, written in 1684 and republished by Dover Publications, Inc., New York) wrote in their journals that the best landfall when sailing for the coast of Darien was to sight the Isle of Pines and lie in peaceful haven there. The Kuna call the island Tup-Pak, meaning whale island; it resembles a whale in profile.

Approach the island from the SE and come in on Point Mami Mulu, the low SW point of Tup-Pak. Beware of a submerged rock, difficult to detect, ½-mile S of the SE point.

A delightful, protected anchorage will be found in 3 fathoms off Mami Mulu, an attractive beach with a small village. Fresh drinking water may be obtained from a spring a short walk into the coconut grove. The channel between Tup-Pak and the low-lying mangroves on the mainland is navigable for vessels drawing up to 6 feet. Freshly baked Kuna bread can usually be obtained at Tup-Pak village, 1 mile to the N.

Tup-Pak to Plyón Chico (BA1278)

This route skirts approximately 60 miles of coastline dotted with tiny islands and hundreds of uncharted reefs. The writer has conducted ten years of hydrographic surveying in this area and expects to publish the charts early in 1976. Meantime, it is hardly possible to explain safe passage among the reefs without those charts.

In general, the treacherous barrier reefs, not always visible, extend up to 6 miles offshore. We suggest departing at daybreak, circling to the S of Tup-Pak and giving Pajaro Tupu (Isla Pajaro) a berth of at least 1 mile to port. Take the blue-water route to the NW, maintaining a comfortable distance outside the reefs, arriving at Snug Harbor, the beginning of the upper San Blas, before sundown.

Upper San Blas Islands (26061)

Snug Harbor (26042), a spacious landlocked anchorage, was a favorite of the Yankee square-rigged merchant ships that came to the San Blas to trade for coconuts and tortoise shells a century ago. Today it is just as delightfully uninhabited. The bay is protected by an assemblage of Ratones Cays, the largest and westermost being Tia Tupu, so called because fresh water may be obtained by digging a hole several feet into the sand.

Frankie Kilu, who cultivated the coconut grove here and comes from the village of Plyón Chico 3 miles to the E, told us stories of the windjammers that formerly visited the harbor and of the old vessels wrecked on the coast. His testimony led us to bronze pieces from an ancient wreck on a reef near the village of Irgandi.

Enter Snug Harbor from the W, steering 075°T on the SW point of Tia Tupu. Beware of a submerged and uncharted reef that juts out about 75 yards from the midside of Tia Tupu. Pass Aquadin, the charted reef, close on your starboard side (it breaks in all but a calm sea), then round the SW point into the lee, and anchor most anywhere you please. The holding ground is good and the water deep. Mooring closer than 100 yards to shore here—or, for that matter, any other parts of the coast of Panama—you may attract a few sand fleas in the late afternoon.

Nargana, or Rio Diablo Village (26063) and the island of Corazón de Jesus are connected by a long wicker-and-plank bridge. These two villages with their contrary names are an interesting example of the impact of Christianity and its brand of civilization upon the Kuna way of life. In 1920, Anna Coope, using fiery evangelistic tactics, was the first missionary to force the Bible upon this community. So great was her zeal that she brought about insurrections among the villagers, who objected to her teaching such new, non-Indian philosophy to their impressionable children. But today, an imposing church, a covered gymnasium, and a cement hot-dog stand are evidence of the accultural evolvement and the Kunas' acceptance of this non-Indian culture.

On an adjacent island, E of Nargana, there is an airport office and a landing strip. Light-commercial air service is maintained daily with Panama City.

Limited supplies of diesel, gasoline, cold beer, and canned goods may be purchased in several shops near the bridge.

The white cement belfry of the church at Corazón de Jesus is easy to spot from seaward. On this mark, enter from the N, passing three picturesque cays on your port hand, which you may care to return to later for a picnic and swim. Favor the channel close to the E side of the villages, and anchor in 4 fathoms due E of the bridge. The mud-sand bottom provides excellent holding ground, and the anchorage is free from swells.

Pider Tupu (26063) has become a favorite anchorage for visiting yachts. There's a small beach resort of cane cottages run by a cordial American, Tom Moodie, and his wife. A tasty meal ashore on the Moodies' cheerful dining verandah might be a welcome change from the ship's food.

The anchorage, with good sandy holding ground, about 75 yards E of the cottages and dock, appears to be open to the N, but the swells are broken somewhat by an outlying reef just to the N.

Visiting guests arrive from Panama City by daily air service. The gravel airstrip lies 3 miles S of Pider Tupu and may be handy for flying into the "big city" for a desperately needed replacement part, for help for a sick crew member, or for a change of crew. The fare is about $25 round trip, and the single-engine flight over the cloudy Continental Divide is a thrill to remember.

The village of Urgandi (Rio Siedra) is 1½ miles S of Pider Tupu, where fresh bread and the usual Kuna supplies may be found.

Carti Keys (KSK-7, 26063) are a group of seven inhabited islands representing the largest concentration of Kuna life in Panama. There's a constant stream of sailing *cayucos* and coastal chuggers engaged in agrarian commerce, and it might be said that this is the metropolis of the San Blas. Although a number of cement structures have been built here, the traditional Indian culture generally prevails. The making and selling of *molas*, and the wearing of gold nose rings and *wini* leg bands, are typical of the women's way of life in this unique matriarchal society. Strangers to this group of islands are tolerated, if not welcomed.

Approach the Carti Keys from any direction, since the reefs can be distinguished in good light. The waters of the anchorage are surprisingly clear, considering the close proximity of numerous muddy rivers along this coast. The most accessible anchorage is 80 yards due S of the island of Yan Tupu, where the sand and coral bottom at 3 fathoms or more provides very good holding, free from swells.

A visit to the San Blas wouldn't be complete without ascending at least one of the larger rivers to experience the awesome nature of the jungle and to see the wild life and the Indian cultivations. Permission, or better still a young Kuna guide, is required before entering the Carti Tummadi River with your dinghy. The water hole, where the villagers obtain their drinking water in calabashes, is at the end of the navigable section of the river; just before the water hole is the spectacular "washing beach," where visitors may do their laundry alongside jovial women bathing and washing their *molas*.

Mandinga Keys or Robeson Islands (KSK-8, 26064) are a group of nine islands and numerous detached reefs offering a multitude of picturesque and roll-free anchorages. Here are good spearfishing, lobstering, or just plain snorkeling in the relatively clear, protected waters of the Gulf of San Blas.

Anchor on the lee (southern) side of most any of the larger reefs, where the holding is good on a sand-coral bottom. The prevailing wind is N, but during the rainy season, from June to December, you may expect the *mandi-purwar*, a local west wind, to grace the anchorage on showery afternoons and evenings. However, this breeze is generally not enough to cause discomfort in the anchorages.

Each year in February, Mandinga is host to a small but colorful regatta. Kuna dugout *cayucos* compete under sail in and around the Mandinga Keys.

Tia Tupu in the Holandes or Kaimau Keys (KSK-6, 26063) is a favorite yacht anchorage. Drop your hook about 100 yards W of this island, where a few Kuna coconut retrievers live. Here, and on the nearby islands of Tigre Tupu and Moro Tupu, are some beautiful, small sand beaches. The SW end of Tigre Tupu is especially pleasant for swimming, free of weed and coral. Towering coconut trees gracefully shade the beach. In general, the Holandes Cays have clearer water than anchorages closer to the mainland because the nearest river mouth is 16 miles away. Closer to the San Blas rivers, especially in the rainy season, the water is more murky.

Porvenir (26064) is the port of entry for the Comarca de San Blas, or Kuna Indian territory, and is the residence of the *intendente*, who acts as governor and liaison between Panama and the triumvirate Kuna government.

Cruising vessels, even the Kuna coastal carriers, must stop here in any event to show their previous clearance and a crew list, which is all that is required, or a transit pass (*pas y salvo*) if proceeding westbound from Obaldía.

Kaimau Keys, typical of the San Blas

On this tiny island, which lies 2 miles E of San Blas Point, is a much-used landing strip providing daily commercial air service to Panama City.

The anchorage just S of the *intendente's* residence, about 75 yards offshore in 8 fathoms, is well protected in all weather and provides very good holding in sand, free from swells. There are several entry possibilities somewhat encumbered with dangers, so (for clarity's sake), enter the E channel heading WSW on the S tip of Porvenir, and anchor just clear of the air-strip approach. Marking the S side of the channel is a conspicuous wrecked barge.

Further W, and easy enough to visit by dinghy, are the island villages of Wichupwala and, beyond that, Nalunega. Both are reasonably cordial. In fact, Nalunega once received a government tourist citation for friendliness to visitors.

Porvenir to Colón (26065, 26066)

The Coast from Porvenir to Isla Grande (26065) is exposed and subject to seas that roll in from the N. We recommend an inside passage westbound—that is, inside the chain of Escribanos Shoals, keeping a comfortable 2 miles or so offshore to take advantage of the westbound current. Closer inshore, there is less current and so the best track for eastbound small craft. This coast is navigable in all weather for sturdy vessels, but beware the 2–4 fathom string of shoals, which break with the heavy winter swells. Escribanos Reef itself is now marked with a lighted buoy.

Isla Grande (26066) has a powerful lighthouse and may be approached at night. The preferred passage is to enter close to the S side of Los Magotes, a remarkable haystack-shaped rock. Turn SW and keep to the center of the Isla Grande Channel, which is deep enough, although the swells in rough weather can be frightening, especially if you are unfortunate enough to be towing a dinghy. The swells diminish as you pass the settlement of Isla Grande. We suggest anchoring 200 yards E of the beach on the SW point, where the sand-mud bottom gives fine holding. The current here usually runs 1 knot to the SW. Bananas, plantains, limes, and occasionally tomatoes are available in the nearby village of Magote.

This anchorage was frequently used by early navigators taking shelter from adverse weather. Columbus spent ten days here tending his ships, and named the island Isla Bastimentos. On the SE side of the neighboring Isla San Joaquim is an extremely tranquil, landlocked anchorage.

Cruising to the W, depart through the wide channel W of Isla Grande, favoring a course rather close to shore, where the current is less. There is usually a strong N-to-NE-setting current off Isla Grande. For this reason, we recommend the inside passage.

Porto Bello (26067) is a spacious yet uniquely snug harbor, flanked on three sides by land and wide open to the W. The unknowing navigator would expect the anchorage to be untenable in case of a wester—but relax, this has simply never happened! In fact, the last turmoil recorded here was the storming of Iron Castle Fort at the harbor mouth in 1741, when Admiral Vernon took Porto Bello, as he had promised, "with six men-of-war only."

Porto Bello has a fantastic past. For nearly two centuries it was the western terminus of the Spanish Plate Fleet. The gold and other treasures of South America were transported here by mule train over the Camino Real from Panama City. Every other year, a large and roisterous fair was held. Cacao, vicuña wool, and quinine were traded for cloth, rice, and furniture that the fleet had brought from Europe. In turn, the armada of galleons stacked their holds with precious metal and set sail back to Spain. In *Buccaneers of America*, John Esquemeling described Porto Bello just prior to Henry Morgan's sacking of the city in 1668:

The city which bears this name in America is seated in the Province of Costa Rica, under the latitude of ten degrees North, at the distance of fourteen leagues from the Gulf of Darien, and eight westwards from the port called Nombre de Dios. It is judged to be the strongest place that the King of Spain possesses in all the West Indies, excepting two, that is to say Havana and Cartagena. Here are two castles, almost inexpugnable, that defend the city, being situated at the entry of the port; so that no ship or boat can pass without permission. The garrison consists of three hundred soldiers, and the town constantly inhabited by four hundred families, more or less. The merchants dwell not here, but only reside for awhile, when the galleons come or go from Spain; by reason of the unhealthiness of the air, occasioned by certain vapours that exhale from the mountains. Notwithstanding, their chief warehouses are at Porto Bello, howbeit their habitations be all the year long at Panama, whence they bring the plate upon mules at such times as the fair begins, and when the ships, belonging to the Company of Negroes, arrive here to sell slaves.

Today, Porto Bello is a sleepy little town, invaded only on weekends by tourists who come to photograph the moss-covered ruins, especially San Geronimo and the treasury building. A public bus runs to Colón in less than an hour, convenient for replenishing your supplies of fresh meat and vegetables.

An "Ice for Sale" truck calls every morning, but you need a sharp eye to catch him. Local shops carry a limited supply of canned goods, bananas, limes, and bread. There is also a local *abbatoir*, where fresh meat is sold twice a week, early in the morning.

Two anchorages are suggested. The first is 100 yards N of Fort Gloria and the dilapidated town dock, where there is good holding in green mud in 3 fathoms. The second is a more secluded anchorage away from town to the N, in about the same depth, 100 yards off Fort San Fernando.

Yachts frequently rendezvous here, some to spend a week or more. In addition to its historical significance, this harbor holds the dubious distinction of having the greatest average yearly rainfall, 240 inches, of any place on the North American continent. Even in the dry season it may rain twice a day, so don't plan to catch up on any varnishing until you move on to the Canal Zone or the San Blas.

Colón (26068), is not, of course, in the Canal Zone and until recently was seldom considered by yachtsmen, since the American port of Cristóbal and the Panama Canal Yacht Club (also called Cristóbal Yacht Club) were so close at hand. However, better political relations and improved facilities have changed this attitude, especially in the case of yachts not intending to transit the Canal. Colón may indeed be a better choice; a new Canal Zone regulation limits yachts to five days dockage at the Panama Canal Yacht Club, a very disappointing turn of events. Besides having no time restrictions, other points in favor of Colón are the expanding facilities and the cordial welcome extended to visiting yachts by the Club Náutico, a welcome personally endorsed by a fellow member and yachtsman, President Lakas of the Republic of Panama.

Colón is entirely surrounded by Canal Zone territory. The exact boundaries of jurisdiction may be confusing, but the important point is that there are two distinct ports. Commercial shipping and large yachts should anchor or dock on the W side of Colón, but the preferred anchorage is 75 yards E of the Club Náutico dock on the E shore of Colón.

The sand-mud bottom provides good holding in 2 fathoms, and shallows to 6 feet on the bar and 6½ feet at the dock. During a winter norther, the anchorage is rough but not untenable. Clearance from foreign ports may be arranged through the yacht club. Gasoline and fresh water are available there, while ice and diesel fuel must be ordered. Just prior to departure from Panama, certain items of food and liquor may be purchased in bond, with substantial savings, through the Colón Free Zone.

In Folk's River, 1 mile S of the yacht club, is a marine railway capable of hauling vessels up to 100 tons with drafts to 10 feet. One block W of Club Náutico is a convenient bus stop for a 10¢ ride to the center of town.

CHAPTER SEVENTEEN

The Panama Canal to Swan Island

In running up or down the western Caribbean, the wind and current patterns should be your primary consideration in deciding whether to stay offshore via San Andrés Island, or to hug all or part of the relatively dull coastline of Costa Rica and Nicaragua. Although this stretch seems to present an uncomfortable lee shore, it does afford some reasonably quiet anchorages in the lee of capes and off-lying cays. For reasons that will become evident later, we recommend pivoting on San Andrés northbound and following the coast southbound. The distances are nearly equal either way.

A compromise route north (especially from May to September, when the winds are down) is to run from San Andrés to Man of War Cay and thence through the Miskito Channel to the Vivario Cays. This track is of course especially desirable when making for Roatán.

On the offshore route, the wind is generally NE to E between the Canal and Swan Island; a southerly component works into the pattern from there northward. On the other hand, particularly from November through March, the wind along the coastal route is likely to be N as often as it is NE or E, and Force 5 is not uncommon.

From November to early April, this whole area is unfortunately subject to the long reach of northers that sweep across the Gulf of Mexico at a rate of one a week and sometimes even more frequently. Although the *Sailing Directions* note at one point that their strength tends to diminish with the latitude, a statistical table in another section shows a higher frequency of northers of Force 7 or more between Cabo Gracias a Dios and Cristóbal than in the sea area from the Cabo to Cozumel. Then, there is a distinction drawn between "true northers" and "intensified trades," the latter being, as the name implies, the cumulative result of a norther combined with strong NE trades.

In *Yellow Bird's* passage from Cristóbal to San Andrés, we ran into seas of 20 feet or more just off the bow, and while winds of Force 8–9 howled around our wheelhouse, we could hear distress messages from big ships further north where it was blowing Force 11; in fact, we were later to see salvage operations underway on one of those vessels, which had blown high on the Quita Sueño

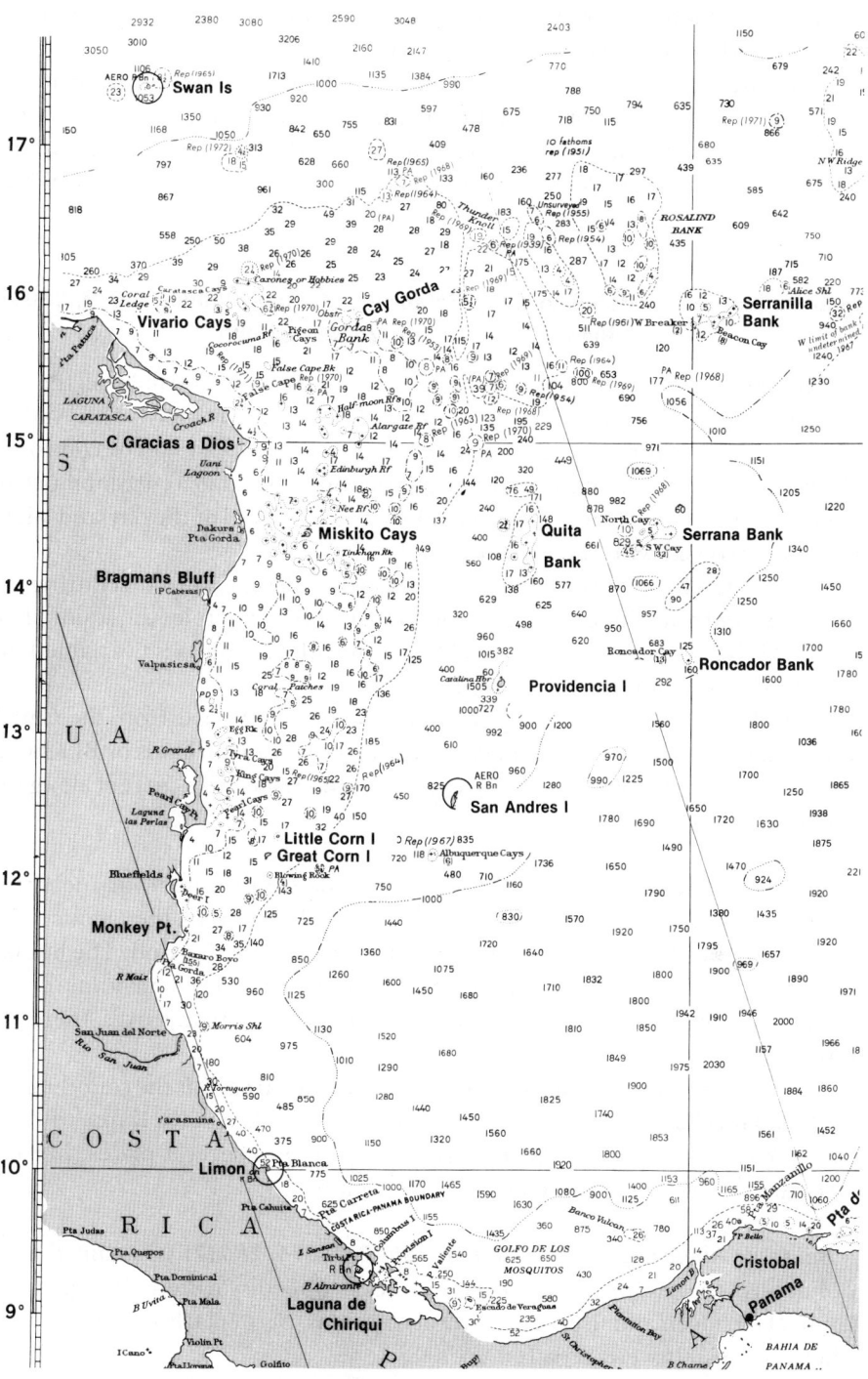

Cristóbal to Swan Island, with offshore islands and banks

Reef. Undoubtedly we were caught in a "true norther," but the distinction becomes rather academic when you are actually at sea in such a gale.

On the offshore route, you will benefit from the full sweep of the Equatorial Current when making for the Yucatan Channel. Along the Miskito Coast, a somewhat inconsistent countercurrent makes south but becomes regular and stronger in its counterclockwise movement along the coast southeast of San Juan del Norte.

Inshore Route, Cristóbal to Swan Island or Roatán (26000, 26069, 28041, 28048, 28061, 28081, 28101, 28000)

Running direct to the Corn Islands, this passage is about 560 miles all the way to Swan Island and only about 10 miles shorter than the route via San Andrés and Gorda Cay. From the standpoint of wind direction, it should be comfortable during spring and summer, although you will be bucking a current much of the way. Then, too, it offers overnight anchorages instead of the day-and-night running involved with the offshore route.

On the other hand, this is a hot and steamy coast all year, but worst during the wet season, from June through December. For example the rainfall at Bluefields is 250 inches per year, and the littoral of Nicaragua is not named the Miskito Coast without good reason!

We will now list the most useful layover places northward from the Canal, although you would do well to make directly for the Corn Islands or Bluefields rather than buck the worst of the perpetual counterclockwise current along the Costa Rican coast.

Laguna de Chiriqui (28042) is easy to enter and offers numerous anchoring possibilities, the most sheltered being in the NW section of the lagoon. The shoreline is mostly mangrove and a clear sand beach is hard to find. The human inhabitants are scarce but the area abounds in herons, terns, pelicans, crabs, oysters, iguanas, and some 'gators; and where there are mangroves, there are usually insects.

The chart is unusually well detailed for so wild an area, but the soundings in the Split Hill Channel (see also chart 28043) are not reliable. Kit Kapp, with the ketch *Fairwinds,* drawing 6½ feet, grounded here in several places, but not seriously for the bottom is merely sand or mud.

Bahía de Almirante (28043, 28044, 28045, 28046, 28047) was named after Columbus, the Admiral of the Ocean Seas, who discovered this spacious, landlocked haven and used it on several occasions, particularly Careening Cay, where his vessels were repaired.

The main settlements are Almirante and Bocas del Toro, the latter being a

P.O.E. and a quiet little town of Victorian frame houses with leaky, wooden water tanks, and a general appearance of "has-been" prosperity. Fruit is available and fresh meat if you get there early enough on slaughtering days. Supplies in general are scarce, especially drinking water. You may be able to tie to the public quay but commercial coasters are given preference.

Almirante is a fruit company town with a population of about 3,000. The commissary and hospital are open only to company employees, but you may be able to make an "arrangement" with a local resident who has commissary privileges. Fresh water, and usually ice, are available at the large banana-loading wharf.

Puerto Limón (28049) offers little shelter and constant swell but good holding in mud. The town lacks charm but is a place to replenish your supply of meats, vegetables, and ice.

Apparently, the economy of the area has not recovered from a blight that necessitated destroying the banana trees some years back. However, it is Costa Rica's only port on the Atlantic side and is the railhead for the Northern Railroad to the capital of San José.

Incidentally, this Toonerville-type transportation is your golden opportunity to see Central America at close hand, as well as a chance to gain some welcome relief from the heat and humidity of sea-level living. For 5 hours and 103 miles, this little train winds its clacking, narrow-gauge way through tropical forest, across spidery trestles, and along verdant mountainsides until it crosses the Continental Divide and ends its tortuous journey in the blessed coolness of San José, 4,000 feet up on the plateau that gives Costa Rica its second climate.

If, after a night's rest in what we think must be the cleanest city in the world, you're still game for more railroading, you can take a similar ride down to the Pacific Ocean at Puntarenas, as described in Chapter Three.

Along the beach some 50 miles N of Limón, at isolated Tortuguero, green turtles come from all over the western Caribbean to breed and lay as many as a hundred eggs at a time in pits in the dark sand, then to wriggle their 200–300 pounds back to their natural habitat, the sea. Although the turtles habitually use this particular 22-mile stretch of beach, the whole shoreline of Costa Rica is protected by law against poachers. Nevertheless, they still come by night, goaded by the high prices that turtle meat commands, to tip as many of these female turtles as they can onto their backs, where they lie helplessly until picked up by boats for transport back to Limón.

San Juan del Norte, or Greytown (28062) was the terminus of a canal project which would have linked the Atlantic and Pacific Oceans via the San Juan River and Lake Nicaragua. In fact construction carried on from 1889 to 1893 when the private company, having run through $4 million, was unable to persuade the U.S. Government to invest $100 million more to keep the project alive.

Kit Kapp advises that the entrance to the river mouth is, for all practical purposes, closed. In calm conditions, local coasters occasionally pick up light cargo and passengers which are brought across the bar in canoes or small lighters. To take even a shallow draft yacht across the shifting bar into the river would be tricky and hazardous.

Monkey Point (28063) is well protected from W through N to E, and the high bluff makes it a particularly good refuge in a norther.

Approach the anchorage cautiously, especially when within a half-mile of the shore. Although the chart gives no such indication, the Niemeiers of the powerboat *Shield* report reefs and shoals in the bay, and Kit Kapp of *Fairwinds* tells us he hit bottom where the chart showed 17 feet. Under the circumstances, the large-scale chart noted above is not really needed; 28061 should suffice.

Bluefields (28082) will carry 4½ feet all the way into the town dock, but you should engage a local pilot, at least the first time.

There is no need, however, to proceed beyond the deep-water anchorage just inside Casaya Cay, whence you can easily dinghy into the town, which is neither quaint nor modern. Report to the Port Captain's office on El Bluff. Some English is spoken here and at other places from here northward.

There is a slipway capable of hauling the shrimpers that base here.

Rio Escondido is navigable by scheduled passenger boats for 55 miles to the town of Rama. This might make an interesting side cruise for a yacht.

Great Corn Island (28083) is ringed with white sandy beaches, literally rustles with coconut palms, and is lightly sprinkled with friendly and cooperative people who make their living primarily from fishing—and they all speak English. In addition to the banana and coconut plantations, the island is base for a huge shrimper and lobster fleet, with an attendant cold-storage plant. If in need of repairs, you will find a good machine shop and expert mechanics and electronics technicians ready and willing to help you.

Brig Bay is the preferred anchorage, but if the swell is uncomfortable you might be better situated in Southwest Bay near the end of the airstrip. If caught in the early stages of a norther, go around into Long Bay. Beware Scylla Rock—it has less than 6 feet over it and lies about a mile 250°T from West Point.

Little Corn Island (28083) affords good shelter in Pelican Bay due S of the light. Only about 50 people live here, and if you are only stopping overnight and want to forego the Nicaraguan entry formalities, this might be a better choice than Great Corn.

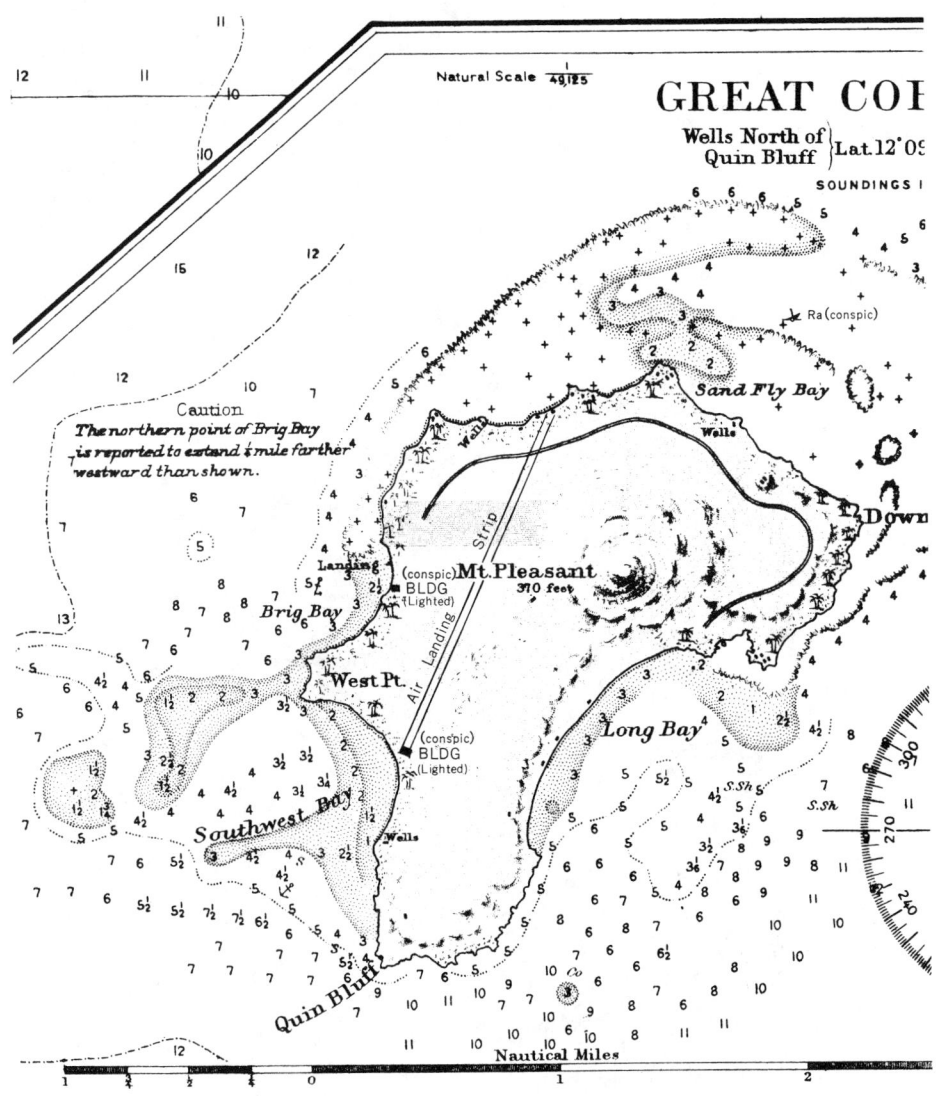

Great Corn Island, Nicaragua (soundings in fathoms)

Tungwarra Cays (28083) are favored by the fishermen as an anchorage, which of course is a pretty good recommendation. From the SW, approach the anchorage between Buttonwood and Little Tungwarra Cays and anchor in the vicinity of the mooring buoy.

Obviously, there are other suitable anchorages in this area known as the Pearl Cays, but very cautious piloting is required because the water is too murky for eyeballing.

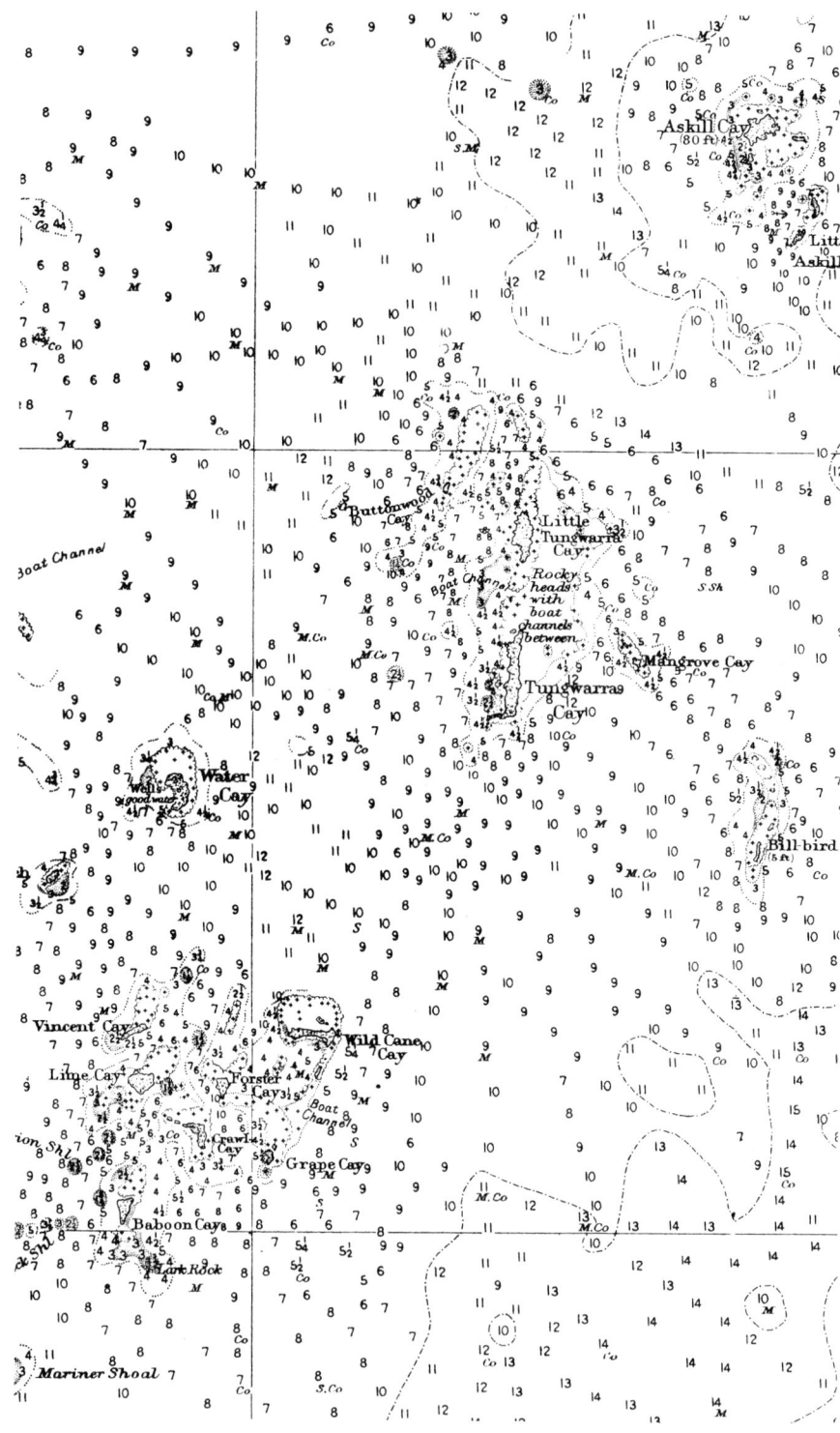

Tungwarra Cays or Pearl Islands (soundings in fathoms)

Man of War Cays (28081) once served as a loading port for fruit, which was lightered out from the mainland. The ships lay along pilings in a cove on the W side of the westernmost islet, where shelter is adequate from NW through N to E. Some shelter may also be found just S of the cluster of easternmost cays.

Puerto Cabezas (Bragman's Bluff) (28102), with its dilapidated long wooden pier, is an impoverished port town devoted to the shipping of bananas and timber and has nothing to attract yachts except in emergencies. The roadstead is open, the pier pilings don't break the sea, and mainland Nicaragua is not noted for its hospitality toward yachtsmen. Entry and clearing formalities have been reported to cost $25, although there is no consistency in such charges in any Central American ports.

Miskito Channel to Cabo Gracias a Dios (28101) presents a low swampy shoreline with no identifiable objects to check your progress; judging distance off is very deceptive. When rounding the cape itself, stay at least 2 miles off but never in less than 5 fathoms, and even further off in bad weather, since the seas are then actually breaking in 4–5 fathoms.

If you're caught by a norther, you can take shelter in Sunbeam Bay, S of Cabo Gracias a Dios, but expect a bad roll.

Cabo Falso (28101) is imperfectly charted, low-lying, and as dangerous as its name implies. Give it a wide berth.

Vivario Cays (28103), which lie about 50 miles N of Cabo Gracias a Dios and 100 miles S of Swan Island, have become a popular stopping place for the few yachts that come this way. The approach is easy, the protection rather remarkable, and the setting idyllic, for here you lie in the lee of a 2-mile-long natural breakwater of exposed or awash reefs interspersed with a chain of tiny islets.

Anchor in the lee of Grand Vivario itself, where the palms give shelter from the wind. You may find better holding about 6 cables S of the northernmost cay, where the shrimpers usually anchor to rest after their all-night trawling operations.

When the husky powercruiser *Eventide* passed through here in 1968, Esther Newmark, in an article in *Yachting*, wrote eloquently of this lonely haven in the middle of the sea:

> Gratefully we sighted Grand Vivario Cay at 0600 one morning. A semi-circle of reefs forms a lee from the easterly trades and seas, and it's always a source of wonderment to me to find a patch of calm water in the open sea created by those walls of coral.
>
> One of the cays was a natural bird sanctuary, the prominent specie being

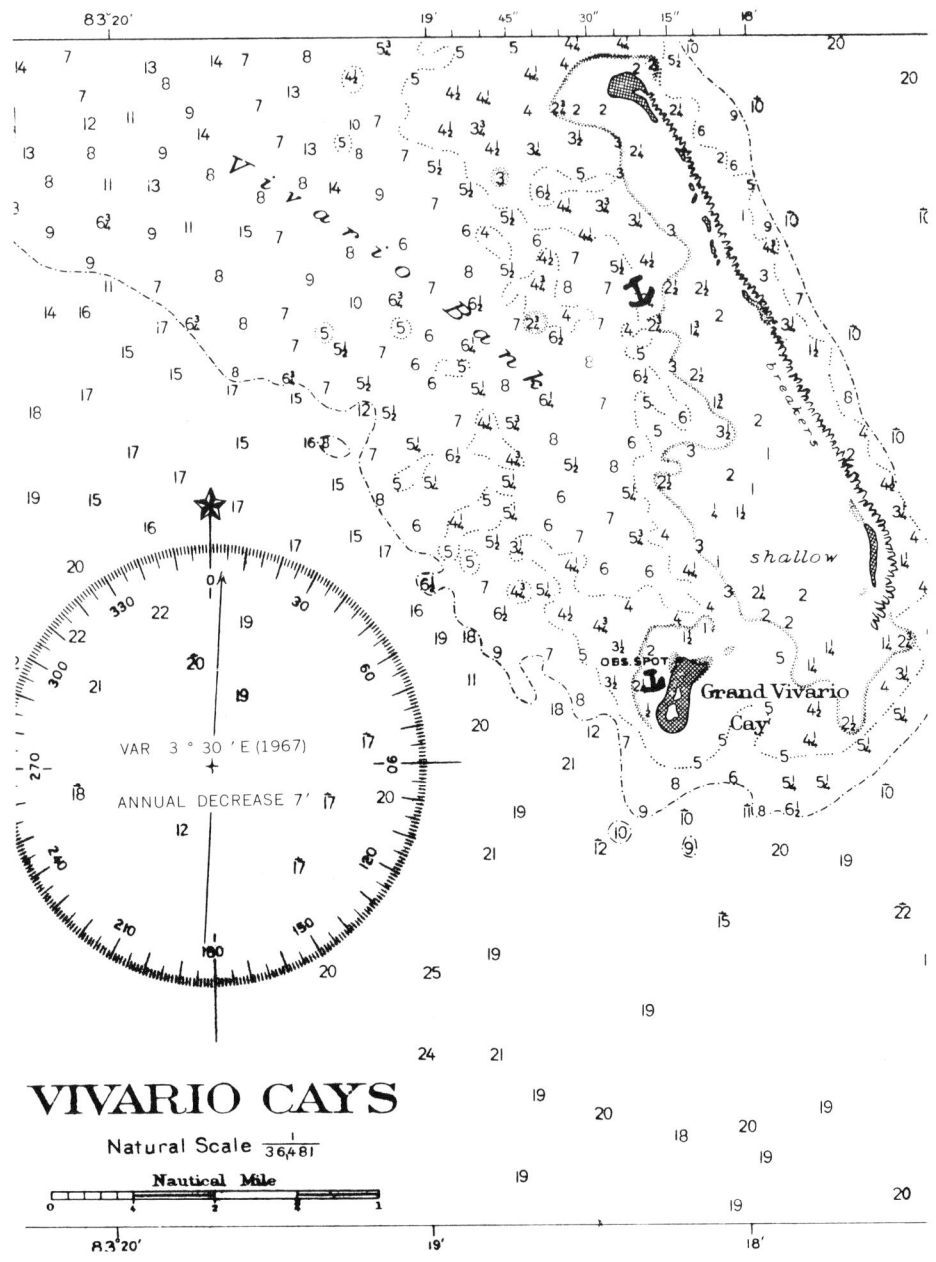

VIVARIO CAYS

Natural Scale $\frac{1}{36,481}$

Nautical Mile

Vivario Cays (soundings in fathoms)

the black man-of-war frigate. Even though it was December, it must have been "spring" to them, for the males were blowing up their beautiful red pouches and flying back and forth among the females, not at all disturbed by us in the Whaler.

Shrimp boats from Guanaja, the mainland of Honduras, and elsewhere, anchored here during the day. Usually the first one in after the night's shrimping drops a hook, then the succeeding arrivals merely toss a line to be secured to the stern of the preceding boat. As many as seven would tie up in this fashion. We traded some canned goods and paperbacks for buckets of shrimp and lobsters. For those who like the serenity of a lonely seascape, with only the call of the birds and the sound of seas breaking on reefs, and the breathtaking beauty of an unmarred sunset, Vivario Cays is such a place.

Swan Island (28121) which lies about 100 miles off the NE shoulder of Honduras and about halfway between San Andrés and Cozumel, could hardly have been set down in a more convenient spot for yachtsmen. Actually, there are two of these little coral limestone islands, each about 1½ miles long and only 60 feet high, and separated by a narrow channel that may or may not be foul.

Gitano and *Yellow Bird* docked at Swan Island's western end

In 1972, they were ceded by the U.S. to Honduras under the announced claim that, since they had once been a part of the Spanish Empire, they should belong to the nearest formerly Spanish country. It's a little hard to digest this argument, and probably the U.S. can afford to be gracious, but we hope it doesn't set a precedent for Puerto Rico and Culebra.

Anyway, now that Honduras has achieved its long-standing wish, life goes on unchanged on Swan except that the officer in charge of the U.S. weather station, who is an American, represents Honduras in customs and immigration functions. It is his duty to report the comings and goings of vessels and the names and nationalities of persons aboard.

In the prevailing NE to SE winds, the bight at the western end of Great Swan gives adequate protection, provided you go all the way into the concrete quay. For some reason, the swell seems to dissipate down in this corner, but anchored off, the motion is very uncomfortable. When we were there, the wind came in from the SSE, setting up a dangerous surge at the quay, and we had to move around to an anchorage on the NW side of uninhabited Little Swan, about 150 yards off, where it was smooth and well sheltered from the wind. In a strong norther, shelter may be taken along the S shore.

The half-dozen members of the weather station crew are a hospitable bunch to whom the arrival of a vessel from anywhere is an event of some significance. You will probably want to watch one of the twice-daily launchings of weather balloons into the upper atmosphere, and you will very likely be invited to their airconditioned mess, where you can look forward to a real rib-sticking American meal.

Swan's only marine frequency is 2738 kHz, over which a forecast is broadcast daily at 1205 EST.

Since Swan is such a small speck in the ocean, an early morning approach is helpful, in order to take advantage of the aircraft beacon visible for some 30 miles in clear weather.

A walk around the island will show only traces of the old plantation days when United Fruit harvested coconuts from some 15,000 trees. Hurricane *Janet*, in 1955, wiped this all out.

Besides the American foreigners, some 15–20 people from the Caymans and the Bay Islands of Honduras live here, raising cattle and a few crops.

Offshore Route, Cristóbal to Swan Island or Jamaica (26000, 28000, 26010)

This 570-mile route to Swan, with San Andrés the first stop, takes the current on the beam for the first 215-mile leg. From Providencia on, you begin to feel the powerful effect of the steady current that sweeps through the Caribbean and up through the Yucatan Channel. It is perfectly safe for night passaging, whereas the inshore route is encumbered by the Miskito Cays.

The deserted Quita Sueño, Serrana, and Serranilla Banks project themselves ever so slightly above the surface to offer a small measure of protection for overnight stops, particularly if you're bound for Jamaica.

San Andrés Island (26081) is only a flyspeck in the middle of the western Caribbean Sea, yet this little Colombian possession has more to offer in facilities and amusement than anyplace for hundreds of miles in any direction. Any ordinary mechanical or electrical repairs can be effected here, and should it be parts you need, there is almost daily air service nonstop from Miami. As for amusement, the resort atmosphere is pleasantly low key.

Lying within the protecting arm of the long barrier reef that creates the harbor, the water is so transparent and the colors are so exquisite that the rather numerous brown bars stand out sharply against the sandy bottom, and just to make it easier in poor light conditions, the channel is well buoyed as far as the commercial dock (where there is too much activity and dirt for a yacht). Coming in after dark, you would have to anchor near the entrance buoy, where you are somewhat protected from the surge—and you might possibly raise a pilot by blinking toward the near shore.

The yacht anchorage lies NNE of Cotton Cay at the N end of the harbor, reached by a wide and obvious channel rounding S and then E of Cotton Cay.

San Andrés Island. One ship that didn't quite make it over the bar.

This little cay itself is surrounded by shoal water, but the anchorage, in spite of the chart, has 2 fathoms with plenty of room to swing and absolute protection from the sea. The reef, of course, offers no buffer to the wind, but this keeps the bugs under control and the ventilation is welcome.

On the beach N of the anchorage, a stranded barge serves as a very, very rustic bar, restaurant, and dinghy landing called, for some obscure reason, HK-3. Cappy Salazar, who runs the establishment, is most obliging and knows where everything is in town.

Turn left from HK-3 and you come shortly to a well-stocked supermarket and the beginning of the commercial part of town, which is mostly an endless succession of shops devoted to the sale of radios, china, watches, cameras, and all the other geegaws that entice tourists to a free port—which San Andrés is. After a session of what we thought was very sharp bargaining in one of these stores (the clerk even telephoned the boss for his approval to sell at such a low price), we bought a portable Japanese radio for keeping in touch with the weather and news, only to find when we got back to the States that we'd saved only $2 on the list price!

Turning to the right from HK-3 brings you to the beach front and the hotels, bars, and bistros that line such places the world over. No Hiltons, Sheratons, or Holiday Inns yet, for this is basically an unsophisticated resort frequented mostly by Colombians. With the new air service from Miami, this modest state of affairs probably won't last long, especially considering that this is a truly beautiful island with wide, white beaches, palm-covered sandy islets just offshore, and a smooth bay of clear aquamarine enclosed by a fringing reef. All add up to a convincing South Sea-island impression.

If you rent a car, drive up on the hill behind the town where two-storied clapboard houses with brightly painted balconies line the road. The views of the bay through the waving trees are rewarding. Then continue on around the island, where still-working plantations provide vistas of slanting coconut palms and orderly rows of banana trees. Here today is a remnant of the West Indian scene as it was on most of the Caribbean islands a quarter-century ago, before the concerted tourist assault.

That almost-respectable buccaneer, Henry Morgan, was here, too, and no wonder, because San Andrés sits exactly astride the route of the gold- and silver-laden galleons that plied from the ports of the Isthmus through the Yucatan Channel on their way to Spain. A cave, purported to be one of his lairs, is just off the road on the W side of the island.

We were held up on San Andrés for several days waiting for the wind to drop, and liked every minute of our stay. A couple of good restaurants will be found along the playa: the Oasis for one, and off on one of the side streets is the relatively elegant Romano's, serving the finest food in town.

Entry formalities change as port captains and their assistants come and go. In our case, we had to hire a taxi to go halfway down the island to enter, and again to get our *zarpe* when it came time to depart. Better ask Cappy Salazar at HK-3 whether the Port Captain is likely to seek you out or whether you should seek him; sometimes an official may be on duty at the commercial docks, anyway.

On the opposite side of the island from town, Southwest Cove is a snug anchorage, but on an airless evening, we suspect the bugs would make it uncomfortable.

Providencia (26083, 26082), within an easy day's sail of San Andrés, is obviously of volcanic origin. Its jagged peaks rising to 1,200 feet make this almost forgotten island, also a Colombian possession, an easy target from almost 20 miles at sea. Yachtsmen have long recognized Providencia as a convenient and secure stepping-stone in the vastness of the western Caribbean. There are now regular tourist flights from San Andrés, so the island is gradually losing its reputation for isolation.

The 4,000 islanders, who eke out a living through fishing and cattle-raising, proudly trace their ancestry through Negro, Spanish, and English blood to that great ruffian, Henry Morgan, who was so widely respected by the British and just as widely hated and feared by the Spaniards.

In those mid-17th-century days, pirates took this strategic island from the Spaniards to use as a base for savage forays upon Spanish colonies on the mainland and upon shipping that had to pass their way. They also took advantage of the richness of the land to grow vegetables and to raise cattle to provision their fleets. It was called Santa Catalina then, referring more specifically to the small island at the NW corner of Old Providence, where the fortifications stood.

Two avid cruising people, Bob and Rosie Cullen of *El Sonador*, became so entranced with this primitive island that they stayed for almost two years. Our visit was only overnight, so we prefer to let the Cullens describe the place:

Port Isabel has a very secure anchorage with sand bottom and is sheltered from the NE trades that continually bathe the island. The village consists of four small general stores and a new 3-story hotel building housing the government offices, the post office, and a bakery—in addition to its 14 guest rooms.

A road circles the island and transportation is by horse and 8 pick-up trucks. Cattle graze on the green slopes and cows and pigs join the traffic on main street. In case of a news event, a town crier circles the island on horseback, stopping at intervals to shout the news.

The settling of Providencia has resulted in a multi-colored society, ranging from almost white to almost black. There are no color barriers, and the children can only be described as absolutely beautiful. Six names of English origin dominate: Archibald, Newball, Howard, Rankin, Robinson, and Taylor, but inbreeding has not produced the serious effects that it has elsewhere. The people speak English, but with a dialect that is sometimes difficult to understand. Spanish is also spoken. They are without doubt the most friendly people Rosie and I have ever met.

Another who liked Providencia enough to stay for several months was Ginnie Higman of *Tormentor III*. Commenting on how small the island is, she observed that it takes only 5–6 hours to sail around it in a dinghy. She also tells us:

At Fresh Water Bay, a lovely, coconut-bordered white-sand beach on the SW side of Providencia, there's a public building with two adequate fresh-water showers which yachtsmen may like to know about. Via dinghy from Isabel Village it's about 2 miles.

The Cullens also report that for years ships have sailed hundreds of miles out of their way just to obtain a pair of Providencia crickets, which are said not only to help greatly with a cockroach problem but bring good luck to the ship as well.

Indeed, the enticements of Providencia seem truly overwhelming!

The entrance to Catalina Harbor via the south channel, as shown in 26082, is quite simple after you have finally identified Black Point, and with the afternoon light behind you, you should have no difficulty.

Bob Cullen, however, has given us a sketch of the south approach (which first appeared in the SSCA *Bulletin*), which he says is the best when coming from San Andrés and the one that the islanders use all the time. Since the navigation light is out most of the time, and the structure difficult to see against the

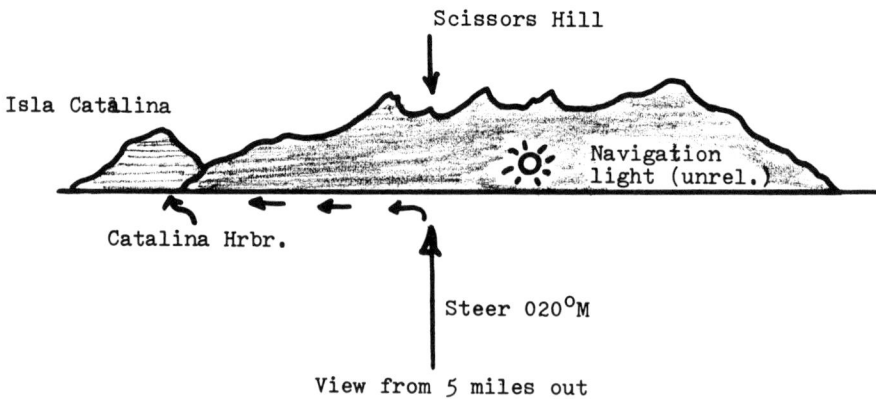

Approach to Isla Providencia from the south (inshore route)

greenery anyway, he advises entering on Scissors Hill on a heading of 020°M, this being the small hill in a saddle between two sharp and prominent peaks. Continuing Bob's instructions:

> The last mile before reaching the island you will be over 2–3 fathoms but you can read the water as it is crystal clear. Go right up to within 200–300 feet of the island and turn to port. Go up the western shore, staying in close. Enter the harbor and anchor anywhere E of the cement wharf.

The extensive breaking reef and Low Cay, some 7 miles N of Catalina Island, will be your reference mark when approaching Providencia from the N. The harbor approach on a southeasterly course, as shown in 26082, is not as difficult as it may appear, because Morgan Head is prominent and Lawrence Reef is barely covered and thus easily seen.

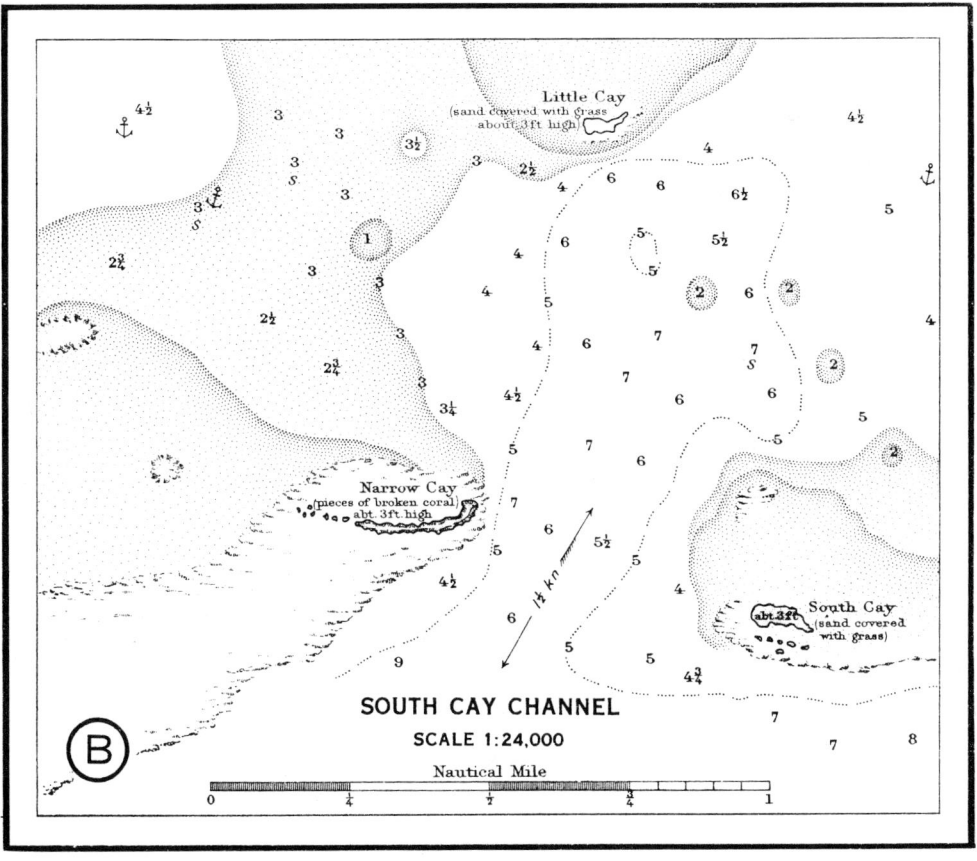

Preferred anchorage on Serrana Bank (soundings in fathoms)

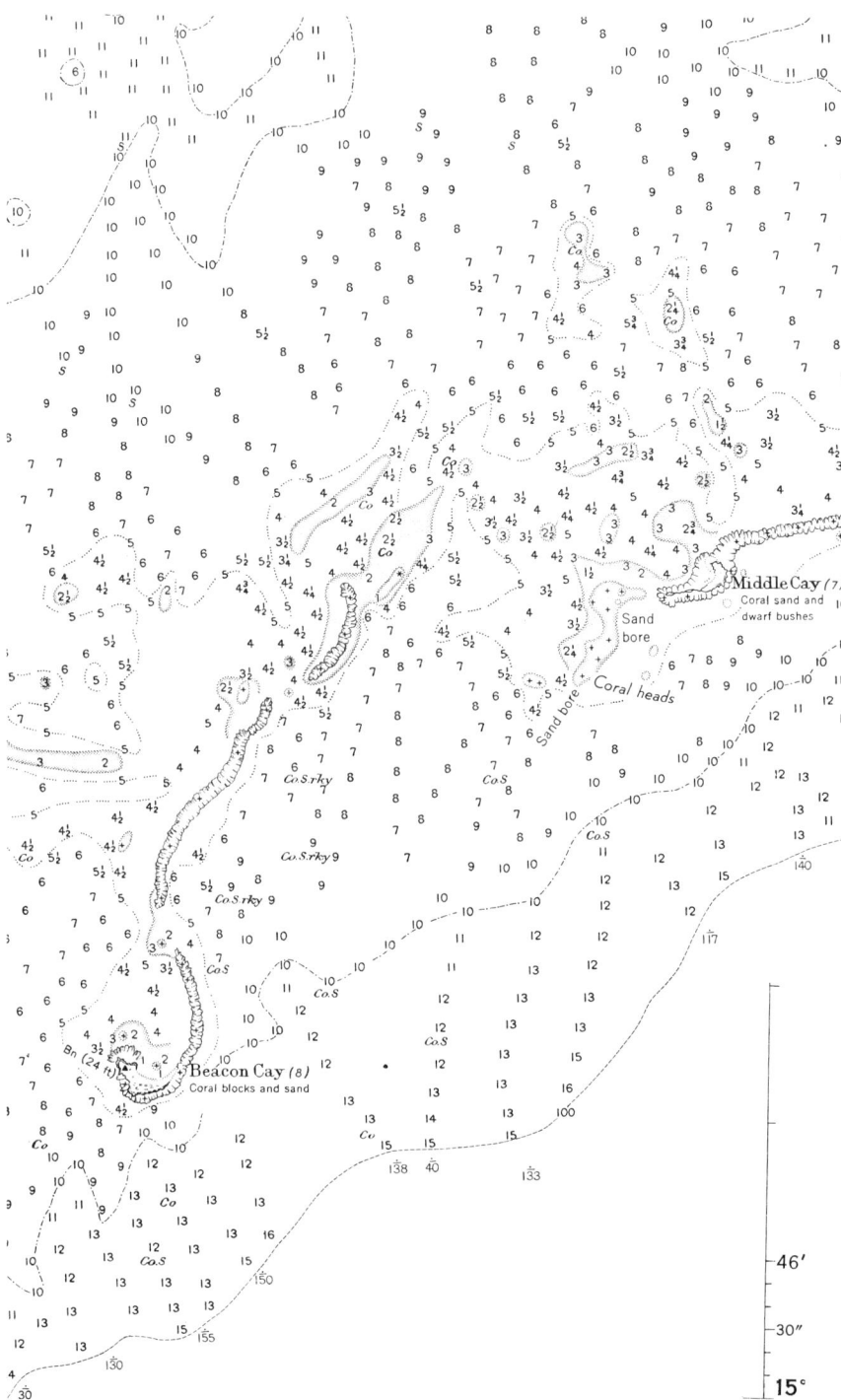

Serranilla Bank, best anchorage in lee of Beacon Cay (soundings in fathoms)

Quita Sueño Bank (28000) may hardly seem appropriate as an anchorage, lying as it does 120 miles off the mainland and some 60 miles N of Providencia; yet the low reef, barely awash in places, breaks up most of the sea, and you can at least expect a reasonably comfortable sleep literally miles from nowhere.

The "landmarks" here are the wrecks along the weather side of the reef, but it is nearly impossible to know which wreck is which on the chart, if indeed they are all shown. We anchored in approximately 14°15′ N, 81°11′ W, in 6 fathoms, sand. A new stranding, still with steam up, lay about 1½ miles from us across the reef, and there were two other wrecks in sight, to the NE and SE of us. There may be more now, for the reef is very steep-to on its eastern side, the currents are strong, and the whole area is a trap for the unwary.

Serrana Bank (26101) lies about 50 miles E of Quita Sueño and actually offers some solid land in the form of a half-dozen tiny cays widely scattered over its 17-by-8-mile area. The largest is Southwest Cay, standing all of 32 feet high with a light structure and a couple of palms, but the best anchorage is in South Cay Channel, within the triangle of three tiny cays that are hardly more than sand piles. The ½-mile-wide, unobstructed entrance is 10 miles NE of Southwest Cay. Be prepared for a 2–3 knot current.

On passage to or from Jamaica and the Canal, this is a useful and surprisingly good shelter. Some of these cays are occasionally inhabited by lobster and turtle fishermen.

Serranilla Bank (26102) is another useful overnight stop when bound to or from Jamaica or the Caymans. Anchor in the lee of the curving reef that makes out from the 8-foot-high Beacon Cay, the most southerly of the three cays that protrude from the vast underwater plateau extending from Cabo Gracias a Dios irregularly to Jamaica.

Still another stepping-stone is Southwest Cay on the Pedro Bank, mentioned in Chapter 23.

CHAPTER EIGHTEEN

The Gulf of Honduras and the Bay Islands

Just from looking at the charts, you would have to say that the Gulf of Honduras must be an interesting and challenging Caribbean cruising area. Bypassed by most yachts making a direct passage between Florida and the Panama Canal, the Gulf and its Bay Islands are not only off the beaten track but are probably the least-known cruising areas in the entire Caribbean. Even the geographic position was unfamiliar to many otherwise knowledgeable yachtsmen until Hurricane *Fifi* pinpointed the north coast of Honduras on its destructive passage through the Gulf in September, 1974. Yet within this offbeat area, at most times of the year, you will find pleasant weather and some of the best cruising waters anywhere in the tropics, with a rich variety of islands, cays, atolls, jungle rivers and lagoons.

The Gulf of Honduras occupies the western part of the huge bight that cuts deeply into the coast of Central America north of Cape Gracias a Dios (Lat. 15°) and south of Mexico's Yucatan Peninsula. It covers a triangular-shaped water area of approximately 10,000 square miles, bordered on the south by the mountainous coast of Honduras, on the west by the low, sandy coastline of Belize and its outlying barrier reef, and in the SW corner by Guatemala's short coastal region, with its spectacular Rio Dulce tucked in between them at the apex of the triangle.

Inside the triangle, there are three quite different subregions, each of which has its own distinctive characteristics and cruising attractions. In this chapter we discuss two of the subregions—the Bay Islands of Honduras and the Rio Dulce basin of Guatemala—and the navigational problems likely to be encountered in approaching them from sea. The third area, Belize and its barrier reef, is covered in Chapter 19.

APPROACHES TO THE GULF OF HONDURAS (28000)

No one planning to cruise the Gulf of Honduras in his own boat should take lightly the navigational problems of getting there or the skills required to pilot

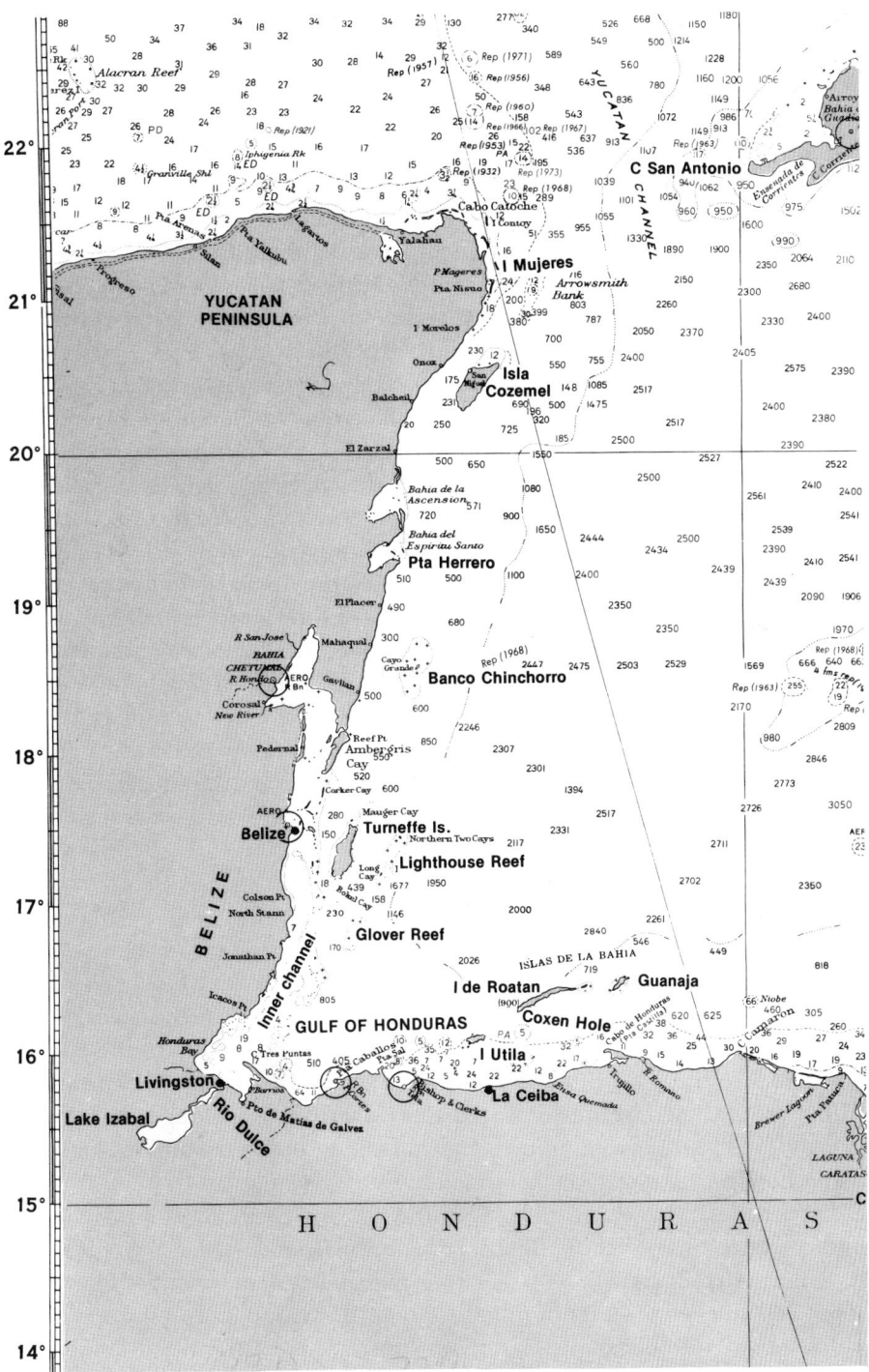

The Gulf of Honduras to the Yucatan Channel

safely in this extensive area of outlying reefs and shoals. It's not that the Gulf is geographically remote. Actually, Belize and the Bay Islands are closer to Florida than Puerto Rico and the Virgins are—it is only about 615 miles from Key West to Belize by way of Cozumel and the Yucatan Channel, plus another 100 miles or so to the Bay Islands, compared with about 900 miles from Miami to Puerto Rico or about 1,000 miles direct to the Virgin Islands. But the westward passage around Cuba and southward through the chain of reefs off Yucatan and Belize can be more taxing than the straightforward ocean passage to the Virgins, particularly when winter northers sweep across the Gulf of Mexico, affecting both the direction and intensity of ocean currents that are erratic and difficult to judge even under the best of conditions.

The northern route can be done in relatively easy stages by making the first leg from Key West to Cozumel, off the northern end of the Yucatan Peninsula, a distance of 395 nautical miles; then proceeding down the coast of Yucatan inside the Chinchorro Bank and Turneffe Islands to English Cay and the Eastern Channel across the bank to Belize Harbor, a track distance of about 220 miles. The chief problems are likely to arise in northers and periods of unsettled weather, when you have to be concerned about poor visibility and erratic currents. You must also constantly keep track of your position in the vicinity of three particularly dangerous reefs that are inadequately charted and not visible until you are close upon them. These areas are described in Chapter 19.

Yachts making a direct passage offshore from Cozumel to the Bay Islands should note that the current generally sets strongly to the NW and W. A few vessels (including more than one yacht) have failed to take this into account and have made landfalls at Puerto Cortéz on the coast of Honduras instead of at Roatán.

Eastern and Southern Approaches (28000)

In periods of unsettled weather, it might almost be easier for yachts heading south from Florida to make their approach from the eastward to Swan Island, keeping clear of the banks and reefs, or to cruise through the Bahamas, round the eastern end of Cuba through the Windward Passage, and then run back west with the trade winds to Swan Island and the Bay Islands of Honduras. Although the latter route would be more than twice as long—about 1400 miles—it holds promise of more downwind sailing and opportunities for short, island-hopping passages via Jamaica and the Cayman Islands.

Approaches from eastward and southward are generally free of dangers until you are close to the outlying reefs. Swan Island, which has a weather station and strong radio beacon, lies approximately 240 miles east of Belize and about 200 miles east of Lighthouse Reef, outermost of the offshore reefs, but it is only about 150 miles northeast of Roatán, largest of the Bay Islands, with nothing but deep water in between. We'll have more to say about the inadequacies of existing charts, but here it is sufficient to note that even the most recent U.S. and British editions are based largely on surveys made between 1830 and 1841, and are of limited use in identifying island landmarks or determining the course of channels through the reefs.

For yachts approaching the Bay Islands from the south and eastward, however, there are no serious problems in making a landfall under good weather conditions with average visibility—the islands are relatively high and can be seen from 15 or 20 miles at sea. If you are coming north from Panama, you have a choice: you can stand well off the coast of Central America until clear of the shoals northeast of Cape Gracias a Dios before turning westward for the Bay Islands, or you can follow the coastline of Honduras from the Cape as it trends northwesterly for about 125 miles to Cape Cameron. From there you continue on much the same course; it takes you offshore another 60 miles until the mountains of Guanaja, most easterly of the Bay Islands, become visible over the horizon. Columbus made the first recorded approach to the Gulf of Honduras on his last voyage to the Caribbean, in 1502, when he felt his way cautiously through the reefs to an anchorage off those same mountains of Guanaja. As Guanaja is not an official port of entry today, yachts following this route will have to continue westward to Roatán, largest of the Bay Islands, where the port of entry is Coxen Hole on the south coast.

THE BAY ISLANDS—ROATÁN, UTILA, GUANAJA (28000)

Although Columbus claimed the Bay Islands for Spain when he put his brother Bartolome ashore at Guanaja on July 30, 1502, the Spanish failed to settle there and showed little interest in the islands until after buccaneers of five nations had made them a base for raiding treasure ships homeward bound from the Spanish Main. The Brethren of the Coast found the reef-locked harbors and lagoons perfect hideouts for their fast ships, and established some of the first permanent settlements in the islands.

The first British settlement on Roatán was established by the Providence Company in 1638, but the site has not been found. By the mid-1650s, British, French, and Dutch buccaneers had established footholds they successfully defended against Spanish attacks from the mainland. Henry Morgan was only one of many British buccaneers who used the Bay Islands as a base prior to the sacking of Panama in 1671. By the middle and late 1700s, British colonists had a number of permanent settlements throughout Bay Islands as well as along the coast of British Honduras. But in 1859, the British negotiated a treaty returning the islands to Spanish Honduras.

Today the islands are no longer as isolated as they once were, though they have not yet been caught up in the Caribbean tourist current. The islands can

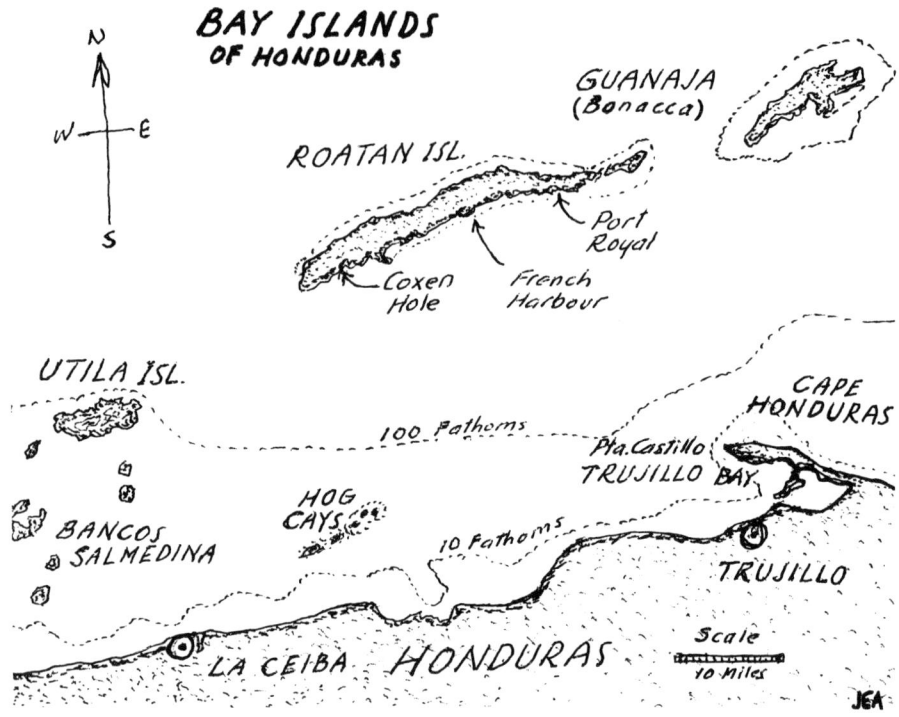

The Bay Islands of Honduras

be reached by air in a few hours from Miami and New Orleans, but the outlying reefs and shoals still make them difficult of access by sea.

There are three main islands, three smaller inhabited islands, and scores of islets and cays in this enticing group that rises steeply from the blue-green sea close behind the fringing reefs. Roatán, the largest of the group, occupies the central position, between Guanaja to the east and Utila to the west. The entire chain extends for 75 miles on its east-west axis, 20–30 miles off the mountainous northern coast of Honduras, forming a cruising ground of approximately 1,750 square miles, considerably larger than that of the Virgin Islands area.

Each of the main islands is easy to identify on approaching from sea. Roatán and Guanaja are heavily wooded and hilly or mountainous, with numerous distinguishing peaks and rocky outcroppings, some of which are shown in sketch views in the British *Pilot*. Utila is the lowest of the group, but has a rim of hills near its only harbor at the eastern end. All of the main islands are surrounded by reefs and banks, which rise steeply from the sea bed. The principal openings are shown on the charts, but the scale is not adequate for close-in piloting around the reefs, and yachts must depend largely on their own careful soundings and eyeball navigation.

Aids to navigation are few and far between, and currents in the area are extremely uncertain. But inside the reefs there are many fine harbors comparable to the best in the Virgin Islands or the Grenadines. Here you will find a small segment of the Caribbean that still looks much as it did half a century ago. You won't find marinas or plush shoreside hotels, or TV or telephones, and you may have to anchor out in most of the harbors and lagoons. Provisions and ship supplies are hard to come by in the small villages that cluster around the harbors, but if you carry your own basic supplies you won't have too much trouble supplementing them with an assortment of imported canned goods and native staples usually available at the local stores. Rice, beans, potatoes, and cabbage are the main staples.

There are other drawbacks, too, ones you are likely to find in most of the tropic isles. Pests, for example: mosquitos in the mangrove swamps, sandflies on sandy beaches, and "no-see-ems," which appear mysteriously at dusk with a hunter's instinct for exposed flesh and yachtsmen among their preferred targets. Roatán seems to have a particularly aggressive breed, although the native population is virtually immune. When we asked for an effective preventive lotion at a store in French Harbour, the proprietor looked surprised and said, "Oh, they don't bother us none." Fortunately, the faithful trade winds keep most of the insect pests a safe distance from your boat, and if you select an anchorage where the breeze blows at night, you are unlikely to be bothered. Some cruising boats don't bother to carry screens, and we've been more pestered by mosquitos on the Chesapeake than in the Caribbean.

The people in all the islands are friendly and eager to help visiting mariners. The population of about 10,000 is a mixture of British, Spanish, Black Carib and Creole, speaking both English and Spanish. The Honduras government requires Spanish in the public schools, but almost half of the population trace their ancestry to the British bucanneers and colonists and are proud of their English-speaking heritage. They resist interference from the mainland and support English-speaking church schools in many of the villages.

In the following sections, we take a closer look at each of the three main islands and cruising conditions in the area.

Roatán Island (28141, BA1219)

Isla de Roatán is not only the largest of the Bay Islands but its many fine harbors make it the most attractive of the group to cruising yachtsmen. Its eastern tip lies about 15 miles W of Guanaja, across a deep channel with soundings of 700 fathoms close to its fringing reefs. The island is about 28 miles long and 2–4½ miles wide, with densely wooded hills and ridges rising to heights of 700 feet or more toward the E end and a peak of 900 feet toward the W end. Three small inhabited islands lie off the easternmost tip of Roatán, so close together within the same encircling reef that they seem to be a part of the main island. They are called Santa Elena, Morat, and Barbareta.

For vessels entering Honduran waters, Coxen Hole on the S coast of Roatán is the only port of entry in the islands. Roatán is the official name of the town, which is the capital of the Bay Islands. Known locally as Coxen Hole, this little bight is named after Capt. John Coxen, a British buccaneer who made the port his private hideaway. It lies about 4½ miles E of West Point. Entry procedures are not difficult, but there have been numerous complaints in the past about delays and often exorbitant (or illegal) charges imposed on visiting yachts. In February, 1969, Pat and Leo Miner entered Coxen Hole after a passage from Swan Island in their 42-foot motor sailer *Myna Bird* and reported "a three-hour wait for the arrival of eight officials and their kids" resulting in assorted fees and charges totaling $38.50, including a cruising permit. Apparently that was more or less normal at the time, and the charges may or may not have involved any illegal fees. In October, 1974, the skipper of another U.S. cruising yacht, the *Maggie Fury*, reported to SSCA that "on entering and clearing Roatán the multitude of local officials demanded a total of $87.13." In this case, the skipper, Dr. Kenneth Tucker, complained to the Minister of Tourism for Honduras, who responded by reprimanding the officials and having the illegal fees and all other charges refunded. Conditions seemed to be improving in 1975, as a 65-foot Pacemaker cleared in at Coxen Hole on April 5 with her papers in order and was charged only $18!

The usual customs and immigration forms have to be filled out. It's necessary to have passports and health certificates for all persons aboard, and a crew list prepared in advance saves time. Regular hours for customs at Coxen Hole are 9 AM to 5 PM weekdays, 9 to 12 Saturdays, with overtime charges for entering at other hours and on Sundays and holidays. The Customs House is located on the main street of Coxen Road, facing the harbor near the center of the bight. Anchorage may be found a hundred yards offshore, and your flag should bring a boarding party in due course. The officials are Spanish-speaking Hondurans from the mainland, but some of them usually have enough English to conduct the necessary entry business without trouble. We found them friendly and courteous, and the procedures here are undoubtedly simpler and less time-consuming than in the larger ports of entry on the coast.

You will probably be visited by customs even if you have already made your official entry at a mainland port. Nelson and Jane McClary brought their Baltic trader *Josefine* to Coxen Hole after entering at Puerto Cortés on the mainland, but soon found it was necessary to get an additional cruising permit to visit other ports in the islands. "The officials searched through our documents, as is customary," they wrote, "gesturing like fly fishermen about to cast, before finally putting their official signatures on the paper clearing us for Port Royal."

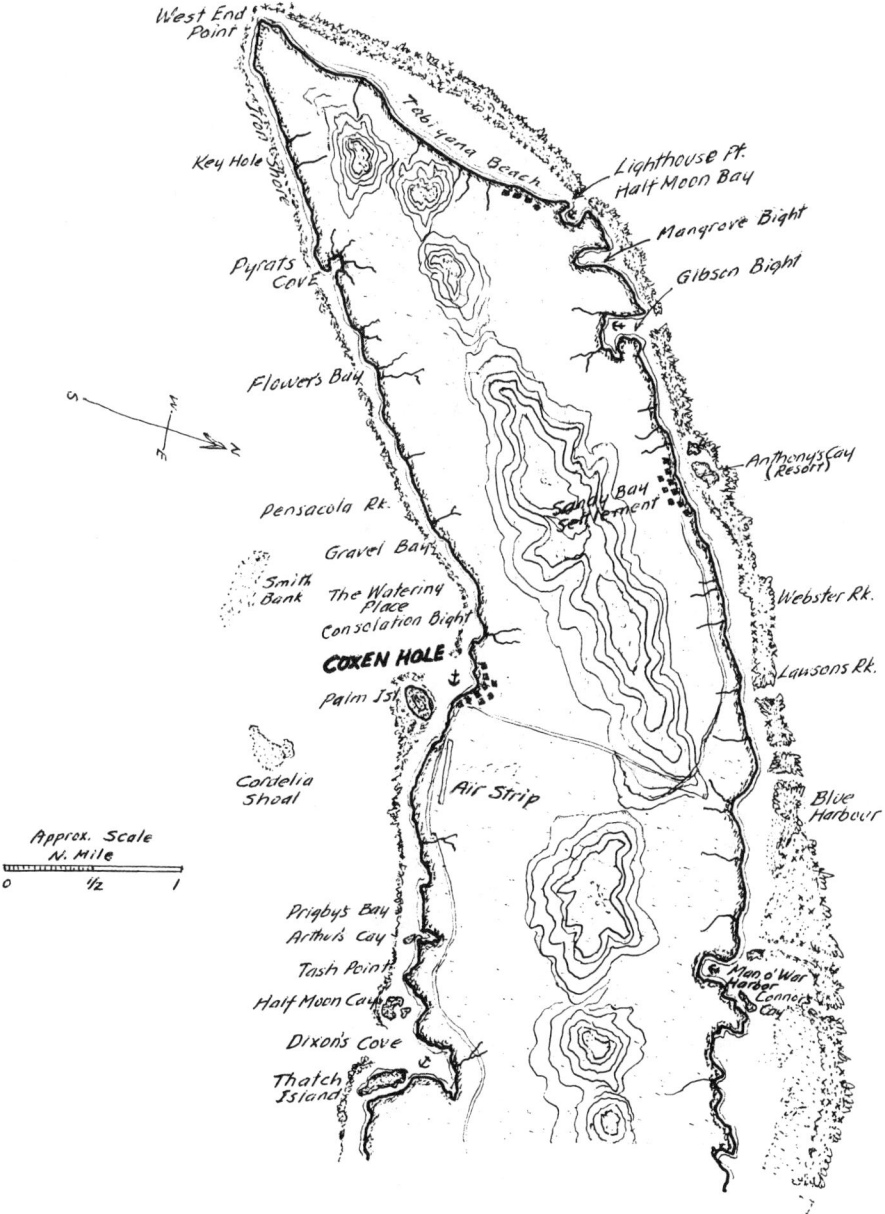

Plate 1: Roatán, west end to Thatch Island

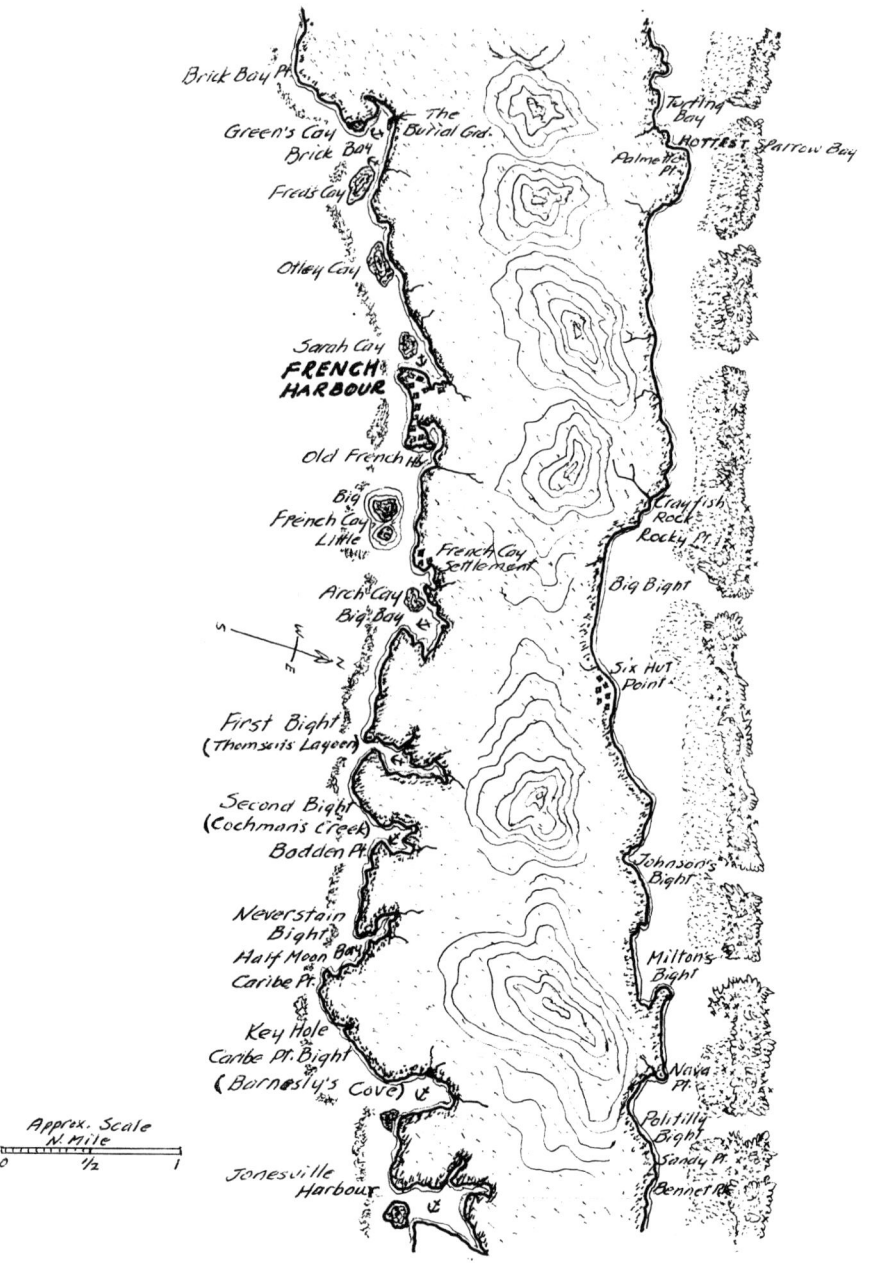

Plate 2: Roatán, Brick Bay to Jonesville Harbour

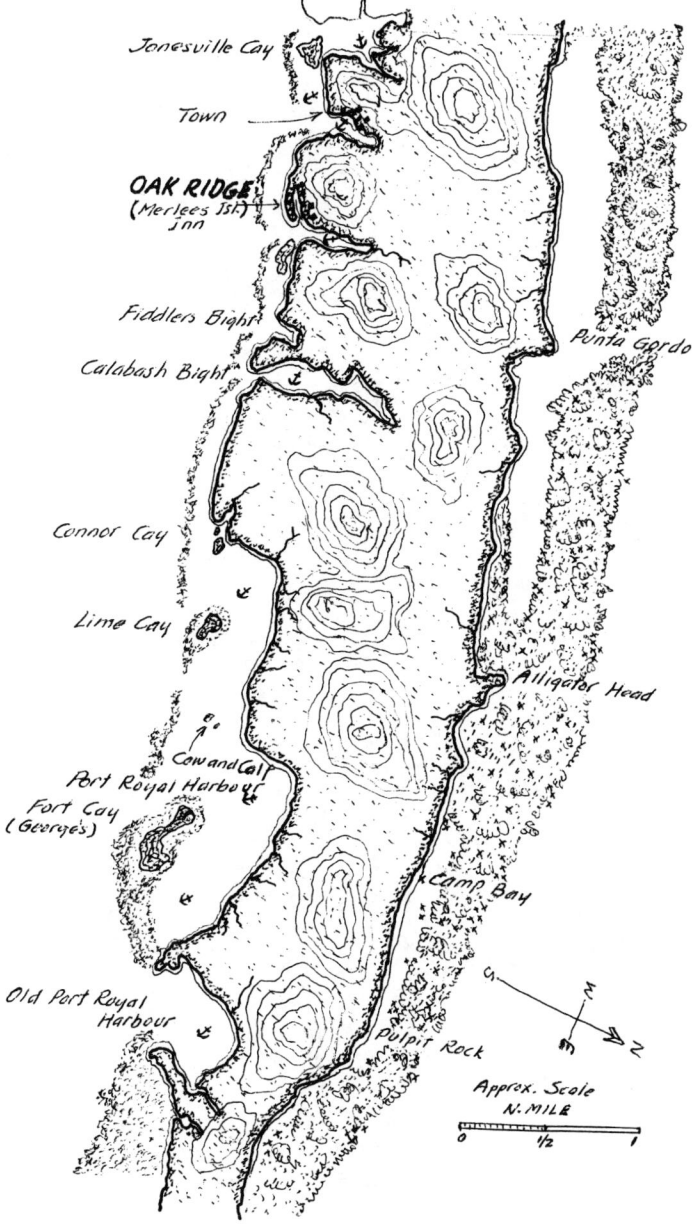

Plate 3: Roatán, Oak Ridge to Old Port Royal Harbour

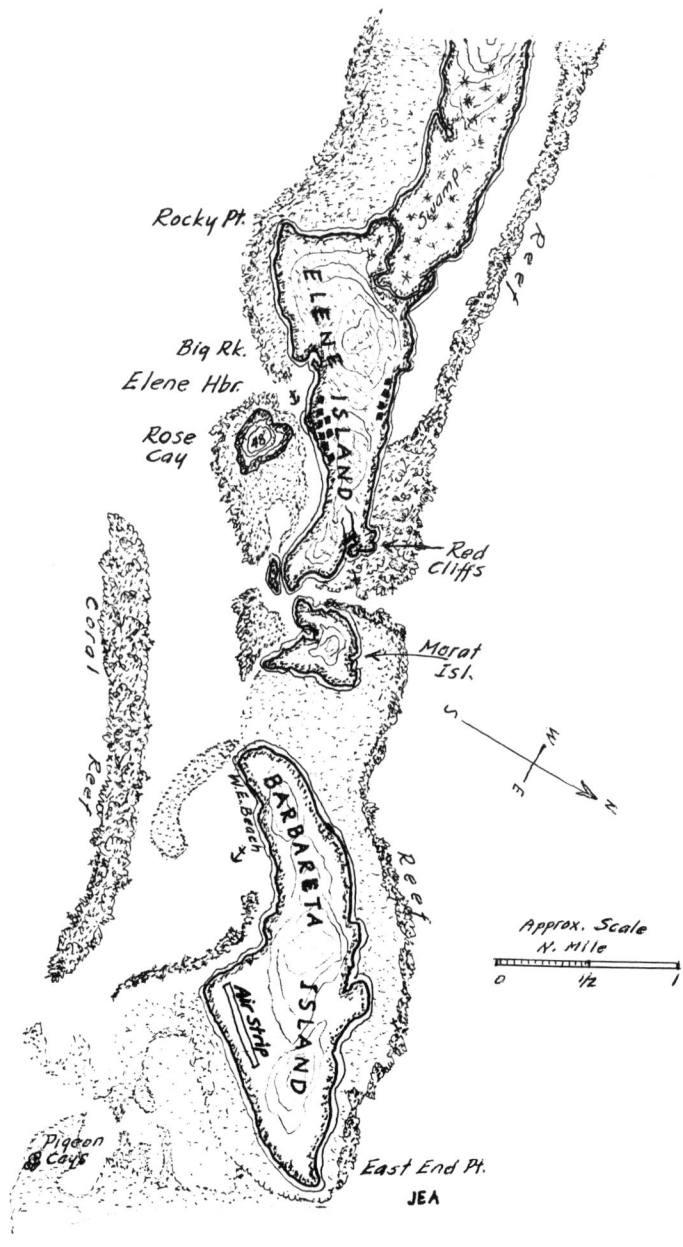

Plate 4: East end of Roatán, Santa Elena and Barbareta Islands

Harbors and Anchorages

Coxen Hole is by no means the best harbor on Roatán; in fact, it is hardly more than an open bight protected from the prevailing trade winds by Coxen Cay and Reef. The town is picturesque when seen from a distance in the harbor but dusty and bedraggled when inspected at close hand. Most of the houses facing the harbor are built on stilts over the water, with out-houses at the end of rickety piers extending into deeper water. Not long ago most of the island's travel was by boat, and Bay Island dories, fishing smacks, and small interisland freight boats are still much in evidence. Two airlines, SASHA and LANSA, have daily flights into Coxen Hole's unpaved airstrip at the eastern end of the harbor. Both lines use ancient DC-3's that call daily at each of the three main islands.

You will find limited supplies and provisions in the small shops along the half-mile "downtown" shopping street. Groceries seem to consist chiefly of canned goods and such staples as cabbage, rice, and beans. Diesel and gasoline are available on the waterfront, but ice and fresh drinking water are harder to find. Since most of these basic necessities are also available at other harbors a few miles away, you too may wish to start your further exploration without delay.

Few islands in the Caribbean have more harbors, coves and protected anchorages than Roatán. With one or two exceptions, all the best harbors are to be found along the south coast, in the 24-mile stretch between Coxen Hole and the eastern end of the island. Here you'll find more than a dozen all-weather harbors, protected from northers by the high ridges and wooded hills that extend the full length of the island, and sheltered from other directions by small cays and connecting reefs close in along the south shore. None of the U.S. or British charts provides enough detail for small-boat piloting, and the *Sailing Directions* and British *Pilot* describe only major anchorages for larger commercial vessels. The sketch maps shown on pages 465–68 should not be used for navigation, but they indicate topographical features of the island and locations of the principal harbors. We have suggested additional anchorages in coves and bights that are easy to enter with careful eyeball navigation.

Here is the overall picture, based on our own observations by plane and small boat and advice by local boatmen and others who know the area well.

Reefs and Entrances

With the exception of the western end of the island, which is steep-to, Roatán is completely surrounded by a reef that rises abruptly from the deep sea bed. The entire island lies outside the 100-fathom curve of the Honduran continental shelf, with recorded soundings of 1,000 to 2,000 fathoms a few miles north of Roatán. The barrier reef lies about one mile off the north coast of the island and continues (with only a narrow opening at the eastern end) around Isla Barbareta. As early as 1704, a map by Thomas Jeffreys warned unwary mariners that "The N side is bounded, in its whole extent, by a Reef of Rocks that have not few passages through, and these of small note. . . ." While it is possible to take shoal-draft boats through several small openings in the north reef, we do not recommend attempting to enter for the first time anywhere along that coast without a local pilot. In poor visibility and high seas, this reef is quite impassable.

Most of the south coast of Roatán is, by contrast, relatively free of dangers with many entrances into the principal harbors. From the eastern point of Barbareta, the edge of the reef extends at least 3 miles offshore, curving around to the southeast and south, then trending west to Isla Elena, close off the southeast end of Roatán. While there are several delightful small-boat anchorages inside the reef between Barbareta and Roatán, they should be reserved for exploration by dinghy, at least until after the visiting boat has become familiar with reading depths in these waters. In any case, the remainder of the south coast is bold and clear, with well-defined channels between the small cays and through connecting reefs that lie close inshore.

Protected Coves and Lagoons

Without writing an entire book about the harbors of Roatán it's impossible to describe all of the sheltered coves and lagoons that invite inspection by cruising boats with time to explore. Here's a brief inventory of what you might expect to find in the course of a week's leisurely cruising around the island.

Port Royal Harbour (28141; BA1219 Plan, KSK-9) is one of the finest anywhere in the Caribbean. It is said to have been used by Henry Morgan as a major base for his freebooting raids on the Spanish Main; Morgan's fortifications, or what remains of them, may still be found on George Cay, locally known as Fort Cay, guarding the main entrance to the harbor. The channel is about 200 yards wide, with depths of 18–27 feet between a short reef, just W of Fort Cay, and Long Reef, extending about ¾-mile W. Both reefs are visible, and parts of Long Reef are exposed and almost dry at low tide. There are two other charted entrances W of Long Reef, but both are narrower and more intricate than the main channel. A good landmark for vessels approaching from the S is the conspicuous 735 foot peak about three quarters of a mile W of the harbor entrance.

Good anchorages may be found almost anywhere inside the protecting reefs, in depths that range from 12 to 60 feet or more, over a bottom that provides

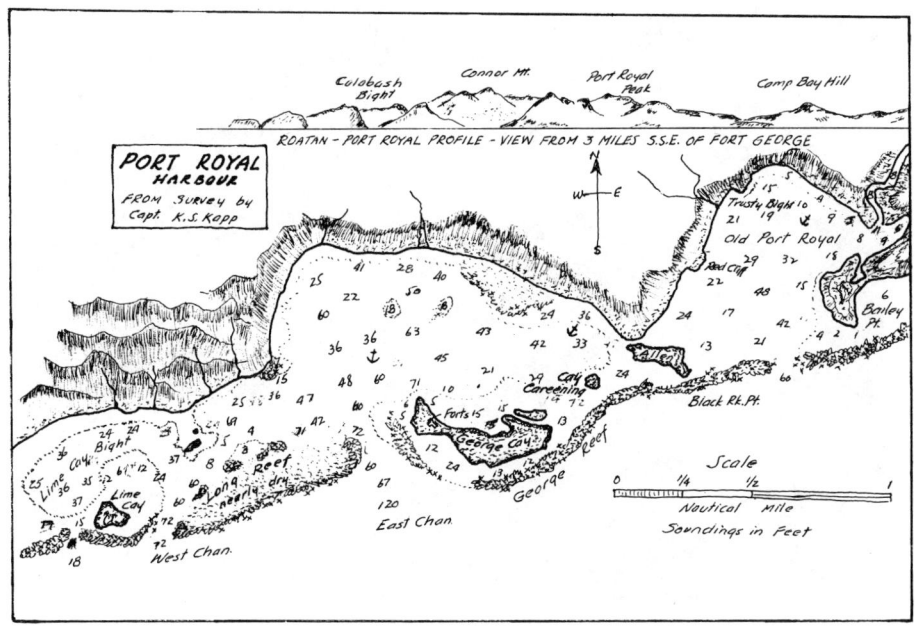

good holding. Six feet can be carried close up to the beaches on the northern and western shore. In buccaneer days, large fleets of privateers based in the harbor and careened their ships on the gently sloping sand beach inside the eastern rim of George Reef. Careening Cay is the name of the small islet with coconut palms at the E end of the reef, and it's still used for that purpose by native boats. The wreck of *Rambler*, an oceanographic research vessel lost in a December storm in 1972, lies hard in the sand nearby, and many earlier wrecks are hidden beneath the sand.

Speaking of wrecks and ocean research, Port Royal Harbour is the site of current archeological exploration by a group of scientists who have uncovered a wreck so ancient that it could possibly turn out to be of pre-Columbian origin. The date of this controversial hulk is still being debated by universities and research institutions while "The Pirates of Port Royal," as they are affectionately known on the island, continue their excavations. Their story, as we heard it, is interesting.

The first discoveries were made in 1968 by a cruising yachtsman from the Pacific Northwest named Michael Johnston, who attracted a number of adventurous divers and marine scientists to the site and negotiated an agreement with the Honduras government sanctioning further exploration. The group, known offically as *Oceanographicos de Honduras*, developed its own techniques for identification of subsurface sites and found evidence of 11 wrecks in the harbor, one of which turned out to be the remains of a 120-foot hull deep

Josefine lies at anchor in the deserted harbor of Port Royal, once a hidden base for the pirates of five nations.

under the sand bottom of the harbor, close by Careening Cay. For many months, the divers dredged sand from the hulk, laboriously moving ballast stones and finding perfectly preserved sherds that proved—believe it or not—to be about 40 large unbroken amphorae, or Mediterranean jars, with insignia that could not readily be identified. Samples were sent to the government of Honduras and to scientific institutions in the U.S., including the University of Pennsylvania's Museum and Applied Science Center for Archeology. Results of tests based on a modern thermoluminescence technique dated the pottery samples from as early as 570 A.D. to as late as 1470, plus or minus 150 years! Later tests and "corrections" by the Pennsylvania Center suggested other possible dates between 1510 and 1716, but noted that "dating is not very precise at the 'modern' endpoint of the scale."

When we visited Port Royal in 1974, the scientific leader of the group, James L. Radawski, was still seeking verification of the age of the wreck and its pottery jars, while continuing the search for other archeological finds in the harbor. The group has had its ups and downs, losing two research ships in tropical storms and weathering more than one financial crisis. They know their operation is not all cakes and amphorae, but they still believe they have only scratched the surface of the harbor floor. Their attractive Roatán Lodge on a bluff overlooking the harbor has facilities for a limited number of amateur archeologists, scuba divers, and armchair explorers as paying guests. They also serve meals and sell beverages and groceries.

Today there are few visible reminders of the old Port Royal, where the Spaniards once destroyed 500 houses in the town in retribution for buccaneer attacks on their ships. The Port Royal Farms Company, owned by Roy and Eric Anderson, holds extensive acreage around the shores of the bay and has plans for developing the property as a resort, with marina and other waterfront facilities; we're glad we saw it in its pristine beauty.

Port Royal offers good protection in a norther and is frequented by local shrimp boats, fishing vessels, and occasionally by visiting yachts. One interesting anchorage for small boats is just north of the two rocky cays known as Cow and Calf, toward the western end of the harbor, where you'll find the remains of buccaneer gun emplacements. N of Lime Cay, other good anchorages may be found in Old Port Royal Harbour, about 1½ miles E of the Fort Cay channel entrance.

Oak Ridge Harbour, or Pitt's Lagoon as it was once called, is located about four miles W of Port Royal, providing a deep-water harbor entered through a narrow channel with depths of 12 feet over the bar. The channel opens into two forks of the inner harbor, with depths of 12 to 30 feet. The channel over the bar is marked by a light structure (seldom lighted at night) on the E side, and by the bow section of a wreck stranded on the reef W of the entrance.

Oak Ridge settlement, with a population of about 1,000 in 1974, is an active shipping port built close around the shores of both forks. The E harbor directly N of the entrance channel is lined with small clapboard houses built to (or over) the water's edge. There is a shipyard and marine railway, operated by Tom Garcia, with facilities for hauling large shrimp boats. This yard, which has hauled yachts up to 80 feet in length, has a well-equipped machine shop, and in 1975 Tom planned to build several new slips for visiting yachts. Another machine shop and outboard repair facility is located at the E entrance, owned and operated by Al Albertson and Harvey Mayer, a retired Californian who has built a home on the harbor. Bill Kepler's Reef House Lodge has several guest cottages on the palm-fringed cay.

The W fork of the harbor has depths of 8 to 20 feet, with numerous private piers and the docks of a shrimp-packing plant recently purchased and reactivated by an American group from Palm Beach, Florida. When we visited Oak Ridge in 1974, the 72-foot Baltic ketch *Josefine* was lying alongside the bulkhead dock near the entrance to the W fork. Owned by Nelson and Jane McClary of Middleburg, Virginia, *Josefine* was built in Denmark in 1895 and sailed for more than half a century as a Baltic cargo boat before her conversion to a yacht. We'll have more to report about her cruise in the Gulf of Honduras later in this chapter.

Harvey and Bunny Mayer live on the point at the entrance to the western lagoon, and are friendly advisers to visiting yachtsmen. Harvey built his own 29-foot Bartender sportfishing boat at the Albertson–Mayer shop across the entrance. Fuel, ice, water, and groceries may be obtained at Rex Gough's dock nearby.

French Harbour is the second commercial harbor on the S shore, 7 miles WSW of Oak Ridge. The entrance is marked by a light (unreliable), which you leave to starboard in rounding the town point. The channel is deep enough for ocean steamers as far as the Hyber Shrimp Company docks and packing plant at the W side of the harbor, where a fleet of shrimp boats will usually be seen. This is a locally owned firm that packs and ships frozen shrimp (and crayfish, in season) from Honduras to Miami twice a month in its own refrigerated vessel, the *Hyber Transport*. The Elwin Shipyard, with two marine railways, lies just W of the Hyber docks, with facilities for handling vessels up to 100 feet. Gasoline and diesel fuel are available at a Texaco dock at the head of the harbor, just N of the Hyber plant; groceries and other supplies may be had at the docks and stores alongside the E shore of the harbor.

The town of French Harbour, with a population of approximately 1,000, is almost completely surrounded by water, as a deep lagoon lies back of the settlement with its entrance to the E. While the entrance channel to this lagoon is deep enough for the large, deep-draft schooner we found moored inside at the time of our visit, the unmarked approach should be explored by dinghy before attempting to enter the first time. Despite its name, French Harbour is populated by McNabs, Dixons, Elwins, and Archs, who trace their ancestry to the first English colonists. The Elwins are descendents of Thomas Elwin, the first English governor, and the McNabs, who operate the public bus service (jeeps and Land Rovers) between Coxen Hole and French Harbour, look back to even earlier buccaneer days. There's an attractive guest-house lodge on a hill overlooking the harbor and lagoon, the Carib Inn, run by Nancy Lange. She serves excellent homecooked meals. A small restaurant on the waterfront is operated by a member of the Arch family. The Buccaneer Inn has been recently refurbished and a new restaurant on the waterfront across the road serves good food and drinks at moderate prices.

Coves and Anchorages on the South Shore

In cruising the south shore, you will be able to identify at least a dozen more coves and lagoons that invite closer inspection. All of these inlets may be entered through narrow openings in the reef, which lies close to shore in the 20-mile stretch between Old Port Royal Harbour and Coxen Hole. The prevailing trade winds make this a downhill run for yachts heading westward, and a close beat to windward eastbound. But the orientation and distance between ports are comparable to Sir Francis Drake Channel in the British Virgins; the coves are even more protected, though there are not as many good beaches. Here are some of the best.

Calabash Lagoon lies between Port Royal and Oak Ridge. Vessels running outside the reef must keep a sharp lookout for the narrow, unmarked entrance to this mile-long lagoon that indents the coast. Inside the entrance channel, you can find protected anchorages almost anywhere in the deep bight (also known as Manatee Lagoon), completely surrounded by green hillsides rising steeply from the water.

Fiddler's Bight is an intriguing little cove between Calabash Lagoon and Oak Ridge. A connecting shoal-draft channel leads inside the reef and back of the mangrove keys to Oak Ridge Harbour, and is used by local dories and outboards. However, don't try to enter with more than 3-feet draft.

Jonesville Harbour, once known as Falmouth Harbour, is a two-pronged basin providing several safe anchorages off the town of Jonesville. Island trading boats call regularly at the town docks. Limited supplies are available ashore, but fuel and water are more conveniently obtained at Oak Ridge or French Harbour.

Caribe Point Bight, also known as Barnsley's Cove, is a large bay that must be approached cautiously, since the reef extends S and W beyond Moley Key before revealing its narrow, unmarked opening. A more protected anchorage may be found in the next bay to the westward.

Neverstain Bight lies half a mile W of Caribe Point. Here the reef opens into a tight little anchorage close to shore, known also as Darmple's Bay.

First and Second Bight are two deep indentations W of Neverstain Bight. Yachts proceeding in deep water outside the reef should be able to identify two narrow openings leading into these protected bays, known respectively as Thompson's Lagoon and Cochman's Creek. Both should be approached with caution, as the entrances are narrow, unmarked, and difficult to read in poor light. First Bight (Thompson's) leads through a winding channel (which should be explored by dinghy before entering for the first time) opening into a completely landlocked lagoon that looks like a mountain lake.

Arch Key and Big Bay are too intricate for strangers to enter safely, although there are inside channels behind Arch Key and Big and Little French Key leading to Old French Harbour and the lagoon mentioned above. Several sandy beaches are visible from beyond the reef, with a small settlement inside the French Keys.

Brick Bay, also called English Harbour, lies about two miles W of French Harbour, halfway to Dixon's Cove, with a tiny islet at the N end known as the Burial Ground.

Dixon's Cove was once a favorite anchorage of British buccaneers, rivaling Coxen Hole three miles to the W. The entrance channel lies between the two easternmost keys. It is marked by the edges of the reefs, which are clearly visible on both sides. Depths up to 15 fathoms are found in the ship anchorage near the center of the cove. Yachts can anchor in 12–18 feet close to the shores, which are fairly steep-to.

West of Coxen Hole, the coastline is steep and provides no all-weather anchorage for almost 4 miles to West End Point. Pyrates Cove, a small bight 1½ miles E of the point, is not recommended as an overnight anchorage, although it may be entered by shoal craft in settled weather.

The North Shore of Roatán

As already noted, there are very few harbors on the N coast of Roatán that can be entered safely through the continuous line of reefs, and none we recommend attempting for the first time without a local guide or pilot. However, there are several interesting bays and bights used by boatmen, scuba divers, and sportfishermen who know their way around the reefs and can guide visiting yachts to safe anchorages. Here are the principal bays, from west to east.

West Bay is not really a bay at all but a three-mile-long bight (Tabiyana Beach), rising steep-to at West End Point, with deep water off the sandy beach and bluffs that trend NE to Lighthouse Point. The bight provides protection in the easterly trades but is wide open to northers and occasional westerly winds. It's not a good overnight anchorage, although boats can lie safely off the beach in settled weather. Halfmoon Bay is entered through a narrow opening in the reef just N of lovely little Lighthouse Point. It's a cove just as attractive as its name.

Mangrove Bight, also known as Cahoon Hole, is larger than Halfmoon, but it's not recommended as an anchorage for cruising yachts. Tom Fool Bight, as the name suggests, is a place to keep clear of.

Anthony's Cay resort, on the north coast of Roatán

Gibson's Bight affords protected anchorage in the middle of the bight, which may be entered in settled weather a mile NE of Halfmoon Bay.

Sandy Bay and Anthony's Cay are the center of scuba-diving activity on Roatán. A charter yacht, the 40-foot sloop *Starfinder*, sailed by Dean and Mary Swain Clarke, was based at Anthony's Cay when we were there in 1974, along with several sportfishing and reef-fishing boats operated in conjunction with the resort. The entrance channel through the reef is extremely narrow and should be attempted only in good weather; there is a strong tide-rip on both flood and ebb tides. A small anchorage basin lies just inside Anthony's Cay, with 13–18 feet of water. It is protected in almost any weather, but a 2½-knot current sets across the basin, making two anchors advisable. Anthony's Resort runs a small ferry between the palm-fringed area (where its cay guest cottages are located) and the beach on the main island, where the central lodge and dining room are perched on a steep hillside overlooking the cay and reef. A small native settlement and resort-type lodge, the Pirate's Den, are situated close by at Sandy Bay.

Man-O-War Harbour lies about 4 miles E of Anthony's Cay and provides temporary and fair protection behind Man-O-War and Conner's Cays. Our repeated caution about entering through the narrow openings in the outer reef holds especially good from here to the eastern end of the island, despite the tempting names along the 20-mile stretch of coast, names like Turtling Bay, Hottest Sparrow Bay, Polittily Bight and Barbarossa Bay. A resort hotel located on Spyglass Hill commands an impressive view of this section of the N coast.

Islas Barbareta, Morat, and Santa Elena

These three small islands lying within the reef off the east tip of Roatán should be approached only from the south, as the break in the northern reef leads one into strong tidal currents and uncharted shoals and coral heads. About 1½ miles S of Barbareta, on the edge of the reef, there are two small cays between which an opening leads northward (toward the high land at the center of island) into a clear basin in the protected bight between West End Beach and Pelican, or Pelham Rock. The island is privately owned. Another opening in the reef lies about half a mile S of Elena and E of Rose Cay, leading NE toward a narrow channel into the S end of Morat. Elena harbor is entered through a channel W of Rose Cay, which leads to a small settlement. While these channels are visible to the eye in good weather, they should always be approached with caution, using depthfinder, lead-line or sounding pole. The canal at the E end of Roatán is navigable only by canoe, dory or small outboard.

Isla Guanaja (28123; BA1718)

Most easterly of the Bay Islands, Guanaja (shown on British charts as Bonacca) lies about 15 miles ENE of Roatán and 24 miles off the mainland of Honduras. Columbus is believed to have anchored here in 1502, and Guanaja's green hills, rising to heights of 1,200 feet, are easily identified, and provide the first landfall for vessels approaching the Gulf of Honduras from the east. Visiting yachts should not attempt to put in here unless they have previously cleared at Coxen Hole, as there is no port of entry on Guanaja. For vessels with time to visit all the Bay Islands, Guanaja is worth returning to, even though it usually means a windward beat across the channel from Roatán. Like all the main islands, Guanaja rises from a very steep coral bank and is completely surrounded by a barrier reef that extends several miles offshore on the northern and northeasterly sides.

The island is about 8 miles long and 2½ miles wide at its widest point, but it has few harbors comparable to Roatán. Its charm lies in the rugged, heavily wooded hills that rise steeply from the water's edge and the lines of palm-fringed cays that lie just inside the reef along the southwestern shore.

The principal town and anchorage are at the southwestern end of the island, where a large fleet of shrimp boats may often be seen at anchor in the roadstead

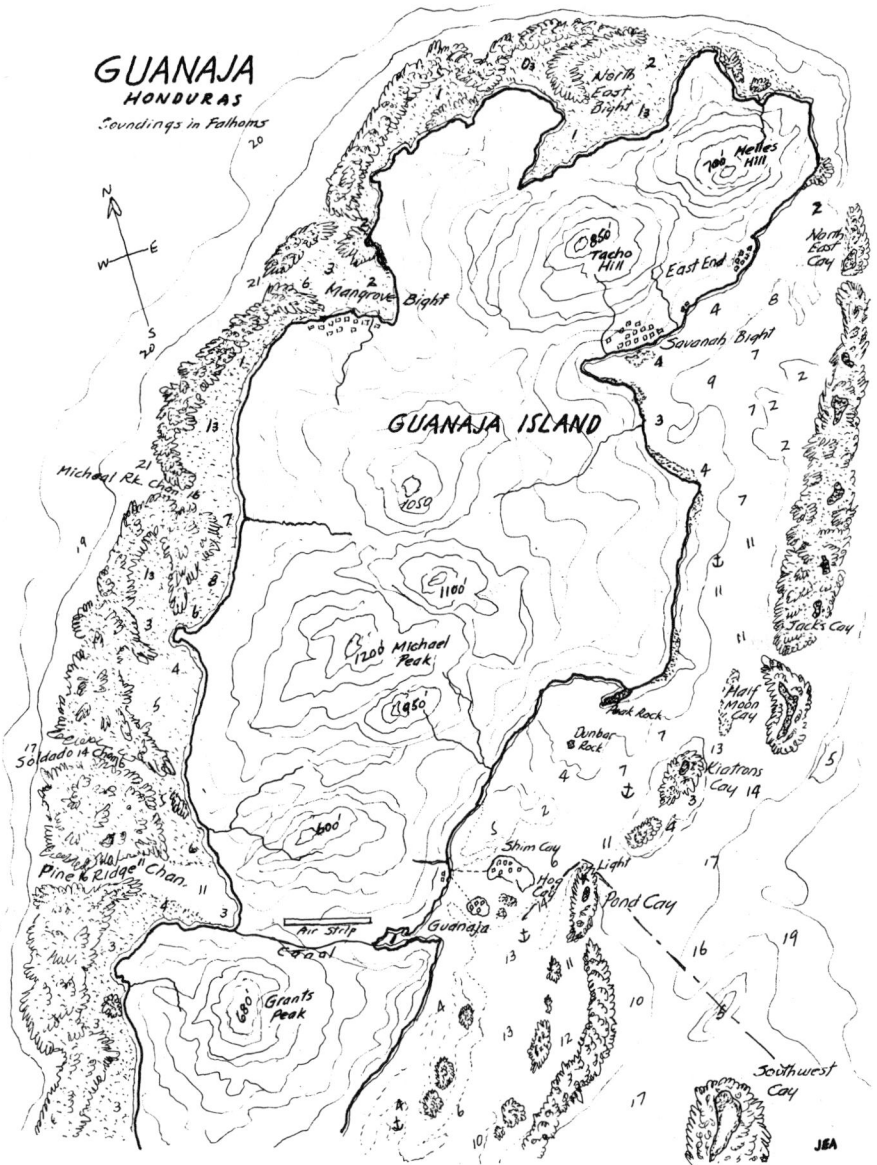

Isla Guanaja and southwest anchorages

or tied up alongside the docks of the settlement. There are depths of 20–60 feet in the anchorage, but the surge is uncomfortable in northers, and there are numerous shallow banks and sand bores. Two deep channels lead through the reefs, which are clearly visible in good weather but may be confusing when entered for the first time. Pilots are not required, but can be obtained if needed.

BA 1718 and the British *Pilot* provide adequate directions for entering. A light standing 30 feet high on a metal column just E of Pond Cay marks the inner entrance leading to the town, which is situated on two small sandy islets named the Sheen Cays.

Most of the population of Guanaja, estimated to be about 3,500 in 1974, lives on these tiny cays in what must be one of the most unique coastal settlements in the Americas. The highest "land" on the islands is scarcely 18 inches above high water, and most of the frame houses are built on poles extending over water. Bridges and narrow causeways connect the two islands. Storms and hurricanes have submerged the town more than once, but it has been quickly rebuilt on the same low site—"to avoid flies and insects," as they say on the higher shores of the main island. Good water is piped in from the main island. There are two "downtown" hotels and numerous small shops, churches, bars, and restaurants along the crowded main street and alleys. Spanish and English are both spoken, although Spanish seems to be more prevalent here than on Roatán. Fishing, chiefly for shrimp and crayfish, is the principal occupation. Daily airline service is maintained between the island and La Ceiba on the mainland. The airstrip is on the main island, at the end of a lagoon that provides the only fully protected small craft harbor, half a mile from the town. Small ferries ply between the lagoon and the settlement, and to some of the outer cays that have small villages. There was only one small beach lodge on the outer cays when we visited there in 1974, and no cruising yachts were in the harbor at that time. However, we counted more than 50 shrimp boats in the anchorage.

Isla de Utila (28143, BA1632)

Smallest of the Bay Islands, Utila lies at the southwestern end of the group, about 19 miles offshore and 16 miles WSW of Roatán. It is lower than the other islands; its ridge of wooded hills reaches a maximum height of about 290 feet at the northeastern end, where a red framework tower (no longer lighted) provides a distinctive landmark. The principal harbor, Puerto Este, is located at the southeastern end of the island, in a natural bight that provides good protection in northers and the prevailing trades. While it's exposed to the S and SW, a fringing reef affords sufficient shelter except in severe weather. The entrance should be approached from the SW, and vessels entering from N or E must be careful to keep well outside the fringing reef that extends for at least a mile and a half southwesterly from the dark, reddish cliffs that mark the southeastern end of the island. A light is usually visible from a small wooden building about 400 yards from the eastern side of the entrance, but the channel must be navigated carefully by eye to avoid the two shallow ledges, on either side of the 300-yard-wide entrance, and two small submerged coral heads with 6 feet or less over them inside the harbor. A controlling depth of 20 feet can be carried

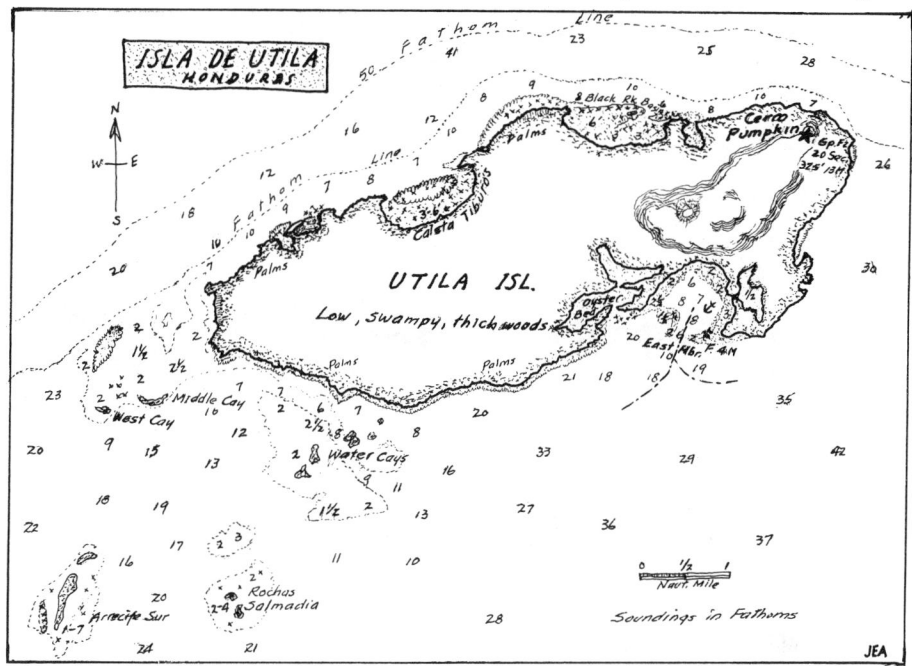

all the way into the harbor. Local pilots use a range of 020° formed by a church steeple and a conspicuous tree. Yachts can find good anchorage in the north-western side of the harbor, in 10 to 20 feet; most of the eastern side is shallower, with foul ground and coral heads.

The Utila settlement, built around the shores of the harbor, is smaller then Coxen Hole on Roatán, and is not a port of entry. It boasts several general stores where limited provisions may be found; gas and diesel fuel are available, but should be filtered before you fill up. There is plenty of good water, but ice is hard to find. A small resort hotel, run by a California couple, Brian and Ida Mommsen, rent scuba, snorkeling, and fishing gear, and have outboards for exploring the reefs and cays. There are several local boarding houses; they serve home-cooked meals at reasonable prices. Daily air flights from La Ceiba are beginning to bring a few tourists, but the island and its settlement remain much as they were 50 years ago. Both English and Spanish are spoken.

There are other anchorages for cruising yachts in the small cays that extend off the southwestern end of the island, and there is plenty of water in the narrow, winding channels that lead between the sandy shoals. Here you can find one or two sheltered pools and basins with room to anchor a good-sized ship in 50–60 feet, and yachts requiring 6 feet or less can take their choice of several tiny basins that look as though they were just waiting to be discovered. Although the principal cays, shoals, rocks, and ledges are clearly shown in the

View of Utila, westernmost of the Bay Islands, a boat-building and deeply religious
community

large-scale charts, we recommend exploring the area first, by dinghy or with a local guide.

The northern side of Utila is fringed by reefs that extend up to 400 yards offshore, with only a few narrow entrance channels, which are hard to identify from seaward. Inside the reef, however, there are two shallow basins or lagoons used by local fishermen. They are worth exploring with a guide. Black Rock Basin, the eastern one, is entered through a channel that lies about midway between Black Rock and the east end of the reef, where it converges with the shore. Depths of 6 feet can be carried over the channel bar, and anchorage inside may be found in 6–18 feet S of the entrance. The basin shoals rapidly at the western end.

Utila is a pleasant place to linger for a few days. It was a favorite port of call for Nelson and Jane McClary, who cruised the Bay Islands for five years (1969–1974) in their 72-foot Baltic trader, *Josefine*, and have shared their knowledge of the area with us.

Islas de Cochinas (28143; BA 1219)

These little wooded islands lie on a rocky bank between the mainland and Roatán, about 20 miles south of Coxen Hole and about the same distance northeast of La Ceiba on the coast. In settled weather, they can be reached under sail in a few hours from Roatán, and offer an interesting overnight anchorage. The two principal islands rise steeply from the bank: East Island, the larger, is 430 feet high and wooded. West Island, about ½-mile to the SW, rises to a conical peak about 500 feet high. Good anchorage may be found under the lee of East Island, over a coral and sand bottom, but be careful to find a clear sandy spot to drop your hook.

THE NORTH COAST OF HONDURAS

Some of the most exciting scenery in the Caribbean is found along the mountainous north coast of Honduras, but the steep-to shorefront provides almost no protection along the 130-mile section between Cabo Honduras and the border of Guatemala to the west. The prevailing trade winds make this an uncomfortable lee shore for most of the year; winter northers can be danger-ous for small vessels, and during the hurricane season it would be one of the worst places imaginable for any vessel to be caught. Although most of the hurricanes recorded during this century have turned north before reaching the Gulf of Honduras, there have been notable exceptions, like Hurricane *Fifi* in 1974, which caused great damage along this coast and in the interior of Honduras. Coastal areas fared better in this instance than mountain districts, where torrential rains created flash floods that took a heavy toll of life, while the Bay Islands suffered relatively little damage.

The principal ports on this section of the coast are open roadsteads, with only one partially protected harbor, Puerto Castilla, really worth considering.

Puerto Castilla (28142) is a small port on the south side of Cabo Honduras on the peninsula that forms Bahía Trujillo. It provides shelter from northers and easterly winds. Anchorage may be found off the town about 2 miles SE of Pt. Castilla. This was once a major shipping port, but the old pier is in ruins and the town largely abandoned. The lagoon at the eastern end of the bay makes an excellent all-weather boat harbor for vessels that can clear the shallow bar off the entrance channel, where depths vary after each major storm.

Puerto Trujillo (28142) is a port of entry on the south side of Trujillo Bay. It has little to offer visiting yachts, and the anchorage is exposed to all but southerly winds.

La Ceiba (28144) is one of the principal ports of Honduras and a growing commercial city of about 40,000. It has a 1,400-foot pier for loading bananas and lumber, but no facilities for yachts. The anchorage is an open roadstead, and during northers vessels must put to sea. There is daily air service to Roatán and the Bay Islands. Water and fuel are available at all of the major mainland ports, but the process of fueling yachts may be time-consuming.

Puerto Tela (28161) lies about 32 miles westward of La Ceiba, in a section where the low coastal plain rises a few miles inland to jagged mountain peaks that are often lost in the clouds. Rivers flow down from the mountains, spilling over their banks in the rainy season and disgorging tons of yellow silt into the blue Caribbean Sea. The anchorage at Tela is another open roadstead off the commercial pier.

Punta Sal (BA 1219) is a bold rocky promontory on the coast between Tela and Puerto Cortés which affords protection from the prevailing trades in a small cove and lagoon on the western side of the point. The eastern side of the point provides shelter from northers and is sometimes used as a harbor of refuge by native coasters who have been forced to leave the exposed roadstead at Tela.

Puerto Cortés (28163) is a major banana port about 15 miles E of the Guatemalan border and 30 miles W of Tela. Cortés is a principal port of entry for Honduras. Our friends the McClarys entered here on a passage from Guatemala to the Bay Islands in their Baltic trader *Josefine*, but reported later that "This was a mistake. Anyone bound for the Bay Islands should bypass the mainland and clear at English-speaking Coxen Hole on Roatán." Finding no one among the officialdom who could speak English, and having no one aboard with much more than high-school Spanish, the McClarys were delayed 48 frustrating hours, ended up paying $130 in assorted fees and gratuities, and narrowly avoided a fine for not having five stars in the center of their home-sewn blue-and-white Honduran courtesy flag. Their warning to other visitors by sea: "Be sure you have the proper flags for all of the countries you intend to visit."

The town of Cortés, with a population of about 25,000, straggles along the shoreline of a deep bay that extends SE of Punta Cabellos for about 2½ miles. There are two commercial wharfs, one of which is a 960-foot banana-loading facility with a moveable crane and conveyor belt, and a T-headed oil pier. Fuel and water are available at both piers, but don't expect pumping facilities for yachts. The anchorage off the town is protected from northers and the easterly trades, but is exposed to the westward. Yachts bound for Guatemala should be sure to get their clearance papers before leaving Puerto Cortés; it is the last port on the Honduran side of the border.

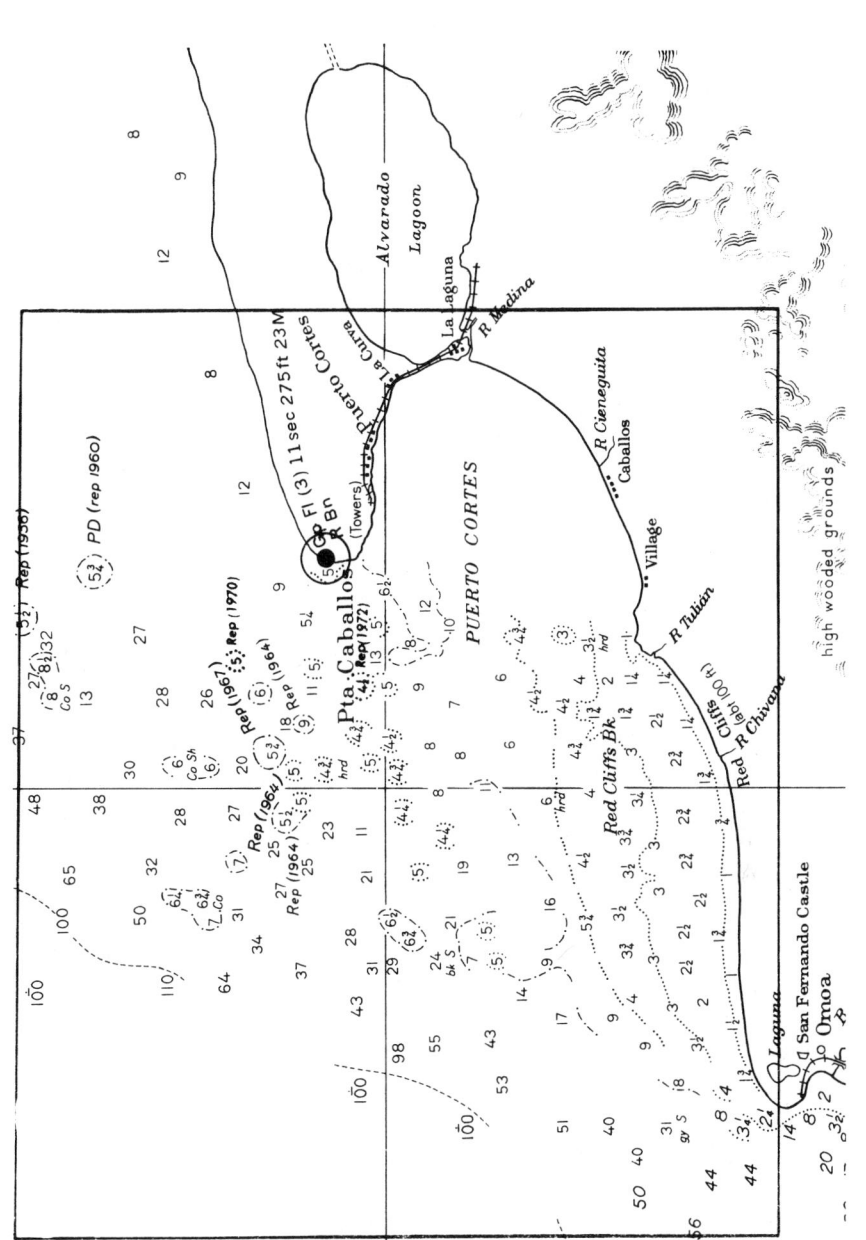

Approaches to Puerto Cortes (soundings in fathoms)

EAST COAST OF GUATEMALA TO THE RIO DULCE (28162, BA1219)

The ultimate destination of every cruising yacht entering the Gulf of Honduras is bound to be the Rio Dulce, that fabulous Guatemalan river that empties into the Bahía de Amatique at the head of the gulf. But before reaching that destination, navigators should familiarize themselves with coastal features of this area and keep their charts and *Sailing Directions* handy for eyeball piloting in the shoaler bank waters, which are a distinct change from the steep-to coast of Honduras.

The coastline of Guatemala is scarcely 45 miles long, as the crow flies, from the eastern border on the Rio Motagua to the boundary with Belize on the Sarstoon River in the northwest—but it's almost double that distance if you follow the winding shoreline that meanders inland around Bahía de Amatique and the three smaller bays that form this estuary. From the mouth of Rio Motagua, the coast is low, swampy, and bordered by dark sand beaches that have few distinguishing features for about 27 miles, until you sight the lighthouse and water tower on Cabo Tres Puntas at the eastern entrance to Amatique. Vessels approaching the bay are cautioned against deceptive currents that vary in direction and strength.

Bahía de Amatique (28162; BA1573)

The entrance to this large bay (also called Honduras Bay) is over 13 miles wide between Cabo Tres Puntas and Punta Gorda, with depths of 6–18 fathoms, shoaling to less than 2 fathoms near the shores and on several sand banks within the bay. Ox Tongue Shoal, the largest of these banks, extends about 7½ miles off the eastern shore and is at its western end marked by a light buoy with radar reflector. All three of Guatemala's east-coast seaports are situated on estuaries of Amatique Bay. Anchorage may be found in Ox Tongue Bight, north of the shoal in the lee of Punta Manabique and clear of the steamer lanes that lead to Puerto Barrios and Santo Tomás.

Puerto Barrios (28165) is the largest commercial port in Guatemala, exporting bananas and timber and handling most of the country's imports. The town, with a population of about 35,000, lies on the eastern shore of Bahía de Santo Tomas de Castilla about 14 miles SSE of Cabo Tres Puntas.

Puerto Santo Tomás (28165) is almost an extension of Puerto Barrios and is reached through the same dredged channel that leads into the Bay of Santo Tomás and continues about 2½ miles southward to the end of that bay. There are berthing facilities for commercial vessels at both ports, and a naval installation at Santo Tomás with facilities for lifting 60–80-foot patrol boats. The McClarys found anchorage W of the naval station and clear of the channel. In an emergency, they were told, private vessels might be lifted for repairs if the facilities were not being used by the navy. Most yachts are likely to prefer Livingston, however.

Livingston (28164, BA 1573) is a small river port at the mouth of the Rio Dulce on the western shore of the Bay of Amatique, but it's also an official port of entry with a Customs House and a Port Captain who is somewhat used to dealing with visiting yachts. The charter yacht *Tongaroa* was a frequent visitor here in 1973–74, and our friends the McClarys had their 52-ton *Josefine* hauled at the government shipyard and marine railway. In fact, customs and clearance formalities are conducted more easily at Livingston than at most Central American ports, according to the McClary's, our principal source on this interesting area.

Once known as the Gateway to Guatemala, Livingston was a bustling center of shipping and commerce at the turn of the century, when coffee, bananas, and timber came down the river by boat from the plantations and hardwood forests of the interior. Planters and the wealthy German owners of the coffee and banana *fincas* traveled by the sternwheeler that carried mail and passengers across Lago de Izabal and down the winding gorge of the Rio Dulce. Today the town has lost all traces of its earlier glamor, and the population has dwindled to an estimated 1,500—predominantly Mayan, Ladino, and Black Carib. The Caribs are descendants of early settlers who had been forcibly transported to the Gulf of Honduras from St. Vincent in the eastern Caribbean during the 1770s, and then had migrated here to establish the first community, which they named Labuga, "Mouth of the River." Half a century later, Guatemala's President Francisco Morazan renamed it Livingston after a then-famous Louisiana lawyer who wrote a new penal code, which Morazan adopted, introducing trial by jury to Guatemala in 1823.

Now the little town has surrendered its trade and commerce to Puerto Barrios and Santo Tomás across the bay, but it retains the advantages of its geographic position at the mouth of the Rio Dulce and continues its intimate association with the unique waterway that still carries native small craft between the interior and the seacoast of Guatemala. It can be reached only by boat—no roads connect it with the interior—and its principal activities are two shipyards: Blanco's and the government-owned Ferropazco, where *Josefine* was hauled by an antique donkey engine belching clouds of black smoke.

A ferry-tug runs between Livingston and Puerto Barrios, and if you are in doubt about how to cross the 6-foot bar off the river's mouth, just wait for the ferry and follow its course to the public dock. Here is Jane McClary's description of the town and its people:

> The main thoroughfare rises from the public dock, past the stall presided over by the "Marquesa," so-named because of her regal manner, who sells fruit (avocados at 2 for a nickel in season) and vegetables, wrapping them carefully and decoratively in banana leaves. Stalls along the roadside sell tomatoes, onions, and potatoes. Fish, available at the waterside market, is generally sold out by 9 AM. We learned to intercept the *cayucos* (the dugout canoes used by the Indians for fishing and transportation) from upriver and deal directly with the fishermen. In order to buy meat it was necessary to find out when one of the steers, brought in by boat, was being butchered and to stand by. . . . Canned goods, very expensive and occasionally rusted beyond edibleness, are available at one or two stores. During the times we were in Livingston we bought lunch from Marguerita, who came daily to the public dock at noon carrying her woven tray of home-baked bread and pork sandwiches on her head.

The Rio Dulce to Lago Izabal (BA1219)

When we were in the Bay Islands, the marine archeologists at Port Royal said of the Rio Dulce: "The Mississippi is longer, the Amazon wider, the Yukon colder, but the Rio Dulce is the ultimate!"

There are several practical problems for yachts planning to cruise the Rio Dulce. One is the 6-foot controlling depth over the extensive bar at the mouth of the river, where the mean rise and fall of the tide is less than a foot. However, the afternoon sea breeze may produce greater depths by backing up the river stream about ½-foot or more on a rising tide. *Josefine* needed the assistance of the tug *Rio Dulce*, aided by a second tug, *Guatemala*, to clear her 7½-foot draft over the bar, but yachts drawing 6 feet or less should not have serious trouble.

Another problem is the lack of nautical charts. The inland waters of Guatemala are completely uncharted, and the U.S. charts don't go beyond the river delta and a few miles upstream. BA1219 includes the lake but is almost too small in scale to be usefu!. However, Rio Dulce and Lago Izabal have been navigated for more than three centuries by all manner of deep draft vessels, and yachtsmen who have cruised the area had little difficulty in piloting by eye and sounding their way to the headwaters of this fascinating river-and-lake system almost 50 miles inland from the Caribbean Sea. The McClarys found it useful to carry a set of aeronautical charts produced by the U. S. Air Force (series ONC J-24, Belize, Guatemala, Mexico) and distributed by the Defense Mapping Agency's Aeronautical Chart and Information Center, St. Louis,

Josefine being towed over the bar off Livingston

Missouri 63118. While these show no water depths, they do indicate the course of the river and the topographical features around the lake.

Once you are safely across the two sandbars at Livingston, the river flows for about 8 miles through a winding gorge between steep limestone cliffs backed by heavily wooded hills, with midchannel depths of 16–60 feet. Jane McClary wrote:

> Suddenly the sea lay behind us, we were enclosed in shadow, by walls of living green. Waterfalls cascaded from the sheer cliffs, hundreds of feet high, wreathed in mist. Graceful clusters of mauve candelaria and other rare varieties of *Bromeliad* grew to the water's edge. Here and there branches were hung with the curious nests of the *Oropendula*, the orioles that build their hanging compartments, sometimes as many as a hundred to a single tree. The river twisted and turned, changing direction so sharply that we virtually boxed the compass. Occasionally, in an angle of turns, the rising sun lit the leafy walls with scorching force, only to vanish again leaving us in dense shade. We saw caves in the limestone cliffs. The graffiti of generations decorated the rock where it was exposed. Our boys wondered if the pirates who beseiged the fortress guarding the Spanish ships anchored in Lake Izabal had left their mark. These, the buccaneers of the Honduran coast,

followed in the wake of the Spaniards soon after Pedro de Alvarado, a 34-year-old captain in Cortés' army, subjugated the Indians of Guatemala in 1526.

El Golfete suddenly comes into view around a bend in the river as the mountains recede into the distance. It is a "sweet-salt" basin about 9 miles in length with an average width of 2 miles and depths of 12–24 feet. There are several small islands that afford protection in their lee and are well worth exploring. At the western end, the basin narrows and the river continues its winding course through wooded hills, with depths of 12–36 feet in the channel, for about 6 miles where it connects with Lake Izabal. A substantial current flows through the narrow sections of the river at most times of the year, becoming stronger in the rainy season, when you must keep a sharp watch for floating logs.

There is almost no traffic on the Rio Dulce, other than an occasional Guatemalan gunboat patrolling the interior and the *cayuco* fishermen, who cast their lines and nets out of the current under overhanging rocks in the shadows of the steep cliffs. El Golfete, "the little gulf," is bordered by the jagged splendor of the Mico Mountains to the southeast, the jungle and foothills of the Sierra de Santa Cruz to the northwest. The crocodiles and turtles that oldtimers

Hotel Catamaran on the Rio Dulce

say consorted in the shallows are no longer in evidence. But the McClarys found it possible, literally, to run into manatees, the sea cows that the Caribs feature in their dance, Pio Manati. These beasts may be seen feeding on water plants. Along the shores you pass the thatch-roofed huts of the Indians, half hidden amidst coconut palms, with their small plots of corn and beans nearby. For the Indians, writes Jane McClary, "life flows on, like the river, its course unchanged for centuries." According to tradition, the Indians believe that the river is a vein in God's body, providing the fish they eat and the water they drink, clean, and sweet—*dulce*!

The last mile of the river before you reach Lake Izabal and the ferry landing is full of surprises. It discloses, of all things, a modern marina-hotel on a lush little island, owned and operated by an American couple, Louisa and Kevin Lucas. It's called Catamaran, and has a good anchorage, a dockside bar topped with palm thatch, a swimming pool, and a group of hotel units that can accommodate 36 guests. Kevin Lucas was a Navy pilot in 1962 when he met and married Louisa, daughter of a United Fruit Company official; in 1969, after Kevin had left the service, the couple bought the island and became the first Americans to own and operate a hotel in that area.

Catamaran is a fine base for exploring the lake and surrounding country. Fresh water and fuel are available at the Lucas' marina, and at the Marimonte Marina and Hotel dock across the river. Food may be bought at the little marketplace of Relleno, at the ferry landing 10 minutes away by dugout canoe. Catamaran is now accessible from Guatemala City, 165 miles by the new road that opened in 1971, linking the capital with Tikal in the Peten rain forest, where the great city of the Mayan civilization is being restored. One may travel by bus, an experience no intrepid traveler should miss, or charter Kevin Lucas' plane for trips to the historic capital of Antigua, the market at Chichicastenango, and Lake Atitlan.

Lago de Izabal and Castillo San Felipe de Lara

After the breathtaking grandeur of the Rio Dulce, the 23-mile-long Lake Izabal seems flat and exposed, with almost no good all-weather anchorages around its shores. There are general depths of 36–48 feet in the central part of the lake, shoaling to 6 feet or less around the shores. The McClarys found only one fully protected anchorage, at Ensenada de Balandros, about 7½ miles W of the village of Izabal on the southern shore, with depths of 2 fathoms or more behind a long spit. (The British *Pilot* calls this place "Puerto Refugio.")

Castillo San Felipe de Lara, which stands at the entrance to Lake Izabal, has been rebuilt on its original foundations from plans found in the Spanish archives. The restoration offers a somewhat Disney-type tourist version of the colonial outpost that once played an important strategic role in defending the

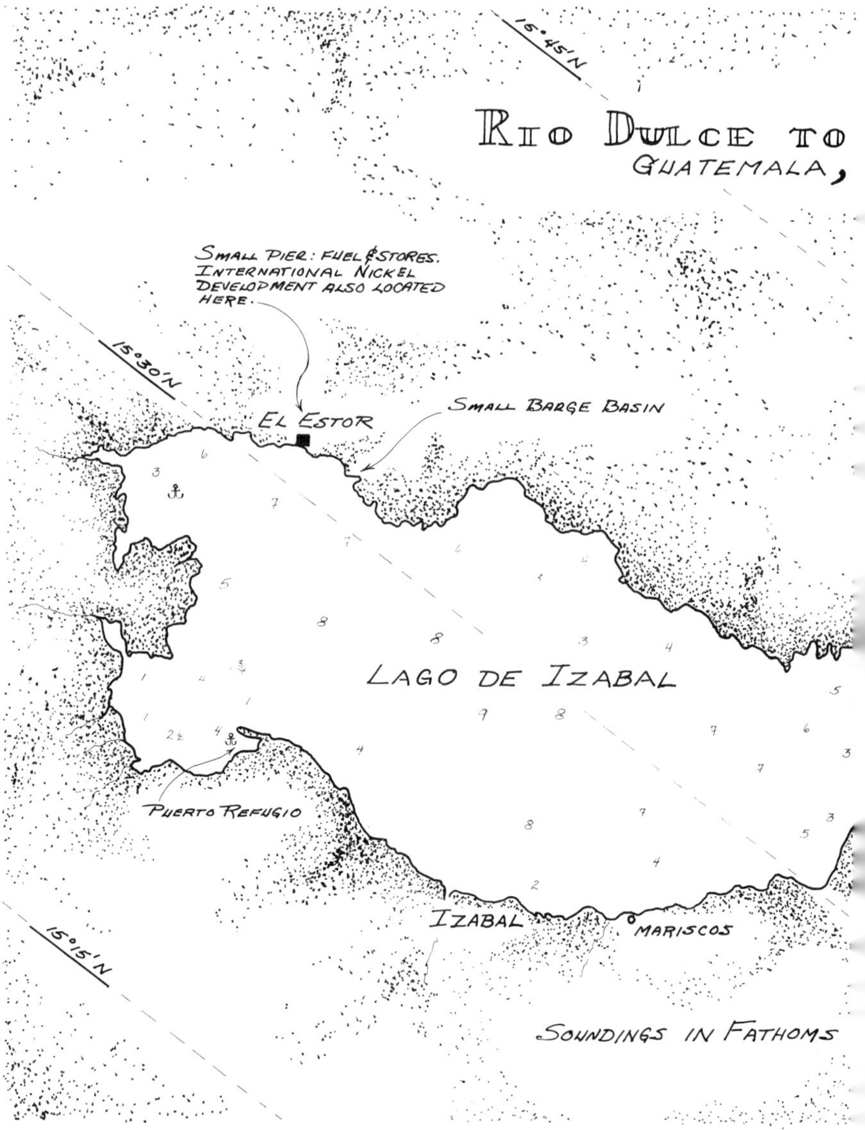

SMALL PIER: FUEL & STORES.
INTERNATIONAL NICKEL
DEVELOPMENT ALSO LOCATED
HERE.

15°30'N

EL ESTOR

SMALL BARGE BASIN

3   6

7

7

5

8

8   8   3   4

LAGO DE IZABAL   5

7   8   7   6

3

5   4

2 2   4

4   8   7   3

PUERTO REFUGIO   5

2

IZABAL

MARISCOS

15°15'N

SOUNDINGS IN FATHOMS

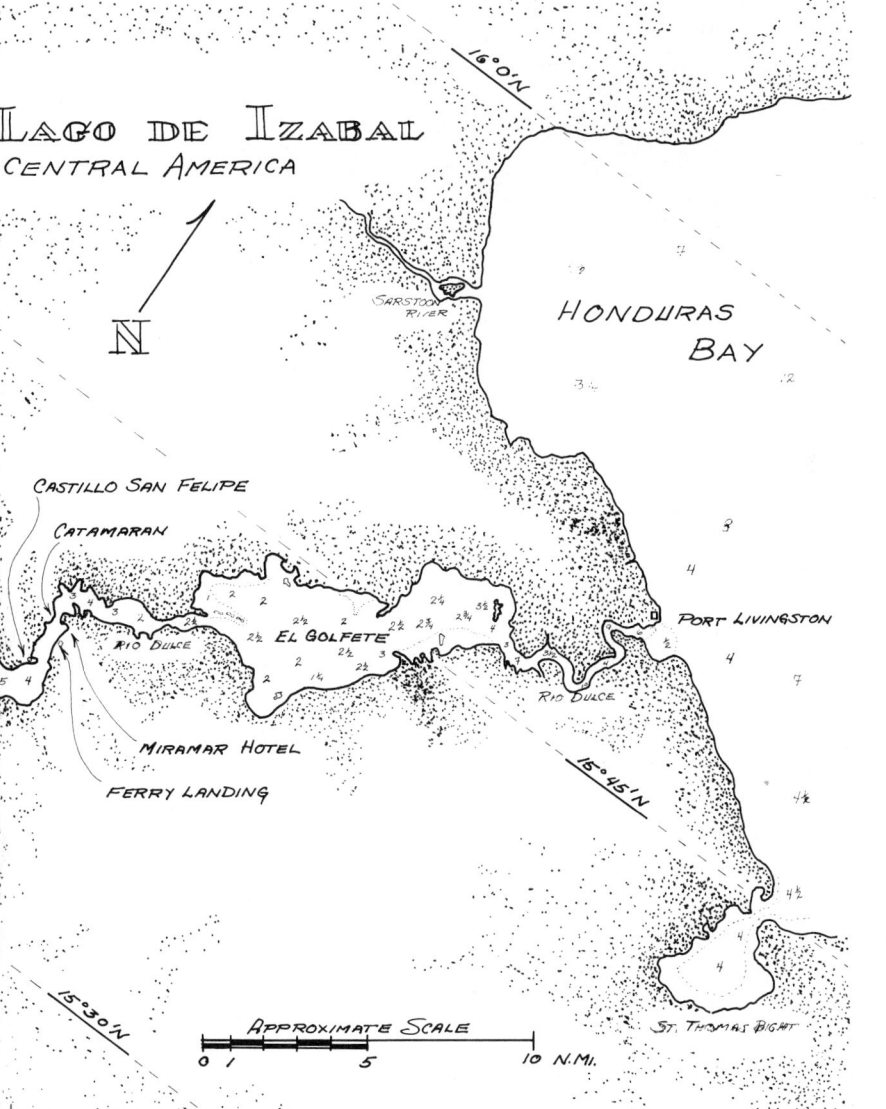

LAGO DE IZABAL
CENTRAL AMERICA

N

SARSTOON RIVER

HONDURAS
BAY

CASTILLO SAN FELIPE
CATAMARAN

RIO DULCE
EL GOLFETE

PORT LIVINGSTON

MIRAMAR HOTEL

FERRY LANDING

RIO DULCE

16°0'N

15°45'N

15°30'N

ST. THOMAS BIGHT

APPROXIMATE SCALE
0 1   5   10 N.MI.

Castillo San Felipe on the shores of Lake Izabal

treasure ships that loaded here awaiting shipment to Spain. Today, for a modest fee, you may see dungeons, tunnels, bronze cannon dredged from ships that sank in the river, and links from the original chain that was stretched across the channel to prevent pirate ships from sacking the vessels laden with loot at anchor in the lake.

John L. Stephens, the intrepid discoverer of Mayan ruins, who traveled through Central America in 1839, was fascinated by the river and the lake, which he described as "a fairy scene of Titan land, combining exquisite beauty with colossal grandeur." Since Stephens' day, the town of Izabal, then the jumping-off place for mule trains over the Sierra de Las Minas to the interior, has dwindled to a handful of thatched huts along the south shore of the lake about 17 miles SW of Castillo San Felipe. Mariscos, the only other present-day settlement on the south side, is known as a "tough" town, rumored to be a hangout for guerrillas who come down from the hills for supplies.

El Estor is the only town on the north shore of the lake. The McClarys anchored *Josefine* off the mining property of the International Nickel Company, which is building a plant expected to be in operation by 1976, despite much argument over the danger of polluting the lake. The western end of the lake is fed by a number of delightful rivers; this compensates to some extent for the lack of protected anchorages. Fortunately, the prevailing NE winds are generally moderate during the winter months, when cruising conditions are best. From May to September, the winds are frequently strong, with heavy thunder squalls at night during the rainy season. Hurricanes are rare, but *Fifi* did considerable damage in Guatemala after it passed through Honduras in September, 1974.

Coastal waters between Livingston and Sarstoon River

There are no protected anchorages in the coastal waters between Livingston and the Sarstoon River, which forms the boundary between Guatemala and Belize (formerly British Honduras). Most of this 10-mile coastal section is low, with little to attract cruising yachts; about 2 miles inland the Santa Cruz mountains rise to a height of 1,395 feet.

The Sarstoon River (28162) is navigable for about 10 miles above the entrance, but the banks are so low, swampy, and covered with mangroves that it's difficult to land anywhere along its shores. The bar at the entrance carries about 6 feet, and the sea generally breaks heavily in the prevailing onshore winds. Vessels bound for Belize usually proceed directly to Punta Gorda, about 16 miles NNW of Livingston, or the Snake Cays, which provide a number of sheltered anchorages another 15 miles to the NE.

CHAPTER NINETEEN

Belize and Its Barrier Reef

Quite different types of tropical cruising are in store for those who make the Inner Channel passage between Punta Gorda and Belize City, a distance of just under 100 miles, and for those deepwater skippers who may choose to sail outside the great barrier reef that stretches 118 miles northward to Ambergris Cay at the foot of Mexico's Yucatan Peninsula. The reef lies 10–22 miles off the sandy Belize shoreline and provides a broad belt of protected bank water with a wide choice of good anchorages. The entire length of the reef is skirted by small sandy cays and coral heads, inside of which lies the Inner Channel, the main southern approach to Belize City.

Outside the barrier reef, which drops off almost perpendicularly to the 100-fathom line, there are two large isolated reefs atop submerged plateaus that rise from the deep sea bed to form atolls much like those found in the South Pacific. These are Lighthouse Reef and Glover Reef, which lie 10–30 miles seaward of the barrier reef in the eastern approaches to Belize. Another group of submerged islands, Turneffe, lies beyond the 100-fathom curve between Lighthouse Reef and the entrance channel to Belize City.

Each of these areas is described in the following sections, starting with the Inner Channel, which is the preferred route for small coastal vessels and yachts making the southern approach to Belize. The northern and eastern approaches are discussed in connection with the barrier reef and the outlying reefs and islands.

THE INNER CHANNEL—PUNTA GORDA TO BELIZE CITY

With a few zigs and zags, the 100-mile Inner Channel runs almost due north and south across the easterly trade winds, in generally protected waters with controlling depths of 24–30 feet in the fairways. For the most part, the coastline is low, with long stretches of palm-fringed beaches indented by small streams, jungle rivers, lagoons, and coastal salt ponds, some of which provide lovely sheltered anchorages. There are several small coastal towns and villages, with a

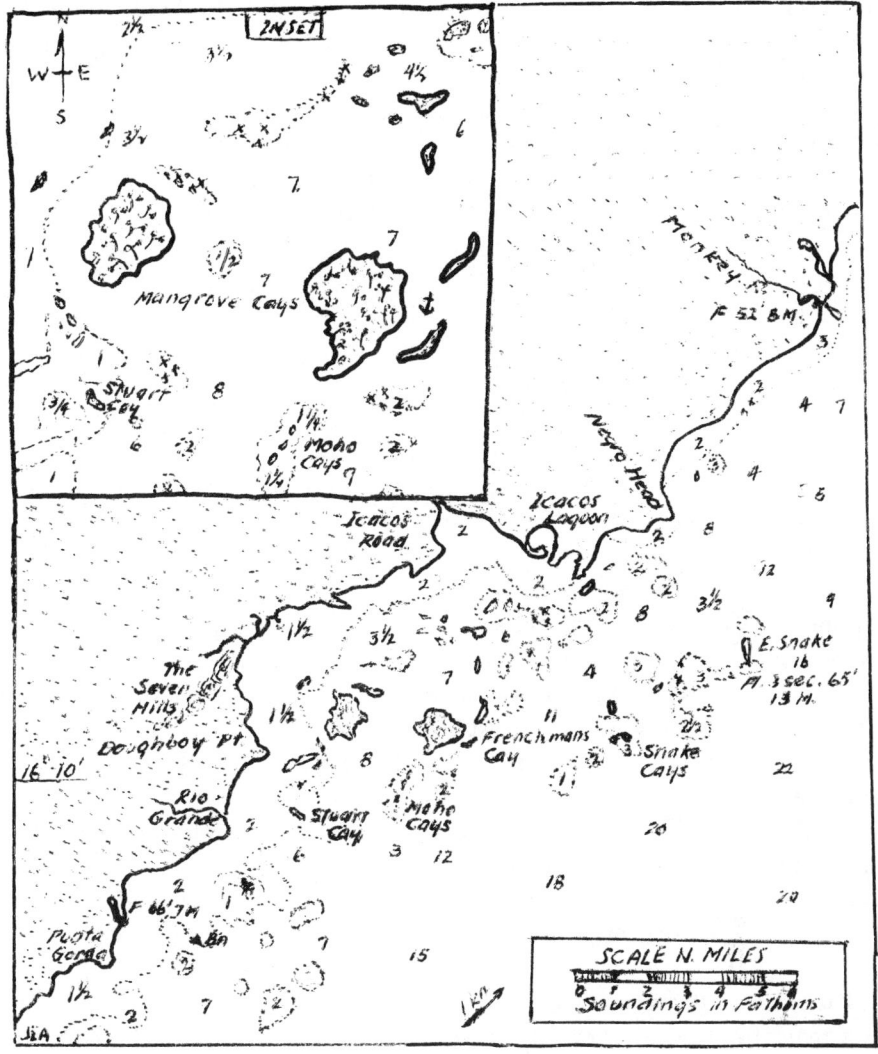

Coast of Belize, Punta Gorda to Monkey River, and outlying cays

friendly English-speaking population of mixed Indian–African–European stock. Most make their living from the sea or as plantation workers. Here the dugout canoes are called dories; they range in size from 12 feet to 30 feet or more and are used for fishing and all forms of water transportation. Some have outboards, some have sails, some are only paddled.

Most of the villages have one or more small piers, but don't expect to find fuel pumps or other yacht facilities along this waterway. Fresh water and limited provisions are usually available, but the water should be boiled for drinking purposes. There are a few small hotels or lodges along the coast, and fishing camps in the cays, but as Dorwin Teague wrote after cruising the area, "If you aren't happy unless you can get a room in a plush hotel on your vacation, don't go. Epicures will be wasting their time as the food is rough and ready, service is haphazard and supplies of most kinds are hard to obtain." On the other hand, if you are not too finicky, you will find much of interest on this primitive coast and among the unspoiled islands and cays along the waterway.

From Punta Gorda to Placentia (28160, 28166)

This section of the coast trends northeast for 38 miles, indented by several bays, rivers, and lagoons. They provide good anchorages in 2–6 fathoms. Additional anchorages may be found in the lee of numerous small cays that lie only a few miles off the shore on the eastern side of the channel. The shorefront is generally low except in the southwest where it is backed by hills that rise to heights of 400 feet to 728 feet at Gorda Hill north of Punta Gorda.

Punta Gorda (28162) is the largest town on the southern coast of Belize, with a population of about 2,000 in 1974. The anchorage is exposed to the prevailing sea breeze, and the holding ground off the T-head pier is reported to be poor. Vessels approaching the town should steer for a flagstaff behind the pier, on the grounds of the District Commissioner, or the 56-foot light on the point north of the Commissioner's residence. A depth of 5 feet may be carried alongside the pier, with 6 feet in the approach channel marked, in 1974, by a single day-beacon. The town is connected by road with the interior, and a local airline provides daily flights to and from Belize City. The town market is well worth a visit on market days. Sugar, rice and bananas are grown in the area, and the market even sells iguanas.

The Seven Hills shown on the chart a few miles NE of Punta Gorda provide a landmark for vessels entering the large bay of Port Honduras, which is sheltered from the easterly sea breeze by two groups of low islands and sandy cays. The Mangrove Cays at the SW entrance to the bay offer a number of anchorages in depths from 1–6 fathoms. The McClarys visited here in *Josefine* and found an intriguing anchorage in the lee of Frenchman's Cay, just east of the Mangrove Cays (see sketch), where an American ex-Navy man named Dick Moore has a house surrounded by all sorts of exotic plants and livestock. He's a colorful character and a first-class cook. Approach from NE on 235°, lie off the island, and sound your horn.

The Bedford Cays lie about 3 miles N of Mangrove and Frenchman's Cays with anchorage in 2–4 fathoms.

Main Street, Punta Gorda, on a showery day

The Seven Hills near Punta Gorda, Belize

Icacos Point is the southern tip of a long tongue of land that extends S of Punta Negra to form a snug little cove on its western side with depths of 9–15 feet inside and pine trees along the shore. Just westward of the cove is a narrow channel with 7 feet in the entrance leading into Icacos Lagoon, a completely landlocked basin.

The Snake Cays are four little wooded islets about 3 to 5 miles SE of Icacos Point, surrounded by a number of detached shoals providing temporary anchorage in settled weather. East Snake Cay is marked by a 65-foot concrete lighthouse.

Monkey River lies about 7 miles NE of Punta Negra, with a conspicuous light on a 54-foot white mast at the river mouth. The stream is blocked by a 2-foot bar across the entrance, and the anchorage off the small town of Monkey River is exposed and uncomfortable in strong on-shore winds. Great Monkey Cay, NNE of the town, is too small to offer much protection.

Placentia Lagoon (28166) provides some of the best anchorages on this section of the coast, with a fascinating little village on the Placentia peninsula, a sandy crescent beach, and a number of small cays on both sides of the Inner Channel. The southern approach is straightforward, with the main channel leading through The Narrows between Bugle Cay (marked by a 52-foot light) and Placentia Cay off the southern end of the peninsula. If you are making an approach from the N, you can enter through the narrow but deep channel between the crescent beach on the peninsula and the tall palm trees on Placentia Cay. Once inside, you can anchor anywhere south of the town pier and westward of the cay in 12–18 feet of clear blue water over a good-looking sand bottom. When we were there in 1974, a seagoing ketch lay quietly at anchor in the harbor, and coasting vessels often stopped on their way up or down the channel.

The town pier is usually crowded with local fishing boats, dories, and dugout canoes and there may not be room to tie alongside, although you'll be welcome for a few hours when the fishing fleet is out working on the banks. There is a refrigerated-fish storage plant at the inner end of the pier, where a narrow sandy road leads to the village between tall, waving palm trees. If you are interested in a shore meal, you will probably be directed to Mrs. Leslie's boarding house, a four-bedroom hostelry with a wide veranda overlooking the sandy beach and a central dining room where fine home-cooked meals are served by one of the Leslie granddaughters. Sea-turtle soup and fish chowders are specialties of the house. Mr. Leslie owns and operates the general store across the street, and one of the Leslie boys, a seaman anxious to get into the U.S. Navy, was working at the bar and liquor store when we were there. The

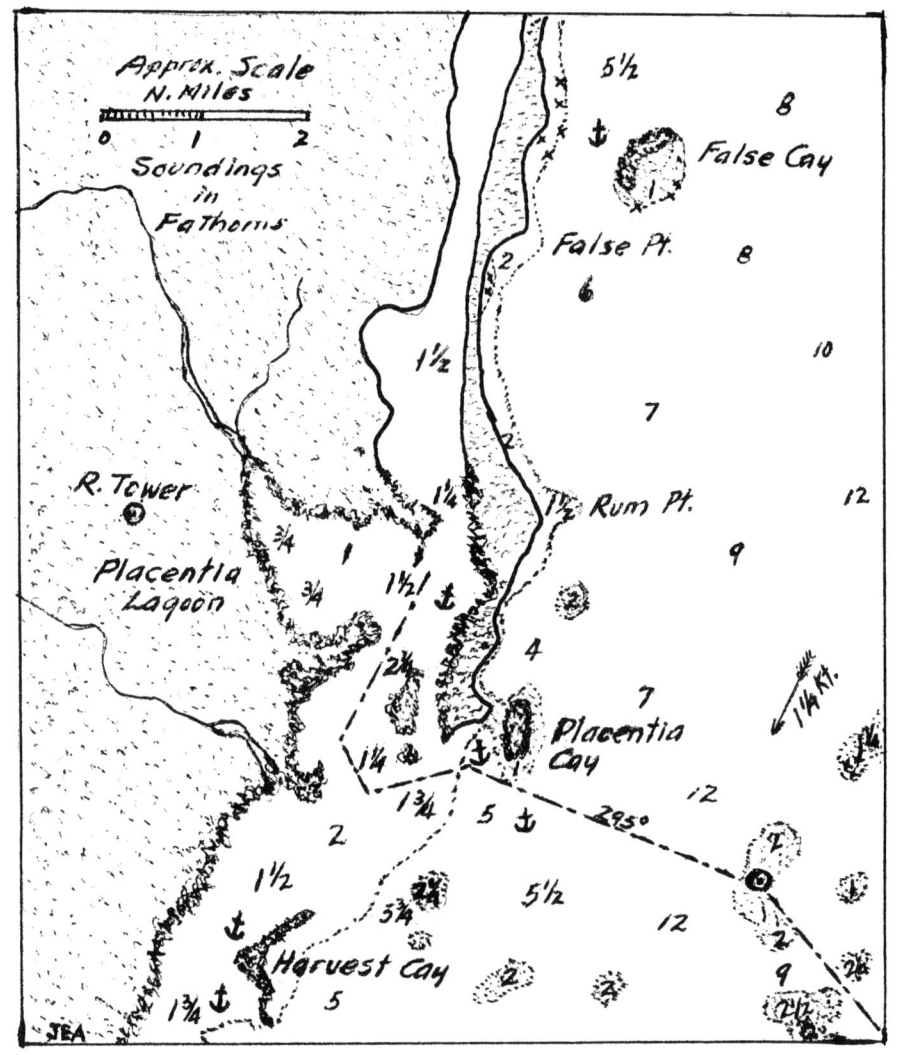

Placentia Lagoon, coast of Belize

Leslie family are of English–German ancestry and are obviously leaders in the community.

The village of Placentia occupies the sandy spit behind the crescent-shaped beach; most of its white framed houses are perched high above the ground on piles to keep them from flooding when tropical storms sweep across the penin-sula. The houses are laid out in neat rows on either side of the "main street"— actually a sandy path traveled by nothing larger than a jeep or Land Rover— with separate cookhouses, out-houses, and sheds scattered round about. The population, about 400, is typical of the coastal villages—a mixture of English,

Scotch, Irish, Spanish, Black Carib, Mayan, and African stock. Fishing and processing frozen fish for market are the principal occupations. Many families have relatives living in the U.S. or working abroad, and some of the men are employed on the large banana plantation recently acquired by the United Brands Company.

At the north end of the white crescent beach, there is a small tourist resort owned and operated by Jim Gavagan, an American, who also has a Howard Chapelle-designed charter schooner, *Leprechaun*, which is known all along the Belize coast. Jim is undoubtedly one of the best authorities on cruising this area, and should be consulted about anchorages and navigational problems if you can find him. Unfortunately, we missed seeing him on our visit in 1974, and he's often hard to find if he's out cruising in *Leprechaun*. An American family owns the conspicuous waterfront house on Rum Point, NE of the Gavagan cottages.

The lagoon at Placentia is a long, shallow estuary extending about 10 miles N and S behind the sandy peninsula. The shoreline near the entrance and well into the lagoon is low, swampy and covered with mangroves, but affords good all-weather protection that is particularly welcome in a norther or strong

The anchorage in Placentia Lagoon off the Town Dock

easterly trades. Chart 28166 shows depths ranging from ½ to 2 fathoms in the southern part of the lagoon, but we found too many discrepancies to use the chart with any assurance. (Big Creek, which is used by commercial vessels, is not shown at all.) However, with careful sounding it is possible to take vessels drawing 6 feet to protected anchorages far into the lagoon. Starting from the deep water westward of Placentia Cay, we kept about 100 yards S of Little Harvest Cay (identified only as "Cay" on the chart) before turning northwesterly for ½-mile toward a conspicuous clump of tall palm trees on the western shore, then heading NNE for about 2 miles into the lagoon. But we'd recommend using a local guide for your first trip into the lagoon.

The channel into Big Creek is marked with day beacons and carries 7 feet over the bar, with depths of 9–12 feet in the creek. There's a wooden wharf near the airstrip about a mile upstream. Maya Airways had daily flights to Belize when we were there.

Other interesting anchorages in the Placentia area may be found S and W of Harvest Cay, which is easily identified by the tall stand of palm trees SW of the Big Creek entrance channel, with sandy beaches and unspoiled tropical foliage. The Bugle Cays, 3½ miles SE of Placentia Cay, are four little wooded islets providing temporary anchorage on the eastern side of the Inner Channel.

Placentia to Belize City (28166, 28167)

The 60-mile coastline between Placentia and Belize City is generally low and marshy in spots, with long stretches of yellow sandy beachfront intersected by small rivers, creeks, and lagoons backed by wooded hills a few miles inland. From Placentia northward, the Inner Channel widens gradually into a broad sound, free of hidden dangers and sheltered by the barrier reef and its fringing islands, cays, and rocks. For coasting schooners and cruising yachts, it's an exhilarating daylight sail up or down the channel, with the trade winds abeam, a blue sky overhead, and sparkling clear water on the bank. In settled weather, the channel is relatively simple to navigate, despite the paucity of navigational aids, and one has a choice of safe temporary anchorages along the coast or under the lee of islands and cays on the reef. In a winter norther or hard easterly blow, however, there's no good protection on the reef and very few all-weather anchorages on the coast. Cruising skippers should be particularly careful to keep track of their position at all times in this area, and to know what anchorages may be within reach during an unexpected blow.

Sapodilla Lagoon (28166) is the only fully protected harbor on this section of the coast. It's about 16 miles N of Placentia. Its narrow entrance is difficult to see from midchannel, but the general location can be identified by houses in the small village of All Pines about a mile N of the entrance and by the extensive pine ridges, 50 to 100 feet high, behind the lagoon. There are depths of 6–12 feet inside the entrance, with good anchorage just west of the southern sandy spit or near the tiny cay N of the entrance. The lagoon is fed by a fresh-water stream known as Cabbage Haul Creek.

Sittee Island (28166) is a small cay off the mouth of the Sittee River about 4 miles NE of the entrance to Sapodilla Lagoon. It provides some protection in a norther. It is marked by a 30-foot light. Coastal vessels anchor SW of the island and S of the river bar in depths of 18–30 feet. Yachts drawing up to 6 feet are much better off in Sapodilla Lagoon.

Stann Creek (28166) is the largest town on this section of the coast, fronting the Inner Channel about 10 miles NNE of Sittee Island. There is a 400-foot jetty at the N end of the town that is used by local boats. The anchorage off the town is exposed to winds from N to E to S, but is not uncomfortable in settled weather. Limited provisions are available in the town, which extends along the waterfront for about a mile. The District Commissioner has his office here, and there are several small tourist facilities that serve meals. North of Stann Creek the coast trends NNW past Colson Point and the Manatee River, which leads into a large lagoon, but the entrance bar is very shallow and prevents access to boats drawing over 3 feet. There are no anchorages in the 30-mile coastal section between Stann Creek and Belize City.

Islands and cays on the eastern side of the main channel provide shelter for vessels making the passage between Placentia and Belize City, and those closest to the channel may be approached safely in fair weather with good visibility. They carry intriguing names like Coco Plum Cay, Crawl Cay, Sandfly Cay, and believe it or not, Wee Wee Cay! Not all of them are as attractive as they sound, for a goodly number of them are low mangrove islets often surrounded by flats and coral heads. In local parlance, these are known as "wet" cays. Dorwin Teague described the difference between "wet" and "dry" cays in an article in *Yachting* (March, 1970): "Dry cays are those like Laughing Bird cay, all sand and palm trees; wet cays are mangrove-covered and impenetrable, with the mangrove growing directly out of the water."

We'll have more to say about wet and dry cays when we describe the barrier reef in a later section of this chapter. Here it is sufficient to say that there are several good dry cays on the channel side of the reef bank. We don't attempt to name them individually, because they are difficult to identify from the chart and even more difficult to distinguish one from another when seen from a distance. The British *Pilot* gives a good description of some of the best cays in its sections covering the reef and Inner Channel, and the charts often indicate

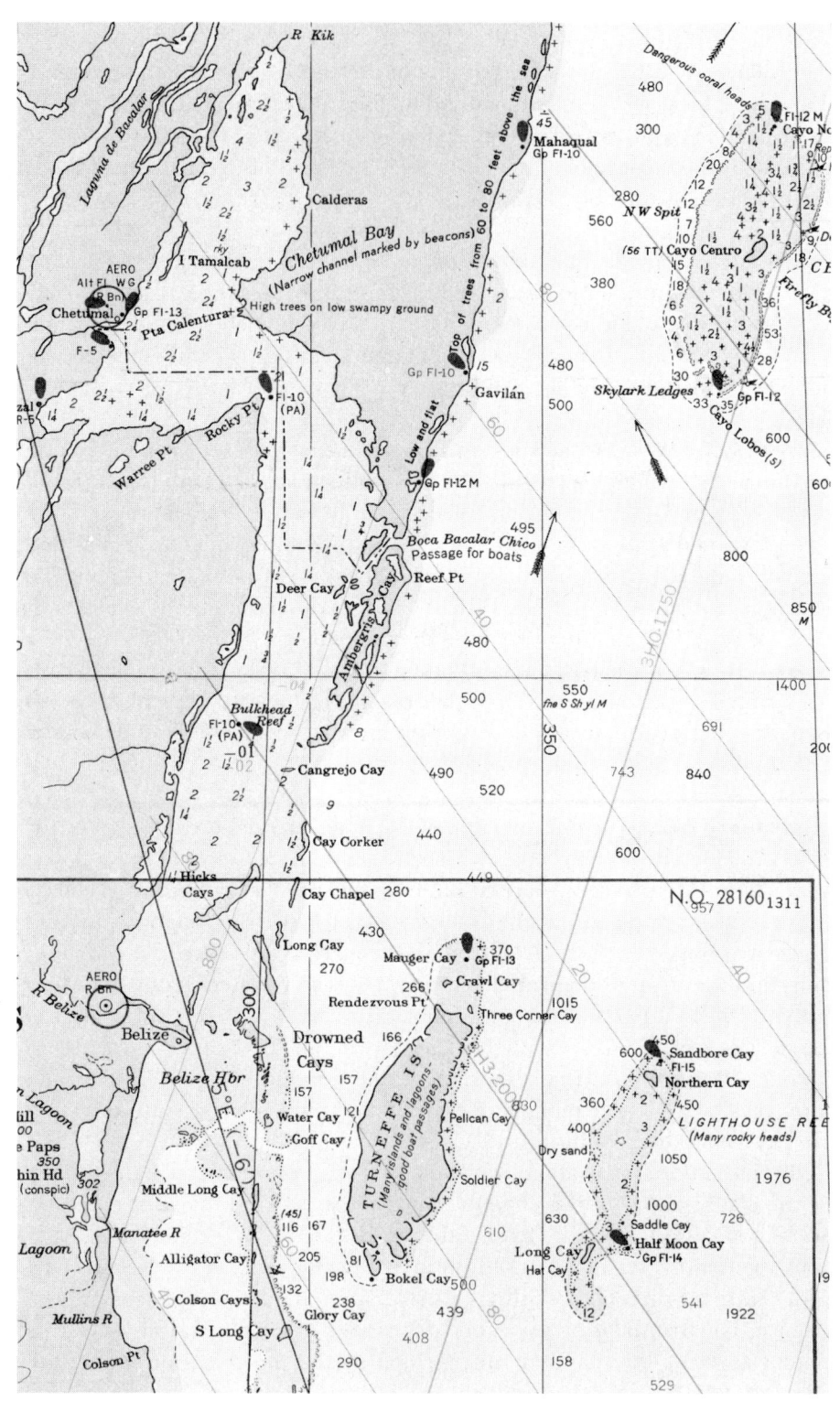

Belize's off-lying reefs and cays

those that have conspicuous palms or other trees, showing that they are more than wet mangrove cays. But as we've pointed out before, the charts cannot be depended upon and are unreliable guides once you are off the fairways of the Inner Channel. The configuration of many of the islands has changed radically in the century or more since the original British surveys were made in the 1830s and 1840s. Several large islands north of Belize have actually been cut into two or more small islands, so that you may now follow a deep channel directly across what the chart still shows as dry land.

We don't want these necessary words of caution to discourage you from keeping a sharp lookout for tall palms and sandy patches of beach if you sail along the eastern side of the fairway. Some of your most likely sightings may turn out to be the tall trees on Crawl Cay, about 4 miles E of the main channel line opposite Rocky Point on the Placentia peninsula, where our friend Dave Kimball once found boa constrictors, or the 50-foot trees on the largest of the Pelican Cays, about 4 miles northward. Kimball, who explored the cays for two months from an inflatable outboard boat, found hundreds of boobies, pelicans, and other water birds nesting on tiny Man-of-War Cay, a mile E of Coco Plum Cay.

APPROACHES TO BELIZE CITY (28167)

The approach from the south on the Inner Channel is clearly marked and presents no problems. North of Stann Creek the main fairway is wide and clear, with depths ranging from 6 to 10 fathoms until you sight the 42-foot light N of Grennels Cay, where soundings drop off to 2 to 5 fathoms for the remaining 8 miles through Belize Harbor and the roadstead off the city.

If you know the worst about Belize Harbor and its open roadstead before you arrive, perhaps the anchorage and shoreside facilities may not seem as disappointing as they do to most visiting yachtsmen. But after cruising in clear bank waters or arriving from a hard ocean passage outside the reefs, you're bound to feel somewhat depressed when you drop your anchor in the dirty, murky-brown waters off the mouth of Haulover Creek and scan the dilapidated waterfront in search of the Customs House. Even with forewarning, it's hard to believe that this is the principal port of what was formerly British Honduras. Deeper-draft vessels are required to anchor from 1½ to 2 miles off the entrance SW of Fort George on the north shore of the river, but yachts drawing 6–7 feet can approach to within 400 yards of the white light tower on the point or about the same distance off the Fort George Hotel. The Customs House is just inside the mouth of the river, readily identified by its flagstaff and orange-red rooftop. A patrol boat or pilot vessel is usually moored in the entrance, with small boats lying alongside the Customs House wharf and bulkhead.

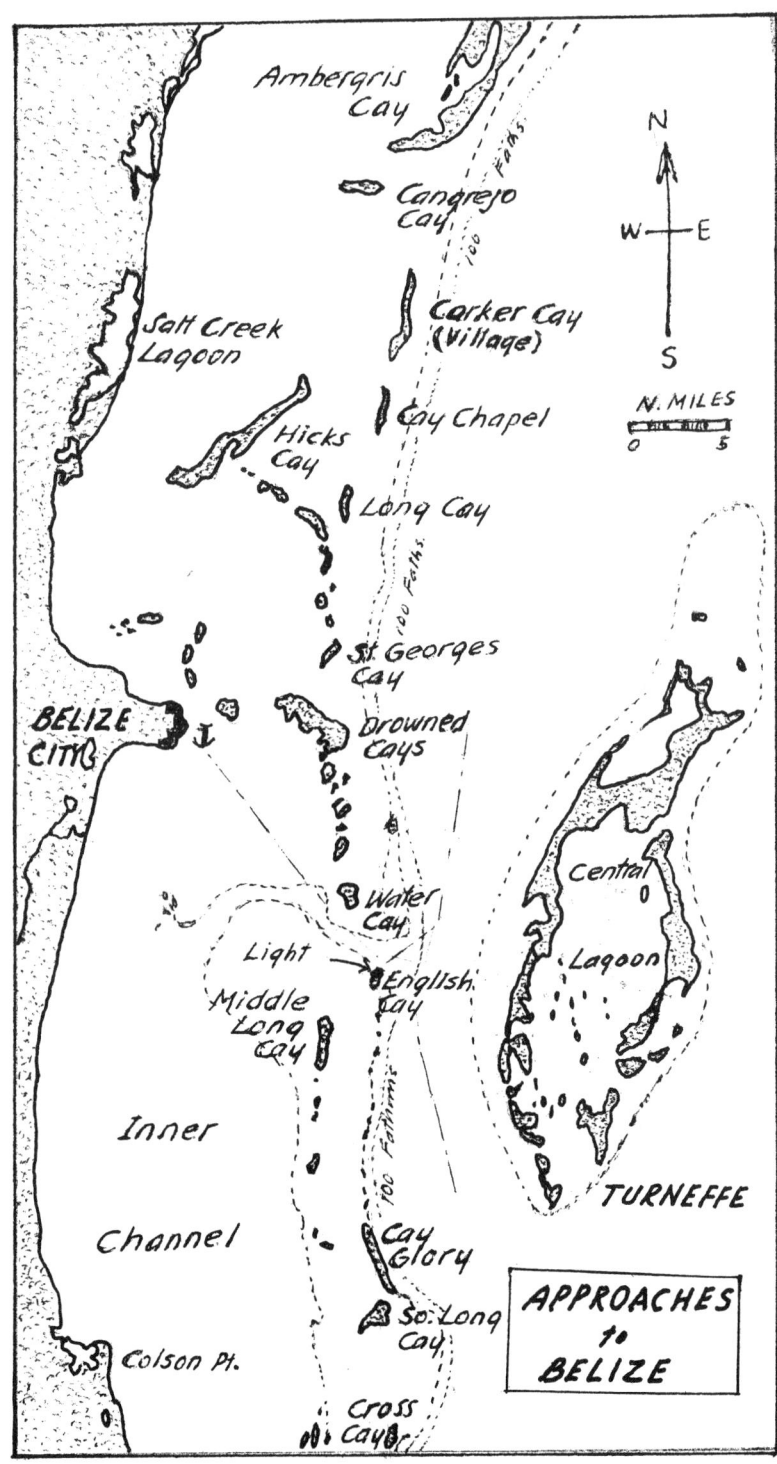

Ambergris Cay

Cangrejo Cay

100 Fms

N
W   E
S

Carker Cay
(Village)

Salt Creek
Lagoon

Cay Chapel

N. MILES
0   5

Hicks
Cay

Long Cay

100 Faths.

St. Georges
Cay

BELIZE
CITY

Drowned
Cays

Central

Water
Cay

Light

English
Cay

Lagoon

Middle
Long
Cay

Inner

100 Fathoms

TURNEFFE

Channel

Cay
Glory

APPROACHES
to
BELIZE

Colson Pt.

So. Long
Cay

Cross
Cay

Clearance procedures are handled rather better here than in some other Central American ports. Yachts are encouraged to give advance notice of their expected time of arrival, by mail or radio when possible, and advised to remain at anchor until cleared. We went through the routine with Nick and Judy Hylton, skipper and mate of the charter yacht *Tongaroa*, which arrived when we were there in February, 1974. After waiting several hours for the customs launch to come alongside, Nick went ashore by dinghy and checked through customs without too much delay. But the immigration office is located in town on the other side of the river. Hoping to save time, Nick took his dinghy across the river and presented his documents at the immigration office, only to find that the official had already departed for the Customs House on his bicycle. Nothing could be done until he returned. So we ran back to our dinghy and returned to the Customs House to intercept the official before he left—only to find, alas, that he had already returned to *his* office. In the end, it took only a couple of hours to catch up with him and complete the business with a final and congratulatory drink at the bar in the Fort George Hotel.

The Eastern Channel to Belize Harbor (28168) is used by vessels entering from seaward through a wide opening in the barrier reef NE of English Cay, a small island with a 62-foot light structure visible for 13 miles. The winding channel is marked by lighted beacons for about 9 miles to One Man Channel, leading NW into the harbor. Yachts drawing 7 feet or less can steer a course of 325°T from the second beacon W of English Cay across "The Flat" directly to Fort George, a distance of about 8½ miles, as shown in the accompanying sketch. Licensed Belize pilots have a station at English Cay.

Fort George Anchorage is protected from the easterly trade winds by the Drowned Cays, a group of low mangrove islands 5 miles to the E behind the reef, but it is exposed to northers and uncomfortable in a blow. The current generally sets southward through the harbor at about 1½ knots, but during northers the rate may increase to 2½ or 3 knots. Under such conditions, yachts may find it more comfortable in Siburn Bight, SW of the city. Northers are most apt to occur during November and December, according to the *Sailing Directions*, but they may come with a cold front at any time during the winter months and last two or three days. We encountered one with Force 8 winds in late February, preceded by several days of almost flat calms.

Belize City, formerly the capital of British Honduras, has a population of about 40,000, nearly a third of the total population of the country. The city is built on low, swampy land, in some places no more than 2 feet above sea level, and has suffered severely from hurricanes. Hurricane *Hattie* swept a 10-foot tidal wave over the city on October 31, 1961, causing such great damage and

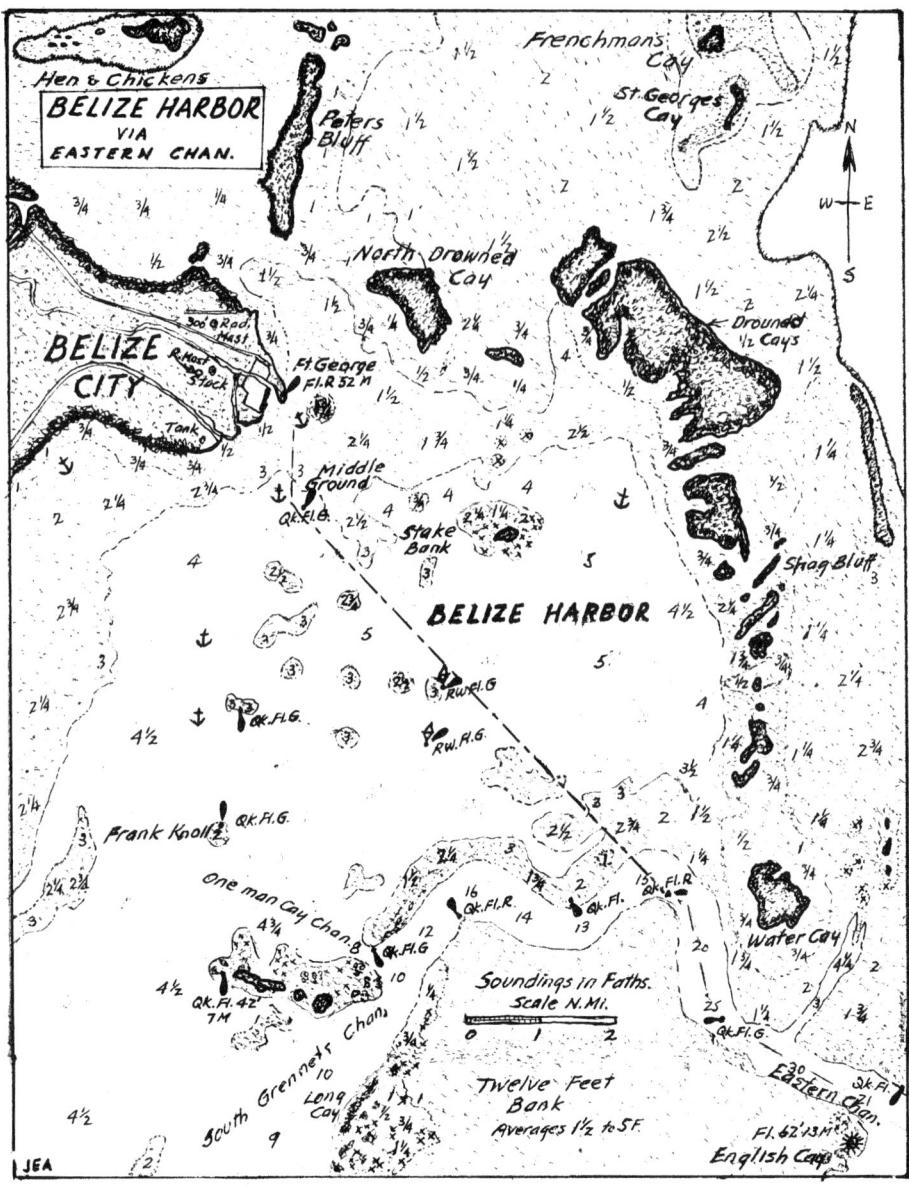

loss of life that the capital and many government offices were moved 50 miles inland, where the new capital is still under construction at Belmopan. Most of the people remained in the old city, however, rebuilding their clapboard houses on piles and mahogany posts on the same narrow streets on both sides of Haulover Creek. Two bridges connect the two parts of the city, with the town center and market on the south side and larger residences and several foreign consulates on the north side. There are two tourist hotels, the Fort George on

The bridge over Haulover Creek, Belize City

the north point and the Bellevue facing the river on the south shore. The Fort George has a small landing dock that may be reached by dinghy from boats anchored off the point.

English is the official language, although Spanish is widely spoken throughout the city and countryside. The people are of mixed racial origins, with African and Afro-Europeans accounting for about 60 percent of the total population; Mayan and Mestizo (Spanish-Maya) 26 percent; Afro-Carib about 7 percent; British and other European 4 percent, and East Indians and Asiatics the remaining 3 percent.

Boat facilities are limited, despite the large number of local fishing craft, canoes, dories, tugs, barges and lighters seen in the river mouth. Fishing sloops up to 40 feet in length are moored bow-and-stern to stakes below the first bridge in the river, and lighters unload cargo at wharfs along the north shore. Sugar is loaded onto barges at a large dock and warehouse between the Customs House and the bridge. Fuel and water may be obtained at two filling stations, both on the north side of the river, one below the bridge, the other just above it. We don't recommend bringing yachts into the river, which is shallow, crowded, and very dirty. There is seldom room to tie alongside the bulkhead at either of the filling stations, or at the market dock on the south side by the bridge, except with a dinghy. So if you require fuel, it's best to carry your own

Native fishing boats moored off the market, Belize

portable tanks, have them filled at the gas station, and take them back to your boat by dinghy.

There are several shipyards with repair facilities above the first bridge on the river. Belize has had a reputation for boatbuilding, and most of the yards have had some experience in building or repairing yachts. The fine Honduras mahogany of former years is becoming scarce but is still available in limited quantities, and skilled carpenters and shipwrights have not yet disappeared entirely. When we were there, the U.S. Consul, Robert Driscoll, was having a classic Atkin-designed sloop built at one of the yards; he hoped to sail it back to the States at the end of his tour of duty. The hull we saw would compare favorably in workmanship with anything we've seen done by the few remaining wooden-boat builders in the U.S. All parts, machinery, and fittings have to be imported, however, and if your own spare-parts kit doesn't have what you need, you'll have a difficult time indeed in getting replacements of any kind in Belize.

The cays north of Belize (28167) are worth exploring if your boat draws no more than 5 feet or if you have access to a shoal-draft outboard. The Inner Channel ends just S of Belize, and the entire bank shoals rapidly to depths of 1 and 2 fathoms over sand and mud bottom for about 25 miles on a northeasterly track a few miles inside the reef. There are no recent charts of this area, and the positions and configuration of islands shown on 28167 bear little resemblance to what you will see today. Yet these cays are interesting historically and for their close proximity to the edge of the barrier reef, where some of the finest reef fishing is found. Archeological research has disclosed evidence of early aboriginal fishing sites on several cays that were later occupied by buccaneers in the early 1600s and permanently settled by the British in the 1760s. We'd recommend using a local pilot on your first venture into these shallow waters. We found the following cays of interest.

St. George's Cay, about 7½ miles NE of Belize and 2 miles N of the Drowned Cays, was used as a buccaneer stronghold before 1650, when turtling was a favorite occupation. The earliest map of the island, in 1764, when it had been settled by British colonists, shows five large turtle pens and more than 70 houses and other structures on the tiny island, which is used today as an offshore beach colony by well-to-do residents of Belize.

Hicks Cays are an uninhabited group of mangrove cays on the flats about 9 miles NE of Belize, with little to distinguish them from dozens of other "wet" cays, except for an Indian mound that has provided rich archeological evidence of a very early pre-Columbian settlement that must have existed a long time. This is one of the best examples of how hurricanes can change the configuration of low islands and cays: the southeastern island of the Hicks Cays group was cut apart by Hurricane *Hattie* in 1961, and the main channel now leads directly through the middle of what is still shown as a single 4-mile-long mangrove cay on Chart 28167. The new channel has a controlling depth of about 5½ feet. Tugs tow barges through this cut, which is on the main water route to Chetumal Bay and the ports of Corozal and Chetumal. Someone must have had trouble squeezing through, however, as the cut is shown as "Port Stuck" on local sketch charts!

Cay Chapel, about 5 miles NE of the cut through Hicks Cays, is the first of two inhabited "dry" cays, complete with sandy beaches and waving palm groves and close to the edge of the barrier reef. Cay Chapel is the site of another aboriginal Indian village and the present-day location of a self-contained fishing and snorkeling resort. Guests are transported to the island by seaplane or boat from Belize.

Cay Corker, or "Caulker" as it was called in earlier times, is the northern of the two reef-edge cays, and the site of a native fishing village that has managed to survive successive hurricanes, keeping alive a way of life that can't be too different from that of the Indians and early European settlers. Prior to Hurricane *Hattie*, most of the 100 or more houses in the village were built along a sandy path close to the exposed eastern shoreline and a few feet back of the sandy beach. Many of these older houses were swept away in the space of 15 minutes during the 1961 blow by a series of huge surge waves that came roaring in from the reef not much more than a mile off the beach; others have replaced them, and today the "main street" has been relocated nearer the middle of the narrow neck of the island, with new houses, outbuildings, and community structures clustered along both sides. A map of the village, made during a 1965 study (*The Geography of Fishing in British Honduras*, conducted by Alan E. Craig), shows 101 structures at that time, including a "hurricane-proof" school, a "cricket pitch," a fishermen's cooperative warehouse, and several wooden piers and docks.

The village looked much the same when we were there in 1974, a few months before two hurricanes bypassed Belize but swept all the reef cays with gale force winds and high seas. We enjoyed meeting Frank Bozzell, a native of Colorado who settled on Cay Corker in the late 1960s and operates a small fishing and snorkeling camp called the Lone Jib Lodge. There you are put up in native-style houses built on piles a few yards back of the beach. Frank took us out to the edge of the reef in his small outboard on a clear calm day; you could see the beautiful coral heads rising from the sandy bottom in 2 fathoms of crystal-clear water only a stone's throw from the precipitous drop-off ledge, with depths of 100 fathoms a few hundred yards beyond. There are depths of 1½ to 2 fathoms between the reef and the eastern shore of Cay Corker, where it's safe to anchor, in settled weather, and take your dinghy ashore to one of the small piers. In a northerly or easterly blow, fishing vessels move around to the western side of the island, where there's good holding ground in an anchorage within the bight west of the village. Sometimes you'll see a sizable fleet of Creole smacks and small trading vessels lying at anchor or tied to the pier in the bight.

Fishing remains the principal occupation in all of the reef islands, and each village has inherited its own individual method of fishing from earlier times, each insisting that its system is the most successful, and refusing to change. The McClarys, who cruised here in *Josefine*, found all the people of the cays friendly and hospitable. "Theirs is a 'three-fish-a-day' culture. Living on rice and beans and fish, they are relatively untouched by 20th-century civilization."

Bahía Chetumal (BA 1204), which extends northwestward from Cay Corker to Corozal and the Rio Hondo and forms part of the border between Belize and Mexico, is a large, very shallow bay. It is poorly charted and not covered at all by any published U.S. Navy chart. Although local boats and shoal-draft barges carry cargo between Belize and Chetumal, it is not an area to attract yachts, and we have made no attempt to include sailing directions to the few ports that might be reached by cruising boats.

APPROACHES TO THE BARRIER REEF (28166, 28167)

However it is approached, whether from the N or E or S, the great barrier reef of Belize is impressive. It may not be the longest barrier reef in the western hemisphere, as the tourist brochures say, but its 118 miles of coral-fringed shelf at the edge of the Belize coastal bank offers a more formidable challenge to mariners than any comparable shorefront we know about in the Caribbean or Bahamas. For amateur skippers cruising this coast, there are three major navigational challenges: (1) to be sure of your precise position at all times in the vicinity of the reef, (2) to be able to identify small islands and cays on the edge of the bank, and (3) to pinpoint those in the vicinity of the few openings that provide safe channels onto the bank. We suggest you keep a copy of the *Pilot* aboard as a constant necessity!

Openings are shown on the charts, but as we've mentioned before, the features of the cays are so similar that it's often difficult or impossible to determine the location of critical entrance channels. The British *Pilot* for the east coasts of Central America gives a detailed description of the principal openings, but cautions its readers that the information is "only given with a view to assisting a vessel in case of necessity."

Zapotilla Cays to Gladden Spit (28160; BA 1573)

The Zapotilla Cays are a group of small islets at the southern end of the long barrier reef, about 30 miles eastward of Punta Gorda. Vessels proceeding northwestward from Puerto Cortés, on the coast of Honduras, may enter the Inner Channel through Zapotilla Cut, an opening about half a mile wide NE of Zapotilla Cay, which can be identified by a clump of coconut palms. The cut has a controlling depth of 24 feet in the channel, bounded on the NE by Low Cay and a 57-foot light structure on Hunting Cay half a mile northward. One can anchor W of Hunting Cay in 9 to 12 feet. Fishing and diving boats from Guatemala are often found here. Both cays are inhabited, and there are likely to be fishing nets and fish traps in the area.

Ranguana Entrance (28166) is the next navigable opening, about 14 miles NNE of Hunting and Nicolas Cays, in a section of the reef presenting few distinguishing features along the edge of the bank. We would not care to be caught here in a norther or a hard squall with poor visibility, since the 50-foot trees on Ranguana Cay provide the only identification nearly a mile W of the breaking edge of the reef. However, this entrance and two others to the NE are used by local vessels approaching the Inner Channel at Placentia, 15 miles NW of Ranguana entrance.

Queen Cay and Gladden Entrance (28166, Plan A) are the two most easterly openings on the entire barrier reef, about 22 miles E of Placentia. They are not easy to identify from seaward, as the edge of the reef rises steeply from depths of 400 to 600 fathoms, and the only distinguishing landmarks lie almost a mile westward of the Queen's entrance. These are the three low sandy islets covered with bushes, known as the Queen Cays. The large-scale Plan A inset is helpful, but please note that the bushes on the three cays are only 10 feet high and that the chart is based on a British survey of 1840. There are depths of 18 to 24 feet in the mile-wide Queen Cay channel and similar depths in Gladden Entrance about 3 miles NE, but the bank within both entrances is so studded with shoals, cays, and isolated coral heads as to make navigation hazardous. "Neither channel," says the British *Pilot*, "should be attempted without local knowledge or a local pilot." Yet given a competent pilot, you'll find some of the most interesting cays anywhere around in this wide section of the bank on both sides of Victoria Channel and the Inner or Main Channel.

Victoria Channel (28166) is a wide, clear waterway that starts about 5 miles westward of the Queen Cays and trends NW for about 10 miles toward its confluence with the Inner Channel just N of Crawl Cay. Dorwin Teague has written with enthusiasm of a cruise in this area aboard the 44-foot trimaran *Kyma*, which was owned by Bob Lewis of Maya Beach, a Canadian development just north of Placentia. Although *Kyma* drew only 3 feet, Teague reported several surprise encounters with uncharted coral reefs, fortunately without injury, and harmless groundings on soft sand banks, proving that while careful skippers with local knowledge can't put much dependence upon their ancient charts, they don't necessarily suffer dire consequences from going aground. Commenting on the charts, Teague noted that coral formations are shown very vaguely, and that many spots where the coral actually breaks the surface aren't shown at all. Furthermore, he said, some of the islands disappeared in former hurricanes, many of them are wrongly named on the chart, and none of them has a shape anything like the shape shown on the charts. The following cays are some (but by no means all) of those mentioned by Teague or by Dave Kimball, as being of special interest.

Moho Cay, at the southern end of Victoria Channel, about 10 miles W of Gladden Entrance, is the site of a former Indian fishing village. It's inhabited, and has fresh water.

Laughing Bird Cay, about 3½ miles SW of Moho, can be recognized from afar by its tall palm trees, which rise to a height of 95 feet.

Crawl Cay lies at the N end of a long narrow coral reef at the confluence of Victoria Channel and the Inner Channel, with depths of 75–80 feet right up to the edge of the shore. Here Dave Kimball found turtle eggs, boa constrictors, and many kinds of water birds.

Channel Cay, with its 80-foot trees, lies ENE of Crawl Cay, surrounded by deep channels with depths of 80–90 feet fringed by sand bores and coral heads.

Curlew Cay is a tiny islet with sandy beach and palm trees within a stone's throw of the edge of the reef. Curlew is privately owned by the Bowmans of Stann Creek. It's also been called Caribou and Carrie Bow Cay.

South Water Cay is a larger inhabited islet directly fronting the edge of the reef about 2 miles N of Curlew Cay. It actually forms part of the barrier reef, which drops off into deep water immediately off the beach. South Water Cut is one of the few openings in the 50-mile section of the barrier reef between Gladden Entrance and English Cay, at the entrance to Eastern Channel, which we described above as the eastern approach to Belize Harbor.

Man-O-War Cay, as its name implies, is a nesting place for frigate birds and other water fowl, including brown boobies and pelicans. When Phillips and Nancy Dean came upon this little isle in their Bermuda-40 yawl *Marelle*, they found an amazing sight: "The entire island swarmed with an incredible colony of nesting frigate birds. Anchoring just feet away from the cay, we watched enthralled as the giant birds wheeled over us. It was a nature photographer's dream come true." The cay lies between Coco Plum Cay and the Tobacco Range just S of Columbus Reef.

Tobacco Cay, at the very edge of the barrier reef N of the entrance of that name, first appears "as a sweep of white beach bearing a majestic stand of palms," as the Deans described it. Tobacco is barely a quarter of a mile long and only feet above the water, and fishermen's huts are nestled beneath the swaying trees.

Rendezvous Cay, about 5½ miles S of English Cay and the Eastern Channel, is shown on the chart as a conspicuous island with tall palms and huts, occupying the center of a wide opening in the reef. But Hurricane *Hattie* swept away most of the palm trees, and the island today is little more than a windswept sandspit.

English Cay to Ambergris Cay (28167)

From English Cay, the long, breaking fringe of the barrier reef trends northward for about 35 miles to the south end of Ambergris Cay, which borders Mexico's Yucatan Peninsula at its northern end. The reef in this section is steep-to, with only a few openings for small boats. None are safe to enter from seaward without local knowledge. All the small cays—St. George's, Cay Chapel, and Cay Corker—should be approached only from the bank side, as previously described, although it's possible to take vessels drawing 6 feet or less through several small openings in the reef between those cays.

Ambergris Cay is low and swampy, but has a long sandy beach facing the reef, which is only about half a mile offshore along parts of the eastern side of the island and even closer at the northern end. The island is separated from the mainland of Yucatan Peninsula by a shallow boat-channel called Boca Bacalar Chico, used by local fishing smacks and dories but not recommended for yachts without local knowledge. From offshore, it is difficult to see the opening and the island appears to be part of the coast.

San Pedro, the largest village on Ambergris, is fast becoming a popular beach resort town, with daily air service linking it with Belize City and Corozal. It has an attractive beach fringed with tall palms, several small resort hotels, and close access to reef fishing and snorkeling, but it lacks a protected harbor or facilities for yachts.

OUTLYING ISLANDS, REEFS, AND ATOLLS (28160)

Lying outside the great barrier reef and athwart the principal deep-sea approaches to Belize, are two large isolated reefs and the uncharted Turneffe Islands we spoke of in the introduction to this chapter. Columbus never sighted the reefs when he first approached the Gulf of Honduras in 1502, but for centuries afterward mariners from many nations found them a major navigational hazard, as numerous stranded wrecks still attest. Today they continue to present a challenge to yachtsmen who venture into these waters.

Obviously, these outlying dangers must be approached with great caution. The reefs rise suddenly, without warning, from depths of 500 to more than 1,000 fathoms, and are steep-to on all sides, so that soundings give no advance notice of shoaling. Currents often set strongly around them, and they are so low that they are seldom visible for any distance.

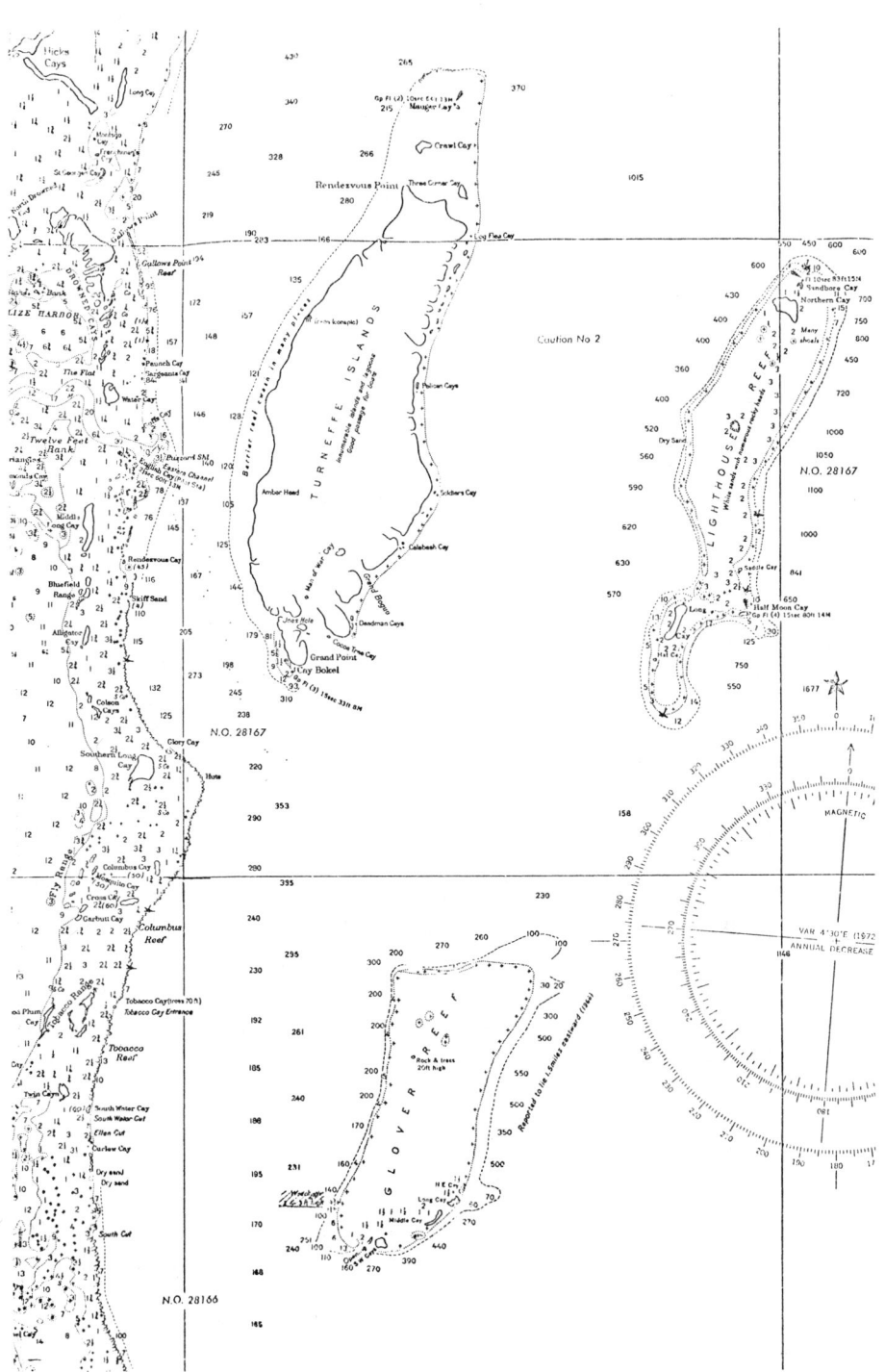

Glover and Lighthouse Reefs and Turneffe Islands and cays

Glover Reef (28166)

Named after an English buccaneer named John Glover, who operated off the coast of Belize in the early 1700s, Glover lies approximately 12 miles eastward of the barrier reef and about 40 miles southeast of Belize City. The reef is some 15 miles long from north to south and 4½ to 6 miles wide, enclosing a shallow lagoon of about 80 square miles. Seen from a high-flying aircraft, it looks more like a South Pacific atoll than anything you are likely to see anywhere else in the Caribbean. Geologically, it was formed by coral growing around the edges of a steep limestone plateau that was flooded by the sea after the last glacial period; as the sea level contined to rise, the coral growth kept pace with it, until today it is 700 feet thick, forming a wall 44 miles long that drops off steeply to the sea bed all around the rim of the reef. Some 24 different species of coral have been identified, and the reef is still growing and changing its shape. The northeast side was reported to be extending eastward in 1969, and must be given a wide berth. In fact, this edge of the reef is now reported to lie 1.5 miles eastward of its charted position!

Inside the elliptical rim of the reef, the pale-green waters of the lagoon show depths of 1 to 3 or more fathoms over a sandy bottom. The only opening permitting entrance into the lagoon is at the extreme southern end of the reef, southwest of five small sandy cays with palm trees and other tropical growth. Phil and Nancy Dean sailed their 40-foot Hinckley yawl *Marelle* out from Belize in the spring of 1972 and were fascinated by the natural beauty of the lagoon and its fringing reef. Here they met Gil and Marsha Lomont, who operate an unusual fishing and scuba-diving resort located at Glover Reef Village on Long Cay about 5 miles northeast of the opening. Here they have built 12 cabins and an open-air dining room just off a sandy spit that drops off steeply to the 100-fathom line. The Lomonts can take up to 24 guests at a time. They have no electricity, flush toilets, or hot water, but offer a lot of privacy, good seafood, and some of the best fishing and reef diving anywhere in the Caribbean. Guests are brought out from Belize by seaplane or boat, and yachtsmen are welcome to anchor off the dock on Long Cay. The Lomonts keep a radio watch on 2638 kHz and 2182 kHz.

Lighthouse Reef (28167)

Situated about 13 miles NNE of the northern tip of Glover, Lighthouse Reef is the outermost of the offshore islands and shoals. Like Glover, it is completely surrounded by its own barrier reef, which forms a lagoon with several islands and small cays. The reef is about 22 miles long and 2 to 5 miles wide; the only navigable openings are at the southern end, west of Half Moon Cay, where there is a lighthouse. The British *Pilot* reminds mariners to ap-

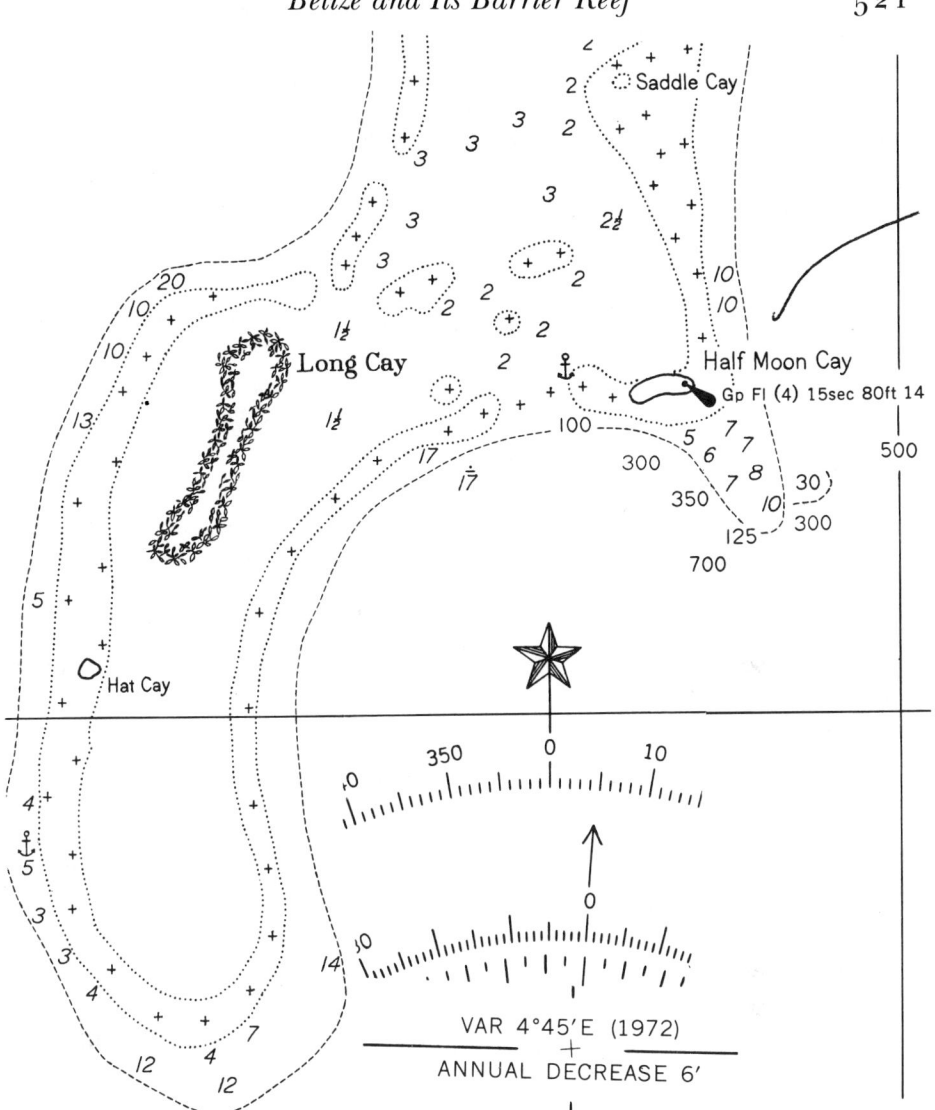

Approaches to Half Moon Cay, Lighthouse Reef

proach with caution, as the only chart of this reef is an enlargement of a survey made in 1830.

Half Moon Cay is about 10 feet high and covered with trees and bushes. The light structure is a 70-foot white metal tower, and there is a lighthouse keeper on the island. The anchorage NW of the island is exposed, with an uncomfortable surge in almost any weather, but there is said to be good holding ground in depths of 2 to 5 fathoms off the sandy beach on the S side of Half Moon Cay, giving better protection from the normal trade winds. The entrance into the lagoon is about half a mile westward of the cay, with depths of 2 fathoms, but keep a sharp watch for numerous coral heads around the cay.

Hat Cay is a tiny sandy islet on the SW side of the reef, where temporary anchorage may be found under the lee of the cay in prevailing easterly winds.

The Blue Hole near the center of the lagoon is a remarkable natural phenomenon, now part of an Underwater National Park. Jacques Cousteau spent a month on *Calypso* here in 1971, filming a sequence for his TV program. The "hole" is a deep circular pit surrounded by a rim of coral that rises to the surface of the lagoon. The hole was originally said to be "bottomless," but lead-line soundings have shown depths of 464 feet, and divers have found a huge underwater cavern with stalactites, some of them 40 feet long, hanging from the ceiling. The rim of the Blue Hole is 1,000 feet in diameter and is clearly visible from aircraft flying over the reef.

Sandbore Cay is a small wooded island at the northern end of Lighthouse Reef, with a red-and-white metal light structure at the end of a jetty off the N shore of the cay. The chart shows what appears to be an opening in the reef ½-mile N of the light, but there is a wreck in the entrance, and a warning note: "Many rocks, shoals, and coral formations exist in the north end of the reef." We don't recommend entering here or exploring nearby Northern Cay without a local pilot, although the chart shows depths of 1 to 2 fathoms in the lagoon.

Turneffe Islands and Cays (28167)

This large group of low mangrove islands and cays lies between Lighthouse Reef and the main barrier reef off Belize. It covers an area almost 30 miles long from north to south and from 3 to 10 miles wide, completely surrounded by its own barrier reef. The mangrove islands are so close together that from seaward they look like a single island. Although there are several openings leading into interior channels and lagoons, they are uncharted and should only be entered with a competent local guide. The only aids to navigation are a 64-foot light on Mauger Cay, at the northern end of the Turneffe barrier reef, and a 33-foot light structure on Cay Bokel at the southern end of the archipelago. The 100-fathom curve is close to the fringing reef, which is awash at many places.

Cay Bokel (28167, Plan) is a tiny islet with sandy beach and palm trees, lying just off the SW corner of the reef, with an anchorage charted from a British survey in 1921. There's a fishing lodge there, operated by Bill Hare. The anchorage looks good on the chart and sounds good from the *Pilot*, but Dorwin Teague's description of their arrival in *Kyma*, in 1969, leaves one with lingering doubts about the approach channel and the nature of the holding ground:

We got to Turneffe around sunset where a long tortuous channel marked by small stakes leads into the very fancy fishing camp of Cay Bokel. We groped our way to within sight of the Cay Bokel docks, where a large cruiser was tied, but finally went hard on the bottom in the dusk a quarter-mile short of our goal. As usual, *Kyma* [drawing 3 feet] churned her way off and anchored in shallow water with a grassy bottom. Sure enough, the wind came up during the night, the anchor dragged again, and we blew aground next to a mangrove island around midnight.

With a bit of kedging, *Kyma* was backed off in the morning without damage, but the grassy bottom and uncharted channels on the shoal bank appear to make Cay Bokel something less than an ideal anchorage. However, it continues to be a popular rendezvous point for Belize sportfishermen, and it was formerly an important anchorage for commercial fishermen, who combed the channels of Turneffe for spiny lobster and turtles.

CHAPTER TWENTY

Mexico's Quintana Roo

This wild and almost roadless eastern part of Mexico's Yucatan Peninsula, its miles on miles of straight coastline made up of powdery sand hills and turquoise lagoons, would hardly be known today were it not for Cozumel, the sportfishing mecca and low-key resort island a few miles off its northeastern shore. But in this day and age, such enticing areas cannot long retain their natural state, and sleepy Cozumel, which recently sprouted its own high-rises and a real marina, is already mightily overshadowed by another island just up the coast, Cancún by name, where big government has masterminded and put up the ante for a huge resort and residential complex: a sort of eastern Acapulco, but without the cliffs and mountainous backdrop.

Mysterious Yucatan, which saw the rise and fall of the mighty Mayan Empire, now lives to see the rise of a tourist empire, with all the civilized trappings this entails, and cruising there will never again be quite the adventure it once was, although there is still the formidable Yucatan Channel to cross to reach it.

Here you will probably contract "Mayan Fever," which is the natural and healthy desire to see, and let your imagination be titillated by, the baffling ruins left by a cultured and progressive people who, having been a nation for a thousand years, simply disappeared from the face of the earth even before the Spaniards arrived to "Christianize" and decimate the Indians. Apparently the Mayans were a hyper-religious people in their own way, for it is said that quite apart from the cities that have been unearthed, the whole Yucatan countryside remains literally unscratched and that temples can be found in the underbrush all over this flat land if only you have the tenacity to hack your way through it. Temples and other remnants of their civilization along the shore have already been vandalized; you have to go further back into the hinterland now. Incidentally, earthmoving for the Cancún development has turned up Mayan ruins.

If you've got a day to spare, a guide can take you on horseback to temple ruins on the weather side of Cozumel, or you can fly to Tulum, on the mainland coast, said to have been a Mayan seaport, although this seems a rather grandiose claim since there isn't even an indentation in the coast here. The ruins themselves have been dutifully excavated; you can get a glimpse of what this walled town

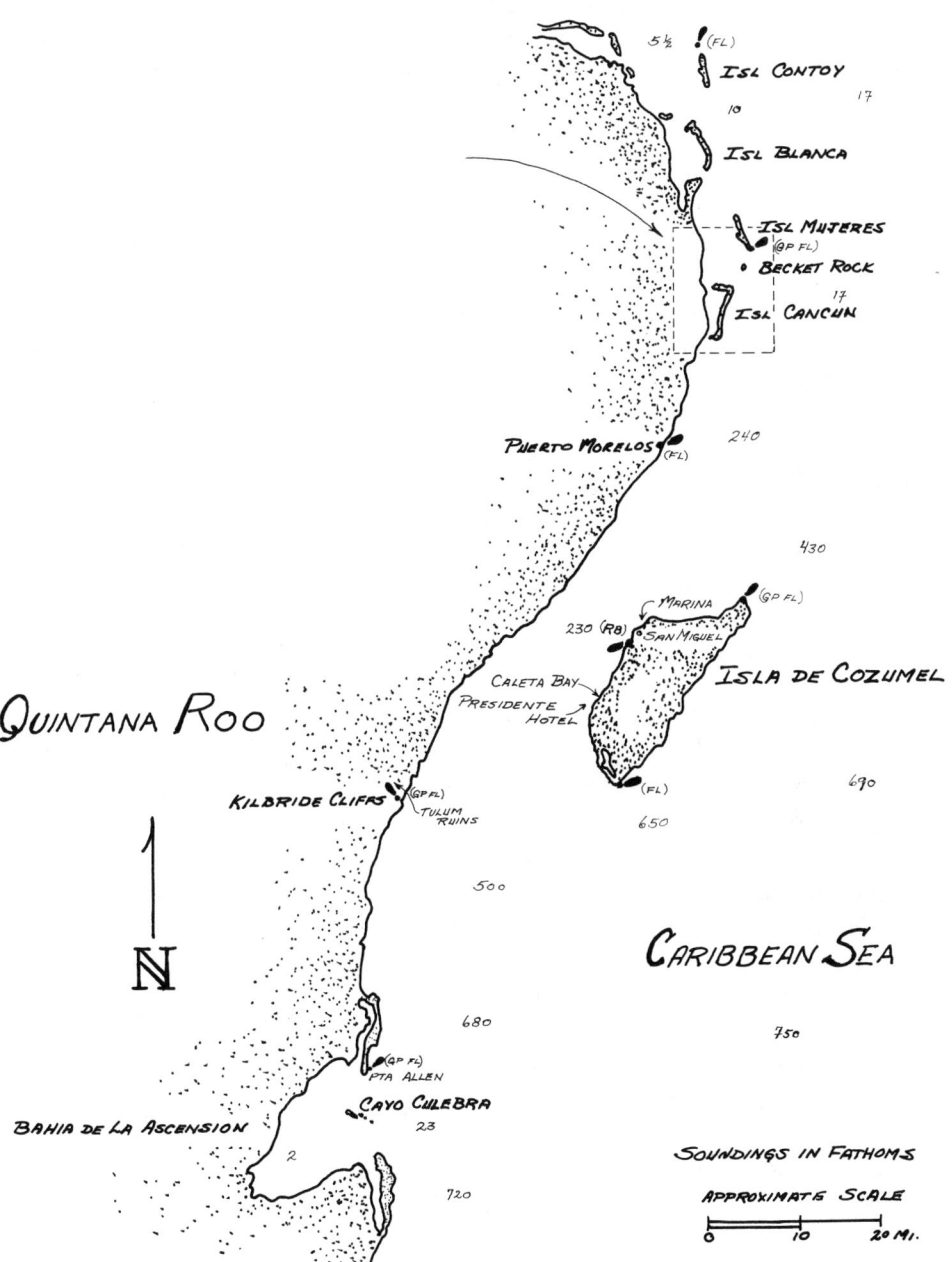

THE YUCATAN COAST

ISLA CONTOY TO CAYO CULEBRA

5½ ! (FL)

ISL CONTOY

17

10

ISL BLANCA

ISL MUJERES
(GP FL)

BECKET ROCK

17

ISL CANCUN

PUERTO MORELOS
(FL)

240

430

MARINA (GP FL)

230 (R B)

SAN MIGUEL

ISLA DE COZUMEL

CALETA BAY
PRESIDENTE
HOTEL

QUINTANA ROO

690

KILBRIDE CLIFFS (GP FL)
TULUM
RUINS

(FL)

650

500

N

CARIBBEAN SEA

680

750

(GP FL)
PTA ALLEN

CAYO CULEBRA

23

BAHIA DE LA ASCENSION

2

720

SOUNDINGS IN FATHOMS

APPROXIMATE SCALE

0   10   20 MI.

might have been like in its heyday. The main temple, with its carvings to the upside-down god, stands high on the cliff and is an inspiring sight.

Further afield, Mérida is the center for sightseeing other Mayan city sites, notably Chichén Itzá, Uxmal, and Dzibilchaltún.

Our search for cruising experiences along the southern part of this coast has been singularly unsuccessful, for most yachts seem to run the 185 miles direct from Cay Corker to Cozumel. There are however, at least a couple of shelters along this route.

Banco Chinchorro (28000 or 28015) obviously offers protection along its western side, but we have no reports from yachts having put in there. The above small-scale charts are of little help, and the U.S. *Sailing Directions* give no directions at all. The British *Pilot*, on the other hand, gives quite a complete description of the bank but does not go into detail on the anchoring possibilities for small craft, except to mention that there are several openings for eyeballing through the reef into the lagoon in a 3½-mile stretch NW of Cayo Lobos, a very low sand and coral islet with a light structure on it.

Skylark Ledges, which dry, lie about ½-mile W of Cayo Lobos. Blackford Ledge, always awash, is about 2 miles WNW of Lobos.

Bahía de la Ascensión (28015) may be entered through a wide opening in the barrier reef N of the group of mangrove cays (Cayos Culebra) which lie in the mouth of the bay. Enter through a position about 2½ miles SE of Punta Nicchehabin, but beware a dangerous rock about 1½ cables SW of the drying reef to starboard of the entrance.

The McClarys on *Josefine* passed through this cut in the.reef "with everyone pointing out coral heads at once, and found a quiet anchorage off Punta Allen," which is Punta Nicchehabin, with a light on a framework tower.

Some 25 miles N of Ascensión stand the impressive and quite well-preserved ruins of Tulum already mentioned. This "seaport" has a short beach N of the highest temple, where hardy canoes could be hauled up through the surf, but we do not recommend anchoring off the reef and mounting a dinghy excursion except in calm conditions. You would do better to make a day of it by flying from Cozumel or taking a tour from Cancún.

Isla de Cozumel (28015) is low, flat and surprisingly dull considering its prominence as a resort, but until Cancún is opened up, it is the last (or the first) port of any consequence between the western Caribbean and Florida.

The anchorage off San Miguel, the only town, is safe and comfortable in settled easterly weather, although it is an open roadstead. In the winter, northers have to be considered. The bottom is hard sand, but the water is so clear you can make a snorkel check to make sure your anchor has dug in.

Tulum—Mayan "seaport"

Perfect shelter will be found in the government-run marina, which has been dredged from a lagoon about 1½ miles N of town and only slightly N of the airport. The entrance is narrow, and allowance must be made for the probability of a strong north-setting crosscurrent. Water, electricity, and fuel are all here, but there is apt to be congestion, since the marina is filled with fishermen and local yachts. So be prepared for some tight maneuvering and the possibility of having to drop anchor and moor stern-to just inside the entrance.

Hang up your Q flag, telephone the Port Captain's office, and wait patiently. At Cozumel you must let *them* find *you*, not the other way around.

If you are adventurous and draw less than 5½ feet, you might try Caleta Bay, which is about 8 miles S of town and a few hundred yards N of the towering El Presidente Hotel. The entrance is narrow and obstructed by some massive boulders; they are, however, easily seen in the clear water. The cove itself is some 200 yards in diameter, with a rocky perimeter to which you will moor Med-fashion. You can use the amenities of the swank El Presidente, rent a car in the lobby there, or use buses and taxis to get to town.

Cancun Resort Area

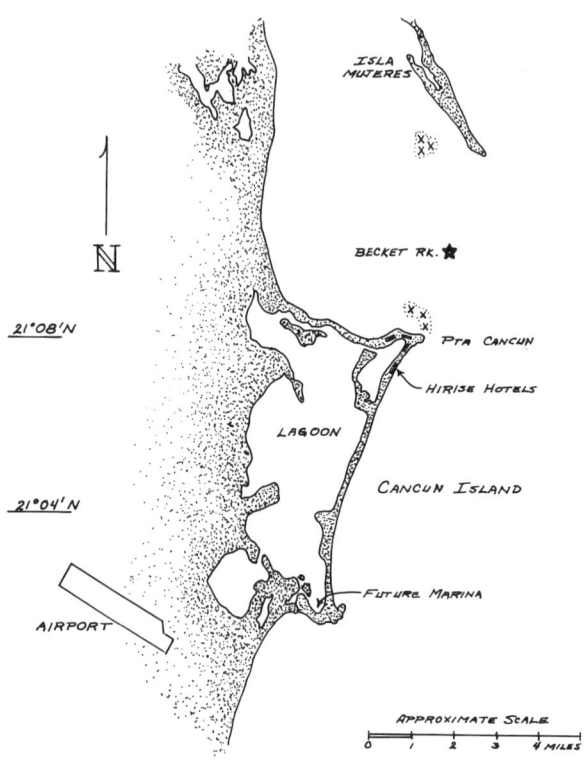

Cancún (28015) is a skinny, L-shaped island about 9 miles long, separated from the mainland by a lagoon and well endowed with beaches of powdery white sand. In coming years it will be of major significance to yachtsmen, at least to those seeking sleek marina facilities and resort amenities on the grand scale.

About nine hotels have already opened their doors, and Fonatur, the government agency which has masterminded this ambitious development, has indicated that some accommodation for yachts will have been completed by the end of 1977. For the latest advice on what to expect here, call the Cancún Information Bureau in New York, (212) 421-9220, or write them at 485 Madison Ave., New York, N.Y. 10022.

Miles and miles of sandy coast stretch S to Tulum and beyond, interspersed with lagoons that appear to be navigable from the sea but have never been charted on a useful scale. With Cancún as the catalyst, we expect that not many years will pass before this now inhospitable coast will be dotted with resort establishments and associated marinas dredged into the lagoons.

Isla Mujeres (28202) may be entered by passing about ½-mile N of the square black rock called The Anvil, then rounding gradually down toward the settlement, where anchorage may be taken anywhere along the shore S of the village.

The more customary entrance, however, is to come in from the S, passing about halfway between the southern end of Mujeres and Becket Rock and steering toward the northern end of the sand hills on the mainland shore until the village bears due N, then turning toward it and eventually picking up the charted range. Give the front range a good berth before turning in to the anchorage.

The Spanish explorers heard of temples on the island decorated with female idols, hence they called the place "Island of Women." The town is typically Spanish and appealingly primitive, with two nice hotels and a charming French restaurant right on the beach, where the meals are truly worthy of the French tradition.

You are expected to go ashore and present yourself with your papers to the Port Captain, which will involve a trip to the hospital for health clearance and to the airport for immigration, then back to the Port Captain for the remaining details. You repeat all that when you are ready to depart.

Isla Contoy (26000) has been described to us as a "nothing place" except as a jumping-off point for the usually boisterous passage to the Dry Tortugas or Key West. The anchorage close under the lighthouse is reasonably protected from N and E.

Yucatan Channel—Crossing Strategy

The Equatorial Current, which has been flowing freely from the Atlantic and through the Caribbean, becomes markedly compressed when it reaches the straits between Yucatan and Cuba. As it enters the Gulf of Mexico, with its axis about a third the distance, or 35 miles, off the Yucatan coast, it spreads out to the west and east. The westerly branch circles the Gulf clockwise, and the easterly branch becomes the Florida Current or Gulf Stream, later augmented by that same clockwise current emanating from the Gulf of Mexico.

Just how far offshore the axis actually is, where it fans out, and how strong it may be at a particular time are of course questions of immense interest to those who race regularly from Biloxi to Cozumel and from St. Pete to Mujeres; but race results and careful post-race study of the relative positions of the boats at different times during the race show that even these astute sailors are easily foiled by the inconsistencies of the stream. Some racers sailing along smoothly at 5 knots couldn't believe their instruments when they discovered that they were actually making no progress over the bottom; they were roundly beaten by others that sailed a long course toward Cuba and back across the channel.

If there is any strategy for the cruising sailor to follow when making from, say, Mujeres to Key West, we would advise a straight track across—but allowing for at least 4 knots of north-setting current until nearly abeam Cabo San Antonio and thereafter a much milder current more or less on the stern.

Going the other way, we would make for the Cuban coast 70–80 miles NE of Cabo San Antonio—but staying 12–15 miles offshore in today's unfriendly atmosphere. There is often a countercurrent along the Cuban shore, perhaps too close in to be reached in safety, but at least you would be avoiding the worst of the head current. Also, when finally out in the channel, we would try to overestimate the rate of the current in order to assure a landfall somewhat south of our target on the Quintana Roo side.

Naturally, the weather pattern must be watched very closely, since 20–30-knot northerly winds against a current and swell from the south can create a mighty uncomfortable, even dangerous, sea condition. On several occasions, yachts have had to take shelter under the lee of Cabo San Antonio, where they have been under the surveillance of Cuban patrol boats but allowed to leave unmolested. Perhaps it's luck or perhaps it has something to do with that common bond that joins all sailors when faced with peril at sea.

CHAPTER TWENTY-ONE

Cuba

With 1,400 miles of conveniently indented coastline fronted by myriads of offlying islets to invite the inquisitive cruising man, it seems a shame that Cuba, which Columbus chose to call "the Pearl of the Antilles," must remain a forbidden cruising ground for Americans—in fact, a dangerous and unwelcoming place now for yachtsmen of any nationality.

The U.S. Coast Guard has warned that vessels approaching within 9 miles of the coast of Cuba may be stopped and boarded by Cuban patrol boats and, further, that if apprehended within the 3-mile limit, their right of innocent passage will not be recognized and they may be "detained," which is a mild way of expressing a nasty situation. In view of this warning, coupled with the advice of a European yachtsman who has lived in Cuba recently and knows the attitudes and operations of the Castro regime, and with the published stories of several yachtsmen who have entered Cuban waters under distress circumstances, our recommendation is to stay completely away.

A 12-mile offing may keep you from the clutches of the Cuban Navy, but there should be no need even to approach that closely unless you are driven there uncontrollably. In that unfortunate eventuality, expect to be met by trigger-happy frontier guards and to be packed up in a hotel under house arrest, at your cost, while repairs to your boat are carried out without your direction and at astronomical expense.

Should you feel the need of a drink in such unhappy circumstances, be prepared to pay $84 for a bottle of whisky, and a fifth at that. Things are expensive in Cuba today!

Having someone aboard who speaks Spanish would of course be a great help. Then, with the language barrier broken, the 2760 kHz frequency on your radio (in case you had some rare premonition to have such a crystal installed) would enable you to explain your predicament to a Cuban coast station and request permission to enter a specific harbor, so that you would not necessarily be treated as part of an invading force.

But enough of such catastrophic thoughts!

In the meantime, in case the spirit of *detente* contines to soften the bearded

Cuba, so near and yet so far

man in the green fatigues, and to whet your anticipation of a new turn of events, we have drawn up an itinerary of ports and places worth seeing around Cuba. It has been distilled from a series of fascinating articles that appeared in *Yachting* during the Batista days.*

We have made assumptions right and left. We cannot know of course whether the three yacht clubs at Havana, the once busy establishment at Santiago, or the posh yacht basin at Kawama Lagoon near Varadero Beach will ever be reactivated after all these years of repression and confiscation of everything that smacked of wealth. In fact we cannot speak assuredly of *any* facilities that may be available when that fateful day comes that yachts will again be allowed in Cuba's wondrous waters. But the land configurations that produce the maze of sheltered passages and idyllic anchorages have not changed, and we give you these now, not only for dreaming purposes but also to serve in some later revision of this Guide as an outline for a properly documented chapter to help you cruise Cuba, the largest by far of all the islands of the Caribbean.

Since most of the island is canted in a SE–NW direction, and the prevailing winds are a little north of east, it follows that a circumnavigation should be counterclockwise; and since Havana is a logical port to enter after a 90-mile open water passage from Key West, we shall start from there.

Havana to Cabo San Antonio

Havana to La Mulata (27084, 27101) is an exposed passage with three nicely spaced and completely landlocked bays along the way: Mariel, Cabanas, and Bahía Honda, all of them free of any dangers in entering.

Laberinto de los Colorados (27101, 27121), which you will enter at La Mulata, is a barricade of reefs affording protection in any weather all the way to Cabo San Antonio. This should present no difficulty to skippers with a trained eye for piloting through reef areas, but if you don't feel confident, a pilot may be picked up at Morrillo, La Mulata, or Cayo Paraiso. Esperanza and Santa Lucia are easy to enter, but the best port along this stretch is La Fé.

La Fé (27121) affords excellent protection and is the last possibility for food, fuel, and water until you get all the way around to La Columa in the Gulf of Batabano.

Ensenada Cajon (27121) or, more specifically, the arm of the Cayos de Lena, is the last anchorage before rounding Cabo San Antonio. Depths are ample and the protection is complete, even in a strong NW blow.

* Ernesto Aguilera, "Cruising Around Cuba," Dec., 1956; Edward and Mary Stevenson, "Island of Enchantment," Apr., May, and June, 1953.

Golfo de Batabano

La Coloma (27141) is the first real shelter following an exposed passage of over 80 miles. This tuna and lobster fishing port has a marked channel, fuel, and some supplies.

Batabano (27142) lies some 85 miles further E across the comparatively shallow gulf via the Hacha Channel. Exposed to southeasterly winds, this small port has supplies and a commercial pier used by coasters.

Ensenada de la Broa (27142) is the mouth of the Hatiguanico River which is entered via a staked channel. The Stevensons, on *Sea Eagle*, anchored for a week up in one of the tributaries of this large river that flows out of the Zapata Swamp, concentrating on the superb tarpon fishing. During the rainy season, the mosquitoes are said to be "a torment."

Isle of Pines (Isla de Pinos)

Nueva Gerona (27142) is the principal port for the island, now called Isle of Youth because some 50,000 teenagers are currently encamped here learning how to farm. Supplies and fuel are available at the village, 1½ miles up the river. There is also a boatyard with a large slipway here.

Rio Jucaro (27142) on the E side of the island may be entered for several miles until the river narrows abruptly. Depths are ample, the banks are high, and there are mangroves and palm trees to moor to in case of a hurricane.

Ensenada de los Barcos (27141) offers splendid protection in normal weather.

Bahía Siguanea (27141) is said to have one of the finest beaches on Cuba's south coast, with a protected anchorage at the southern end in the deep coves, if you can get in over the bars between the caylets.

Puerto Francés (27141), just around the point of that name, gives perfect protection from the NW; Caleta Grande, just beyond, is said to be safe in all winds except from W and N.

Southwest Coast

Isle of Pines to Cienfuegos (27142, 27161) requires some delicate navigation via the Canal del Ingles to a point just S of Cay Palanca, thence 102°T to the

Diego Perez Channel and on past the famous, or infamous, Bay of Pigs to Cienfuegos.

Cienfuegos (27161) was, and perhaps still is, a thriving modern city and one of the best and largest ports in Cuba. Four miles up the river there were once two yacht clubs with safe water and ice and a capability for most repairs, a good base for resting and refitting. Expect a 2-knot current in the entrance, twice that in the rainy season.

Casilda (27181) is a must stop. The oldest and most picturesque town in all Cuba, Trinidad, lies 3 miles inland, while the port itself was the scene of Hernan Cortés's departure for the conquest of Mexico.

Trinidad, with its narrow and twisting cobblestoned streets, was settled in 1514 and was once the wealthiest town in Cuba. During the previous regime, it was declared a national monument, and it will be interesting to see what has since become of this remnant of Spanish architecture, which some say is in a class with Toledo in Spain and Taxco in Mexico.

Twelve League Labyrinth (27181, 27184, 27201, 27206) is a vast, relatively shoal area stretching 180 miles from Casilda to Cabo Cruz. Though infested with cays, rocky islets, and banks, it is regularly navigated by large ships loading sugar and other agricultural products from Cuba's central-plains region. The muddy bottom discolors the water, but the charts are detailed and we presume the buoyage is being maintained in the numerous channels leading through the tight spots.

Twenty years ago, Ernesto Aguilera told of bringing *Indra*, a 47-foot Chris Craft, through here, and has left us the following specific directions.

> Depart Casilda by the La Mulata Channel and return to the bank S of the Machos de Afuera Cays, thence to Punta Ladrillo and the large sugar port of Tunas de Zaza. Then run close along the shore past what our guide claims is the most beautiful cay in Cuba, Obispito, on the way to another important sugar port, Jucaro.

From Jucaro, Aguilera's route leaves Flamenco, Flamenquito, and Guasimas Cays to port, passes through the Ana Maria group of cays, then on to the Pinque Channel after leaving Algodon Grande and Malabrigo Cays to starboard on the way.

From the SE end of the Pinque Channel he tells us to run 093°T to Santa Cruz del Sur, an important shrimp port.

Cruising in the Gulf of Guacanayabo beyond Santa Cruz is somewhat less obstructed, with stops suggested at the small sugar-and-molasses port of

Guayabal, where ice used to be available, as well as safe water, which has always been a problem in these parts. Also recommended is the large commercial port of Manzanillo (unsafe water), and lastly Campechuela and Niquero, before turning the corner into the trade winds again at Cabo Cruz.

Southeast Coast

With the five- and six-thousand-foot peaks of the Sierra Maestra dropping sheer to the sea, much like Spain's own south coast, the 220-mile passage from Cabo Cruz to Cabo Maisi is surely the most magnificent along Cuba's coastline. Since the powerful trades draw in upon this exposed coast, it would be a most uncomfortable stretch were it not for several very secure harbors along the way.

Pilon (27221) is strewn with reefs and shoals across the entrance, but their very presence provides excellent protection, and the channel is buoyed.

Santiago (26222) was once the capital of Cuba. In fact, its Morro Castle is even older than Havana's. Through the years, Cortés was the city's first mayor; the slave revolts in Haiti in 1776 sent many Frenchmen here to leave an indelible French influence; Teddy's Rough Riders made history here in 1898 winning the decisive battle for Cuban independence; and Fidel Castro used this mountainous countryside to build his revolutionary movement and gather his faithful adherents about him.

Once inside the 60-yard-wide entrance, the protection is complete and the anchoring possibilities many and varied. Punta Gorda used to be the site of one of Cuba's most active yacht clubs, the Club Amateur de Pesca.

Guantanamo Bay (26222) is a U.S. naval base situated in the midst of an avowedly hostile country. It's one of the great anomalies of the world today, but it stands in fact upon land that has been leased for this purpose since 1903, shortly after Cuba won her independence from Spain with immense assistance from the United States, military and otherwise.

Even after a healing of U.S. and Cuban relationships, it's doubtful that the port would be open to small craft except in emergencies. Needless to say, the shelter is more than adequate.

Puerto Baitiquero (26235) is a landlocked inlet completely surrounded by high hills with a 10-foot-deep channel only 50 feet wide between the awash reefs on each side.

Cabo Maisi to Nuevitas (26241, 26244, 27041)

This portion of the northeast coast is a sailor's delight when traveling counterclockwise, with the wind on the beam and a snug harbor every 25–30 miles; and many of these ports are commodious coves entered via narrow, winding channels that completely filter out the swells. Ernesto Aguilera of *Indra* has recommended Baracoa, Moa Bay, and Tanamo, this last having such a twisting entrance that it cannot be seen until you are almost on it. Landlocked Nipe Bay is so huge that the problem is to find a shelter for the particular conditions at the time. If you must have your daily swim, better go elsewhere, because Nipe Bay is famous for its shark population.

Puerto Banes, Vita, and Puerto Padres are all sugar and molasses ports with circuitous, high-walled entrances. The one at Banes, in fact, is called "The Canyon." Currents run strong in these entrance canyons, and there is of course the danger of meeting a big ship where you least want to find it. Food and fuel should be available in any of these ports and some repairs as well, since all the sugar mills have machine shops and mechanics.

Nuevitas Bay to Havana

Nuevitas to Caibarien (27041, 27045, 27047) poses a 45-mile run along the Bahama Channel to Cayo Verde, where you can duck inside the reef to anchor on a sandy bottom, with reasonable protection even in a norther. The next anchorage in northeasterly winds is under the light at Paredon Grande.

The mainland port of Caibarien lies some 15 miles in from the line of the outer reefs and is hardly worth the detour unless you are desperate for provisions. Better to go on to Isabella.

Isabella (27061) is only 6 miles in from the open sea. Before Castro, it had a special pier maintained by Amigos del Mar, an association devoted to the "development of seamanship and love of the sea among Cubans," with several chapters around the island.

Cardenas (27081) marks the end of the long chain of offlying cays that has stretched 215 miles from Cayo Verde. Few yachts would however be likely to use this huge sugar port considering the nearness of Kawama.

Kawama Lagoon (27081), in the former balmy days of tourism, used to contain the most modern yacht basin in Cuba, right next to the famous resort center of Varadero Beach.

Havana (27084) was like this to the Stevensons when they came up to the coast in their 46-foot power cruiser, *Sea Eagle*, one day in 1952 after a bumpy passage from Key West:

> We were able to see the wide stretch of Havana suburbs and the lovely homes along the shore including the Havana Yacht Club, the Biltmore Yacht and Country Club—an amazing community.
>
> We eased into the channel to Havana Harbor on the lookout for the Club Náutico Internacional, of which we had heard a great deal. We could see the traffic on Avenida del Puerto and hear the constant blare of horns from the busses and autos. Suddenly the club came in view, a modern building completely clean in character, an incongruous sight in this ancient harbor.

How many years will pass before the next foreign yacht enters past El Morro, and what will he find when he gets there? Let's hope that *something* will happen in the near future to open up Cuba's beautiful coastline for the enjoyment of yachtsmen, who by the very nature of their life on the water are often the best ambassadors of (in this case) pent-up good will.

CHAPTER TWENTY-TWO

The Cayman Islands

Almost in dead center of the western Caribbean, yet off the usual sailing routes to anywhere, the Caymans seemed to have been hardly worth fighting for, and were very late in being settled. Even Columbus missed them until he was returning from the Isthmus on his fourth and final voyage, and he sighted only the Lesser Caymans, which lie some 80 miles east of Grand Cayman. Sugarcane had no part in the development of this island group; in fact they are so low and thus so subject to hurricane destruction that agricultural enterprises have hardly had a chance.

Although the Caymans take their name from the Spanish word for crocodile, and these reptiles have been seen on Little Cayman (the island most visited in the early days), it was the turtle that for many years provided these islands with their livelihood. In fact, had it not been for the availability of turtle steaks, and water from wells deep in the limestone, few of the early sailors would have bothered to set foot in these remote islands. In 1592, the log of a Capt. William King, sailing from Jamaica to Grand Cayman, tells us:

> . . . we found no people, but a river of fresh water, and there we turned up three score great tortoises or turtles. Two of these, with their eggs, fed ten men for a day.

Since the Caymans were so isolated and provided such good sustenance, the pirates of the early 18th century quite naturally made good use of them. This in turn made the island quite unsuitable for God-fearing settlers. It was not until 1734 that the first grant of crown land was made in Grand Cayman—to the first of the Boddens, who, with two pages in the telephone book, have been a prominent family in the islands ever since, exceeded only by the slightly more prolific Ebanks, who fill three pages.

The lack of big plantations led to a more limited need for slaves than on the other West Indian Islands, with the result that the races were about evenly divided when slavery ended in 1834. There has since been enough intermarrying among the population of 12,000 to make racial tensions almost nonexistent. And so the Caymans have slumbered their way into modern times, sending

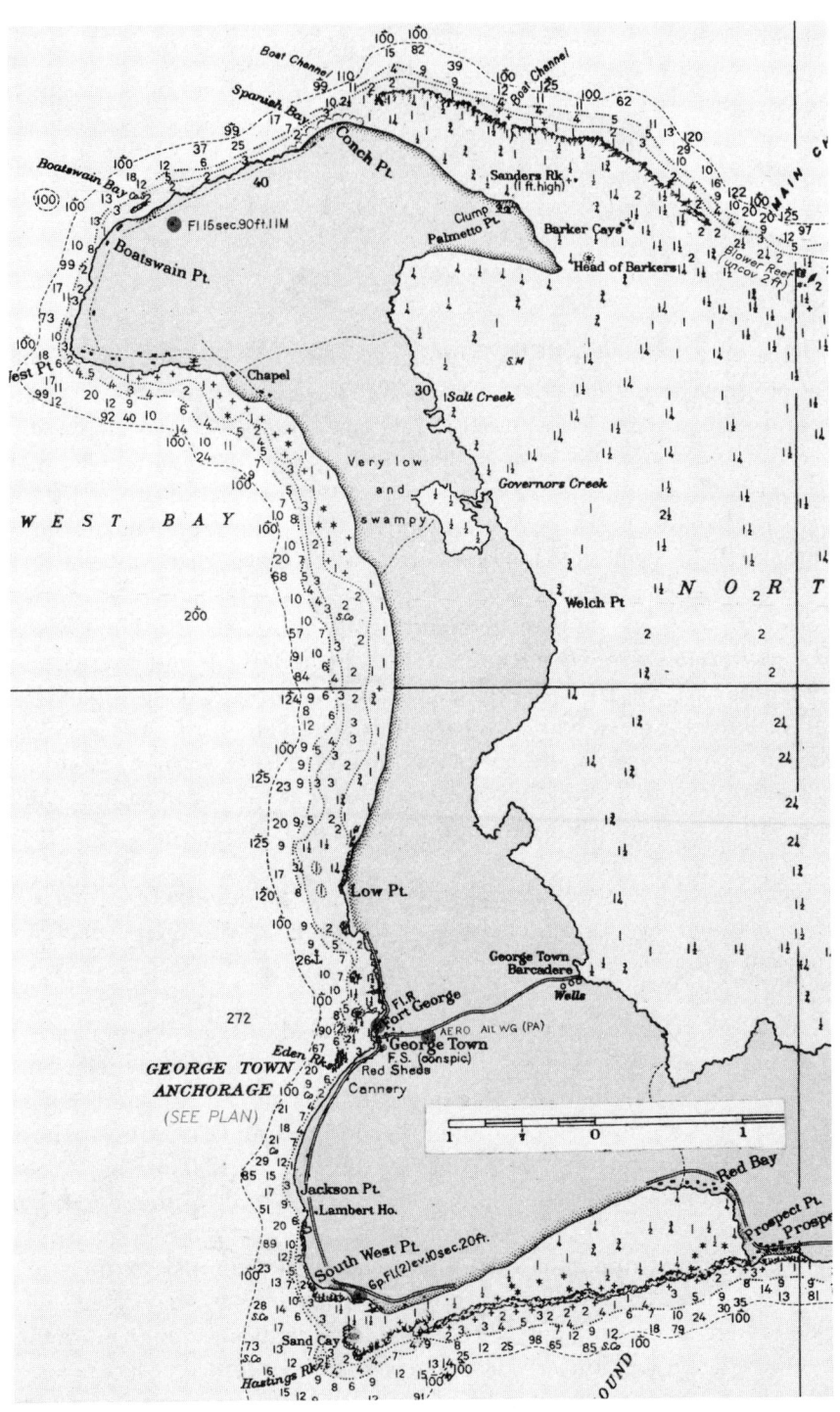

Grand Cayman, western end (soundings in fathoms)

their men to seek the turtle as far as the Nicaraguan coast and to serve, in great demand, among the merchant fleets of the world.

Rediscovery of Grand Cayman has come about only in the last few years, and already a "Gold Coast" is building up along its beautiful western beach. Furthermore, George Town has suddenly become a tax haven for offshore money, in competition with Nassau, which is feeling the effects of the financial community's distrust of the present Bahamas government. Stark white and cream-colored bank buildings are creating a skyline where once the town's tallest building was a red-roofed, two-story Customs House.

Though Grand Cayman can hardly be classed as a cruising ground in itself, it has enough amenities and facilities to attract yachts for a safe and restful stay of several days or weeks along the gorgeous beach on its generally sheltered western end, or within the expansive North Sound, protected by a formidable barrier reef.

George Town (27141) is an open roadstead, yet is perfectly protected from the prevailing northeasterlies. Anchorage may be taken anywhere clear of the commercial traffic. The town quays are in almost constant use by small freight and passenger vessels and would be uncomfortable for a yacht anyway because of the constant surge. A tiny cove with a pile of rocks in the middle is directly off the town's center and has a convenient beach for landing the dinghy. The Customs House, where you will have to report upon arrival, is only a hundred yards N along the waterfront.

Passports are not required of U.S. and Canadian citizens, but some proof of citizenship, such as a birth certificate or voter-registration card, is necessary. As in most British and formerly British islands, dogs and cats are subject to 6-months' quarantine.

In 1975, construction was slated to begin on Cayport, an enlargement of the docking space for the small freighters that supply the island with most of its needs, but even when the new quays are built, the port will be untenable in northwesters and all vessels will have to continue to seek shelter in Southwest Sound, where the usual anchorage is as close under the shore as draft permits, between Spot Bay and the hamlet of Prospect.

These northwesters, which are most prevalent from November through April, are a part of the storm systems that sweep across the States throughout the winter. Unlike the northers in the Bahamas, which are presaged by a wind shift through S with a fair blow from the SW on the way around, these storms come in with little warning to strangers, sometimes right out of a blue sky. The local people seem to have a sixth sense about these blows; perhaps they feel the shift in direction of the swell, or notice the sea fans beginning to bend toward the SE, or maybe they've simply heard the 1205 forecast from Swan Island on 2738 kHz. In any case, if there is a general exodus of vessels from George Town

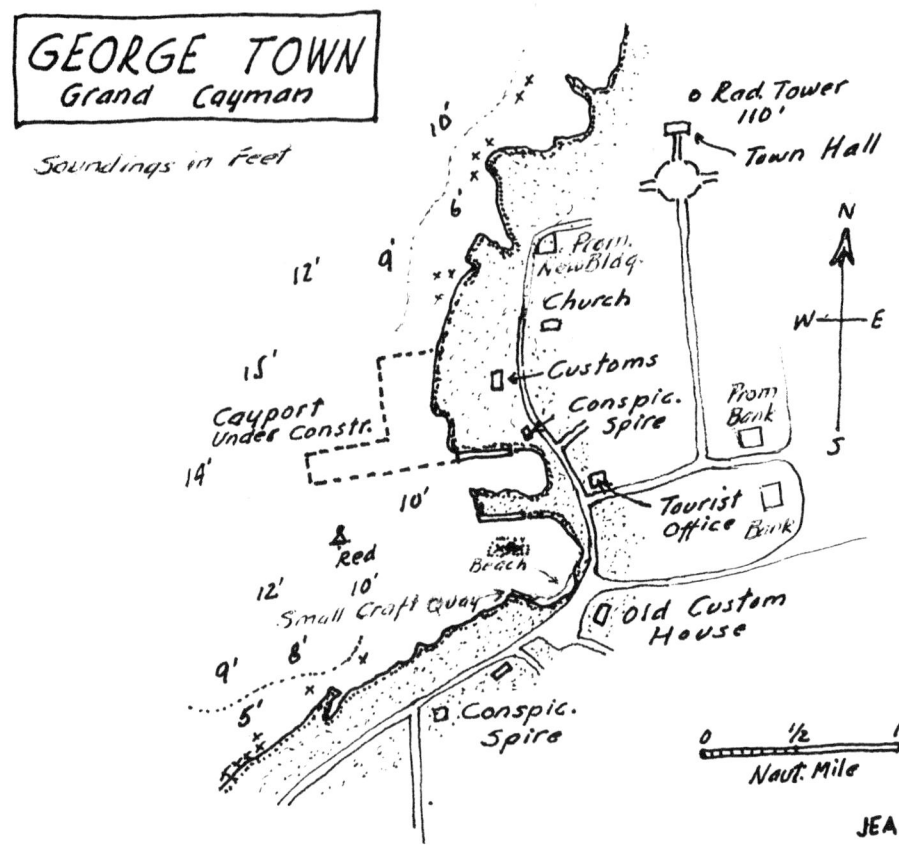

or West Bay around the corner to Southwest Bay, by all means follow the crowd! And remember, the colder the forecast for Miami, the more violent the northwester will be.

West Bay (27241) is made beautiful as an anchorage by Seven Mile Beach, which is really only 4 miles long. Already this gorgeous strip of white sand is pocked with hotels and more are abuilding. Anchor anywhere along here, according to the chart and your draft. Mosquitos may bother you, especially from May to October, so it may be best not to anchor too close in. Mosquitos are a very real problem here. Although they are being vigorously attacked, they're far from being under control.

If you want to rent a car or hire a taxi, you will find it convenient to anchor off the Holiday Inn at 19°20.3′ N.

A short distance N of the village of West Bay is one of the prime attractions of the island, the only sea-turtle farm in the world, operated by Mariculture Ltd. Having been fished practically out of existence, the turtles are (quite appro-

priately) back in the Caymans now, 120,000 strong, being bred in tanks, where
the survival rate of hatchlings is about 85 percent, compared with 1 percent
under natural conditions. Conducted tours and a gift shop are part of the act
here.

Reef Entrances to North Sound (27241) are not difficult to negotiate by
anyone familiar with piloting in such waters, for the bottom is clearly visible and
the barrier reef itself is very distinct.

The Big Channel shown in our sketch is actually the one entitled "Main
Channel" in 27241; we have simply used the name by which it is known locally.
On your first approach you will be coming from George Town, having cleared
customs there. After passing Conch Point, stand along the barrier reef to its
conspicuous termination about 2 cables NW of Blower Reef. You should
further orient yourself by noting Barker Cay, which is a single, low rock easily
identified off the Head of Barkers. Other prominent objects against a rather
featureless shore are a dish-shaped microwave antenna (not shown on the
chart) at 19°22.2′ N, and Welch Point.

Leave the end of the barrier reef fairly close to starboard while heading into

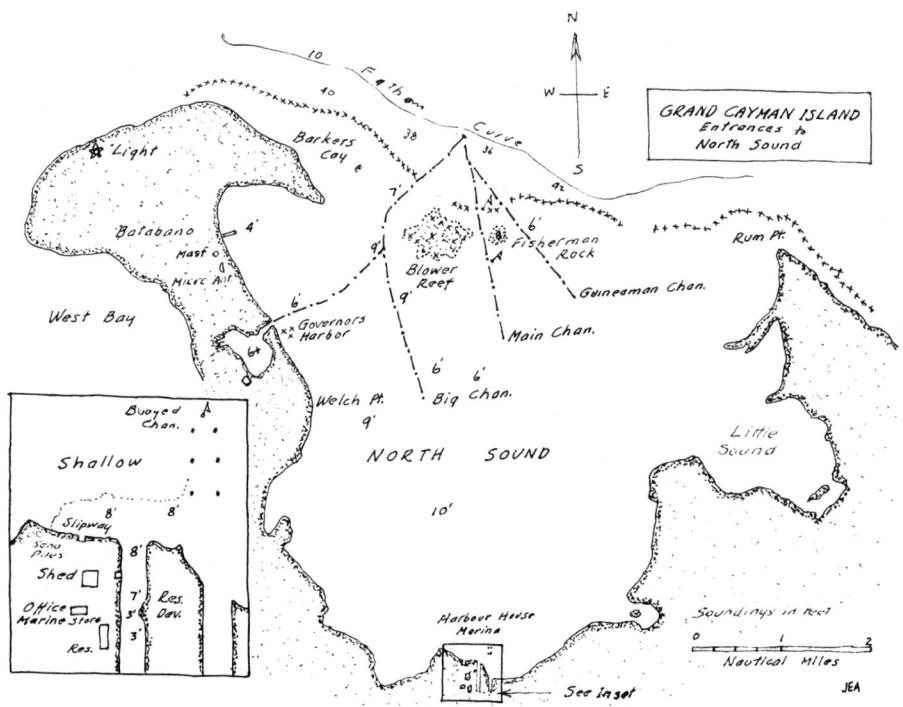

The three reef channels into North Sound, Grand Cayman

the sound on a southwesterly course, until Barker Cay bears about NW, then take up about 172°T toward some sand piles to be seen on the far southern shore. After clearing Blower Reef, there are essentially no other dangers within North Sound except for the shallowness near the shores and the 1-fathom patches near the center.

The Main Channel, as it is called locally, enters just W of a short breaking reef, which itself is about 60 yards W of the continuation of the barrier reef. The key to this channel is Fisherman Rock, which is a jagged nubbin of coral not more than 2 feet high. Pass the above-mentioned short reef patch close on the port hand, on a course about S by E, calculated to pass Fisherman Rock about 50 yards to port. On the outer reef patch, there may or may not be a red flag buoy, and there may be a similar buoy with a black flag some 40 yards SW of Fisherman Rock.

Guineaman Channel starts where the barrier reef recommences, on a SE heading toward the center of Little Sound. Leave the end of the main breaking reef close to port, a small reef patch close to starboard, and carry on in with a sharp eye to starboard for the brown bar that surrounds Fisherman Rock. This channel is narrow at the start and carries barely 6 feet just inside in places.

While we have described and sketched three channels, we urge that only the first (Big Channel) be used for the first time. This is the first prominent break in the long reef that you will come to and is by far the widest. Note, however, that Blower Reef is very dangerous; it covers a wide area, it does not always break conspicuously, nor does it have the continuity of the outer reef line, which is very obvious.

Do not try to come into North Sound even in the early stages of a northwester. Take shelter instead along the island's S coast as described earlier.

Batabano (27241) is situated at the termination of a road crossing the peninsula from West Bay, just N of a microwave antenna and red-and-white radio mast; neither is shown on the chart. Anchorage may be taken in 4 feet about 50 yards off the dock and the weirs, but we would be inclined to anchor in deeper water further out to avoid the bugs. The shoreside surroundings are not attractive.

Governor's Harbour is a blossoming real-estate development with some "waterfront" homes already built on its conventional, Florida-inspired canal system. By publication time, there may be some facilities for yachts, but if not, there is plenty of room to anchor and lie snug while a northwester blows around your ears. On a still evening in the mosquito season, this anchorage would be a horror, since the creek is almost surrounded by mangroves.

Stand in for the entrance at a right angle to the shoreline, to avoid shoal water that will appear on your port hand and to miss a sunken wreck to starboard about 100 yards off the shore. Hold to the center of the entrance creek, which has been dredged to 6 feet. Once inside, there is plenty of water except on the eastern side.

Harbour House Marina in 81°20.0′ W can be identified at the bottom of North Sound by the dredging and land-development operations on each side of it.

The place is more a boatyard than a marina; in fact, the only dock space is along the W side of the dredged canal. Go no further S than the owner-manager's house, where a rock ledge with about 3 feet over it has stalled further deepening. Although plans are afoot for bulkheading and breakwatering, the dock space is rather open to the wide expanse of North Sound, and a small chop funnels into the canal with the afternoon trade wind. In a bad northwester, a dangerous sea would roll in here.

Electricity comes from the island's modern powerplant but the dock wiring (110V–240V, single-phase, 60-cycle) is at present crude. Water is very limited and brackish.

A 40-ton Tami lift will accommodate about 60-foot length, 18-foot beam, and 8-foot draft. Hull and mechanical repairs can be handled, but not finish work or rigging repairs. A fuel dock, a rather sparsely stocked marine store, and a small cafe complete the facilities list. Since George Town is about 5½ miles away, a rental car would be necessary if you headquartered here.

The marina monitors 2738 kHz from 0800 to 1700 daily. Other contacts on this frequency at Grand Cayman are: West Point Radio, Delworth Esso at West Bay, and Shelby Hyde, the shipping agent. The last two also have SSB facilities.

The Lesser Caymans (27241)

Lying almost 80 miles dead to windward from Grand Cayman, and considerably off the direct route from Jamaica to the Yucatan Channel, these two slim islands hold little attraction for a yachtsman, except perhaps to his more adventurous spirit. Separated by a 4-mile strait, lacking any significant indentations along either coasts, and pointed almost directly into the prevailing wind, these island slivers offer minimal protection, and the selection of an anchorage (in any case at the western end of either island) depends on whether the wind happens to be blowing a little N or a little E of NE.

Less than 20 souls live on Little Cayman, where the feeling of remoteness is almost overwhelming. The action, if it can possibly be called that, is at the Brac, meaning "bluff" in Gaelic, where some 1,200 people live, mostly along the northern shore. In normal weather the usual anchorage here is at Scott Bay, on the north shore at the extreme western end of the island, near the airstrip and the only hostelry, the Buccaneer's Inn.

CHAPTER TWENTY-THREE

Jamaica

A huge and impressive island with almost 300 miles of coastline, her 7,000-foot mountain peaks usually wreathed in clouds, Jamaica (26120) boasts no less than 14 truly authentic and neatly spaced harbors giving shelter to yachts. Furthermore, she is, via the Windward Passage, one of the easiest islands to sail to from Florida, and back again.

The Arawaks called her Xaymaca, or "Isle of Rivers"; indeed, a number of the harbors we will describe stand at the mouths of small rivers or streams. Jamaica is much too big to miss; Columbus was here, of course, probably bitterly disappointed that he had found yet another island instead of the mainland of Asia. The Spaniards did little with Jamaica during their long occupation but probably wished later that they had realized the island's strategic position, for in 1655, after an abortive attempt on well-defended Santo Domingo, the British took over the island for the specific purpose of establishing a West Indian base from which to try to topple the Spanish supremacy in these parts, a plan which succeeded admirably with major help from the cutthroat Brethren of the Coast, who knew no laws at all.

Like so many Caribbean islands, Jamaica prospered mightily from the sugar industry until 1805, when, mostly through absentee ownership and attendant mismanagement, the bottom fell out of their market. But sugarcane is again a very major crop, along with bananas, cocoa, and some coffee. As you coast along her eastern and northern shores, you will see a verdant island with a patchwork of plantations made luxuriant by the rains brewed in the mountains. In other places, however, you will see land laid open in brick-red scars where massive bauxite mining operations are in full swing. And some parts of the south coast, especially in the vicinity of Kingston, are parched and dusty, the lower hillsides drab and eroded.

The prevailing wind is north of east, with a southerly component thrown in during the summer. Unfortunately, Jamaica's proximity to the North American mainland brings dreaded northers in the winter season to the western and northern coasts, where many of the harbors offer little protection from this quarter.

Taking advantage of the way the island presents itself to the prevailing winds, you will find it far more comfortable to circle Jamaica counterclockwise.

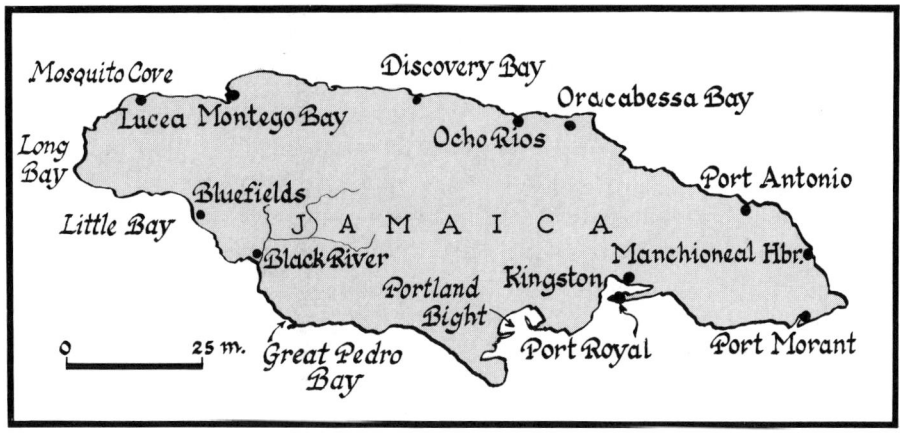

This puts the wind and sea on your stern along the exposed north coast, and after rounding the west end, you will have some lee at least as far as Great Pedro Bay.

Most yachts coming from the Bahamas or the east will make for Port Antonio, which is a convenient as well as pleasant place to enter. We will, however, start our circular cruise from Kingston, since it is the capital and chief port.

Kingston Harbour (26128) is so expansive and so ruffled by the afternoon breeze that a yacht can only consider berthing at Morgan's Harbour Club, next to old Port Royal, or at the Royal Jamaica Yacht Club, about a half mile E of Manly Airport.

Before proceeding to a berth, anchor off the customs dock at Port Royal with your Q flag flying and you will be promptly boarded by courteous customs officials. Firearms, drugs, and animals are their main concern. Cats and dogs must remain on board, but parrots seem to go unnoticed. Immigration officials, on the other hand, come from the airport in their own good time—maybe today, maybe tomorrow. If you tactfully request permisssion by phone, you may be allowed to bring your crew list and all other necessary papers by taxi to the airport, which will save you a lot of time for more interesting activities. You will have to clear with them again at the airport before you leave.

Morgan's Harbour, at the end of the Palisadoes, the long, low spit of land that creates Kingston Harbour, is a 12-mile taxi ride from the city center (although there is a 25¢ ferry service across); the R.J.Y.C. is only 8 miles from town. Both places are safe and quiet and afford a magnificent view of the towering Blue Mountains. And unless you have some pressing reason to go to town, Kingston offers little attraction today. The traffic is intense, the waterfront is undergoing urban renewal, slums and shantytowns abound, and judging from hearsay and one first-hand account, the city is not safe to walk in day or night. In fact, the same perils that years ago caused the wild Maroon country of central Jamaica to be called the "Land of Look Behind" could now be applied to the city of Kingston itself. So be as wary here as you would be in some parts of New York City.

You will be welcome at the Royal Jamaica Yacht Club if you are a member of another recognized yacht club. The new out-of-town premises (17°56.5' N, 76°46.5' W) were built in 1971 and include an attractive clubhouse, bar, and clean swimming pool overlooking a dredged basin set about with mangroves. Most of the 70 or more slips are occupied by local boats. The entrance channel is good for at least 9-foot draft and the basin is perfectly protected. Fuel and electricity are laid on, and a marine railway will take modest-size boats. You may also anchor just outside the basin in reasonable comfort.

Morgan's Harbour Club, at Port Royal, is a small hotel-and-restaurant establishment that has changed little in the 20 years since we were first there. Adjacent is a fuel dock and small-boat marina with what appears to be a rather improvised marine railway. Mooring at the club is stern-to at the wooden dock fronting the bar and restaurant; it's best to use your anchor rather than tie to the rotted pilings off the dock. There is at least 6 feet alongside, but even if there is plenty of room, we recommend mooring off because of the slight swell and the wakes of passing boats.

Royal Jamaica Yacht Club, Kingston; Blue Mountains in the background

For convenient sightseeing, Morgan's Harbour Club stands literally in the outskirts of what was old Port Royal, a prominent port for supplies and repairs. It was also the scene of such debauchery among the hard-living, devil-may-care buccaneers who frequented the place between their seagoing forays, that it was called the wickedest city in the whole world. An earthquake in 1692 unceremoniously dumped most of the town into the bay, with the loss of 2,000 lives and a lot of booze. This was followed up by a fire in 1703, a severe storm in 1722, another fire in 1816, and a second earthquake in 1907, which seems like divine justice with a vengeance.

Of the original three forts that guarded Port Royal in the days of Henry Morgan, only Fort Charles, which controlled the outer channel, has survived. Its brick walls and interior buildings are slowly being restored to make it an imaginable point of historic interest, but much more needs doing. A plaque on one of the parapets draws attention to the memory of Admiral Lord Nelson, who, at the ripe age of 21, commanded this fort for a time. In grave tones is inscribed: "You who tread his footsteps, remember his glory."

About the Kingston area in general, here are the comments of Al and Sandy Humphers of the cutter *Elan*:

We haven't objected at all to being stranded here; it's been delightful. However, in need of sail repairs and marine supplies (we lost our taffrail log), we found Jamaica sadly lacking in anything resembling yacht equipment, including hardware, canvas, and dacron and nylon line. This stems from the government's attempts to improve its balance-of-payments position by not allowing merchants to import any goods defined as "luxuries," a category that seems to include anything associated with a yacht. In provisioning the boat we found that even mayonnaise and green beans are in the luxury-import group.

Even sail repairs are difficult. After much searching we finally found Jamaica's only sailmaker, of sorts, a sewing-machine repairman named David Roberts who has only recently started making a few sail repairs because he has a suitable machine. He did a nice job for us on our minor repairs on the spinnaker and staysail panels. When we picked up our sails he said his fondest hope was to someday get a book on sailmaking so he could become more professional.

For a brief respite from the sea and your galley chores, go up into the cool of the mountains for a delicious dinner at the Blue Mountain Inn. Elegant, expensive, and worth it.

British charts are obtainable from R.S. Gamble & Son Ltd., a shipping agency on Harbour Street, where Kingston's waterfront used to be.

Port Morant (26129), near the E end of the island, has a well-buoyed entrance into a quiet harbor in a lush tropical setting with clear, clean water. There are no facilities, no small-craft docks, in fact few signs of any habitation or activity except the Bowden Dock of United Fruit Ja. Ltd., where small freighters load sugar and bananas from plantations served by a narrow-gauge railroad that runs 7 miles back into the hinterland.

We suggest anchoring slightly beyond the Bowden Dock, where protection is complete and free of surge.

Manchioneal Harbour (Plan from cancelled BA 459) is partly protected by a breaking bar that makes out from the northern arm of this small bay. Run well up into the N end, where a stern line may be run ashore to hold your bow against the river current and into the swell. The village is rather slovenly, but otherwise the surroundings are pleasant. Small freighters used to load bananas here, so there is plenty of depth and room to maneuver.

Blue Hole is a gorgeous and justly famous spot, well protected by high, steep hills all around, but the entrance is limited to 4 feet over the bar and a local pilot is essential. You can engage one in Port Antonio.

Port Antonio (26130) is two harbors divided by the Tichfield Peninsula, but the eastern one is sufficiently exposed to the prevailing wind and swell to be completely ignored. Take the channel into the W harbor between the peninsula and Navy Island (privately owned), toward the Boundbrook commercial wharf. Swing to port and ask for a berth at the Eastern Jamaica Anglers' Association dock, or anchor off the market area about 100 yards further E.

Yachts entering from foreign ports may not dock until cleared by customs, while foreign-registered boats that have already cleared at another Jamaican port may dock but must still report to Port Antonio customs within 24 hours. All foreign yachts must also clear with Port Antonio officials even when departing for another Jamaican port.

If these regulations seem overly stringent, remember that *ganja* (marijuana) has been an illegal but rather abundant crop for years, and the government is finally taking stern measures to halt this trade, which is also linked with gunrunning. When we were last there, a 35-foot sloop sailed by a young couple was inspected by customs officers every day for ten days and finally told to leave the port.

Note that dogs and cats are subject to a 6-month quarantine regulation, as is the case in most of the formerly British islands.

The E.J.A.A. dock has 110V-220V electricity, but at 50 cycles. It also has hose connections, although the water may be heavily chlorinated. You will also find a fuel dock and a comfortable clubhouse with bar and immaculate shower rooms.

EAST COAST

MANCHIONEAL
HARBOUR

By Lieut! T. F. Pullen, R. N.

assisted by Lieut^te W.C.H.Hastings and M.H.Smyth.R.N.1879.

+ Nettle Pt. Lat. 18º 2.15 N. - Long. 76º17' 5."W.

MagVar.ⁿ 0°10 E.(1959) decr⁹ ab.ᵗ 4'ann⁹⁷

Natural Scale 18160

10 Cables or
1 Sea Mile (6052 f ᵗ)

This plan no longer appears in current charts and is reproduced from cancelled chart BA 459 with the sanction of the Controller, H. M. Stationery Office, and of the Hydrographer of the Navy.

The narrow wooden docks have at least 8 feet alongside, but you will probably elect to Med-moor, as is customary here. Bryan Smith was the hospitable manager of the club when we were there.

E.J.A.A. Dock, Port Antonio

Navy Island is being developed as the "Windjammer Club" by American interests and will, we understand, also cater to yachts.

For a remarkable view and a breath of cool air, take a taxi to Bonnie View Inn, a half-mile ride "straight up" from town. It's a toss-up whether the panorama or the ride will thrill you more.

Port Antonio is a deservedly popular yacht stop, well protected in all weather and picturesque when seen from the water. Although Columbus didn't come here, Capt. Bligh, R.N., did—with the first shipment of breadfruit from the South Seas.

Welshwoman's Point (26120) makes a welcome lee when making for Port Antonio in heavy weather.

Oracabessa Bay (26130) is undergoing extensive harbor development to make it safe for banana ships against the northers that are the bane of this coast, but none of this shows on the charts as just yet. As our sketch indicates, breakwaters have been built atop the reefs, and the channel and basin have been dredged deeper than now charted.

The late Ian Fleming wrote the James Bond 007 thrillers at his estate here.

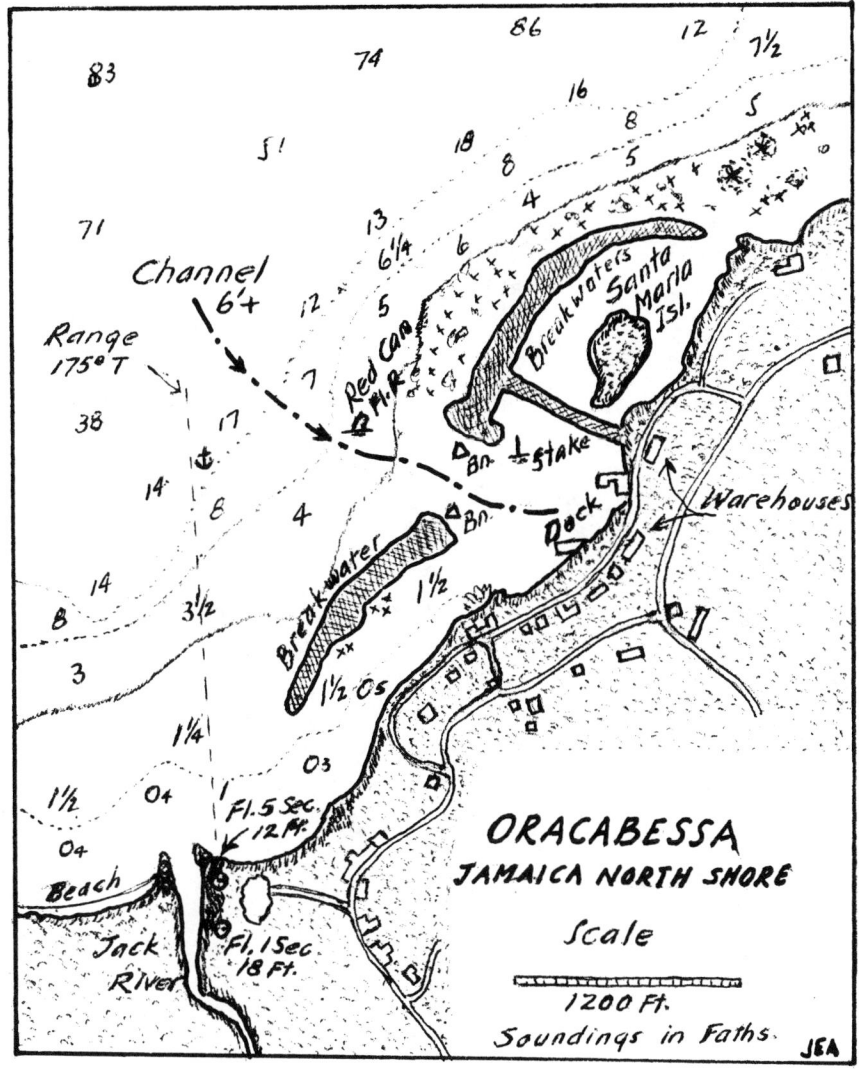

83

74

86

12

7½

71

5!

16

8

5

S

Channel
6'+

13

6¼

6

18

8

4

Breakwaters

Santa
Maria
Isl.

Range
175° T

12

5

Red Can
Fl. R.

38

17

7

Bn. + stake

14

8

4

Warehouses

Dock

14

3½

Breakwater

Bn.

1½

8

1½ Os

3

1¼

O3

1½

O4

Fl. 5 Sec.
12 Ft.

O4

Beach

ORACABESSA

JAMAICA NORTH SHORE

Jack
River

Fl. 1 Sec.
18 Ft.

Scale

1200 Ft.

Soundings in Faths.

JEA

Rio Nuevo Bay (26123) provides a good lee, but it may be necessary to set a stern anchor to hold your bow into the swell against the river current.

Ocho Rios (26130) has now been breakwatered against the northerly blows, but still is too open for comfort in such conditions, and some swell will be felt even in normal weather. Apartments and a shopping plaza are springing up all around this harbor; this is not the place if you prefer natural surroundings.

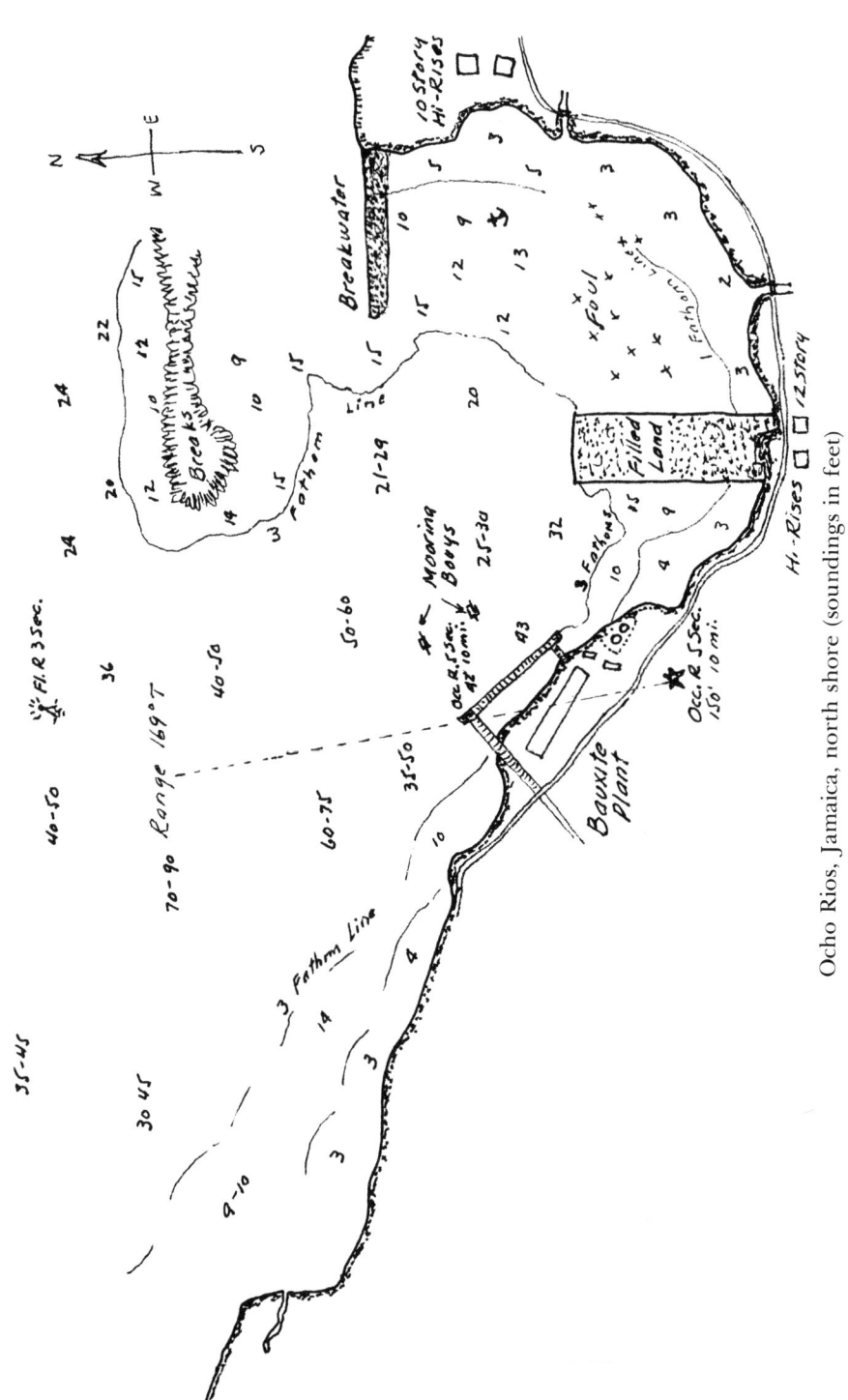

Ocho Rios, Jamaica, north shore (soundings in feet)

St. Ann's Bay (26130) presents an easy entrance through the reef, as the chart shows but, with its rather messy waterfront and muddy water, can hardly qualify as a yacht stop.

Discovery Bay (26122) is named after who else but Columbus, who landed here during his second voyage in 1494, when the accompanying royal historian recorded for Queen Isabella that Jamaica "is the fairest island that eyes have beheld; mountainous and the land seems to touch the sky . . . and all full of valleys and fields and plains. . . ."

Ten years later, on his fourth and final voyage, whereby the "Admiral of the Ocean Sea" hoped to regain favor with the King and Queen, Columbus was forced to beach his last two worm-riddled ships at St. Ann's Bay. Having lost almost all his influence, he and what was left of his company spent a year in this area before he was able to arrange passage in another ship back to Spain.

Discovery Bay is surely one of the most attractive anchorages on the whole northern coast, especially close under the shore in the SE corner adjacent to the park.

An interesting phenomenon is the fresh-water spring that bubbles up in the W side of this bay near the 46-meter sounding NE of the white flasher.

Rio Bueno (26122) is excellent shelter in normal weather. The smoothest anchorage is under the hill on the E side, near the range beacons. Here again a stern anchor will be helpful to counter the river current, which tends to lay you broadside to the swell. For those interested in native art, there are two galleries in the village exhibiting the work of local artists.

Falmouth (26130) lies in a low, swampy area surrounded by mangroves and infested with insects. We suggest avoiding this unattractive place, which isn't even good shelter in a norther.

Montego Bay (26122) boasts a fine headquarters for yachts in the new Montego Bay Yacht Club, located in the new port area. Although 3½ miles from town, the club and grounds are pleasant and tidy with all the customary facilities. Shelter is complete, and a cooling breeze comes into the basin. Notify customs when you come in and they will clear you at the club.

If there are no northers in the offing and you want to be near town, come in on the Casa Blanca Hotel immediately S of Sandy Reef and the famous Doctor's Cave Beach. This beach is named after one Dr. McCatty, who, near the turn of the century, when swimming meant bathing in full costume and shoes, felt so strongly about the therapeutic value of this daring sport that he donated the beautiful white beach that he owned for the establishment of *Doctor's Cave Bathing Club.*

When a hurricane threatens Mo' Bay, yachtsmen take their boats into the Bogue Island area to moor among the mangroves in the extreme SE portion of this bay. The charted beacons clearly show the way in.

Mosquito Cove (26122) with its 500-foot-wide opening is surely Jamaica's finest gunkhole. Keep to midchannel and proceed straight in for excellent protection. To avoid Buckner Reef when entering or leaving, be very sure of your distance off before turning along the coast.

Lucea Harbour (26122) is an agreeable place to drop anchor for a night, though the town is uninspiring. Pronounce it "Lucy."

Negril Harbour (Bloody Bay) (26123) affords good anchorage in the middle and southern parts of the bay. The bottom is flat and 2 fathoms extend for quite a long distance off the beach. For a more snug anchorage, tuck in behind the rock in the northern corner of the bay.

Negril (or Long) Bay (26123) is unquestionably one of the most beautiful stretches of beach on the whole island, a fact which has only lately been appreciated by resort developers. In addition to the original Sundowner Hotel, several new ones are under construction, while down at the village of Negril itself, British interests had a huge shopping center and villa complex nearing completion in 1974.

The most attractive anchorage for yachts is at the N end of the strand. Keep 150 yards off Booby Cay and come in by eye toward the Sundowner Hotel (18°19.5' N). Though you will be crossing solid reef, according to the chart, actually there is a 17-foot channel all the way in. However, if you prefer to be conservative, enter this NE corner of the bay by passing S of Sandy Reef which is clearly visible.

Little Bay (26123) requires caution entering. Hug the shoreline as you enter from the SE, and go into the anchorage behind the rocks at the extremity of the bay. Stay only 50 feet off the shore and do not be deterred by the fact that the passage is only 30 feet wide. The bottom is mud and grass.

Savannah la Mar (26123) is an important commercial center, but is drab and dingy and definitely no place for a yacht.

Bluefields (26123) is a pretty spot with high hills all around and attractive beaches. The approach is straightforward with no hidden dangers, the snuggest anchorage being close under the point with the fort ruins.

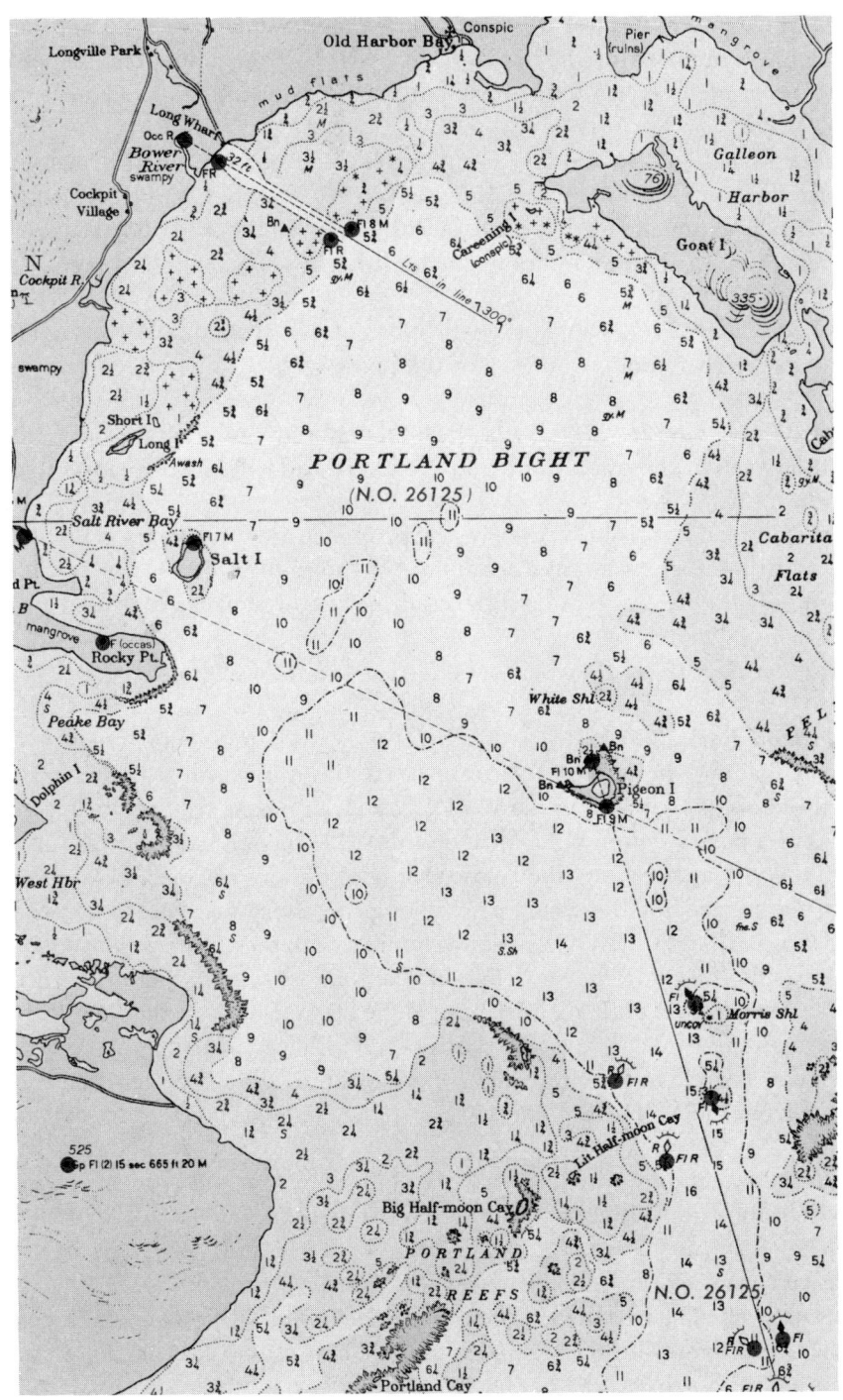

Portland Bight, Jamaica (soundings in fathoms)

White House Point (26123) offers similarly good shelter with no approach problems. You may drop the hook within 20 yards of the point. This section of coast is extremely beautiful with its sloping pasture land and high hills beyond.

Black River (26123) should be entered via the northern half of the bay, toward the church spire, then angling slightly S to the river mouth, which you may actually enter and tie to the wall on either side, being prepared of course to maneuver in a current. Or simply anchor off the village, as convenient.

Parotte Point (26123) anchorage must be entered from due W through the break in the reef about ¾ mile N of the point itself.

Great Pedro Bay (26123) is the last real shelter before turning the corner into the full sweep of the trade wind, and even here you will feel the constant and sometimes heavy swell.

From here, if not from further W, the proper strategy is to start in the small hours of the morning to take advantage of the night breezes, which will be flowing off the land and at least neutralizing the regular trade wind.

Alligator Reef (26124) affords a better lee than one might suspect.

Portland Bight (26125) is a delightful area and quite unmarred by the bauxite-loading operations of Alcoa at Peake Bay and Alcan at Port Esquivel. On the shore, about a half mile W of Old Harbour Bay, are the conspicuous stacks of a power station not shown on the 1974 chart. Entrance to the Bight from the W may be safely taken close around the shore of Portland Point, but with due regard for the rocky patch along the shore just before you come abeam of Portland Cay. Those who are familiar with these waters even enter in darkness by following the shoreline of the point until on a line between the forward range light on Pigeon Island and the 20-mile light on Portland Ridge, thence to a pretty anchorage off a sandy beach with waving palms on the N side of Pigeon Island. In judging your swinging room, allow for the usual night breeze from the N. The bottom is grass, so care must be given to setting your anchor.

Alternate anchorages are NW of Little Half Moon Cay and W of Wreck Reef although the latter (26121) is considerably more exposed.

Pedro Cays (26120), some 50 miles S of Jamaica, provide fair shelter, but expect a swell. The best anchorage is in the lee of South West Cay, where you will see the huts of fishermen from Kingston. These cays make a useful rest stop when bound north, via the banks, from Providencia.

Morant Cays (26129) lying 35 miles SE of Port Morant, offer good shelter from the E, and better fishing. The run from Jamaica is best made at night, when the wind is down and advantage may be taken of the lights on Morant Point and the cays themselves, since the arcs of visibility come within 5–6 miles of overlapping.

APPENDIX A

Leeward and Windward Islands and Vice Versa

When the West Indies were first a "Spanish Sea," the islands were grouped as Barlovento and Sotavento, or Windward and Leeward. The Leewards, quite logically, were the large islands from Puerto Rico toward the west; the Windwards were considered to be all the island chain east of Puerto Rico.

Later, when the British secured most of the previously termed Windwards, they divided their islands into Windwards and Leewards for administrative purposes. Dominica and the other British islands to the south were in the Windward group; the cluster from Montserrat and Antigua north were administratively the Leewards. However, the modern division, geographically, puts Dominica and the islands north of it among the Leewards, and all the islands southward, beginning with Martinique, in the Windwards. How this classification came into being is not at all clear, for it depends where you are sailing from. Since most landfalls from Europe were (and still are) made on Barbados, it follows that the Leewards were just that, but this doesn't explain the designation of Windwards except as you beat back from the Virgins.

The term "Antilles" is also bandied about, deriving from the name of a legendary "island of the Seven Cities," which appeared in very early charts of the waters west of the Azores and which Columbus believed he would sight on his voyage to the Indies. Today, the Greater Antilles are known as the Leeward Islands of the Spaniards and the Lesser Antilles are the Spaniards' Windwards, that is, from Puerto Rico to the east.

If this explanation clears up all the confusion so far, we are happy; but now bear in mind that the Dutch islands of Saba, St. Maarten, and Statia are called the Dutch Windwards, although they lie among the formerly British Leewards. This appelation, however, makes some sense because the Dutch Leewards—Aruba, Bonaire, and Curaçao—definitely lie to leeward of their cousins to the north.

APPENDIX B

Nautical Charts from K. S. Kapp Surveys, 1962–1972
(See chart index page 427.)

KSK-1 Republic of Venezuela North Coast Anchorages
11 small port plans: Carenero, Pto. Azul, Ocumare, Cato, Chiao, Pto. Colombia, Maya, La Cruz, Barcelona, Isla Coche, and Cubagua.
Average scale: 1:15,200   Size: 28″ × 18″

KSK-2 Colombia and Venezuela Anchorages
10 remote ports: Isla Larga, Chichiriviche, Ríohacha, Manaure, Tucacas, Isla Suanchez, La Vela, Pto. Estrella, Santa Ana, and Guaranao.
Average scale: 1:15,200   Size 28″ × 18″

KSK-3 Republica Colombia, Costa Norte
5 anchorages: Bahía Cinto, Nenguange, Gayraca, Chengue, Ancon Concha.
Scale: 1:21,150   Size: 30″ × 16″

KSK-4 Islas del Rosario Anchorages, with inset: Isla Tesoro
Scale: 1:15,200   Size: 26″ × 20″

KSK-5 Republica Colombia, Costa Norte, Fondeaderos, Golfo de Uraba
Features anchorages of the Conquistadores: Zapzurro, Turbo, Bahía Gloria, Necocli, Titumate, Pinololo, Trigana, and Goleta.
Scale: 1:14,500   Size: 22″ × 15″

KSK-6 Kaimau Keys (Holandes Cays), San Blas Coast, Panama
Scale: 1:34,500   Size: 26″ × 20″

KSK-7 Carti Keys, San Blas Gulf, Panama North Coast
Locale of the Republic of Tule Indian war in 1925.
Scale: 1:8,500   Size: 24″ × 20″

KSK-8 Mandinga Keys (Islas Robeson), San Blas Gulf, Panama North Coast
Inhabited isles of the Kuna Indians.
Scale: 1:8,500   Size: 24″ × 20″

KSK-9 Port Royal Harbour, Isla Roatán, Honduras
Includes profile from seaward and historical notes of this pirate haven.
Scale: 1:10,400   Size: 28″ × 18″

All charts $3 each, or $22 for the complete folio postpaid, when ordered from:

K.S. Kapp Publications, Box 121, Northbend, Ohio 45052

These charts are also stocked by:

Panama Canal Yacht Club, Cristobal, Canal Zone

Johnson & Joseph, Shelter Island Drive, San Diego, Ca. 92106

Bahía Mar Marine Store, South Atlantic Blvd., Ft. Lauderdale, Fla. 33316

BIBLIOGRAPHY

Government Publications

Defense Mapping Agency. *Atlas of Pilot Charts, Central American Waters and South America.* Philadelphia: D.M.A., Hydrographic Center Depot, 1955 (with later revisions).

———. *Catalog of Nautical Charts, Region 2.* Philadelphia: Hydrographic Center Depot, published annually.

———. *Sailing Directions, Vol. 20.* Philadelphia: D.M.A., Hydrographic Center Depot, 1952 (with supplements).
Comprising Colombia and the east coast of Central America.

———. *Sailing Directions, Vol. 21.* Philadelphia: D.M.A., Hydrographic Center Depot, 1958 (with supplements).
Comprising the Bahamas, Turks and Caicos, Hispaniola, Puerto Rico, Cuba, Jamaica, and the Caymans.

———. *Sailing Directions, Vol. 22.* Philadelphia: D.M.A., Hydrographic Center Depot, 1963 (with supplements).
Comprising the Lesser Antilles and Venezuela.

Hydrographer of the Navy. *East Coasts of Central America and Gulf of Mexico Pilot.* Taunton, Somerset, England: Hydrographic Dept., 1970 (with supplements).
Comprising Costa Rica, the Miskito Coast, the Bay of Honduras, and the Yucatan Peninsula.

———. *South America Pilot, Vol. IV.* Taunton, Somerset, England: Hydrographic Dept., 1969 (with supplements).
Comprising Trinidad and Tobago, the A-B-C Islands, and the Spanish Main as far west as Almirante Bay.

———. *West Indies Pilot, Vol. I.* Taunton, Somerset, England: Hydrographic Dept., 1971 (with supplements).
Comprising the Bahamas, Florida Straits, Hispaniola, Cuba, Jamaica, and the Caymans.

———. *West Indies Pilot, Vol. II.* Taunton, Somerset, England: Hydrographic Dept., 1969 (with supplements).
Comprising the Mona Passage, Puerto Rico, and the island chain to Grenada.

National Ocean Service. *Coast Pilot, Vol. 5.* Riverdale, Md.: Distribution Div. C44, N.O.S. Published annually.
Comprising Puerto Rico, Culebra, and the U.S. Virgin Islands.

National Oceanic and Atmospheric Administration. *Worldwide Marine Weather Broadcasts.* Revised annually. For sale by the Superintendent of Documents, U.S. Government Printing Office, Washington, D.C. 20402. Price $1.45. The principal source of information on marine weather broadcasts for ships, replacing H.O. 118, formerly published by the Naval Oceanographic Office.

Cruising Guides

Auger, Raymond N. *Westward from the Virgins*. Aspen, Colo.: Columbine Books, 1971. Paperback.
Covers eastern Puerto Rico, Vieques, and Culebra.

Cary, C.G., and E.A. Rainold. *Virgin Anchorages*. Road Town, Tortola, B.V.I.: The Moorings, Ltd., 1974. Paperback.
Air views, in color, of the most popular anchorages in the Virgin Islands.

Kline, Harry. *Yachtsman's Guide to the Bahamas*. Coral Gables, Fla.: Tropic Isle Publishers, published annually. Paperback.

———. *Yachtsman's Guide to the Virgin Islands, Puerto Rico, Republic of Haiti, Dominican Republic*. Coral Gables, Fla.: Tropic Isle Publishers, published annually. Paperback.

———, and J. Linton Rigg. *Bahama Islands*. New York; Charles Scribner's Sons, 1973.

Roscoe, Robert S., and Fessenden S. Blanchard. *A Cruising Guide to the Southern Coast*. New York: Dodd, Mead, 1974.
Covers the east coast "jumping-off" points to the Caribbean.

Street, Donald M. *A Cruising Guide to the Lesser Antilles*. Boston: Sail Books, 1974.
A thorough description of ports and places from Puerto Rico to Trinidad, together with a wealth of general information.

Wilensky, Julius M. *Cruising Guide to the Abacos*. Tenafly, N.J.: C.S.Y., Ltd., 1976. Paperback.

———. *Yachtsman's Guide to the Windward Islands*. Tenafly, N.J.: C.S.Y., Ltd., 1973. Paperback.

Cruise Accounts

Cottman, Evans W. *Out-Island Doctor*. London: Hodder and Stoughton, 1963.
The adventures of a doctor sailing his Bahamian ketch among the islands to minister to his isolated patients.

Eggleston, George T. *Virgin Islands*. Princeton, N.J.: D. Van Nostrand, 1959.

Fenger, Frederic A. *The Cruise of the Diablesse*. New York: Yachting, Inc., 1926.
A classic pre-World War I account of a cruise by schooner from Boston to Tobago and back.

Hiscock, Eric C. *Atlantic Cruise in Wanderer III*. London: Oxford University Press, 1968.
Chapters on the trade-wind passage from the Canaries to Antigua, thence through the Turks and Caicos Islands and the Bahamas.

———. *Sou'west in Wanderer IV*. London: Oxford University Press, 1973.
Chapters on crossing to Barbados, thence to Antigua, Grenada, the Panama Canal, and coastwise to California.

———. *Voyaging Under Sail*. London: Oxford University Press, 1970.
Useful chapters on planning a transatlantic passage to the West Indies.

Mitchell, Carleton. *Islands to Windward*. Princeton, N.J.: D. Van Nostrand, 1955.
From Trinidad, *Carib* sails the island chain north to Annapolis. Includes useful appendices on pilotage and routes.

———. *Isles of the Caribbees*. Washington: National Geographic Society, 1966.
From Grenada to the Virgins, with the usual top-flight color photography.

Niemeier, Jean. *Wild Blue Water*. Portland, Ore.: Metropolitan Press, 1962.
The powerboat *Shield* cruises from the West Coast to the Great Lakes via the western Caribbean.

Puleston, Dennis. *Blue Water Vagabond.* New York: Doubleday, Doran, 1939.
  Chapters on a passage from England to Antigua in a 31-foot yawl and of cruising in
  the West Indies in the early 1930s.
Robinson, Bill. *Over the Horizon.* Princeton, N.J.: D. Van Nostrand, 1966.
  Chapters on the Virgin Islands, the Windwards and Leewards, and the Bahamas.
———. *Where the Trade Winds Blow.* New York: Charles Scribner's Sons, 1963.

History and Background

Craig, Alan K. *Geography of Fishing in British Honduras and Adjacent Coastal Waters.* Baton
  Rouge, La.: Louisiana State University Press, 1966. Paperback.
  A study of fishing in the area of the barrier reef, with chapters on the development of
  fishing techniques and boat building from the colonial period to the present, with
  maps.
Craton, Michael. *A History of the Bahamas.* London: Collins, 1962.
  From the Ice Age to the 20th century.
Davidson, William J. *Historical Geography of the Bay Islands.* Birmingham, Ala.: Southern
  University Press, 1974.
Esquemeling, John. *The Buccaneers of America.* New York: Dover Publications, 1967.
  Paperback.
  Written in the late 17th century by an eyewitness to events at the time of Henry
  Morgan, this fascinating book purports to be "A true account of the most remarkable
  assaults committed of late years upon the coasts of the West Indies by Buccaneers of
  Jamaica and Tortuga (both English and French)."
Harman, Carter, and the Editors of *Life. The West Indies.* New York: Time, Inc., 1963.
  An overview of the history of the region, the impact of slavery and European culture,
  and the economic and political aspirations of the people.
Johnston, Michael C., and James L. Radawski. "Marine Archeological Investigations of
  the Bay Islands and North Coast of Honduras, 1968 to 1975." Roatán: Ocean-
  ographicos de Honduras, 1975.
  A report presented at the Sixth International Conference on Underwater Archeolo-
  gy, Charleston, S.C., Jan. 7–11, 1975.
Lewisohn, Florence. *The Romantic History of St. Croix.* Christiansted, St. Croix: St. Croix
  Landmarks Society, 1964. Paperback.
———. *Tales of Tortola and the British Virgin Islands.* 1966. Paperback.
Macpherson, John. *Caribbean Lands—A Geography of the West Indies.* London: Longmans
  Group, Ltd., 1973. Paperback.
  An easy-to-use reference book on the formation and development of the West Indies.
Masefield, John. *On the Spanish Main.* Annapolis, Md.: Naval Institute Press, 1972.
  A somewhat disjointed but extensively researched word picture of the prowess of
  English adventurers, from Drake through Morgan, as well as the life style of the
  buccaneers. Engrossing background reading for those who will cruise the western
  Caribbean.
Morison, Samuel Eliot. *Admiral of the Ocean Sea.* Boston: Little, Brown, 1942.
  The Pulitzer Prize-winning biography of Columbus.
———. *The European Discovery of America—The Southern Voyages, 1492–1616.* Boston:
  Oxford University Press, 1974.
  The concluding volume of Morison's monumental study, with much new material on
  the voyages of Columbus, Magellan, Drake, and other early explorers.

————, and Mauricio Obregon. *The Caribbean as Columbus Saw It.* Boston: Little, Brown, 1964.

An informative narrative retracing, by airplane, the routes of Columbus, with nearly 300 air photographs of harbors and landmarks.

Morley, Sylvanus. "Yucatan, Home of the Gifted Maya." National Geographic Magazine, Nov. 1936.

Pearcy, G. Etzel. *The West Indian Scene.* Princeton, N.J.: D. Van Nostrand, 1965. Paperback.

The physical, social, and economic aspects of the Antilles.

Waugh, Alec. *A Family of Islands.* Garden City, N.Y.: Doubleday, 1964.

A readable and informative history of the West Indies from 1492 to 1898.

White, Robb. *Our Virgin Island.* Garden City, N.Y.: Doubleday, 1953.

The trials and successes of a penniless young couple who made their home on Marina Cay in the B.V.I. in the days before tourists and charter yachts.

Fiction

Forester, C.S. *Admiral Hornblower in the West Indies.* Boston: Little, Brown, 1957.

Wilder, Robert. *Wind from the Carolinas.* New York: G. P. Putnam's Sons, 1964.

An historical novel that traces the fortunes of a Loyalist family forced to move from the Carolinas to the Exumas, cleverly woven into Bahamian history from the Revolution to Prohibition.

INDEX

Page references for charts are in italics.

Jane in love. She shook her head, smiling, as she entered the foyer. The telephone was ringing and she automatically picked it up before Haney had a chance. "Hello?"

"Caroline, Granger."

"Yes?"

"I've spoken with Rink. He'll arrive some time this evening."

There were a million things to be done in the afternoon, a million people to notify. Roscoe had no living relatives save his son and daughter, so there was no family to be concerned with. But everyone in the county, and many in the state of Mississippi, would want to know of Roscoe's illness. Caroline divided the list with Granger and spent a great deal of time on the telephone.

"Haney, you'd better get Rink's old room in order. He's coming home tonight."

At that the housekeeper burst into copious tears. "Praise God, praise God. I've been praying for the day my baby would come home. His mama is dancing in Heaven today. She surely is. All that room needs is fresh bed linens. I've been keeping it clean against the day he'd come back to it. Lordy, Lordy, I can't wait to clap eyes on him."

Caroline tried not to think of the moment

23

when she would have to look at the prodigal son, speak to him. She busied herself with the myriad tasks at hand.

Nor did she think of Roscoe's imminent death. That would come later, in private. Not even when she visited the hospital late in the afternoon and sat by his bedside did she let herself dwell on the thought that he would never leave the place. He was still a captive of the anesthetic, but she thought a small pressure was applied to her hand when she took his and squeezed it in good-bye.

At dinner, she told Laura Jane about Rink's coming home. The girl jumped out of her chair, grabbed Haney and began to dance her around the room. "He promised he would come back someday, didn't he, Haney? Rink's coming *home!* I've got to tell Steve." She raced out the back door toward the stables, where Steve had an apartment.

"That girl's gonna make a nuisance out of herself if she doesn't leave that young man alone."

Caroline smiled secretly. "I don't think so." Haney cocked one inquiring eyebrow, but Caroline didn't elaborate. She picked up her glass of mint-sprigged iced tea and went out onto the front veranda. As she sat down in a wicker rocking chair, her head fell back onto the flowered cushion and her eyes closed.

This was the time she loved best at The Retreat, the early evening, when lights from inside the house shone through the windows and made them look like jewels. Shadows were long and darkly hued and melded into one another so that there were no sharp angles or distinct shapes. The sky overhead was a rare and lovely shade of violet, dense and impenetrable. The trees were looming black etchings against it. Bullfrogs down on the river channel croaked hoarsely and cicadas filled the breezeless, humid air with their shrill soprano notes. The rich delta earth smelled of fecundity. Each flower gave off a unique and heady perfume.

After long moments of rest, Caroline opened her eyes. That was when she saw him.

He was standing motionless beneath the branches of a sprawling live oak. Her heart rocketed into her throat and her vision blurred. She didn't know if he were real or a mirage. Dizziness assailed her and she gripped the slippery iced-tea glass hard to keep it from sliding through her cold, stiff fingers.

He nudged himself away from the trunk

25

of the tree and moved, pantherlike and silent, coming closer until he stood at the brick steps leading up to the porch.

He was only a shadow among many, but there was no mistaking the clean masculine lines of his shape as he stood with his feet widely separated. Physically the years had been kind to him. He was no less trim than the first time she had seen him. Darkness hid his face from her, but she caught the shine of straight white teeth as he smiled slowly.

It was an indolent smile if it matched his tone of voice. "Well as I live and breathe, if it isn't Caroline Dawson." He placed one booted foot on the bottom step and bent at the waist to prop his arms on his knee. He looked up at her and the light from the entrance hall fell on his features. Her heart constricted with pain . . . and love. "Only it's Lancaster now, isn't it?"

"Yes, it's Lancaster now. Hello, Rink."

That face! That face had haunted her dreams and filled her fantasies. It was still the most marvelous face she had ever seen. Good in his twenties, he was magnificent in his thirties. Black hair, the Devil's own, intimated the wildness of his spirit with swirling strands that defied control. His eyes, which had mystified her from the first time she had seen them, intrigued her anew. People with no imagination would call them light brown. But they were gold, like the purest dark honey, the finest liquor, like sparkling topazes.

The last time she'd seen him, those eyes were blazing with passion. *Tomorrow. . . . Tomorrow, baby. Here. In our place. Oh, God, Caroline, kiss me again.* Then: *Tomorrow, tomorrow.* Only he hadn't returned the next day or ever again.

"Funny," he commented in a tone that left her to believe it wasn't funny at all, "us sharing the same last name."

There was no answer for that. She wanted to shout that they could have shared the same last name years ago if he hadn't been a liar, if he hadn't betrayed her. Some things were better left unsaid. "I didn't hear your car."

"I flew in, landed on the airstrip and walked from there."

The landing strip was about a mile away. "Oh. Why?"

"Maybe I didn't know what kind of welcome I was going to get."

"This is your home, Rink."

His curse was vicious and rank. "Yeah, sure it is."

She wet her lips with her tongue and

wished she had the courage to try standing. She feared to, afraid her legs wouldn't support her. "You haven't asked about your father."

"Granger filled me in."

"You know he's dying, then."

"Yes. And he wants to see me. Wonders never cease."

His scathing remark brought her out of the chair without having to think about it. "He's a sick old man, Rink. Not at all the way you remember him."

"If he's got one breath of life in his body, he's exactly the way I remember him."

"I won't argue with you about this."

"I'm not arguing."

"And I won't have you upsetting him or Laura Jane or Haney. They're looking forward to seeing you."

"*You* won't have? My, my. You do consider yourself mistress of The Retreat, don't you?"

"Please, Rink. The next few weeks are going to be difficult enough without —"

"I know, I know." His long sigh reached her where she stood tensely on the porch, her hands clasped tightly together. She had set her glass of tea on the porch railing for fear of dropping it. "I can't wait to see them, either," he said and glanced toward the stables. "I saw Laura Jane come out of the house a while ago, but didn't want to suddenly appear out of the dark and scare her. I remember her as a little girl. I can't believe she's all grown-up."

An image of Laura Jane and Steve kneeling in the hay of the stall together, his rough fingers brushing her cheek, came to Caroline's mind. She wondered what Rink would think of his sister's romance. It made her uneasy to surmise. "She's a woman now, Rink."

She felt his eyes on her, touring, analyzing, assessing. Like warm brandy they poured over her and touched everywhere. "And you," he said softly. "You're all grown-up now, too, aren't you, Caroline? A woman."

She was remarkably unchanged. The beauty of the fifteen-year-old girl he had known had only mellowed. He had hoped to find her fat, disheveled, frumpy, with lackluster hair and heavy thighs. Instead she was still reed slender, with a waist that looked like a strong Gulf breeze would snap her in two. Her breasts had matured to a soft fullness, but they were still high, round and achingly touchable. *Damn her!* How often had his father touched her?

He took the steps up to the porch slowly,

like a predator who wasn't hungry but only wanted to torment his prey. The golden eyes, gleaming through the darkness, held hers. The wide sensuous lips were fixed in a sly, knowing smile, as though he knew she was remembering things she wished she could forget, like how his lips felt on her mouth, on her throat, on her breasts.

She spun on her heel. "I'll call Haney. She'll be —"

His hand flashed out to manacle her wrist and she was jerked to a halt. He forced her around to face him. "Hold on a minute," he said silkily. "After twelve years, don't you think we can greet each other more cordially?"

His free hand wrapped around the back of her neck and brought her face up dangerously close to his. "Remember, we're kinfolks now," he whispered tauntingly. Then his lips swooped down on hers, hard and angry. He took them brutally with his mouth, punishing her for all the nights he had had to think about her, his unspoiled Caroline, sharing her bed, her body, with his father.

Her fists dug into his chest. There was a roaring in her ears. Her knees went to jelly. She fought him. She fought herself harder. Because she wanted to fling her arms around him and hold him close, to know again the thrill of being in his embrace.

But this wasn't an embrace, it was an insult. She struggled for all she was worth to tear her mouth free.

When she succeeded, he slid his hands into his jeans pockets and grinned with mocking triumph at her outraged expression and bruised lips. "Greetings, Mom," he drawled.

Chapter 2

Caroline gasped, her breasts heaving with anger and humiliation. "What a wretched thing to say! How can you be so horrible?"

"How could you marry that rotten old man who just happens to be my father?"

"He isn't rotten. He's been good to me."

His laugh was a short barking sound. "Oh, I can see how good to you he's been. Are those pearls in your ears? Diamonds on your hand? You've come up in the world, haven't you, Caroline of the river? You live in The Retreat now. And didn't you tell me one time you'd give anything to live in a house like this?" He leaned over her and spoke in a low growl. "Let me guess what you gave my father before he married you."

She slapped him hard. It happened before she could measure the wisdom of it. One instant he was grinding out his insults and the next her palm was cracking across his hard cheek. It made her hand burn and she hoped his cheek felt the same sting.

He backed away, grinning a sardonic smile that made her angrier than his deprecating words. "Whatever I gave him, it was more than you did these last twelve years. He was heartbroken, living alone in this house, pining for you."

He laughed again. "Pining? That's good, Caroline. Pining." One knee bent so that his weight was shifted to his other leg in an arrogant stance. His arms crossed over his chest and he tilted his head. "Why is it so difficult for me to envision my father pining over anything? Especially my absence."

"I'm sure he wanted you here."

"He was as glad to see the last of me as I was of him," he said harshly. "Spare me any more sentimentality. If you attribute it to Roscoe, I assure you, you imagined it."

"I don't know what your quarrel was, but he's sick now, Rink. Dying. Please don't make things harder than they already are."

"Whose idea was it to notify me, yours or Granger's?"

"Roscoe's."

"That's what Granger said, but I don't believe it."

"It's the truth."

"Then he sure as hell has an ulterior motive."

"Roscoe wants to see his son before he dies!" she exclaimed. "That's motive enough."

"Not for Roscoe it's not. He's a cunning,

manipulative bastard and if he got me here to watch him die, believe me he has a reason."

"You shouldn't speak to me this way about him. He's my husband."

"That's your problem."

"Caroline? Who's — Oh, my Lord. *Rink!*" Haney barreled through the screen door and embraced Rink in a hug that would have squeezed the life out of a less brawny man. He hugged her back just as hard. Tears came to Caroline's eyes as she watched the bitterness and derision leave his face to be replaced by a wide grin of pure joy. His golden eyes were now lit with happiness, his teeth gleamed whitely behind a broad smile.

"Haney! God, how I've missed you."

"You could have written more often," she sniffed, drawing herself up and trying to look indignant.

"I apologize," he said humbly, though his eyes were as mischievous as they had been every time the housekeeper had caught him with his hand in the cookie jar. He'd always gotten away with it. He did now.

"I see that you've met Caroline," Haney said, beaming at the two of them.

"Oh, yes. I've met Caroline. We've been getting to know each other."

34

The housekeeper missed the glance he gave Caroline. "You haven't been eating right, I can see that. Making money hand over fist, picture showing up in the newspaper all the time, and still you look like you never get a decent meal. Well, get on inside. I've got supper warmed over for you."

"And pecan pie. I can smell it from here," he teased, pushing her through the door.

"I didn't bake it special for you."

"Now, come on, Haney. You and I both know better."

"And it's a coincidence that we had chicken gumbo for supper, too."

For weeks after Caroline had moved into The Retreat as its new mistress, she had felt like a visitor who didn't really belong. But months had passed. Laura Jane had accepted her as a friend. Haney had come to like her. But now, seeing Rink in his home, hearing the sound of his boots on the antique hardwood floors and hearing his voice echo through the high-ceilinged rooms, Caroline once again felt like an interloper. Rink belonged here. She didn't.

By the time she had followed them into the kitchen, Haney had Rink sitting at the large round oak table with a heaping plate of food in front of him. He was surveying the room. "Nothing's changed," he said warmly.

"I had the kitchen painted a couple of years ago," Haney told him. "But I told Mr. Lancaster that I wasn't going to change the color. I wanted everything to stay the same for the day when you came home."

Rink swallowed and moved a forkful of food around his plate. "I'm not home for good, Haney. Only until Daddy . . . gets settled down again."

Haney's busy hands paused in their endless tasks. She looked down at the man as though he were still a young boy in her charge. "I don't want you to go running off again, Rink. This is where you belong."

His eyes flicked toward Caroline then back down to his plate. "There's nothing here for me anymore," he said angrily before shoving another bite into his mouth.

"Yes there is . . . Laura Jane," Caroline reminded him softly. Rather than hovering inside the door, she forced herself to enter the kitchen. She didn't want Rink to know that his presence intimidated her in her own house. She wasn't Roscoe's widow yet, and as his wife she certainly had a right to be here. Going to the refrigerator, she poured herself another glass of iced tea which she really didn't want.

"Bless her heart, Rink," Haney contributed as she polished an already gleaming glass. "She beats me to the mailbox every day looking for a letter from you. On her account you shouldn't have stayed away, no matter the bad words between you and your daddy."

"I hated not being here for her. Is she all right?"

"Sure, sure. Pretty as a picture."

"That's not what I mean."

Haney thumped the glass onto the counter. "I know what you meant," she said tightly. "And yes, she's fine. I know by the way you've asked about her in your letters that you have no idea what Laura Jane is really like, Rink. She may not have been much for book learning, but she's smart as a whip about some things. You didn't stay around to watch over her, but you're as possessive as a mama bear with her cub. Watch out. She's a grown-up lady now and might not take kindly to being treated like a breakable object. She's a beautiful young woman. If folks got a chance to meet her, few would even realize she was different."

"But she is," he insisted.

"Not so different," Caroline said. "She knows exactly what's going on in the world, but her emotions are fragile. I worry more about her vulnerability than what mental deficiencies she has. If someone she loves

37

should disappoint her, she might never recover."

His eyes never left hers as he wiped his mouth with a linen napkin, tossed it down and pushed his chair away from the table. "Thanks for the sermon, Sister Caroline. I'll try to keep it in mind."

"I didn't necessarily mean —"

"Of course you did," he snapped and reached for the coffeepot, sloshing a generous amount into his cup.

"Rink Lancaster, you've got no call to light into Caroline that way." Haney was shocked by the automatic antipathy between these two. They hadn't known each other for five minutes, yet each time they looked at each other sparks flew. Apparently Rink didn't cotton to the idea of his daddy taking a bride as young as Caroline. But he'd been gone for twelve years. What difference had Roscoe's marriage made to him? Unless it had something to do with The Retreat. "Where are the manners your mama and I drilled into you? You remember that Caroline is your daddy's wife and deserves your respect as such."

Rink, his eyes still on Caroline, lifted one corner of his mouth in a mocking smile. "My stepmother. I keep forgetting that."

"Here comes Laura Jane," Haney said,

glancing worriedly at the two in the kitchen. "Don't upset her, Rink. She's already had one shock today and she took it well."

Laura Jane's soft voice trailed through the screen door before she pulled it open. She froze, her willowy body poised like a Grecian statue in the doorway as she spied her brother. For a moment her face remained blank, then it began to glow and the glow spread to her eyes, over her cheeks and became the most radiant of smiles. "Rink," she whispered.

She launched herself against him, folding her thin arms around his neck and burying her face in his shirt collar. His arms went around her and he rocked her back and forth while hugging her tight. His eyes were squeezed shut against the emotions that assailed him. Laura Jane was the first to pull back. With fingers that looked too fragile to have life in them, she explored her brother's face, his hair, his shoulders, as though to reassure herself that he was truly there.

"You're so tall," she remarked. "And strong." She laughed, gripping his biceps.

"You're beautiful and so grown-up." His eyes took in all of her, a beautifully delicate young woman. Then they both started laughing with the sheer joy of seeing each other. They hugged again.

"Daddy's going to die, Rink," Laura Jane said solemnly when they finally released each other. "Did Caroline tell you?"

"Yes," he said softly and ran his finger along her chin.

"But now you're here. And Haney and Caroline and Steve . . . Oh, my goodness! I forgot to introduce you." She turned to the stable manager, who had walked with her back to the house and who was now standing just inside the screened back door. Laura Jane took his hand and pulled him forward. "Steve Bishop, this is my brother, Rink."

Steve had to disengage his fingers from Laura Jane's in order to shake hands with Rink, who was staring at him with guarded eyes. "Mr. Lancaster, nice to meet you."

"Call me Rink," he said, shaking Steve's hand with a firm grip. "How long have you worked here?"

"A little more than a year."

Rink glanced at his sister and then back at the stable manager. "Laura Jane has mentioned you in her letters."

"One of the mares had a foal yesterday, Rink," Laura Jane informed him excitedly. "Steve helped her."

"And I need to get back to them," Steve said.

"Why don't you stay and have a piece of pie with us?" Haney offered.

He looked at Rink, then away. "No thank you. I need to check on that filly."

"I'll be over to see her in the morning, Steve. Is that all right?" Laura Jane inquired, taking his hand again.

"Sure," he said softly, smiling down into her guileless face. "She'd miss you if you didn't come to visit."

He pulled his hand free and went to the back door. "Good night, Steve," Laura Jane called.

"Good night, Laura Jane," he replied. Then he touched the brim of his straw cowboy hat in a salute to everyone else and disappeared into the darkness, limping slightly.

Rink stared after him, bracing himself in the doorjamb. Haney bustled around, slicing generous portions of pecan pie and scooping vanilla ice cream on top.

"None for me, thank you, Haney," Caroline said. From the corner of her eye, she saw Rink turn around to look in her direction. "It's been a long day. I think I'll go upstairs."

"Do you need anything?" Haney asked, concerned.

"A good night's sleep," Caroline said.

41

She leaned over Laura Jane and brushed a kiss on her cheek. "Good night. Tomorrow we'll go to the hospital and you can see your father."

"Yes, I want to. Good night. Isn't it wonderful that Rink's home, Caroline?"

"Yes, it is." Caroline straightened and met Rink's eyes. "Haney has your room ready for you. Good night, Rink."

Before he could respond, she was out the door and making her way through the dining room and up the stairs. Being in the same room with him was proving too much for her. Besides, he and Laura Jane and Haney, who had been a mother to them after Marlena had died, deserved some time alone together.

Her tread down the upstairs hallway was muffled by the Oriental runner that extended its length. Her bedroom was softly lighted by two bedside lamps. She switched one of them off. Darkness seemed comforting tonight, as though it hid what one didn't want to see, didn't want to think about. She went to stand at the wide window that looked out over the back acreage of The Retreat and down the grassy slope to the river channel. The moon was only half full, but she could see it reflecting on the water in the distance. Everything

42

looked so peaceful.

Caroline was anything but serene. She had suffered three shocks today. She had learned that her husband was going to die. She had seen that Steve's affection for Laura Jane went beyond friendship or even compassion. And Rink had come home.

With a long sigh, she moved away from the windows and began to undress. After running a deep, hot bath, she gratefully sank into the scented bubbles and closed her eyes. Only then did she let herself cry. For Roscoe. He had been frustrated by his illness yet stubbornly refused to see his doctor. A man of his vitality couldn't tolerate being ill. Perhaps it was better that the end would come soon. Forcing a man of Roscoe's spirit and ambition to lie useless and ailing in a hospital bed for months would be inhumanly unkind.

She lay in the tub for a long while until her tears dried and the water cooled. She prepared for bed. The house had grown quiet. When the gentle knock came on her door as she was pulling back the bedcovers, she jumped in a startled reaction.

Opening the door only a crack, she peered into the shadowed, silent hallway. "What do you want?"

"To talk to you."

Rink pushed his way through the door. Unless she wanted to create a scene, she had no choice but to let him in and close the door behind him. He stood in the middle of the floor and pivoted slowly, taking in the furnishings of the room. He crossed to the window and trailed his hand down the draperies, as though remembering the feel of them from long ago. He surveyed the items on the antique dressing table. He stared at himself in the beveled mirror over it. Was he looking for the little boy he had once been?

"This was my mother's room," he said at last.

Caroline's hands found each other at her waist and clung together moistly. "Yes, I know. It's a lovely room. One of my favorites in the house."

"It suits you," he said, studying her reflection behind his in the mirror. "Just as it did her. It's a totally feminine room."

As he continued to stare at her, Caroline became uncomfortably aware of her attire. The nightgown and robe were no competition for the burning gaze Rink subjected her to. She was conscious of her nakedness beneath her nightclothes, even though she was covered from chest to toes. And most unnerving of all was the knowledge that Rink was conscious of it, too.

His venturing eyes made pointed stops at her breasts, her waist, below her waist. As though responding to some silent summons, those erogenous places awakened and stirred to life. Her nipples tightened. Her womanhood flowered. Caroline condemned them, condemned herself, yet was powerless to stop the currents of arousal that flowed through her with each glance of those dark gold eyes.

He was holding a tumbler of bourbon in his hand and took an appreciative sip. He savored it as the liquor slid like silky fire down his throat and into his stomach. "Daddy still likes expensive whiskey," he remarked. "And pretty women. You look very pretty in this room, Caroline, with the lamplight on your hair." He gave her one more thorough going-over in the mirror, then turned away.

He walked to the chaise in the corner of the room and stretched out on it. It was made for a much daintier figure than Rink's. His boots hung off the end. He balanced the tumbler on his stomach, holding it with one hand while he put the other arm beneath his head, watching Caroline like a hawk. She stood nervously in the same spot where she had been standing when he'd entered the room.

"Mother and Daddy never shared this bedroom," he said idly, but Caroline wasn't deceived. Rink never said anything just for the sake of conversation. "I remember like it was yesterday the day he told her not to bother moving back into his bedroom after Laura Jane was born. Mother cried for hours. He never slept with her again." He sipped the whiskey and laughed harshly. "I don't think he ever forgave her for Laura Jane."

"He loves Laura Jane," Caroline protested. "He's always done what he thought was best for her."

He laughed again, more scathingly this time. "Oh, yeah, he's good at that. Doing what he thinks is good for somebody."

Caroline forced herself to move. She went to the bed and sat down on the edge of it, twisting the cord belt at the waist of her robe through her fingers. "Is this what you wanted to talk to me about?"

"About husbands and wives sleeping together?" he asked, one black brow arching. "Or about Laura Jane?"

He was being deliberately provoking. Where had all his sweetness gone? All that tenderness he had showed her when they'd met in secret and poured out their hearts to each other? He was someone she didn't know, yet was so very familiar with.

His shirt was unbuttoned and lay open. His chest rose and fell with each breath. She remembered how he had looked the first time she'd seen him, river water streaming down that muscular chest and matting the dark hair. His stomach was just as hard and flat now, corded with muscle. A black stripe of hair divided it into two perfect halves before disappearing into the waistband of his jeans. Behind the fly of the snug-fitting jeans was profound evidence of his sex.

Flustered, Caroline's eyes flickered away from him. "Why do you want to talk to me about any of it? I don't want to get involved in the argument between you and your father."

He found that extremely funny and chuckled for long minutes while he leisurely finished the whiskey. Then he got off the chaise and stalked toward her. The single lamp cast shadows on his dark features. He was satanic, dangerous and illicitly appealing as he stood there, looming over her. His knees were almost touching hers, he stood so close. She forced herself not to shrink away from him in fear. Not fear for what he might do to her, but fear of how she would respond if he did.

"I'll need a car in the morning. I came to

ask if I might borrow yours."

"Of course," she said on a breath of relief. "I'll get you the keys." She moved off the bed, avoiding brushing up against him as best she could. But as she squeezed past him, for one heart-stopping moment her thigh rubbed his and she felt the hard muscles contract. She moved away quickly and went to the dresser where her purse was. With shaking fingers, she fumbled for the keys, finally extracted them and dropped them into his palm. "Where are you going in the morning?"

"I want to see the doctor before I see my father. I'll come back midmorning to drive you and Laura Jane to the hospital if you like."

"Yes, that will be fine. I have some business to attend to here first thing in the morning."

"Cotton gin business?"

"Yes. I do the bookkeeping."

"So I understand from Granger. He said you became indispensable to Daddy before you married him." He came a step closer. His breath was warm and fragrant with expensive bourbon as it wafted over her face.

"Granger often goes overboard with his compliments." She tried to move aside, but he merely followed her with a matching

48

sideways movement of his own. If anything, her avoidance tactic had brought them closer.

"I doubt that. I bet you're indispensable to Daddy in a lot of ways, aren't you?"

Her eyes flashed like lightning as she glared up at him. "Why do you insist on making these snide innuendos, Rink?"

" 'Cause it just tickles the hell out of me to get a rise out of you, that's why. Caroline, so young, so sweet, so demure, so . . . pure." He snarled the word.

She lifted her hand, but he grabbed it and twisted her arm behind her, hauling her against him. Her breasts were flattened against his hard chest. She stubbed her bare toes on the toes of his boots. His face came down to within an inch of hers. When he spoke, each word was pushed from behind clenched teeth.

"I let you get by with that once, but if you ever slap me again, you'll wish to God you hadn't."

"What would you do? Slap me back?"

He smiled with evil mischief. "Oh, no. That's not how I'd get retribution. I'd do something you wouldn't like at all." He pulled her tighter against his aroused body so she would understand his implication. He brought his head down closer. "Or would you like it very much, Caroline? Hmmm?" His belt buckle gouged through her nightclothes to bruise her stomach. "You may be Mrs. Roscoe Lancaster to everybody else, but you're still just Caroline Dawson to me, a girl walking through the woods in the summertime on her way to work . . . and driving me into a slow madness in the meantime."

Caroline stared up at him. Her expression was one of defiance. Her eyes were dark, like a storm cloud blowing up from the Gulf that carried with it rain and wind and lightning. The hair he had complimented earlier fell away from her face to hang down her back in a rich cascade. "Then you *do* remember, Rink. I was wondering if you had any memory of it at all."

Rink's eyes went wide for an instant before they narrowed. They scanned her face hotly, lingering long on her mouth, sliding down her throat to her breasts, which swelled in the opening of her robe, then going back up again. In those eyes was turbulence, the sign of an internal battle being waged.

"Yes," he said roughly. "Yes, goddammit. I remember."

She was released so suddenly that she reeled and caught herself against the dressing table. By the time she had regained her balance, he had stridden angrily from the room.

Damn! He wished he didn't remember.

Back in his room, he tore off his shirt, re-filled the tumbler from the bottle he had pilfered from the liquor cabinet in his father's study and flung himself down into the leather easy chair that had always stood next to the windows. He took a swig of whiskey, but it had lost its charm and he set it aside in distaste. He bent down and pulled off his boots, dropping them with soft thuds onto the rug.

Leaning back, he rested his head on the chair's deep cushion and let his mind go back, back to that summer day when he had taken all he could of the gin, his father's harping and the humid Mississippi heat. He had gone to the river, stripped to the skin and plunged into the stream where it ran cold. It was after he had gotten out, shaken himself dry and pulled on his jeans that he had seen her. . . .

"God Almighty!" Rink exclaimed. His fingers fumbled to zip up his jeans quickly. "How long have you been standing there?" He almost laughed out loud at her expression. If he was surprised at seeing her, the girl was absolutely paralyzed at seeing him.

He didn't think she was going to answer; then she stuttered, "I . . . I just got here."

"Well it's a damn good thing, because I've been skinny-dipping. If you had come along any sooner, we would both have been embarrassed."

His grin was wide and confident, with more than a trace of conceit. She was still shaking in her bobby socks and penny loafers, but she managed a timid smile. "I hope I didn't disturb you," she said with a politeness that, under the circumstances, amused him.

"No. I was finished. It's been so hot. I had to take a swim."

"Yes, it is hot. That's why I was walking down here by the channel. It's cooler than on the road."

He was curious about her from the beginning. Not only was she a strikingly beautiful girl, she was different. Her skirt was cotton, clean and pressed, but unfashionable. Her white cotton blouse smelled of laundry soap and starch rather than Youth Dew, which was what all the girls seemed to be wearing these days.

Beneath the blouse he could see the outline of a white brassiere that must have been as confining as a straitjacket. Most of the girls he knew wore something called a demicup push-up bra, which did just that, he was certain, with the sole intention of driving their dates crazy.

He dragged his eyes away from her chest, ashamed of himself for imposing on her the analysis he gave to every woman he met. She was just a kid. Fifteen? Sixteen? At most. And she still looked scared half to death of him.

But God, she was a looker. Clear skin; eyes the color of the fog that rode low over the bayous; a neat, trim body with a softness about it that was all female. Her hair gleamed darkly, like polished mahogany wood. Every time a breeze stirred the limbs of the trees overhead, dappled sunlight shot sparks of fire through the heavy strands.

"Where are you going?"

"Into town. I work at Woolworth's."

He didn't know any girls who actually worked during the summer. Most lay out by the swimming pools, private or public, cruised the main drag until they saw someone they knew and organized parties for the evenings.

"I'm Rink Lancaster."

She was looking at him strangely and it occurred to him that her fascination was

53

with his state of undress. She was fighting her curiosity, but her eyes kept flickering to his chest, his stomach and to the as yet undone snap of his jeans. Normally that would have boosted his confidence that this was going to be an easy conquest. He would have taken such an appraisal as an announcement that the woman was willing and available. But the innocence in this girl's eyes made him irritatingly self-conscious. With her eyes constantly returning to his fly, Rink was dismayed to feel unwelcomed arousal enlarging him.

Trying to keep an air of propriety, he stepped forward to offer her his hand. She flinched momentarily, then shyly placed her palm in his. "Caroline Dawson," she said tremulously, lifting her eyes to meet his.

They stared.

Time ticked by, insects hummed around their heads, an airplane whined high overhead, the channel water lapped the mossy rocks lining its banks. It was long moments before they moved and dropped their hands.

"Dawson?" Rink asked at last and wondered why his voice sounded as it had ten years prior when it was "changing." "Pete Dawson's daughter?"

Her eyes dropped to the ground and he

saw her shoulders sag. Damn! Why had he asked in that incredulous tone of voice? Everyone knew Pete Dawson. He played dominoes all day in the pool halls, begging money off anyone dumb enough to stop and talk to him, until he had enough to buy a bottle of cheap whiskey to get him through to the next day.

"Yes," she said softly. Then, shaking slightly and raising her head with an air of pride that made Rink's chest feel warm and full, she said, "I've got to be going or I'll be late for work."

"It was nice to meet you."

"Nice to meet you, too."

"Be careful walking through the woods."

She laughed. "What's funny?"

"You telling me to be careful when you just went swimming in there." She pointed at the channel. "There could be water moccasins and Lord knows what else in there. Why didn't you go to the swimming pool in town?"

He shrugged. "I was hot."

He was hot. God, was he hot. When she had laughed, her head had gone back, making her throat look white and vulnerable and inviting. Her hair had shimmered over her neck and shoulders. Detergent and starch were beginning to smell better than any fancy perfume his nose had ever come in contact with. The fragrance blended so well with the clean fresh scent of her skin. Her laughter, husky and genuine, had seemed a tangible thing that reached out and stroked him. It stroked him right where it felt damn good and right where it hurt like hell.

Yes, he was hot. Burning up with heat. "What time do you get off work?" He was as surprised as she by his question.

"Nine o'clock." Cautiously she began to back away.

"After dark? You walk home after dark?"

"Yes. But then I don't go through the woods. Only in the daytime."

He pondered that. This girl was like none other he had ever met, here in Winstonville or at Ol' Miss.

"I'll be late for work," she repeated and backed away farther, though he sensed in her a reluctance to part, too.

"Yeah, sure. Don't be late. Be seein' you, Caroline."

"Good-bye, Rink."

There was more said in that parting than either had verbalized. He counted on their meeting again. She never thought they would.

He had walked back to his convertible

and vaulted behind the wheel without opening the door. He made the drive to The Retreat in record time and went immediately to his room, bounding up the stairs two at a time, and . . .

Now, as then, thoughts of Caroline swirled through his mind. He could see himself entering this very room that summer afternoon twelve years ago. He had tossed his discarded clothes onto the floor and fallen into this same chair. He had sat in the same slumping posture then as he did now, the same woman filling his mind. She was still a mystery, still elusive and haunting and obsessive.

And now, as then, he knew that no matter what he might do, there was little hope of easing his aching, throbbing desire.

Chapter 3

It was early when she awoke. She had hoped to sleep longer, to put off waking up and facing the crises of Roscoe's illness and Rink's return to Winstonville.

From downstairs she heard the front door open and close quietly. Throwing off the covers, she went into the hall and out onto the second-story balcony. The sun wasn't yet up over the tops of the trees, though a peachy glow painted the eastern sky. One star and a half-moon were still vividly bright against a vermilion sky. Mist rose from the dewy grass in trailing wisps. It would be another humid day.

Below her, Rink stepped off the porch. He lingered on the bottom step and studied the landscape that Caroline knew he loved. This land was as vital to him as breath. She pitied him for all the years he had banished himself from the home he loved.

Slowly he walked to the car parked in front of the house. He had on jeans and a sportcoat, a pretentious combination for drugstore cowboys but exactly right for him. The jeans were fashionably faded but had been starched and pressed to knife-blade creases down the front of his legs. Caroline watched as he dug into the front pocket for the car keys.

He swung open the car door. That was when he accidentally caught sight of her standing there watching him from the balcony. Propping his arm on the top of the car, he stared back up at her.

She stood perfectly still, didn't speak, didn't greet him, except with her eyes. They locked with his and held. And held. For long moments, in the pinky gold of the dawn, they stared at each other. The hazy morning light surrounding them seemed unreal, outside of time. In that silent moment of intimacy they could let down their defenses. They could indulge themselves. There existed nothing else in the world save the two of them.

Then at last, without speaking a word, he got into her Lincoln and drove away. Dejectedly Caroline returned to her room and dressed. She looked at herself in the mirror and asked, "How could this have happened?"

The only man she had ever loved, or had ever come close to loving, was Rink Lancaster. For only a short while they had shared something special and rare. At least to her it had been. She had allowed herself to dream that the implausible might be possible. She had been duped into believing all he'd told her that summer. His words had been meaningless. She had been nothing more to him than a novelty.

Now, by some whimsical twist of fate, she was married to his father. His *father!* When Roscoe had asked her to marry him, it had seemed the answer to all her dreams. She would have respectability, money. People who had looked down on her all her life would treat her with deference.

Rink had been gone, never to return. Why hadn't she considered that he might come back and how she would feel if he did? Had she been completely honest with herself? Had she married Roscoe not because she'd wanted to make him happy and help him with his business, to be a friend to Laura Jane, but because she'd wanted to make Rink jealous and sorry that he had deserted her? Was she trying to pay him back for the heartache she had suffered when he left? Had she secretly hoped that he would hear about the marriage, remember that summer twelve years ago and be outraged?

She smiled sadly at her reflection in the mirror. "He's merely amused, Caroline. Amused and disgusted."

Haney was already in the kitchen when Caroline came down a short time later to pour herself a cup of coffee. "Good morning."

"You're up bright and early," the housekeeper remarked over her shoulder.

"I have to get the payroll out and I want to do it early and leave the rest of the day free." She sipped the coffee. "You're up earlier than usual, too."

"I want to cook a fine breakfast for Rink."

"He's already left, Haney."

She whirled around and confronted Caroline to verify what she'd heard. "Already?"

"Yes. About an hour ago."

Haney shook her head, making *tsking* sounds. "He's not eating right. Here I was waiting to make him his favorite breakfast and he's hightailed it out of here before I even got a chance."

Caroline placed a comforting hand on her arm. "Why don't you fix it for Laura Jane? Call Steve over to share it with her. I'm sure they'd like that."

"Okay," she mumbled. "But it won't be the same without Rink. Nothing in this house has been the same since he married that gal and left town."

Haney was right about that, Caroline thought as she made her way toward the back of the house and into Roscoe's study. Painfully, she remembered the day Rink hadn't showed up at their rendezvous. Disconsolate, she had gone on to work only to overhear the town buzzing with gossip that Rink Lancaster was going to marry Marilee George, one of Winstonville's prominent debutantes. Caroline's world had never been the same.

She whipped through the bookkeeping without having to think too much about it. When she telephoned the gin, the morning shift foreman told her things were running smoothly.

"Got one machine that's being ornery, but it's nothing you need to worry about at a time like this."

"I'll count on you to carry on as though nothing's out of the ordinary, Barnes. As long as he's alive, Roscoe is still in charge and I report directly to him."

"Yes, ma'am," the foreman replied before he hung up.

She was sure some of the men balked at the idea of taking orders from a woman, especially ol' Pete Dawson's daughter. But if they did, they never vocalized their feelings. They feared Roscoe too much. But what would happen when he was gone?

"Problems?"

Her head jerked up to see Rink lounging against the door frame. She realized that her brow was creased with worry and she relaxed it. "Minor ones. You know how it is at the gin."

"Actually, I don't." He sauntered into the room. His sportcoat was hooked over his index finger and slung over his shoulder. The first three buttons of his plaid shirt had been left undone to reveal a tanned throat and a wedge of dark hair. "I left town before I had much to do with the running of the gin." By now he was at the edge of the desk. He leaned far over it until his face was on a level with hers. "Why don't you tell me what it's like, boss lady?"

Seething with anger, she surged to her feet, sending her chair rolling backward on its casters. They faced each other like adversaries in a boxing ring waiting for the bell to begin the round.

"Rink, Haney sent me in here after you. Breakfast is just now ready and she wants you to eat." Laura Jane happily skipped into the room to hug her brother. "Good morning. Caroline, I'm supposed to bring you, too. And Haney said no excuses."

Another argument had been thwarted, but Rink wasn't going to let her off easily. He extended his hand to her. "Caroline."

She had no choice but to place her hand in his and let him lead her around the desk. Nor did he release her hand until they reached the dining room. That he was also holding Laura Jane's hand didn't matter. Where his palm touched hers, where his fingers curled possessively through hers, Caroline's skin tingled.

Despite Haney's sumptuously prepared brunch, it wasn't a pleasant meal. Rink didn't seem too happy to find Steve sitting next to Laura Jane. Steve cast uneasy glances around the table, as though he might be asked to leave at any moment.

The hostility between Rink and Caroline was palpable, though they went out of their way to be polite to each other. Haney couldn't figure it out and she was huffy because the tension between them was ruining all her efforts to make this a special homecoming for Rink.

"Why is everybody mad?" Laura Jane asked suddenly.

They all looked at her, dumbfounded. She alone was happy, enjoying the presence of those she loved. But her perception was keen and she had picked up on the antagonism that crackled around the table.

It was Caroline who finally spoke. "We're all just worried about Roscoe," she said gently, reaching across the table to pat the young woman's hand.

"But Rink's here. And Steve." She blessed him with a look radiant with love. "Let's all be happy."

She shamed them into it. Rink stopped staring suspiciously at Steve and tensing every time he looked at Laura Jane. He and Caroline stopped glowering at each other and even got into a conversation about the townsfolk that Rink had known years ago. She informed him about who had married whom, who was divorced, who was prospering and who wasn't.

When they were done, Steve stood and thanked Haney, then headed toward the kitchen. "Just a minute, Steve," Laura Jane announced. "I'm coming with you to see the filly."

"We're going to the hospital, Laura Jane," Rink said curtly.

"But I want to see the foal. I promised Steve I would come to the stables this morning."

Steve shifted self-consciously from one booted foot to the other. "Laura Jane, your daddy will be disappointed if you don't go see him. That filly's not going anywhere," he teased. "You can come see her another time."

65

"All right, Steve," she acquiesced softly. "I'll come see you as soon as I get back."

Steve nodded, thanked Haney again and left quickly. He didn't look directly at Rink before going.

Caroline stood hastily. "I'll be ready in a few minutes, Rink. Laura Jane, do you want to freshen up before we go?"

"I guess so."

They came back downstairs a few minutes later. Rink was waiting for them in the foyer. Haney stood beside him, holding a vase of fresh-cut roses. "Haney wants to follow us in her car and take Daddy the roses. Then she'll come on back. Laura Jane, why don't you ride with her and hold the flowers so they won't spill."

"I'll do that," Caroline offered hurriedly. Rink's hard look said otherwise.

"I'd like to talk to you on the way." Imperiously he helped her into the Lincoln while Haney drove the station wagon that belonged to The Retreat but was left at her disposal.

"Did you see the doctor this morning?" Caroline asked to break the tense silence.

"Yes. He told me what he'd told you and Granger."

"Did . . . did he say when it —"

"Any time."

They were on the highway, heading toward town, before Rink said another word. "Who is this Steve?"

"Steve Bishop." Caroline was automatically on the defensive. She thought she knew what was coming and she wasn't going to like it.

Irritation thinned Rink's lips. "Can you elaborate on that a little?"

"He's a Vietnam War veteran."

"Is that why he limps? A war injury?"

"He lost his left leg from the knee down." She turned to him as she imparted that piece of news. He continued to stare out the windshield, but she saw his hands grip the wheel and the muscles in his arms bunch. His face was set in hard lines that bespoke an iron will and dogged determination. And pride. So much pride.

She knew he wanted to dislike Steve. Knowing he was permanently handicapped wasn't going to make it easy to do. "He was bitter and surly when he applied for the job. I believe his attitude was a defense mechanism against being rejected. He's conscientious, hardworking, honest."

"I don't like the attachment Laura Jane has for him."

"Why?"

"You have to ask?" he demanded, swiveling his head around. "It's unhealthy and dangerous, that's why. She has no business hanging around a single man all the time."

"I see no harm in it. She's a single woman."

"And innocent about sex. Totally. I doubt if she even knows the difference between men and women and why the difference is there."

"Of course she does!"

"All right, then, all the more reason why she doesn't need to spend so much time in his company. Because I can guarantee that he knows the difference."

"I think he's good for her. He's kind and patient. He's been hurt and not only physically. He knows what it's like to be an outcast and feel rejected as Laura Jane always has been."

"What if he took advantage of her fondness? Sexually."

"He wouldn't do that."

Rink scoffed. "He damn sure would. He's a man and she's a beautiful woman, and plenty of opportunities present themselves."

"You ought to know all about that, shouldn't you?"

The heated words were out of her mouth before she could halt them. He braked the car jarringly in the parking space at the hospital and swung around to face her. His face was as angry as hers. She had gone to the water's edge, she might as well plunge in.

"You should know all about taking advantage of an innocent girl, lying to her, making promises you don't intend to keep."

"Are you referring to that summer?"

"Yes! I've never understood how you could be with me the way you were and still get Marilee pregnant. You must have exhausted yourself. Or was I merely the warm-up act for your big finish?"

He broadened her vocabulary by several choice words before he shoved the car door open and slammed it behind him. Only then did Caroline realize that Haney and Laura Jane were already at the hospital entrance and were watching them expectantly. Caroline's fingers were icy as she clenched them, but she forced herself to relax when Rink opened her door and helped her out. Her features were schooled into a mask of composure by the time the group traversed the lobby of the hospital and entered the elevator.

The nurse at the desk on Roscoe's floor informed them that they could go in together if they didn't stay too long. "He had a rough night. A lot of pain," she told them sadly.

"Maybe I'd better go first and tell him you're here," Caroline said. No one objected. Rink was rigid and remote. Haney was uncharacteristically subdued. Laura Jane was wide-eyed and looked like she might bolt at any moment.

Caroline pushed open the heavy hospital room door and went into the room. It was the largest, most expensive private suite the hospital had to offer. Florists' arrangements already lined the window ledge and TV table. Much as she hated to admit it, Roscoe inspired little love in the people his life touched. But many revered or feared him, as evidenced by the abundance of cards and flowers.

He didn't look intimidating now as he opened his eyes and saw her. His skin had the gray-yellow, pasty look of death. Dark shadows ringed his sunken eyes. His lips were tinged with blue. But his eyes were as dark and alive as ever.

"Good morning." She bent over him, took his hand and kissed his forehead. "The nurse said you had a rough night. Did you get any rest?"

"Don't patronize me please, Caroline." He shook off her hand. "I'll have a whole goddamn eternity to rest." He laughed wheezingly. "Or to burn, I'm sure some

70

hope. Did you get the payroll done?"

"Yes," she said, stepping away and taking his rejection of her affection pragmatically. He was gravely ill. He was allowed some contrariness. "This morning. I'll deliver the checks to the gin this afternoon."

"Good. I don't want them to think I'm dead yet." He laid a hand on his stomach and winced with pain, cursing viciously.

When he subsided, Caroline said softly, "Are you up to having visitors?"

"Who?"

"Laura Jane and Haney."

"Haney! That hypocritical bitch. She's hated me since the day she first saw me. Thought I married Marlena for her money and for The Retreat. Blamed me for Rink's leaving. Blamed me for every goddamn thing that went wrong with this family."

Caroline played devil's advocate. "Why didn't you fire her years ago?"

He cackled. "Because I liked jousting with her. Kept my wits sharpened. Now she's come to snivel over my deathbed. Ha!"

Caroline had seen him in this kind of mood before, but she had always ignored it until it passed. She regretted that he chose to be this way during their last days together. "Please, Roscoe. Don't be angry.

Haney picked some flowers from the rosebeds for you."

He growled his consent to see the house-keeper. "Laura Jane has no business in here. This place'll scare her silly. Does she know I'm not coming home?"

Caroline looked away from the razor-sharp eyes. "Yes. I told her yesterday."

"What did she say?"

"She said you'd go to Heaven and be with Marlena."

He laughed until pain wrenched him again. "Well, it would take a simpleton to think that."

His choice of words offended Caroline greatly, but she held her peace. Few ever argued with Roscoe over anything, even his way of putting things. "Shall I tell them to come in?"

"Yes, yes," he said, waving a thin hand weakly. "Let's get it over with."

"There's someone else, Roscoe."

Her quiet tone brought his eyes snapping back to her. He stared at her hard, searchingly, making her unaccountably uncomfortable. "Rink? Rink's come?"

She nodded. "As soon as Granger called him."

"Good, good. I want to see my son, to say some things to him before it's over."

Caroline's heart swelled with gladness. It was time these two strong-willed men settled their differences. She hastened toward the door, missing the cold, shrewd calculation in Roscoe's eyes as he watched her go.

Laura Jane was first in the room. She ran toward the bed and flung her arms around her father's neck, hugging him hard. "I miss you at home, Daddy," she said. "We have a new filly. She's beautiful."

"Well, that's fine, Laura Jane," he said and gently pushed her away. Caroline watched, wishing just once that he would return the spontaneous affection his daughter showed him. "Been picking the rosebushes, I see," he grunted crossly as he peered up at the housekeeper from under scowling brows.

Haney had been bullied by him for years. She wasn't the least intimidated now. "Yes. These are only half of them, too. The others are on the dining room table."

Roscoe appreciated her spunk. They had waged a cold war for over thirty years and he considered her a worthy opponent. "To hell with flowers. Bring me anything to eat?"

"You know you're not supposed to have anything the hospital doesn't cook."

"What the hell difference does it make?" he roared. "Huh? Somebody tell me."

One by one he treated the women to baleful stares and then turned his head to meet his son's steady gaze. For an interminably long time the two men stared at each other. No one moved. Finally Roscoe's chest began to shake with a low, rumbling laugh. "Still mad at me, Rink?"

"I got over being mad a long time ago, sir."

"Is that why you came back? To make peace with your old man before he croaks. Or for the reading of the will?"

"I don't need anything in your damn will."

Haney stepped forward diplomatically. She had feared the reunion wouldn't be pleasant. "I'm taking Laura Jane home now. Laura Jane, kiss your daddy and let's go." The girl complied dutifully.

Roscoe barely noticed them leave. His eyes were still boring into those of his son. Caroline was left alone with two generations of Lancasters who had far more than years separating them.

"You turned out to be a good-looking man, Rink," his father said analytically. "Hard and mean, too. The meanness doesn't show up in all those smiling newspaper pictures, but I figured it was there."

"I had a good teacher."

74

That same laugh, a hideous laugh, filled the room again. "You bet you did, sonny, you bet you did. Only way to get on in this world. Be mean as hell to everybody and no one'll ever get the best of you." He gestured impatiently. "Sit down, both of you."

"I prefer to stand, thank you," Rink replied. Caroline sank into an available chair. She'd never seen Roscoe quite this acerbic. No wonder Rink had been forced to leave his home. She had known the antagonism between them was strong but nothing like this.

"From what I read, that airline of yours is making you rich."

"My partner and I had great expectations for Air Dixie from the first. So far all our goals have been exceeded."

"Smart philosophy you've got. Herd the passengers on, herd them off, low fares, keep the planes flying. You've profited when others are going out of business."

If Rink was surprised to learn that his father had followed the success of his commuter airline, he gave no indication of it. "As I said, we've been pleased with our success."

A nurse came in carrying a stainless-steel tray with a hypodermic needle on it. "I've come to give you a shot for your pain, Mr. Lancaster."

"Stick it in your own ass and leave mine alone," Roscoe shouted at her.

"Roscoe," Caroline said, shocked by his vulgarity.

"Doctor's orders, Mr. Lancaster," the nurse said firmly.

"I don't care what that quack said. This is my life, what's left of it, and I don't want any damn shot to relieve my pain. I want to feel everything. Understand? Now get out of here."

The nurse's lips pursed in severe disapproval, but she left the room.

"Roscoe, she's only doing —"

"Stop mothering me, for God's sake, Caroline!" The tone of his voice was like none he had used with her before. She shrank back as though he'd struck her. She fell silent, her lips compressed. "If all I'm going to get from you is insipid pity, don't bother coming back."

Breathing hard, Caroline hastily grabbed up her purse and left the hospital room with regal dignity. As soon as the door closed behind her, Rink whirled on his father.

"You sonofabitch." His golden eyes flashed fire. Each hard muscle in his athletic body was strained with fury. "You've got no right to talk to her in that way, I don't care how much pain you're in."

Roscoe chuckled, an evil sound, as evil as his calculating expression. "I have every right. She's my wife. Remember?"

Rink's hands balled into fists on his thighs. He made a feral sound deep in his throat before he spun on his heels and stormed from the room.

At first he didn't see Caroline. Then he spotted her at the end of the corridor. Slumped against the wall, gazing sightlessly out a window. He came up behind her. He raised his hand to touch her, paused to reconsider, then thought, To hell with it, and placed his hand on her shoulder. She reacted instantly, stiffening reflexively.

"Are you all right?"

Oh God, she thought. Why had he asked that, in that particular tone of voice? It was exactly the way he had asked her that same question another time. The same words, the same inflection, the same gentle concern in the husky timbre of his voice.

She turned slightly to look up at him over her shoulder. Tears formed in her eyes. They could have been put there by the humiliation she had suffered at her husband's hands. But that wasn't the reason for them. They were tears of remembrance. She gazed into his eyes and was transported back, back to that first night. . . .

★ ★ ★

The car lights came up behind her and she hurried her footsteps. She didn't particularly like walking home alone. Of course, she could wait for Papa, but Lord knew when he'd likely start home. Besides, in his condition he would be of no help if she were to be attacked.

She had almost died of shame that afternoon when Rink Lancaster had figured out that she was the town drunk's daughter. He would know that they lived in an old ramshackle house and that her mama took in laundry to keep food on the table and secondhand clothes from her customers on Caroline's back.

She had recognized him instantly. Everybody knew the Lancasters. She had seen Rink many times from afar, driving like a bat out of hell in his shiny red sports car with the convertible top down, the wind whipping his black hair around his head. Usually there was a girl with him, her left arm draped over his shoulders. The radio would blare. He would honk and wave at everybody he knew, including the sheriff's deputies, who overlooked his flagrant disregard of the speed limit. Everybody knew Rink Lancaster, football hero, basketball team captain, track star, heir to The Retreat and the largest cotton gin in five counties.

He had occupied her thoughts during the hours she worked at Woolworth's. Now she hurried home so she could crawl into bed and think about him and all he had said to her that day. Of course he probably wouldn't even remember —

"Hi, Caroline." The car that had been cruising behind her crept to her side. Incredulously she looked into Rink's smiling face as he leaned over the passenger seat and opened the door. "Get in. I'll drive you home."

She glanced up and down the road as though she had been caught doing something she shouldn't. "I don't know if I should."

He laughed. "Why?"

Because boys like Rink Lancaster didn't drive girls like Caroline Dawson around in their sports cars, that's why. But she didn't say that. She didn't say anything. Her heart, pounding in her throat, left no room for words.

"Come on, get in," he said with an irresistible smile. She slid into the leather seat and pulled the door closed behind her. The seat swallowed her in luxury and it was all she could do to keep from running her hands over its softness. The dials and gadgets on the dashboard winked at her in myriad colors.

"Do you like chocolate milk shakes?"

She had only had one in her life. One day after Mama got paid they had stopped at a lunch counter in town and bought one to share as a special treat. "Yes."

"I stopped at the Dairy Mart. Help yourself." He tilted his head and indicated the paper cup propped between the seats on the console. It had a lid on it, but the straw was sticking up out of the hole in the top.

"Thank you," she said timidly, picking it up and sucking on the straw. It was cold and rich and delicious and she smiled her pleasure. He smiled back.

The radio wasn't playing loudly and the canvas top was up on the car. He didn't want anyone to see her with him. She understood and didn't mind. He had come to pick her up; he had bought her a chocolate shake. That was enough.

"How was work?"

"I sold a set of dishes."

"Yeah?"

"They were ugly. I don't think I'd like eating off them."

He laughed. "Then you don't plan to sell dishes all your life?"

"No."

"What do you want to do?"

Go to college, she thought with that desperation of the hopelessly hopeful. "I don't know. I like math. I was on the honor roll two years in a row."

She felt a need to impress him with something, tell him something that would make him remember this night, because she knew she would never forget it for as long as she lived. She, Caroline Dawson, riding around with Rink Lancaster! Why had he bothered? He could have his pick of girls, girls older and far more worldly than she. Girls who wore pretty clothes and went to club meetings, girls whose mothers served on committees and drove long cars, girls who would never deign to speak to Caroline Dawson.

"Math, huh? Maybe I could have used your help up at college. I barely squeaked through my math courses."

"Did you like college?"

"Sure. It was a blast. But I'm glad to be out."

"You graduated?"

"Six weeks ago."

"What's your degree in?"

"It was a toss-up between agriculture and engineering. I thought I already knew a lot about agriculture, so I majored in engineering."

"That should be helpful at the gin."

"I guess." Without asking directions he turned off the highway onto the county road that led to her house.

"You don't have to take me all the way," she said hastily.

"It's darker than pitch out here."

"I'm not scared to walk the rest of the way, honest. Please stop."

Without an argument, he braked the car. She didn't want him to drive her all the way home. There would then be explanations to make to her mother. This day was too special. She didn't want to share it with anyone. Mostly, she didn't want him to come face-to-face with the squalor she lived in.

After the motor had been cut, everything went silent. He turned off the headlights and let the convertible top down. The moon bathed them with a silvery-white glow. A breeze flirted with their hair.

He propped his arm on the back of her seat. His knee bumped into hers as he turned to face her. He didn't move it away. She could smell the cologne he was wearing, see the faint shadow of a beard. He wasn't a boy, he was a man. She had never had a date before, never been alone with a man of any age.

Self-conscious because he wasn't saying anything, she continued to suck on the straw. He watched her intently. With every pull of her lips on the straw, she was aware of his eyes on her mouth. The straw made a loud slurping sound when she reached bottom and she looked up at him in mortification.

He was smiling. "Enjoy the milk shake?"

"Very much. Thank you." She handed him the empty cup and he bent to shove it beneath his seat.

When he straightened, he leaned forward slightly so that they faced each other. As it had that afternoon, conversation gave way to ravenous curiosity. She studied him as intently as he did her. She could see his eyes roving over her face and hair and neck and chest, and it made her feel warm and funny on the inside, weightless. Yet there was a gathering heaviness in the lower part of her body. A heat, unfamiliar and delicious, forbidden and heavenly, began to pump through her veins.

He placed his thumb lengthwise under her lower lip, touching the border of it with his well-trimmed nail. She thought she might die of suffocation. Suddenly she couldn't breathe.

"You're very pretty," he said huskily.

"Thank you."

"How old are you?"

"Fifteen."

"Fifteen." He muttered a curse under his breath and looked away from her. Then, as though he couldn't control them, his eyes came back. "I thought about you all day after I saw you in the woods." His hand was lying along her cheek now and his thumb was hypnotically stroking her bottom lip.

"You did?"

"Mmm," he murmured. "All afternoon you were on my mind."

"I thought about you, too."

That seemed to please him. He grinned lopsidedly. "What did you think?"

Her cheeks flamed and she was grateful to the darkness for hiding her girlish blush. To avoid his eyes, she looked down at his throat in the open collar of his shirt. "Things," she said hoarsely, shrugging with feigned indifference.

"Things?" He smiled. But it was a slight, fleeting smile, not one that distracted him from his intent perusal of her face. "Did you think about . . ." He seemed to search for the proper words.

"Making out" was what came to her mind. That was what kids did when they went on dates, wasn't it? Wasn't that what they whispered about in groups that she was never invited to enter?

But that was not what Rink said. He said, "Did you think about us . . . together? Maybe touching?"

"Touching?" she repeated breathlessly.

"Kissing?"

Her lips parted, but no sound came forth. She heard nothing but the beating thud of her own heart.

"Have you ever been kissed?"

"A few times," she lied.

"You're so damn young," he groaned, squeezing his eyes closed momentarily before opening them quickly. "Would you be afraid if I kissed you? Would you like it if I kissed you?"

"I'm not afraid of you, Rink."

"And the other?" he prodded gently, touching her hair.

"I . . . I think I'd like you to . . . kiss me."

"Caroline," he whispered, moving closer. She felt his breath on her face first and her eyes closed. Then his lips touched hers — soft, still, hesitant. When she didn't pull away, he tilted his head to one side and pressed more firmly. Again and again his lips collided with hers in brief, light kisses, soft pecks that made her hungry from the bottom of her soul for something she couldn't name. Even "making out" didn't apply. Because anybody could do that and this was something she knew no one had ever experienced before.

He cupped her face with both palms and laid his mouth, lips open this time, firmly over hers. She felt the moistness of his tongue just a breath away from her lips, then on them, flicking lightly.

He moaned softly before he pressed his tongue against her lips. Caroline's eyes went wide with shock. She froze. Then the pleasure of what he was doing vanquished her resistance and her lips parted. His tongue slid between them. It touched the tip of hers, rubbed, stroked, pushed deeper.

When his arms closed around her, she grasped handfuls of his shirtfront and clung. Her insides were in chaos, tossed about and tumbling with what she didn't know yet was arousal. She knew a compelling urge to gravitate toward him. The need to touch his body with hers was an obsessive desire she could barely keep under control. She both craved and feared the impulses he had awakened her to.

He pulled back regretfully, kissed her moist lips tenderly, then separated himself from her and put hateful space between them. His hands returned from her back to rest on either side of her face. Her eyes were closed and when she raised the heavy eyelids, it was with a lassitude that had invaded her entire body.

"Are you all right? . . ."

Now, in the chilly hospital corridor, she answered him as she had twelve years ago on a warm balmy night after that first kiss. "Yes, Rink, I'm all right."

Rink, too, seemed caught up in a memory. He gazed down at her for a long time before he brusquely turned away and said, "We'd better go."

Chapter 4

"She's so pretty."

"So are you."

Laura Jane's hands stilled on the filly's neck as she lifted her dark liquid eyes to Steve, who had spoken with soft fervency. "Do you really think I am?"

Her expression made him curse himself. She was vulnerable, took everything literally. He shouldn't speak aloud the things he thought. Her feelings were fragile and could be easily shattered.

He levered himself up from the hay-strewn floor of the stall, bracing his weight on his good leg. "You're very pretty," he said tersely and turned away from her, leaving the stall.

Putting space between them was becoming necessary more frequently. She had no idea what her nearness, her flowery scent, the warm smoothness of her skin did to his senses. Had she known the responses she elicited from his body, she would have been terrified of him.

Ha hauled a saddle from the tack room wall. Rink had told him that afternoon that he wished to ride the following morning, and Steve wanted everything to be perfect. He knew the reason for Rink's apparent dislike of him. The man wasn't blind. Nor was he insensitive. Rink would recognize longing when he saw it. Steve knew his desire for Laura Jane was as evident as a neon billboard hanging around his neck.

He didn't blame Rink for his suspicions. Laura Jane was his sister, a very special sister who had required special care all her life. If Steve had had anyone in his life like her, he would have been as fiercely protective as Rink was.

Still, he couldn't help loving her, could he? Love wasn't something he had gone looking for. He hadn't expected to ever love anybody. But he did and he missed Laura Jane every moment of the day that she wasn't with him. She was standing close beside him now as he applied saddle soap to the saddle. Each time his elbow moved with the sawing motion of his cloth, it almost touched her breast.

He bent to his task with renewed vigor and tried not to think of what her breasts would feel like beneath his callused hands or how soft her throat would be beneath his lips.

Laura Jane, vaguely disappointed that

Steve hadn't gone on talking about how pretty she was, had patted the foal farewell and followed him. "Is your leg hurting?"

Without looking up, he answered. "No. Why?"

"Because you're frowning, the way you do sometimes when your leg hurts."

"I'm just working hard, that's all."

She moved closer. "I'll help you work, Steve. Let me help you."

He moved away from her, ostensibly to get another rag. His blood was pounding. She was so sweet, so sweet, but the feelings she aroused in him were far from sweet. Around her he felt like a slavering savage within touching distance of the sacrificial virgin. "No. You don't need to help. I'll be through in a minute."

"You don't think I can, do you? No one thinks I can do anything."

His head came up quickly and he dropped his polishing cloth. "Of course I think you can."

He saw the hurt on her face, the pain in her dark, fathomless eyes. She shook her head and her soft brown hair swished over her shoulders. "Everybody thinks I'm stupid and useless."

"Laura Jane," he groaned miserably and placed his hands on her shoulders. "I don't think any such thing."

"Then why won't you let me help you?"

"Because this is dirty work and I don't want you getting messed up."

With a childlike need to trust, she peered up at him. "That's the only reason? Promise?"

"Promise."

He didn't release her as he should have, but kept his hands on her shoulders. Her upraised face was bathed with the soft amber glow of the stable lights. She looked like an angel except for the flame burning steadily in her eyes. If he hadn't known better, he would have thought that flame had a carnal origin.

"I know I'm not bright. But I'm smart about some things."

"Of course you are." God! Her lips were soft and moist and pink as they formed her words. He wanted to taste them. What he'd give to press her close, to feel that beautiful dainty body against his hulking, scarred, deformed one. It would be like applying a healing balm to his aching body, his aching spirit.

"I notice things. For instance I know Rink isn't happy. He laughs and tries to act happy, but his eyes are sad. He and Caroline don't like each other. Have you noticed that?"

"Yes."

"I wonder why." Her face wrinkled with concentration. "Or maybe they like each other very much, but are trying to make everyone think that they don't."

Steve smiled at her perception. That had been the conclusion he had drawn after eating brunch with them that morning. They looked ready to either fight or love. He thought the scale tipped strongly in favor of the latter. He chucked Laura Jane under the chin. "You may be right."

She smiled up at him and moved closer. "You think I'm smart? And pretty?"

His dark eyes roamed her face. "You're beautiful."

"I think you're beautiful, too." With fingers as flawless as china, she reached up and traced his hard cheekbone, then trailed her fingertips down to his chin.

He felt her touch on more than his face. The sensations it created rocketed straight to his loins. He sucked his breath in sharply and stepped away from her, dropping his arms to his sides. "Don't," he said with unintended harshness.

Laura Jane recoiled as though he'd slapped her.

"Oh, God, Laura Jane, I'm sorry. I'm sorry." He reached out to touch her comfortingly but couldn't bring himself to. She had covered her face with her hands and was weeping softly. "Please don't cry."

"I'm a terrible person."

"Terrible? You're far from terrible." He had never felt so wretched in his life. He was damned if he touched her and damned if he didn't. It was suicidal to show her any affection; Rink would kill him if he found out. On the other hand, how could he hurt her this way, make her feel rejected, unloved, unwanted? "You're wonderful," he whispered urgently. "You're all that everyone should be."

"No. I'm not." She lifted her tear-streaked face to his. "I've loved Rink for as long as I can remember. I thought that if he came home, everything would be all right. I thought he was the strongest, most beautiful man in the world. But now that he's home, I see that he's not." She wet her lips with her tongue. "You are." Her small breasts trembled beneath her summer dress. Teardrops rolled down her cheeks. "Steve, I love you more than I do Rink!"

Before he could react, she flung herself against him, kissed him swiftly on the lips and ran from the stable.

He could count the racing heartbeats as they thudded in his eardrums. He was both elated and miserable. God, what could he do about this?

Nothing. Absolutely nothing.

He turned off the lights in the stable and went into his well-maintained but painfully lonely apartment at the back of the building. Flopping down in his narrow bed, he covered his eyes with his forearm. He hadn't felt this kind of despair since he had awakened in the army hospital to learn that he was going home . . . with half of one leg missing.

"Oh, I'm sorry, Rink. I didn't see you out here."

"It's all right," he said from the shadows. "This is your house."

Caroline let the screen door close behind her and sat down on the wicker glider. She breathed deeply of the cool evening air. Her eyes closed tiredly as she leaned her head against the wicker back. "This is your house, Rink. I'm only a visitor for as long as —"

"As my father lives."

"Yes."

He didn't make a reply. He was weary of arguments. "You didn't go back to the hospital."

"I called. They had finally talked him into

94

a shot and it put him to sleep. The doctor said there was no reason for me to be there. Roscoe wouldn't know one way or another. I felt I could be more useful here at home doing some business for the gin. It'll soon be picking time and we need to make sure we're ready."

"I'd hate to be at the hospital when Roscoe wakes up and discovers he's lost a day."

Caroline rubbed her forehead as though she already had the headache his angry shouting would bring on. "So would I."

"Does he often treat you the way he did today?"

"No. Never. I've seen him lose his temper with other people. I've gone behind him and placated them. Today was the first day I've been the target."

"You've been lucky, then," Rink said. "He was that way with my mother, constantly on her case about some trivial something he had trumped up. God" — he slammed his fist against the arm of his chair — "there were days when I wanted to smash his foul mouth as hard as I could with my fist. Even as a little kid, I used to hate him for making her unhappy when she had given him everything. Everything."

He glanced up at her and she got the impression that he was embarrassed by revealing so much emotion to her. "Can I make you a drink?" he asked shortly.

"No thank you."

He sighed in the darkness. "Sorry. I forgot. You don't drink, do you?"

"After growing up in Pete Dawson's house? No," she said with a soft laugh. "I don't drink."

"Then I won't, either." He leaned over the arm of the chair where he was sitting and set his highball glass on the floor.

"No, please. I don't mind. It doesn't smell on you the way it did on him."

It was far too personal a comment to make. She looked at him to see if he had read anything into what she had said. His golden eyes captured hers from across the darkness that separated them. She was the first to look away.

"Haney told me that your daddy died," Rink said at last. He left the glass untouched on the porch.

"Yes. They found him dead one morning in a ditch on the highway. The coroner said it was a heart attack. I think he finally succeeded in poisoning himself."

"And your mother?"

"She died a few years ago." Her eyes were unseeing as she stared into the twilight. Her mother had been barely fifty. Yet she was a stooped, wrinkled old woman when she gratefully died of exhaustion and despair.

Rink got up from his chair and came to sit closer to her on the top step of the porch. Crossing his ankles, he leaned back and propped himself up on his elbows. His shoulder touched the frame of the glider, dangerously close to her calf. "Fill me in, Caroline. What happened to you after that summer, after I left?"

She yearned to reach down and touch his hair, to sift through the thick dark strands with her fingers. His body was long and lean, the male power within it just as evident in repose as in movement.

"I finished high school and got a scholarship to college."

"A scholarship? How?" He yanked his head around and bumped against her shinbone with his chin. He pulled back quickly.

"I don't know."

He sat up and looked at her inquiringly as he turned slightly. "Don't know?"

She shook her head. She couldn't organize her thoughts. They had scattered like autumn leaves in a whirlwind at his touch. He was now sitting with his knees raised, his arms looped loosely around them. The dangling fingers of his left hand had but to extend to touch her leg.

He was waiting for an explanation, so she collected herself and spoke, haltingly at first. "One day the high school principal called me into his office. It was just a few days before graduation. He said I had a scholarship from a donor who wished to remain anonymous. It paid for everything. I even got an allowance of fifty dollars a month for mad money. To this day I don't know who was responsible."

"God Almighty," he said under his breath. Haney had told him in one of her gossipy letters that "the Dawson girl" had gone to college ("You probably don't remember her. She was several classes behind you. Old Pete Dawson's girl. Anyway, she's left town to go to school and everybody's wondering how she managed it.") And much later he had received a letter from Laura Jane ("Daddy told me today that somebody named Caroline Dawson has married a boy at college. He said she used to live here and that you might know her.")

"After I got my degree, I moved back to town," Caroline continued.

"Your marriage must not have lasted long."

His studiously casual observation baffled Caroline. "Marriage?"

"The guy you met at school."

She stared at him as if he had lost his mind. "I don't know what you're talking about, Rink. I didn't even *date* anybody, much less get married. To keep the scholarship, I had to maintain a B average. I studied all the time. Where in the world did you get the idea I'd been married?"

Rink, too, was shocked. Had Laura Jane made that up? No. Laura Jane hadn't even known Caroline until she'd started working for Roscoe.

Roscoe.

A worm of suspicion entered his mind. What occurred to him was too diabolical even to contemplate. But where Roscoe was concerned . . . "I heard that you'd gotten married. I forget who told me."

"Whoever it was told you wrong. I didn't marry until I married . . ."

"My father."

After a long awkward silence, Caroline asked what had been on her mind for years. "What happened between you and Marilee?"

"World War Three," he said with a short laugh. Caroline didn't say anything. She sat stiffly, her fingers knotting together. "It was doomed from the beginning. She didn't want that baby any more than I did. She used it as a means to trap me into marrying her, and after Alyssa was born, we started divorce proceedings."

"Do you ever see the child? Alyssa?"

"No. Never," Rink said. His face was inscrutable, but the tone of his voice indicated clearly that the subject was closed. It hurt Caroline to the quick that he didn't love his child, his only child. How could he be so unfeeling? For years after that magic summer, she had wished she had had his baby. It would have been something of his left for her, some part of him to love since he wasn't there.

"After the divorce was finally settled — it took years — I began to concentrate on getting the airline started."

"I'm very proud of it for you, Rink," she said in a voice so soft and sincere that it brought his eyes up to hers.

His smile was wry. "Yeah, well, I worked like hell to make a go of it. It was something to occupy my mind and keep it off . . . other things."

"What other things? Home?"

His eyes remained pinned on hers for a long moment. They were hard and piercing. "Yes," he said shortly and stood. Giving her his back, he propped his shoulder against one of the pillars. "The Retreat. Laura Jane.

100

My father. The gin. Winstonville was home. I never intended to leave it."

"You made a new life for yourself in Atlanta."

"Yeah." Such as it is, he could have added. His house was too new, too ostentatious. It had no character or gentility. The parties were too raucous. The women . . . The women were too glitzy, too cosmopolitan, too phony. He saw through them just as they did him.

The life he led now was a charade. Not that he wasn't happy with Air Dixie. He was. The airline was certainly something to take pride in because it had taken years of hard work to get it where it was.

But the accoutrements of success had never meant a damn to him. His roots were here, in this town, in this rich bottomland, in this house. Any other life was just pretense. He would never forgive his father for driving him away. Never.

Suddenly he whirled on Caroline. "Why did you marry him?"

She almost cowered at his fury. "I won't discuss my private life with your father with you, Rink."

"I don't want to know about your private life. I only asked why you married him. He's almost old enough to be your grandfather,

101

for God's sake." He strode forward and leaned over her, bracing his hands on the arms of the glider and imprisoning her between them. "Why? Why did you even come back to this town after you graduated from college? There was nothing for you here."

Her neck hurt as she arched it back to look up at him. "My mama was still alive. I came back, got a job at the bank and within a few months had saved up enough to get us out of that pigsty and into a rented house in town. I met your father in the bank. He was nice to me. When he asked me to come to work for him at the gin, I did. He doubled the salary I was making at the bank, which allowed me to bury my mother with some semblance of dignity."

His breath came in rapid gusts on her face. Dark locks of wavy hair fell over his forehead. His shirts seemed never to remain fully buttoned for long. This one wasn't now. Her eyes were on a level with his muscular chest. He was male; he was virile; he was attractive, dangerously so. She wanted to close her eyes against his appeal.

"After a while I started coming here to The Retreat to work rather than going to the office at the gin."

"I bet you loved that, being invited to The Retreat."

"I did," she cried defensively. "You know how I've always loved this house. For that naive girl walking to work through the woods, it was like the castle in a fairy tale. I don't deny that, Rink."

"Go on with your story. I'm fascinated. Was my father the Prince Charming of this fairy tale of yours?"

"Of course not. It wasn't anything like that. After Mama died, I spent more time here. He came to rely on me in business matters. Laura Jane and I became friends. Roscoe encouraged that since she didn't have any friends her age."

Hurriedly she wet her lips. Greedily his eyes charted the action of her tongue. "It was something that happened gradually. It seemed right since I was already spending so much time here. When he asked me to marry him, I said yes. He could give me everything I'd always wanted and never could have any other way."

"A new name."

"Yes."

"Clothes."

"Yes."

"Money."

"Yes."

"A beautiful house."

"The one I'd always loved."

"For all that you sold yourself to my father!" he hissed.

"In a way I suppose I did." His repulsion made her feel dirty. She groped for justifications. "I wanted to be the constant friend Laura Jane needed. I wanted to help your father."

"So your motives were purely unselfish."

"No," she confessed, lowering her eyes. "I wanted to live in The Retreat. I wanted the respect that would go along with being Roscoe's wife. Yes, I wanted all that. And you'd have had to grow up in a shack, lived hand to mouth every day of your life, worn shabby clothes when other girls had dyed-to-match sweaters and skirts, worked every day after school and on Saturdays when all the other kids were riding around in convertibles and going to the Dairy Mart and football games, been the daughter of the town drunk before you'd understand that, Rink Lancaster!"

On speaking his name she bolted off the glider, but he didn't budge. She was brought up soundly against his body. His hands closed firmly around her upper arms and secured her against him. Their breathing was harsh and labored as though they had both been running hard.

She wouldn't lift her head and look at

him. If she did, she didn't know what she would do. So she stared into the V at the base of his throat, at the rapid pulse beating there. Her lower body felt heavy and thick, weak with passion. Her lips were rubbery as she tried to form words on them. "Please let me go, Rink. Please."

He ignored the plea. Instead he buried his face in the side of her neck. Helplessly, her head fell back. His lips rubbed back and forth over her skin, leaving behind the moist vapor of his breath to cool and excite.

"Knowing that you're my father's wife, knowing the reasons you married him, why do I still want you?" With frantic desperation his head moved to the other side of her neck. Her head tilted to accommodate him.

Feebly she protested her own responses. "No, no, Rink, don't."

"I want you so much I hurt." He kissed her neck with hot urgency. His teeth nipped her lightly. "I want you. Why, damn you, why?"

Caroline groaned. "Oh, God, help me," she breathed. More than anything, she wanted to surrender herself to him. She needed him as he needed her, to ease the years of misery they had both suffered. For a few precious moments, they wanted to forget everything but each other.

But it was impossible. That knowledge gave her strength to resist and she renewed her efforts to get away from him.

Just as quickly as he had embraced her, his hands released their grip and fell to his sides. He stepped backward, breathing rapidly and hard. Hastily she went to the front door.

"Caroline." His voice halted her and commanded that she turn around. "I've always had difficulty accepting things I didn't like. I had no right to grill you that way. It was none of my business."

His image blurred through her tears. She knew the pride it had cost him to admit that. She smiled at him softly, a smile that said much that couldn't be spoken aloud. "Wasn't it, Rink?" she asked quietly. Then she let herself in and went upstairs.

Lying on her bed, still clothed and too apathetic to undress, she stared up at the ceiling. And remembered. She hadn't known whether to expect to see him the next day or not. But he had been there. . . .

"Hi."

"What are you doing here?"

"Fishing." He cocked his head toward the cane pole that was stuck in the mud near the riverbank. The line trailed in the water. He wasn't fishing very ambitiously. "You're earlier than yesterday."

She blushed and looked away from his dazzling smile. When she had left home half an hour early, she had sworn to herself that it wasn't on the outside chance that he might be in the woods and that she would have some time to spare with him if he were. She had taken great care in dressing, wearing her best skirt and blouse, brushing her hair after she washed it until her scalp tingled, inspecting her fingernails.

She had run home in the dark after leaving his car the night before. He had kissed her. And he had been tender afterward, asking if she were all right. But she hadn't anticipated ever seeing him again.

Only now he was here, sitting under the willows in short cutoff jeans and a sleeveless T-shirt and looking as confident and handsome as a movie star. The muscles of his athletic arms and legs bulged. The dusting of body hair on his limbs intrigued her, but when she looked at him too long at a time, her stomach began to do flip-flops.

"I had Haney, that's our housekeeper, pack some sandwiches. Do you like smoked turkey?"

"I don't know. I've never eaten it."

"Well, you're about to," he said, grinning. He spread a quilt on the grass and asked her to sit down. Then he opened a hamper and handed her a plastic-wrapped sandwich. They chatted as they ate.

"Are you going to start working in the gin? Smoked turkey is delicious, by the way."

"Glad you like it." He rested his back against the trunk of the tree as he munched. "I guess I will," he said thoughtfully. "If Daddy and I can ever come to terms on some things." She wanted to ask what things but didn't. He would think she was meddling in his business.

But he glanced at her, saw her intent listening posture and went on. "See, Daddy doesn't want to dip into the profits to make the gin better. He's satisfied with it as it is. There are many ways we could improve it, update it, make it a safer place to work for our employees. I haven't convinced him that some expensive investments right now would pay off in the long run."

"Maybe you could compromise with him on a few for a start."

"Maybe," he remarked doubtfully. He reached into the hamper and pulled out a can of soft drink. He winked at her. "I'm dying for a cold beer, but I was afraid if I got caught drinking beer with someone as young as you, I'd be arrested."

If they were caught together, what they were drinking would be the least of their worries and they both knew it. They finished their lunch and Caroline conscientiously helped him put the leftovers back in the hamper. She took his place leaning against the tree trunk and he stretched out on his side and propped his head on his elbow. He looked up at her.

"What are you thinking about?" he asked.

Her eyes found his. "Your mama."

"Mother?" The surprise in his voice couldn't be disguised.

"I was sorry to hear when she died, Rink. She was a very nice lady."

"When did you meet her?"

"I never did, but she used to come into Woolworth's now and then. I always thought she was the . . . cleanest person I'd ever seen."

Rink laughed. "Yes, she was. I don't ever remember her being less than immaculate."

"She was beautiful, and always dressed up so nice." Her expression was soft. "What did she die of, Rink?"

He studied the hem of her skirt, ran his index finger along the row of tiny handmade stitches. "A broken heart," he said in a low voice.

Caroline saw the sadness on his face and

109

it tugged at her heart. She wanted to press his head into her breasts, to comfort him, to run her fingers through his hair. "How could anyone be brokenhearted living in a house like yours?"

He ignored her question and asked one of his own. "You like The Retreat?"

Her eyes sparkled. "It's the most beautiful house in the world," she said worshipfully and he laughed. She blushed. "Well, at least it's the most beautiful one I've ever seen."

He seemed surprised. "You've been inside?"

"Oh, no, never. But I've walked past it many times. I love to just stand and look at it. I'd give anything to live in a house like that." She looked away self-consciously. "You probably think I'm crazy."

He shook his head. "I love The Retreat, too. I never get tired of looking at it either. I'll invite you to see the inside sometime."

They both knew he wouldn't, and for the next moment they couldn't meet each other's eyes. Finally Caroline said, "Your little sister is pretty. I saw her with your mother a few times."

"Her name is Laura Jane."

"I've never seen her at school. Does she go to a private school?"

Rink plucked a blade of grass and bit into its stem. His teeth were very straight and very white. "A school for retarded children. She's not severely retarded, but her mind was slow in developing. She doesn't learn as quickly as other children."

Caroline's cheeks burned. "I'm . . . I'm sorry . . . I didn't —"

"Hey," he said, taking her hand. "It's all right. Laura Jane is a wonderful little girl. I love her very much."

"She's lucky to have a brother like you."

He propped his head on his hand again and looked up at her roguishly. Sunlight glistened on the black fringe of his eyelashes. "You think so?"

"Yes."

They lapsed into one of those staring spells when words were superfluous. His eyes fell to her hand resting on her thigh. He lifted it, turned it over and lightly examined the faint lines etched in the palm. His finger trailed from her palm to the sensitive hollow in the bend of her elbow. His touch made her tingle all over. There was an uneasy fluttering in her chest and she marveled at her nipples, which were becoming hard and swollen.

"I've got to go soon," she said breathlessly.

"I wish you didn't have to," he said huskily. His eyes traveled slowly up to meet hers. "I wish we could spend the day here, like this, talking."

Her heart was thudding. There was a roaring in her ears that blocked out all other sound save his voice. "I'm sure you could find plenty of your friends in town to spend the day with. They talk to you, don't they?"

"They outtalk each other," he said. "No one listens, just listens, like you do, Caroline."

With his golden eyes locked onto hers, he sat up slowly. His hand lifted her hair off the back of her neck and closed around the slender column. He drew her close and she went without a hint of resistance until his mouth met hers. They melted together, murmuring their harmonizing groans of gratification.

His lips were as gentle as the night before, but her sweet acceptance of them aroused him quickly. The kiss became more fiercely insistent.

Caroline was carried along by his passion. Her soul spun crazily, caught up in his taste, his smell, the pressure of his body against hers. Soon she was lying across his bare thighs and he was bending over her. His tongue thrust madly into her mouth while her fingers tangled in the wild mass of his hair.

He raised his head, panting for breath, dropping hot kisses on her face. "Caroline, fight me, say no. Don't let me do this." He moved the collar of her blouse aside and slipped his hand inside. Her skin was warm and silky against his palm. He toyed with the strap of her brassiere. His fingertips brushed against her flesh and he moaned. "You're just a kid. A *kid*. God help me. You're not old enough to know better, but I am. We're playing with fire, sweetheart. Stop me. Please." He kissed her again, deeply and thoroughly.

A restlessness deep within claimed her. Her legs shifted in agitation. Her breasts throbbed achingly and she wanted to cover them with her hands. With his hands. She looped her arm around his neck and strained upward.

But he pulled away, gulping for air, his eyes squeezed tightly shut. "This can't go any further, Caroline. If we don't stop, things are going to get out of hand. Do you understand what I'm talking about?"

Dumbly, she nodded, wishing he would hold her again, kiss her some more, touch with his hands all the places on her body that were feeling swollen and warm.

He pulled her to her feet. She swayed against him and he held her close, stroking her back, whispering lovely words in her hair. Unashamedly, naturally, her arms went around his waist. When he pushed her away from him, his smile was rueful. "I would never forgive myself if I got you fired from your job," he whispered.

"Oh, my goodness!" she exclaimed, slapping her palms to her flaming cheeks. "What time is it?"

"You've got time if you leave right now."

"Bye," she said, stuffing her blouse back into her waistband and shaking her hair to straighten it.

He clasped her hand. "I won't be able to pick you up tonight."

"I didn't expect you to, Rink," she said earnestly.

"I *want* to, but I already had plans for tonight."

"It's all right. Truly." She began backing out of the clearing. "Thanks for the lunch." Turning, she dashed through the trees. He went tearing after her.

"Caroline!" He called out so masterfully that she stopped in her tracks and turned around.

"Yes?"

"I'll see you tomorrow. Here. Okay?"

Her face rivaled the sun for brilliance as she smiled at him. "Yes," she had called back, laughing. "Yes . . . yes . . . yes . . ."

He had come the next day and the day after that and the day after that and for most days for the next few weeks. And when he could, he picked her up at some point on her walk home.

Caroline rolled to her side and stared at the moon through the branches of the trees outside her window. How glorious those days had been! She had lived in a haze of excitement, savoring the feelings his kisses generated and miserable because she yearned for something more. He shared his dreams of the future with her and she confided her secrets. They communed on a level that neither had known with anyone else.

Every stolen hour they had spent together had been golden and only partially because of the summer sun. Because one day when they met, it had rained.

That day had been the most golden of all.

Caroline hiccuped a sob and let the tears stream unchecked from her eyes. She prayed for forgiveness but didn't think she was absolved. Because she tried to weep for Roscoe, her husband, but her tears were all for Rink, her love.

Chapter 5

Caroline slept later than she had intended. She put on a robe and went down to the kitchen for a cup of coffee before going into the library to work. Haney was humming as she stood at the sink washing dishes. She disdained the automatic dishwasher.

"Good morning. You sound happy."

"Rink ate a good breakfast," she said, beaming.

Caroline smiled. The housekeeper talked about him as though he were a four-year-old. "He's already up and about?"

"Yep." Haney nodded at the back door and Caroline wandered toward it, sipping her coffee as she went. Rink was standing beside one of the Lancaster prize horses talking to Steve. As she watched, he vaulted into the saddle, swung his long leg over it and secured his booted foot in the stirrup. The stallion pranced arrogantly before Rink pulled sternly on the reins. The horse responded immediately and after Rink nodded his thanks to Steve, horse and man went bounding across pastureland toward the road.

Caroline watched for as long as she could see him. His hair was as black and shiny as jet in the early morning light. Thigh and back muscles rippled as he effortlessly jumped a fence and guided the horse into the trees.

When Caroline turned away, Haney was staring at her curiously. Nervously Caroline's hand went to her throat. "I need to make some calls, so I'll be in the library," she rattled off before hastily leaving the kitchen. She couldn't help her absorption with Rink, but she would have to guard against anyone else becoming aware of it.

The nurse's station at the hospital had little to report when she telephoned. "He isn't awake yet. He slept through most of the night. He woke up once but we immediately gave him another sedative."

"Thank you," she said before breaking off the call and dialing Granger. "Is there anything I should be doing that I'm not?" she asked the attorney. "I don't want to presume that I have anything to do with Roscoe's professional or private dealings, but I want to be useful if I can be."

"I would never think you presumptive," Granger said kindly. "And it's your right to be concerned."

"I'm not concerned for myself. I just want

to make certain that Laura Jane's affairs are taken care of. And Rink's, of course."

The attorney remained silent and Caroline knew he was reminding himself of professional discretion. "I don't know all of Roscoe's intentions, Caroline. Swear to God I don't. He made up a new will several years ago, but he's asked to see me about it. I'm sure some provision will be made for you. I don't think there will be any surprises."

She fervently hoped not, too, but didn't express her anxiety that there might be. After discussing a few minor business items, they said their good-byes.

As soon as she hung up, the telephone rang again. "Hello?"

"Miz Lancaster?"

The racket in the background told her the call was originating at the cotton gin. "Yes."

"This is Barnes. 'Member that gin stand I was telling you about the other day? This morning she sounded like she was grinding her guts out, so we shut her down."

Caroline rubbed her temple. This was a breakdown they couldn't afford with cotton picking time approaching. The gin stands separated the lint from the seeds. With even one breakdown during harvest, hours of production time could be lost.

"I'll be right there," she said briskly.

Hurriedly swallowing what was left of her cooled coffee, she dashed upstairs. Within half an hour, she had bathed and dressed efficiently in a poplin skirt and pullover knit top. Her shoes were low-heeled. She had pulled her hair back into a ponytail at her nape and tied a bright printed scarf around it. She never went to the gin dressed in her finest. One reason was because it wouldn't be practical. The other, the main one, was because she wanted the workers to consider her one of them and not merely the boss's wife.

She called out her good-bye to Haney, explaining where she was going. Then, catching up her purse, she ran out the front door. Rink was just reining in the stallion. When he saw her, he handed the stallion over to a waiting Steve and jogged over to her.

"Where are you going in such a hurry? The hospital?"

By his expression, Caroline knew he thought the cause for her haste was that his father had taken a turn for the worse. Despite the antagonism between them, she thought, Rink cared for his father and hated the agony he was suffering. She relieved him quickly. "No. I called earlier. Roscoe wasn't awake yet, but they said he had a fairly peaceful night. I'm going to the gin."

"Problem?"

"Yes. With one of the stands."

He nodded. "Bad?"

"I think it might be. The foreman had to shut it down." She could all but see the wheels of his brain whirring and before she could weigh the wisdom of her impulse she asked, "Would you come with me, Rink?" His eyes flew to hers and she swallowed hard. "Maybe if you looked at it, you could tell what's wrong. I would trust your judgment. Anyone else might try to take advantage of me right now."

He stared at her so long and so thoroughly that she thought he was going to refuse. Then he held out his hand. "I'll drive."

She dropped the keys to the Lincoln into his palm and they each ran to the car, getting in on opposite sides. He drove as he did everything else, aggressively. The car roared out of the curved drive, leaving behind it a shower of gravel and a cloud of dust.

"Have you been having problems with this machine?" he asked her.

"Some, yes."

"Recently?"

"Yes."

She wished they could keep the conversation going. His nearness was wreaking havoc on her senses. He smelled of fresh morning air, of wind, of horseflesh, of a brisk cologne and of man. The image of him on horseback kept creeping back into her mind.

With stark clarity, she remembered the day he had showed up at their rendezvous riding bareback. She had shrunk from the horse, which had looked enormous to her. Rink had laughed away her timidity and insisted that she ride with him. He had easily hoisted her across the horse's back. Luckily she had worn a full skirt that day so she had been able to sit astride.

Even now she remembered the feel of the horse's bristly hide against her bare thighs, of Rink's middle against her hips as he pulled himself up behind her, the bunching and flexing of his thighs against hers, the strength of his arms as they went around her to hold the reins. His body had been warm and faintly damp with healthy sweat. He had rested his chin against her hair. She could even now feel his breath on her cheek, on her eyelids. He smelled the same today as he had that day twelve years ago.

She didn't remember much of that horseback ride beneath the canopy of low-hanging trees, only the pounding of her heart as his hand rested just beneath it. She remembered being afraid of nothing save that he might not like the way she felt when his hand brushed against her breast. She couldn't afford the lacy confections the other girls wore for underwear. Her lingerie was basic, white, functional and unattractive. She had wanted to feel soft and alluring and sexy beneath his hand. She had feared she didn't.

Now, she looked at his hands as they steered the car. Beautiful hands. Dark and strong, lean and tapered. His nails were bluntly clipped straight across. Dark hairs bristled on his knuckles, the back of his hand, the wrist bone.

"Let me help you down," he had said, raising those hands up to her.

She had swung her leg over the horse's back and leaned down to rest her hands on his shoulders. His hands had cupped her underarms as she slowly slid from the animal's back. But long after her feet touched the ground, he kept his hands there, the heels of them pressing into the fleshy sides of her breasts. And he had spoken her name.

"Caroline. Caroline."

Now, she jumped, realizing that his voice wasn't a part of her mental meanderings but reality.

"What?" She looked at him, her agitation evident. Her eyes were smoky and dilated with remembrance of the heady kiss that they had shared then. Her chest was rising and falling rapidly, just as it had that day when his hands had moved to cover her breasts, to massage them with slow, rubbing circles that had brought her nipples to peaks.

Rink looked at her strangely. "I asked if there's any special place you park."

"Oh. Y-yes. By the door. It's marked."

He steered the car into the space where her name was stenciled on the concrete and cut the car's motor. She was treated to another analyzing stare. "Ready to go in?" He didn't sound certain that she was.

But she had to escape the car, the memories. Almost shouting her yes, she shoved open the car door and nearly fell out of it in her haste to leave.

The din and dust of the gin were welcome familiarities. She entered with Rink and led him toward his father's office.

Rink saw that little had changed. Most of the workers who clustered around them were familiar.

"Barnes!" he exclaimed. "Still here?"

"Till they bury me." He pumped Rink's hand. "It's good to see you, boy."

Others greeted him just as enthusiastically and he inquired after family members by names that another man might have forgotten. But these people were part of Rink's heritage. They would be as much a part of him as his life's blood for as long as he lived.

"What's the problem?" he asked Barnes, walking toward the broken gin stand that stood in a row of many.

"Age, mostly," the foreman replied uneasily. "Been patching up these machines for years, Rink. Don't know how much more rigging they'll stand. Especially if this year's crop is as good as it's supposed to be. We'll be going day and night."

Rink picked up the cotton fibers that were the last out of the machine and rubbed them between his fingers. There were bits of leaves and burrs enmeshed in the fibers. Both Barnes and Caroline avoided his eyes as he looked at them sharply. "What grade cotton is this?"

"Middling," Caroline finally admitted when Barnes remained silent.

"Lancaster gins have always produced good-to-strict middling. What the hell is going on here?"

"Let's go into the office, Rink," Caroline suggested softly. She turned and led the way, hoping that Rink would follow her and

124

not make her appeal to him in front of the men.

She was seated in the leather chair behind the desk when he came through the office door and slammed it behind him, rattling the frosted glass in its top half.

"This used to be one of the finest spot markets in the state," he began furiously and without preamble.

"It still is."

"Not if that's the best grade of cotton we can produce, it isn't. If I were a planter I'd sure as hell take my crop to some other gin. Why aren't we producing better than that?"

"I told you we're having some trouble with the equipment. It's —"

"Ancient," he cut in. "Dammit, hasn't Daddy done one damn thing to improve or update?"

"He didn't see the need," she replied softly.

"The need!" he shouted. "Look at this place. It's a dinosaur compared to modern gins. We're not being fair to ourselves or to the growers. It's a wonder they haven't started taking their crops to other —" He broke off suddenly and his eyes narrowed. "Or are they?"

"We lost a few last year, yes."

He hooked the toe of his boot around a

chair leg and pulled it toward him. Sitting down, he leaned across the desk and said in a voice she couldn't disobey, "Tell me about it."

"A few of Lancaster Gin's dependable planters have started taking their cotton to other gins, paying the fee to have it ginned and then selling it to the merchants directly."

She squirmed uneasily in the squeaky leather chair as he studied her. "So they'd rather go to all that trouble and expense rather than let us buy their crop, gin it, bale it and sell it to the merchants." She nodded and he vocalized the rest of what they were both thinking. "They can make more money doing it that way than by letting us gin it, because we're paying them for a lesser grade of cotton."

"I suppose they think so."

He got out of the chair and went to the window. He turned his hands palms out and slid them into the back pockets of his jeans. He seemed to be studying the landscape, but Caroline knew that he wasn't seeing it at all. "You knew all this, didn't you? Didn't you?" he repeated, spinning around when she didn't answer him immediately.

"Yes."

"But you didn't do anything about it."

"What could *I* do, Rink? At first I was only the bookkeeper. I learned about the ginning process and the marketing by listening, studying, making a nuisance of myself around the workers. I don't make executive decisions."

"You're his wife! Doesn't that give you a vote in anything?" He held up both hands. "I take that back. Wives of Roscoe Lancaster don't criticize him or anything he does, they just remain meekly at his beck and call and administer . . . wifely comforts."

Her chin went up as she balled her hands into fists and crossed her arms at her waist. "I told you once that I wouldn't discuss my relationship with Roscoe with you."

"And I told you once that I don't give a damn what you do in his bed."

They both knew that wasn't true. Rink almost looked embarrassed for telling such a bald lie. Caroline wisely chose not to challenge it. "If insulting me is the best you can do by way of helping, then I'll ask you not to bother."

He spat an expletive and raked frustrated fingers through his hair. Their eyes battled until they tacitly declared a truce. "I'll do whatever I can," he grumbled.

"Can you repair the stand?" she asked,

putting aside her pride.

"I'll need some tools, but I think I can. I've torn airplane engines apart and repaired them. Surely this can't be any more intricate than that. But I'm not promising anything, Caroline. What repair I do won't be an answer to your problems."

"I understand that." She softened considerably, letting her rigid posture relax as she smiled that shy, apologetic smile of hers. "Whatever help you can give me, I'll appreciate."

This time his curse was even more vile, but silent. And it was aimed at himself for his own culpability. He wanted nothing more at that moment than to hold her, protect her, meld her lips to his, graft his body to hers. What a damn fool he was. It drove him to distraction to think of her body entwined with that of his father. God! Sometimes he thought he'd go mad thinking about it.

Yet, he couldn't despise her, much as he wanted to. Every time he looked at her, he wanted her more. He should leave. Immediately. Before he did something to disgrace himself. He couldn't do that, either, for so many reasons. Laura Jane. His father. But mostly Caroline. Seeing her after twelve years, he couldn't bring himself to voluntarily leave so soon.

"You'll know where to find me," he said on his way out the door.

Caroline worked in the office doing paperwork while Rink commissioned the workmen's help in seeking out the necessary tools. An hour later, she came up behind him where he was studying the entrails of the huge machine. "Rink, I'm going to the hospital for a while. You can ask one of the men to drive you home if you get done before I get back."

He smiled wanly. "Not a chance. I'll be here for a while yet." She grinned and he had the notion that her half-raised hand was going to touch his arm. Instead, she muttered a rapid good-bye and left.

The hospital was cool and quiet after the noise and confusion in the gin. Roscoe was lying in bed, his eyes glued to the television screen, though he had turned the sound off. Tubes were feeding him and ridding his body of wastes. Monitors blinked and beeped and recorded his vital signs. He was pitiable to behold, but Caroline smiled brightly and bravely as she came in.

By an act of will, she forced yesterday's encounter from her mind. He was in tremendous pain. He couldn't help his behavior. She had been merely a convenient scapegoat for the terrible frustration he felt.

"Hello, Roscoe." She kissed his chalk-white cheek. "How are you feeling?"

"It's too crude to say to a girl of your sensibilities," he growled. Eyeing her attire, he asked, "Have you been to the gin?"

"Yes. All morning in fact, or I would have been here sooner. We have a problem with one of the stands."

"What kind of problem?"

"I'm not certain. Something mechanical. Rink's taking a look at it. These flowers from the Sunday school class are lovely."

"What the hell do you mean, Rink's taking a look at it?"

She had been looking over the flower arrangements delivered in her absence, collecting the cards so she would know whom to acknowledge. But at his words she spun around in alarm. From their dark sockets, Roscoe's eyes gleamed fiendishly. She had never seen him look so menacing. Or was it merely his illness that gave him that malevolent expression?

"Answer me, damn you!" he roared with far more strength than she had expected. "What is Rink doing anywhere near that cotton gin?"

She was flabbergasted and had difficulty

getting the words out of her mouth fast enough. "I . . . I asked him to look at the broken equipment. He's an engineer. He could tell —"

"You took it upon yourself to ask my son back into the gin?" He struggled to sit up. "He gave up any rights he had to Lancaster Gin when he left here twelve years ago. I don't want him in the gin, *near* it. Do you understand me, woman?" Sweat had popped out on his brow. His eyes bulged with fury.

Caroline was afraid, both of his ire and for his life. "Roscoe, please calm down. All I did was ask Rink to look at a broken machine. He's not asserting any rights over the business."

"I know him. He'll start finding fault with everything down there, telling you how to spend my money." He pointed a gnarled finger at her and said stridently, "You listen to me and you listen good. You're not to spend one damn cent on that gin without my approval."

She wanted to slap down that finger, which unfairly accused her. "I never have, Roscoe," she said levelly.

"Rink's never been around, either."

"And whose fault is that?"

Her unwise question reverberated off the

131

sterile walls of the room and came back to assail her. For several seconds she failed to breathe, only glared back at the wasted form of her husband, who in his weakness appeared dangerous, like a normally tame animal who had been wounded and would now destroy anyone trying to help him.

He laughed that horrible laugh as he collapsed against the pillows. "Is that what he told you? That I sent him away in disgrace for knocking up that George gal?"

Caroline's eyes dropped to her hands. Her fingertips were frigid and the hospital's air-conditioning was only partially responsible. Her palms were slick with perspiration. "No. We didn't discuss it," she said honestly.

"Well, just so you don't go getting the wrong notion, I'll set it straight. I didn't ask Rink to run off and stay away for twelve years. He knew I was mad as hell at him, but not for getting that gal pregnant." He chuckled. "I expected mischief like that. Boys will be boys. They'll take it where they can get it, won't they?"

She turned away. His words were like lances stabbing into her. "I suppose so."

His laugh was snarling. "Oh, believe me. A man will do anything, say anything, to get under a girl's skirt. Especially if she's halfway obliging."

She closed her eyes, willing away the tears, willing away his words, willing away her own shame.

" 'Course, they don't like getting caught at it the way Rink was. When Frank George came to me and said Rink had knocked up his Marilee, I told him right off Rink would marry her. That was the honorable thing to do, wasn't it?"

"Yes." It hurt to speak the word.

"Well, that scoundrel said he wasn't having any of it. That was the real disgrace. Not that Rink had been caught with his pants down, but that he wouldn't face up to his careless mistake. He told me then that if I forced him into marrying that girl, he'd leave and never come back."

He sighed as though the memory pained him. "I had to do what was right, didn't I, Caroline? I had to make him marry that gal. It was his choice to stay away after that, not mine. So don't go feeling sorry for Rink, no matter what he tells you. He made his bed, and for the rest of his life he'll have to lie in it."

He fell silent and for a long while she remained staring out the window. If she turned around, he would see her despair, he would know. When she had collected herself, she returned to his bedside. His eyes were closed as she leaned over him and she thought he was asleep. Softly she made to leave, but his hand shot out with uncanny speed and strength and clamped around her wrist. Startled, she gasped.

"You're still behaving like a wife, aren't you, Caroline?"

His smoldering eyes terrified her, as did his question. "Of course. What do you mean?"

"I mean that you'd regret it if you did anything that wasn't in keeping with a grieving, inconsolable wife watching her husband die." His fingers twisted over the fragile bones of her wrist until she thought they would crack. Where did he get the strength?

"Please don't talk about dying, Roscoe."

"Why not? It's a fact. But you remember this." Again he tried to sit up. Spittle gathered in the corners of his blue-tinged lips as he hissed at her. "Until I'm dead, you're my wife and you'd damn well better act like it."

"I will," she vowed frantically, trying to pull her hand free. "I mean, I do."

"I never put much stock in religion, but one thing I do believe. Thinking of disobeying a commandment is the same as doing it. Did you learn that in Sunday school?"

"Yes," she cried desperately, terrified of him and not knowing why.

"Have you been thinking of disobeying any commandments?"

"No."

"Like committing adultery?"

"No!"

"You're my wife."

"Yes."

"You'd better remember it."

All the strength went out of him then, and he fell back onto the pillows, struggling for air. Caroline wrenched her hand free from his death grip and ran to the door. She was bent on escape but remembered herself just in time and went for a nurse. "It's my husband," she panted. "I . . . I think he needs a shot of something. He's terribly upset."

"We'll take care of him, Mrs. Lancaster," the nurse said kindly. "If I might say so, you look in bad shape yourself. Why don't you go home for now?"

"Yes, yes," Caroline said, trying to restore her wits. Her heart was racing. She was trembling with fear. Why had she become so afraid of her own husband? "I think I will."

Granger was getting off the elevator as she got on. "Caroline, is something wrong?" He was alarmed by the state she was in.

"No, no. I'm going back to the gin. Trouble there, but please don't mention it to Roscoe. He's upset." Breathing raggedly, she backed against the wall of the elevator as though it were a hiding place from some unnamed terror that stalked her.

"Can I help —"

"No," she said, shaking her head furiously as the doors began to close. "I'll be fine. Go to Roscoe. He needs you."

The doors closed between them and she brought her hand up to her mouth, covering it to stifle the whimpers she felt welling up in her throat. "God, God," she repeated, wondering how he could have frightened her so. Her stomach was churning. Her body was flashing hot and cold.

She forced herself to walk through the first-floor lobby without a visible sign of her distress. By the time she reached her car, the most violent of her trembling had subsided. Lowering the car windows, she drove out of town along the river road. The wind beat through her hair, carrying with it all the scents of summer. There was little traffic and she drove fast, ridding her mind of the fears of moments ago.

She had let her imagination get the best of her. Roscoe couldn't possibly have known about her and Rink that summer. Rink wouldn't have told him. She certainly hadn't. No one had ever seen them together or there would have been gossip all over town. No, Roscoe couldn't know. Nor would he guess they were attracted to each other. To his mind, they had only met a few days ago.

His veiled threats and warnings were products of her own imagination and guilty conscience. Maybe his carefully chosen words hadn't been threats at all. No, she shook her head. They had been, much as she would like to think otherwise. But why had Roscoe made them?

How else could he occupy himself? He had nothing more to do than to think, to speculate, to become paranoid and suspicious. A man with a brain as active as Roscoe's would loathe lying in bed all day. He would despise that kind of inactivity. So mental power was the only thing he had left and his mind was working overtime to compensate for his wasting body.

Pain and anguish were magnifying everything in his mind, building mountains out of molehills. He had a wife more than thirty years younger than he. He had a strong, good-looking, virile son. For the time being they were living in the same house. He had put together a combination of facts that added up to a horrible suspicion.

He was wrong! She'd done nothing a wife shouldn't.

On the other hand, he was right. Thinking about making love to Rink was as grim a transgression as the act. And she never stopped thinking about it.

She must force that thought from her mind. Maybe if she treated him more like a friend, as ludicrous as it seemed, more like a friendly stepmother trying to keep peace in the family, memories of times past would fade. She had to put things into a new perspective, into the here and now and forget all that had happened before.

When she returned to the gin, the afternoon sun was slanting across the floor from the windows high on the walls. She looked around her in dismay. The place was deserted save for Rink, who was lying on his back, one knee bent, inspecting the workings of the gin stand. He was banging against the metal with a wrench. The ringing sound echoed loudly and drowned out her footsteps. "Where is everyone?"

The racket ceased. His head came out from under the piece of equipment and he sat up. He wiped his sweaty forehead with a handkerchief. "Hi. I didn't hear you come in. I took the liberty of sending everyone home an hour early. There was nothing much to be done while I was trying to get this back in shape." He hitched a thumb over his shoulder to indicate the machine. "Dust was flying everywhere. With some of the faulty wiring in this place, that could create a dangerous situation."

She should have berated Rink for closing early when it wasn't his place to do so, but she didn't. On her long drive, she had decided that Roscoe's decision-making ability had been affected by his hospitalization. The thought of doing something he wouldn't approve of behind his back was loathsome, but she had reasoned that what he didn't know wouldn't hurt him. In the long run, what was good for Lancaster Gin was what he would want her to do.

She squatted down next to Rink. "How's it going? Find the problem?"

"Yes, and it's a doozy."

"Can it be repaired?"

"Temporarily." He sighed and made a swipe across his brow with his sleeve. "How is Daddy today?"

The reminder of the scene in the hospital room made her shiver. "Not so well. About the same." He studied her closely, but she didn't give anything away with her composed expression. Changing the subject quickly, she asked, "Have you had anything to eat?"

"No. I'm too hot and dirty to eat." It was true he was dirty. His face was grimy and sweat-streaked. It made his teeth look even whiter when he smiled. "Besides, I didn't want to take the time."

She smiled and reached into the white paper sack she had carried in with her. "I brought you a late lunch. You won't have to stop working — you can drink this lunch." She poked a straw into the plastic lid on the paper cup.

"What is it?"

She thrust the tall frosty cup into his hand and stood up. "A chocolate milk shake."

Chapter 6

What did it mean?

Damned if I know, Rink answered his own questions as he reached into the shower stall to turn on the taps. He peeled off the sweaty, oil- and dirt-streaked clothes. He sipped his drink and set it on the dressing table.

First there had been the chocolate milk shake. It was as obvious a friendship-making token as a peace pipe. All afternoon she had remained at the gin. She had said she had paperwork to do in the office, but more often than not she was kneeling down beside him asking if there were anything she could do to help, if there were something she could get him. With the efficiency of a surgical nurse, she had passed tools to him when he'd extended his hand.

They talked about inconsequential things. Most of those topics they agreed on. They talked about family matters. On none of those did they agree.

"Did you see Laura Jane today?" she asked him.

"No. Did you?"

"No. Yesterday she seemed depressed. I wonder if she's just now realizing the severity of Roscoe's condition."

"Maybe. But it could have something to do with Bishop."

"Why do you say that?"

"Hand me that screwdriver again, please."

"The one with the red handle or the yellow?"

"Red. Because this morning when he brought that horse around for me, he was as touchy as a hungry crocodile."

"Maybe you just intimidate him."

"I hope to God I do."

He expected an argument. Though he could tell she didn't like what he'd said, she didn't comment. Since the floor of the gin was dusty, she had pulled a stool near him — too near. Even when his head was buried in the machinery, even when he wasn't looking at her, he was constantly aware of her presence. Her fragrance was as all-pervasive as the afternoon heat. Beneath his clothes, perspiration beaded and formed pools and trickled down his body in rivulets. But when his hand came in contact with hers, it was cool and dry. He wanted to press it to his face, his neck, his chest.

Cursing his recollection of the afternoon,

142

he took another sip of his drink. That had only been the beginning of where he would like her hands to be.

On the way home, she had been chatty. As soon as they'd come through the front door she had turned to him and said, "Take your time in the shower. I'll tell Haney to hold dinner until you've had time to cool off and relax. Let me fix you a drink to take up with you. What would you like?"

What he would like was for her to explain what the hell she was up to with this friendly camaraderie routine. Was this something Roscoe had put her up to? Or had she thought of it all by herself? Why all of a sudden was she acting like a new step-mother trying desperately to win the approval of the stepchild?

Well, whatever her game, it wasn't going to work, he thought as he stepped under the shower's spray. He was never going to think of her as a stepmother, and if she thought he ever could, then she didn't remember anything that had happened that summer. That summer. The merest thought of it set his heart to pounding.

He scoffed at himself. Twelve years later and he was still acting like a besotted moron. He, Rink Lancaster, heartbreaker. Ha! He had never had problems with women except how to get rid of one once he was tired of her. Was it any wonder that his feelings for Caroline had come as a rude awakening?

That summer was a time of conflict. He was both happier than he had ever been and more miserable than he could remember. When he wasn't with Caroline, he counted the minutes until he could be. When he was with her, he cherished every second but dreaded the time they would have to say good-bye. He was frustrated because he couldn't take her somewhere on a normal date and terrified that someone would see them together. He was starving all the time but wanted nothing to eat. He went around in a perpetual state of sexual arousal, but there was no appeasing it. He wouldn't with Caroline and he didn't want another girl as a substitute.

He wanted Caroline Dawson. He couldn't have her.

Night and day he had argued with himself. She's a little girl, for God's sake. *Fifteen!* You're asking for trouble, Lancaster. Big trouble.

But every day had found him waiting for her in the woods, holding his breath out of fear that she might not come. His anxiety wouldn't leave him until he saw her standing among the trees in a shower of sunlight.

But one day, that last day, the sun didn't shine. It had rained . . .

It was sunny when he left the house. That day, even more than most days, he was anxious to see her. He and his father had had an argument that morning. Roscoe was bending the regulations of the cotton exchange. What he was doing wasn't so much illegal as unethical. When Rink had hesitantly pointed that out to his father, Roscoe had flown into a rage. How dare his still-wet-behind-the-ears son presume to tell him how to run his business or live his life? He hadn't brought Lancaster Gin to where it was by being Mr. Nice Guy.

Rink was heartsick over the things he saw happening but was powerless to do anything about. He needed to talk to Caroline. She listened.

She was already there, sitting under a tree with her legs primly folded beneath her. Her face lit up when she saw him rushing toward her. Without a word he dropped to his knees in front of her, cradled her face between his hands and kissed her. His tongue plowed deeply into her mouth, finding a wellspring of sweetness there so different from the ugliness between him and his father. Her kisses always took him far from the gloom that shrouded his beautiful home.

When at last he released her mouth, he muttered, "God, it's good to see you." Then once again his mouth came down hard on hers. Gradually and without preliminary, he lowered her to the ground, onto a bed of soft fern and moss. Compliantly she lay down and he stretched out beside her, pressing one thigh over hers.

He raised his head and gazed down at her. Her gray-blue eyes were languorous behind sooty lashes. Her lips were dewy and full from the ardor of his kisses. Her hair was fanned out behind her head like a dark silk mantle on the green undergrowth. A rising wind flirted with the wisps on her cheeks.

"You're beautiful," he whispered. He bent down and kissed her eyelids.

"So are you."

He shook his head in denial. "I'm a selfish bastard. Who do I think I am, coming on to you like this, kissing you, taking for granted that you want to be kissed, without even so much as a hello? Why do you let me?"

A graceful hand came up to brush back the hair that was falling low over his eyebrows. "Because you needed me this way today," she said.

He laid his head in the curve of her shoulder and her arms folded loosely around his neck. "You're right. Daddy and I had a helluva shouting match this morning."

"I'm sorry."

"So am I, Caroline." His voice had the ragged, tearing sound of desperation in it. "Why can't he and I love each other? Or even like each other?"

"Don't you?"

He took his time, considering the answer carefully. He knew then how important it was. "No. We don't. Not even a little. I hate it, but that's the way it is."

"Tell me."

"He married my mother for her family name and her money. He didn't love her and she knew it. He's to blame for her un-happiness in life and her premature death. I meant it when I said she died of a broken heart. And he doesn't like me because I see him for what he is and he can't stand that. He's got so many fooled, but he can't fool his own son and that galls the hell out of him."

Her comforting fingers continued to sift through his hair. "Perhaps you judge him too harshly. He's a man, Rink, not a god. He has faults. Are parents supposed to be without flaws?" She stroked down his cheek and applied light pressure to his jaw until he lifted his head and looked at her.

"I think you're a bit intolerant. Forgive me for saying so. You demand perfection and can't abide failure within yourself. But you expect the same from everyone else and that's unfair, Rink. It's unjust to impose your standards on the rest of us. We're all no more than human."

She stroked his lips with her fingertips. "I'm so sorry that the relationship between you and your father isn't what it should be. Despite what my father is, I can't help but love him. Mainly because he needs love so much." She smiled up at him. "Go slow, Rink. Don't be so impatient. Your father has lived one way for a very long time. It won't be an easy conversion." Her eyes filled with unshed tears. "But I admire you so much for the uncompromising stand you take on what's right, even if it means angering your father."

His smile was slow and infinitely tender. "You're something, you know that? How do you make everything seem better? Hmmm? Why is it that when I'm with you things don't look so dark, so hopeless? Why do I feel like I have all the answers when you're around? At the same time you're slapping

148

my hand, you restore my self-confidence."

Her pleasure in what he said was evident. Her eyelids lowered with unintentional coyness. "Do I do all that for you?"

The gold in his eyes turned molten. He moved closer and lifted himself over her. He was hard and full. "You do a lot of things for me," he said thickly, rubbing his front against hers. Her eyes went wide and she shivered. Cursing himself, he moved away from her. "Damn! What's the matter with me? I shouldn't do things like that with you. I'm sorry."

Reaching for him, she said, "It wasn't that." She held her arm up and showed him the gooseflesh. "It's turned cooler. I think it's going to rain."

The words had no sooner left her mouth than raindrops began to fall lightly on her face. He rolled off her onto his back and watched as the clouds opened up. The rainfall rapidly increased to a downpour and they laughed like carefree children as they lay on their backs and let it deluge them. The fury of the sudden summer storm was soon spent and the rain once again subsided to a gentle shower.

Rink raised himself on an elbow and looked down at Caroline. Her complexion hadn't suffered from being washed of the frugal amount of makeup she wore. It was glowing with youthful loveliness. His eyes moved down her neck, farther. The breath caught in his throat. Her white blouse was wet and clung to her breasts. Today she hadn't worn a brassiere.

He looked at her in stunned inquiry.

Her voice was low and husky with embarrassment. "I don't have anything pretty to wear. I thought . . . if I didn't wear anything, it wouldn't be so ugly . . . I . . . oh . . ." She made a whimpering sound and crossed her arms over her breasts. "I didn't mean —"

"Shhh," he said, slowly lifting her arms aside. For a long moment, while the only sound around them was the dripping rain, his eyes appreciated her. The wet blouse detailed everything, the soft mounds, the puckering areolas, the peaked nipples.

"I think I hear thunder," she whispered tremulously.

He lifted her hand and laid it against his own wet shirt. "No. That's my heart beating."

He bent over her and placed his mouth on hers. The kiss was soft and sweet, exquisite in its tenderness. His tongue lightly flicked the corners of her lips, delicately traced their shape. From her throat a low purr reached his ears. "Oh, Caroline," he rasped.

The kiss changed character. It was no longer gentle. His lips slanted over hers, opening them. He pressed home with his tongue and it sank into the recesses of her mouth. His hand settled on her waist, squeezed lightly, then inched up slowly, slowly, until it covered her breast.

Nothing in his life, nothing, had ever felt so good and right as having her breast, still immature but already full, beneath his hand. He plumped the tender mound, pressed soothing circular motions into it. He explored with enough finesse not to alarm her but with enough technique to coax all the sensuality in her into play. She moved against him, each movement inadvertently seductive and inviting.

When his fingers found her nipple, her back arched off the soft grass. The sensitized flesh beaded with passion. His fingers played with it gingerly until it hardened more. And what his fingertips were doing to her nipple, his tongue was doing to the tip of hers. Sounds he wasn't even aware of issued out of his throat and his breath was hot and quick on her face and neck.

His hand went to the buttons of her blouse and he undid them swiftly. Caroline gasped softly and clutched at his hand and the wet fabric he was loosening. "Rink.

151

No," she whispered, meaning yes. She flung her head from side to side. Her teeth made tiny dents in her lower lip.

"Baby, baby," he murmured. "I won't hurt you. I just want to see you, touch you."

His mouth fastened onto hers again with a sweet suction. He drew life and love from her as he parted the blouse and slid his hand inside to cover the soft globe of her breast. When he felt her flesh against his palm, he exploded with new fire, hotter and more rampant than any sexual stimulation he had known in his life.

And he knew then that no other woman in the world would ever complement him as this one did. He had found her, the woman who would make him complete.

He fondled her, pushing her breast high with his hand, rubbing the nipple with his thumb. He inched down her body dropping light, quick kisses on her throat and chest. Then he took one rosy pearl into his mouth and sucked gently. Caroline sobbed. She grabbed handfuls of his hair and held his head fast. His heart burst with love at the moans of pleasure his loving elicited from her.

Her knees were raised, instinct having placed them so with no conscious thought from Caroline. He laid a hand on her bare

152

knee and caressed it. Her thighs were long, silky, as his hand smoothed its way up. The full cotton skirt she was wearing didn't deter him. He didn't stop his quest until he touched the elastic leg of her panties.

Her back arced still higher and she gripped his shoulders. "Rink, Rink." Her cry carried both rapture and panic and he understood both.

"It's all right, sweetheart. I'd never do anything to hurt you. I swear I won't."

His touch was feather light. The strokings continued on and on until there was no longer cloth between them. His fingers touched the soft hair, the soft flesh, her feminine mystery.

"Oh, my God," he moaned, burying his lips in her neck. "You're so sweet. Oh, God."

His fingers strummed, parted, discovered. When she quickened beneath him, he knew he had found the source of the magic. Deftly he applied just the right pressure as he circled and stroked until her throat arched, her head went back, the petals of flesh closed around his fingers and her cries mingled with the rustling wind in the rain-drenched trees.

He studied her face, gloried in its sublime expression. He watched as her eyes blinked open, as she righted her world and gradually returned to reality from that realm where all is bliss.

With the reality came confusion. She shoved down the skirt bunched around her waist. "Rink?" she asked on a high note. "Rink, what happened to me? Hold me. I'm frightened."

He lowered himself over her, sheltering her with his body. He held her close, hands on each side of her head. His lips nuzzled soft kisses over her face as he reassured her. "Don't you know what happened to you, Caroline?" Emotion roughened his voice.

She searched his eyes, pondered his mouth, touched it, as though she marveled over the miracle he was and what he had brought about. "But you didn't . . . I mean . . . you weren't . . . inside me."

Groaning, he pressed his forehead against hers. "No I wasn't. But I wanted to be. I wanted to be deep inside you, filling you with myself, giving you everything that I am." He kissed her, making love to her mouth with his tongue, pressing it deep inside her mouth. But the kiss was too evocative a reminder of what he couldn't do and he raised himself off her.

She was weeping. Her tears mingled with what remained of the rain. He wiped them off her cheeks with his thumbs. "Don't cry." He got to his feet and pulled her up with him, holding her close. Still she cried. "Why are you crying, Caroline?" God, if he had broken his promise and hurt her in some way, he would never forgive himself. Would she despise him now, be frightened of him? "Please tell me why you're crying."

"You won't be back. Not after today. After what I did . . . you'll think I'm trashy."

Relief flooded through him. "Oh, sweetheart," he whispered fiercely and gathered her even closer to him. "I love you."

Slowly she lifted her head to look at him. "You love me?"

"I love you," he vowed, because he knew it to be true. If he didn't love her, they would still be lying in the grass and he'd be doing what his loins ached to do. "I love you and would risk hell or high water to come back tomorrow." He hugged her hard, kissing her breathless. Then, as he held her with fierce possession, he whispered directly into her ear, "We're in a helluva mess, Caroline." Pushing himself away from her, he searched her eyes. "You see that, don't you?"

"Of course!" she cried softly. "I've always known that anything between you and me was hopeless."

"Not hopeless. I'm going to do something about the situation. Tonight."

"Tonight? What?"

"I'll see to it that we can go on proper dates, be with other people and stop all this hiding."

She gripped his upper arms. "No, Rink, don't do anything. Let's just keep on as we are for as long as we can."

"I'll die if we keep on as we are."

"Why?"

"When we're all alone like this, it's too hard for me not to finish what we start."

She was still and silent for a long moment, staring at the base of his throat as her fingers lightly trailed up and down the collar of his shirt. She wet her lips. "Rink, I wouldn't mind if you . . . I'd let you if you wanted to . . . uh . . ."

A finger tilted her chin up. "No." His voice was quiet but adamant. "I don't like the back street flavor of all of this. There's no way I'll complicate matters, risk hurting you, by making love to you." He lowered his face to within kissing distance of hers. He closed his eyes tightly and released a breath between clenched teeth. When he opened his eyes he said, "I want to. God, I want to. But I told you, didn't I, that I would never do anything to hurt you?"

"Yes. And I believe you."

"Then leave everything to me. Don't worry about anything. I'll get this straightened out and then we won't have to meet in secret like this ever again."

"Are you sure, Rink?" The worry was still stamped on her face and he knew the worry was for him, not herself.

"I'm sure. Tomorrow I'll have good news. Tomorrow, baby. Here. In our place." His hands folded around her face. "Oh, God, Caroline, kiss me again." His lips seared hers, but it wasn't a lengthy kiss. He didn't trust himself to uphold his promise. He wanted to take her and damn the consequences.

"Tomorrow, tomorrow," he repeated as he backed away, stretching his hand to reach her outstretched one until the tips of their fingers finally fell apart. He ran through the rainy woods to where his car was parked, anxious to get home. . . .

"You fool," Rink said to the fogged mirror as he stepped out of the shower. His image was blurred, which he thought appropriate to describe what he had been like since that day twelve years ago. "Whatever made me so naive as to think that it would all go as I planned?" He threw the last of his drink down his throat with no regard for its mellow taste. He only regretted that the ice had diluted the bourbon's punch.

Thinking of that night when he had gone into his father's study asking for an interview still turned him inside out. Like a residual poison, hate and resentment crept through his body every time he remembered how stupidly confident he had been. What a sap. What an idiot. He had been a young David facing Goliath. Oh, he had had the courage. But he hadn't had the slingshot and stones. And Roscoe had had a cannonball.

He had stridden into the study and announced, "Daddy, I've found the girl I'm going to marry."

"You're damn right you have," Roscoe had growled, rolling his fat cigar from one corner of his lips to the other. "Frank George called me this evening. Marilee's pregnant. Three or four months gone. According to him she's bawling her eyes out because you haven't been around to see her. Congratulations, son. You're about to become a husband and father."

Even now his father's words made his gut feel as tight as a steel spring. That bastard. That hateful, manipulative, conniving bastard.

And Caroline, *his* Caroline of the river and the rain, was his father's wife. Now it was he she listened to, talked with, gave solace and encouragement to. With Roscoe she shared that sweetest of mouths, those breasts, those thighs.

Rink dug into his eye sockets with the heels of his hands as image after image of them together flickered like an obscene slide show across his mind. Thinking about it was almost more than he could bear.

Everything inside him hurt. And there wasn't one damn thing he could do for the pain.

"Thank you, Steve."

"You're welcome."

"Rink said that toaster was done for and Haney should just buy a new one. But she said there was no use getting a new one when this one could be fixed. Rink was going to fix it but he's been busy at the gin. I said for him not to worry about it. I'd ask you to. You didn't mind, did you?"

"Of course not. I'm glad I could get it working again." He busied himself with straightening up the worktable in the garage where small tools were kept.

"Are you mad at me, Steve?"

He stopped what he was doing and looked

down at Laura Jane. She was wearing a halter sundress and her skin looked as soft and creamy as a magnolia blossom. Desire hit him like a sledgehammer. He turned away brusquely. "Why would I be mad at you?"

She drew in a shaky breath and perched on the top level of a stepladder. Restlessly her fingers fiddled with the tie belt at her waist. Her head was bent so low her chin almost touched her chest. "Because I kissed you the other day," she said softly. "Ever since then, you've been mad at me."

"I said I wasn't mad."

"Then why won't you look at me?"

He did then. Her shouted, angry demand brought his shaggy head around and he stared at her in speechless awe. He had never known her to lose her temper or raise her voice for any reason. There was little of the child in the face that was defiantly staring back at him. Her expression was that of a woman scorned.

He swallowed with difficulty. "I look at you."

"Your eyes slide over me. They never stop to look anymore. Why, Steve?" she asked, getting off the ladder and approaching him. "Why? Don't you like the way I look?"

His eyes gorged on her, taking in everything from the crown of her soft, heavy brown hair to her slender sandal-clad feet. When his eyes lifted to hers once again he said huskily, "Yes, Laura Jane, I like the way you look very much."

She smiled, but it faded rapidly. "Is it the way I kissed you? Didn't I do it right?"

He slid his hands up and down the outsides of his thighs, drying his damp palms on his jeans. "You did it just fine."

She drew her face into a worried frown. "I don't think I did. The women on television kiss the men for a long time. They move their heads from side to side. I think they open their mouths when they do it."

His whole body groaned. "Laura Jane," he said on a hoarse whisper, "you shouldn't talk about this to a man."

"You're not 'a man.' You're Steve."

"Well, you shouldn't talk about kissing to me, either."

She was genuinely puzzled. "Why?"

"Because there are some things that a man and woman who aren't . . . aren't . . . married shouldn't discuss."

"It's all right to do them, just don't talk about them?" she asked quizzically.

He snorted a laugh in spite of the seriousness of the situation. Laura Jane was making more sense than he was. "Something like that."

She glided toward him and laid her hands on his chest. Her head fell back as she looked up at him. "Then let's not talk about them. Let's just do them." Her voice was as light as the breath that landed on his throat.

His hands covered hers. "It's not proper for us to do them, either."

"But why, Steve?"

Anguish tore at his vitals. It took every ounce of discipline he had to pull her hands from him and gently set her aside. "Because it isn't." He went back to the table and picked up the bridle he had been working on when she'd called him from the tack room.

Disconsolately she watched him leave the garage and cross the yard. Taking up the toaster, which had only been an excuse to see him, she headed back toward the house. When she saw Caroline's car turn into the driveway, she paused to wait for her.

"Hello, Laura Jane. What are you doing with that out in the yard?" Caroline asked, gesturing toward the toaster as she alighted.

"Steve fixed it for Haney. I was on my way back to the house."

Something in the girl's tone caught Caroline's attention. "How is Steve? I haven't seen him in several days."

Laura Jane's slight shoulders lifted in a

shrug. "He's okay, I guess. He acts funny sometimes."

"Funny?"

"Yes. Like he doesn't want to be my friend anymore."

"I doubt that."

"It's true. Ever since I kissed him."

Caroline stopped in her tracks. "You kissed him?" She glanced around worriedly, hoping that no one else had heard and offering up a small prayer of thanksgiving that Rink wasn't around.

"Yes." Laura Jane's eyes were guileless and calm as she stared into Caroline's dismayed face. "I love him."

"Did you tell him that?"

"Yes. Was that bad?"

"Not bad, exactly." Caroline knew that she must choose her words carefully. This was Laura Jane's first and probably only romance. How did one caution and yet keep from intimidating? "Maybe you were too hasty. You probably took Steve by surprise. He might have wanted to kiss you first."

"I don't think he would have and I couldn't wait."

Caroline smiled. "Given enough time, I think he would have gotten around to it."

"Do you think Rink will get around to it?"

"Get around to what?"

"Kissing you. He wants to."

For the second time within the same sixty seconds, Caroline was dumbfounded. "Laura Jane, you mustn't say such a thing! He wants nothing of the sort."

"Then why does he stare at you?"

Her mouth went dry. "Does he?"

"All the time when you're not looking. And he works so hard at the gin for you."

"Not for me. For everybody, for the workers and the planters who use it, and for your father."

"But you're the one who asked him to. I didn't think he was going to at first, did you?"

Caroline thought back to that night after he had repaired the gin stand. She had tried all afternoon to establish a new rapport with him and thought that she had succeeded. But after they'd returned home, when he'd come down to dinner after his shower, he'd been more hostile than ever. She'd refused to acknowledge it. What little ground she had gained, she wasn't about to surrender.

During the evening meal and later in the living room with Haney and Laura Jane, she had killed him with kindness until he no longer scowled each time he looked at her. Finally she'd garnered enough courage to ask him to check out several more things that she'd thought warranted attention at the gin. He had grudgingly consented. For the past three days he had worked as hard as any of the salaried laborers.

"I'm grateful that he's here to help out while your father's sick. He's working hard."

"So are you. You look tired, Caroline."

She was tired. Very tired. She was still walking a tightrope with Rink, hoping to keep the channels of communication open between them without hinting at intimacy. And Roscoe. His verbal abuse became more vitriolic every time she visited him, which was at least once a day, twice if she could stand it. She didn't tell him about the work Rink was doing at the gin because she knew he wouldn't approve. Nothing else she did suited him. He criticized her on everything from the way she was dressed to the way she took his doctor's orders as law engraved in stone.

"I am tired," she admitted to Laura Jane. "About Steve," she said, returning to the original subject, "maybe he's just in a bad mood. Don't crowd him. Generally men don't like that. I think the next time you kiss, if you do, it should be his idea, not yours."

"I guess," she mumbled, her head hanging low.

Caroline thought she knew the reason behind Steve's sudden coolness. Apparently he was in love with Laura Jane but didn't want to do anything to encourage her at the risk of incurring Rink's wrath. Her sympathies were with all of them. "Let's go get some supper," she said kindly, taking the younger woman's hand.

"Where's Rink?"

"I don't know. He said he'd be along —"

She was cut off by the loud honking of a horn, and when she and Laura Jane turned around they saw Rink pulling a shiny new pickup truck to a stop behind the Lincoln. He bounded out of the cab.

"Well, what do you think?"

His exuberance reminded Caroline so much of the young man she had met in the woods that she almost ran to him and heedlessly threw her arms around him.

"Is it yours, Rink?" Laura Jane asked, hopping up and down happily and clapping her hands. "I like the color."

"Cavalier blue," he said, sweeping her a low bow. "I needed my own transportation as long as I'm here and I'd been giving some thought to a pickup. How I'll get it and the airplane both back to Atlanta, I haven't figured out yet."

They all laughed and Caroline's heart

melted at the sight of him, hair windblown, eyes dancing.

"I'm starving. Is dinner ready?" He looped one arm around Caroline's shoulders and the other around Laura Jane. "Let me escort you ladies into the dining room."

Before they reached the front porch, Haney came running through the screen door shouting, "Caroline, Rink! Thank God you're here. The doctor just called. Mr. Lancaster's taken a bad turn. He said you two better get to the hospital fast."

Chapter 7

Only one dim light over Roscoe's bed illuminated the room. It was a directional fixture. The metal shade was pointed down so that the light fell harshly and eerily on the man's pain-ravaged features. A nurse was bending over him when Rink and Caroline entered the room. With his arms trailing IV tubes, he waved her away querulously.

"Get out of here and leave me alone. There's nothing you can do."

"But Mr. Lancaster —"

"Get out," he hissed nastily. "I want to talk to my wife and son." The titles were slurred in a way that made them sound like insults.

The nurse left, the rubber soles of her shoes squeaking faintly on the vinyl floor. Caroline went to Roscoe's bedside and took his hand. "We came as soon as the doctor called."

Dark eyes, like iron pellets, bored into her from blackened sockets as intimidating as the barrel of a gun. His face was ugly. He had a look of decay about him that wasn't physical but spiritual, a rottenness that had eaten at him for years from the inside and was only now making itself manifest on the surface. "I hope I didn't drag you away from anything important," he said snidely and snatched his hand from her grasp.

Caroline refused to be provoked. Calmly she answered him. "Of course not, Roscoe. You know I want to be here with you."

He grinned maniacally. "So you'll know the instant I'm dead? So you'll know the very second you're free of me?"

Her body flinched as though she had sustained a blow to the head. "Why do you say things like that? Do you truly think I want you to die? Didn't I urge you to see the doctor long before you consented to? I've never given you any reason to doubt my devotion to you."

"Only because you lacked the opportunity." His eyes slid to Rink, who stood at the foot of the bed, his shadowed face giving away no emotion.

"W-what do you mean by that?" Caroline stammered, bringing Roscoe's eyes back to her.

"I mean now that the man you really wanted is living under the same roof with you, you might be tempted to be unfaithful to the husband you claim such devotion for."

All the breath left her body. She stared speechlessly at her husband. That sly grin was still riding his lips. His eyes were gleaming like the lights of hell.

"Are you talking about Rink?" she asked.

"Rink?" he repeated, mimicking her. "Rink, *Rink*. Yes, goddammit! Of course I mean Rink."

She wet her lips with her tongue. "But Rink and I . . . we haven't . . . we never —"

"Don't lie to me." He came to a sitting position and snarled at her like some fearsome demon chained to the bed by plastic tubes. "Don't pretend with me, little girl. I know all about you and Rink."

Caroline backed away from him, hunching her shoulders forward, folding her arms protectively across her midriff. Wildly her eyes sought Rink's. He hadn't moved. He was still standing rigidly at the foot of his dying father's bed, his eyes glowing with hate. He was the first to break that terrible silence.

"You knew about Caroline that night you told me Marilee was pregnant, didn't you?"

Roscoe collapsed onto the pillows. His breathing sounded like paper crackling in his chest. Physically it had cost him to shout his triumphant message, but his face was smug with satisfaction as he directed those malevolent eyes to his son.

He laughed. "I knew. Everything," he sneered. "You should have known you couldn't go sneaking off into the woods every day without arousing my curiosity. I gave you credit for being smarter than that."

"So you followed me one day and saw us together," Rink supplied in a quiet and level voice.

"Hell no." Roscoe sounded amused. "I wouldn't have troubled myself with anything to do with you. I just wondered what mischief you were up to. I sent some flunky after you and what he had to report was very interesting. You were meeting some trashy girl down by the river every day."

Caroline made a pitiful crying sound. Roscoe didn't even look in her direction. His fight was with his son, always had been. She had been a convenient pawn.

"This girl you were sneaking off to see was just a kid, the man said, but as juicy as a ripe peach." Roscoe smacked his lips. Caroline closed her eyes and fought off nausea. Rink rocked back and forth slightly in an effort to control the rage that tore through him. "We had a good laugh when we found out your ladylove was ol' Pete Dawson's girl." He winked at Rink. "But I had to admire that streak of lust in you, boy. She was jailbait, but you were willing to risk it, weren't you?"

"Let's get on with it," Rink snapped. "You knew that wasn't my baby Marilee was carrying, didn't you?"

"I thought it was just as likely yours as it was anybody's, and you couldn't prove otherwise. Everybody in town knew she wasn't all that discriminating as to whom she took to bed."

"The child wasn't yours?"

Rink's head snapped around and his eyes met Caroline's full on. Her voice had cracked with a combination of incredulity and . . . something else. Joy? Her eyes were swimming with tears. "No, Caroline," he said. "The child wasn't mine."

"You'd been with Marilee, though, hadn't you?" Roscoe asked from his bed.

Rink kept his eyes on Caroline as he answered. "Yes. But it was long before she became pregnant. I wasn't with anyone that summer after I met Caroline. Alyssa was not my child." He turned back to his father. "And you damn well knew it. I told you the baby didn't belong to me, that I hadn't slept with Marilee for almost a year. But you forced me into marrying her anyway. Why?"

"How conveniently you forget that you chose to marry her."

"Because you threatened to put Laura Jane in an institution if I didn't!" Rink yelled, finally giving vent to the anger that had simmered until it had to boil over.

"Oh, my God." Caroline covered her face with her hands. Would this nightmare never end? Roscoe had blackmailed Rink into marrying a girl carrying another man's child? How could he have?

"Why was it so damned important to you that I marry Marilee? Why didn't you laugh in her daddy's face when he suggested that I was that baby's father and send him packing? Surely you weren't afraid of the scandal it might cause. You never cared a fig for social niceties. And I know you weren't intimidated by old man George. Why did you make me marry her?" His voice had risen to a shout and the question hung in the air a long time after the words had left his mouth.

"Money," Roscoe said laconically. "He had money. I needed it. It was as simple as that. I sold you, boy, for twenty-five thousand dollars."

Rink was stunned. Even knowing the worst about his father, it had never occurred to him that something as commonplace as money had been behind the coercion. "But you didn't stop the divorce once Alyssa was born," he said, perplexed.

"There was no time stipulation to the deal. George only wanted a husband for that sorry gal of his and a daddy for her kid. He wanted a respectable name slapped on the birth certificate."

"Respectable," Rink scoffed, throwing his eyes toward the ceiling. He swore. "We reek of respectability, don't we?"

"Besides," Roscoe continued smoothly, "it seemed a convenient way to keep you from making a big mistake."

"What kind of mistake?"

"Taking up with trash, that's what." Roscoe cocked his head in Caroline's direction.

"Leave her out of this," Rink said threateningly. "This has nothing to do with Caroline."

Roscoe chuckled maliciously. "It has everything to do with Caroline. I couldn't have you knocking up a little gal like her, now could I? That would have been one helluva fine mess."

"It wasn't like that." The words were forced through Rink's clenched teeth.

"From what my informant told me, it was getting close. He said you could barely keep your hands off her." Roscoe's eyes narrowed as he glared at his son. His lips curled with contempt. "You fool. Do you know how hard it was for me to keep from laughing when you said you'd met the girl you were going to marry?"

Caroline jerked in reaction and her eyes flew to Rink. He glanced at her, but this wasn't the moment to dwell on the fathomless inquiry in her gray eyes.

Roscoe went on relentlessly. "Marilee was a hot little slut. She'd let just about anybody crawl between her legs, but at least she came from a respectable family." His eyes slithered to Caroline. "At least she wasn't the town drunk's kid."

"Then why did *you* marry me?" Caroline demanded, breaking her silence at last. Roscoe was responsible for all the heartache she had suffered. All this time she had believed that Rink had fathered Marilee's child while he had been seeing her. Roscoe's machinations had been skillfully executed. He had gotten away with deliberately ruining both their lives. She had nothing to lose now by fighting back.

"I married you because I wanted to make good on my investment," Roscoe stated bluntly.

"What do you mean?" She had a sinking feeling that she didn't want to know any more. But she had to know. This was a night of revelation. She didn't think she could survive another encounter like this. It would be better to learn everything at once. "What investment?"

"I'll be damned," Rink said softly as the truth dawned on him.

"You figured it out, did you?" Roscoe cackled.

"Will one of you tell me what we're talking about?" Caroline cried.

"I think you've been living with your mysterious benefactor, Caroline," Rink said softly.

She stared at him until the fog of misapprehension began to lift and she saw what had always been apparent if only she had looked for it. "The scholarship?" she asked hoarsely, staring down at Roscoe.

"I wanted to keep you out of town in case Rink, once his divorce was settled, decided to come back for you."

"You paid for my schooling?" She was trying to assimilate what was quickly unfolding. "It was that important to you that I not taint your son and his family name?"

"Oh, it wasn't just that," Roscoe drawled. "You had to be made suitable for the final step of the plan."

"Which was?" she asked on a thread of air.

"Which was that you become Mrs. Lancaster. Mrs. *Roscoe* Lancaster."

Clutching her stomach with both arms, she bent at the waist. Humiliation pumped through her with every agonizing beat of her heart. "You planned all this years ago? You made it happen?"

"How do you think you got that job at the bank so soon out of college? Did you think it was an accident that I met you there? I made available the job at the gin when the time was right. Want me to go on?"

"But why?" she cried. "Why?"

Roscoe said nothing, only slid his cunning eyes from her to Rink. It was Rink who answered. "Because I wanted you. And he knew it. And he would have done anything, no matter how unscrupulous, even marry you, to keep me from having you."

"You always were a smart boy." Roscoe leered.

"You told Laura Jane to write me that Caroline was married."

"That was easy enough to do. She would do anything to please me and then forget it within hours. You could have learned a lot about devotion and respect from your simpleminded sister, my boy."

"Respect." Rink spat the word.

"For years you manipulated all our lives

because of some grudge you had against Rink?" Caroline said, still not believing that a man could be so obsessed with hate. "I wasn't good enough for him, but you married me. You gave me your name, brought me to live in The Retreat. I can't understand it."

"You were easily seduced, my dear. I knew that coming from your background, we Lancasters and The Retreat would represent all that you'd never had. The house and family name were bait you couldn't resist, weren't they? Even if that house and name belonged to your long-lost love. Actually there were times when I was grateful to you for making it so simple. You were articulate and clean, which was a bonus. You're refined. God knows where that came from, but it was a benefit. You're good to look at, which made it easy for folks to believe that a dirty old man like me could be taken with you. Yeah, Caroline, thank you for making it so easy."

She turned her back in mortification. She had been used abominably. But oddly it was herself she blamed more than the twisted mind of her husband. If she hadn't been so gullible. If she hadn't been so quick to judge Rink. If she hadn't been so ambitious in her own right. If, if, if . . . What could Roscoe have done to hurt her more than she had hurt herself?

The dying man's eyes were lively as they darted between the two. "What's it been like living in the same house? Torture? This week has been the most fun of all, watching you squirm. You thought no one knew, didn't you? Oh, it's been entertaining watching you trying to hide it, watching you trying to keep from looking at one another and giving yourselves away."

His eyes lit on Rink. "You've been wanting her again, haven't you, boy? Got a twitch between your legs you can hardly stand, hmmm? Have you been thinking about her in my bed and what we do there?"

Caroline whirled around, outraged and offended. "Stop this, Roscoe!"

"Look at her, sonny. She's got a terrific body, doesn't she?"

"Shut up," Rink ground out.

"All woman. Every silky inch, female."

"Don't talk about her that way, damn you!"

Roscoe chuckled evilly. "I'm not saying anything you haven't been thinking. Have you been thinking about how you'd like to kiss her? Hold her? Undress her? Sleep with her? Been wanting your daddy's wife, boy?"

"Oh, *God!*" Devastated, Caroline ran from the room.

Roscoe laughed as he watched her go.

"You sonofabitch." Rink addressed his father with deadly calm.

"You're right about that." With an effort Roscoe pulled himself up and propped his weight on his elbow. "I'll burn in hell and love every miserable minute of it because you'll be more miserable here on earth. Ever since you were born you've been a thorn in my side."

"Because I saw all the ugliness in you. Because you killed my mother as surely as if you'd put a bullet through her brain."

"Maybe, maybe. She was a weak woman. Never stood up to me. But you did. You did, all right. I never could stand your eyes looking at me with such righteous reproach. And the older you got, the worse it got. You appointed yourself my conscience and I didn't want a conscience."

He pointed a shaking, skeletal finger at his son. "Well, I got you back, son of mine. It took me years, but I've repaid you in full. You'll never have that woman now, Rink. I know you. Your damned stubborn Winston pride won't let you have her." He paused significantly, then added, "Because I had her first. You remember that. She was *my* wife and I had her first!"

★ ★ ★

The four in the limousine were silent as it glided beneath the trees on the lane that led to the cemetery. Rink and Caroline stared out the windows by which they sat. Laura Jane, sandwiched between them, threaded her handkerchief between her fingers. Haney, on the jump seat, analyzed them all but kept her peace. At least as long as she could.

"Looks like a good turnout," she commented, peering out the back windshield at the procession of cars following the hearse and limo.

No one spoke. Finally Caroline said, "Most everyone in town, I think."

"I don't remember much about Mama's funeral. Do you, Rink?" Laura Jane asked timidly. When Rink's eyes looked as hard as they did now, he frightened her.

"Yes," he said bitingly, "I remember it." Then, realizing he was speaking to his sister, he turned his head and gave her a soft smile. Taking up her hand, he kissed the back of it and clasped it warmly between his. "A lot of people came to it, too."

"I thought so," she said, smiling tremulously, glad that he wasn't staring into space with that cold, foreboding expression on his face any longer.

"Folks are going to talk," Haney said prophetically. " 'Cause you aren't holding a funeral service in the church. The preacher was shocked. Everyone else was, too."

"Then they'll just have to be shocked and I don't care if they talk," Rink said bluntly.

"You don't have to live here," Haney snapped. "We do."

"No church service," Rink said gratingly. "All right, Haney?" His spearing eyes and the imperious edge to his voice rendered her submissive.

"Yes, sir." She drew herself up huffily. He turned his eyes out the window.

Caroline's heart went out to Haney and Laura Jane. Innocent as they were to the true nature of Roscoe's spirit, they couldn't understand Rink's remarkable coldness over the loss of his father. For herself, they thought that grief had stupefied her.

Haney had taken her hand and said, "You're a brave soul, Caroline, but the crying will come. When you're alone and all the hubbub is over, then you will cry."

Haney was wrong. Caroline would shed no tears for the man who had been her husband. Her eyes had remained dry from the moment she had run from his hospital room in abject humiliation. Rink had followed her out a while later, looking like he had been in hell and visiting with the Devil himself. His visage had been terrible, stony. It had stayed that way.

Through the long night they had kept vigil in the plastic-and-chrome waiting room chairs. They didn't speak. They didn't look at each other. So many times she had wanted to apologize for thinking he could have betrayed her love with Marilee. She had wanted to touch him, to hold him, to grieve with him for all the years they had been kept apart. But they were apart still. Every taut line of his body and tense angle of his face told her so. She kept her distance and held her silence.

Roscoe had been heavily sedated after Rink left his room. Once the doctor had come to Caroline and knelt in front of her, taking her hand. "It won't be long. You can go in if you wish, but he won't know you're there."

She had shaken her head. She never wanted to see his face again. When at last the doctor had come to tell them that Roscoe had died, she left the hospital with Rink, dry-eyed and empty-hearted.

Now she must play the role of the bereaved widow. The limousine pulled to a halt. She was helped out of the backseat by the solicitous funeral director and led to the

183

temporary tent that had been set up at the gravesite. She took the chair he indicated and sat stiffly, Rink beside her, Laura Jane next to him. Haney chose to stand behind Laura Jane, her comforting hands on the young woman's shoulders.

Caroline closed her ears to the minister's eulogy. Her eyes stared right through the casket with its blanket of white roses. When the service was over, she accepted the condolences of those who came to speak to her and Rink with formal graciousness.

"Isn't she holding up well?" they murmured to each other.

"Not a tear."

"Of course, since he had that exploratory surgery she's known it was only a matter of time."

"Yes. She's had time to prepare herself."

"Still, she could be carrying on something awful. You know how those people are. They tend to get emotional in public."

"I wonder what will happen to the gin?"

"She'll go on running it, I reckon."

"What about Rink?"

"He'll stay."

"He'll go back to Atlanta."

"I don't rightly know."

She heard the whispered speculations as she returned to the waiting limousine, and she was unmoved by them. The magnitude of Roscoe's deceit was still in the forefront of her mind. If she let any of her control slip, she would lose it all and disgrace herself by screaming like a madwoman. So she let them think her stoic. She would neither pray nor weep for the soul of Roscoe Lancaster. He had hurt not only her, but the only man she had ever loved. There would be no forgiveness in her heart for meanness so profound.

"Thank God that's over," Rink said as he sank into the backseat after shaking hands with the minister one last time.

But it wasn't over. All afternoon The Retreat was filled with people who had ostensibly come to pay their respects to Roscoe's survivors. Caroline thought most of them had come out of curiosity. Did they want to see what changes she had made in Marlena Winston Lancaster's house? She got the impression that most of them were disappointed to find it unaltered. Had they expected scarlet wallpaper and fringed lampshades?

They were insatiably curious about Rink and his life in Atlanta. He was grilled about his business, his private life, the years he had been away from them, his future plans. He handled the subtle inquisition adroitly.

185

They were equally curious about Caroline. From where she sat in somber dignity, she watched her visitors covertly study her and wondered what they expected. Had they expected her to wear something besides a sedate black dress? Did they expect her to be weeping uncontrollably? Or did they expect her to be laughing now that her rich older husband had died? Just as they were disappointed with the unchanged house, she felt they were disappointed in her. The Dawson girl hadn't given them anything to talk about later.

At last the callers began to leave, until finally the house was empty. Lengthy evening shadows came through the shutters to stripe the hardwood floors. Haney went about clearing up used glasses and paper napkins, emptying ashtrays.

"Will anybody be wanting supper?"

"Nothing for me, thank you, Haney," Caroline responded desultorily.

"No thanks." Rink splashed a draught of bourbon in a highball glass. "Go on to bed, Haney. It's been a long day for you."

She hoisted up her laden tray. "As soon as I get these things washed up, I may take you up on that. Is there anything you need, Caroline?"

Caroline smiled her thanks and shook her

head. "Good night, Haney."

"Well, there's plenty of food in the refrigerator if anybody gets hungry. Good night."

She left the two alone in the front parlor. Caroline leaned her head back on the sofa cushions and massaged her temples as she closed her eyes. She unbuttoned the top button of her dress and slipped off her shoes, sighing in relief.

Having taken off the jacket of his dark suit and rolled up his shirt-sleeves, Rink stood at one of the tall windows. One hand was in his pants pocket, the other periodically raised the glass to his lips. This was the first time they had been alone together since they'd left the hospital two nights before. It seemed they still had nothing to say to one another.

Caroline's eyes drifted open and she studied him from across the room. She indulged herself and greedily soaked up the sight of his dark silhouette against the indigo evening.

His black hair was a startling contrast against the white collar of his shirt. His shoulders were wide and she followed the tapering shape of his vested back to his waist. His buttocks were narrow and taut beneath the tailored slacks, his thighs hard and lean and long. She wanted nothing more than to go to him. She could almost feel her arms sliding under his and around that firm torso to a stomach she knew her hands would find flat and corded. Her breasts ached to be pressed against the strength of his back. She wanted to lay her cheek against his shoulder and drink in his scent, every nuance of him.

Then, as she watched, his body tensed and she heard his muffled, "What the hell?" before he slammed the glass down on the antique sideboard and stormed from the room, his face set in hard lines. Alarmed, Caroline jumped from the sofa and hurried to the window.

Steve and Laura Jane were on the lawn. They were making slow progress toward the house. His arm was around her shoulders as he held her securely close to him. Her head was nestled against his chest. His head was bent protectively over hers. Caroline saw his lips moving as he spoke to her softly. Then she saw his lips rest fleetingly on her temple in a gentle kiss.

Spinning on stockinged feet, she raced from the room, knowing now what Rink had seen. She must catch up with him before —

But even as she thought it, she heard the front door screen bang closed behind him and his heels on the front porch. "Laura Jane," he called out.

Caroline ran after him, bounding down the front steps. "Rink, no."

Laura Jane raised her head from Steve's chest, but she made no effort to move away from him. Instead she carried him along with her as she obeyed her brother's summons. Caroline could see the reluctance in Steve's footsteps. He wasn't as naive as Laura Jane and had recognized the rage in Rink's voice immediately. But he didn't avert his eyes from the other man as they came forward.

"Yes, Rink?" Laura Jane asked.

"Where have you been?"

"I've been in Steve's apartment watching television." She smiled up at the stable manager. "He was trying to take my mind off Daddy's funeral."

Fury radiated off Rink like heat from a stove. "Well, it's getting late. You'd better get upstairs to bed."

"That's what Steve said, too." She sighed. "Good night, everybody." She bestowed upon Steve a private smile before she glided toward the front door.

Rink let several seconds tick by after they heard the door close behind her. Then he took a belligerent step forward. "Keep your hands off my sister, understand? If I see you pawing her again, you'll be out of a job and off this place so fast your head will spin."

"I wasn't pawing her, Mr. Lancaster," Steve said levelly. "I was comforting her. She's upset by your father's death and . . . other things."

"Well she doesn't need your kind of 'comforting.' "

"Rink," Caroline interrupted and laid a cautioning hand on his arm. He shook it off.

"What's that supposed to mean?" Steve asked.

"You know damned good and well what it means. You could get by with a helluva lot under the heading of comforting."

Steve gnawed his lower lip and Caroline knew that only fear of losing his job and having to leave The Retreat and Laura Jane prevented him from lashing back at Rink.

"You can think whatever you like about me, Mr. Lancaster, but this you can write down as fact. I've never done anything to hurt Laura Jane, nor will I ever."

Rink glared at him balefully. "Then we don't have a problem, do we? But just to make sure I don't ever misunderstand anything you do, stay away from her." With that he turned away and stamped back into the house.

After casting an apologetic glance in Steve's direction, Caroline rushed after

Rink. She caught up with him in the wide foyer and, grasping his arm, spun him around. "You bully! Did taking your anger out on Steve give you any satisfaction? Do you feel better now?"

"Not quite."

He reversed their roles and became the aggressor. Taking both her upper arms in fists of iron, he pushed her into the parlor and slid the door closed behind them. Pressing her into the wall with his body, bending his face close over hers, his breath labored, he demanded, "How could you have slept with him? How, Caroline?"

Chapter 8

The kiss that followed was brutal. His mouth twisted over hers and forced her lips to part and admit his tongue. His hips thrust forward and ground into hers. One hand released her arm and covered her breast. He squeezed it without tenderness. It was a caress intended to debase.

She fought him. Her free hand alternately pushed against his unyielding chest and pounded his shoulder. She tried to drag her mouth free of his assaulting lips, but to no avail. Her screams were nothing but high-pitched garbled noises that were muffled by his mouth.

This wasn't Rink. Caroline knew that he didn't want to hurt her this way. He was crazed with an anger that had been building all his life. His enemy was dead and that left him with no one to fight. Frustrated, he was taking out his rage on her, because unwittingly she had been a part of Roscoe's scheme. She understood then that her best defense was not to fight him at all. She went limp in his arms.

It was several moments before Rink came

to his senses and realized that she was no longer struggling against him. His lips gentled and the tempestuous kisses became sweet nuzzlings against her mouth. The hand on her breast ceased its insulting groping and after touching her tenderly, apologetically, was withdrawn.

It was this sweetness that she had to fight. The violent caresses of a moment ago weren't from the man she had known and loved but a man torn asunder by deceit and bitterness. Now, his touch was painfully familiar, achingly reminiscent of that summer when every touch had been enchanted.

"Rink." His name was a soft groan, carrying with it yearning and hopelessness.

"Did I hurt you?"

"No."

"I didn't mean to."

"I know."

He leaned forward and placed his arms from elbow to fingertips against the paneled wall behind her. His forehead pressed into the wood as he rested it close above hers. His breath stirred her hair. "Why do I want to make love to you more than I want to breathe? Why haven't I been able to forget you? After all this time, why am I still obsessed by you?"

He inclined toward her until they were

touching in one unbroken line. Their position was so blatantly sexual that their hearts hammered against each other. "We could be lying in a bed in this same position, couldn't we, Caroline?"

"Oh, God." She burrowed her nose in his neck. "Don't talk about it, Rink."

"That's what you're thinking. That's what I'm thinking."

"Don't think about it."

"I'll always think about it."

Their bodies heated one another. Her breasts flattened softly against his hard chest. Their bellies massaged each other with every shallow breath. He adjusted himself against her so that she might feel the strength of his desire. His sex nestled in the receptive hollow of her femininity. Their thighs pressed against each other.

Fully clothed, standing, not moving, they were intimate. They made love. It was a mental intimacy, not physical. But each was thinking about the act so potently that it couldn't have meant more had it been performed.

Rink turned his face into her hair, burying his nose in it. He whispered her name repeatedly. Their emotions were so undisciplined that they trembled with them. Then they were still.

Minutes passed and they neither moved nor spoke. They just stood there, relishing the nearness of one another, regretting what had never been and lamenting that it could never be.

Gradually Rink began to back away until they were no longer touching. His eyes pored over her face, hot and compelling. She raised hers to meet them. "How could you have been with him, Caroline?" he rasped. He pushed himself away from the wall and ran his hand through his hair. He didn't ask again, but his stern expression demanded that she answer him.

"He was my husband." It was a simple statement that should have explained everything. Instead it provoked fresh anger.

"How could you have married him in the first place? How, for God's sake? After what had been between us, how could you have married *him?*"

"That's not fair, Rink!" she said heatedly. "You deserted me, not the other way around."

"You know why I married Marilee."

"Not until two days ago I didn't."

He put his hands on his hips and faced her angrily. "Then you actually thought that I was screwing somebody else while I was defying everything, even my own common sense, to be with you?"

His vulgarity shocked her into flaring back. "How was I to think otherwise? You were gone without a word. I heard that you were getting married to Marilee George because she was pregnant. What was I supposed to think?"

He cursed and turned away to avoid her sound reasoning. "I couldn't come to you with the truth. You wouldn't have believed me any more than anyone else did."

"I might have."

"Would you?" he asked, rounding on her. Her eyes fell beneath the accusation of his. "No, you wouldn't have," he answered for her. "You would have thought just what everybody else did, that the baby was mine."

He went to the couch and flopped down on it, extending his legs far out in front of him. He rubbed his eyes with his thumb and middle finger. "Besides I was afraid you might become involved somehow if I tried to see you again. I knew the town was buzzing with gossip and that I would be watched like a hawk. Anything I did would be duly reported. I didn't want to risk getting you mixed up in the mess."

She went around the room plucking cards from the numerous flower arrangements that had been delivered before the funeral.

"Who was the baby's father, Rink?" Disinterestedly he named the man. Caroline turned to him in surprise. "But that was the man Marilee married after your divorce."

He laughed mirthlessly. "She could hardly wait to run back to him. But first she had to bleed me dry financially. That was my punishment for not wanting her."

"You wanted her at some point," she said in an almost inaudible whisper, remembering what he had said that night in Roscoe's hospital room.

His head snapped up. "Are you going to hold that against me? My God! I was just a kid, Caroline." He was irritated and it showed. "Sewing wild oats. Yeah, I was with her a few times. Every guy in town was. But I had sense enough to take precautions so she wouldn't get pregnant. A couple of romps in the backseat of my car sure as hell didn't mean I wanted to marry her."

She looked down, studying her thumbnail. "And it's true that you weren't . . ."

"Caroline." Her head came up at his soft beckoning. "Do you want to know if I was with her at the same time I was seeing you?" Her eyes brimmed with emotion as she stared back at him. "No," he said with soft emphasis. "I wasn't with anyone else that summer."

"Did you really tell Ro . . . your father . . . that you wanted to marry me?"

"Yes. I told him I'd met the girl I wanted to marry."

Their eyes locked and held and it was a long while before her head fell forward and she turned away. "The baby, Alyssa?"

The corners of Rink's lips lifted in a brief smile before his face became sad. "She was a great little girl."

At his mellow tone, Caroline faced him again. "You loved her," she said with no inquiring inflection.

Unashamed he looked up. "Yeah," he said, laughing softly. "Crazy, isn't it? But once she was born, I wanted to keep her."

Caroline's heart wrenched with love for him. She sat down beside him on the couch. "I'm not prying, Rink. But if you want to talk about it, I'll listen."

His eyes roamed her face. "You always were good at listening. Tell me, did you sit at my father's feet and listen as he poured his heart out to you?"

She uttered a strangled cry as she leaped to her feet. He caught her wrist and checked her retreat. "I'm sorry. Sit down." When she strained to pull her arm free, he gave it a swift, light jerk that brought her back down on the sofa. "I said I was sorry. That was un-called-for, but habits are hard to break. If you want to know about my ill-fated marriage, I'll tell you. You know about all the other garbage in my life, you'd just as well know about that, too."

"I said I wasn't prying."

"And I believe you," he snapped. "Okay?" When she bobbed her head once in terse agreement, he released her hand. "Marilee didn't love me any more than I did her. Roscoe was right about that. She only claimed the baby was mine to keep her family from disowning her. Anyway, when we left here, which she hadn't bargained for, we went to Atlanta. I had to find work because I wouldn't take a cent from my father. The marriage deteriorated, but I loved Alyssa. As soon as she was born her real father showed up and he and Marilee picked up where they had left off."

"You didn't mind?"

"Hell no. I couldn't wait to get her off my hands. But I worried about the baby. Marilee wasn't the most conscientious of mothers. When she filed for divorce on the grounds of mental cruelty, I didn't contest it, but she wasn't done yet. She demanded an outlandish settlement. At one point I was actually supporting her and her lousy boyfriend. To make a long story short, I had to work day and night for years to buy her out of my life. I hated losing Alyssa, but Marilee insisted on having custody of her."

"Did Alyssa ever know that you weren't her father?" Caroline couldn't bear the thought of the little girl pining away for a father who never saw her.

"Oh, yes," he said with disgust. "Alyssa was about three when the divorce became final. She was crying, clinging to me while Marilee pulled her out of my arms. They were coming back to Winstonville and I was staying in Atlanta. Alyssa was calling me Daddy, crying that she wanted Daddy. Marilee told her that if she wanted her daddy she'd have to go to Winstonville to find him because I wasn't her daddy."

"Oh, Rink," she murmured, shivering at the thought of such a terrible scene.

"She's eleven now and I hear she's as wild as a March hare, the scourge of Winstonville Junior High." He shook his head sadly. "It's a shame, because she was such a sweet little girl. As you know, she's had a succession of 'stepfathers.' I doubt if she even remembers me."

After a long silence Caroline said, "Had Air Dixie started by this time?"

"Not quite. I had gotten my pilot's license my first semester at college. By the time I moved to Atlanta I had gotten in enough flying time to hire on as a charter pilot. I kept logging hours, upgrading my classification to fly larger airplanes. I met my partner and we started thinking about a charter service of our own. When one went bankrupt and was selling cheap, we managed to scrape enough together to make a down payment on it. We began doing so much business we paid off our loan years ahead of time and couldn't keep up with our demand. We bought a larger plane, then another, then another."

"And it went from there."

"Yes."

The lamplight formed a halo around them. Her dark hair fell to her shoulders and blended with the black dress she wore. Only her face and throat shone creamy and pale in the golden light. Her eyes were shadowed but luminous as they gazed back into his.

"Caroline?" he asked softly.

Her heart began to thrum behind her breasts. It was disgraceful to feel the way she did on the day of her husband's funeral, but she knew that if Rink made one overt move, she would flow toward him and there would be nothing she could do to stop herself. She still loved him, had never stopped. But she no longer worshiped him as an adolescent does an idol. She loved him as a woman loves a man. Despite his temper, his intolerance of human weakness, his fury over her relationship with Roscoe, she loved him.

"Yes, Rink?"

"Did you ever think of me when you were making love with my father?"

He couldn't have hurt her more if he had plunged a dagger into her heart. She cried out in agony and bolted off the sofa. "You bastard! Don't ever say anything like that to me again."

He came off the couch to stand facing her. His proud chin jutted forward. "I want to know. Didn't it prick your conscience just a little to marry my father when we had come so close to being lovers ourselves?"

"I was willing to be your lover, remember. You weren't willing to be mine. You weren't willing to take the risk."

"That's right. I wouldn't risk hurting you."

"I wanted you to hurt me." She spoke with so much emotion it sounded like a sob.

He gnashed his teeth and his voice lowered to a rumble. "I wanted to hurt you that way, yes. I wanted to be the first, to give you that instant of pain that would make you mine forever." He came a step closer, seething with pent-up emotions. "But I had some misplaced sense of nobility. More the fool, I wanted you to be set apart from the other girls I'd been with."

"And there were many, weren't there?"

"Yes."

"Before and since."

"Yes."

"Then how can you blame me for marrying Roscoe?"

"Because you said you loved *me!*"

"Did you love all those other women, Rink? Did you?" He turned away abruptly but not before she saw the guilt on his face. "You weren't here, Rink. You were married to someone else. For all I knew I had only been a casual plaything for you to while away those lazy summer hours with. You could have written, called, anything. I doubted that you even remembered me except perhaps because I was so unsophisticated compared to the women you were used to."

"You know why I couldn't contact you. I didn't want to involve you in that mess with Marilee. By the time it was over you were in college and I was informed that you were married. I gave up the hope of ever seeing you again. Then the next thing I know you're sharing my father's bed!"

She covered her face with her hands. She could feel his resentment coming toward her in incessant waves. Her hands fell from her face and she bravely met his angry eyes. "We can't go on this way, Rink," she said softly. "We're destroying each other."

His shoulders sagged and again his hair was punished by raking fingers. "I know. I'll be leaving in the morning."

Her heart dropped to her feet like a lead weight. She hadn't intended to run him off, she had merely wanted to make peace between them. "You don't have to leave. I will. This is your house. My residence was temporary. I knew that after Roscoe's death I wouldn't belong here."

"If you left and I stayed, how would that look to everybody? It would look like I had run off my daddy's widow. No. I'll return to Atlanta tomorrow."

"But the reading of the will and the cotton gin . . ." She groped for a plausible reason for him to stay. It was hopeless between them, but she couldn't stand for him to leave her again. Not yet. Later, but not now.

"I'll come back for the reading of the will. We'll decide then on the living arrangements. I'll feel better knowing you're here with Laura Jane. As for the gin" — he smiled sardonically — "carry on as you did under Roscoe's supervision."

The bleak look on her face vexed him. He took the steps necessary to bring them together. He wrapped his arms around her and hauled her against him. Her head fell back as he bent low over her face.

"Don't look at me like that. Do you think I want to leave? My home? My house? Laura Jane and Haney?" His voice dropped significantly. "*You?*" He pulled her closer and moaned as her body molded to his. "Damn you. Damn you, Caroline."

His mouth came down hard and demanding on hers, but she was waiting for it. Her lips opened and invited him inside. His tongue burrowed into the hot sweetness of her mouth. He kissed her long and deeply, his head tilting first to one side then another to taste all of her. His hands closed about her face as his mouth fused intimately with hers.

Then he broke it off with a suddenness that made her dizzy. His voice was gruff, torn from a throat constricted with the pain of wanting. "Damn you for belonging to him first."

A heartbeat later she was alone.

"Laura Jane?" Steve knelt down in the hay and touched her shoulder. "What the hell are you doing here?"

"Hmmm?" She stirred in her sleep and rolled from her side onto her back. "Steve?" she murmured. Her eyes blinked lazily, then came slumberously awake. "Is it morning?" she asked softly, stretching languidly, arching her back and lifting her breasts toward him.

"Barely morning," he said, tearing his eyes away from her chest. "What are you doing in here?"

She sat up and shook hay from her hair. Faint sunlight shone into the stable onto her bare shoulders. The air was still night-cool, but the hay on which she had slept was warm and pungent. Horses in the various stalls were nickering, hungry for their morning ration of oats. Dust motes floated in the air, catching the sun's first rays.

Laura Jane's sleepy eyes focused on Steve. She smiled and touched his cheek, which was pink and shiny after his recent shave. "Last night Caroline and Rink argued. I could hear them shouting all the way in my room. Haney was already asleep so I couldn't go to her. I had to get out of the house. Why are Caroline and Rink always so angry with each other? I don't understand it, Steve."

She leaned forward, laying her head on

his chest and wrapping her arms around his waist. "Anyway, I came out here. The door to your apartment was closed and all the lights were out. I knew you were already asleep, too, and didn't want to bother you. I curled up here in the empty stall and went to sleep. I felt better just being close to you."

She snuggled closer to him and his insides were pitched into chaos. He had cursed Rink Lancaster and his threats after the scene in the yard. Did Lancaster actually think he meant any harm to come to Laura Jane? Couldn't that bullheaded brother of hers see that he loved this woman/child, that to him she embodied everything that was pure and good in a world he had thought rancid with hate and killing and blood and war?

He had sworn last night never to be alone with her again, never to touch her. Because to be caught at it would mean that he would have to leave for good. That he couldn't have borne.

Now, however, he knew that he would not be able to heed Lancaster's warnings. The nearness of Laura Jane's soft body was blotting them from his mind. Without his planning it or weighing the consequences of such a move, his arms closed tightly about her.

"I'm sure they were both upset by your father's funeral. They'll iron out their differences. It's natural for a household to undergo some stress when someone in it dies."

"I love them both so much. I want them to be friends."

He laid his cheek against her hair. His large, scarred hands smoothed her back. She had on a soft cotton nightgown with a daintily smocked bodice across her breasts. Thin straps tied it onto her shoulders. The light robe she had covered herself with had been cast aside when she sat up. Her skin was warm and soft.

"When things settle down, they'll be friends. They won't argue anymore. I promise."

She lifted her head from his chest to look at him. Her brown eyes were trusting and loving. "You're so good, Steve. Why can't everybody be as good as you are?"

"I wasn't good," he said thoughtfully, trailing a finger down her cheek. "Not until I met you. Whatever goodness I have, you gave to me."

"I love you, Steve."

His eyes closed with internal anguish and he drew her close, pressing her head under his throat. "Don't say that, Laura Jane."

"I want to. Because I do love you. I think if you love somebody you should tell them, don't you?"

"I suppose so, yes," he whispered. The dike behind which his emotions were damned was cracking up. The pressure was getting to be too much. He would have to find an outlet for them and when he did, God help him.

She pulled back and stared at him compellingly. Lashes as long and luxurious as a feather brush surrounded the eyes that had cured a man as hard and cynical as he of all callousness. She stared back at him expectantly and the choice was taken from him. He had to speak the words aloud.

"I love you, too, Laura Jane."

Smiling, she launched herself at him, throwing her childishly thin arms around his neck and hugging him hard. "Oh, Steve. I love you. I love you." She covered his face with kisses as soft and fleeting as the beat of butterflies' wings. "I love you." She came to his mouth and hesitated, remembering Caroline's words of caution.

He inhaled her breath, felt the trembling excitement in her body so close to his. He was like a drowning man going down for the third and final time. What the hell? he asked himself. Lancaster couldn't do anything to him that hadn't already been done. When one has faced death a hundred times, one comes to mock it, dare it.

And besides all that, he loved this woman.

His mouth met hers gently and held. The tiny tremors that shimmied from her breasts up to her throat matched the flutterings in his own body. The way he felt about her was like nothing in his life before. He was well acquainted with women, but not this kind of woman, not one who was loving and trusting, innocent and eager, sincere and unselfish.

Quite naturally her lips parted beneath his and he groaned. His tongue tentatively ventured between her lips, tested, tasted. She pressed her mouth more firmly against his and edged closer until he felt her breasts and their small pointed nipples against his chest. His embrace became stronger as his tongue deflowered her mouth.

They swirled together in an orgy of discovery. It was as significant a learning experience for Steve as it was for Laura Jane. Together they fell back onto the hay. He laid his good leg over her thighs and her slender legs twined around it.

"Laura Jane." He sighed into her neck. Valiantly he tried to get a grip on his rioting sexual impulses, but her breast was beneath his hand and it was firm and ripe with passion. The peak responded with such enthusiasm that he couldn't keep from loving it with his fingertips.

"Steve, Steve," she panted. "Oh, Steve, make love with me, Steve."

His head jerked up and he looked down into her shining face. "I can't," he said softly. "Do you know what you're saying?"

"Yes." Her fingers moved adoringly over the blunt features of his face. "I know about what men and women do together. I want us to do it."

"We can't."

She wet her lips and her eyes filled with uncertainty. "You don't love me?"

"I do. That's why I can't. I couldn't do that with you unless you were my wife."

"Oh." She was vastly disappointed. Her eyes went to his mouth. Her fingers touched it. "Do we have to stop kissing?"

Smiling, he bent down and brushed his mouth against hers. "Not yet," he whispered. "Not yet."

"Good morning." Caroline entered the kitchen and headed straight for the coffee maker. She poured herself a generous cupful. As she carried it to the table, she avoided looking directly at Rink, who was already there.

"I'm calling the doctor this morning," Haney said, stirring the scrambled eggs in the skillet.

"Doctor? Why?"

"You look terrible, that's why," the housekeeper said without compunction. "I know you didn't sleep well. Look at those circles under your eyes. Can't you see them, Rink? You need a sleeping pill or tranquilizer or something."

"No I don't," Caroline said, sitting down across from Rink. Even though he had been included in the conversation, she didn't look at him and he remained silent.

"Don't be so brave," Haney said chastisingly. "No one is handing out prizes for the most courageous widow of the year. No one would blame you if you broke down and got all that grief out of your system. It's natural to grieve when you lose your husband."

At that point Caroline hazarded a glance at Rink. He was staring at her over the top of his coffee mug. She was the first to look away. "I don't need a doctor."

Haney sighed, not bothering to hide her exasperation. "Well, eat a good breakfast, at least." She piled the eggs onto a plate and set it in front of Caroline. "Go on and start. I'll go up and wake Laura Jane later. I thought it best to let her sleep."

"She's not sleeping," Caroline said, stirring cream into her coffee. "I stopped by her room before I came down." She had wanted the girl to accompany her downstairs, to act as a shield against Rink's mood, whatever it might be this morning. "She wasn't there."

Rink lowered his fork to his plate. Haney turned from the countertop, a plate of toast in her hand. "Where is she? You haven't seen her this morning?" he asked Haney.

"Didn't I just say I thought she was still asleep?"

Rink tossed his napkin down on the table and stood up. He stamped to the back door and tore it open. "Rink!" Caroline shot out of her chair and went after him. By the time she had run down the back porch steps, he was striding purposefully toward the stable. "Rink!" she called after him and increased her pace.

At the door of the stable he turned on her. "Be quiet!"

"You can't spy on them, Rink," Caroline objected, though she kept her voice to a whisper.

"Stay out of it."

She was interfering when she knew it would be wiser not to, but she couldn't let him destroy Laura Jane's chance at happiness. "She's not a child."

"With what he has in mind, she is." He eased the door open. Thanks to Steve's careful maintenance, it didn't make a sound. Rink stepped into the dim building with Caroline following close behind him. His boot made a grinding sound on the floor as he reached the stall where Steve and Laura Jane lay.

They heard it and, seeing the enraged expression on Rink's face, sprang apart. Unfortunately Rink had already seen the intimate way Steve was kissing his sister, the way her body was curved into his, the way his hand was caressing her breast.

Rink's cry of outrage curdled Caroline's blood. He lunged at Steve, grabbed him by the front of his shirt and yanked him jarringly to his feet, a maneuver that Caroline knew must have nearly torn the prosthesis from his stump.

Rink plunged his fist into the veteran's stomach and sent him falling backward against the side of the stall. Then, before he had a chance to recover, Rink's fist slammed into his chin.

Laura Jane screamed and scrambled to her feet. She flung herself toward the fighters, but Caroline grabbed her and pulled her out of the way. Steve's instincts as a guerrilla fighter had been awakened and he came back at his attacker with a vengeance. When a well-aimed fist brought blood to Rink's nose, Laura Jane screamed again and ran from the barn.

"Stop it!" Caroline shouted. "Stop it, both of you."

Fists and feet were flying. They grappled against the stall, striking stunning blows at each other.

Caroline rushed into the two-man melee and wedged herself between them. "Stop it now. Both of you. My God, have you both lost your minds?" At last she was standing between the two fighters, who were panting for breath and swabbing at bleeding cuts.

When Rink had finally regained his breath, he glared malevolently at Steve. "I want you gone by noon."

"He stays." Caroline turned her back on Steve and resolutely faced Rink. "He stays until I fire him. Roscoe told me to hire him and I'm the only one who can fire him. At least until the will is read and you take possession of The Retreat. In the meantime, as Roscoe's widow, I make the decisions concerning the estate."

"Like hell you do," Rink snarled. "This has to do with Laura Jane, not The Retreat. She may be your stepdaughter, but she's my sister."

"I agree. This has everything to do with Laura Jane." Caroline's breasts were heaving with exertion and emotion. As she faced him defiantly, she loved him fiercely and ached for the bleeding bruises on his face. But she wouldn't back down. "Steve wasn't taking advantage of her. He was loving her, Rink. She wanted him to."

"She doesn't know what she's doing."

"Yes, she does. She loves him. Are you so hard-hearted and immune to human emotions that you can't see what's so plainly obvious? If you send Steve away, how do you think she'll feel about you? You're her god. She worships the very ground you walk on. It will destroy her if you break her heart by doing this. I beg you not to. Please."

"It's for her own good."

"How do you know what's best for her?"

"I know."

"Just like Roscoe knew what was best for you? Would you keep them apart the way he did us?"

Rink reacted as though she had landed a blow better placed and more dreadful than any of Steve's. His eyes bored into hers, but she held her ground. Finally he sliced his eyes toward Steve, who was unconsciously rubbing his aching thigh. Rink glared at him but said nothing before he strode from the stable.

All the life and spirit went out of Caroline then and her body sagged. She stood for a long time, staring at the hay-strewn floor through blurred eyes. She had backed Rink into a corner and he would hate her for it. Sighing, she raised her head and turned to Steve. His face was distorted with rapid swelling.

"Will you be all right?"

He nodded, dabbing at a disfigured lip with a handkerchief. "I've had worse." He tried to smile but grimaced with pain.

"I'll send Haney out to tend to you."

He nodded and Caroline turned. When she reached the door of the stable he called out to her. "Mrs. Lancaster." She faced him, and he took two limping steps toward her. "Thanks. No matter how it turns out, I appreciate your taking up for me."

She smiled wanly and headed toward the house. When she reluctantly went through the back door, Rink was sitting at the kitchen table holding Laura Jane on his lap. Her face was buried in his neck and she was crying uncontrollably. "You're mad at me. I know you are."

"No," he said gently, stroking her back. "I'm not mad. I just don't want anything bad to happen to you, that's all."

"What Steve was doing wasn't bad. I love him, Rink."

Rink's eyes met Caroline's over his sister's head. "I'm not sure you know what it is to love a man, Laura Jane. Or what it means for him to love you."

"I do! I love Steve and he loves me. He would never do anything to hurt me."

Rink wasn't going to concede that he had been wrong. "We'll talk about it later. I'm sorry I lost my temper."

But Laura Jane wasn't going to be placated, either. She raised her head and gripped Rink's shirtfront. "You won't fight with Steve anymore. Promise me you won't."

Rink couldn't hide his surprise. He stared into his sister's determined eyes and finally said, "I promise I won't fight with him anymore."

Slowly she released his shirt and sweetly kissed his cheek. "I'll go help Haney find the bandages." For Laura Jane the crisis was over. She left the kitchen and skipped up the stairs.

"I won't be leaving today after all," Rink said in measured tones when they were alone.

Caroline's heart jumped with gladness, but it was a momentary reaction. Her chin went up defiantly. "What changed your mind? Are you afraid that in your absence I'll corrupt your sister and ruin the family's reputation?"

He gave her body a deprecating, leisurely inspection before saying, "Something like that."

Her eyes smarted with unshed tears. He knew how to hurt her. "To you I'm still that white trash girl, aren't I, Rink? I'm good enough to kiss when you feel like kissing, but not good enough to be a part of your family."

"I'm not leaving."

That was all he said before he sauntered from the room.

Chapter 9

"Morning, Miz Lancaster."

"Miz Lancaster, nice day, ain't it?"

Caroline acknowledged the greetings called to her as she entered the gin. Harvesttime was upon them. The men were already working overtime to handle the first crops brought in. The hours were long, the shifts tiresome, dusty, hot and noisy. Yet there was a spirit of pride among the gin workers that hadn't existed for years. It was no secret where this feeling of unity came from.

Rink.

There was no denying that all the equipment, due to a recent overhaul, was operating in prime condition. Farmers who in seasons past had been seeking other spot markets for their cotton were returning to Lancaster Gin. There was no secret why that was so, either.

Rink.

In just the few weeks he had been around, the gin had undergone a radical change. Most of its employees had welcomed him back. Those who wanted to work hard were given a raise in pay. Those who were habitually late or shirked duty were fired. Caroline recognized those who had been fired as perpetual agitators. They were men Roscoe had employed for specialized jobs, jobs she surmised she was better off not knowing about. The one and only time she had suggested that Roscoe get rid of a certain employee, she had learned not to venture into the no-man's-land of Roscoe's private affairs.

"He's a troublemaker," she had said.

Roscoe had smiled benignly. "He does . . . errands . . . for me, Caroline. If he makes trouble with one of the gin workers, do me a favor and look the other way."

"But he's a gin worker, too."

"That's the way it's supposed to look." At her disbelieving expression he had diplomatically added, "I'll speak to him if he causes you any more problems."

She realized now that such a man must have been sent to spy on Rink that summer.

Rink, with her sanction, hadn't wasted a minute cutting off the dead wood and raising the salaries of trusted, loyal workers. They respected him. Rather than working for Rink out of fear, as they had his father, they stayed on because they liked the man. He had a knack for motivating them. He criticized constructively. He praised when it was deserved. He worked and sweat right along with them. It was no wonder to her that he was such a successful businessman.

Ten days had gone by since the eruption in the stable between Steve and Rink. Rink spent most of his time at the gin. Caroline loved having him there. He gave her confidence. She knew that a few of the men had been fired because of their criticism of her.

Though they hadn't specifically laid down the terms, a peaceful truce existed between the two of them.

One morning at the gin she was working on the endless stream of business correspondence when he entered the office without knocking. "Caroline, there's someone out here I'd like you to meet if you're not busy."

She smiled up at him and spread her arms wide over her littered desk. "Oh, no, I'm not busy."

He grinned lopsidedly. "It's important or I wouldn't have interrupted you."

Standing, she asked curiously, "Who is it?"

"A surprise."

With his fingers riding lightly on the small of her back, he ushered her through the teeming gin and out onto a loading dock where five-hundred-pound bales of cotton awaited delivery to the warehouse.

A rotund man in a startling white suit and Panama hat — he looked like he belonged in a Tennessee Williams play — was pinching samples of cotton off the bales and stretching them between his thumbs and fingers. He was chomping on a cigar that fleetingly and unpleasantly reminded Caroline of Roscoe. But there was nothing of Roscoe's dominating personality in the man who looked up and smiled congenially when he saw her coming toward him with Rink.

"Mr. Zachary Hamilton, this is Mrs. Caroline Lancaster."

"Mr. Hamilton." She extended her hand. It was swallowed by his and heartily shaken. Had she ever known a grandfather, she would have wanted him to look like Mr. Hamilton.

"It's a pure pleasure to meet you, Miz Lancaster. A pure pleasure. Your . . . uh . . . er . . . stepson, Rink, here, was telling me that under your careful management Lancaster cotton has improved considerably."

Her cheeks flushed becomingly as she glanced first at Rink, then back to their guest. "Rink is giving me more than my due, I think. But I'm proud of the product we're producing now."

"Mr. Hamilton is a buyer for the Delta Mills in Jackson."

Caroline was looking at Rink, so only he saw the instantaneous lift of her eyebrows and the small circle of surprise her mouth formed. His eyes were dancing mischievously. It was with difficulty that he didn't burst out laughing.

"I . . . I see," she stuttered and turned back to the cotton merchant. Everyone in the South who grew cotton or sold it knew about the Delta Mills. They supplied the world with textiles of the highest quality.

"We'd be privileged to have you sample our cotton, Mr. Hamilton," she said as calmly as she could. She was beside herself with nerves and excitement. Adrenaline had begun to pump through her. If she and Rink could sell to Delta Mills, it would be a business coup.

"Thanks to Rink's hospitality, I've been sampling it." He pinched off a wad of cotton from the bale and began the stretching process until he could determine the average length of the fibers. "This is prime cotton," he said musingly. "Has a good staple length. I think you could sell us some."

Both Caroline and Rink had to force themselves not to whoop with glee. "We've got a lot already committed to other buyers," Rink said with shrewd evasiveness.

"I can appreciate that, Rink," the buyer said. "How many compressed bales can you sell me?"

As Caroline stood by, shifting anxiously from one foot to the other, Rink bargained with the man. Finally they settled on the number of bales to be delivered and the price per bale. It was the best deal Lancaster Gin had ever made.

"Of course, we'll be delivering the cotton by air," Rink said offhandedly as he escorted Mr. Hamilton to Caroline's office to sign a contract.

"By air?" Mr. Hamilton stared up at Rink in awe. But he was far less astounded than Caroline.

"A service we provide only for our most preferred customers." Rink's teeth flashed whitely and when Mr. Hamilton turned to go into the office, he winked at a stunned and speechless Caroline.

After Mr. Hamilton had left, she was still staring at Rink with dismay. "By air?" she asked in a thin, high voice. "Whatever happened to the railroad?"

He laughed and began opening desk and file cabinet drawers in a mad rush to find something. "Nothing happened to it," he said absently. "Ah-ha! I knew it had to be here." He pulled a bottle of bourbon from the bottom drawer of a file cabinet. "Got any glasses? Oh, to hell with glasses." He uncapped the bottle, threw his head back and took a long pull from the bottle. He made a face as the burning liquor went down. "I've got an old freight airplane that I've reconditioned myself. We want to impress Delta Mills, don't we? Do you think they'll forget the company that delivered their cotton by air?"

"But the fuel costs alone . . . Rink, it'll be incredibly expensive."

"Not if I load the cargo and fly it myself," he said, flashing her a broad grin. "It'll cost us fuel and a few hours of my time. But a standing contract with Delta Mills will be well worth the investment, I think. To us." He saluted her with the bottle before taking another swig of the bourbon, then pushed it toward her. "Here."

Caught up in the spirit of his celebration now, she eyed the bottle, tempted. "I couldn't," she said with false coyness and glanced nervously over her shoulder toward the door.

"Of course you could."

"What if someone comes in and finds us drinking?"

"They'd understand. We just pulled off a

helluva deal. Besides I've put the word out that no one comes through that door without knocking."

"You do it all the time."

He assumed an annoyed stance. "Are you going to drink some of this or not?"

Boldly, she took hold of the bottleneck and, imitating him, threw back her head and took a large swallow. She came up coughing and sputtering, her eyes tearing and her insides flaming. Rink took the bottle from her as she bent at the waist to cough. He thumped her back with his open palm, laughing uproariously.

"Better?" Slowly she straightened, drying her weeping eyes with the backs of her hands.

"I think so," she croaked and they both laughed at the unfamiliar hoarseness of her voice.

"God, Caroline. My heart was in my throat," he said with boyish enthusiasm. "I was so afraid he was going to say no or leave us hanging without a firm commitment."

"Why didn't you tell me he was coming?"

"I didn't want to get your hopes up."

"I'm glad you didn't. I loved the surprise."

"Did you?"

"Yes." She smiled up at him and her smile

widened when she realized again what they were celebrating. "Yes, yes, yes."

It was unplanned. Entirely unplanned. He caught her about the waist, lifted her several inches off the floor and whirled her around. They were both laughing. His head was thrown back as he looked up at her. She smiled down on him from her elevated position and put her hands on his shoulders.

"We did it! We pulled off the best deal ever in Lancaster history. Do you realize what that means, Caroline? New buyers will come snooping around. Planters will check us out," he said, answering for her. "Not this year, but next. We may have to expand." He held her, spinning her around in an impromptu waltz.

When he set her down it seemed perfectly natural for him to kiss her. His mouth met hers firmly and squarely. It wasn't a lover's kiss. It was a kiss between friends, a celebration of a job well done.

But the instant their lips made contact, that changed. They couldn't touch without it being the touch of lovers. When he felt the soft, moist acceptance of her lips beneath his, desire shot through him like lightning. He raised his head to judge her reaction.

His eyes greedily toured her face, taking in every feature. The high color in her cheeks, her auburn hair, the sparkles that made her eyes look like glistening raindrops on slate, her mouth, all caught his attention.

She waited expectantly, feeling his breath accelerate, watching his eyes grow hot.

He wanted her. God, he wanted her. He wanted to devour her, to make her his finally and everlastingly. But she had pledged faithfulness to his father till death parted them. And Rink knew that dead as his father was, his influence reached beyond the grave. She still belonged to Roscoe and for that reason he wouldn't take what he longed for so badly. Desire smothered him, yet he clawed free of it and released her.

He didn't want to. First his hands moved from the back of her waist to the sides, then fell away completely. As though an invisible adhesive held them together, their bodies pulled apart slowly before he took a severing step backward. Last to release her were his eyes, which stayed on hers until he forced them away.

She was disappointed and shaken but tried not to show it as he turned back to her before opening the door.

"I thought I'd invite the whole crew out for a beer in celebration. It'll be an incentive for them to produce the cleanest cotton possible for the Delta Mills."

"I think that would be a wonderful gesture, Rink. I'll see you at home?"

He nodded. "I won't be late."

It was at the supermarket that she got her first inkling that people were talking.

Haney had called the gin and asked if Caroline would stop at the store on her way home. Caroline made a list of items as Haney reeled them off. "Thanks. I'll appreciate it."

"No problem," Caroline said. "I'll be home shortly. Rink is going out after work, so you might want to plan dinner a half hour later than usual."

She was pushing her grocery basket down the aisle, checking off the things on her list when she spotted two townswomen eyeing her with undisguised interest. She recognized them. One was touted to be the most malicious gossip in town. She had a daughter the same age as Caroline, who was now married to a factory worker. It was said that because of a drinking problem, he had difficulty keeping a job. The daughter had been popular, one of the "in crowd" from which Caroline had always been excluded. How it must rankle that the Dawson girl had married so well! The other woman ran the dry cleaning store and dealt out gossip with each exchange of dirty clothes to clean.

There was no avoiding them, though Caroline wished she could. Her chin went up a notch and she deliberately steered her basket so she would have to pass right in front of them.

"Hello, Mrs. Lane, Mrs. Harper."

"Mrs. Lancaster," they said in unison. The effusiveness of their greeting was transparent. "You poor dear," one said. "How are you making out now that Mr. Lancaster is gone?"

"I thought it was a lovely funeral. Lovely," the other said.

"Thank you. I'm doing fine." She would have pushed on then, having satisfied the dictates of politeness, but one of them rushed to engage her in conversation.

"It must be such a comfort to you to have Rink home at a time like this."

Careful, Caroline, she warned herself. These are piranhas and they'll tear anything you say to shreds. "Rink's return to The Retreat meant a lot to Laura Jane and Haney, our housekeeper. Despite the circumstances, they were glad to have him at home again."

They virtually smacked their lips at every morsel she doled out. "How long will he be staying, now that he's a bigshot in Atlanta and all? We must seem like hicks to him."

"Rink loves Winstonville. The town is named after his mother's family, you know. The Retreat will always be his home."

That seemed to whet their appetites even more. They moved in closer, like beasts of prey anxious for a kill. "But what about you? Since you married Mr. Lancaster, isn't The Retreat *your* home? Or do y'all plan on living there together? Like one big happy family?"

"That's what we are," she said, smiling coldly. "One big happy family."

"Oh, of *course*," they agreed enthusiastically.

"Give my regards to Sarah," Caroline said to her classmate's mother as she moved off. "I hear she had another baby."

"Her fourth." Colorless eyes enviously raked Caroline's slender figure in her trim linen dress. "It's a shame Mr. Lancaster didn't leave you with a baby. A child would provide such a comfort to you in your grief." It was the most insincere display of pity Caroline had ever seen. If she weren't shaking with anger, she would have laughed at the inept performance.

"What does she need with a baby, Flo?" Another pair of eyes, just as mean, just as prejudiced, slid over her. "She's got Rink living in that big house to keep her company and give her all the comfort she needs."

"Oh, yes, Rink. We mustn't forget that he's there with her."

"Good afternoon, ladies," Caroline said quickly. She forced herself to pick up the last items on her list before going through the checkout and leaving the store. Tears of humiliation burned her eyes.

As long as Roscoe was alive no one would have dared speak to her that way out of fear of reprisal. Roscoe Lancaster's wife had commanded their respect, no matter how grudging. Apparently his widow did not. She had gone back to being Caroline Dawson and it seemed that the stigma of her background would live with her forever. It didn't matter how cleanly you lived; if you grew up poor trash, your morals were suspect.

Why didn't she leave this place of small-minded, bigoted people?

For the same reason Rink couldn't. Their roots went too deep. He was at the highest echelon of society and she the lowest, but her place here was as solidly entrenched as his. It was infuriating to be assigned a place at birth, with no hope of changing it. Didn't it matter that she was managing one of the finest, certainly one of the largest, cotton gins in the region? Didn't it count that she had gotten a college degree? Or did her accomplishments only feed their jealousy?

Why punish herself this way? Why not go somewhere where she wasn't known?

The Retreat.

For as long as she could remember, she had dreamed of living in The Retreat. And now, when Rink claimed it as his inheritance, what would she do? Leave town? Never come back?

No. She would find another house in Winstonville and go back to dreaming of The Retreat. But she could never leave it entirely. Never.

She was quiet throughout the evening meal. They ate the fried chicken dinner in the formal dining room, Rink having declared this an official celebration of the Delta Mills deal. Haney and Laura Jane shared his gaiety. Caroline was finding it hard to be festive after the subtle persecution she had been subjected to in the supermarket.

She noticed Rink looking at her quizzically and roused herself from her disturbing musings. For the rest of the meal, she doubled her efforts not to let her distress show.

After dinner she went for a stroll around

the grounds. The evening was cool and clear. A rare breeze fanned the full summer leaves of the trees overhead. She went to sit on the bench swing hanging from the huge pecan tree in one corner of the property. It was one of her favorite spots at The Retreat. The river channel gurgled nearby. Moss dripped almost to the ground from the trees. The undergrowth was lush. With the toe of her shoe barely pushing against the soft grass, she idly rocked herself in the swing.

But her indolence reversed itself when she saw a long, lean shadow separate itself from the trunk of a tree and move toward her on silent feet. He pushed aside draping wisteria vines and bent to walk under the sprawling arms of a live oak until he stood just in front of the swing.

"What's wrong, Caroline?"

"You must have Indian blood. You're always sneaking up on me."

"I didn't come down here to discuss bloodlines. Answer me. What's wrong?"

"How did you find me?"

"I found you." Taking hold of the swing's ropes in each hand and stilling it, he bent over her. "Now, dammit, I'm asking you one last time. What's wrong?"

She shifted uncomfortably. "Nothing."

"Something. What?"

"It's nothing."

"I'm not budging from this spot and neither are you until you tell me. And the mosquitoes can get ferocious around here after dark. So unless you want to be carried off by a swarm of the bloodthirsty little suckers, tell me now what's bothering you. Something at the gin? Me? What?"

"This town!" she exploded and stood up. Rink was forced to let go of the ropes. Her burst of temper was so sudden that he moved aside and gave her room. The swing rocked crazily behind her. She went to the massive trunk of a tree, crossed her hands on it and laid her forehead against them.

"What about this town?"

"It's full of petty people."

He laughed softly. "Are you just finding that out?"

"No. I've known that since I was old enough to walk behind my mama pulling her wagon as she delivered fresh laundry. I've always known they were prejudiced and judgmental." She turned and braced her shoulders against the stout tree trunk. "It's just that I thought a college degree, a good job, a new name would elevate me enough in their eyes so that I wouldn't be considered trash anymore."

"You should have known better. Whatever you're born to around here, you're stuck with."

"How well I know. And lest I forget, I was reminded today."

"What happened?"

She pushed her hair back and let her eyes flicker toward him before looking away again. "It's too silly and insignificant to get upset about."

"So tell me and we won't get upset together."

Sighing, she named the two women who had spoken with her in the supermarket. Rink made a rude sound. "I don't like it already. Go on."

"They . . . they commented on how lucky I was to have you around after Roscoe's death, living in the same house with me. They made a point of stressing that. They intimated . . . well, you can guess what they intimated."

"They intimated that there was more to our living together than sharing an address. Is that it?"

She looked up at him. "Yes."

He cursed softly. "They hinted that all might not be proper."

"Yes."

"That something illicit might be going on."

"Yes."

"That we might be more than stepson and stepmother."

She didn't reply but merely nodded. Stillness surrounded them. Cicadas sang cheerily. Bullfrogs croaked mournfully. They found it impossible to drag their eyes away from each other. Her breasts vibrated with pounding heartbeats. She could swear the pulse in Rink's temple matched the tempo of hers.

"Forget what those crows said, Caroline. Gossip is their favorite form of entertainment. If it weren't us, it would be somebody else they were raking over the coals. As soon as the newness of Roscoe's death wears off, they'll find something else to occupy their busy little minds."

"I know that. Rationally I know it. But I still can't stand their nasty innuendos. I don't like being the subject of their vivid imaginations." Their eyes met again briefly, hotly, before they darted away. What the gossips had suggested wasn't all that vividly imaginative.

"It would be ridiculous for one of us to move out until all the legalities are settled," Rink reasoned. "Wouldn't that cause even more talk?"

"I suppose so. Everyone would wonder who had driven whom off. They would say you hadn't approved of me."

"As my father's wife, you mean."

Caroline could have bitten her tongue for bringing that up. "Yes."

"Why would they think I don't approve of you?"

"Because of who I was when I was growing up." She shifted uncomfortably against the tree. The bark snagged her dress. "Because of the age difference between Roscoe and me."

When their eyes met this time, there was no pulling them apart. "They would be right," he whispered, leaning close to her. "I would never have approved of you as his wife."

"Don't, Rink." She wanted to back away, but escape was blocked by the tree.

"Why do you worry about gossip, Caroline?" he asked smoothly, coming even closer. "Your conscience is clear, isn't it? You know there's nothing improper going on at The Retreat."

"Of course."

Closer still. "There's nothing illicit going on between us, is there?"

"No."

"Liar."

The last word came out raggedly. He placed his thumbs lengthwise along her throat and enclosed her neck with eight strong, lean fingers that interlaced at her nape. With the pads of his thumbs, he tilted her head up.

"Tell me there's no chemistry between us." Moaning softly, she tried to turn her head aside. He wouldn't permit it. "Tell me that every time you look at me you see only a stepson. Tell me you don't remember what it was like with us. Tell me you don't remember that day it rained. Tell me never to kiss you again. Tell me you never want to feel my touch. Can you tell me that, Caroline?" Her only reply was a whimper. "That's what I thought," he growled.

His mouth clamped hard and sure over hers. Her arms flailed uncertainly until the heels of her hands came to rest on his shoulders where she made feeble attempts to push him away. His body only pressed more intimately against hers. Like the pieces of a puzzle designed to lock in place, he fit them together. His mouth moved over hers, willing her lips to obey his command. His tongue probed the seam of her mouth.

"Kiss me back, Caroline. You want to. You want to."

And she did. With a slight murmur of surrender, her arms circled his neck tightly. Her lips yielded to the persuasion of his tongue. It entered her mouth with no resistance and met only a welcoming warmth and entrapping sweetness. He stroked her mouth, dipping into each recess with so sexual a cadence that Caroline felt the last vestiges of her resistance melting.

Mercilessly he aroused in her a desperate need for him. His kisses were evocative and thorough. The pressure of his virility between her thighs created in her such a hunger that she couldn't bear it. She wanted him to fill that aching void. It was of his making and only he could make it whole.

He freed the buttons of her dress and slipped his hands inside the bodice. Her breasts were covered with a lacy camisole. His senses roared as he slid his hands over their full warmth. He massaged them with lazy motions that hypnotized and seduced.

From his lips flowed curses and prayers in a thrilling litany that fell like love songs on her ears. She heard in his voice the desperation of her own soul, the hunger, the agony of unfulfilled desire. He fondled the lace and satin-covered breasts, sought and teased the crowns with his fingertips. The caress gave her immense pleasure. The sensitive flesh grew hard in response. He dipped his head and touched one nipple with his lips.

Caroline felt the kiss in her womb, deep in her innermost self. Her whole body contracted with an intense need and she made an anguished sound. She knew if she didn't stop now, she would be lost.

She pushed herself free of his embrace. "No, Rink, no," she cried. She covered her breasts with her hands, willing her heart to stop its erratic racing. "I can't. We can't."

His chest rose and fell alarmingly with each breath. His hair had been mussed by her pillaging hands. His eyes, dilated with passion, blinked back into focus. "Why? Because of my father?"

She shook her head, sending her hair flying wildly. "No, no," she protested miserably, pulling her dress together. "Because of the people in town. Because I don't want to be what they expect me to be. I can't do what their sordid minds accuse me of doing, seducing first Roscoe, now his son."

"I don't give a damn what they think."

"I do!" She realized she was crying. Tears were rolling down her cheeks. "Just as you said, we remain what we're born as. You were a Winston and a Lancaster. No matter what you do, it would be considered above reproach. They wouldn't dare criticize you.

But me, I came from trash and that's what I'll always be to them. I have to care what they think."

While the seconds ticked by, they stared at each other. Rink was the first to turn away and when he did, it was with a blasphemy. "I can't live in the same house with you and not want to make love to you."

"I know."

"Well, I've admitted it. Isn't that what you wanted to hear?" he shouted.

"No, Rink. I didn't need to hear it to know it." When he whirled around and looked back at her she said softly, "It's the same for me. Did you think that it wasn't?"

It may have been a trick of the moon, but she thought his eyes looked suspiciously moist. His mouth worked but no words came out. At his sides, his fists clenched and released reflexively. His body was taut with suppressed emotions. He looked barely capable of containing them.

She swiped at the tears on her face. "Do you see why I can't be with you, Rink? They're right. I do want you. But just as you can't forget it, neither will they. I was Roscoe's wife."

He turned, giving her his back for several minutes. When he faced her again, his expression was hard, bleakly resolved. "What will you do after the will is read?"

She made no effort to conceal the tears that filled her eyes. "The only thing I can do, what I always knew I must do. I'll leave."

He nodded his head once, jerkily, before he turned and thrashed his way through the woods. Caroline sank onto the swing and buried her face in her hands. She wept.

Neither of them saw the shadow flitting through the trees as it moved away from the site.

Chapter 10

"Steve?"

There were no lights on in his apartment, but the portable black-and-white television was shedding flickering silver light on the walls.

"Laura Jane?" he said incredulously.

"I wasn't sure you were here. Were you asleep?"

Self-consciously Steve pulled the plain white sheet over his naked chest. He was lying on his back in the narrow bed. When she squeezed through the door, opening it only wide enough for her thin frame to slip through, he propped himself up on his elbows. "No I wasn't asleep, but what in the world are you doing here? If your brother finds you here —"

"He won't. I just saw him driving away in his new truck. He and Caroline . . . Oh, Steve. I don't understand anything!" She flew across the room and flung herself over him. Automatically his arms went around her. Crying, she buried her face in the hollow of his neck.

"What's the matter? What happened?

What don't you understand?"

"Rink. I don't understand him at all. He got in a fight with you because you were kissing me. He made me feel like we'd done something shamefully wrong. But if it's wrong, why do he and Caroline do the same thing? If it's wrong for us, why isn't it wrong for them? They're not married either."

"You saw them together? Kissing?"

"Yes. Down by the old bench swing. They didn't see me."

He combed his fingers through her hair. He didn't want to upset her any more than she already was, so he answered carefully. "I think you saw something you weren't supposed to see."

Laura Jane raised her head. "I shouldn't have stayed and watched, should I? Haney said you're not supposed to watch people and listen to them when they don't know you're there."

"It's impolite, yes."

She plucked at the edge of the sheet like a contrite child. "I know it was wrong. But I heard them, so I followed the sound of their voices. When I got there, Rink was kissing Caroline. They were standing against a tree so close together that I couldn't tell them apart."

As her fingers filtered through the dense

hair on his chest, he became increasingly aware that he was wearing only his underwear beneath the sheet. Laura Jane was sitting on the edge of the bed, her hip fitting into the slight indentation of his waist.

She told him how Caroline had ended the kiss. "She said they weren't supposed to be kissing because people would think they were bad. Rink listened to her, standing very still. He looked like he wanted to hit something, not Caroline. He looked like he wanted to go on kissing her."

Laura Jane's voice wavered. "Caroline said as soon as the will was read, she'll leave." Leaning from the waist, she laid her head on Steve's chest. "I don't want her to leave. I love her. I love Rink. I want us all to go on living the way we are now forever."

With one hand he cupped the back of her head comfortingly. With the other he rubbed her back. He had pieced together the whole story. Hadn't he heard Caroline remind Rink about Roscoe keeping them apart? At some point in time, they had been important to each other. But Rink had left and she had married his father. Now, still attracted in spite of themselves, they were trapped in an untenable situation. "It's a helluva mess all right," he murmured against Laura Jane's hair.

She lifted her head and gazed down at him. "Do you know what I wish?"

He touched her face with exploring fingertips, marveling over the unspoiled beauty of it, the purity of her mind, the lack of guile and meanness. Such qualities were precious to him because he had seen so little evidence of them. Until he had met Laura Jane, he'd thought human nature was putrid, including his own. "What do you wish?" he asked softly.

"That they could love each other the way we do."

He longed to laugh, he longed to cry, he longed to kiss her. He thought about the two former, he did the latter. Pulling her down gently, he pressed a tender kiss onto her parted lips.

"Steve?" she whispered.

"Hmmm?" He kissed her face, amazed that skin could be so fragile and still hold a body together.

"You're not wearing your plastic leg."

He ceased his nuzzling instantly and followed her eyes to the end of the bed where he had propped the prosthesis. "No," he said sharply. "I'm not."

"Let me see your leg. Please." She reached for the sheet to pull it back.

He grabbed it and held it taut over his body. "No."

His tone was colder, harder, than he had ever used with her. For a moment it frightened her, but only for a moment. She laid her hands over his and tried to work his fingers off the sheet. "Please, Steve. I want to see you."

Angrily he flung her hands off. He raised his hands from the sheet and threw them over his head. She wanted to see? All right, better to let her see. Better to let her get disgusted now before he fell any more in love with her than he already was. Better that she should run from him shrieking in fear and revulsion now than later. He was hideously deformed and the sooner she realized it, the better for them both.

In anguish, he felt the sheet slide away from his body. The cool air from the window air-conditioning unit touched his body. His jaws ached from clenching them. He stared at the ceiling, trying to concentrate on the dancing patterns of light the television cast there. He didn't want to see the look of horror on her face. He wished he could close his ears to any sound of repulsion she might make.

He wouldn't blame her, of course. She had been sheltered from ugliness. Her world had been soft and beautiful, a chrysalis of gentility and graciousness. The world he came from, the jungle war he had lived through, were as foreign to her as life on another planet.

"Oh, Steve."

It wasn't the kind of reaction he had expected. Her voice was breathless, tremulous; her tone emotional, reverent. Tucking in his chin, he looked down the length of his body just in time to see Laura Jane's hands reaching out to touch his pink, puckered thigh. Even though he could feel the shy, light touch, even though he could see her hands gliding over the hair-roughened skin, he didn't believe it. His flesh quivered beneath her sweet tribute, but his heart exploded.

"Steve, you're beautiful." As she looked down at him her eyes were liquid with tears. He searched them but could find no trace of repugnance, nor even pity, only undiluted love and admiration.

With a strangling sound, he reached for her and pulled her down onto his chest. His hands cradled either side of her face, holding her hair back as she bent toward his mouth.

He kissed her with a new ardency. His tongue pressed into her mouth deeply. It swirled, gathering up all her sweetness.

Learning from him, she nibbled at his lips, sucked lightly when he introduced his tongue into her mouth again and went on a darting expedition between his lips with her own tongue.

"God, God, Laura Jane." He held her head tight against his shoulder to stop her ardent kisses and to regain his breath and common sense. His sex was full and surging behind his underwear. Everywhere her skin touched his, he was burning. He thought to ease himself by touching her breasts. But their full soft weight in his palms only made him want her more, not strictly in a carnal sense but for all the healing succor she offered.

"I feel funny on the inside," she confessed. Her hand feathered over his chest and stomach.

Mirthlessly he laughed. His loins were throbbing. "So do I."

"My heart's beating fast." Taking up his hand, she pressed it over her left breast.

His hand closed softly over the delicate mound of flesh. He gritted his teeth. "So is mine."

"Is this how you feel when you make love?" she whispered.

He couldn't vocalize an answer but nodded.

251

"We can't make love because we're not married, right?"

He moaned and hugged her closer. "No, baby, no. We can't. It wouldn't be fair to you." Nor to him. If he had her once, he knew he would want her every day for the rest of his life.

Sitting up, she smoothed her hand over his cheek. "Then, Steve," she said with simple logic, "let's get married."

It was a subdued group that gathered in the front parlor of The Retreat. The day was equally gloomy. Moisture-laden clouds hung heavily over the landscape. It hadn't rained. Rain would have been a welcome relief from the oppressive humidity.

This day had been both anticipated and dreaded. Twice Granger Hopkins had set a time for the reading of Roscoe's will. Twice it had been postponed. On the first occasion, Rink had been unexpectedly called back to Atlanta to handle some Air Dixie business. Granger himself had asked for the second postponement. Another client had demanded his immediate attention.

Caroline was secretly glad for these delays. She had been promising herself for weeks to start looking for another house, someplace small but with character, someplace away from town but not too remote for a woman living alone. But she felt no ambition to get started on the project. She used the gin as her excuse.

They had ginned more cotton than ever before. She and Rink went early every morning and came home late every evening. The majority of the season's crop had been ginned, baled and was waiting in the warehouse ready for shipment to the various merchants. The Delta Mills order had been flown to Jackson as Rink had promised.

They shared a feeling of supreme satisfaction, but also one of unspoken loss. Without the constant demands of the gin, they had no reason to spend so much time together. Since that night by the swing, there hadn't been a romantic interlude between them, but the desire was there, a living thing, constantly flowing between them.

Granger coughed behind his hand to get their attention. "I guess we're ready." He was seated beside a small table where he had laid a manila envelope.

Laura Jane and Rink were sharing an heirloom love seat. Their hands were clasped affectionately. Caroline sat in a wingback chair at their left. Haney, who had also been invited, sat to their right and slightly behind them in a lyre-back chair.

Granger took a pair of wire-rimmed eye-glasses from his breast pocket and settled them on his beefy nose. Carefully opening the envelope, he took out the multi-paged document and straightened the stiff sheets. He began to read.

Roscoe had never been philanthropic. He had begrudged every cent his wife Marlena had given to charity. What donations he had made in his lifetime had not been made out of a spirit of generosity, but rather for an income tax advantage. In his will, however, he had bequeathed a sum of money to the church he had been an unfaithful member of and to various other community charities.

Granger paused, poured a glass of water from the pitcher Haney had left on the table for him, sipped it and proceeded. He read in an unemotional voice, but with a detectable reluctance. As the terms of the will were methodically read, the reason for that reluctance became appallingly clear. When he was done he folded the papers and stuffed them back into the envelope. He removed his glasses and replaced them in his breast pocket.

The other three in the room remained motionless. Even Laura Jane, who couldn't fully understand the implications of her father's will, comprehended the unfairness of it.

"He didn't leave anything to Rink." Laura Jane addressed Granger, but her eyes made a slow sweep around the room and finally fell on her brother, whose face seemed to be carved of stone . . . or ice.

"That old bastard," Haney said under her breath as she left the room in a huff. She would refuse to accept the money left to her for "years of devoted service to Laura Jane."

Caroline slowly stood and took a hesitant step toward the love seat. "Rink, I'm sor—"

His head snapped up and his golden eyes blazed at her, halting the words before they could leave her mouth. Rink leaped off the love seat with all the sinuous grace of a panther and had the same deadly look of carefully contained violence about him. He left the room without a word. Remorsefully Caroline stared after him. Laura Jane nervously twisted her handkerchief between her fingers.

Granger went after Rink and caught up with him in the foyer. "Rink, I'm sorry." He grabbed for Rink's sleeve and succeeded in stopping him on his way out of the house. "I hated like hell to be the one to read that will. I begged Roscoe to reconsider."

"You should have known better and

saved your breath," Rink said bitterly.

"I tried to persuade your mother to keep this house and estate in her name. Long before her death, she signed it over to Roscoe, making it his after she died. At the time I didn't think that was a good idea. Of course, now . . ."

"For the first time in history, there's not a Winston at The Retreat. It belongs to a Dawson now." His tone was scathing as he spoke the name.

"If you think Caroline had anything to do with Roscoe's decision, you're wrong."

"Am I?"

"Yes," the lawyer said emphatically. "She was as ignorant of this as she was of that scholarship."

Rink's head jerked around. "How do you know about that?"

"I know," Granger replied in a low voice. "Just as I know about everything he secretly did for her. I couldn't understand it. I would have thought he was her sugar daddy, except . . . well, he had other girls for that." He eyed Rink keenly. "I finally figured it out. Only lately, though. For years he'd been using her to get to you, hadn't he?"

Rink was admitting nothing. Apparently the lawyer had put together an accurate picture of things, with one vital piece missing.

He didn't know about Rink and Caroline those long years ago. "Well, if that was his dying wish, it's been granted. Because he's sure as hell gotten to me this time."

He stalked out, letting the door slam behind him.

In the parlor Caroline watched him go. She had what she had always wanted. The Retreat. But at what price? The man she loved.

"Caroline, what will I do with the cotton gin?" Laura Jane asked in bewilderment as she came up behind her stepmother. "I've only been there a few times in my whole life."

Compassion for the confused young woman acted as a distraction from Caroline's own heartache. She embraced Laura Jane. "You don't have to worry about the gin any more than you ever have. Your father only willed you the profits from it."

"What about you?"

"I'm to be paid a yearly salary for watching over it for you. Granger will advise us both and keep track of everything. So stop worrying. It'll be just as it was before."

"You'll stay here, won't you? You won't leave?"

"You heard Granger. Your daddy gave The Retreat to me." She laid her cheek against Laura Jane's hair and let it absorb the tear that trickled from her eye. She wasn't fooled. Roscoe's motives had been far from benevolent. He had known that by giving her The Retreat, he could ensure that Rink would despise her. She now owned his mother's house. If Rink had ever loved anything, it was The Retreat.

"You'll stay, but Rink won't," Laura Jane said miserably.

"No, Rink won't stay." Then Caroline sent the girl to Haney so she could cry alone.

"What are you doing up?"

"Waiting for you."

"Should I feel honored?"

"I thought we should talk."

"About what?"

"Don't be obtuse, Rink."

"Obtuse?" he asked, his dark brows arching high over his eyes. "Now that you're the lady of the manor you've started using fifty-cent words."

The foyer was dim. It was late. He hadn't returned for dinner and Caroline had no guarantee that he would come back at all. Except for Laura Jane. He wouldn't leave without saying good-bye to her. So she had waited up until she'd heard his pickup in the driveway, then had run downstairs to confront him when he came through the front door. She was standing on the second step. He was on the first. He was looking up at her belligerently.

"I don't blame you for being angry."

"Thanks. I'm glad I have your blessing."

"Rink, please don't."

"Don't what?"

"Don't blame me for Roscoe's will! I had nothing to do with it. I was as flabbergasted as you. Why don't you contest it?"

"Give Roscoe and the town the satisfaction of knowing how much it bothers me? No thank you."

Roscoe's dead! she wanted to scream. When would the war between father and son end? With forced calm, she said, "No matter what that piece of paper says, The Retreat belongs to you, Rink. It always will. You can live here for the rest of your life if you want to."

He laughed, but it wasn't a happy sound. "The terms of the will only stipulated that Laura Jane could live here for the rest of her life, not me, too. Your hospitality is commendable, Mom," he said, bowing slightly at the waist.

She flinched against his ugly words, but she tilted her chin up. "I can see you're determined to hurt me. All right. If it makes you feel better, go ahead. Call me dirty names."

With lightning reflexes, his hand shot out, caught the tie belt at her waist and hauled her against him. The impact drove the breath out of both of them. He twisted the belt around his fist, grinding his hand against her stomach. His jaw was rigid and hard as he clamped his teeth tight. He closed his eyes.

For only an instant, a heartbeat, he laid his head on her breast and groaned almost soundlessly. Then he released her with a terse expletive.

"I'm sorry, Caroline, I'm sorry." He sighed. "Yes, I'm mad as hell. But not at you. At him. What makes it worse is that there's no getting him back. He's dead and I'm powerless to fight the sonofabitch. There's no way to release the rage inside me."

He banged his fist on the oak banister. Instinctively she reached out to comfort him but withdrew her hand before it could make contact. He would only misconstrue her love as pity and would hate her for it.

"Where did you go tonight?" she asked softly.

He drew in a deep breath that expanded

his chest and opened his unbuttoned shirt to reveal a mat of dark curling hair. "Driving. Just driving around town." He looked at her. "This is my home, Caroline. Despite its flaws, I love this town. I could no more turn off my love for it because the people in it aren't perfect than I could love Laura Jane less because she's not perfect. I'll miss it all over again when I have to leave."

"You are leaving, then?"

"In the morning."

Pain knifed through her heart and she clutched her hand to it. Her face crumpled. So soon! He would be gone and this time he might never come back. Now he could send for Laura Jane when he wanted to see her. "Rink, what kind of monster was he? What kind of man leaves no legacy to a son like you?"

He saw her tears and her pain and knew that it was for him, for all that hadn't been. He wanted to hug her to him. He wanted to bury his head between her breasts and breathe the scent of her flesh. He wanted to press his lips into her skin. He wanted her loving comfort. He wanted the temporary forgetfulness making love to her would bring him. At that moment he could almost have begged her for it. But he remembered the words he had been intended to remember.

You'll never have that woman now, Rink. I know you. Your damned stubborn Winston pride won't let you have her. Because I had her first. You remember that. She was my wife and I had her first.

"He left me a legacy, Caroline," he said roughly. "A helluva legacy."

He brushed past her and went upstairs. Slowly she followed and went into her room. Peeling off her robe, she lay down on the bed, thinking that there was no way she would ever rest again.

But when the telephone rang a while later, she was bemused and disoriented with sleep as she picked up the receiver and brought it to her ear.

"Hello."

She listened for no more than an instant before dropping the phone and racing for the door of her room, not even taking time to put on her robe. Her bare feet flew over the hardwood floors in the dark hallway. She barged through the door of Rink's room and raced toward the bed. Her hands landed in the middle of his bare back.

"Rink, Rink, wake up."

He rolled over and stared up at her in disbelief. Her eyes were dilated, her hair was wild, her breasts were heaving, almost spilling out of her nightgown. "What —"

"The gin's on fire!"

Both his feet hit the floor at the same time, almost knocking her over in the process. He grabbed up a pair of jeans that were folded over a chair. "How do you know?"

"Barnes called."

"Is it bad?"

"He couldn't say yet."

"What about the fire department?"

"Already notified."

"What the hell is going on in here?" Haney demanded from the doorway as she knotted the sash of her robe around her waist. "It sounded like y'all were playing basketball and —"

"The gin's on fire."

"Lord o' mercy."

Caroline left Rink's room at a run. He was almost dressed and she intended to go with him. She pulled on the first clothes her hands came into contact with, an old shirt and a pair of denim cutoffs. She crammed her feet into a pair of sandals. Not exactly a firefighting outfit, but she could already hear Rink's boots thudding down the stairs. She bounded after him.

"Rink, wait!"

"You stay here," he shouted over his

shoulder as he ran out the front door.

"Like hell." She was right behind him.

"What's going on?" Laura Jane, looking like a doll with her pale pink nightgown and wide eyes, trailed down the stairs.

"The gin is on fire and Rink and Caroline are going to see that it's put out right away," Haney explained.

"The gin is on fire?" she repeated.

Rink's curses would have burned the ears off a sailor as he pumped the motor of his pickup to life. Haney and Laura Jane stood together on the porch, their arms around each other, while Caroline demanded that he unlock the passenger door.

"You're not going!" he roared.

"If you don't open this door, I'll just follow in my car and then you won't know where I am."

Obscenities poured from his mouth, but he pushed open the door and she climbed in.

Steve had heard the ruckus and was crossing the yard with his limping gait. He was pulling on a T-shirt. "What's going on?"

"A fire at the gin," Caroline shouted back.

"I'll help."

"No, Steve!" Laura Jane cried.

"Steve, you stay with Laura Jane and Haney," Caroline told him through the cab window.

"That's right. You stay," Rink said succinctly. The truck was idling now, but Steve was holding onto the door handle and Rink couldn't accelerate.

Meeting Rink's eyes squarely Steve said forcefully, "You'll need my help more than they will. I'm going."

"Steve!" Laura Jane catapulted herself off the porch and flung herself toward him, wrapping her arms around his waist. "Don't go. I'm frightened for you."

"Hey," he said, tilting back her head. "I'm counting on you to keep Haney calm and to have a big breakfast waiting for us when we get back. Okay?"

She beamed up at him. "Okay, Steve. Be careful."

"I will." He kissed her swiftly on the mouth then gently pushed her away before ducking into the cab next to Caroline.

For a moment Rink stared hard at the man, then he jammed the toe of his boot onto the accelerator pedal and the truck screeched out of the drive.

They had much to be grateful for. The fire was a small one and it was contained in only one part of the building. Thanks to Barnes's quick action, the fire engines were already there when Rink arrived.

Heedlessly, Caroline ran into the building to make sure the bookkeeping ledgers were secure in the office. Rink ran after her, caught her around the waist and pulled her out, kicking and protesting. When she was somewhat subdued, he grabbed her by the shoulders and shook her hard.

"Don't ever do anything that stupid again. You scared the hell out of me." After seeing the fierce expression on his face, she wouldn't have thought of disobeying him.

There was plenty to do. Rink supervised the volunteers in moving the bales of cotton still on the loading dock out of harm's way. Steve, despite his leg, worked harder than any of them. Caroline kept spectators out of the way. She reassured them that no one had been in the building. In two hours the flames had been doused.

She and Rink were summoned by the fire chief and sheriff. "It was arson, Rink," the fire chief said. "They made it happen, but your antiquated wiring helped it along."

Rink ran a blackened hand through his hair. "Yeah, I know it was in sad shape. Was there much damage?"

"Nothing compared to what it could have been if we hadn't caught it in time."

"Thank God most of the cotton had already been baled and sent to the warehouse." Now that she had stopped moving, Caroline realized how tired she was.

"Do you know who might have set the fire, Mrs. Lancaster?" the sheriff asked her.

"I do." It was the foreman, Barnes, who answered. "It was one of 'em who set it that called me. I figured he realized what he'd been a part of and chickened out at the last minute. He didn't identify himself, but I'm sure it was one of the guys you fired a few weeks back, Rink."

At the sheriff's request Rink named the men whom he had fired. The peace officer scratched his ear. "Mighty unsavory bunch. What were they doing working for you?"

"They didn't work for me. They worked for my father," Rink said. He glanced down at Caroline and saw the droop of her shoulders. "If that's all for now, I'd like to take Caroline home."

"Sure thing. We'll be in touch when we have something."

Steve opted to ride in the bed of the truck on the way home. He sprawled on his back and didn't move until Rink pulled the pickup to a stop outside the back door. Haney and Laura Jane tumbled out of it as though they'd been waiting for the first sign of them.

Rink went around to open Caroline's door and she all but fell out of the cab and into his arms. Steve eased himself off the tailgate just in time to catch Laura Jane as she ran into his arms, disregarding the soot and grime that covered him.

"Are you all right, Steve?"

"Sure, I'm fine."

"Well, you don't look fine," Haney snapped. "Lordy, Lordy, look at the three of you. I never saw such a motley crew. Y'all go get a bath and I'll have breakfast waiting for you."

They straggled toward the house. Laura Jane released Steve reluctantly and he headed toward his apartment.

"Steve." The veteran halted and turned to face Rink, who had stopped on his way through the back door to address the man. "Thanks," Rink said.

"You're welcome," Steve replied.

Their eyes held for a long time, then they smiled broadly at each other.

Laura Jane's eyes melted with love for her two heroes. Haney sniffed back threatening tears. Caroline squeezed Rink's arm in approval.

Upstairs in her room she peeled off her

clothes and let them fall to the tile floor of her bathroom. She would have to throw them away. The smell of smoke would never wash out. She only hoped she could get it out of her hair.

Several doses of shampoo accomplished that. She stood under the shower's pulsing spray and let the warm water wash away the filth and stench of the fire. When at last she turned off the taps, she felt herself again. Stepping over the pile of clothes, too weary to pick them up, she wound her hair in a towel. She had just wrapped herself in a terry-cloth robe when someone knocked on her door.

"Come in."

She had expected Haney or Laura Jane. That it could be Rink never entered her mind. But that was who stepped into her room, holding a tray laden with a steaming carafe of coffee and a glass of orange juice.

"Haney thought you might want to start with this before you come down."

His mind wasn't on what he was saying. The words found their own stumbling way out of his mouth because all his concentration was devoted to the woman with her hair wound in a damp towel and a wrapper barely concealing the curves of her body. Her skin was dewy. She smelled of honeysuckle-scented soap. Her eyes were large and luminous in her face as she stared back at him. There was a slight catch in her voice when she spoke.

"Thank you. The coffee smells good."

She, too, was distracted. Rink's hair was wet and clung in sculpted strands to his head. He was wearing only a pair of tight, faded jeans that rode low beneath his navel and emphasized his sex. His muscled chest was furred with dark, damply curling hair. His eyes glowed warmly as they watched her.

He set the tray on the table, but made no effort to leave. Later it was difficult to say who had moved first. Had he raised his arms a fraction, spread his hands wide as if to receive her? Or had she taken a tentative step first? They didn't remember. All they could recall was that suddenly she was in his arms and he was holding her tight.

Tears streamed from her eyes and she clung to him. All the fear and anxiety of the last few hours rained from her eyes. He whipped the towel from her head and dropped it to the floor. His hands plowed through her wet hair and pressed her face against the hard warmth of his chest. His head bent over her.

"We have unfinished business, you and I, Caroline."

She raised her tear-glossed eyes to his. She smiled softly. "Yes, we do."

"And it's long overdue," he said quietly, letting his thumbs brush the tears from her flushed cheeks.

"Too long overdue."

Reaching behind him, he pushed the door closed.

Chapter 11

The catching of the door latch was the only sound in the room. There were no artificial lights on. The sun was just beginning to tint the eastern horizon and only that ethereal light came through the sheer drapes. The lemony perfume of magnolia wafted in from the large tree outside.

She went into his arms, no longer a girl but a woman needing what he had to give, needing to give of herself.

He was warm. So warm. There was a vibrancy in his body that she had recognized the first time she'd seen him. She had always gravitated toward it. She did so now. Wanting that energy to surge through her as it did him, she snuggled close, folding her arms around his lean waist. The hair on his chest tickled her nose. Against the hard curve of his breast, she smiled.

Rink held her tight. His eyes closed with sublime contentment. He explored her through touch. His hands examined the slender curves of her back. They slid below her neat waist to the soft fullness of her derriere. He cupped her gently in his hands, squeezed lightly, stroked soothingly, pressed arousingly.

His manhood reacted and they both felt it. Their soft gasps of pleasure echoed each other.

"Caroline, Caroline," he breathed into her wet hair before he pushed her away only far enough to duck his head and seal her open lips with his. Their mouths melded together with soft moistness. Their tongues touched. She allowed him the male privilege of dominance and his tongue slid into her mouth. It was a symbolic possession and he made no apology for it. His tongue loved her with lazy thoroughness, darting and flicking, delving and feathering.

All her senses whirred to life. They hummed softly deep inside her. Then, gaining momentum with each thrust of his tongue, they spun faster and faster until her whole body was singing a new song.

She was inundated with sensations. His hair coiled around her fingers as she caressed the back of his head. The soap he had showered with, his brisk, clean cologne, his own special scent, filled her nostrils, her head, intoxicatingly. With gentle plucking motions of her lips against his, she tasted the minty flavor of toothpaste. The soft moans of arousal and the love words he rasped with ragged breaths thrilled her and made her confident.

And she knew that even without intercourse, she was one with this man. Always had been, always would be. Fate had decreed it. From the moment she first saw him twelve years ago, her destiny had been charted.

Lifting his head, he placed his hands on her shoulders and separated himself from her by several inches. Her smoky eyes shimmered as she looked up into his, which were hazy with swirling gold. Slowly, he unzipped his jeans and pushed them down over his hips. Then, his eyes never leaving hers, he peeled them off and tossed them aside. He stood before her naked.

Her eyes drifted over him. Had she been a man, she would have envied him his physique. He was hard and lean and lithe. His chest was magnificently proportioned. The dark hair that covered it grew in intriguing patterns her fingers longed to explore. The wide fan of body hair tapered to a sleek black ribbon that bisected his flat stomach, whorled around his navel and disappeared into the dense thatch that surrounded his manhood.

It was hard, full, as proud as the man.

Rivers of life coursed through her heart as

she studied him. Momentarily she closed her eyes against waves of dizziness. She felt faint. A desire so intense that she thought she might die of it seized her. It was an honest lust, one sanctioned by love because it was only part of why she loved him.

"Are you all right?"

She opened her eyes and saw him smiling down on her. She laughed in a maidenly, shy way. "Yes. Yes, Rink. I'm all right. It's just that you're so very beautiful and I want you so much."

He kissed her lips with chaste tenderness. "Thank you for the compliment. I'll see what we can do about the other."

He sought the sash of her robe and caught it between his fingers. He tugged on it and it came undone. Moving with deliberate slowness, he inserted his hands beneath the wide lapels and eased the robe aside.

"My God, look at you." His murmur was all but soundless as he gazed at her breasts. As though he couldn't believe all of her could be as perfect, he quickly divested her of the robe and let his eyes roam freely and eagerly over her nakedness. His eyes were wildly excited as they devoured her.

Then his fingertips, lightly, so lightly she could barely feel his touch, took the same path as his eyes. They skimmed the creamy flesh of her breasts, the smooth expanse of stomach, belly and hip. They fanned the dark nest of hair between the slender columns of her thighs. "God, you're beautiful. Beautiful and sweet."

She felt the earnestly whispered words against her flesh as he dipped his knees to lower his face to her breasts. Worshipfully he cupped one in his hand and massaged it. She raised her hands and laid them softly on his hair. She inclined toward him, swaying slightly.

He kissed her. With his thumb he outlined the areola, touched the nipple. It flushed beneath his deft strokes. He looked at it, smiled a quick, fleeting smile, then leaned forward and applied his tongue. Again and again, his tongue circled over the velvety button.

"Rink." His name was a pleading sigh. He heeded it.

He took her nipple between his lips and suckled it. Caroline emitted a sharp, startled cry and arched her back to give him greater access. His cheeks flexed as he drew on her gently. He treated her other breast to the same delicious torment until she was whimpering and clutching at his hair.

"Sweetheart." He buried his face between her breasts as he had longed to do so many times. Splaying his hands wide over her back, he drew her as close as they could get. He hugged her hard for endless moments, then straightened. Adoringly his eyes wandered over her face. He lifted one of her hands to his mouth, kissed the palm and spoke against it. "Touch me. Please."

He carried her hand to that part of him that strained with life, life he wanted to share with her. When he withdrew his hand, hers remained. With her heart in her throat lest she do something displeasing, she closed her fingers around him.

"Ah, God." Whispering her name and endearments like a chant, he covered her hand with his own and instructed her on what gave him pleasure until he couldn't bear any more. His breath was loud in her ear when he groaned, "Caroline, darling . . . better stop."

Trapping her face between his hands, he kissed her fiercely, his tongue plunging deeply. Not ending the kiss, he lowered her to the bed and followed to cover her body with his. She accommodated him and he nestled his hips in the cove of her parted thighs. His belly meshed with hers, his chest settled against the mounds of her breasts.

The kisses he planted on her throat and

neck were hot and moist. "If I wait much longer —"

"Don't wait," she said quickly, arching against his hardness.

But it had taken twelve years to get there and Rink wanted to experience all of it without rushing. His hands glided over her breasts. Her nipples were ripe for the tender finessing of his fingertips. He replaced his fingers with his mouth, kissing and licking and nuzzling her breasts until she was almost delirious.

He levered himself above her. His hand smoothed down her stomach, her abdomen, marveling at the fabulous texture of her skin. Then his fingers encountered her fleecy delta and luxuriated in it. He laid his palm over it and let his fingers curve downward between her thighs. They came away dewy with her desire.

He leaned away from her and guided himself to the very threshold of her femininity. They watched each other, watched the play of intense feeling flicker across one another's faces each time the velvety tip of his manhood touched that magic spot. Beyond pride and shame, she touched her hands to his chest and curled her fingers into the mat of hair.

"Now, Rink, please."

His whole body straining, he introduced himself into the warm harbor between her thighs and lowered himself upon her. He pressed deep, deeper, until . . .

His whole body went rigid and his eyes, suddenly clear, speared down into hers. Rapid breathing made a bellows of the chest suspended above her as he braced himself on his arms.

"Caroline." She read her name on his lips. He had spoken it almost inaudibly in his disbelief. "You're a virgin."

"Yes, yes," she cried gladly. Locking her fingers around his neck, she implored him with a sustained pulling motion. "I've always been yours, Rink. Only yours. Claim me."

He paused a moment; then, making a groaning sound of immense gratification, he covered her again and pressed her into the bedding. His thrusts were gentle but imperative. The extended foreplay had made her ready. When her body yielded to him, it caused her but fleeting pain. Her slight gasps were captured by his mouth. They sighed together with supreme emotion as he sank completely into her.

He filled her. She gloved him. And for long moments neither of them moved. They savored the feel of being one, of being as intimate as two separate beings can be, of being grafted together by love and desire and pain.

"I can't believe it. Sweet heaven. Oh, God, Caroline, don't let this be just another of my dreams about you."

"It's no dream, Rink," she whispered into his shoulder. "I can feel you inside me."

Raising his head, he smiled down at her. He kissed her lips lightly. "Can you?" he whispered, and made certain that she could.

Her throat arched as she made a purring sound. "Yes, yes."

He began to move. Out of deference to her, his thrusts were shallow and slow, but no less potent as they drew her closer to a magical sphere.

"Am I hurting you?"

"No, my love, no."

"Caroline . . . Caroline . . ." He could repress his mounting passion no longer. Reaching the summit, he experienced the highest level of ecstasy he had ever known. It went on and on as his lifeforce pumped into her. And when it was over, he collapsed, spent and sated and loved, into her welcoming arms.

"It sure is taking Caroline and Rink a long time to get down here," Laura Jane complained. She was afraid the breakfast she had helped Haney prepare would get cold and therefore be ruined for Steve.

"Why don't you two go ahead," Haney said.

"I don't mind waiting," Steve offered.

"No. You're starving. I know you are." Laura Jane spooned a heap of fluffy scrambled eggs onto his plate. "How many slices of ham do you want?"

"Two," he said.

"Three," she amended.

Haney set her coffee cup on the countertop. "I'll mosey upstairs and see if I can't hustle them along. I'm sure they'll want to get some sleep, but they really should eat first after being up half the night." She went on her grumbling way, but Steve and Laura Jane barely missed her. They were engrossed with each other.

At the top of the stairs, Haney looked curiously toward Rink's bedroom door. It was open, but when she stuck her head inside he was nowhere to be seen. Nor was he in the adjoining bathroom. At least he didn't answer her when she softly called out to him.

"Humph!" she grunted, planting her hands on her hips. "Now where do you suppose . . . ?" She glanced toward Caroline's room. The door was closed.

The housekeeper's eyes narrowed in contemplation. "I send him up here with a tray for her. Now the tray's disappeared and so has he. Her door is closed and I feel in my bones that it's supposed to stay closed for a while."

She turned toward the stairs again. "Well, it sure isn't any of my business what they're doing in there, but I didn't hear any conversation." At the bottom of the stairs, she glanced back up, nodding her head in approval. "Makes more sense for her to be with Rink than it did for her to marry his daddy, that old buzzard," she muttered as she made her way back to the kitchen.

"Are they coming down?" Laura Jane asked.

"No. Not any time soon, anyway." Haney turned away and began to wash the dishes.

"Why not?"

"They're sleeping, that's why not."

"But they should eat something first. You said so yourself. I'll go wake them and tell them —"

"You sit yourself back down," Haney commanded, turning away from the sink and trailing soapy water onto the floor with an indomitable finger. "They're tuckered out. Now, you mind your own business and see to that hungry young man sitting there."

Hurt by Haney's stern tone, Laura Jane slowly returned to her chair. Steve caught the housekeeper's eye and looked at her inquiringly. He cast a glance toward the ceiling. Haney watched his face as he gradually began to comprehend the situation.

Steve's eyes glinted mischievously. "Laura Jane, after breakfast why don't you come out to the stables with me? You haven't been to see the filly in days."

Laura Jane looked up at him, her light-heartedness returning. "But I thought you would need to sleep this morning."

"Naw," he said expansively. "I'm not tired. If Haney can spare you, I'd like for you to spend the morning with me, help me do some chores."

"Oh, Steve," she said, pressing her hands together. "I'd love that."

Haney exchanged a look with Steve and he winked at her.

"Why didn't you tell me?" Taking up a strand of her hair, Rink whisked it back and forth over his mouth. He was lying on his back. Caroline was on her stomach, leaning over him.

She tweaked clumps of chest hair and traced the swirling patterns with her fingertip. "Because I had to know how much you loved me. If I had told you that your father and I had never been intimate, would you have believed me?"

"I might have. I would have known soon enough."

She shook her head. "I didn't want our first loving to be a test."

His eyes fondly surveyed her face. "I see your point. But what if I had wholeheartedly believed you?"

"Then it would have been easy for you to come to me, Rink." She touched his nipple and watched it bead in response. "But I would never have known the extent of your love. Since you came to me, believing the worst but still loving me, I know that you were willing to sacrifice your pride for your love."

Drawing her down to him, he kissed her long and deeply. When he finally ended the kiss he said, "Not that I particularly want to discuss this right now, but why didn't you ever sleep with Roscoe? Don't tell me any nobility on his part kept you a virgin."

"No, I wouldn't try to convince you of that. I think he intended to consummate the marriage on our wedding night." She closed her eyes and shuddered. "He came into this room. I didn't know how I was going to survive it, loving you as I did." She brought his hand to her cheek and absently rubbed the backs of his fingers over it. "But I had made a bargain and I was willing to live up to it."

She fell silent. Rink stared at the ceiling, not even wanting to think of her sharing the same space, the same air, with that foul old man. "What happened, Caroline?"

"He kissed me several times. That's all. Then he left me without a word. I was confused. I didn't know what to think. It wasn't too many days later that I began to notice that he was ill. I saw things that I wouldn't ordinarily have seen if I hadn't been living with him. He took huge quantities of stomach remedies, things like that.

"I realized when he didn't come to my room again that he was more than likely impotent and that this stomach ailment was responsible. Of course, I know that for a fact now. We never spoke of it. It would have been such a blow to his ego to try and fail that he never tried. We lived platonically."

After a brief silence, he asked, "Would you have ever told me?"

"You mean, to spare us all that antagonism? I don't know, Rink. I asked myself that every day. Why didn't I just tell you and put an end to it?" She ran her finger down the length of his nose. "I have my pride, too.

I wanted you to love me in spite of everything."

"It was tough. I wanted you. But every time I thought of you and him, I —"

"Shhh," she said, stopping his words by laying her index finger lengthwise over his lips. "I know. I understand what you were suffering."

"Do you know what he told me after you left the room the night he died?" She shook her head. "I told you he left me a legacy. It was this. He told me that I would never have you because my pride wouldn't let me." His eyes melted into hers and one corner of his lip lifted in a half smile. "He was wrong, wasn't he? He didn't count on my loving you this much." He touched her face. "Then he told me always to remember that you had been his wife, that he had had you first."

She stared at him, astonished. "You mean he deliberately led you to believe that —"

"Yes."

"Oh, my darling." She kissed his cheek softly and brushed strands of hair off his brow. "I thought you just *assumed*, but to think he died wanting you to believe that lie."

Rink laughed scornfully. "He knew me well. It almost worked to keep us apart."

"I'm glad it didn't."

"God," he whispered savagely, "so am I." He wound a handful of her hair around his fist. "When I think of all the hours I tormented myself over it. Every time I thought about you with him, my guts would wrench so hard it hurt. And all that time, you were the same." He touched her lips. "My Caroline of the summer woods. The same. The very same."

He pulled her down and kissed her until they broke away from each other breathlessly. "The same, but different."

She could tell by his softened expression that the discussion about her marriage to his father was over. "Different? How so?" she asked impishly, bending her knees and then raising her feet in the air. She pointed them daintily, like a ballerina. He watched them. They were beautiful feet, slender, high-arched. Her toes were polished a frosty coral shade. He had erotic plans for those toes.

He responded to her flirtatiousness. "For instance . . ." He wedged his hand beneath her. "Your breasts." He took one in his hand and kneaded it.

"What about them?"

"They're larger." He rolled the nipple between his thumb and finger. "This is darker.

Not much. But slightly."

"Anything else?"

"You're softer, rounder, much more womanly, but with the same fawnlike grace of a girl. You're everything I've dreamed about for years. More."

"You're not disappointed?"

He dragged his tongue along her collarbone and hotly kissed the top curve of her breast. "No, God no." He glanced up at her. His eyes were regretful. "But I'm afraid you were."

"Not I, Rink Lancaster." She kissed his eyebrow. "Not I."

"But you didn't . . . you know. What all the ladies' magazines say you're entitled to."

Her three middle fingers played with his lips. "And it didn't matter a bit. I experienced yours. I watched it, felt it inside me, knew what it was like for you. I wanted to witness you loving me."

His arms closed firmly around her. "I do, you know. Love you. Even though I've acted like a bastard the last few weeks, said things, insinuated things. The more I loved you, the more rotten I behaved."

Laughing softly, she laid her head on his chest and rested her hand low on his stomach. "You don't have to remind me how rotten you've been at times. But I knew why. And I forgive you. I love you."

He covered her hand and moved it down. "Mind?"

She cupped her hand over him. "Not at all. I love touching you."

His hand went to her breast and treasured it. "Let's sleep for a while."

"You want to sleep?"

"Not really. But I want to wake up with you."

It was shortly after noon when they came downstairs. Arm in arm, they were smiling at each other, so they didn't see Laura Jane and Steve until they reached the wide foyer.

"Steve wants to talk to you, Rink," Laura Jane announced. She looked like a little girl about to burst for having to keep a birthday secret. Her eyes were shining. She couldn't stand still.

Rink looked first at her, then at Steve, who was nervously rotating the brim of his straw cowboy hat between his fingers. "Caroline and I are starved. Can it wait till after lunch?"

"Yes." "No." They answered in unison.

Caroline, sensing what might be on Steve's mind, diplomatically intervened. "I'm sure we'll all feel better after lunch."

Giving Rink a loving look, she disengaged her arm from his and went to Laura Jane. "Does Haney have it ready?" She steered the young woman toward the dining room. "What does Steve want to talk to Rink about?" she asked softly.

"Us getting married," Laura Jane whispered back.

"Then I suggest we wait until after he's had something to eat." Caroline squeezed her arm in affectionate support.

During lunch, Haney brought the cordless telephone extension into the dining room. "It's the sheriff."

He had called to say that the arsonists had been arrested. One of them, the one who admitted to calling Barnes and warning him of the fire, had broken down and confessed, implicating the others. "It won't do them much good to plead innocent. I figure we'll have formal confessions from the other three by suppertime."

"Thanks, Sheriff. Be sure that their families are taken care of, food, rent money, whatever they need for the next several months and send me the bill."

He hung up and reported the news to the others. As soon as the sherbet dishes had been cleared away, Laura Jane excitedly herded everyone into the study. "Go ahead,

Steve," she said, nudging him.

His Adam's apple slid up and down as he swallowed. "Rink, with your blessing, I want to marry Laura Jane."

Giving away nothing of what he thought of the request, Rink sat down in the deep leather chair behind the wide desk. He took a sip of his iced tea, which he had carried with him from the dining room. "And without my blessing?"

Steve's eyes never wavered. "I still want to marry her."

Rink studied the man for a long, tense time. Neither pair of eyes moved from the other. Finally Rink said, "Ladies, will you excuse us please? And, Caroline, please close the door behind you."

"How did you know I'd be here?"

"A hunch." He pushed aside the branches of a pine sapling and came into the clearing. She was sitting beneath a tree, her legs tucked under her, a book resting on her lap. She hadn't been reading it but had been staring into space when he came through the trees. He went to the tree, propped his hand on the trunk and looked down at her upturned face. "Don't you know it's dangerous for you to be out in the woods alone?"

"Why? These are my woods."

"But some sex-crazed man might come along and ravish you."

"That's what I'm counting on."

Laughing, he dropped down beside her and gathered her in his arms. He kissed her lightly several times all over her face, then pressed his mouth with firm possessiveness over hers. She indulged him for only a moment before pushing him away. "Wait. First I want to know what you told Steve."

"I told him if he ever did anything to hurt her, I'd kill him."

"You didn't!"

He shrugged and grinned at her devilishly. "Well, I said it in a nice way."

"But you did consent to their getting married?"

"Yes, I did," he said solemnly.

She hugged him hard. "Rink, I'm so glad."

He eased her away to look at her. "Are you? Do you really think that will be best for Laura Jane?"

"Yes, I do. She loves him. And you don't have to worry about him hurting her. He idolizes her. He's never talked about his past, but I get the feeling that it was dismal. Then the war and losing his leg. I'm sure Laura Jane is like a fairy princess to him. He can't quite get over being allowed to touch her."

"He sounded sincere," Rink said musingly. "I made the condition that Laura Jane would always live at The Retreat. I don't think she'd adjust to another home. He agreed, but insisted that he be given more responsibility. He's touchy about her being an heiress and him a hired hand."

"I would expect that of him. He works harder than anyone to compensate for his handicap."

"He made no bones about the way he feels. He told me, or maybe *warned* is a better word, that their marriage would be a real one." His brow furrowed. "Do you think Laura Jane can tolerate sleeping with a man?"

Caroline laughed and burrowed her nose in his neck. "I get the impression that Laura Jane has been chasing Steve around the stable for months and that he's been the one trying to save her virtue."

"But does she understand the responsibility that goes with sex?"

"Rink." Placing her hands on his cheeks and capturing his full attention, she said, "Laura Jane was born with a deficiency for learning. But she has a woman's emotions and a woman's body. No one should deprive her of what that body needs, any more than it should be deprived of nourishment or air. She'll be happier now than she's ever been. He loves her. He'll cherish her. They'll work the rest out between them."

She could feel his tension ebbing, and the taut lines in his face began to relax. It thrilled her to know how much he valued her opinion.

"What about you?"

"Me?" she asked.

"What about your needs all these years and the deprivation you imposed on yourself?"

"I survived on memories and dreams. Memories of you in this place. Dreams of what I thought could never be."

He inched down onto the soft grass with her and began to unbutton her blouse. "You thought about me? Every once in a while?"

"Every day. Every hour. And even if I had never seen you again, I would have been thinking of you the moment I died."

His eyes closed briefly with the emotion that swept him. When they opened, they shone down into hers. "I hear thunder. Or is that my heart?"

She smiled. He had said almost those

exact words once. "Thunder. It's going to rain."

"Do you mind?"

"I prefer it."

"Sweet, sweet," he whispered across her mouth. "God, I love you."

She helped him take off his shirt. He stood and she was an avid audience as he unbuckled his belt, unzipped his slacks and stepped out of them. Hooking his thumbs in a brief pair of light blue underwear, he peeled it down his hard, sinewy thighs.

His nakedness matched the wilderness setting. In the darkening light, a harbinger of rain, his body stood bold and primeval. Even as she watched, raindrops began to fall on his bronze skin.

Kneeling beside her, he pulled her to a sitting position and took off her blouse. Her brassiere was lacy and sheer, a contrast to those she had worn years ago. Through the silk confection, he touched her breasts. He teased the nipples until they strained against the tenuous veil.

"Look at what you've done," she said scoldingly as she shimmied out of the garment after he had unsnapped it. "Aren't you ashamed of yourself?"

"Yes," he replied contritely, looking anything but.

He unbuttoned her full peasant skirt and pulled it off, leaving her only in her panties. Then he bent to work on the leather thongs of her sandals, which wound seductively around her ankles. When her feet were free of the sandals, he caressed them, massaging her arches and wringing the toes between his strong fingers. She propped herself on her elbows and watched this loving ritual in wonderment. But when he lowered his head and his tongue touched the tips of her toes, her breasts trembled with passion.

"Rink," she cried softly, and fell back onto their bed of verdant undergrowth.

He braced himself above her. She caught handfuls of his now damp hair and twisted it around her fingers as his mouth fused hotly with hers. He enjoyed her mouth as he would a piece of luscious fruit. Then, as softly as the falling raindrops, his lips skidded across her face, paused at her ears. His tongue darted playfully about her earlobe. He kissed her neck, her chest.

The rain fell on her breasts, making them shine wetly. He sipped up the gathering moisture. Against her cool skin, his mouth was hot when it drew a budded nipple inside. "I never forgot the way you taste. Never."

Restlessly, she shifted beneath him,

making a cradle of her femininity to hold his hard maleness. They fit together and their sighs spiraled above them. He rubbed against her suggestively but didn't claim her. She called his name plaintively.

"Not yet," he whispered against the quivering flesh of her stomach. "This is for you."

He moved lower, counting each rib with a kiss. His mouth drifted down to her navel and blessed it with a kiss that made her arch and moan. The tip of his tongue dipped into the shallow dimple repeatedly. Then, employing his teeth and nose and chin, he nudged her panties down over her hips and thighs and legs until she could kick them free.

Caroline felt she would shatter from the pressure building inside her. She didn't think she could stand any more. But he had only begun. His lips drifted over the tuft of dark hair, disturbing it with his light, rapid breath. His tongue discovered the grooves where her thighs joined her abdomen and followed their slanting decline.

"Rink . . ." His name stumbled from her trembling lips as she clutched at his hair.

Gently his hands positioned her, parted her, touched her. But nothing could have prepared her for the sweet kiss he pressed there. His lips were loving, his tongue daring, and together they brought her to a pitch of ecstasy that robbed her of thought. He tantalized and tasted until her whole body began to quake. He had kindled a volcano inside her. When he knew it was about to erupt, he rose above her and drove himself deeply inside.

The hands that gripped his hips, the thighs that enclosed his, the ragged words of love she spoke were his encouragement. His body pulsed inside hers, sparing nothing, driving them higher and higher with each thrust until they exploded together in a shower of dazzling light.

When the crisis passed and they returned to the world, the light had faded. They were in a welcome world of shadow and cloud. They were hidden by a silvery fog that whirled as crazily as had their hearts and minds only moments ago. And their entwined bodies were bathed by the softly falling rain.

Chapter 12

The bride wore white. The silk dress was simply cut but exquisitely fashioned for her slender figure. She didn't look consumed by it as she might have in a traditional wedding dress with yards of fabric and lace. She wore pale stockings and white slippers. The sides of her dark hair were pulled away from her center part and held back by twin white camellias, her favorite flower. She was loveliness personified. Her eyes were glowing, testifying to her happiness. She showed no signs of nervousness.

Her groom did. He fidgeted and constantly cleared his throat and shifted to support himself on his good leg. He tugged at the knot of his necktie, unfamiliar apparel for him. It had been suggested that he not bother dressing up for the occasion, but he had insisted. He wanted this day to be a memorable one for his bride. He wanted everyone to know that this wedding was official and that both of them were well aware of what they were doing and proud of it.

Caroline touched Steve's arm reassuringly as they stood below waiting for the bride. He smiled at her gratefully. But when the minister's wife began to play the wedding march on the grand piano in the back parlor, Steve had eyes only for Laura Jane. And she for him. Her huge brown eyes sought him out in the foyer and stayed on him as she descended the curving stairs on her brother's arm.

Few had been invited to witness the nuptials. Rink and Caroline. The minister, who had so recently officiated at the bride's father's funeral, and his wife. Granger. And Haney, who wept through the entire recitation of vows. Fortunately, the ceremony was brief.

Steve pressed a tender kiss on his new wife's lips and immediately discarded his necktie.

"Steve." He turned and took Rink's outstretched hand. "Welcome to the family."

Steve's face wrinkled into a broad grin as he pumped his brother-in-law's hand. "Thanks, Rink. I'm very glad to be a part of it."

"Congratulations, Steve," Caroline said and kissed him lightly on the cheek. "Laura Jane." Caroline hugged the young woman tight. "Always be happy."

"I will, I will," she said eagerly, bobbing her head. "Let's have refreshments now. I think Steve needs a cold drink."

Everyone was laughing as they filed into the dining room, where Haney had outdone herself with a buffet of ham and turkey, innumerable salads, vegetable casseroles, a traditional three-tiered wedding cake and other desserts. There was coffee and a citrus punch. When Rink was seen spiking Steve's punch glass from a decanter of bourbon, even the minister laughed. It was a festive, lighthearted party, and for Laura Jane's sake, Caroline was glad.

After everyone had eaten, the photographer grouped them for formal pictures. Steve's discarded necktie had disappeared and had to be found and replaced. Caroline brushed Laura Jane's hair and touched up her lip gloss. By the time the photographer was done, no one could see for the spots that danced before their eyes.

The guests departed and the family was left with the ravaged buffet. The bride and groom retired to the upstairs. During the week preceding the wedding, Steve's things had been moved into Roscoe's old room. The couple would share it since it was larger than Laura Jane's bedroom. Caroline planned to redecorate it and make it more appealing and personally theirs.

After they had helped Haney clean up,

Rink and Caroline went to a movie in town. When they came in, the house was quiet and dark. They crept up the stairs, hoping not to disturb the newlyweds. They went into Rink's room. After closing the door behind them, he switched on a dim lamp beside the bed.

"I'm getting tired of all this sneaking around," he complained. "I hate one of us having to get out of bed and run across the hall at dawn. Why can't you just move into this room with me, or let me move into yours?"

"Because."

"That's a real good reason." He had already taken off his boots and shirt and was working on his pants. "Maybe I should write it down so I'll remember it."

"Please don't make fun of me. I don't want anyone to know yet."

"They already know," he said. He was down to his underwear. He collapsed into the leather easy chair that was his favorite spot in the house.

Caroline drew her sleeveless cotton sweater over her head and peered at him in astonishment. "Do you think so?"

Speechlessly, he nodded and watched her carefully fold the sweater and drape it over the back of a chair. Her brassiere was flesh-toned. There was a rose woven into the stretchy sheer fabric. Its petals flowered open around her nipple. As though to make up for all the years she had had nothing pretty, she always wore beautiful lingerie.

Finding his voice, Rink said, "Steve and Haney know for sure. They'd be blind not to, Caroline. For twelve years I've had to keep it a secret that I love you. I don't think I've been too discreet the last few days. I'm happier than I've ever been in my life. And it shows, dear heart."

She blushed as she stepped out of her skirt, revealing a pair of tap pants that matched her brassiere, a lacy garter belt and a pair of silk stockings. His manhood responded significantly.

"I don't like the sneakiness either, but for my sake let's not let everyone in on the secret. I'm flouting decency as it is."

She picked up her hairbrush and lifted it through her hair. The lamplight caught the falling strands and burnished them with red highlights. Her back was to him. It curved with supple grace down either side of her spine. The lace border on the tap pants barely concealed the bottom curve of her derriere. Between that lace and the top of her stockings was an expanse of thigh he ached to touch. "How are you flouting decency?" he asked with a thick voice.

Taking a small plastic bottle from her purse, she dropped a dollop of lotion in her palm. She rubbed it into her hands and smoothed it onto her arms. God! She was driving him insane.

"Because legally you're my stepson."

"And illegally?"

She turned toward him, saw him sprawled in the chair, saw his body, hard and male. Her smile was both shy and wanton. "Illegally, you're my lover."

"Come here." Quickly he freed himself of the underwear and threw it to the floor.

She went to him and stood docilely as he rid her of the tap pants, leaving the garter belt riding low on her hips and the garters stretching down the columns of her thighs to the top of the stockings. He squeezed his hand into the top of one stocking and gently pinched the tender flesh. Her fingers curved around his ears as he leaned forward to kiss her thighs, her belly, her stomach.

He guided her down to straddle his lap and his hard virility was sheathed by her mystery. Her arms went around his neck and her back arched, bringing her breasts to his seeking lips. He kissed the rose design, probed its center with his tongue until it gave birth to another bud. His lips closed around the hard bead and he massaged it with his tongue. The brassiere finally fell away beneath his deft fingers. He buried his face in the fragrant cleft.

Her thighs tightened around his as she rocked above him with slow rotations of her hips. His hands stroked up the backs of her thighs to her hips, where he caressed the soft flesh and held her fast. Clasping his head tightly to her breasts, she bent low over it and whispered love words in tempo to his upward thrusts. He reached higher and higher, to the very gate of her womb. Then, when she trembled with her fulfillment, he melted her with his fire.

Caroline slumped against him and for long minutes they didn't move. Finally he ran one hand down the back of her head. He kissed her shoulder. When she still didn't move, he asked softly, "Is something wrong?"

"In a chair? What have I turned into?"

Smiling, he nuzzled her ear. "A generous, gorgeous, loving woman with all the sexual passion a young man dreamed of." He hugged her tightly. "I used to sit in this chair and dream of you. This is where I did most of my fantasizing of what it would be like when I made love to you." He brushed her cheek with his knuckles. "It's far superior to my fantasies, Caroline."

She raised her head. Her eyes looked like still, moonlit lakes. "Is it?"

"Yes." He touched her hair, her mouth, her breasts. "I still can't believe this is real."

"I can't believe this is *me,* behaving like this. But then you've always been a bad influence on me."

The loving glow in his eyes was replaced by a mischievous gleam. "Aren't'cha glad?"

"Uh-huh." Matching his light mood, she rolled her hips forward.

He groaned theatrically. "Good God, Caroline. Are you trying to kill me? Can't we at least get to the bed first?"

Later, wrapped together under the light covers, Rink found her ear in the darkness and whispered, "You know, if Haney had a bed partner, we could make this into a club." She yanked several chest hairs and he yelped softly. "I only meant that with Steve and Laura Jane in one bedroom and us —"

"I know what you meant." Her smile turned into a yawn. "I can imagine how Steve is feeling right now, but I wonder what Laura Jane thinks of marriage."

They didn't have to wait long to find out. The next morning the newlyweds joined Caroline and Rink at breakfast. They stood in the kitchen doorway with their arms around each other. Steve was wearing a comically sheepish grin. Laura Jane was absolutely radiant. To them all she enthusiastically declared, "I think everybody in the whole world should get married."

Reconstruction had already begun on the gin. Caroline was grateful that Rink was around. She wouldn't have known where to begin the cleanup after the fire. No sooner had that been accomplished than he began to talk about refurbishing. He went over all his plans with her, and she approved them. They included scrapping the old equipment and buying new, replacing the wiring and generally making Lancaster Gin one of the most modern mills in the country.

"We've made a tremendous profit this year. The bank is willing to grant us a long-term loan for the improvements at the lowest interest rate possible. We should take advantage of their generosity."

"I agree."

They worked long hours in the sultry summer heat, but it was invigorating to them both. Too often they had to control their urges to touch each other. They were watched and they knew it and they didn't want to give people any more to talk about than they already had. Gossips were speculating as to why Rink hadn't yet gone back to Atlanta. That worried Caroline, too.

"Rink?" They were taking a short break in the office at the gin.

"Hmmm?" He rubbed a cold soft drink can back and forth over his forehead.

"When are you going back to Atlanta?" She tried to sound casual but knew she had failed when he lowered the can and looked at her sharply.

He took a sip of his drink. "Trying to get rid of me?" he asked teasingly.

Her eyes softened with love. "Of course not," she spoke quietly. "I just wondered why you're doing all this for the gin. I'm being paid a salary, but there's no reason for you to put so much time and energy into it."

He set the can down on a coffee table piled high with outdated trade magazines. Standing, he stretched and went to the window where he could see workers unloading building supplies from a flatbed truck. "This gin means a lot to me whether Roscoe wanted it to or not. I don't profit from it financially, thanks to his will, but it's still of vital interest to me. The gin belonged to my mother's family before Roscoe took it over and put his name on it. Since it's part of my heritage and bears my name, I have to care about it. And if those reasons don't

308

seem valid enough, let's just say that I'm protecting my sister's legacy."

"I love you."

He turned swiftly to face her. Her pronouncement was unexpected and seemingly out of context. "Why? I mean, what made you say so now?"

"Because any other man would have left long ago, bitter and enraged over the circumstances."

"That's what he wanted me to do. Even now I refuse to buckle under to him."

"Is that the only reason you're still here, to defy Roscoe?"

He smiled and came to her. Taking her hand, he pulled her to her feet and backed her into a corner between the wall and a file cabinet. The narrow space afforded them a modicum of privacy from anyone who might come in. "You have a little to do with my hanging around," he drawled and began to kiss her.

He tasted salty. He was sweaty. He was thoroughly masculine. She loved the sheer maleness of him. Everything feminine about her responded to it. Inching closer, she pressed her aroused body to his. His lips slid to her neck to nibble and tease. His hand covered her breast and caressed it.

"You can't take that kind of liberty," she

murmured. "I'm the boss."

"Not my boss. I don't officially work here, remember?"

She moaned softly as his fingers idly traced her nipple through her blouse. Bending his head, his teeth pulled free the first button and his mouth savored the warm flesh beneath. "But I still exercise a certain amount of control," she said breathlessly.

"Not over me you don't." Her hand went to the fly of his jeans and pressed the hardness there. "All right. So I lied," he said roughly. "You exercise a helluva lot of control."

"I always thought this place was a honkytonk." Caroline looked around the dim interior of the tin building.

"It is. But it has the best barbecue east of the Mississippi. An old family recipe imported from Tennessee. What will you have, baby back pork ribs or sliced beef brisket?"

"Can I lick my fingers?"

"Sure."

"Then I want the ribs."

They smiled as the waitress sashayed off with their order. They had to shout over the blaring music coming from the gaudy jukebox in the corner. Couples danced on a sawdust-strewn dance floor, bobbing a two-step or swaying together in a clenching embrace, depending on how romantically involved they were.

A cloud of tobacco smoke hovered just under the ceiling. From the cheaply paneled walls, flashing pink-and-blue neon lights touted various brands of beer. A model with a smile as voluminous as her hairdo and bosom adorned a poster for a radiator shop. Behind the bar, the face of a clock wavered beneath a moving waterfall. That electrically animated marvel made Caroline slightly nauseated if she looked at it too long.

She and Rink were enjoying themselves. They had made a habit of inventing places to go for a few hours every night just to give Steve and Laura Jane time alone in the house. Steve had told them confidentially that he had mentioned a honeymoon to Laura Jane, but the thought of traveling too far afield was frightening to her. She had adjusted to married life beautifully. He didn't want to make an issue of a honeymoon.

"Did you come here often?" Caroline asked, resting her forearms on the table and leaning toward Rink.

"All the time. When I was in high school and too young to buy beer, all of us guys would pile into one car and come out here. They didn't have any qualms about selling it to us. Daddy told me —" He broke off suddenly and Caroline knew it was because he had called Roscoe by the familiar form of address.

"Go on," she prodded gently. "What did he tell you?"

"He told me that during Prohibition this place was a hotbed of bootlegging. More illegal whiskey was run in and out of here than anywhere else in the state."

He became meditative as he absently toyed with the salt shaker. Caroline covered his hand, bringing his eyes up to hers. "It wasn't always bad between the two of you, was it? Weren't there a few good times that you could remember and forget the rest?"

He smiled sadly. "There were a few, yes. Like the time I wanted to smoke one of his cigars. I was about twelve. He let me. I got sicker than a dog and he thought that was hilarious. He teased me about it for years later, but I didn't mind. Then there was the time I got caught painting 'Go Wildcats' on the rival school's team bus. Roscoe defended the whole bunch of us to the school board, reminding them that boys were supposed to raise hell or they wouldn't be normal."

312

His brow wrinkled. "There's a pattern here, Caroline, that I've never thought of before. If I was involved in some kind of mischief, Roscoe approved. He liked me best when I was in trouble. It was when I stood up for something right that he couldn't stomach me. He wanted me to be like him, a mover and shaker just a little beyond the pale of morality. I don't claim to be a saint, but I've never swindled anybody or hurt anyone just for the hell of it." He met her eyes full on. "I want you to know this. I regret very much that he and I didn't love each other."

"I know you wanted to love him, Rink."

"If I ever have sons or daughters, I'll love them for what they are. I'll never try to change them. I swear that."

They clasped their hands tightly across the table and didn't release them until their food arrived.

By the time they had eaten, the place was getting rowdy. There were more drinkers and dancers than diners. The noise level had risen to a din. As soon as Rink got their check from the waitress, they made their way to the cash register at the end of the bar. Their tab was being tallied up when Caroline heard the first slurred voice.

"Must be nice, huh, Virgil, to move right

in where Daddy left off?"

Rink's hands, which had been leafing through a roll of currency, became ominously still. Caroline saw the vein in his temple begin to tick and his jaw bunch in anger.

Virgil giggled. "Reckon you're right, Sam. Ain't nuthin' like havin' your own daddy work out all the kinks for you, so to speak."

Rink calmly laid his money on the bar. "Rink, let's go." Caroline grabbed his arm. He shook her off like a pesky fly. She glanced around self-consciously. Someone had turned down the volume on the jukebox. All the dancers were suddenly still. Others at the bar moved away from Virgil and Sam, who were obviously too drunk or too stupid to know that they had just ignited a very short fuse. As Rink turned to face them, his eyes smoldered with a yellow light that made Caroline shrink in fear.

"What did you say?" His lips barely moved as he asked his simple question in a deadly quiet voice. One of the men poked the other and they fell against each other laughing.

"Mr. Lancaster, sir," the manager of the tavern ventured, "they're new to town. They don't know nothing about your family. They're just shooting off their mouths. Don't pay them no mind. I'll throw them out."

He could have saved his courage and his breath, for Rink ignored him. "What did you say?" he demanded more loudly. He advanced on the two men, who were teetering on their barstools.

"Well, we was just sayin' how lucky you was to have had your daddy warm up your bed for you before he kicked off."

Caroline raised a trembling hand to cover her mouth and tried to avoid the curious eyes that were aimed at her. She knew they were remembering that for all her finery, she was still Pete Dawson's girl. Trash.

Virgil could barely talk for laughing at Sam's clever way with words. "I'll bet the sheets didn't even cool off none before you moved right in. Did your daddy teach her some good tricks, sonny? Does she do for you what she —"

Virgil never got to finish his question. He never remembered even starting it. Rink's rocketing fist crunched into his chin, lifted him off the stool and sent him flying into the ring of spectators. He was unconscious before he hit the floor.

Sam watched his friend's misfortune with openmouthed astonishment. He got off his stool waveringly. He smiled sickly at Rink.

"He . . . he . . . we didn't mean nuthin' by it, Mr. . . . uh . . . Lancaster, sir. We was just funnin' with —"

He saw the fist coming, tried to dodge it and took the blow full on his cheekbone. He howled in pain and fell to his knees. Rink stood over him, feet braced wide apart, breathing harshly, his fists balling and releasing at his sides.

"Apologize to the lady," he said in a soft rasp. "Now."

Sam rocked back and forth in agony, both his hands clutching the side of his face as though to hold it together. The only sounds he could utter were guttural whines.

"Apologize to the lady," Rink roared.

Caroline rushed to him and grabbed his arm. "Please, Rink," she pleaded earnestly, "let's go. He can't speak. It doesn't matter. Just get me out of here. I can't stand everyone looking at me. Please, let's go!"

He shook his head as though to clear it. Then he abruptly turned toward the cash register, angrily tossed down a handful of bills and, while stuffing the rest of his money into his jeans pocket, took Caroline's upper arm and dragged her with him as he pushed through the door.

He sped home, but the pickup lacked the

responsive engine of his sports car. He cursed it when it sputtered and choked and wouldn't go as fast as he wanted. When they got home, he came around to her side and opened the door but didn't wait for her to get out before he stamped into the house. She followed and found him pacing the library like a caged cat. Judiciously she closed the door behind her as she entered the room and dropped her purse into the nearest chair.

He glared up at her. "Do you see what everybody thinks? They think you slept with my father."

"I was his wife. What are they supposed to think?"

He cursed imaginatively and ran his hands through his hair. "I guess I'm the laughingstock of the whole damn town. What a kick everybody must be getting out of this. Me taking over where my old man left off."

His selfishness overwhelmed her. "Have you given any thought to how *I* feel, to what they think of *me?*" She splayed a hand wide over her chest. "They all thought I had seduced your father into marrying me. Now they think I've seduced my stepson. Whatever they say about you can't compare to the ugly things they say about me. I'm poor trash, remember? To them I always was and always will be. And it has nothing to do with how moral I am or am not. It's a stigma I was born with."

"But as Roscoe's wife you were about to overcome that stigma, weren't you?"

She tried to avoid answering, but when she saw the smirking knowledge on his face, she had to respond. "Yes."

"Well, maybe for your sake it's a damn shame he died," he said cruelly. "At least you came out on top financially. I'm sure the contents of his will are common knowledge by now. Everybody knows I was left out of it. The whole town probably thinks I'm mooching off you because you've got The Retreat."

"Be reasonable, Rink. That's impossible. Everybody knows how successful your airline is."

"They all know how much I love this place, too. They probably think I'm playing your stud just so you'll keep me around."

She recoiled as though he had slapped her. "I hate it when you talk like that."

"Why not talk about it? Let's face facts. Isn't that what I'm doing?" he asked. "What purpose am I serving around here? Laura Jane's got Steve to take care of her. Haney bustles around them like a mother hen. All

318

I'm doing is keeping the mistress of the house happy in bed."

"Don't you dare sound self-sacrificing. You're happy, too." She cursed the tears of anger and hurt that filled her eyes.

"I was until I realized that everybody thinks I'm taking Roscoe's place in your bed."

"But you're not! You know that, Rink."

"The net effect is the same."

"Because everyone thinks I slept with your father?"

"Yes." The word exploded from his mouth like a missile. The aftershock that followed was a deadly silence. Finally Rink said, "Even dead he's keeping us apart."

Caroline rounded on him, indignation lifting her head to a haughty angle. "Not him. *You.* Your damned pride. Your pride is keeping us apart this time."

"And what about yours?" he flared back.

"Mine?" she asked, aghast.

"Yes, yours."

"What have I ever had to be proud about?"

"That you went off and got yourself a college degree. That you married the richest man in the county. That you live in his mansion. That you're socially above all those who used to look down their noses at you."

"I told you when you first came back that I loved living here."

"But what if everyone knew that the only reason Roscoe married you was to get back at me, that your marriage was a sham? Could you hold your head quite so high then?"

Her guilty silence was as good as a confession. She sank into a chair. Rink's shoulders sagged. In a calmer voice he said, "I can't stand their thinking you were my father's lover and you couldn't stand their knowing otherwise." He threw his head back and laughed. "God, what a wizard of revenge he was. If his first trick didn't work, keeping us apart by assuring me he'd slept with you first, he had this to fall back on."

He went to the door. "Much as I hate to admit it, Caroline, we've played right into his hands. Just as he knew we would."

There was a heart-wrenching finality to the way he pulled the door closed after leaving the room.

Chapter 13

"I'd like to turn that boy over my knee, that's what I'd like to do," Haney grumbled as she stripped the linens from Caroline's bed. "If any young'un ever needed a whipping . . ."

Caroline sat at her dressing table, trying to massage away a headache. It wasn't working. Her whole body ached as though she had been bludgeoned. And she had been. By her argument with Rink.

The housekeeper heaped the linens in the middle of the floor and unfolded fresh ones. They popped crisply as she flapped them over the bed. With military neatness, she tucked them under the mattress. "Didn't he say anything to you last night, give you any indication that he was going to sneak out of here like a thief in the night?"

"No, he . . . uh . . . We talked for a while. He came upstairs, and a few minutes later I went to bed. I didn't know he was gone until you woke me this morning."

"I taught that boy better manners and his mama did before me. Imagine just packing up and leaving without so much as a how-dee-doo. Driving that new pickup to the landing strip and taking off in his airplane. I swear to goodness, I don't know what got into him."

Caroline wished that for once the housekeeper wouldn't be so talkative. The last thing she wanted to talk about was Rink. Her wounds were too new. Every mention of his name opened them up and made her heart bleed. "I'm sure he had neglected his business in Atlanta for as long as he felt he could."

Haney threw her a sardonic look. I knew which way the wind was blowing, she wanted to tell the younger woman. She was dying to know what had happened between them to cause Rink to leave so suddenly. For weeks they had been walking around all goo-goo-eyed toward each other. Something had caused Rink to hightail it, and that something had to do with Caroline. She bent down and hoisted up the load of laundry. "I don't know what I'm going to tell Laura Jane. It'll break her heart that he didn't even say good-bye."

"You said he left her a letter."

"That isn't quite the same, is it?"

Caroline's graciousness had worn out. She stood and went to her closet, gathering up clothes to take into the bathroom, silently hinting that she wanted to be left alone. "She won't mind Rink's leaving so much, now that she has Steve to take care of her."

"And who's going to take care of you?"

Caroline halted on her way through the bathroom door and spun around to face the intuitive housekeeper. Haney only gave her an arch look before ambling out with an air of superiority, her arms full of bed linens.

Caroline showered and dressed mechanically. She wasn't interested in how she looked. Rink wouldn't be there to see her. She would go on as normal, go to the gin and check on the progress of the reconstruction. It would be more important than ever for her to appear in charge and to stand firm on every decision. Some employees might use Rink's abdication as an excuse to slack off on the work.

When she arrived at the gin, she learned that Rink hadn't been all that impulsive when he'd left for Atlanta during the night. Barnes met her in the office.

He stood when she entered, shuffling his feet uneasily and never letting his eyes meet hers. "Rink — Mr. Lancaster, that is — called me from Atlanta first thing this morning."

She tried to appear unaffected by the news, but her hand was trembling when she pulled open the desk drawer to put her purse inside. "Oh?"

Barnes cleared his throat. "Yes, ma'am. And he said that I was to help you in any way I could to keep things running smooth, and all. He told me to call him if anything irregular-like came up."

"Thank you, Barnes," she said quietly. He hadn't completely deserted her. He still cared enough to see that she wouldn't be left with an inoperative gin. On the other hand, he could merely be protecting Laura Jane's inheritance.

The foreman twisted his hat in his hand. "You know, me and the guys . . . well, we sorta got used to having Rink around again. 'Course he was just a kid when he left here the first time, but we all liked him even then. He was always looking out for us, know what I mean? Not like his daddy, meaning no disrespect. But Rink was always taking up for us workers."

"Yes, I know what you mean, Barnes."

"Well," he said, backing toward the door and mentally cursing himself. Hell, he hadn't meant to make her cry. "If you need anything, you just holler, you hear, Mrs. Lancaster?"

"Yes. Thank you."

When he was gone, Caroline went to the

window and surveyed the landscape. Summer's demise was imminent. The flowers and trees were no longer lush. They were drying up, curling and brittle with fatigue, waiting to die. That was how she felt. For those precious weeks she and Rink had been together, her heart had celebrated life. Now it felt as shriveled as the last brave blossoms of summer clinging to life.

"It was never meant to be, Caroline," she whispered to herself. Were they the proverbial star-crossed lovers, doomed before they were even born? Did fate arrange such human catastrophes? Or were they paying for the sins of their fathers, living out a biblical prophesy?

The cause didn't matter because the end was irreversible. Rink had been right. They were both too proud. She had liked what being a Lancaster meant. Rink knew her well enough to know that she wouldn't want to give that up. And for fear that it would look like begging, he would never come to her as long as she owned The Retreat.

Her head came up. Her heart began to pound.

As long as she owned The Retreat.

Could she give it up? What did the house mean to her without Rink in it? That had always been part of its mystique, part of what drew her to it. It was where Rink Lancaster lived. Even when she shared the house with Roscoe, she would walk the halls and imagine Rink there, as a child, as an adolescent, as a young man. Without him it was just a collection of lovely rooms surrounded by four walls.

It had never belonged to her. Always to him. Legal jargon written down on a piece of paper would never change that.

But could she give it up?

A soft knock on the study door brought her head up from the ledgers. "Come in."

Granger stepped into the shadowed room where only the green-shaded lamp on Roscoe's desk shed any light. "Haney said you were in here. I hope I'm not disturbing you."

Caroline smiled at the attorney. "Come in, Granger. I welcome the interruption."

"You're burning the midnight oil. Is that necessary?"

Yes, it was necessary. Because when she didn't bury herself in work she thought of Rink. She thought of him anyway, but at least staying busy helped alleviate the pain. In the month since he had left, the pain had become less sharp, changing into a steady dull ache for which there was no relief.

"This bookkeeping has to be done some-time. At the gin I'm constantly interrupted, so I can get more done here after hours. Did Haney offer you something? A drink, coffee?"

"No thank you." He seated himself across the desk from her in the straight-back chair. "How are things at the gin?"

"Busy, chaotic, fine. But you know that. You were out there yesterday. Is there some problem, Granger?" He looked like a man on his way to the gallows. "Why did you come to see me?" Her face paled. Rink. *Something's happened to Rink.*

Granger was sensitive to her rising panic. "No, no. I didn't mean to alarm you. It's nothing tragic." He studied the rug beneath his chair for a moment. "It's just that you've been extended an invitation and I don't know how you're going to take it."

"An invitation to what?"

"An invitation to accept a plaque desig-nating Roscoe as Citizen of the Year at the Fall Festival."

He referred to the citywide celebration sponsored each year by the Winstonville Chamber of Commerce. Caroline couldn't imagine herself having anything to do with the festival, nor Roscoe. "They want to give the award posthumously? Why? Why not honor someone who's living?"

Granger scratched behind his long, droopy ear. "That's what I asked. Not that I wasn't honored on Roscoe's behalf," he rushed to add, ever loyal. "But it seems that the award committee voted on him last spring. They don't see fit to change their minds and want you to accept the plaque at the opening ceremony of the festival."

She stood and, wrapping her arms around her waist, went to stand at the window. It was raining, a dreary September rain. It fell heavily, despondently. Not at all like a soft summer rain that kissed and caressed naked skin even as hands and mouths did. She pressed her forehead against the cool pane of glass. Would she ever get over missing him?

His picture had been in the newspaper the day before yesterday. Steve had seen it and Laura Jane had come running to show Caroline. Another city had granted Air Dixie access to its airport. In the photograph Rink was shaking the mayor's hand, smiling, his white teeth flashing in his dark face. His hair was falling on his forehead. She had ached to touch it, brush it back.

"You miss him, don't you?" Granger asked quietly.

"Roscoe?"

"Rink."

She turned. "You know?"

His basset-hound face wrinkled into a wistful smile. "I think there was something between you and Rink long before he came home. No" — he held up his hands when he saw she was about to speak — "I wasn't fishing for details. In fact, I'm probably better off not knowing. But that day I was here for Laura Jane's wedding and saw you two together, I was fairly certain you were in love with each other. Am I right?"

"Yes."

She returned to her stance at the window and they were silent for a moment. "Would I be nosing in where I don't belong to ask why he left?"

She shook her head. "You've always been a good friend to me, Granger. When Roscoe married me, I knew you were surprised, but you never treated me with anything less than the highest respect and courtesy. I don't know if I ever thanked you properly for that." She faced him again. "I thank you now. So as a friend I can tell you that there was too much antipathy between Rink and me for him to stay."

"Namely his father."

"Precisely his father. And my marriage to him."

"Rink's proud."

"Oh, yes, I know." She smiled. Then she looked at the attorney and said levelly, "My marriage to Roscoe was never consummated."

"I figured that, too."

She laughed softly. "You're full of surprises tonight. I thought you'd be shocked."

"I'm relieved. You were too good for him, Caroline."

She sank back into the chair behind the desk. "He did some terrible things, the worst of which is what he did to Rink."

"I agree."

"You knew about all his machinations?"

"Far more than you can count."

"Then why did you stay his friend for so many years?"

"His *attorney*. Roscoe had no friends. He wouldn't let anyone be his friend. I stayed with him partially to keep him in line. I took a lot of abuse from him, but I hate to think of what he would have tried to pull if I hadn't watched over his business affairs."

Caroline placed her elbows on the desk and leaned her head on her fingers, rubbing her temples. "He doesn't deserve that award."

"Do you want my advice?"

"Please."

"Accept it, smiling graciously."

"And be a hypocrite?"

"Don't disillusion them, Caroline," he said, speaking of the entire town. "They need their public figures to love and hate and envy and emulate. Give them what they want. For one hour, let Roscoe be what he should have been in reality."

"I guess you're right."

He stood and she joined him on the other side of the desk. Arm in arm, they walked to the door. "I'll tell them tomorrow that you'll accept the award on Roscoe's behalf."

"Granger." She paused at the door. "What would it take, legally, to sign over the deed to The Retreat to someone else?"

This time she had succeeded in shocking him. "You're not thinking of selling it?" he asked, flabbergasted.

"No. I'm thinking of giving it away."

He studied her face and saw the resolution there. It prevented him from prying further. As he pondered her question, he pulled on his earlobe, stretching it even longer. "The Retreat is yours to do with as you wish. I think it might have been an oversight on Roscoe's part, but there was no stipulation that you couldn't give it away, only that Laura Jane be allowed to live here the rest of her life."

"I understand. This wouldn't affect that."

"In that case there would be no problem in your giving it away. If you're sure that's what you want."

Musingly, she nodded her head. "When is the Fall Festival?"

"The third week in October. About a month away." He placed his hand on the doorknob. "They asked for Rink's address. I'm sure they intend to invite him."

Her eyes flickered away from his. "Could you have a new deed drawn up by the third week in October?" When she raised her eyes again, he was smiling down on her fondly.

"You know, if it weren't for these Lancaster men always getting in the way, I think I'd be a little in love with you myself."

"Hey!"

Caroline stopped on the sidewalk and peered over the top of her grocery bag at the young girl who had so rudely addressed her. "Are you talking to me?"

"Aren't you Mrs. Lancaster?"

"Yes." The girl couldn't have been more than twelve, but she had on garish purple eye shadow and blue eyeliner that had been applied with a heavy hand. Her dark hair had been cut to stick up from the top of her head. One earlobe had three holes pierced in it. A colored paper clip dangled from each of the holes. The other ear bore a large, glittering star. Her mouth was a slash of white lipstick.

Her clothes were as outlandish as the makeup, a green miniskirt over a pair of orange mesh hose, a white sweat shirt with a huge pair of red lips and an obscene tongue emblazoned on it. Caroline thought she must be in costume for some bizarre play. What kind of parent would allow a daughter on the streets looking like this? In any event the girl had gained her attention. "How do you know me?"

"I knew Mr. Lancaster. Rink Lancaster. But it was a long time ago. My name's Alyssa."

Caroline's eyes widened in surprise. This was Marilee's daughter, the one Rink had grown so fond of before her mother cruelly separated them. "How are you, Alyssa?"

"Okay, I guess. You were married to Rink's old man, weren't you?"

"To Roscoe. He died a few months ago."

"Sure, I know that. Everybody knows that. A while back I saw you and Rink at the Dairy Mart."

"Why didn't you come over and speak to him?"

She shrugged insolently. "Didn't feel like it. He probably don't even remember me."

"Doesn't."

"Huh?"

"I'm sorry. I was rudely correcting your grammar."

"That's okay. My mama does it all the time, but it don't . . . doesn't seem to do no good."

Caroline laughed in spite of herself. But she sobered when she cast a glance at the group Alyssa had been with. She could well imagine that peer influence was stronger than parental guidance in this case. The girls accompanying Alyssa looked like escapees from a reform school.

Caroline was immediately ashamed of herself for forming an opinion based on appearance alone. She had put labels on the girls just as people had at one time labeled her. However, when one of the girls, no older than Alyssa, lit a cigarette, she couldn't help but be appalled.

"How is your mother?" Caroline remembered Marilee as petite and buxom, with long blond hair, china-blue eyes and a petulant pout.

"She's got a new husband. He's a jerk. Worse than the last one. I don't hang around there no more than I have to."

Then, as if realizing she had revealed too much of herself, she pulled herself erect and said, "Well, I gotta be goin'."

"Wait!" Caroline surprised herself by saying. When the girl stared at her through lashes gummed with black mascara, she was at a loss for what to say. In those overdecorated eyes she saw rebellion, suspicion and a great deal of vulnerability. It was as though a little girl was living behind the lurid mask and wanted desperately to be coaxed out. "Why don't you come to see me at The Retreat sometime? I'd like to get to know you."

Alyssa scoffed with a crude snorting sound. "Like hell."

"No, really, I would." Why Caroline persisted she couldn't say. The girl had touched her heart in some unfathomable way. Rink would hate to see the child he had loved so lonely. If Caroline could help, she wanted to. "I'd like for us to become friends."

The dark blue eyes wavered. "Why?"

"Because I've heard Rink speak of you so often."

"Yeah? What does he say?" Her chin was tilted at a belligerent angle, but Caroline could tell she had been surprised and was interested.

"He talks about what a sweet baby you were, how much he cared for you and hated to give you up."

"He wasn't my daddy."

"I know. But he loved you just the same." The girl began to gnaw at the white painted lips and Caroline thought for a heart-stopping moment that she might cry. "Rink will be here in a few weeks for the Fall Festival. Why don't you come out and see him?"

Her shoulders lifted in a noncommital shrug. "Maybe. I'm real busy."

"Oh, I understand. It's just that I think Rink would love to see you. Your mother has made that difficult."

Without answering, Alyssa glanced over her shoulder at her friends, who were waiting for her with growing impatience. "Look, I gotta split."

"It was nice to meet you, Alyssa. Please think about coming to see me."

"Yeah, okay."

Caroline watched the girl's slinking retreat down the sidewalk. She was a pathetic sight. Yet Caroline's heart was lighter than it had been in weeks.

"Are you proud of me, Steve?"

"I'm always proud of you."

Laura Jane and her husband of two months were lying together in the king-sized bed in what used to be Roscoe's suite. The rooms were barely recognizable as such now. Caroline had redecorated them for the newlyweds' wedding present. The wallpaper was new but still in keeping with the antebellum architecture of the house. There were new drapes on the windows, new towels and fixtures in the bathroom, new area rugs on the hardwood floors. A chaise and an easy chair with a tea table between them had replaced the rolltop desk in the sitting area.

Laura Jane snuggled closer to her husband. Idly her fingers stroked his stomach. "But I mean especially proud since I bought those things all by myself today. I got the correct change back and everything, didn't I?"

His arm tightened around her. After two months of sleeping with her, he was almost convinced that she wouldn't break in his embraces. "You did everything just right. I knew you could."

He had taken her to the feed store with him. When he'd first suggested that she handle the transaction, he had seen the trepidation in her eyes. But she had studied the bill the clerk had handed her and painstakingly counted out the correct amount of money, then waited until she had been given her change. When they'd left the store, she'd beamed up at him like a child who had done well at her first piano recital.

"I was afraid to try. I remember Rink used to take me to town. He wanted to teach me to do things on my own, but I was always afraid I'd do something wrong and he'd be disappointed in me. I wouldn't even try."

Steve slid his head across the pillow so he could look down at her. "You aren't afraid of disappointing me?" He was teasing and she buried her nose in the hollow of his shoulder.

"Of course not. I want to please you more than I ever wanted to please anybody. That's why I was willing to try my best. I know I'm not as smart as other people. I don't ever want you to be sorry you married me."

He rolled to his side and hugged her against him. "My darling," he whispered into her hair. "How could I ever be sorry about that? I'll always love you no matter what you do, or don't do. You don't have to earn my love, Laura Jane. You have it already. Forever."

"Steve," she murmured, touching his chest lightly. "I love you so much." Sitting up, she pulled her nightgown over her head and tossed it to the foot of the bed.

It was endearing, her lack of modesty. She was childish in her unconcern over nakedness. Because her spirit was so pure, she felt no shame about her body. Like an Eve before the apple, she was free of conscience and restraint. Such spontaneity continued to delight her husband, and he was almost ashamed of the way he enjoyed her lack of inhibition.

She had taught him something about his own body. He had hated to look at it after the loss of his leg. He had despised it. It amazed him that Laura Jane took such pleasure in his body. She continually invented excuses to touch him. Her chinalike hands soothed when he'd thought there was no healing power left on earth. She thrilled him with her curious examinations and aroused him to heights he had never known before. Each caress was a demonstration of the unselfish way she loved him. In his whole life, he had never known such care from another human being.

Now, with a quiet smile on her lips, she lay back down beside him and threw her thin arm around his waist. He threaded his fingers in her long straight hair and brought her face up to receive his kiss. It wasn't long before their hands began to wander. He caressed her back as she rolled atop him. She laid her palms on his cheeks and kissed him repeatedly on the face. Her kittenish tongue teased his ears, something she had learned from him.

She inched down his body and dropped kisses on his throat and chest. Then her lips opened over one of his nipples and she tested its texture with the tip of her tongue. He almost vaulted off the bed.

"Laura Jane," he gasped.

"Hmmm?" she murmured, not stopping.

"When you do this to me, it feels good. Doesn't it feel good to you? If it doesn't, I'll stop."

His hands tunneled through her hair and his fingers closed about her head. "No, don't stop," he gasped. "Not until . . ." He positioned her over him and with a slow, easy movement made them one.

Bracing herself on her arms, she leaned forward and placed one of her breasts against his lips. He kissed the tiny pink nipple until it pearled. His tongue curled around it. She sighed her pleasure.

The tempest inside them continued to build until he clasped her hips between his hands and strained into her. She nestled his head against her small breasts as their bodies shuddered together. Long after it was over they held each other. Then softly she kissed his forehead and lay down beside him.

"I'm glad you taught me how to make love," she said.

He chuckled. "So am I."

"I wish everyone in the whole world were as happy as we are."

"I don't think that's possible. No one could be as happy as I am." He pressed a gentle kiss on her mouth.

"I wish Caroline was happy. Since Rink left, she hasn't been happy." Her perception should have surprised him, but it didn't. He thought that sometimes she was more sensitive to emotions than other people. "Do you think she misses Rink?"

"Yes I do, sweetheart."

"So do I." She fell silent for a moment and he thought she had gone to sleep. Then she said, "I'm afraid she's going to die like Daddy did."

Steve caught her beneath the chin with his fingers and tilted her head up. "What in the world are you talking about?"

"Caroline's sick."

"She's not sick. She's certainly not going to die."

"Daddy used to rub his stomach when he thought no one was looking. Or he'd close his eyes like he was hurting somewhere."

"What does that have to do with Caroline?"

"She's doing the same things. Late yesterday evening when she came home from the gin, I was watching her from the parlor. She hung up her jacket on the coat tree and went up the first two stairs. Then she stopped and leaned over the banister. She rested her head on her hands for a long time. It looked like she couldn't get her breath. I was just about to run and help her when she pulled herself up. It seemed to take all her energy to get to the top." Concern marring her perfect features, Laura Jane bent over him. "Steve, she's not going to die, too, is she?"

"No, no, of course not," he reassured her, smoothing back her hair. "She was probably just tired, that's all."

"I hope so. I don't want anyone else to die until I do. Especially you," she said, hugging him hard. "Don't ever die, Steve."

He held her close and soon he felt her gentle breathing against his skin and knew she was asleep. He pulled the covers over them and continued to hold her. But he didn't sleep. He stared into the darkness, his brow furrowed. He had been worried about Caroline, too. And what Laura Jane had told him only fed that worry.

Chapter 14

Fall Festival was blessed with a good weather forecast. The morning of the opening ceremony dawned clear and brisk. Caroline decided to wear her new suit. It would be cool enough.

Following a discreet tap on her door, Haney came in carrying a tray. "I hated to disturb you. You should sleep late more often. But I knew you wouldn't appreciate it if I let you sleep through the shindig."

"Thank you, Haney." On the tray was a pot of tea, which she had begun drinking recently instead of coffee, a glass of orange juice and two blueberry muffins. "I wasn't sleeping. Just being lazy."

"That's good for a body now and then. Especially since today is probably going to wear you out. Do you need me to press anything? Want me to run your bathwater?"

"My clothes are ready," Caroline said, sinking down into a chair beside the table where Haney had set the tray. She poured a cup of tea. "A hot bath sounds nice. It's chilly outside."

Haney went into the adjoining bathroom,

343

keeping up a stream of chatter about the coming events of the weekend. Caroline barely listened as she sipped her tea meditatively. "Your bath's ready. Why haven't you eaten those muffins?"

"I'm not hungry." Every time she thought of standing up in front of the whole town to accept that blasted plaque, her stomach lurched in protest. Putting any food into it would be risky.

The housekeeper watched the young woman as she rose and went to her closet to get a terry robe. Through the batiste nightgown she could see that her mistress had lost a significant amount of weight. The figure that had been fashionably slender was now downright skinny to Haney's way of thinking. "Do you think he'll be there?" She bent to straighten the covers on the bed.

"Who?" Haney tossed Caroline such a reproachful look that she lowered her head and answered, "I don't know." She went into the bathroom and closed the door, just as effectively closing the topic of Rink.

When Caroline came down the stairs an hour later, Steve whistled long and low. Laura Jane clapped her hands. Haney's expression was somewhere between concern and pride.

"Man, that's class!" Steve said.

Caroline laughed and the three watching her were grateful for the fluting sound. She wasn't given to laughter lately. "Do you like it?"

"You look beautiful, Caroline," Laura Jane said enthusiastically. "Oh, you're gorgeous."

"She's too skinny," Haney grumbled, but lovingly picked an imaginary piece of lint from Caroline's shoulder.

"I thought as long as they're going to talk — and they will — I would give them something to talk about. Besides, we're representing the Citizen of the Year. We should dress the part."

Her two-piece suit was of cream-colored wool crepe. Her blouse was dove gray, almost the exact shade of her eyes. She had tucked all her hair under a soft felt hat the same color as her suit. Its low, dipping brim flirted with her brows. Her makeup was sedate and had been carefully applied to camouflage the violet shadows beneath her eyes. Pearl earrings were in her ears. Her stockings were pale ivory. She wore bone-colored suede pumps and carried a pair of matching kid gloves.

"You all look spiffy, too," Caroline commented as she surveyed them proudly. Laura Jane was in pale blue and looked like

345

a collector's prized doll. Steve was in his wedding suit, but Caroline had seen to it that he had a new necktie for the occasion. Haney, too, was in her Sunday best.

"The carriage awaits," Steve said, formally offering his arm to Laura Jane. "Lady Laura Jane, Lady Caroline." He turned and she took his other elbow. "Haney, if you please," he said, and they left The Retreat.

The high school auditorium was jampacked. No one remembered it ever being so crowded, not even when the commencement exercises had been rained out of the football stadium and moved into the auditorium.

Caroline sat up on the stage, flanked on one side by her family and Haney, whose presence she had insisted on, much to the officials' chagrin, and on the other side by those same officials.

To keep her panic at bay, she tried to focus on the American flag standing sentinel in the corner of the stage. The stars seemed to buzz like gnats over the field of blue. The stripes waved. The flag was perfectly still.

Caroline was sick.

She glanced out over the audience and all she saw was a sea of swimming faces staring at her with avid interest. Diverting her eyes to her lap, she noted that her palms were shiny with perspiration. If she put on her gloves, her hands would be too hot, though now they were icy cold. She swallowed the nausea in her throat and wished that she hadn't tied the bow at her neck so tightly.

Her stomach was growling as it rolled from side to side. Why hadn't she eaten those muffins? If she had, she would have thrown them up. But she was going to throw up anyway. She was going to disgrace herself in front of the whole town.

Why was it so damn hot in here? Her skin was clammy. She looked around. No one else seemed uncomfortable. Steve and Laura Jane were speaking quietly to each other. Haney had found one of her church friends and they were gaily chatting. The mayor, against the rules of the building, was puffing on a cigar as he talked loudly and expansively to the county judge. The odor of the smoke turned her stomach.

As she watched the mayor, he excused himself from the judge and went marching toward the back of the stage. "Well, well, we can get started now. I was afraid you weren't gonna make it, boy. How are you, Rink?"

Caroline swallowed and began breathing

347

through her mouth with shallow pants that were supposed to control nausea. Her whole body went cold, then flushed hot. Her earlobes seemed to be on fire, they burned so.

She heard his voice as he greeted those around her. From the corner of her eye, she saw Haney advancing on him militantly. He stopped the tirade he saw coming with a sound kiss on her cheek. She jerked back, as flustered as a young girl, then squeezed him in a bear hug. Laura Jane vaulted from her chair and ran to embrace him. Steve stood and the two men shook hands.

Then she saw his brown pant legs moving toward her. He stood directly in front of her. She could feel heat and energy radiating from him. And because the whole town was watching, she drew her lips into a stiff smile and raised her head to look at him. "Hello, Rink."

Rink stared down at her and was only partially successful in hiding his shock. Her eye sockets were deeply shadowed. Her cheeks were gaunt. She was pale. She looked like she could stand about seventy-two hours of uninterrupted sleep and about five hearty meals.

But she was beautiful.

It took every ounce of self-control he possessed not to take her in his arms and hug her to him fiercely. The last two months had been hell. He could recount every miserable second of them because he had done nothing but think of her, miss her.

Damn his temper. Damn his pride. He had gotten angry because two drunken jackasses in a tavern had shot off their mouths. He had taken out his angry frustration on her. This time, she had given it back tit for tat. That had both surprised him and angered him more. Mostly because what she had said had been right on target. Roscoe could no longer be blamed for keeping them apart. He was bringing this misery on himself, on her. He had left without a word. What kind of behavior was that for a grown man?

For a man in love?

Ah, but being in love made you mean and crazy. Love made you act like a fool even when you knew you were acting like a fool and couldn't help yourself from acting like a fool. Love made you take a hand so cold it was shocking and say an insipid, "Hello, Caroline. You look lovely," when what you wanted to do was throw your arms around her, beg her forgiveness, claim her as yours and defy heaven and earth to try to come between you again.

Rink sat down beside her. The hem of his trouser brushed her leg and she circumspectly moved it aside. He watched her hands tug self-consciously on the hem of her skirt as she sat with rigid posture on the stage. God, she was precious. She was still the girl in the woods, the Dawson girl, trying so hard to gain approval. His heart ached with love for her. He wanted to shout at her, "What the hell do you care what they think of you? You're head and shoulders above any of them."

Then it struck him that he was as bad as she. He wanted her more than he wanted to live till tomorrow. Yet he had let public opinion keep him from her. She had been his father's wife. So what if everybody thought it had been a normal marriage? He knew better. And even if he didn't . . .

He turned to her so quickly he startled her into looking straight at him. Their eyes collided.

He studied every feature of her face. He cataloged every minute detail. She was as beautiful to him as the first time he'd seen her. He loved her a thousand times more now than he had that summer twelve years ago.

And he knew in a blinding instant that if he had had to go through eternity not knowing her true relationship with his father, he would still want her. He loved her to the exclusion of all else, more than he minded public ridicule, more than he resented his father, more than anything, he loved Caroline Dawson.

"So I'll now ask Mrs. Caroline Lancaster, Roscoe's widow, to come to the podium."

Rink's eyes flew to the speaker's microphone where the mayor had just introduced Caroline. He hadn't been listening to the flowery speech. Apparently neither had she. When the audience burst into loud applause, she jumped.

Rink watched as she visibly collected herself and stood gracefully. She placed her purse and gloves on the seat of her chair, then walked to the podium with more poise than a queen bred to such ceremony. The smile she gave the mayor was tremulous and the audience took her evident emotion to be reaction to his speech. Rink scanned every face in the crowd. She needn't have worried. They approved of her.

She accepted the plaque with one hand and shook the mayor's hand with the other. Moving aside, the mayor offered her the microphone. "Roscoe would have been honored to receive this token of appreciation from you. I and all his family accept it for him and say thank you."

There was nothing hypocritical in her short acceptance speech. Everything she had said was the truth. She hadn't added to the litany of praise the mayor had heaped on Roscoe. She had merely accepted the tribute in Roscoe's stead. She had given these people what they wanted, a hero for the day. To Rink's way of thinking that was well and good.

He watched her turn. Her face was as pale as the bone china in the cabinet at The Retreat. She paused and closed her eyes briefly as she seemed to struggle for breath and equilibrium. She took another step and swayed. The mayor's hand went to her elbow and he spoke her name.

Rink bolted up from his chair. She looked toward him, blinking rapidly as though she were trying to focus on him. Then slowly her eyes drifted closed, her knees folded beneath her and she collapsed to the floor.

A murmur of surprise and alarm rose up from the audience. Laura Jane cried out and clutched Steve's hand. Haney cried, "Lord o' mercy!" and clasped her hands over her enormous bosom. Those closest to Caroline surged around her, dropping to their knees on the stage.

Rink, wild with fear, began plowing

through them, shoving men twice his size out of the way. "Get away from her. Get — *Move!* Let me through. Dammit, get out of my way!"

At last he reached her. He fell to his knees and grabbed her hand. It lay lifelessly in his palm. "Caroline, Caroline. For God's sake, would someone call a doctor? Caroline, sweetheart. God, speak to me!"

He clawed at the bow on her blouse and ripped open the first few buttons. He pushed aside her jacket, wreaking havoc on the expensive ensemble. The hat was whipped from her head and sent sailing. Her dark hair tumbled free. With smart, swift pats, Rink slapped her cheeks. Her eyes fluttered open and he gave a soft cry. "Just rest, darling. What's wrong? What's the matter? No, don't talk. Someone's calling a doctor."

"Rink," she whispered, smiling drowsily and serenely. "Rink."

"You fainted, sweetheart." Weakly she raised her hand and touched his cheek, his hair.

As though on cue, those ringed around them raised their eyebrows. Someone was heard to mutter, "Well, I'll be damned."

"You're going to be fine. I promise. I'll see to it." Rink carried her hand to his mouth and pressed the palm against it. He gathered her into his arms so she was lying across his lap rather than on the floor. "A doctor will be here soon."

"I don't need a doctor."

"Don't talk. You fainted. It was the excitement, that's all. You'll —"

"I'm pregnant, Rink."

Her soft interruption halted his rapid flow of words and he stared down at her speechlessly. She laughed softly at his blank expression. "That's all that's wrong with me. I'm going to have a baby."

Her eyes roamed around the curious circle of faces bending over her. The leaders of the community were all listening avidly as the drama that would feed the gossipmongers for months unfolded before their very eyes. It was people like these who had labeled her and her family trash. It was these people she had tried to impress, whose approval she had made a career of seeking.

Now she wondered why she had devoted so many years to such an empty goal. Her eyes went back to Rink's. Golden eyes that had always stirred in her passion and desire and love. Placing her hand on his cheek, she said, "I'm going to have your baby, Rink."

His eyes shimmered with emotion. Tightening his arms around her, he bent his head and put his lips to her ear. "I love you," he whispered. "I love you, Caroline."

Then, like a whirlwind, he surged to his feet, swooping her up into his arms. "Let us through. You heard the lady, she's pregnant. I'm taking her home. Mayor, put out that damn cigar. It's making me sick and I'm only the father, not the expectant mother. Haney, please get Caroline's things there on her chair. Steve, if you would be so kind as to bring the car around, please. Laura Jane, are you okay? That's my girl."

All the while he was issuing orders, Caroline's head was resting comfortably against his chest. He maneuvered them through the crowd, assuring everyone that she was fine, that she had fainted from the excitement, the heat in the building and the lack of a proper breakfast. "I'm taking her home now to feed her and put her to bed. Everybody go on and have a good time. She'll be fine. I understand pregnant ladies do this a lot."

He smiled down at her, and with the whole town watching as they left the building, she wound her arms around his neck.

"Waking up already?" Rink leaned down and pressed a sweet kiss on her forehead.

"Have you been here all this time?" She

had fallen asleep with him holding her hand.

"Every second."

"How long have I been asleep?" She stretched languorously.

"Several hours. Not long enough. I intend to keep you in bed for the next few days."

Her eyes opened wide. "Just to sleep?"

"Among other things." He growled menacingly and hugged her tightly. For a moment he nuzzled his face in the fragrant softness of her neck, then raised his head to kiss her.

His lips met hers with tender pressure. With his tongue he examined the seam of her lips lightly, and when they parted he pressed it deep into the sweet hollow of her mouth. Her arms looped behind his neck and she pulled him down closer.

He surrendered to an urge he had suppressed for hours because it might disturb her. He stretched out beside her on the bed and held her sleepy-warm body against his. Their mouths played with each other. They couldn't stop smiling. But eventually Rink did and looked down at her seriously.

"When were you going to tell me, Caroline?"

He was fully clothed, but his shirt was unbuttoned. She slid her hand inside and laid it flat against his chest. "After this weekend.

If you hadn't come home for Fall Festival, I would have called you."

"Would you?"

"If I hadn't, Haney would have."

"She knew?"

"I think she suspected. And Steve. They hadn't said anything, but I could feel them watching me all the time."

"It didn't take me but one look to see that something was wrong. You've lost so much weight." His hand coasted down her ribs to her hipbone.

"The doctor said that was normal. I haven't been eating much. What little I did eat often came up."

"Why didn't you tell me? I don't know whether to beat you or kiss you."

"Kiss me."

He granted her request. With his palm, he massaged her stomach. "My baby's in there. God, what a wonderful miracle," he said, hugging her boisterously. He kissed her again, a hearty kiss that mellowed to one of desire.

His hand slid up to her breast. He had left her in only a silk slip when he had stripped off the rest of her clothes and ordered her into bed as soon as they'd arrived home. The silk was warm with her body heat. He filled his hand with her breast, pushing it up until it stretched the slip's lace cup. He kissed her through the lace, taking teasing love bites of the firm flesh. "Caroline, will you marry me?"

She sighed. His mouth closed hotly around her nipple and sucked. "How could I refuse? You have such a nice way of asking."

He raised himself over her, capturing her face between his hands. "I want you to know something, something I didn't realize until today." His eyes probed deeply into hers. "If you *had* been a wife to my father, I would still love you and want you for myself just as much as I do now."

He actually saw the tears welling up in her eyes. He watched as they overflowed and rolled down her cheeks. "I love you." She caught the back of his head in her hand and urged it down for another kiss. "Yes, I'll marry you."

"Soon?" he prodded. "It's only been four months since Daddy died. People will talk."

She tossed her hair on the pillow and laughed. "After the episode this morning, that's an understatement." She gave her abdomen an affectionate pat. "I'd say the sooner the better."

"This week?"

"Tomorrow," she whispered and he smiled. "What are we going to do after we're married? Where will we live?"

"Here at The Retreat. I'll have to shuttle between here and Atlanta for business."

"I'll shuttle with you."

"Not afraid to fly with me?"

"I've never been afraid to do anything with you."

That earned her another kiss. "While we're here, what are we going to do, switch bedrooms every few nights?" he teased.

"Why don't we use your bedroom and convert this one into a nursery?"

His eyes surveyed the room, then came back to rest lovingly on her. "My mother would have liked that."

Their mouths melted together again. "I can't get enough of you. God, I missed you."

His furred chest moved against her breasts, still damp from his mouth's caresses. His hand covered hers where it lay on her lower abdomen and pressed. The warm sensations of desire spread through her belly and thighs like melting butter. Feathering her lips over his throat, she purred, "Rink, take off your clothes."

"Damn!" he cursed and sat up. His cheeks were flushed and his pulse was pounding in his temple. "I can't. We'll have to postpone our reunion. I promised Haney

I'd bring you down for supper as soon as you woke up."

"Oh, golly!" Caroline said, throwing off the covers and thrashing her legs to get off the bed. "I just remembered. We're having company for supper."

"Company? Who?"

"It's a surprise. Find me something to wear." She dashed to the dressing table, picked up a hairbrush and began to drag it through her hair. "Do I look like we've been . . . you know?"

Worriedly she studied herself in the mirror as she patted her kiss-abraded lips with a powder puff.

He tossed down the soft challis dress he had selected from the closet, came up behind her and reached around to take a breast under each hand. His fingers outlined the tight beads of her nipples. "Uh-huh. You look exactly like we've been . . . you know."

He buried his face in her neck, just behind her ear, and nuzzled the erotic spot. Groaning, she breathed, "Rink, I'll never get ready if you don't stop."

"I'm ready." He pressed his swollen masculinity against her bottom. "I've been ready for hours. Do you know how beautiful you are when you're asleep?"

360

"You know what I mean. Ready for dinner."

"Oh, dinner. Hell." Sighing theatrically, he dropped his hands and stepped away from her.

When they were somewhat composed, they went downstairs to join Steve and Laura Jane in the parlor. Without asking, Steve fixed Rink a bourbon and water and brought it to him where he was seating Caroline on the sofa with comical carefulness.

"Thanks," Rink said, accepting the drink. He looked at his brother-in-law and smiled. If he had had any remaining doubts about Laura Jane's marriage, he had only to look at her and Steve together. Laura Jane glowed with happiness like a beacon. Steve was relaxed, no longer tense and defensive. He had some terrific plans for making the stables more productive. He now spoke to Rink as an equal. The men were getting to know and like each other.

When the doorbell chimed, Caroline, much to Rink's consternation, jumped up and ran toward the foyer. "I'll get it. Enjoy your drink."

"How does she expect me to enjoy anything with her hopping around like a jackrabbit?" Rink complained. "She's supposed to be taking it easy these first few months, isn't she?"

"I can't believe Caroline's going to have a baby," Laura Jane said to her brother.

"What I can't believe is that I'm the last to know." Rink looked accusingly at Steve. "Why didn't you call and drop me a hint?"

Steve shrugged unrepentantly. "It wasn't my place to."

Rink frowned. He had more to say but was halted by Caroline's appearance in the doorway. "Rink, someone's here to see you."

The young girl's eyes darted nervously around the strange room. She gnawed on her lips, which Caroline was relieved to see were free of freaky lipstick. Gone, too, were the paperclip earrings and the makeup. Her clothes were more traditional, a simple dress with a full skirt. The hair was still spiked, but it had been brushed down in a pixie style around her face.

"She said it was all right for me to come," Alyssa said defensively, jerking her head toward Caroline. "I said you probably wouldn't even remember me, but she said you did, so . . ." She ended on a shrug.

Caroline watched Rink's face go from wonder to shock to delight. He spoke the girl's name under his breath, then repeated it more loudly, gladly. He stretched out his arms as he came toward her. But he didn't rush her. He stopped before he reached her, still with his arms widespread.

Caroline looked down at Alyssa, who had arrived at The Retreat in the town's only taxi. She saw the girl's lips begin to tremble, saw tears in her eyes. Alyssa tried very hard to put up an uncaring front, but she failed. Throwing off the last vestiges of toughness, she plunged headlong into Rink's arms, mashing her face into his chest as her arms went around his waist.

"She's not a half-bad kid."

They were in Caroline's bedroom, undressing for bed.

"Not at all. Only misdirected. Correction. I don't think she's had any direction at all. You should have seen her the first time I met her. She looked like something out of a horror movie."

"How long has this friendship between you two been going on?" He sat down on the bed to take off his shoes and socks.

"A few weeks. We've met twice in town for milk shakes. I invited her here tonight for dinner on the outside chance that you'd be here." She turned from the closet where she'd just hung up her dress. "I'm glad you were," she said with soft significance.

"So am I," he responded. "You've given me another reason to love you. Thank you, Caroline."

"You're welcome." Emotion made her voice as husky as his.

"Did you see the look on her face when we invited her to go to the fair with us to-morrow? That bitch Marilee. I'll bet she's never taken that poor kid anywhere."

"You'll be a good influence on her."

"Not near as good as you'll be. I want us to see her as often as we can."

"So do I. But are you sure you want to go to the fair tomorrow?"

"Why not?" he asked, stepping out of his trousers.

She faced the mirror and with feigned nonchalance fluffed back her hair. "Everyone in town will be there. After today —"

She never got to finish. He came up behind her, turned her around and sealed her lips with his. Finally, he raised his head. "I'm going to parade you all over those fair-grounds. We're going to talk to everybody. And I'm going to tell anybody who wants to know and some who don't just how much I love you and that I can't wait to get our baby here."

She dropped her forehead against his chest. "I love you so much. You're wonderful."

"You're wonderful," he whispered, gently setting her away from him. His eyes wandered over her body with leisurely pleasure. Her Charmeuse slip clung seductively to the curves of her body, detailed her breasts and their pert crowns, formed a shallow cup around her feminine delta, conformed to her thighs. "You're beautiful, Caroline."

He touched her through the satiny fabric, sliding over her form with his gentle, talented hands. Her nipples responded to the provocative fanning of his fingertips. The backs of his knuckles rubbed over the faint triangle and made her thighs tingle.

She knew in a moment she would be lost to all else. "Rink, wait." His hand opened over her and his thumb skated across the satin-covered delta. "I . . . I have something to give you."

"I have something to give you, too," he murmured as he dipped his head. His tongue touched her nipple at the same time his thumb searched and found. "Can yours wait?"

"I . . . I supp . . . suppose so."

"Mine can't," he grated softly as he took her hand and guided it to his sex, which was hard and full and straining against his briefs.

He hooked his fingers under the straps of

her slip and pulled it down so she could step out of it. She stood before him naked and quaking with arousal. Lifting her against him, he carried her to the bed. As she lay back, he peeled off his underwear and stretched above her in naked splendor.

He knelt between her thighs. "I love you. I've always loved you, Caroline. I used to dread every dawn because I'd wake up thinking of you, wondering where you were, what you were doing, wanting you, aching for just the sight of you. Now I look forward to every new day because I'll wake up loving you and knowing that you love me."

He touched his lips to her abdomen, knowing his baby slept securely within the body of the woman he loved. She placed her hands on his beloved head in wonder that life had afforded them such happiness. His lips drifted over the cluster of dark curls. Desire and love spiraled through her like a lazy zephyr.

With his hands on her breasts, he lowered his head farther and kissed the velvety petals of her womanhood. His tongue bade them open. He withheld nothing, gave everything.

"I won't hurt the baby?" He rose above her and settled his manhood snugly against her creamy warmth.

"No."

He possessed her with a fierce passion tempered by love and caring. His taut hips rose and fell rhythmically as he plunged deeply but gently. Ever attuned to her needs, he withdrew, stroked lightly the portal then sleekly delved again. She closed about him tightly, milking him with the walls of her body. They gave and they responded equally in a tempestuous physical exchange of love. When the tumult came, they shared it, hurtling off the edge of the universe in each other's arms.

It was a short while later, as they dried each other after a shower, that she said, "You never did let me give you my present."

"You mean there's more?" Playfully he smacked her bottom as she returned to the bedroom. "It couldn't be any better than what I've already had."

"This is serious." She went to an antique bureau and pulled open a drawer. Out of it she took a folded piece of paper. Handing it to him, she went to the window, giving him her back.

The harvest moon shone a silvery light down on the wide expanse of grass. The river channel could be seen winding through the trees in the distance like a spar kling ribbon. How she loved this place. Bu she loved the man more.

She heard the paper rustling, knew that he was reading the deed that transferred The Retreat to him. His footfalls were muffled by the area rug as he came up behind her.

"I can't accept this, Caroline. The Retreat is yours."

She turned to him. "Never mine, Rink. Always yours. That was why I loved it so much. Without you in it, having it meant nothing. You're its heartbeat. Just as you are mine."

She took a step toward him and rested her hand on his chest. "I love you enough to give up the thing I thought I wanted most in the world. Love me enough to put your pride aside and accept it. Please."

He looked at her for a long moment, then at the paper in his hand. He folded it carefully and set it on the bureau. "I accept. With one condition. That you promise to share The Retreat with me for the rest of our life. Promise that we'll love here and have babies here and that we'll never dwell on the tragedies that happened before."

Her smile was radiant. "I promise."

He sealed the covenant with a kiss as warm as the pledge. Then, lifting her into his arms, he carried her back to their bed.